McDONALD INSTITUTE MON(

C000137142

# A woodland archaeology
## Neolithic sites at Haddenham

By Christopher Evans & Ian Hodder

*With contributions from*
David Atkinson, Chris Caple, Edward Cloutman, Chantal Conneller,
Richard Darrah, Natasha Dodwell, Mark Edmonds, Charles French,
Duncan Garrow, Kasia Gdaniec, Dafydd Griffiths, David Gurney,
Robert Johnson, Glynis Jones, Jonathan Last, Frances Lee, Anthony Legge,
Mark Knight, Robert Middleton, Ruth Morgan, Peter Murphy, William Murray,
Michael Parker Pearson, Joshua Pollard, Sylvia Peglar, Jon Price, Tim Reynolds,
Paul Shand, Maisie Taylor, Jennifer Wakeley & Leo Webley

*Principal illustrations by*
Crane Begg, Marc Berger & Andrew Hall

## The Haddenham Project Volume 1

*Published with the aid of a grant from*

ENGLISH HERITAGE

# Contents

# The Assembly of Context

# Preface & Acknowledgements

Extending from 1981–87, the project's fieldwork spans the later phases of the Fenland Survey project. Originally occurring as a University of Cambridge training excavation supported by English Heritage, between 1985 and 1987 it was funded by the Manpower Services Commission (MSC), with the excavation of the Foulmire Fen long barrow being almost exclusively sponsored by English Heritage. In this capacity the support of J. Coles, G. Wainwright and P. Walker is gratefully acknowledged; H. Evans, then of Cambs. County Council, organized and provided the MSC liaison. During the course of the fieldwork, variously the local interest, support and co-operation of D. Hall and F. Pryor, and also J. Alexander, C. Hills, A. Taylor and M. Young, as well as the late T. Gregory and T. Potter, proved invaluable.

We are grateful for the support that was shown to the project by the Earith and Haddenham Parish Councils, who at different times respectively provided a village hall and a school for our use. We would also like to thank Dr D. Wilson, then of the Cambridge University Committee of Aerial Photography, and Squadron Leader M. Young of RAF Wyton for providing additional aerial photographic cover. Dr B. Devereux kindly gave permission to reproduce photographs from the Cambridge University's Collection of Air Photographs.

Although at times run on a financial 'wing-and-a-prayer' — and the accounting skills of Terry Hoare verged on the wondrous — given their Cambridge connections, the excavations attracted quite a list of luminaries, including R. Boast, S. Cogbill, J. Ette, A. Herne, N. James, P. Lane, C. Lewis, M. Johnson, R. Matthews, N. Merriman, P. Rowley-Conwy, N. Schlanger, M.L.S. Sørensen, S. Stead, T. Taylor and G. Woolf. The involvement of M. Alexander, J. & S. Finney, J. Hutchinson, C. Rochester, M. Samuels, G. Taylor and D. Went is also to be acknowledged, as indeed are the many hundreds who joined the excavation crew at one time or another, each of whose contribution was significant. Often serving as site supervisor in the latter years of the project, P. Reeve's contribution must be singled out. We are especially grateful to J. Miller, F. Hivernel and J. Marshall for their organization of the project's finds. J. Dawson of the Fitzwilliam Museum provided crucial conservation advice, and J. Price of the Ancient Monuments Laboratory undertook in-field conservation. Also to be singled out is P. Shand, who as field director of the long barrow excavations displayed considerable 'grace under pressure'. T. Whitelaw's and O. Bone's perseverance in undertaking the test-pit sampling programme must be gratefully acknowledged, as should also be the participation of G. Owen (photography) and C.A. Shell (surveying and geophysics) of the Dept. of Archaeology, University of Cambridge.

Concerning the production of these volumes, Hodder produced the first draft of this volume, which was then amended by Evans; in the case of the second, this process was reversed. Yet there is no intention here of trying pretend that they are 'seamless' or 'interchangeable'. Each reflects the diverse interpretative interests of its prime author, *viz.* the interrelationship of theory/practice and long-term process/'events' or history. Books — like projects — come 'into being' and eventually cannot be otherwise, but hopefully these differences of approach only contribute a sense of breadth and scope to the series.

The ultimate stimulus to push these volumes finally through to completion owes much to T. Williams and P. Walker at English Heritage, with their production monitored by K. Buxton; we are sincerely grateful for their patience and support. The delay in the volumes' production can only be regretted. Their lengthy gestation has, nevertheless, proven advantageous in terms of the provision of much-needed regional site context through excavations by the Cambridge Archaeological Unit, and we are grateful for information provided by, and discussion with, many colleagues at the Unit. In the final production of these volumes, the graphic skills and computing support of M. Abbott, C. Begg and M. Berger has been invaluable, and in this capacity A. Hall's contribution must certainly be singled out; additional artefact drawings were undertaken by M. Brudenell and R. Parkin. The text has been read by R. Bradley, M. Edmonds, F. Healy, I. Kinnes and N. Sharples, and has only benefited from their comments. Beyond this, now long-term discussion and 'mulling over of things' with Richard (Bradley), Mark (Edmonds) and Ian (Kinnes), and also J.D. Hill, M. Knight, G. Lucas, J. Pollard and M.L.S. Sørensen must, with pleasure, be acknowledged. L. Webley greatly assisted with the final production of this volume.

Aside from Mike Church's co-operation (see citation below), we are grateful to the local farmers for tolerating our mis-use of their lands: specifically in the case of this volume's investigations, the Palmer family for the Foulmire Fen excavations, and John and Peter Dennis of Willow Hall Farm for allowing us to probe the Hill Row Doles mound.

We are particularly grateful to those colleagues who provided us with information concerning relevant parallels for this volume's sites. This includes A. Whittle for discussion of his Peacock's Farm investigations, S. Needham for information relating to Runnymede's Neolithic horizons and C.A. Shell for the image of the Swaffham barrow. D. Jennings and A. Barclay at the Oxford Unit facilitated access to the Raunds manuscript. The latter was provided by F. Healy, who also kindly drew together Hambledon's artefact densities for inclusion in Chapter 5, and D. Mackreth gave us access to the Orton Meadows manuscript. Similarly, C. Ellis of Wessex Archaeology supplied a draft of the St Neots long barrow report and A. Oswald (English Heritage) provided unpublished details of his causewayed enclosure researches. P. Rowley-Conwy, B. & J. Coles and B. Layton also provided crucial source information.

Apart from the named contributing specialists, we would like to thank R. Palmer and R. Bewley for matters aerial photographic, and P. Miracle of Cambridge's Department of Archaeology for his comments on the human bone. D. Haddon Reece of the Ancient Monuments Laboratory organized and oversaw the project's radiocarbon dating. Subsequently, A. Bayliss arranged for additional radiocarbon determinations. We are grateful for her calibration of, and comments upon, the project's dates relevant to this volume. Beyond this, F. Pryor has withstood (with grace) a barrage of queries on a range of matters, just as M. Taylor and R. Darrah have been patient in the face of sustained wood-related interrogation — we are most grateful to them all.

Of the specialists contributing to this volume, Charles French would like to thank R.I. Macphail and the Department of Human Environment, Institute of Archaeology, London. Edward Cloutman's work was funded by a SERC research grant awarded to Professor A.G. Smith. He wishes to thank Professor Smith for critically reading the manuscript and Dr A.C. Groenhof and Dr D. Sweetnam for assistance in the field.

Ruth Morgan's study was funded by grants from HBMC and carried out in the Archaeology Department of the University of Sheffield, and she thanks Prof. K. Branigan and J. Hillam. She is grateful to J. Price and M. Macqueen, who worked so hard to lift the wood and arrange its transport, and gave help with sampling and technical problems. The material was stored and studied at the Technology Transfer Unit in Shepherd Street, Sheffield, and B. Cartwright gave continuous assistance. Morgan was aided in her work by students, E. Scott-Davies and F. Jolley, without whom the project would have proceeded very slowly, as well as C. Ward and V. Toulmin. Finally, her thanks go to M. Baillie and D. Brown, who put much effort into trying to date the chronology, and to R. Darrah for many invaluable discussions and J. Hillam for commenting on this report.

Richard Darrah would like to thank P. Harding for providing the tree-felling data and especially express his gratitude to L. Hooper for editorial assistance. For their participation in the Minsmere experiment, C. Choules is thanked for finding the tree, K. Cross for its felling, and B. Powell, J. Sorenson, F. Pryor, M. Taylor, V. Fenwick and S. James for their help in converting the tree, and L. Hooper for her help in editing his contribution.

For her study of the human bones Francews Lee thanks the following for their support and advice: Dr K. Manchester and K. Dobney of the Calvin Wells Laboratory, Bradford; Dr J. Wakely of the Department of Anatomy, Leicester; and finally N. Garland of the Department of Pathology, University of Manchester.

Of the phosphate surveys, David Gurney gratefully acknowledges the help of Dr P. Craddock of the British Museum. Glynis Jones would like to thank P. Rowley-Conwy and M.I.I. Robles who, together with the author, were responsible for the sieving programme in 1981; P. Halstead also commented on an earlier draft of her report.

Finally, in terms of dedication — this is the point at which we should thank family, kin and loved ones (respectively, Evans: Marie Louise Stig Sørensen, Megan and Kim Michael; Hodder: Christine Hastorf, Chris, Greg, Kyle and Nicky) — but spanning decades as the project has and as something that has involved us for so long, it seems to evade the personal and almost falls into a sense of disciplinary time. Therefore, on the verge of their retirement (whatever that specifically implies in their cases), for support, friendship and stimulation in the long run, this accolade is bestowed on David Hall and Francis Pryor, and also Michael Church, the Hermitage Farm manager who for so long put up with so much from us.

# Summary

The two volumes outline the results of the University of Cambridge's seven-year-long campaign of research excavations in the marshland environs of Haddenham, Cambridgeshire along the lower fenland reaches of the River Great Ouse. Their key concern is with the long-term construction of the cultural landscape, regional environmental adaptation, and the changing inter-relationship and constitution of ritual/settlement over time. Matters of methodology and the archaeological process are highlighted throughout, including sampling strategies, resource and population modelling, the hermeneutics of study and the nature of sequence. Equally, amongst its main themes are community resolution, marginalization and representation; in order to provide broader perspective, both volumes are punctuated by inset 'analogical commentaries' drawn from diverse local and international sources.

Aside from a number of smaller-scale evaluations and survey interventions, the fieldwork involved four major 'set-piece' excavations and these are appropriately paired in each of the volumes. The first volume is primarily concerned with the Neolithic, and issues of 'woodland life' (and its cognition) feature. Following review of the area's environmental sequence, including a deep pollen core from the Ouse palaeochannel (with evidence of clearance and agriculture dating to the later fifth millennium cal. BC), the excavation of the Foulmire Fen long barrow is reported. Uniquely, the great bulk timbers of the monument's chamber and façade were preserved, from which detailed 'mass wood' technology and dendrochronological studies arise (the latter tied to the site's series of radiocarbon dates). These provide significant insights into the character of long barrow sequences (e.g. free-standing vs mound/earth-fast mortuary structures) and, particularly, the dynamics of its subsequent collapse upon the mound. Preceded by two primary cremation deposits, six individuals were interred within its main chamber, and one skeleton displayed evidence of skinning/defleshing (there were also two secondary inhumations within the mound itself). The barrow's findings and its sequence are thoroughly reviewed in a regional and national context.

The terrace 'island' on which the barrow was sited also saw Mesolithic utilization and quantities of earlier flintwork were redeposited within its mound. Occurring as a discrete scatter along the terrace's edge, it was there test-excavated; Neolithic and Early Bronze Age material were also present and, sealed by the Fen Clay, a burnt flint mound was in addition recovered.

(Correlating to the maximum inland extent of these marine clays, they are here dated to the first half of the second millennium BC.) The results of the project's extensive, area-wide test-pitting programme and the sample excavation of an earlier Neolithic scatter site at Cracknell Farm are reported, and the character of Early Neolithic settlement is explored at length. This provides crucial background context for the excavation of the Upper Delphs causewayed enclosure. Its single interrupted circuit (augmented by an internal trench-built palisade) encloses some 8.75 ha, making it amongst the largest monuments of this type in Britain. Major exposures of its perimeter occurred over four seasons (with another area also opened within its interior), and variability of deposition, construction and recutting around its circuit are demonstrated. The occurrence of more obviously 'placed' deposits (including human remains) along its straight western side indicate that the enclosure was laid out according to a façade principle, and the distinction of different modes of ditch-/pit-digging could tell of the participation of more than one community group. Whilst probably attesting to some limited degree of localized settlement activity *per se*, the associated finds densities are so low as to suggest that the construction of the enclosure was itself the prime purpose. Statistical comparison is made between its densities and other sites of this type, it being argued that as a category such monuments reflect a wide range of 'use' variability. Following full contextual review of the enclosure's affinities (involving questions of seasonality, 'planning' and enclosure/community resolution), the volume concludes by discussing key themes of Neolithic land-use and 'experience', and considers the role of monuments in the construction of territory/place and identity.

Generally concerned with post-Neolithic usage, central to the second volume is Snow's Farm barrow complex, excavated in 1983. Having been superficially investigated by Bromwich in the 1950s, this saw a Romano-British shrine sited upon a Bronze Age round barrow (itself sealing traces of later Neolithic Grooved Ware occupation). Also having a later Iron Age enclosure located immediately beside it, the Snow's Farm sequence accordingly provides the volume's pivot. Therefore, following the description of its barrow proper (with a primary *in situ* cremation pyre and ten urned and unurned cremations), the sequence of the neighbouring Hermitage Farm barrow is related. The latter proved to be a complex 'small monument', and from it was recovered an important three-vessel Collared Urn cremation. The area's later second-millennium BC landscape 'fragments', including an enclosure and lynchet system (and also a significant Beaker pit assemblage), are then outlined and, relating to the onset of 'wet' conditions, the evidence of its later prehistoric environmental sequence reviewed.

Thereafter attention turns to the Iron Age landscape. In the course of the project's fieldwork, four Middle/later Iron Age enclosures were investigated. By far the most thorough and intense of these occurred on the HAD V riverside compound, whose surface deposits (floors, banks, etc.) were superbly preserved through subsequent flooding, and its waterlogged deep-cut features produced important wood and environmental remains. The site's finds assemblage proved prolific, and its animal bone included a remarkably high percentage of wild species (e.g. beaver and various 'big' birds). Arguably relating to trade/exchange strategies and seasonal wetland resource exploitation (the marsh-proud crowns of earlier barrows being utilized to this purpose), its evidence and that of the other enclosures of the period permits uniquely detailed social and economic reconstruction concerning the establishment of wetland-specific communities.

The area's Roman-British utilization hinges upon the Snow's Farm shrine complex. This involved the enclosure of the upstanding barrow mound, and its primary stone-footed octagonal cella was, in later Roman times, succeeded by a series of timber post ranges focusing on a post-built shrine structure upon its crown. Although the site's 'conventional' finds assemblages (e.g. metalwork and ceramics) were not especially abundant, its animal remains were outstanding. They included a series of votive carcasses and also head-and-hooves deposits (some having coins set in the mouths of sheep) and a wide array of wetland bird species. When added to the evidence of the site's sherd/vessel distributional analyses, this allows for nuanced insights into the operations of rural shrines and, particularly, the nature of sacrifice and ritual transformation.

A sense of wider perspective is provided by a review of Bromwich's earlier findings from the complex, especially a baton handle which matches those recovered from the renowned Willingham Fen hoard. Therefore, following comparison with other shrine sites and the reporting of the Roman agricultural enclosures (and a droveway system) also excavated during the main project, the extensive Roman settlement and field systems south along the Willingham/Over fen-edge are overviewed. Not only does this include the results of subsidiary W.E.A excavations at Cut Bridge Farm and Queensholm, but also re-analysis of Bromwich's extensive *Fenland in Roman Times* fieldwalking collections.

The area's post-medieval enclosure and drainage is then outlined and related to issues of (re-)colonization, the loss of landscape fabric and the broader impact of history upon these 'marginal' lands.

# Résumé

Ces deux volumes exposent les résultats de sept années de campagnes archéologiques menées par l'Université de Cambridge dans les environnements marécageux de Haddenham, Cambridgeshire, dans la région des Fens ('fagne') de la rivière Great Ouse. Les thèmes principalement explorés sont la reconstruction du paysage culturel sur le long terme, les adaptations à l'environnement au niveau régional, ainsi que la constitution et la négociation constante des relations entre rituel et implantation territoriale. L'importance de la méthodologie et du processus archéologique sont mis en avant tout le long de l'ouvrage, y compris les stratégies d'échantillonnage, la modélisation des ressources et de la population, la dimension herméneutique de l'étude et la nature de la séquence. Par ailleurs, d'autres thèmes fondamentaux sont considérés, tels la résolution, la marginalisation et la représentation de la communauté; afin d'élargir les perspectives offertes, les deux volumes comprennent des encarts, sous la forme de 'commentaires analogiques' provenant de diverses sources tant locales qu'internationales.

Outre quelques évaluations de faible emprise et activités de prospection, la recherche sur le terrain a consisté en quatre opérations, traitées deux à deux dans chacun des volumes. Le premier volume traite essentiellement du Néolithique, de la "vie en forêt" et de sa dimension cognitive. Après un examen de la séquence environnementale de la région, comprenant un carottage palynologique dans le paléochenal de l'Ouse (traces de déboisement et de mise en agriculture à la fin du cinquième millénaire avant J.-C.) la fouille du *long barrow* ('tertre allongé') de Foulmire Fen est présentée. De façon tout à fait exceptionnelle, la structure massive en bois de la chambre et de la façade du monument était préservée, autorisant une analyse détaillée de la technologie impliquée et l'obtention de datations dendrochronologiques (ces dernières confirmant étroitement la série de datations radiocarbone réalisées). Ces éléments permettent de cerner la nature des séquences d'événements rencontrés sur les *long barrows* (entre autres structures funéraires à l'air libre ou sous tertre) et, en particulier, la dynamique de la décomposition de la structure sous le tertre. Précédés par deux crémations en position primaire, six individus ont été déposés dans la chambre principale; un squelette présentait des traces de d'écorchage ou de décarnation (deux inhumations secondaires ont également été mises au jour au sein même du tertre). L'ensemble de ces éléments sont ensuite replacés dans leur contexte régional et national.

La terrasse, qui constitue une sorte d'île, sur laquelle ce tertre est implanté présente aussi une utilisation mésolithique. Quantité de matériel lithique plus ancien a été incorporé dans le corps du tertre. Au bord de la terrasse, une nappe d'artefacts de cette occupation a fait l'objet d'un sondage spécifique. Du matériel néolithique et de l'Âge du Bronze ancien était également présent, et scellé par l'argile du Fen, un amas de silex brûlé a aussi été mis au jour (ces derniers éléments sont datés de la première moitié du deuxième millénaire avant J.-C. par corrélation avec l'extension maximale à l'intérieur des terres de ces argiles d'origine maritime). Les résultats du programme extensif de larges sondages et la fouille restreinte d'une nappe d'artefacts du Néolithique ancien à Cracknell Farm sont également discutés. La nature de l'implantation territoriale durant le Néolithique ancien est analysée en profondeur. Ces éléments fournissent un contexte crucial pour la fouille d'un enclos à fossé, sis le long du cours supérieur de la Delphs. Le tracé de cet enclos, interrompu à une seule reprise (et doublé par une palissade fossoyée interne), ceinture une surface de 8,75 ha, ce qui en fait un des plus grands monuments de ce type en Grande-Bretagne. Des fouilles importantes ont été réalisées lors de quatre saisons tout le long de son périmètre (avec une autre surface ouverte à l'intérieur). Celles-ci démontrent la variabilité des dépôts, de la construction et des recoupements de son tracé. La présence de dépôts d'aspect plus 'intentionnel' (comprenant des restes humains) le long de la partie occidentale, au cours rectiligne, indique que l'enclos a été implanté tel une façade. La mise en évidence de différents modes de creusements pour les fosses et fossés suggère la contribution de plus d'un groupe communautaire. Bien qu'elles attestent probablement d'une activité d'implantation pour le moins localisée, la faible densité des découvertes réalisées montre que la construction de l'enclos en tant que tel fut l'objectif principal. Une comparaison statistique a été réalisée entre ces densités et celles d'autres sites de même type; ceci permet de considérer que, en tant que catégorie, ces monuments reflètent une variabilité marquée en termes d'"usage". Après une mise en contexte des caractéristiques de l'enclos (questions de saisonnalité, de "planification" et de résolution de la relation enclos/communauté), le volume se conclut par une discussion des thèmes principaux de l'usage du territoire et de l'"expérience" néolithiques, et considère le rôle des monuments dans la construction du territoire/lieu et de l'identité.

Dédié de façon générale à l'après-Néolithique, le second volume traite du complexe du tertre de Snow's Farm, fouillé en 1983. Etudié de façon superficielle par Bromwich dans les années 1950, ce site comprend un temple romano-britannique implanté sur un tertre circulaire de l'Âge du Bronze (lui-même scellant les traces d'une occupation *Grooved Ware* du Néolithique récent). Présentant également un enclos de l'Âge du Fer final placé à ses abords immédiats, la séquence de Snow's Farm constitue dès lors le pivot du second volume. Ainsi, après la description du tertre lui-même (comprenant *in situ* le bûcher funéraire d'une crémation primaire et dix crémations, placées ou non en urne), une comparaison est menée avec la séquence du tertre voisin de Hermitage Farm. Ce dernier s'avère être un 'petit monument' complexe, qui a livré une importante crémation, renfermant trois vases datés de la période *Collared Urn*. Les 'fragments' de paysage de la fin du deuxième millénaire avant J.-C. connus dans la région, dont un enclos et un système de champs (ainsi qu'un assemblage campaniforme en fosse pour le moins significatif), sont ensuite exposés. Enfin, en relation avec la problématique du début des conditions 'humides', les données relatives à cette séquence environnementale de la préhistoire récente régionale sont passées en revue.

Le paysage de l'Âge du Fer est l'objet de la section suivante. Dans le cadre des activités de terrain du projet, quatre enclos de l'Âge du Fer moyen/récent ont été analysés. L'analyse de loin la plus entière et extensive porte sur le complexe HAD V, localisé en bord de rivière. Les dépôts de surface de ce site (sols, talus,...) étaient exceptionnellement bien conservés grâce à une suite d'inondations, tandis que les structures implantées en profondeur étaient gorgées d'eau et ont donc livré quantité de restes organiques, dont du bois. Les assemblages mis au jour se sont avérés particulièrement riches, avec, entre autres, une faune comprenant une proportion remarquablement élevée d'espèces sauvages (e.a. castor et divers 'grands' oiseaux). Vraisemblablement lié à des stratégies d'échange ou de commerce et à l'exploitation saisonnière des terres humides (usage des tertres sis en surplomb des marécages), les données de ce site et d'autres enclos de la même période permettent une reconstruction particulièrement détaillée, tant du point de vue social que économique, de l'implantation de communautés spécifiques dans ces terres humides.

L'utilisation romano-britannique de la région s'articule autour du temple de Snow's Farm. Ce dernier comprenait à l'origine le tertre et une cella octogonale à soubassement de pierre. Ensuite, à l'époque romaine, celle-ci fut suivie par une série de poteaux, constituant une structure cultuelle implantée sur le pourtour du tertre. Bien que les découvertes 'conventionnelles' (e.a. métal et céramique) ne soient pas particulièrement abondantes sur le site, les restes fauniques étaient, eux, exceptionnels. Ceux-ci comprenaient une série de carcasses votives, ainsi que des dépôts de type 'têtes-et-sabots' (dans certains cas des pièces de monnaie ayant été placées dans la bouche de moutons) et un large éventail d'oiseaux d'ambiance humide. En conjonction avec la distribution spatiale des vases et des tessons, il est possible de proposer une perception nuancée des opérations menées sur les temples ruraux et, en particulier, de la nature des sacrifices et des transformations rituelles.

Des éléments supplémentaires sont fournis par un ré-examen des découvertes plus anciennes faites par Bromwich sur le complexe, en particulier un manche de bâton qui correspond à ceux mis au jour dans le célèbre dépôt de Willingham Fen. Après comparaison avec d'autres temples et présentation d'enclos à fonction agricole de la période romaine (ainsi que d'un système de chemins de pâture) également fouillés durant le projet, les importants habitats et systèmes de champs romains situés au sud du fen de Willingham/over sont discutés. Ceci inclut non seulement les résultats des fouilles connexes à Cut Bridge Farm et à Quensholm, mais également le ré-examen des prospections pédestres publiées par Bromwich dans son ouvrage *Fenland in Roman Times*.

L'emprise post-médiévale de la région et le système de drainage sont ensuite étudiés et mis en perspective par rapport aux problématiques de (re-)colonisation, de la perte de la fabrique du paysage et, de façon plus générale, de l'impact de l'histoire sur ces terres dites 'marginales'.

# Zusammenfassung

Die vorliegende Arbeit präsentiert in zwei Bänden die Ergenbnisse des Haddenham Projektes der Universität Cambridge. Haddenham liegt in Cambridgeshire im Südosten Englands an den Aufeldern des Flußes Great Ouse. Der Schwerpunkt des sieben Jahre langen Haddenham Projektes lag auf der Untersuchung der Marschlandschaften. Insbesondere die Konstruktion und Konstitution der Kulturlandschaft, die regional bedingte Anpassung an die Umwelt und das sich ändernde Verhältnis sakraler und sekulärer Elemente zueinander wurden untersucht. Durch beide Bände zieht sich außerdem eine Diskussion des „archäologischen Prozesses" und archäologischer Methodik. Diese Diskussion umfaßt unter anderem Sampling Strategien, das moldellieren von Resourcen und Populationen, die Hermeneutik des Projektes selbst und die archäologische Sequenz. Darüberhinaus werden folgende Themen angesprochen: die archäologische Resolution der untersuchten Sozialstruktrukturen und Gruppen, Marginalisation und Representation. Um den Inhalt dieser Diskussion in einen weiteren Kontext zu stellen, sind beide Bände mit sog. „Analog-Kommentaren" gespickt, die sich auf diverse lokale und internationale Quellen stützen und beziehen.

Neben einer Reihe von Evaluationen und Surveys, besteht das Haddenham Projekt hauptsächlich aus vier „klassischen" Ausgrabungen; die Grabungen werden gepaart in zwei Bänden präsentiert. Der erste Band beschäftigt sich mit dem Neolithikum und dem „Leben im Wald", sowie den kognitiv-symbolischen Aspekten einer solchen Lebensweise. Der Besprechung der Grabung des Langhügelgrabes im Foulmire Fen steht die Presentation der regionalen Landschaftsentwicklung vor. Dies beinhaltet auch Betrachtungen zu der sehr langen Pollensequenz aus dem Ouse-Paläobett, welches Hinweise auf Rodungen und Landwirtschaft ab dem späten fünften Jahrtausend calBC ergeben hat. Einzigartige Erhaltungsbedingungen waren für die überaus großen Holzbalken der Grabkammer und der Fassade gegeben. Detaillierte Studien über die Holzbearbeitungstechnik solch großer Balken wurden durchgeführt und die dendrochronologische Analyse erlaubt die Korrelation der 14C Datierungsserie mit den einzelnen Balken. Zusammengenommen erlauben diese Einzelstudien Einsicht in die verschiedenen Bauphasen des Grabhügels (z.B. freistehend oder mit umgebendem Hügel), sowie den nachfolgenden Phasen der Dekonstruktion und des Verfalls. In der Grabkammer wurden insgesamt acht Individuen bestattet, davon zwei als Brandbestattungen und sechs als einfache Bodenbestattungen im Hauptteil der Grabkammer. An einem Skelett konnten Spuren von Häutung oder Entfleischung gefunden werden. Außerdem gab es zwei Sekundärbestattungen innerhalb der Hügelaufschüttung selbst. Die Funde aus dem Grabhügel und die archäologische Sequenz werden ausführlich besprochen, sowohl in regionalem als auch in nationalem Kontext.

Die „Insel"-Terrasse auf welcher der Grabhügel angelegt wurde wahr auch Schauplatz mesolithischer Steinwerkzeugherstellung und –benutzung und einige umgelagerte Flintartefakte wurden im Hügel selbst gefunden. An einer Stelle an der Terrassenkante wurde mesolithisches Fundmaterial in höherer Konzentration vorgefunden und Testgrabungen durchgeführt. Dies ergab ein vermischtes Inventar mit neolithischem und bronzezeitlichen Komponenten und einer Ansammlung verbrantem Feuersteins, der von dem sog. Fen Clay bedeckt war. Fen Clay ist mit der Maximaltransgression der ersten Hälfte des zweiten Jahrtausends BC verbunden. Die Ergebnisse des weiträmigen Testgrabungsprogrammes im Rahmen des Haddenham Prjektes werden vorgestellt. Anhand der Ausgrabung einer frühneolithischen Flintkonzentration bei Cracknell Farm wird die frühneolithische Siedlungsgeschichte ausführlich diskutiert. Dies dient wiederum als wichtiger Hintergrund für die Beschreibung der Ausgrabung der unterbrochenen Grabenanlage Upper Delphs. Dieser einfach unterbrochene Graben mit interner Palisade umschließt ungefähr 8,75ha und ist damit eines der größten Monumente dieser Art in Großbritannien. Über vier Jahre hinweg wurden die Außenseite der Anlage, sowie ein kleinerer Teil des Innenareals weitflächig aufgeschlossen. Unterschiede in der Ablagerung, Bauweise und Wiederherstellung der Anlage können demonstriert werden. Das Vorkommen von eindeutig und speziell platzierten Funden, was auch Bestattungen einschließt, entlang der geraden Westseite der Anlage weißt darauf hin, daß sie nach dem Fassadenprinzip angelegt worden war. Darüberhinaus können die Unterschiede in Bauweise und Wiederherstellungsweise dahingehend interpretiert werden, daß verschiedene Gemeinschaften oder Gemeinden am Bau und der Instandhaltung der Grabenanlage beteiligt waren. Obwohl die kargen Funde um die Anlage herum gegen eine ausschließliche Sakralfunktion des einfach unterbrochenen

Grabens sprechen, scheint die allgemein sehr niedrige Fundkonzentration eher darauf hinzuweisen, daß diese Siedlungsspuren mit den Bauphasen des Monuments selbst in Verbindun zu bringen sind. Eine statistische Analyse der relativen Funddichte in und um solche Monumente herum zeigt, daß es nicht möglich ist eine exklusive Funktion dieses Monumentstypuses festzulegen. Nach der ausführlichen Besprechung der Fundgattungen und Kontexte der Grabenanlage (z.B. hinsichtlich von Seasonalität, Aufbau und Struktur, Resolution), ended der erste Band mit einer Diskussion der Schlüsselthemen, nämlich neolithische Landnutzung und „Erfahrung", insbesondere die Rolle von Monumenten für Territorialität/Orts-Sinn und Identität im Neolithikum.

Der zweite Band des Haddenham Projektes dreht sich um die nach-neolithische Nutzung der Region. Im Mittelpunkt steht die Ausgrabung des Grabhügelkomplexes Snow's Farm, der 1983 ergraben wurde. Bromwich legte erste oberflächliche Grabungen in den 1950ern an und fand einen romano-britischen Schrein, der auf einem bronzezeitlichen Rundgrabhügel plaziert worden war. Dieser Grabügel selbst ergab Spuren spätneolithischer Besiedlung mit rillenverzierter Ware. Direkt daneben wurde außerdem eine Befestigungsanlage aus der Eisenzeit entdeckt. Wegen eben dieser multi-phasischen, dichten Besiedlungsgeschichte dient die Sequenz von Snow's Farm als Anker für die Analyse der nach-neolithischen Aktivitäten in der Region. Zuerst wird die bronzezeitliche Grabanlage besprochen. Dort wurden insgesammt elf Bestattungen freigelegt: eine primäre Brandbestattung und zehn Sekundärbestattungen mit und ohne Urnen. Die chronologische Sequenz von Snow's Farm kann mit der vom benachbarten Hermitage Farm korreliert werden. Hermitage Farm ist ein komplexes „Kleinmonument", wo unter anderem eine wichtige Randurnenbestattung mit drei Gefäßen gefunden wurde. Nachfolgend werden die ergrabenen Fragmente der Landschaft des zweiten vorchristlichen Jarhtausends besprochen, so zum Beispiel eine Befestigungsanlage und Äcker sowie ein nicht unwesentliches Vorkommen von Gruben der Glockenbecherkultur. Diese Funde und Monumente werden in Relation zu dem Beginn der „Naßzeit" in der Region und den späteren Umweltveränderungen gesetzt.

Der folgende Abschnitt is der eisenzeitlichen Landschaft gewidmet. Im Rahmen des Haddenham Projektes, wurden insgesamt vier Befestigungsanlagen aus der mittleren bzw. späten Eisenzeit angeschnitten. Die detaillierteste Untersuchung fand an der Fundstelle HAD V statt. HAD V ist eine Siedlungsanlage am ehemaligen Flußufer und wiederholte Überflutungen haben die ausgezeichnete Erhaltung von archätektonischen Strukturen garantiert. Wichtige Klimainformationen wurden aus den Tiefsondagen gewonnen, die mit Wasser vollgesogene Sedimente erreichten. Das Fundvorkommen von HAD V ist umfangreich und die Fauna ist besonders reich an Wildtieren (z.B. Bieber und verschiedene Spezies von großen Vögeln). Das großes Vorkommen von Wildtieren in HAD V könnte im Zusammenhang mit Handelsbeziehungen gesehen werden. Diese umfangreiche Thanatocenose elaubt eine bisher unerreicht detaillierte Rekonstruktion der Lebensweise und Gesellschaftstruktur von Gruppen, die sich in solchen Niederungs- und Aulandschaften niedergelassen haben.

Der oben bereits erwähnte romano-britische Schreinkomplex bei Snow's Farm ist der Mittlepunkt romano-britischer Besiedlung. Der Schreinkomplex umfaßt die Befestigung um den Grabügel. Die primäre achteckige cella mit Steinfundament wurde in spätrömischer Zeit mit einer Serie von Pfostenreihen ersetzt, die sich in ihrer Anordnung auf den hölzernen Schrein auf dem Hügel beziehen. Wider Erwarten kamen konventionelle Funde wie Eisen und Keramik nicht sehr oft vor, dafür aber ist die Fauna hervorragend. Eine ganze Reihe von Tieropfern sowie Kopf-und Hufgaben (einigen Schafen wurden Münzen in das Maul gelegt) und eine Großzahl an hiesig vorkommenden Wasservögeln wurden freigelegt. Zusammen mit der räumlichen Analyse der Keramikfunde erlaubt dies eine äußerst detailreiche Interpretation der Rituale in und um ländliche Schreine, insbesondere mit Hinsicht auf Opferhandlungen und rituelle Verwandlungen.

Die Besprechung von Bromwichs früheren Funden erweitert die Perspektive. Bemerkenswert ist darunter besonders ein Stabgriff der genau mit Funden von der einschlägig bekannten Fundstätte des Hortes von Willingham Fen übereinstimmt. Der Schrein von Snow's Farm wird mit anderen bekannten romano-britischen Schreinen verglichen und im Rahmen einer Besprechung der ergrabenen römischen befestigten Äcker und des dazugehörigen Wegesystems wird ein Überblick über den Umfang römischer Besiedlung entlang und in der Umgebung des Willingham/Over Aurandes präsentiert. Dieser Überblick basiert unter andererm auf den Ergebnissen kleinerer Grabungen bei Cut Bridge Farm und Queensholm, sowie einer Aufarbeitung der Funde von Bromwichs großem Surveyprojekt *Fenland in Roman Times*.

Abschliessend wird die neuzeitliche Befestigung und Entwässerung diskutiert. Diese Maßnahmen werden in Beziehung gesetzt mit dem (Wieder-)besiedelungprozess, dem Verlust des Landschaftsgewebes und dem Einfluß des geschichtlichen Geschehens auf solche „Randlandschaften".

Each time I remember Fragment 91 of Heraclitus: '*You will not go down twice to the same river*', I admire his dialectic still, because the facility with which we accept the first meaning ('The river is different') clandestinely imposes the second one ('I am different') and gives us the illusion of having invented it. (Jorge Luis Borges, 'New Refutation of Time,' *Other Inquisitions*; emphasis added.)

... This is not just any tree. For one thing, it draws the entire landscape around it into a unique focus: in other words, by its presence it constitutes *a particular place*. The place was not there before the tree, but came into being with it. And for those who gathered there, the prospects it affords, which is to be had nowhere else, is what gives it its particular character and identity. For another thing, no other tree has quite the same configuration of branches, diverging, bending and twisting in exactly the same way. In its present form, the tree embodies the entire history of its development from the moment it first took root. And that history consists in the unfolding of its relations with manifold components of its environment, included the people who have nurtured it ... *The people, in other words, are as much bound up in the life of the tree as is the tree in the lives of the people.* Moreover, unlike the hills and the valley, the tree has manifestly grown within living memory. Thus its temporality is more consonant with that of human dwelling. Yet in its branching structure, the tree combines an entire hierarchy of temporal rhythms. ... At one extreme, represented by the solid trunk, it presides immobile over the passage of human generations; at the other, represented by the frondescent shoots, it resonates with the life-cycles of insects, the seasonal migrations of birds, and the regular round of human agricultural activities. (Tim Ingold writing of Pieter Bruegel the Elder's 1565 painting, *The Harvesters*, in 'The Temporality of the Landscape' in Ingold 2000, with emphasis added; see also Ingold 1993).

# Chapter 1

# Introduction: Working Land

The subtle topography of the drained East Anglian fen marshlands can be misread as a blank landscape. These 'flatland' associations appear to mirror a limited temporal depth to landscape history, and superficially the Fenlands are a historically shallow or young landscape (Godwin 1978; Waller 1994). There are few regions of Europe where so many place-names only date back to post-medieval times. Where else in Britain, apart from its drained marshlands, would farms be named America or Australia? Sequential masking of its subtle topography in water, peat and silt has punctuated the region's history, making it episodic and one of marked settlement discontinuities. Yet even today farmers in the fens tell strange tales of wandering tribes or claim to know the location of ancient potting-clay quarries — local knowledge that jolts against the planned, gridiron newness of the landscape.

While there are the tonnes and minutiae of medieval monastic and legal texts, many Books of Sewers and records of the Bedford Level Corporation (e.g. Wells 1830; see Darby 1940; 1956), the Fenlanders themselves are a populace relatively without (institutional) history. That theirs is not entirely a 'silent history' is largely due to the influence of a fen-edge university, and generations of Cambridge academics have migrated into the Fenlands for research and vacation. Since the late medieval period there has, in fact, been something of a peculiar alliance between these two communities as both disputed the drainage of the fens: the Fenlanders for fear of losing their livelihood, the University to protect its river tariffs (Parker 1983, 125).

The uninformed onlooker is relatively blind when it comes to understanding the cultural landscape of the Fenland. Its subtle 'Great Level' topography cannot be read like the palimpsests of earthwork systems on the chalk downlands which bear such obvious witness to the long ancestry of human occupation. But since the drainage of the fens in the seventeenth century and during the course of peat and coprolite digging, quantities of prehistoric implements, animal skeletons and the trunks of submerged forests have regularly been found (Dugdale 1772, 171–5). It has, therefore, been recognized that a drowned terrain lies beneath this blanket of silt and peat. By the range of animal and tree species recovered, it has long been apparent to some that this buried landscape was once a relatively dry and 'fruitful country' compared to the watery morass of medieval times (e.g. Dugdale 1772, 141, 171–2; Badeslade 1725, 15–16; Elstobb 1793, 8; Miller & Skertchly 1878, 29).

Following the ebb and flow of the waters, people come and go and transform their way of life in an ever-changing environment. They adapt to new circumstances they have increasingly helped to create. Yet what can we say of these sequences of activities in time? On the one hand, it can be argued that each phase is an independent moment connected certainly to earlier and later events elsewhere, away from the fen-edge, but disconnected from earlier and later events in the immediate landscape. This is a prehistory of ruptures and our task is to establish the radical 'otherness' of separate historical moments. Certainly we shall see broken sequences, periods of activity interspersed with abandonment or radical changes in the way the landscape was used. But is there continuity over discontinuity? The past can often seem to repeat itself, a returning meander of a flowing river. Sequences in time often seem to involve a *bricolage* of the past; perhaps the ebb and flow has its temporal structures.

Has the 'reality' of life in the fens created a common response over time? Has the proximity to a moving and flooding 'edge' generated continuity? Are the material constraints such as to have forged similar cultures through time? Once we have constructed the environmental sequence of a changing landscape, can the cultural pattern of ebb and flow be predicted? For example, are 'wet' areas or the 'edges' between wet and dry always seen and used in similar ways?

Space is already implicated in the ebb and flow of time and settlement. One of the tasks of this report will be to document the movement back and forth of fen-edge settlement. This will involve an understanding of environmental changes as water flows and Fenland creeps over the landscape, transforming and transformed by economic and social relationships. But these relationships are also embedded in a

1

conceptual world in which secondary, symbolic meanings are assigned. The cleared land and the forested land can also be the domesticated and the wild; dry and wet can easily become metaphors, as they have been historically in the fens.

In early chronicles and Saints' Lives the Fenland marshes were often depicted as some form of primordial hell inhabited by demons and reeking with ill vapours (Darby 1940, 8–10; Summers 1976, 9). In Fenland commentaries, especially in appeals for its drainage, its landscape was often described in terms to suggest that the very elements of nature were there out of balance and running to riot:

> And what expectation of health can there be to the bodies of men, where there is no element of good? the Air being for the most part cloudy, gross, and full of rotten harrs; the Water putrid and muddy, yea full of loathsome vermin; the Earth spungy and boggy; and the Fire noysome by the stink of smoaky hassocks (Dugdale 1772 'To the Reader').

Moreover, despite more than 350 years of landscape engineering, even recent floods have been seen in terms of a 'fight' or a 'battle' of the banks against the unruly waters.

A common theme of Fenland tales is that its marshes were a place of refuge. Its forests and reed beds were for hiding from the world; it was not a landscape in which the great events of history were enacted. This is both a central and yet a somewhat contradictory aspect of Fenland studies, for rebellion has been a key element in the self- and ascribed identities of the Fenlanders. Localized rioting did occur in the post-medieval fens in reaction to drainage activities (usually resulting in the casting down of banks and the destruction of sluices), but as Darby observed, the population of the fens took no part in the main rebellions of the medieval period (1940, 144–6). The fens were rather a centre of resistance for nobles who utilized the strategic isolation of its marshes;

> The role of the Fenland in English history has been passive rather than active. It was repeatedly a region of refuge, rather than a breeding ground of freedom and discontent (Darby 1940, 143).

The medieval Fenlanders, with their common way of life based on pasture, fishing and fowling, were often seen as 'lazy' since their use of the environment did not involve intense management and the taming of nature. The Protestant work ethic and the Christian virtue of 'honest' labour were contradicted by their predatory existence. Outsiders saw them as wild, vagrant, rugged, lawless and poor, either in contrast to the monks and academics of Ely and Cambridge or more generally in contrast to dry-land farmers.

Yet the cultural valuations given to the spatial separation between wet and dry cannot be seen as timeless. While the physical characteristics of marshland may have meant that it was often used in history as a refuge, the characterization of Fenlanders in medieval and post-medieval times as wild must be set in the context of 'dry' landowners with enough capital to drain and exploit the rich soils of the fen and with enough power to dominate the way in which Fenlanders were written about and perceived. Indeed, one of the justifications for the drainage of the fens has been the 'naturally' unruly Fenlanders. Thus, Wells writing in 1830 directly compared the Ancient Britons in the pre-Roman Fenland to the inhabitants who disrupted the post-medieval drainage:

> The manners and feelings of nations endure in a greater or less degree for generations; and it may not be an overstrained deduction, that this ungovernable disposition, these unrestrained habits, this predatory mode of life, continued for after ages, and perhaps, in part occasioned the violence with which the natives of these regions opposed, in more modern times, the persons who undertook to drain and reclaim the fens from the watery element (Wells 1830, 55–6).

In 1634 the Earl of Bedford with thirteen co-adventurers was granted a charter of incorporation to drain the southern fens, for which the Earl from a previous agreement was to receive 95,000 acres (11 per cent of the total area of the Fenland) in payment and recompense (Darby 1956, 40–41). The Dutch engineer, Vermuyden, was engaged by the Corporation and work began in earnest. In medieval times some minor reclamation of the marshes had made piecemeal encroachments upon the fen-edges (Darby 1940, 43–60), and from the thirteenth century 'The Commission of Sewers' sat regularly as a court to legislate upon the maintenance and control of Fenland dykes and embankments (Darby 1940, 155–68). These preliminary reclamations were as nothing when compared to the truly massive scale and organization of the works undertaken by the new Drainage Corporation. Major new drainage works were constructed apace throughout the later seventeenth and eighteenth centuries.

The wealth generated by drainage did not often go into the hands of the Fenlanders themselves. Outside interests transformed an economy based on pastoralism and fishing and fowling to one based on arable farming. The justification for this transformation may often have been couched in terms of progress and improvement — the provision of a rational landscape within which the poor people of the wetlands could be 'civilized'. Yet E.P. Thompson and others have noted that one must be wary of the altruistic sentiments of agricultural improvement and enclosure propagandists ('greater yields to feed a growing population') as higher profits and rents were certainly a major motivation behind land reform (Thompson 1968, 231).

The contemporary view of traditional life in the fens is thus an historical product. The spatial opposition between two ways of life, wet/dry and undrained/drained, is a product of a particular social tension. In this capacity Fenland historical sources — various 'tales' and drainage histories — clearly reflect upon the historical deployment of 'pasts' relevant to the social needs of their contemporary present (Evans 1997b). Bound up with the evaluation of marshes (and forests), this involves the cultural appraisal of lands and peoples — the proverbial linkage of 'waste'/marginality and 'the other'.

## The lie of the land

Including the fenward portions of the parishes of Haddenham, Sutton (south of the Bedford Level), Over and Willingham, the study area falls at the junction of the Ouse river valley and the fen (Figs. 1.1 & 1.2). Its sub-surface topography is dominated by the great oxbow bends of the river's palaeochannel meandering across the lowlands from Earith (and 'The Hermitage') towards Sutton, from where it turns northward towards Chatteris. The course of this, *The West Water*, has been studied by Seale (1980), and Godwin in 1938 took a section across the river upstream at Little Fen, Earith to Crane Fen, Over. (According to Dugdale its 'ancient' line was re-established as Hammond's Eau between 1649–53.)

The flatness of the land today belies its dynamic environmental history; nothing can be assumed here, rivers change the direction of their flow and terrace islands have become lost to peat. The area's palaeo-environment was the subject of much investigation during the project through the auspices of the Fenland Survey. Although these researches are now published in detail (Waller 1994), it would be erroneous to relegate the area's topography and environmental sequence as a given. The discovery of buried land surfaces or masses (i.e. terrace islands) is part of the 'story' of the Haddenham project. Equally, the area's environment is not just a stable or neutral background against which to set the excavations. Like all results it is best framed in the context of its unfolding, as even it is not without interpretative ambiguity.

When standing in the low ground of the Haddenham Level the northeastern horizon is dominated by the marked rise of the Isle of Ely (up to 30 m OD) — the great Fenland island, which was, however, only separated from the 'mainland' in later prehistory (Waller 1994). The main focus of our fieldwork was on the Upper Delphs terrace (Fig. 1.2). Extending over *c.* 70 ha along the southwestern margin of Haddenham parish, this gravel rise, originally a peninsula jutting from the Willingham fen-edge and later 'islanded', lies at *c.* 2–3.00 m OD in contrast to the fen proper whose surface sits at *c.* 1.00 m OD. Although certainly at times a major 'place' in the prehistoric landscape, in post-Roman times it was lost to marsh; due to its topography it came to prominence again in later medieval times when it featured in drainage and common disputes (see James, Volume 2, Chapter 9).

The gravel terrace continues westwards at a reduced height (at *c.* 0.20 m OD) where it is overlain by upwards of 1.00 m depth of organic deposit. The 'ground' rises again to 0.80–1.00 m OD adjacent to the Earith/Haddenham Road, and has accordingly been named the Lower Delphs. Part of the Ouse-side gravel terraces, further to the north these fragment into a series of islands in Foulmire Fen and are separated by the river's backwater palaeochannels.

Since post-medieval times the Ouse has been channelled seaward through the Bedford Level and the Hammond's Eau course has been entirely cut off; much reduced, the river *per se*, the Ely Ouse, flows westwards, isolating the Delphs' terrace as a fen-edge island, and joins the River Cam at Stretham. Originally this branch of the Ouse south of the Delphs and Ely, named the Old West River, drained northwestwards to the river's main channel at Earith and was utilized as part of the Roman Car Dyke canal system (Bromwich, in Phillips 1970). When this length of the river assumed its present course is unknown, but it is thought to have changed to an eastwards drainage before the eleventh century (Hall 1996, 132). The status of these landscape features will largely be dealt with in the second volume (Chapter 8). However, previously unknown, the route of the Car Dyke through the immediate Delphs environs was recognized during our post-excavation researches. The determination of its line (and in knowledge of its 'flow') has implications for the operation of the area's palaeochannels and is, accordingly, considered in Chapter 4 below.

Another major landscape feature that finally warrants notice at this time is Willingham Mere. Located on the southern flanks of the Upper Delphs, in early historical times this large freshwater lake was recorded as covering 32 ha. Marshland developed in this basin during the first millennium BC and its occurrence is particularly important for the terrace's later Iron Age occupation. It is therefore discussed in Volume 2, with its environmental sequence reviewed in Chapter 3 of that volume.

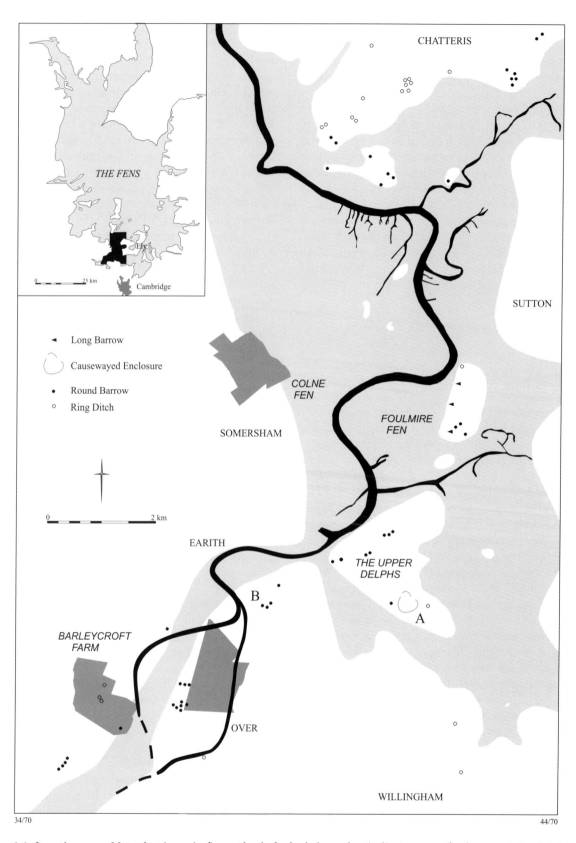

**Figure 1.1.** *Location map. Note that in main figure the dark-shaded swathes indicate areas of subsequent Cambridge Archaeological Unit investigations within quarries adjacent to the Haddenham research area: A) indicates the Delphs causewayed enclosure; B) location of Hall's Over Site 1.*

4

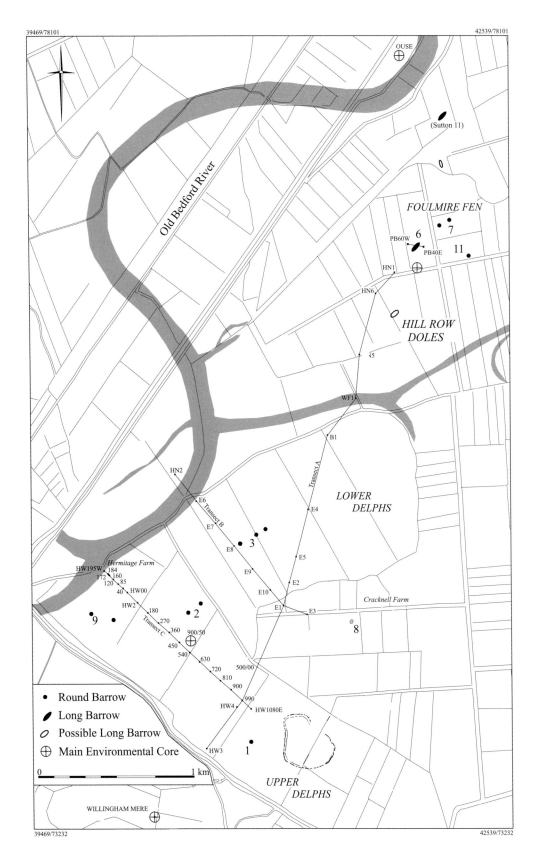

**Figure 1.2.** *Map showing the location of main environmental cores and transects, with the Ouse palaeochannel indicated in grey tone.*

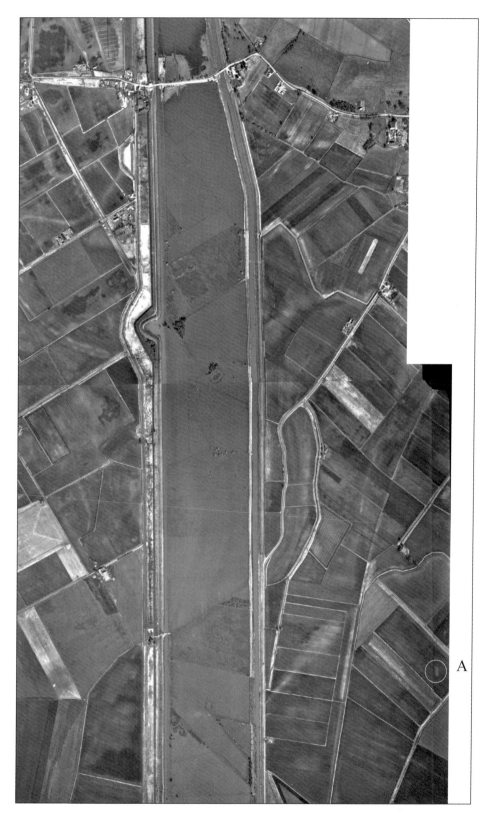

**Figure 1.3.** *The River and the Level: vertical aerial photograph showing the Hammond's Eau/Ouse roddon snaking on either side of the flooded Bedford Level washes. Note in the lower half of the image the line of the roddon has been utilized both to carry the Earith/Hermitage–Sutton Road and to mark field boundaries (cf. Moore's Map of 1658; Vol. 2, fig. 9.1). To the lower right the whitened mound of the Foulmire Fen long barrow is visible (A; HAD 6; CUCAP RC8-EC 121–23).*

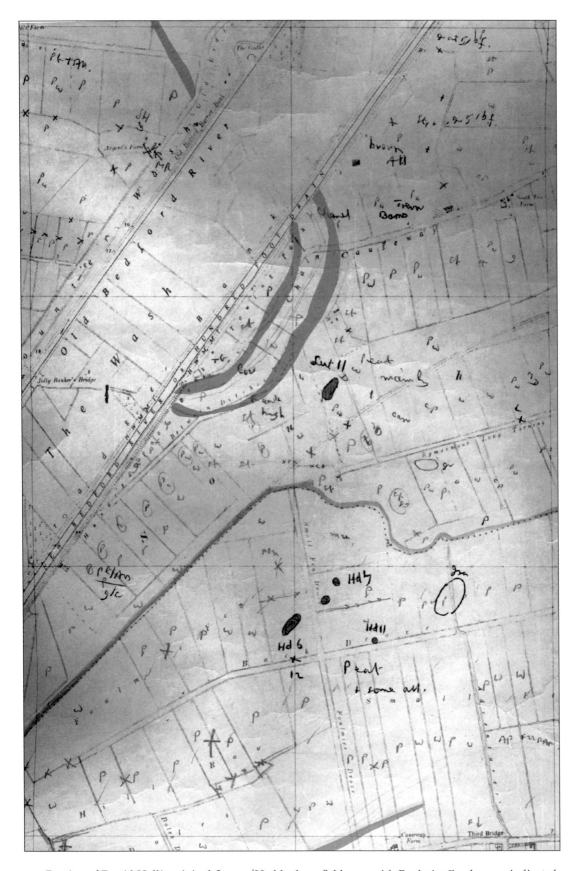

**Figure 1.4.** *Portion of David Hall's original Sutton/Haddenham field map with Foulmire Fen barrow indicated.*

The study area was fieldwalked by David Hall in the course of English Heritage's Fenland Survey during 1978–1982 (see Hall & Coles 1994 concerning the project); the Willingham/Over fen-edge having earlier been surveyed by Bromwich in the course of *The Fenland in Roman Times* researches (hereafter FRT; Phillips 1970; see Volume 2, Chapters 1 & 7). The Delphs terrace had, in fact, first seen fieldwork in the 1950s when John Bromwich undertook limited investigations during the initial ploughing of a Roman 'settlement' (Site 4073, in Phillips 1970). Our 1983 excavations proved Bromwich's settlement to be a Romano-Celtic shrine and, drawing upon his archives, his day-book records are incorporated within Volume 2. (The inclusion of a portion of Hall's original Haddenham/Sutton survey map in this volume, Fig. 1.4, is similarly intended to provide a historiographic dimension and evoke the archival traces of 'discovery'.)

With Hall's survey results now thoroughly published (1996), and that volume also including a full summary of the area's archaeological/historical land-use background, there is no need to repeat its findings in detail. Aside from the recovery of a canoe, probably of Bronze Age attribution and only possibly found in Haddenham North Fen in 1843 (Evans 1881; Fox 1926; see also von Hugel 1887), and the FRT's fen-edge scatter sites and cropmarks to the south, nothing was really known of the archaeology of Haddenham and Sutton low 'fen grounds' prior to the 1970s. It was in 1976 that David Wilson discovered the great causewayed enclosure on the Upper Delphs (Fig. 1.6), although a length of its circuit (not recognized as being of causewayed form) is apparent on an aerial photograph of 1969. Six of the area's barrows at Haddenham Sites 1–3 had been visible prior to 1980. However, it was only through Hall's surveys that the barrow field as a whole was really identified and its true scale appreciated. Apart from the one known on the Upper Delphs terrace (Site 1), the barrows lie in clusters on the riverside terraces southeast of the main Ouse palaeochannel and include a line of three north of the track (Site 3) and four south of the Hermitage Farm drove (two each at Sites 2 and 9). (One of the latter at TL 39989/74502 was a new discovery in the course of the project's fieldwork; it is visible on the aerial photograph CUCAP Rc8 EC 37.) On a separate island/terrace in Foulmire Fen along the northwestern margin of the parish three other round barrows were identified (Site 7 × 2, and Site 11). Also found at that location was a 'long mound' (Haddenham Site 6). Though possibly the combined crowns of two conjoining round barrows, this was suspected to be a long barrow and it indeed proved to be such (see Chapter 3). As discussed in Chapter 2 below, Hall later

identified still another long barrow just to the north in Sutton (Sutton 11) and, through subsequent aerial reconnaissance, another long 'mound' and a ring-ditch have also since been detected in that area. On the other side of the Bedford Level the Ouse-side barrow cemetery continues on islands along the northern margins of Sutton and extending up to Chatteris, though these consist of only round barrows (Fig. 1.1; Hall 1996, 54, 58, fig. 29).

As was indicated through the dyke-section exposure of one of the Hermitage Farm barrows in 1980 (Fig. 1.5; Hall *et al.* 1987, 175–7, fig. 114; 1996, pl. III), these barrows, though upstanding by as much as a metre, are sealed by peat. Consequently, their crowns suffer plough-damage. This is not the case in Over up along the river to the southwest where the Ouse-side barrow cemetery continues (Hall 1996, 147–9, fig. 83). While the northern Over barrow group, Sites 2 and 3 (four round barrows) are also plough-denuded, those in the south of the parish are sealed by alluvium. Over Site 5 denotes a tight cluster of five round barrows (these have been geophysical surveyed, which also shows a Bronze Age field system 'boxing' around them; see below and Evans & Knight 2000, fig. 9.9); a single barrow outlies the eastern side of this group. Just to the north at Site 4 two barrows were identified in the course of the Fenland Survey and another has since been identified on their western side. Although sealed by alluvium, this inundation is of Roman date and the excavation of the westernmost barrow of the Site 5 group has shown no evidence of contemporary waterlogging. Nevertheless their prominent mounds are still well preserved and, based on visual impact alone, they must be classed amongst the most important monument groups in the region. Equally, the Over/Haddenham/Sutton barrow fields must collectively be counted amongst the major discoveries of the Fenland Survey as a whole with only the barrow cemetery at Borough Fen/Thorney in any way comparable (Hall & Coles 1994, fig. 48).

Within the core of the Haddenham project study area only one 'early' scatter site of major significance was identified during the Fenland Survey, Haddenham Site 8 (*Cracknell Farm*, see below), and its investigation is reported in Chapter 4. Lying *c.* 600 m north of the causewayed enclosure, at this locale Hall recovered both Mesolithic and Early Neolithic flints, including a flake from a polished axe (Hall 1996, 61 & 64). Although falling just outside the Haddenham project area proper, given its dating Hall's Over Site 1 is also of importance for the project's results, especially the Foulmire Fen investigations. This lies at the southern end of a markedly raised sand ridge running parallel with the Ouse (Hall 1996, 147, fig.

83). In 1980 both Mesolithic and Iron Age material was recovered from the locale, and Godwin first reported its Mesolithic component in 1938 (Roe 1968 refers to Palaeolithic finds from the location; Hall 1996, 147); this site has recently been tested in the course of quarry-related fieldwork (Evans & Webley 2003). In a similar manner, it is equally noteworthy that Hall discovered two Neolithic scatters (with distinct Mesolithic components) on small islands in the Sutton 'Meadlands' west of the Ouse palaeochannel and the Bedford Level (1996, 54, fig. 29; see also the adjacent Mesolithic scatter U1).

While only relevant for the area's later prehistory and therefore featuring in the second volume's discussions, the proximity of Belsar's Hill 3 km to the southeast of the Delphs should not be overlooked. This univallate 'ringwork' fort, of probable later Iron Age attribution, is located at the Willingham fen-edge and commands the Aldreth Causeway, the shortest route from the 'mainland' to the Isle of Ely. Although, as with the fort, the causeway has distinct late Saxon associations, like the Stuntney crossing on the east side of Ely (Lethbridge 1935) it may well have later Bronze Age or Iron Age origins.

## A fieldwork chronicle

Wilson's extraordinary 1976 aerial photograph of the Upper Delphs (Fig. 1.6) not only well conveys the level plain-like topography of the Haddenham fens, but also attests to

**A**

**B**

**Figure 1.5.** *The Barrow Cemetery: A) Hermitage Farm (1980), looking north with the mound of the middle barrow of the HAD 3 group exposed in a recently cleaned dike section (photograph D. Hall; see Volume 2, Chapter 2); B) the southern Over barrow group as indicated by distinct circles upper right (2003).*

the *fabric* of its early land use. Beyond the line of the causewayed enclosure arcing across the mid-field (with a distinct rectangular enclosure within its interior), the terrace rise is dotted with both sub-square and circular compounds, and even a 'circle-in-a-square' (far left), with the dark patchwork swathe in the middle/upper left marking nineteenth-century quarries. Few of these have any upstanding earthwork imprint and it is only from an aerial perspective that any sense of land-use palimpsest or sequence emerges from the strict grid-iron of the area's present-day fields.

The original focus of the fieldwork was to be the causewayed enclosure. With the Fenland Survey-discovered barrow field looming in the background, it was always the intention to explore the Neolithic enclosure's broader terrace setting. Owing, however, to pragmatic constrains (i.e. funding) and the enclosure's somewhat disappointing initial results, the lure of 'context' proved great. This first led us to other sites on the Upper Delphs themselves and, subsequently, to the Ouse-side terraces. Such are vexed paths of research orientation; the outcome of this was that the

**Figure 1.6.** *The Upper Delphs Terrace. Wilson's 1976 aerial photograph looking north/northwest with the line of the Old West River in the lower foreground and with Cracknell Farm in the upper right background. A) The causewayed enclosure; B) HAD VIII Bronze Age enclosure; C–E) HAD V & VI 'paired' Iron Age compounds with contemporary field system and circular stock enclosure left (HAD VII & X); F) Snow's Farm 'circle-in-the-square' round barrow and Romano-British shrine complex (HAD III) with the HAD IV Iron Age enclosure right; G) area of strip quarries truncating the 'half-circle' of the HAD IX enclosure; H) a 'possible'-only cropmark enclosure to the north of the main study area, an ?ovate rectangle. Note the Upper Delphs terrace (as 'island') edge as marked by the dark peats in the extreme left mid-field immediately west of G (CUCAP BYT 1).*

project's focus broadened to encompass long-term wetland-use and 'place' history, and the cognitive implications of environmental change.

Given the project's immediate background in 'Fenland research', the potential of the area was very much cast in terms of its wetland context. Yet this itself is not without an element of irony. As reflected in the very 'monumentality' of Haddenham's archaeology, the Fenland Survey largely failed to identify wetland-specific sites and, generally, what was discovered were 'upland-type' sites only subsequently buried by peats. Although to some extent a product of the limits to which we could practically survey in depth, it is telling of the character of the area's archaeology that it is only in Volume 2 that the establishment of 'marshland communities' becomes a significant theme.

The motivation to undertake the project in part stemmed from a long-term legacy of the University of Cambridge's fieldwork in the region (e.g. Clark's excavations at Peacock's Farm, Hurst Fen and the Car Dyke at Bullock's Haste). This was furthered by John Coles whose Somerset Levels investigations spurred the Fenland Surveys, in which he played a pivotal role. Nor, moreover, should David Clarke's legacy be ignored. Having earlier published his Glastonbury model (1972), which cited local work by John Alexander (Arbury Camp: see Evans & Knight 2002), with Alexander in 1975 he began to excavate the causewayed enclosure at Great Wilbraham. (Upon Clarke's death, Ian Kinnes co-directed the final two seasons; Clarke's influence is also apparent in C. Tilley's 1979 study of post-glacial communities in the region.)

The Haddenham excavations commenced in 1981 and continued until 1987. Although with funding by English Heritage, it was originally undertaken as an annual University training excavation. Under the supervision of experienced archaeologists, the fieldwork involved 25–40 students for four to six weeks in summers between harvest and sowing. The project continued solely on this basis until 1984, when it was augmented by a Manpower Services Commission project which permitted the long-term detailed excavation of an extraordinarily well-preserved Iron Age enclosure (HAD V). Having a more permanent staff for the next two years allowed for further testing and sample investigations of the Upper Delphs environs (test pitting, trial trenching and dyke survey). This included work on the Foulmire terrace to the north, where a deeply buried Mesolithic site was discovered in the course of dyke survey. The site lies on the edge of the terrace on which the long barrow had been discovered and subsequent trial investigations of the latter's mound revealed that its timber mortuary structure survived. Given the rarity (and fragility) of this finding, English Heritage duly sponsored a major campaign of excavation in 1986–7.

Under the umbrella of the University's investigations, Workers Educational Association (WEA) training excavations also occurred in the vicinity; south of the Old West River at Cut Bridge Farm (A. Herne, Director) and to the east at Queensholme (P. Middleton & D. Trump, Directors). Summaries of these are included in Volume 2.

Drawing together these many strands, a project 'chronology' can be assembled (Figs. 1.2 & 1.7):

| | The Delphs | Environs |
|---|---|---|
| **1981** | Excavation of the north circuit of the Causewayed Enclosure (**HAD I**); test pitting programme | |
| **1982** | Excavation of the east circuit of the Causewayed Enclosure (**HAD I**) and Roman enclosure (**HAD II**); test-pitting programme | |
| **1983** | Excavation of the *Snow's Farm* Barrow and Roman Shrine (**HAD III**), and the adjacent Iron Age Enclosure (**HAD IV**) | Test pitting across *Hermitage Farm* terrace |
| **1984** | Excavation of the southwest Causewayed Enclosure (**HAD I**); excavation of the Iron Age farmstead on southeast margin of terrace (**HAD V**; also an associated **HAD XI** Roman enclosure) | Dyke survey; excavation of *Foulmire Fen* terrace-edge (Mesolithic–Bronze Age); testing of the *Cut Bridge Farm*, Willingham enclosure |
| **1985** | Continuous excavation throughout most of year on the **HAD V** enclosure | Initial testing of the *Foulmire Fen* Long Barrow and terrace test pitting; investigation of the *Hermitage Farm* Round Barrow; *Queensholme*, Willingham excavations |
| **1986** | Sampling of the **HAD VI** Iron Age enclosure; initial testing of the **HAD VIII** enclosure | Excavation of *Foulmire Fen* Long Barrow; *Queensholme*, Willingham excavations |
| **1987** | Trial excavation of the **HAD IX** Iron Age enclosure and **HAD VII** field system (and **HAD X** 'circle'); further exposure of **HAD VIII** (and the Causewayed Enclosure interior); *Church's Drove* test pitting and investigation of the *Cracknell Farm* scatter; excavation of the west circuit of the Causewayed Enclosure and additional trenching of 1981 area of excavation (**HAD I**) | Excavation of *Foulmire Fen* Long Barrow; *Queensholme*, Willingham excavations |

Beginning the project on the heels of the Fenland Survey, many of the major sites within the parish had already been assigned a discrete number which are those used in the publication of the survey results (Hall 1996). However, as a survey gazetteer its entries only essentially extend to finds scatters and upstanding monuments (e.g. barrows). Obviously this is inadequate to cover the many cropmark enclosures recognized in the course of the Haddenham project. It

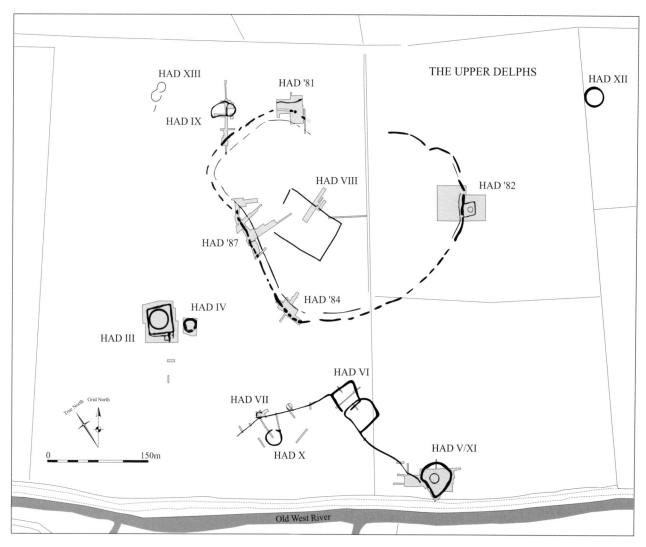

**Figure 1.7.** *The Upper Delphs Terrace: cropmarks and areas of investigation.*

not being our desire to manage a parish-wide system of reference, discrete compounds upon the Upper Delphs terrace were therefore assigned Roman numerals to distinguish them from the Fenland Survey entries. These progress from the causewayed enclosure, which is appropriately entitled HAD I. Including unexcavated cropmarks, they refer to (Fig. 1.7):

*Neolithic:* The Causewayed Enclosure (**HAD I**)

*Bronze Age:* The Snow's Farm round barrow (**HAD III**), the **HAD VIII** enclosure and the **HAD XII** ring-ditch (unexcavated)

*Iron Age:* The **HAD IV** and **IX** enclosures; the paired **HAD V** and **VI** compounds and associated field system (**HAD VII**; and the **HAD X** 'circle'); the unexcavated **HAD XIII** enclosure

*Romano-British:* The **HAD II** compound (and associated trackway that was further exposed in HAD VIII); the **HAD III** shrine complex and the **HAD XI** stock enclosure (overlying the earlier HAD V compound).

This system has its caveats. Firstly, it only applies to the Upper Delphs enclosures; sites investigated on neighbouring terraces are referred to by their Fenland Survey number and/or place-name titles. Secondly, on the Upper Delphs the project's numbering system only extended to discrete enclosures. Admittedly this suffers from normative categorization of what is a site and, as such, is biased to certain monument categories and later prehistoric site types. As a result, the flint scatter investigated along the northern margins of the Delphs terrace, Hall's Haddenham Site 8, has been entitled *Cracknell Farm* (thereby avoiding confusion with our HAD VIII enclosure) and, by this logic, a Beaker pit found amid the HAD VII field system features is not separately distinguished. Nevertheless, it has the advantage that if so entitled, little or no ambiguity relates to the site's integrity — a question must remain, for example, whether the HAD VII

Beaker pit is an isolated 'event' or a site. Of course, evidence of multiple occupation or usage occurred on a number of the Delphs sites and their subsidiary phases are outlined in the appropriate chronological summary sections. In the context of this volume the most pressing concern is the residual recovery of worked flint from the excavation of later enclosures and this material will be presented in Chapter 4.

As in the case of Cracknell Farm scatter, throughout this report and since the first years of the project, invented and 'old' names (variously extant and 'lost' farm titles) have been assigned to major sub-sites (e.g. the *Foulmire Fen* terrace or the *Snow's Farm* complex). To some degree this reflects a long-held disciplinary tradition that significant sites should be mnemonically entitled. (In this capacity only the remarkable HAD V Iron Age enclosure, continuously excavated over a period of two years, is not directly named. While its enumerative reference seems inadequate, in that case there was no obvious immediate place-name alternative.) Yet the appeal of such names also lies in their greater sense of landscape/place resonance, something that gazetteer numerical reference does not convey. This naming equally reflects a sensitivity to 'cultural' topography through long-term working in landscape and its cognitive processes; the scale of modern mapping (and most Fenland farms) seems inadequate to the experience of the landscape — the slight rise that eventually seems a significant landmark and warrants naming. In a landscape so radically transformed as the fens it would be naive to think that our cognitive geographies could have been 'theirs' in prehistory; rather it is just that working (in) the land brings with it its own sensitivity.

Though not intending to dwell in rural sentimentality, in this regard there is no escaping from what seems to be the resonance of nineteenth-century farm names — the 'lost' which until earlier in the last century dotted the fields of the Haddenham level. (The issue of earlier post-medieval land use and its 'new' naming of the drained lands will be dealt with by James in Volume 2, Chapter 9.) The point here is that the choice of pre-twentieth-century names and the appeal of nineteenth-century maps (with their greater density of landholdings) relates to a sense of a 'lived' landscape; one whose usage was more comparable to the past than today's blanket farms and prairie-like fields.

Issues concerning the naming of site-types and their categorization as part of the cognitive processes of excavation will be further considered within these volumes (see especially Volume 2, Chapter 7). Site entitlement and its relationship to place names also reflects upon the recognition (and status) of monuments in the

fen. The fact that most have only emerged to become upstanding from out of the peat over the course of the last two centuries is a phenomenon almost unique to the region's archaeology. What is interesting is that, though many have been apparent and locally known for decades prior to their discovery in the Fenland Survey, they had not been named. As much as anything this reflects upon the character of modern rural communities; farms are distinguished, but not monuments. Why should this be? For this does not just seem to be a twentieth-century phenomenon but also extends to the nineteenth. Sites which should have been noticeable through their finds density and spread of building materials through plough damage (e.g. the Langwood Farm/Chatteris 26 Roman complex: see Evans 2000b; 2003b), or the Wardy Hill Iron Age ringwork whose multiple circuits excavation demonstrated were upstanding in the eighteenth/nineteenth centuries (Evans 2000a; 2003a), were apparently not identified, or at least not named. This may tell of the general nature of the recognition of monuments and the character of post-medieval communities as the naming of a monument requires a degree of group consensus which is quite different than the personal entitlement of private property. If monuments are subtle, how are they to be collectively recognized? Perhaps it ultimately comes down to the motivation of a curious parish priest or minister with antiquarian leanings to give rise to local consensus (and *en masse* 'seeing'); Haddenham was evidently without such a figure (though see Volume 2 concerning Charles Bester's contribution).

**Situating fieldwork**

It is necessary to situate the Haddenham campaigns within their Fenland context and 'time'. Aside from work at Peacock's Farm/Shippea Hill, Hurst Fen, Fengate and the various *Fenland in Roman Times* studies, there had been few earlier investigations; excavations at Maxey, Etton and Flag Fen, and Stonea (and Cardiff's re-investigation of Shippea Hill) were all concurrently on-going. Since the mid/later 1980s there has been extensive excavation in the region. This has seen much fieldwork on the islands of Ely and Chatteris. In 1996 the County Field Unit undertook trial trenching on a 19 ha site in North Fen, Sutton on an island terrace beside the main Ouse palaeochannel. Locally sealed by Fen Clay and with evidence of earlier Neolithic occupation (Last 1997), the site's situation and archaeology has parallels with the Foulmire terrace to the south. However, apart from evaluation fieldwork anticipating the construction of an agricultural reservoir on the southeast end of the

**Figure 1.8.** *Life in woods: A) Bog oak taken from peat at Queen Adelaide Bridge, near Ely, in 1960; 21 m long, its unbranching bole (typical of the Fenland's buried basal 'forest') was radiocarbon dated to 3610–2900 cal. BC (4495±120 BP; Q-589; photograph by J. Slater, reproduced in Godwin 1978, pl. 14); B) 'The tree as dwelling', A. Rooker after S.H. Grimm 'A North West View of the Greendale Oak near Welbeck' in John Evelyn's Silva, 1664; C) The Mesolithic paddle from Tybrind Vig, Denmark, made of ash but in the shape of a lime leaf (of which canoes from the site were rendered): lime, of course, being a singularly 'special' tree as its leaves duplicate the silhouette of its crown (Andersen 1987); D) Kroeber's 'the tree of knowledge of good and evil — that is human culture' (1948, 26): unlike the 'tree of life' branches of knowledge converge and grow together, and not just divide apart; E) 1976 aerial photograph of storm-damaged plantation woodland at Laughton Forest, Lincs. (CUCAP BXC-82); F) Fenland 'buried forest' succession (Godwin 1978, after Skertchly 1877).*

A

B

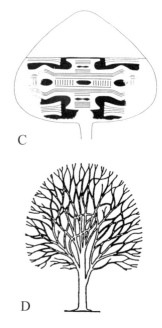

C

D

Delphs at Flat Bridge Farm in 1997 (see Volume 2, Chapter 6), since the project no excavation has occurred within the Haddenham 'level' proper (i.e. in the fen).

Directly arising from the Fenland Survey, the English Heritage-sponsored Fenland Management Project (FMP) of the early 1990s initiated a co-ordinated programme of research-driven fieldwork across the region (see Hall & Coles 1994 for overview). Within the southern Cambridgeshire fens this involved testing of a later Bronze Age settlement at Lingwood Farm, Cottenham (Evans 1999a) and also a Grooved Ware/Beaker-associated scatter at Stocking Drove Farm, Chatteris (Chatteris 37: Wait 2000); larger scale collection took place on major later Mesolithic, Neolithic and Bronze Age scatters at Honey Hill, Ramsey and Eye Hill Farm, Soham (Edmonds *et al.* 1999). Extensive sampling occurred on a massive Iron Age and Roman settlement complex extending over some 10 ha at Langwood Ridge, Chatteris; its latter phase included a major stone-footing building (only

the third known in the Fenland), which arguably was of administrative function and perhaps related to Stonea (Evans 2000b; 2003b). Of particular relevance for work reported in Volume 2 is the fact that as part of the FMP programme a later Iron Age ringwork was fully excavated on Wardy Hill, Coveney (Evans 1992; 1997a; 2003a). A defended settlement of some status (e.g. evidence of on-site metalworking and with a degree of 'elite' goods), the layout of, and assemblages associated with, its roundhouses provides a contextual measure for the Haddenham Iron Age sites. These investigations are all summarized in the FMP summary volume (Crowson *et al.* 2000; for other work in the Ely environs and along the fenward reaches of the

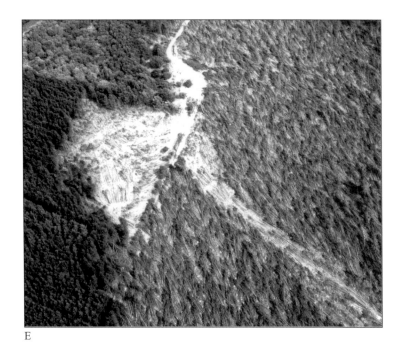

E

WOOD FEN, ELY                    1874

F

the 300 ha of the Ouse floodplain thus far investigated (much of it at and above this Ordnance Datum littoral), little post-Early Iron Age settlement has been found.

Amongst the main discoveries to date at Barleycroft/Over have been extensive and unequivocal evidence of Neolithic occupation. This takes a range of forms, from the 'Early' utilization of tree-throws and a Mildenhall ware-associated pit cluster, to much more robust later Neolithic Grooved Ware pit complexes. Whereas only slight stakehole structures have been recovered in association with the earlier Mildenhall occupation, more substantial post-built 'building' plans have been found in the context of the latter. Of particular relevance to this volume, more detailed presentation of these sites and other early 'clusters' will be made below (Chapter 4).

Aside from these findings, the most singular important discovery has been the scale of Bronze Age land allotment, which was not found to any extent on the Delphs (see Volume 2, Chapter 3). Co-axial field systems have been traced across more than 100 ha on both the Over and Barleycroft sides of the river; an associated settlement swathe was excavated at Barleycroft Farm in 1995, including paired round houses and, quite remarkably, a longhouse (Evans & Knight 2000; 2001). The field system has been found to have had its main axes laid out in relationship to earlier Bronze Age ring-ditches. A pair of these were excavated in their entirety in 1996; one, an elaborated double-ring monument, was found to have a central cremation pit-pyre and a cremation cemetery arranged around its southern sector (Evans & Knight 2000). Another smaller cremation cluster was also excavated within the axes of the field system itself. The cremation practices and particularly the double ring-ditch complex have implications for two round barrows investigated in the course of the Haddenham project, and will be more fully considered within Volume 2 (Chapter 2).

Although occurring a decade later, the limited incorporation of these results is appropriate for a number of reasons. Not least is that the work in these

Cam and Ouse see *Fenland Research* 7–9 and annual fieldwork summaries in *Proceedings of the Cambridge Antiquarian Society*).

More immediately relevant and extensively cited herein will be the Cambridge Archaeological Unit's (CAU) investigations in nearby Hanson quarries: at Barleycroft Farm/Over on either side of the Ouse upstream from Earith, and Colne Fen north of Earith (Fig. 1.1). Seeing two major Romano-British settlement complexes (one possibly qualifying as a small town), the latter is particularly relevant for its dense Middle/later Iron Age occupation. Straddling the wet/dry divide at 2–2.50 m OD, in terms of its fen-edge situation and distributions the Colne terrace is in many ways analogous with the Upper Delphs (see Volume 2, Chapter 6). To date, this pattern markedly contrasts with the Barleycroft/Over investigations where across

quarries has been conceived of as a direct continuation of the Haddenham investigations and involves a similar emphasis on buried soil distributions. Potentially a grand-scale 'hermeneutic' (see below), if all goes accordingly, when the fieldwork concludes at Over in some twenty years time the progress of the quarry will return the work to the southern bank of the Old West opposite the Upper Delphs causewayed enclosure. In effect going full circle in the search for context, collectively these will be the largest in-depth investigations of a buried/wet landscape in Britain.

The inclusion of work in the adjacent quarries is also important by way of contrast. Whilst for its time the Haddenham project involved large-scale excavation, it was curtailed by funding and a need to produce 'solid' results each year in order to ensure further resources. A benefit of developer funding is that it has encouraged in-depth landscape study on an appropriate scale, and it is only through work at such a breadth and sample regularity that 'measurable' negative evidence can be forthcoming. In the course of the work at Haddenham we could not dream of undertaking trial trenching to the extent that the subsequent quarry investigations have allowed. Though justified within the constraints of the time, the early work now seems site-/monument-focused and there was not the scope to tease out and do justice to more 'ubiquitous' site types.

It is largely for the sake of 'domestic balance' that it is essential that the up-river investigations are primarily cited as it provides a context of local Neolithic and Bronze Age settlement. That such sites were not recovered in the course of the Haddenham investigations does not constitute negative evidence (the definite *non-occurrence* of settlement of any one period) and, given these practical limitations, the project results can only be considered in terms of their positive evidence. Of course, in hindsight, there is much which one would wish could be redone at Haddenham, and the programme's shortcomings seem glaringly obvious. Nevertheless, for their time the methodologies employed at Haddenham were innovative, especially regarding the encounter with buried soils, and techniques were developed that only a decade later began to be more extensively employed (e.g. see Evans 2000c for the FMP methodologies). Moreover, despite being largely funded 'on a wing and a prayer', aspects of the Haddenham Project's results still remain unique — the remarkable timber remains within the long barrow (Chapter 3 below) and, featuring in Volume 2, the extraordinary preservation of the HAD V Iron Age enclosure (and its wetland-specific faunal assemblage) and the depositional patterning within the Snow's Farm Romano-British shrine. Over

the intervening 10–20 years nothing has been found in the region which rivals these.

## The Neolithic: life in woods

'Grand-scale' issues are dealt with in these volumes, and we can only anticipate more nuanced readings of the region's settlement sequence. Yet the project's scope (and the text) does not just arise from the formative situation of the fieldwork itself, but also the character of the area's archaeology. The status of the Ouse, the great Fenland river draining the eastern watershed of south-central England, frames the investigations. Against this must be set the causewayed enclosure which, extending over 8.5 ha, is one of the largest enclosures of its type in Britain. Finally, to this must be added the scale of the area's barrow cemeteries and, particularly, the occurrence of long barrows.

This volume essentially concerns the excavation of two main sites, the Upper Delphs causewayed enclosure and the long barrow in Foulmire Fen. The text itself revolves around two structuring metaphors. First, as expressed in Figure 1.3 there is *the river*, snaking through the landscape and both volumes as an ever-changing long-term 'constant'. At a pragmatic level it resonates in the idea of rivers as landscape corridors and, too, the degree to which the archaeology of any period at Haddenham (and other comparable fen-edge locations) is but a lowland expression of broader river valley distributions as opposed to the Fenland *per se* (see e.g. Field 1974). Secondly, and specific to this volume alone, there is a concern with *life in woods* and a woodland-specific archaeology (Fig. 1.8). Representative of the Early Neolithic 'condition' or habitat in general, this is appropriate as causewayed enclosures have themselves been considered as variously defining, mimicking and/or reinforcing forest clearings, with their concentric perimeters ranking a gradation between culture/nature (Evans 1988c; Whittle *et al.* 1999; Brown 2000; see also Austin 2000 concerning the 'architecture' of woodland). Equally, the surviving timber mortuary chamber of the Foulmire Fen long barrow — effectively representing burial within the bulk or heart of a trunk — attests to the symbolic attributes of trees. (Such an identification with woods has also been further explored in relationship to the contemporary usage of tree-throw bowls within the region: Evans *et al.* 1999.)

The experience of lowland forest life, where the horizon is rarely visible, markedly contrasts with the rolling downland landscapes of Wessex's antiquarians or the open tundra and deserts familiar through ethnography. It is a challenging phenomenology (cf. Tilley 1994); the perspective-horizon roots so much of our romantic empathy with landscape, wherein time and experience are identified with distance. Yet only punctuated with trails and scattered clearances, the 'wall of wood' is quite a different matter, and forests evoke primordial dread and disorientation (see Bloch 1995, 65–7 & 75 concerning 'clarity', deforestation and views; see also e.g. Schama 1995). Within western cognitive frameworks individual tree species may be rich in symbolism (e.g. 'hearts of oak') and be employed as metaphor of development/growth and order ('trees of knowledge'; Fig. 1.8.D; see e.g. Fernandez 1998), however collectively they have variously been identified with waste, chaos and the wild.

Living in woods, trees take on quite a different dimension; the forest is not a neutral environmental backdrop but, in effect, a crucial matrix of life (see e.g. Gell 1995). In their variability trees, like plants and animals, can be classified into hierarchical sets. However, they uniquely 'share life' with humans as they appreciably develop and age whilst remaining rooted, and thereby have the capacity to substitute for people. It is in this that their potential for symbolic identity and ritual transformation primarily lies (Bloch 1998; see Garthoff-Zwann 1987 for Dutch ethno-historical wood classifications; Porter 1969, 61 and Evans 1997b, note 8 similarly discuss Fenland wood associations; see also e.g. Coles 2001).

Despite awareness of the dating issues that arise when drawing any parallels with the Darion, Belgium enclosure (Keeley & Cahen 1989; see Bradley 1993b for discussion), Figure 1.9 is intended to visualize the interrelationship between Neolithic houses, long barrows and causewayed enclosures. Barrows are known close to enclosures; at Roughton, Norfolk they lie within 50 m, whereas at Maiden Castle the long mound was sited in and over (i.e. post-dating) the enclosure itself and a long barrow was similarly located within the causewayed outworks at Hambledon Hill. Generally, the dating of causewayed enclosures in Britain seems tight, being essentially an earlier Neolithic phenomenon (c. 3700–3300 cal. BC: Oswald *et al.* 2001,

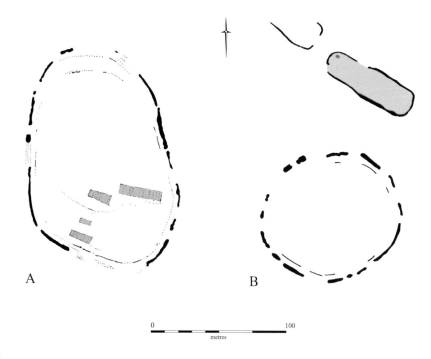

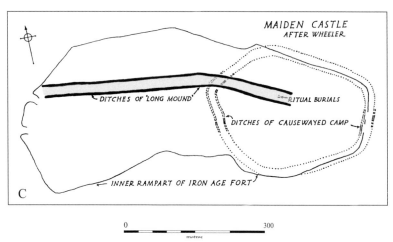

**Figure 1.9.** *'Proximities': Neolithic houses/long barrows and enclosures. A) Darion, Belgium (after Oswald* et al. *2001, fig. 5.5); B) Roughton, Norfolk (after Oswald* et al. *2001, 6.7); C) Maiden Castle (after Piggott 1954, fig. 3).*

2–3, fig. 1.2). The construction of long barrows, on the other hand, shows much greater longevity and clearly continued throughout the later Neolithic (see Kinnes 1992, tables 2.1.2 & 2.1.3 and 2.7.1 & 2.7.3). In the case of Haddenham the long barrow and causewayed enclosure are essentially contemporaneous. Although they lie at a distance of 3 km from each other, here it is presumed that they would have been related. This is further encouraged by the fact that at least one other long barrow is located on the Foulmire island/terrace and, otherwise, the nearest known

17

monuments of this type lie at distances of 15 and 23 km, respectively Swaffham Bulbeck to the southeast (Hall 1996, 112, fig. 57) and westwards up the Ouse at St Neots (Malim 2000; Wessex Archaeology 2001). In other words, by their spatial context the Delphs' enclosure and Foulmire barrows seem to represent a distinct monument grouping. The concurrence of the 'great' causewayed enclosure and these barrows is remarkable and, albeit at a very large scale, suggests that the area was a 'special' or specific locale.

Primarily dealing with 'first monuments', a different sense of context and explanatory framework pervades this volume than the second. Here we must be much more concerned with extra-regional parallels, both national and pan-Continental, whereas essentially covering post-Neolithic developments Volume 2 is much more regionally focused. On the one hand, this relates to the environmental setting of the project's fieldwork and the eventual establishment of marshland-specific communities: yet equally important is landscape 'build-up' and the recovery of historically comparable settlement densities (and sites). From at least the mid second millennium BC, there is simply sufficient regional context to provide a valid interpretative framework. This is not just a matter of landscape 'saturation', but also reflects that with the earlier Neolithic we must be much more concerned with *arrivals* and how ideas were transmitted, be it agriculture, pottery manufacture or the form of monuments.

Although the division of the Neolithic and subsequent sequences between the two volumes is in many ways arbitrary (even if not entirely absolute), it nevertheless is valid in terms of their respective emphasis. Aside from the earlier Bronze Age barrows, a key issue of the second volume is the place of ritual (and any collective inter-group gathering) in relationship to a much more robust domestic record and, by way of contrast, this issue is further realized in the terrace's clearly delineated (and isolated) Romano-British shrine (HAD III). Meanwhile, belying the ready imprint of the Darion longhouses (and reflective of much of the record of the British Neolithic in general), in this volume it is the opposite that poses the primary challenge — the distinction of occupation *per se* to counterbalance the period's hugely evident monuments. Arguably involving modes of residential mobility (and only slight occupation traces), Neolithic settlement is, in effect, *the problem*. This is an issue that runs throughout this volume and is considered at length in Chapters 4 and 5.

## Structure and text

Akin to 'the river', the route by which we encounter the past in the course of sustained landscape research can never be single-stranded or uncomplicated. Variously reflective of personal and academic influences, and the blind alleyways of inspiration, metaphor and evidence, its path is not straightforward. Our texts need to reflect the many routes of this process and, *de facto*, will be multifaceted and effectively meander towards their themes.

The passages that introduce this volume well announce crucial strands of its structure. Yet read them more closely and it becomes clear that what these passages share is a relationship to other sources; Borges discusses the river in relationship to Heraclitus's 'Fragment', whereas Ingold, however much drawing upon the generic tree associations, writes of the pivotal tree in Bruegel's 1565 painting. This epitomises the condition of our studies; a webwork of texts and images stand between us and things — a Foucaultian sense that we are 'beyond origins' and can no longer experience the world afresh but through genealogies of knowledge. This does not, of course, just relate to natural phenomena, but disciplines themselves. In archaeology we cannot see any pristinely 'new past', but only conceive of it through a framework of previous researches, excavations and dominant interpretations. It is in reference to the sense of this wider and/or underlying context that 'analogical commentaries' are inset within these volumes. Drawn from diverse sources (and influences), their intention is to provide resonance beyond the local; their relevance in this capacity being all the greater in Volume 2.

Equally, developing upon Ingold's lead (and a long-standing interest in the interface of art/archaeology and graphic 'languages': e.g. Evans 2003a), the text is punctuated by references to three of Bruegel's paintings. In the final chapter these are drawn together and assembled as if a triptych, which provides a commentary upon the Neolithic and its monuments.

Otherwise this volume involves a number of dynamics concerning the provision of context. These effectively ripple or radiate in relationship to the causewayed enclosure, whose excavation very much lay at the core of the project. Firstly, there is the sequence of work around the enclosure's circuit, which is here considered as an expression of a hermeneutic circle (see Hodder 1992b). Secondly, there is the causewayed enclosure's interrelationship with the long barrow in Foulmire Fen. Despite the fact that the latter is presented first, its excavation was very much framed in relation to the enclosure — a sense of reaching outwards for context. The third dynamic did not actually occur during the Haddenham excavations, but rather has arisen subsequently — a linkage to the Barleycroft/Over quarry investigations — which, as outlined, provides a measure of contemporary

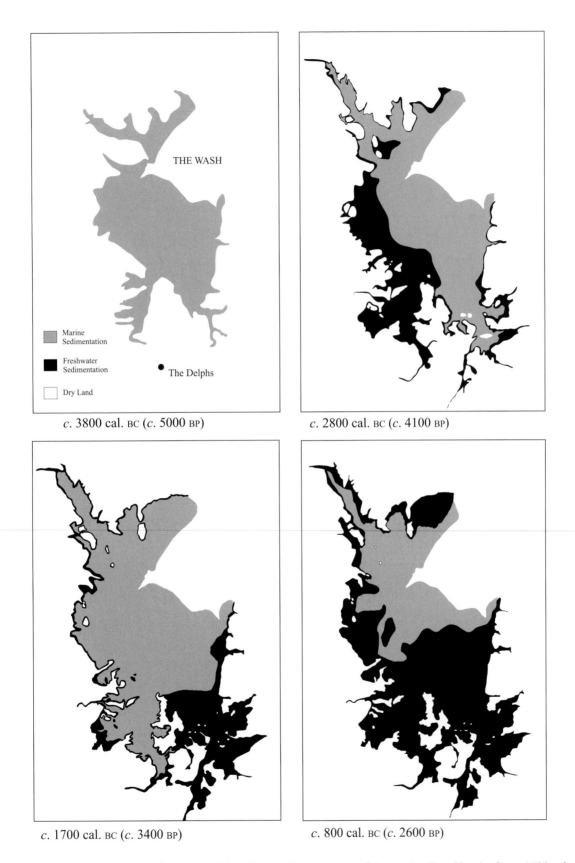

*c.* 3800 cal. BC (*c.* 5000 BP)

*c.* 2800 cal. BC (*c.* 4100 BP)

*c.* 1700 cal. BC (*c.* 3400 BP)

*c.* 800 cal. BC (*c.* 2600 BP)

**Figure 2.2.** *Fenland environmental sequence. Note the maximum extent of the marine Fen Clay in the* c. 1700 cal. BC *map (*c. 3400 BP; *after Waller 1994).*

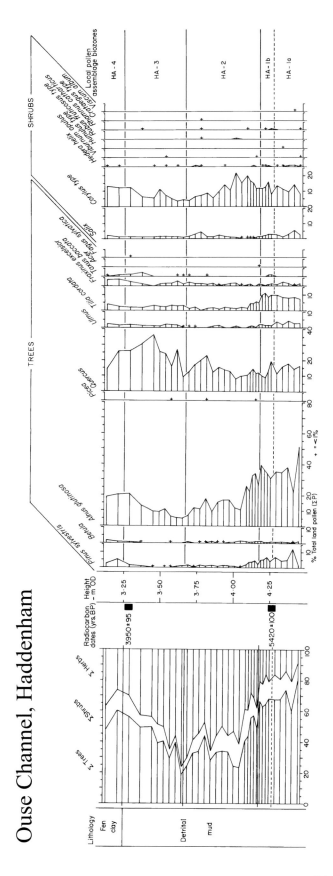

## Ouse Channel, Haddenham

**Figure 2.3.** *Pollen sequence from the Ouse channel.*

next zone (–4.94 to –4.87 m OD) again sees non-arboreal pollen dominant, but pollen occurrence is highly erratic. Dates of 10,650±180 BP (Q-2616) and 8250±120 BP (Q-2815) from the lower and upper boundaries of this zone confirm that the basal assemblage is of late glacial age and support evidence for a hiatus during this zone. The next zone (–4.87 to –4.19 m OD) includes and is equivalent to the HA 1 zone in Peglar's report below which covers the period of immediate interest to the area's archaeology.

It warrants mention in relationship to Zone HA 2, with its decrease in lime and increase in oak, ash and hazel, that the use of immense planks of oak to make the mortuary structure in the long barrow shows that at least some of the oak trees within the dryland 'wildwood' were very different from oaks found in present-day woodland. They were tall and straight with little branching, a trait found in trees growing in quite dense forests. These characteristics are seen in many of the preserved 'bog oaks' retrieved from the Fenland peats. Willis (1961) illustrates a giant oak taken from the 'lower peat' near Ely, with an unbranched straight bole 67 feet in length, which is radiocarbon dated to approximately 3610–2900 cal. BC (4495±120 BP; Q-589). Equally, from the increase in tree pollen in HA 3 suggesting woodland regrowth (but without an accompanying resurgence of *Tilia* values), is it possible that in the environs of Haddenham Neolithic communities had a permanent effect on the forest, altering its overall composition? It is more probable that the rising watertable made some of the areas previously occupied by lime unsuitable for its growth.

### The Ouse Channel Flandrian sequence
by S. PEGLAR

Four local pollen assemblage zones have been defined, prefixed HA (see the percentage pollen diagram in Figs. 2.3 & 2.4). The lowest is further subdivided into two subzones, HA 1a and HA 1b.

*HA 1 (–4.45 to –4.18 m OD) Alnus, Quercus, Tilia, Corylus-*type: Arboreal pollen dominates this zone averaging 70% of total land pollen (TLP) throughout, of which 40% is *Alnus* (alder), 15% *Quercus* (oak), 8% *Tilia* (lime) with some *Pinus* (pine), *Ulmus* (elm), *Fraxinus* (ash), and *Betula* (birch). *Corylus*-type (hazel) attains average values of 12% throughout the zone with some *Salix* (willow). Gramineae (grasses) and Cyperaceae (sedges) are present at *c.* 7% each. Felicales undifferentiated (ferns), *Pteridium* (bracken) and *Polypodium* (polypody) are consistently present with total values of *c.* 10%.

Although *Ulmus* achieves only small values during this zone there is a distinct fall from *c.* 4% to *c.* 2% from –4.29 to –4.25 m OD and this delimits subzone HA 1b from HA 1a. There is also a slight increase in the percentage of total herbs, and *Plantago lanceolata* (ribwort plantain), Compositae and *Solidago*-type (composites) are consistently present in HA 1b.

Dominated by arboreal pollen, the pollen assemblage is indicative of a well-forested environment. Various types of woodland may be envisaged. That closest to the river channel was probably wet alder fen carr with willow and other shrubs including *Viburnum opulus* (guelder rose), *Rhamnus catharticus* (buckthorn) and possibly *Humulus* (hops), and herbs such as *Urtica* (nettle), *Filipendula* (meadowsweet) and *Angelica*-type (umbellifers) as well as grasses and sedges. The ground flora also included Felicales undiff., and *Polypodium* which may also have been growing epiphytically on the alder trees.

Moving away from the river channel, the woodland would have changed as the ground became drier with *Quercus* (oak) and *Fraxinus* (ash) increasing until on the gravel terraces and higher ground the woodland was probably dominated by *Tilia* (lime) as elsewhere in southeastern England, with *Quercus*, *Fraxinus* and a little *Ulmus*. *Corylus* may have been growing as an understorey in more open parts of the forest with *Hedera* (ivy) and *Polypodium* growing on the trees.

When interpreting a pollen assemblage from a relative percentage diagram, a certain percentage of a taxon does not indicate the same percentage of that taxon in the vegetation. Each taxon produces different amounts of pollen and has different dispersal efficiencies. It is recognized that *Tilia* and *Fraxinus* are low pollen producers and poor dispersers, and quite small percentages of their pollen are indicative of high proportions of these taxa within the vegetation. Conversely, *Pinus* is a very high pollen producer and has an extremely efficient dispersal mechanism. Thus although *Pinus* has average values of *c.* 7% during this zone, this is not indicative of pine being present locally and is probably a reflection of grains being blown in from far afield.

Various attempts have been made to produce so-called 'correction factors' by which to multiply or divide pollen percentages to give actual percentages in the vegetation of a particular taxon. Using the correction factors obtained by Andersen (1970), the rough percentages of different tree taxa within the dryland wood, that is the woodland on the terraces and higher ground, before any interference by Neolithic activity, were as follows (level –4.29 m):

|  |  | **Correction factor used** |
|---|---|---|
| Lime | 68% | × 2 |
| Hazel | 12% | w 4 |
| Oak | 10% | w 4 |
| Elm | 6% | w 2 |
| Ash | 4% | × 2 |

It must be emphasized that these correction factors can be taken as only very rough guides to the composition of the woodland, nevertheless the importance of lime is shown.

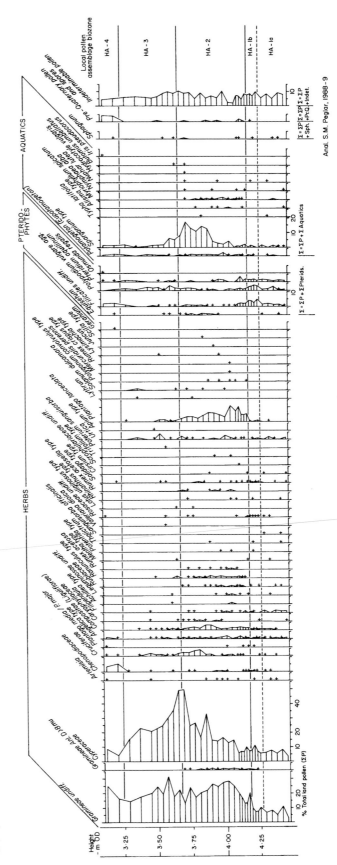

**Figure 2.4.** *Pollen sequence from the Ouse channel.*

*HA 2* (–4.18 to –3.67 m OD) Gramineae, Cyperaceae, *Corylus*-type, *Plantago lanceolata*: Arboreal pollen values drop at the base of this zone to only 24% TLP at –4.01 m, and although they increase slightly above this they average only 35% — half the average in HA 1. *Tilia* drops sharply at the base of the zone from 10% at the top of HA 1, and averages <2% throughout most of the zone. *Ulmus* is only occasionally present. The pollen assemblage is dominated by herbaceous taxa. Gramineae rises to an average 20% and there is a sharp increase in *Plantago lanceolata* to 12% at –4.05 m, and many other herbs are present. Cyperaceae and *Sparganium*-type increase after –3.93 m OD.

The decrease in *Tilia* and other trees seen at the base of this zone together with the appearance and increase of many ruderals (particularly *Plantago lanceolata*), composites, Cruciferae (crucifers), *Ranunculus*-type (buttercups), *Rumex acetosa* (sorrel), *Rumex acetosella*-type (including sheep's sorrel), Rubiaceae (bedstraws), *Polygonum convolvulus* type (including bindweed, knotgrass), Chenopodiaceae (including goosefoots), Caryophyllaceae (including chickweeds and stitchworts) and *Urtica* (nettles), may be equated with a clearance phase (Turner 1962; Behre 1981). This is further supported by the almost continuous occurrence of large pored Gramineae grains within this zone some of which, due to their overall size, are definitely cereals and include two grains which may be referred to *Hordeum* (barley). Charcoal is present within these sediments including large quantities at –4.11 m.

Using the same 'correction factors' (Andersen 1970) on the tree percentages to convert to vegetation percentages after the elm and lime declines (as in level –3.89 m), the following results were obtained:

| | |
|---|---|
| Oak | 44% |
| Hazel | 27% |
| Lime | 16% |
| Ash | 7% |
| Elm | 6% |

**Figure 2.5.** *The Foulmire barrow field, looking north, with HAD 6 long barrow in left foreground (A) and HAD 7 round barrows right (B); C) suspect 'teardrop' mound; D) Sutton 11 long barrow. (Photograph R. Palmer.)*

The drop in *Ulmus* which defines the HA 1a/HA 1b boundary together with an increase in herbaceous pollen may be correlated with the 'elm decline', and has been radiocarbon dated here at 4470–4000 cal. BC (5420±100 BP; Q-2814). This age ties in well with other dated Fenland sites and it is probable that a number of factors (e.g. climate, human impact, disease) were responsible.

It is tempting to envisage some clearance near this site at this time with the first appearance of grass grains with an annulus diameter of >85 (as cereal-type pollen is defined by Andersen 1979), but this category does include some native species of grasses, particularly *Glyceria* spp. which grow in waterlogged situations. Other herbs which may be indicative of open and/or disturbed ground and therefore may be associated with clearance and agriculture, so-called 'anthropogenic indicators', also have a continuous presence in HA 1b (e.g. Compositae (Liguliflorae), *Solidago*-type and *Plantago lanceolata*).

Comparing these with the percentage composition found in the wildwood (see above) it is obvious that the greatest effect was a decrease in lime, with corresponding increases in oak, ash and hazel.

The increase in *Corylus*-type after the 'lime decline' may be indicative of increased flowering of the hazel due to opening of the forest canopy where it had been growing in the understorey, or expansion of hazel into previously cleared areas. Such a '*Tilia* decline' associated with human activity has previously been correlated with the Bronze Age and later (Turner 1962). This Neolithic association is extremely interesting; prehistoric groups are known to have used *Tilia* in different ways, including for timber, leaf fodder and bast fibre.

Towards the top of zone HA 2 an increase in Cyperaceae and *Sparganium*-type, a decrease in *Alnus* and the occurrence of seeds of *Juncus* (rushes), *Carex* (sedges) and *Typha* (bulrush) suggest the replacement in the channel environs of fen carr woodland by sedge fen and reed swamp. This could be indicative of a rise in groundwater level due either to external factors or increased runoff associated with clearance.

*HA 3 (–3.67 to –3.25 m OD) Quercus, Cyperaceae, Gramineae:* This zone sees an increase in arboreal and shrub pollen with a complementary decrease in herbs. *Quercus* accounts for *c.* 30% of the assemblage and *Tilia* 3–4%. *Ulmus* is consistently present at <2%. *Alnus* and *Corylus* type percentages increase towards the top. Of the herbs, Gramineae and Cyperaceae are most prominent at *c.* 17% and 21% respectively. Only two grains of *Plantago lanceolata* are found during this zone and there is a decreased range of other herbs present. *Sparganium* type is much reduced from the high values at the top of HA 2.

The increase in tree pollen and concurrent decrease in herbaceous pollen throughout this zone suggests a regrowth of woodland and a diminution of cleared areas. Although *Tilia* values do increase slightly, they do not attain the values of zone HA 1. It seems that *Quercus* now dominated the woodland with *Fraxinus* and *Tilia*, and with *Taxus* (yew) and *Corylus* as an understorey.

*HA 4 (–3.25 to –3.13 m OD) Gramineae, Chenopodiaceae, Alnus:* The occurrence of Chenopodiaceae at *c.* 4% and pre-Quaternary micro fossils at *c.* 4% is characteristic of this zone. Except for Gramineae (at 18%) there is a paucity of other herbs. *Alnus* and *Quercus* are the main trees with 4% *Fraxinus*. *Corylus* type also increases to *c.* 12%.

An abrupt change in sedimentation occurs at the base of this zone when the detrital muds are overlain by the Fen Clay. A radiocarbon date of 2870–2140 cal. BC (3950±95 BP; Q-2813) was obtained from this transition. This agrees well with other dates from the southern Fenland. The increase in Chenopodiaceae, many of whose genera grow in brackish environs, and in pre-Quaternary microfossils, reworked from ancient sediments, confirm the presence of a marine incursion due to a rise in sea level. The disappearance of the pollen of freshwater aquatic taxa (e.g. *Potamogeton, Alisma*-type, *Myriophyllum spicatum, Nymphaea* and *Nuphar*) supports this view.

*Assessing land: a delta landscape*

In Peglar's account it becomes difficult to evaluate the evidence of the rising watertable in HA 2 and any potential waterlogging of the terraces. There are matters of absolute height to contend with. Even if we accept the greater collapse of organic material within the cored channel, there is more than a 3 m differentiation between the level in the roddon's deposits and the terrace's surface. The core moreover details the river's sequence and not that of the fen generally. In reference to Waller's Fenland map sequence (Fig. 2.2), beyond the establishment

**Figure 2.6.** *The Foulmire barrow field (north). A) looking south to Sutton 11 long barrow, re-oriented to north and enlarged within inset (B); C) suspect 'teardrop' mound (detail inset below); D) ring-ditch. (Photographs R. Palmer.)*

of the immediate floodplain corridor of the Ouse palaeochannel there is no evidence at this time for the onset of general fen marshland conditions in the southern fen. What becomes equally relevant is the character of the underlying sub-strata. Where exposed the low clay 'bedrock' would have always been poorly drained. As has been detailed in the course of the Barleycroft/Over investigations, a factor at least partly determining the 'vertical' limits of settlement is the depth to which well-drained terrace 'mineral'

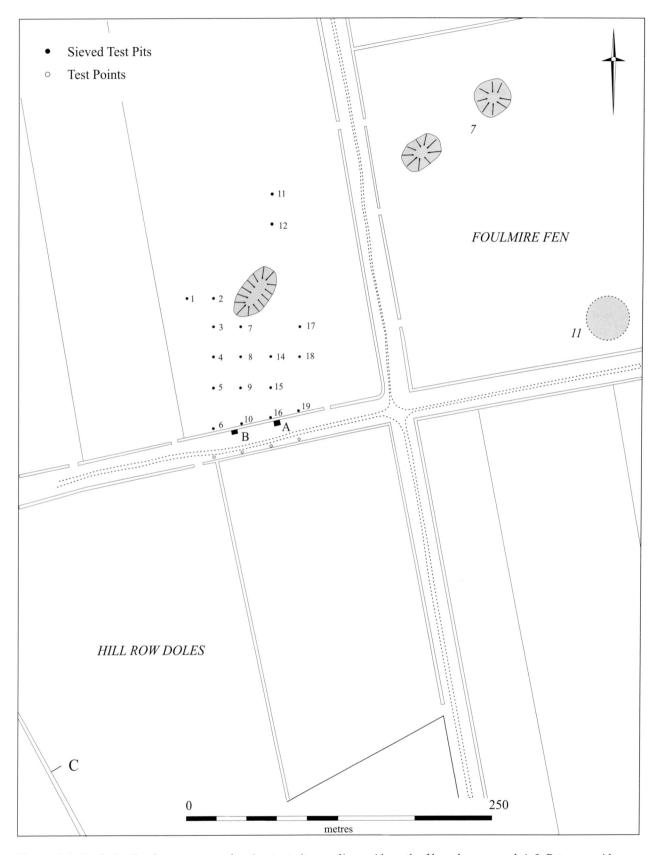

**Figure 2.9.** *Foulmire Fen barrow group showing test pit sampling grid south of long barrow and A & B terrace-side cuttings; C indicates Hill Row Doles mound.*

**Figure 2.10.** *Hill Row Doles dyke survey (1984); note the exposure of the flattened mound in the cleaned eastern ditch side and its shallow flanking 'hollows'. Within the lower profile of the latter, and extending south beyond the southern edge of the gravel terrace, the 'line' of the Fen Clay beds is visible. (Photograph C. Evans.)*

upper profile and the lower flanks of the mound are sealed by Fen Clay. Waller has detailed the environmental sequence through the ditch fill and the overlying deposits. Particularly interesting, and correlating to the Ouse Roddon results (and Cloutman's work at Foulmire, see below), is the high representation of *Tilia* in the peat which accumulated above the ditch fill *per se* before the marine flooding. This is potentially reflective of the occurrence/resurgence of lime-dominated fen woodland (SU-1; Waller, in Hall 1996, 213–16, fig. 109).

Through Palmer's ensuing aerial photographic reconnaissance, a ring-ditch was discovered just south of the Ouse Roddon/road bend 500 m to the north, and still another 'elongated' mound was spotted to the south (Figs. 2.5 & 2.6; Hall 1996, 58). Having a more 'teardrop-shaped' outline and oriented north–south, the latter is unlikely to be a long barrow and probably represents a recent upcast.

During the Haddenham project dyke surveys still another mounded feature was discovered southwest of the HAD 6 barrow in the Hill Row Doles fields (Fig. 2.9). There, cleaning of a dyke section across a peat-sealed terrace (*c.* 60 m wide) revealed a most intriguing feature — a low mound, *c.* 0.50 m high and 15.00 m wide, bedding directly upon the terrace gravels (Fig. 2.10; see also Hall *et al.* 1987, fig. 118). Consisting of light brown to mid yellow sand with fine gravel inclusions, its matrix was remarkably uniform. Its top (sealed by 0.50–0.60 m of undisturbed peat) was generally flat, though it locally carried traces of a mid grey-brown sandy silt loam that was probably a remnant buried soil.

Fen Clay lay along the northern base of the dyke-section and was visible to a thickness of 0.20 m+. Generally its top lay at *c.* –0.05 m OD; it rose up over the flank of the terrace proper (sealing a lower peat) to a maximum height of 0.10 m OD. Only a slight

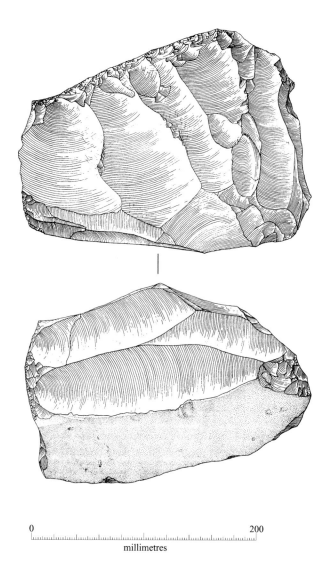

0                                                        200
millimetres

**Figure 2.11.** *Hill Row Doles flint core.*

skim of the clay, lying deeper at *c.* –0.20 m OD, was visible along the lower southern terrace side.

Appearing 'packed', it is difficult to determine the source of the mound material. Slight troughs, 0.15–0.20 m deep and 3.50–5.00 m across, were visible on either side. Although their profile may be exaggerated through outwash, these flanking hollows were probably some manner of quarrying scoops.

At this time there can be no certainty as to the status of this feature, whether it is a mound or ridge (though it appeared to slope down or be terminating westwards as it was only *c.* 0.25 m high in the opposite side of the dyke). A few flints were retrieved from the top of the natural gravel which it sealed; a large 'early' flint core from a buried soil hollow within its bulk is reported upon below. There can be no doubt that the mound was humanly upcast, and the fact that it was

sealed by *undisturbed* peat attests to its antiquity. Given this, the only plausible explanations for it would seem to be either a raised causeway, perhaps of Roman or later date, or, much more likely, a barrow mound of some unusual non-ditched form.

The Hill Row Doles core
by T. REYNOLDS *with* C. CONNELLER
The core is a large three-platformed nucleus for removing blades and blade flakes (Fig. 2.11). Its maximum dimensions are 18 cm long by 11.8 cm wide and 11.4 cm thick. Weighing *c.* 3.3 kg, an area of thin cortex is preserved adjacent to a face where long blades have been removed.

The main flaking face has a platform 12.4 cm long and the flaked surface is 11.4 cm deep. A total of eight removals (over 1 cm minimum dimension) have been struck off. These were all for blade-flakes with irregular edges and have an average length of 8.3 cm. The angle between the platform and flaking surface is about 90° and in places exceeds this. The platform shows no signs of abrasion or preparation and the negative bulbs preserved are poorly developed. The direction of the platform changes after 12.4 cm and it is then prepared with numerous small flakes having been removed from its surface. Removals continue for a further 7.8 cm. Opposed to this platform is a smaller one, also for removing irregular blade-flakes (three in total) and with signs of platform preparation. The final platform is unprepared and unabraded and also has an angle around 90°. It was used to remove two regular pointed blades, one 14.3 cm long and 4.2 cm wide and the second 11.5 cm and 3.1 cm wide. These blades were removed adjacent to an area of cortex.

In summary, the core is multi-platform with two of the platforms opposed and designed for the removal of blades and blade-flakes. Given the intersections of negative flake scars, it would seem that each platform functioned separately for the removal of a small number of blanks.

Unusually for a surface find, the core is in fresh condition, showing no signs of abrasion, rolling, crushing or plough damage, and there is no patination. It is made on a flint which has bands of darker and lighter brown of varying widths. It also retains a substantial area of thin cortex. The flint derives from the chalks that outcrop east and southeast of Haddenham at a distance of some 15–20 km. The author regularly sees worked flint from the region and has only seen a single comparable example, from a Late Mesolithic context at Somersham (7 km to the northwest). Brown flints are, however, a feature of assemblages of Late Pleistocene and Early Flandrian date at Swaffham Prior and elsewhere on the southeastern fen-edge. Given the condition of the cortex, the raw material was obtained from a fresh chalk source. The original nodule has been quartered and then removed for further working.

The dating of a single stray find requires caution as context is lacking. Allowing for the problems of dating stray finds, this piece is a blade core for regularly removing large, broad blades. As such, later prehistoric dates are unlikely for this piece. There are in fact four main candidates for a date, these being Early Upper Palaeolithic, Later Upper Palaeolithic, Early Mesolithic and Neolithic.

An early Upper Palaeolithic date for the core is unlikely due to the lack of other such evidence in the region (Bonsall 1977; Cambridgeshire SMR) and the condition of the core itself. It is improbable that a large piece such as this should come through the Last Glacial Maximum (18,000 BP) unscathed from an open context. Long blade material is known from the southeastern fen-edge at Swaffham Prior, and from the east of Suffolk at Mildenhall and Bury St Edmunds (Barton 1992; 1998; Bonsall 1977). Other later Upper Palaeolithic material comes from Methwold in Norfolk which is also on the fen-edge (Bonsall 1977; Silvester 1991).

## Peacocks Farm: a scientific archaeology

The often-reproduced section and photograph of Clark and Godwin's Peacocks Farm, Shippea Hill excavations has been a dominant image in Fenland archaeology (see Volume 2, fig. 1.2; Clark *et al.* 1933; 1935). Establishing Bronze Age occupation above the marine clays, with Neolithic below, it set the Fen Clay as a near pan-Fenland datum and this 'divide' still pervaded the region's prehistory up to the time of the Foulmire Fen investigations. Beyond this, with its background in the Fenland Research Committee the site had major national significance and, arguably, international resonance. The context of the 1934 excavations and the formation of the Committee has been fully outlined in Smith's 1997 study, 'Grahame Clark's New Archaeology', and the Peacocks/Plantation Farm investigations were certainly its 'flagship' excavation (see also Rowley-Conwy 1999; Fagan 2001).

Formed in 1932, amongst the Committee's august membership were Wyman Abbott, O.G.S. Crawford, Cyril Fox, Christopher Hawkes, Charles Phillips and Stuart Piggott (the core of this group going on to spearhead the formation of The Prehistoric Society to provide a Cambridge counterbalance to the Society of Antiquaries of London). The players were then young ('turks'), with Clark having just published *The Mesolithic Age in Britain* (1932). The Godwins had studied in Sweden to acquire the techniques of pollen analysis, the first opportunity for its application being the peat adhering to the Leman and Ower antler point retrieved from the North Sea. Whereas previously Clark's work was, of necessity, given to typological and distributional approaches, the directive of the Committee was interdisciplinary and involved palaeobotanical, geological and archaeological researches. In effect marking the advent of a scientific archaeology in this country, it was this collaboration that was to foster Clark's own ecologically focused archaeology, as typified by his hallmark 'biome' diagrams that first appeared in *Archaeology and Society* in 1939.

The site's renown was furthered when Clark and Godwin returned to it in 1960 to obtain pollen and radiocarbon samples, the application of the latter then being still very much in its infancy. Published in *Antiquity*, they achieved 12 radiocarbon determinations ranging from 8610±160 BP (Q-588) to 4685±120 BP (Q-499), and the relevant results were set in a table with what few other Early Neolithic dates were then available for the British Isles (obviously without the benefit of calibration). Amongst the authors' conclusion were:

1) We must accept, on a conservative basis, that Neolithic culture was established in these islands by around 3000 B.C., while keeping in mind the idea that it may have begun as early as 3400 B.C. Even on the more conservative figure this would mean that it began a thousand years earlier than Professor Stuart Piggott allowed as recently as 1954 in his fundamental book *The Neolithic Cultures of the British Isles*.

2) It follows that the Neolithic phase in our prehistory lasted around three times longer than Piggott envisaged in his book, on the last page of which he concluded that it was unlikely that 'all three phases together could span more than four centuries' (Clark & Godwin 1962, 21).

The site's legacy was further enshrined through the personal accounts of its chief investigators (e.g. Clark 1989, 53–8; Godwin 1978), and it is telling of the influence or pull of 'great sites' (and genealogies of research: see Evans 1998) that a team from Cardiff would return to it yet again in the early 1980s (Smith *et al.* 1989; see below concerning the results of their work).

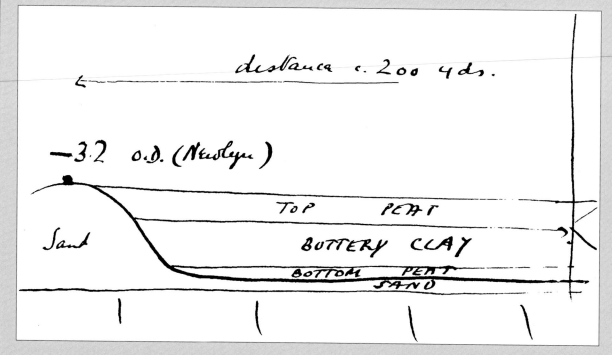

**Figure 2.12.** *Clark's sketch diagram of 'classic' three-phase Fenland sequence from Plantation Farm. (University of Cambridge, Sedgwick Museum archives; reproduced in Smith 1997, fig. 5.)*

Creswellian (thirteenth millennium BP), Hengistbury and Federmesser (twelfth millennium BP) and long or bruised blade (c. 10,000 BP) assemblages are known during the Later Upper Palaeolithic. Barton provides a list of characteristics for these (Barton 1998, 159; see also Barton & Roberts 1996); the size of blades removed, use of high-quality flint and presence of some faceting could support such an affiliation for the Hill Row Dole core. Yet this list was devised for characterizing assemblages and the presence of bruised blades is clearly a significant factor. Both the bruised blade and Later Palaeolithic industries occur on the southeastern fen-edge and the core could be regarded as an outlier of either.

Early Flandrian larger blade-based industries are collectively assigned to the Early Mesolithic and three basic assemblage types have been identified (Reynier 1998). These types are known as Star Carr, Deepcar and Horsham variants. Analysis of a limited data set has shown that the Star Carr variant occurs in the north and west of England and the Horsham variant dominates the south and parts of the west. The Deepcar variant is more widely spread. Absolute dating suggests that the Horsham variant is slightly later than the others, but all are established during the tenth millennium BP. The distribution study has shown that central England, including most of Cambridgeshire, lacks evidence for settlement at this date. Further into East Anglia, Deepcar variant assemblages have been identified on the fen-edge in Suffolk and Cambridgeshire and at Kelling Heath in Norfolk. Haddenham would be the westernmost outlier of such a distribution pattern at present. It may well be that the Greater River Ouse system and the Fen Basin was a barrier for early expansion into central England. However, the find at Haddenham, if Early Mesolithic, suggests incursion as far as the river's eastern bank. It may be, for Cambridgeshire at least, that early sites have not been identified because of the greater than 15 m overburden of later deposits. However, the lack of evidence along the western tributaries draining central England needs explanation. It may be that the middle and lower Greater Ouse system was a bland, brackish and marshy environment with little ecological diversity to attract early human exploitation. Reconstruction of the east of England at the end of the Last Glacial is still at a tentative stage (Coles 1998) and the locally detailed work of the Fenland Project (Waller 1994) still needs to be integrated effectively with the larger regional models.

Alternatively, whilst large cores are not a regular feature characterizing Neolithic assemblages, Saville (1982) has noted the presence of 'giant' cores from that period. He cites two examples from Gloucestershire — one from the Hazelton long barrow, measuring 126 mm in its maximum extent and weighing 750 g; the other from Frocester, near Stroud has a length of 133 mm and weighs 1050 g. Though these examples are smaller than the Haddenham example, Saville states that the Gloucestershire cores are both 'extensively flaked' and so must originally have been larger. A very large Neolithic core is also known from the fen-edge at Honnington (R. Jacobi pers. comm.).

In conclusion, the large blade core derives from a fresh context but one which is unknown and undated. Review of the most likely options for a date would suggest the core dates from the Last Glacial Interstadial, although an Early Mesolithic or even Neolithic date cannot be ruled out. Another option, not considered here, is that the core is a modern product and even this cannot be totally excluded.

The Doles gravel rise would seem to be a small discrete 'island' separated by backwater palaeochannels from both the Foulmire and Hermitage Farm/Lower Delphs terraces. Cloutman's lithostratigraphic results are fully presented in Waller 1994 (164–7; see also Chapter 4 this volume). Within the immediate environs his coring programme struck clay 'bedrock' (though with

mineral particles presumably reflective of terrace-edge outwash) at points HN1 and HN6, and this must reflect the southwestern edge of the Foulmire Fen island (see Fig. 1.2). A 'mineral natural' was reached at HN5, evidently the southwestern continuation of the Doles island terrace.

Only on its southern side has the true extent of the Foulmire island, on which the main barrow group occurs, been formally mapped through coring (Fig. 2.1). Hall & Coles (1994, fig. 52) show it as extending over c. 85 ha. With its ground surface today lying at c. 1.00 m OD, we can be assured of its 'isolation' on its northwest, southwest and southeastern flanks (variously defined through dyke survey and the line of the Ouse roddon). However, its limits have not been established to the northeast towards Sutton and it may conceivably join with the flanks of the Isle of Ely. Regardless of whether a 'fen island' or buried peninsula, having two definite long barrows (and lying at the marked northward bend of the palaeochannel of the Ouse) this clearly was a 'special' place. Apart from its proximity to the causewayed enclosure on the Upper Delphs, this is further attested by the fact that the nearest known long barrows occur at a distance of 15–23 km, and there only in 'isolated' instances (see below).

That these barrows were located on islands amid the braided (palaeo-) courses of the Ouse also seems extraordinary. However, subsequent investigation at Barleycroft/Over immediately upstream of the Delphs terraces has shown this to be a general pattern. All of the main clusters of the Willingham/Over barrow field(s), including the Hermitage Farm/Lower Delphs groupings, lie on islands in the river's delta-like lower reaches.

### The dyke-side investigations

The terrace-edge site was discovered during the course of dyke survey in April of 1984 when a buried ground surface/island was recognized along the exposed southern face of the north dyke of the Backdrove west of Foulmire Drove. During cleaning of the section a quantity of worked and burnt flint was found in sealed contexts beneath the Fen Clay. Because of the quantity and character of the artefacts recovered, and the proximity of 'site' to the HAD 6 long barrow (100 m to the north), the decision was made to conduct limited trial excavations by cutting back the dyke-edge.

This had to be undertaken promptly as the local water level in the dykes was due to rise in early May. Therefore, following recording of the long section, the overlying peat ([1400]) was machined off from two

Samples 2 and 3 are composed of a similar fabric and share similar pedological features, both with each other and Sample 1 above. The main fabric is a relatively dense, partially heterogeneous, quartz sand, which is dominated by very fine quartz sand, with less than 10 per cent fines (e.g. silt and clay) present. Amorphous organic matter is frequent, there are frequent plant residues, a few fine and coarse fragments of charcoal, and textural coatings are rare. Thus, this soil is also 'A'-Horizon material.

The c. 20–30 per cent presence of amorphous calcite crystals as intercalations within the main soil fabric is a secondary feature. The sesquioxide hypo-coating/infilling of former plant stems/roots is also a secondary feature. Both are a consequence of hydromorphism or gleying, presumably as a result of subsequent freshwater and marine flooding which were responsible for the growth of the basal peat and the deposition of the Fen Clay respectively.

Some disturbance of this 'A'-Horizon is evident in thin section. This is probably a result of a combination of plant rooting, alternating wet/dry conditions and freshwater/marine flooding, rather than anthropogenic activity on site. Nevertheless, there is the possibility that the high concentrations of calcium in the ground/flood water, if it does indeed have an upland origin, is a consequence of deforestation and the resultant increased leaching and run-off of exposed soils on the higher ground to the southwest.

In conclusion, the following points can be made:

1. The buried soil at Foulmire Fen is a former 'A'-Horizon.

2. The whole profile, and in particular the uppermost horizon, is greatly disturbed by plant roots growing in the subsequent freshwater/marine fen environments.

3. Although the soil is slightly disturbed, there is insufficient evidence to suggest that it was due to anthropomorphic activity.

4. Soil disturbance was more probably the result of the secondary rooting of fen plants and successive freshwater and marine inundations.

5. The whole soil profile, and especially the uppermost horizon, was subject to the secondary deposition/intercalation of amorphous calcite crystals. Calcite intercalations are only found in strongly hydromorphic or gleyed soil horizons.

6. The secondary hypo-coating/infilling of plant roots and residues with sesquioxides, and in particular amorphous iron, is also indicative of hydromorphism or gleying.

7. The calcite crystals could derive from either or both of two sources: in the ground or flood water carried downstream from the base-rich chalky and clayey subsoils and soils of the uplands to the southwest, and from the drying out of the once base-rich overlying peat.

8. Human action may be seen in both of these sources: firstly, deforestation, increased run-off and leaching of upland soils, and secondly the more recent drainage of the fens.

9. The presence of abundant amorphous calcite crystals at Foulmire could explain the formation of the so-called 'marl' in the ditches of the adjacent long barrow site, especially if there was some localized impedence of the subsoil into which the ditches were cut. Whatever its origin, this 'marl' should be regarded as a secondary formation due to gleying and base-rich ground water conditions.

Pollen analysis
by E. CLOUTMAN

A pollen monolith was taken from a section in in Cutting A in the dyke-side investigations (Fig. 2.9). Its top, the 0 cm point, lay on the archaeological site datum of –0.105 m OD and its base penetrated the basal sands at 26 cm (Fig. 2.15):

| Altitude | Stratigraphy |
| --- | --- |
| –0.105 to –0.185 m OD | Humified deposit with reeds |
| –0.185 to –0.275 m OD | Fen Clay |
| –0.275 to –0.295 m OD | Reedy transition in the Fen Clay |
| –0.295 to –0.365 m OD | Reedy mud containing Phragmites and mineral particles with occasional small stones |
| below –0.365 m OD | Grey sandy deposit |

Two pollen assemblage zones were distinguished:

*ff2* Gramineae–Chenopodiaceae: flooding episode;
*ff1* *Tilia–Corylus*: reed swamp locally, with mostly lime and hazel woodland on dry soils.

The pollen curves hint at several major vegetational changes, but due to the paucity of samples, the diagram has only been divided into two main phases (Fig. 2.15). The basal sample (26 cm) has been included as it gives some idea of the pollen present in the mineral soil, although reservations must be placed on interpretation as only 20 land-plant pollen grains were counted.

*Phase ff1* (–0.365 to –0.30 m OD): Lime and hazel were probably growing on the surrounding dry land areas. The amount of reed in the deposit suggests that the site was colonized by reed swamp. As the phase draws to a close (–0.305 m OD), there is an increase in species diversity (*Prunus/Sorbus*, *Taraxacum*, *Lotus*, *Potentilla*, *Filipendula*, Umbelliferae, Chenopodiaceae) and a fall in the pollen curves of the trees and shrubs, particularly *Tilia* and *Corylus*. This no doubt marks the ecological change caused by the marine incursion (but see also Sub-Phase ff2a).

*Sub-Phase ff2a* (–0.30 to –0.26 m OD): The Phase ff1/ff2 boundary is dated to 2180–1740 cal. BC (3590±70 BP; CAR-829) which places this in the Early Bronze Age. It also marks the start of the marine incursion, a change from mud to Fen Clay in the deposit. The Fen Clay transition is dominated by reeds, thus some of the grass pollen seen in the rising Gramineae pollen curve may be attributable to reeds growing locally. The dramatic decline in the *Tilia* and *Corylus* curves in the previous phase, and subsequent rise in the Gramineae,

*Plantago* and Chenopodiaceae curves is also, no doubt, a response to the marine incursion. It should not be overlooked, however, that some pastoral farming may have been practised.

*Sub-Phase ff2b* (–0.26 to –0.165 m OD): Tree pollen values recover in this sub-phase except those of *Tilia* and *Corylus*. The appearance of cereal pollen indicates that arable farming on the dry soils was now taking place. The marked increase in *Sparganium/Typha* pollen and the abundant reed in the deposit in the –0.165 m OD sample suggest that these plants were growing locally. The Fen Clay, provided that it was not still saline, would have been a good substrate for these plants and by implication the water level must have been relatively shallow. The date for the base of the mud, immediately above the Fen Clay, is 820–400 cal. BC (2520±70 BP; CAR-828) which theoretically dates the top of the Fen Clay to the Iron Age (NB: This assignation would be much too late and either it must indicate truncation of the overlying peats or the introduction of organic material through root action. Equally, given the broader environmental sequence and the low absolute height of these 'deep fen' terraces, it is difficult to see how arable could have been practised in the immediate area at this date.)

## Dating

Because of the importance of absolutely dating the marine transgression a number of radiocarbon assays were submitted. The Cardiff team achieved three dates relating to the Cutting A pollen core:

1) CAR-828  (–0.165 to –0.175 m OD)     820–400 cal. BC     (2520±70 BP)
2) CAR-829  (–0.295 to –0.305 m OD)  2180–1740 cal. BC   (3590±70 BP)
3) CAR-830  (–0.345 to –0.355 m OD)  2030–1630 cal. BC   (3480±70 BP)

The second of these was from just beneath the transgressive contact (i.e. onset of Fen Clay flooding); the first from just above regressive contact.

Within the context of environmental programme of the Fenland Project two further dates were submitted from the sequence within this cutting; the first dating the Fen Clay/upper peat contact and the second from Fen Clay/basal peat contact:

4) Q-2501  (–0.095 to –0.115 m OD)  1690–1420 cal. BC  (3260±60 BP)
5) Q-2502  (–0.505 to –0.545 m OD)  2140–1690 cal. BC  (3550±70 BP)

Another series of samples was also processed to date the sequence in Cutting B:

6) Q-2503  (0.05 to 0.03 m OD)        800–400 cal. BC   (2480±50 BP)
7) Q-2504  (–0.035 to –0.06 m OD)   1390–990 cal. BC   (2950±60 BP)
8) Q-2505  (–0.12 to –0.16 m OD)   1890–1430 cal. BC   (3340±90 BP)
9) Q-2506  (–0.22 to –0.24 m OD)   2870–2300 cal. BC   (3975±70 BP)
10) Q-2507  (–0.26 to –0.275 m OD)  3030–2660 cal. BC   (4260±60 BP)

Q-2503–Q-2505 were from the upper peat, with Q-2505 being from its contact with the Fen Clay; Q-2506 was from the Fen Clay/basal peat contact. As the dates from both cuttings were *c.* 1000 younger than expected, three additional dates were therefore submitted from Cutting B; the first is from the upper peat, the second from the Fen Clay/upper peat contact and Q-2534 is from the Fen Clay/basal peat contact:

11) Q-2532  (0.01 to –0.01 m OD)      1110–790 cal. BC   (2750±80 BP)
12) Q-2533  (–0.18 to –0.20 m OD)  2880–2300 cal. BC   (4020±90 BP)
13) Q-2534  (–0.265 to –0.315 m OD)  3340–2780 cal. BC   (4380±80 BP)

Finally, two further dates were obtained from organic materials deriving from the excavations:

14) Q-2535  (*c.* –0.20 m); from wood in 1610–1310 cal. BC  (3180±60 BP)
     the base of the Fen Clay in Cutting A
15) Q-2536  (*c.* –0.30 m); from bark in 1900–1610 cal. BC  (3430±60 BP)
     basal peat in Cutting B

The implications of these dates are discussed by Waller (1994, 174); it seems likely that in the area of Foulmire Fen the Fen Clay was deposited some time after *c.* 2400 cal. BC (3900 BP), the evidence suggesting that it should date to between *c.* 2000–1500 cal. BC (3600–3200 BP).

In a final effort to attribute the site's occupation more firmly, in 2003 a sample of charcoal form the base of the burnt flint mound in Cutting A ([1433]) was submitted for dating. It generated a date of 3340–2700 cal. BC (Beta-180721; 4340±90 BP), at the cusp of the earlier/later Neolithic.

### The excavations

In Cutting A, though the top of the glacial sand deposits ([1433]/[1419]) generally lay at *c.* –0.10 m below OD, along its southern side its surface bedded between *c.* –0.40 to –0.50 m OD and it sloped down along the southern margin of the trench *c.* 0.30–0.40 m in 1.00–1.55 m (Fig. 2.13). However, in the section on the northern side of the dyke opposite, the sand surface also lay at –0.10 m OD ([1437]), indicating a 'stability' of ground surface towards the north (i.e. the level was maintained). In this cutting the glacial sand deposit was excavated in a series of spits (Table 2.1).

Because of the rise in dyke water level in mid May, it was decided to reduce the area of excavation. Therefore [1429] was dug as two linear strips beside the western and eastern sections (west of the 186 grid line and east of the 189 line), thereby reducing the area by approximately 60 per cent. As the dyke-water covered the trench in the last two days of excavation the final 'spit-strips' beneath [1429] were taken out *en masse*, and were dug by spade and then 100 per cent wet sieved (5-mm mesh). [1431] was excavated west of 186 grid and, on the eastern side, work began on similar strip ([1430]). In the latter however, as the Ampthill clay was immediately reached (which proved unsieveable) only a half metre-square was excavated in which no finds were recovered.

In this trench was found an irregular shallow hollow/cut ([1425]) extending for 2.10 m and 1.65 m, truncated by the dyke. This was 0.12–0.18 m deep with a flat, slightly concave base. On the whole its sides

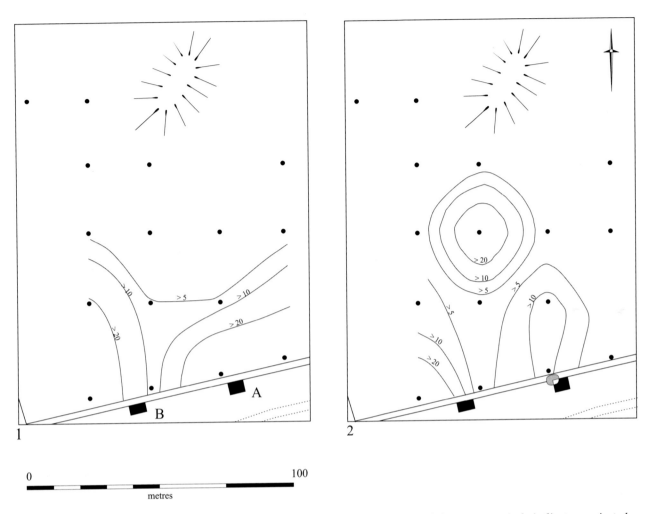

**Figure 2.21**. *Foulmire Fen test pits. Distribution of worked (1) and burnt flint (2); note grey circle indicates projected extent of burnt flint mound in Cutting A.*

bed. Similarly the pieces of irregular workshop waste were accidental removals along planes of weakness within the flint. The low number of such pieces, all of which appear to have derived from the outer parts of the nodules, confirms the high quality of the raw material.

The composition of the assemblage (Table 2.22) indicates the dominance (91 per cent) of waste products. The most common implement types were informally utilized and retouched, with formal tool types present only as singular examples.

A breakdown of the waste flakes to determine their position in the knapping sequence (Table 2.23) suggests that all stages were present, from initial core preparation to unretouched flakes. There was little variation in the proportions of the different types between the test pits, suggesting a lack of spatial differentiation between stages in the knapping process across the landscape. The presence of preparation

flakes, along with the lightly worked core mentioned above, indicates that raw materials were brought to the area in their unworked state.

The technology of the waste flakes is similar to the neighbouring Late Mesolithic assemblage, with a predominance of feather terminations and unprepared and non-cortical platforms. The flake butts show a mix of hertzian and incipient bending fractures, both of which could have been produced with the use of cortical flint pebbles as hammerstones. Core preparation and trimming appears to have been kept to a minimum, reflecting the efficient use of the small raw material that was available.

Although the individual assemblages were too small for metrical analysis, it was noted, on a subjective level, that c. 30 per cent of the unretouched flakes were either blades or broken blades (with a breadth:length ratio of 2:5 or less) with a correspondingly small number of broad flakes (breadth:length ratio of over 5:5). The

**Table 2.22.** *Test pits: overall typology (IWW = irregular workshop waste).*

| Context/ cat. no. | Waste flakes | Cores | IWW | Micro-burins | Utilized flakes | Retouched flakes | Scrapers | Truncated flakes | Points | Flake knives | Totals |
|---|---|---|---|---|---|---|---|---|---|---|---|
| TP 2 28591 | 1 | 0 | 0 | 0 | 0 | 0 | 0 | 0 | 0 | 0 | 1 |
| TP 4 28586 | 3 | 0 | 0 | 0 | 0 | 1 | 0 | 0 | 0 | 0 | 4 |
| TP 5 28588 | 17 | 0 | 0 | 0 | 1 | 2 | 1 | 0 | 0 | 0 | 21 |
| TP 6 28589 | 32 | 0 | 3 | 0 | 0 | 0 | 0 | 0 | 0 | 0 | 35 |
| TP 8 28535 | 1 | 0 | 0 | 0 | 0 | 0 | 0 | 0 | 0 | 0 | 1 |
| TP 9 28581 | 4 | 1 | 0 | 0 | 0 | 0 | 0 | 0 | 0 | 0 | 5 |
| TP 10 28582 | 7 | 0 | 0 | 0 | 0 | 0 | 0 | 0 | 0 | 0 | 7 |
| TP 15 28580 | 4 | 0 | 0 | 0 | 1 | 0 | 0 | 0 | 0 | 0 | 5 |
| TP 16 28584 | 31 | 1 | 1 | 1 | 1 | 1 | 0 | 1 | 1 | 0 | 38 |
| TP 17 28587 | 3 | 0 | 0 | 0 | 0 | 0 | 0 | 0 | 0 | 0 | 3 |
| TP 18 28590 | 2 | 0 | 0 | 0 | 0 | 0 | 0 | 0 | 0 | 0 | 2 |
| TP 19 28585 | 31 | 0 | 1 | 0 | 1 | 0 | 0 | 0 | 0 | 1 | 34 |
| Totals | 136 | 2 | 5 | 1 | 4 | 4 | 1 | 1 | 1 | 1 | 156 |

relatively high number of blades (closely corresponding to the figure of 24.8 per cent from the Late Mesolithic terrace-edge 'cuttings' assemblage) suggests that the bulk of the assemblage was Late Mesolithic in date.

The single micro-burin and worn implements, such as the utilized flakes, indicates both implement manufacture and discard were undertaken in the surrounding area.

Dating
The long time-span of the technological techniques employed and the preponderance of small waste pieces meant that the vast majority of the artefacts could not be individually dated. Despite this, and the small size of the individual assemblages, there are a number of factors which suggest that the bulk of the material is Late Mesolithic in date. These include the relatively large number of blades combined with certain typological indicators including a micro-burin, and a truncated blade and backed blade all from TP 16. There were, however, a number of implements which suggest a Neolithic component, including the large scraper from TP 5 and the flake knife from TP 19.

The overall pattern revealed in the test pits suggests a continuation of the trends noted in the dyke-side assemblage: notably a dominance of Late Mesolithic material, predominantly waste, with later material, mainly implements, in the upper layers. It was proposed above that the later material derived from the situation of the neighbouring long barrow on top of an existing Late Mesolithic assemblage. The distribution of the earlier material suggests that the Late Mesolithic 'site' represents a concentration of material within a landscape covered by a thin scatter of contemporary lithic material. This situation can be paralleled in other Fenland situations, for example in Borough Fen (French & Pryor 1993) and in the March/Manea area (Middleton 1990).

The distribution of this material was not even, with concentrations in TPs 6, 16 & 19 possibly representing individual episodes of flint working and discard. The condition of the artefacts suggested that these activities were undertaken immediately adjacent to the sites of discovery. Within this material was included a few Neolithic artefacts. The sample of flints was not large enough to allow for detailed considerations, but the range of material did suggest a full range of flint-knapping activities, from raw material preparation to the manufacture and discard of artefacts.

**Table 2.23.** *Test pits: waste flake typology.*

| Context/ cat. no. | Unretouched flakes | Dressing chips | Trimming flakes | Preparation flakes | Totals |
|---|---|---|---|---|---|
| TP 2 28591 | 1 | 0 | 0 | 0 | 1 |
| TP 4 28586 | 2 | 1 | 0 | 0 | 3 |
| TP 5 28588 | 10 | 4 | 2 | 1 | 17 |
| TP 6 28589 | 16 | 9 | 4 | 3 | 32 |
| TP 8 28535 | 0 | 1 | 0 | 0 | 1 |
| TP 9 28581 | 2 | 2 | 0 | 0 | 4 |
| TP 10 28582 | 4 | 0 | 2 | 1 | 7 |
| TP 15 28580 | 3 | 0 | 1 | 0 | 4 |
| TP 16 28584 | 19 | 7 | 3 | 2 | 31 |
| TP 17 28587 | 3 | 0 | 0 | 0 | 3 |
| TP 18 28590 | 1 | 0 | 1 | 0 | 2 |
| TP 19 28585 | 20 | 9 | 1 | 1 | 31 |
| Totals | 81 | 33 | 14 | 8 | 136 |

**Table 2.24.** *Sherd totals and weights according to fabric.*

| Fabric | No. of sherds | Weight (g) | Average sherd weight (g) |
|---|---|---|---|
| 1 | 6 | 91 | 15 |
| 2 | 21 (+ frags.) | 278 | 13 |
| 3 | 17 | 64 | 4 |
| 4 | 6 | 28 | 5 |
| Total | 50 | 461 | 9 |

**Table 2.25.** *Earlier Neolithic sherds by context and fabric.*

| Context | Fabric | No. of sherds | Weight (g) |
|---|---|---|---|
| TP 16 | 3 | 1 | 1 |
| *Area A* | | | |
| 1407 | 3 | 2 | 2 |
| 1407 | 4 | 2 | 8 |
| 1408 | 3 | 3 | 2 |
| 1409 | 3 | 1 | 13 |
| 1409 | 4 | 4 | 20 |
| *Area B* | | | |
| 1413 | 3 | 3 | 25 |
| 1414 | 3 | 2 | 5 |
| 1415 | 3 | 2 | 6 |
| 1416 | 3 | 1 | 9 |
| 1417 | 3 | 2 | 1 |
| Total | | 23 | 92 |

**Table 2.26.** *Later Neolithic–Early Bronze Age sherds by context.*

| Context | Fabric | No. of sherds | Weight (g) |
|---|---|---|---|
| TP 1 | 1 | 2 | 5 |
| TP 8 | 1 | 1 | 13 |
| TP 8 | 2 | 19 | 269 |
| TP 16 | 1 | 3 | 73 |
| *Area A* | | | |
| 1407 | 2 | 1 | 8 |
| *Area B* | | | |
| 1415 | 2 | 1 | 1 |
| Total | | 27 | 369 |

## Prehistoric pottery

by J. POLLARD & R. JOHNSTON

Test excavations across the terrace yielded a small assemblage of prehistoric pottery (50 sherds; 461 g), deriving from 11 separate test pits and the two dyke-side areas of excavation. The sherds are in four fabrics; two recognized as earlier Neolithic (Fabrics 3 and 4), with the other two of later Neolithic–earlier Bronze Age attribution (Fabrics 1 and 2) (Table 2.24). The condition of the pottery is variable, ranging from good to poor; the earlier Neolithic material showing the greater signs of weathering.

*Earlier Neolithic*

Twenty-three sherds (92 g) of earlier Neolithic plain bowl pottery were identified on the basis of their form and flinty fabric (Table 2.25). These were sparsely distributed, but with small concentrations (by weight) in [1409] and [1413]. All are small and highly fragmentary, with an average sherd weight of only 4 g, indicating exposure to weathering and post-depositional attrition.

Sherds and crumbs from a minimum of three vessels are present: two or more in Fabric 4 and probably a single vessel in Fabric 3 (Figs. 2.22:1 & 2.22:2). Most are featureless wall sherds, though three rims and two fragments with shallow concave profiles, evidently from the necks of shouldered 'S'-profiled or carinated bowls, were recovered. Of the three rims, two from [1409] and [1407] in Fabric 4 may come from the same vessel. All three rims are simple and everted, one with internal thickening. No decorated sherds were present. Rim and vessel morphology (as much as it is reconstructable), the absence of decoration, and the quality and hardness of the fabrics, suggest the sherds derive from carinated bowls of the Grimston

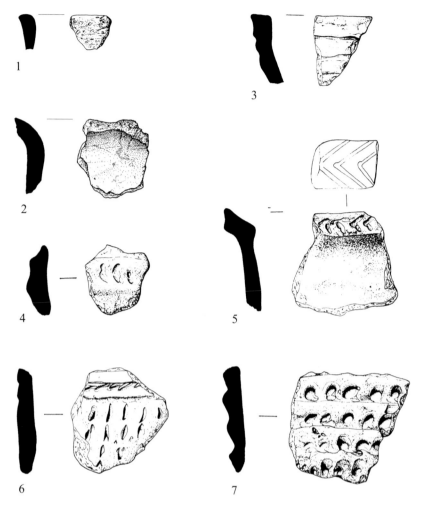

**Figure 2.22.** *Foulmire Fen: prehistoric pottery: 1 & 2) Earlier Neolithic plain bowl; 3) Grooved Ware; 4 & 5) Food Vessel; 6 & 7) Rusticated Beaker.*

was much more localized than that of the Early Neolithic ceramics, most occurring in TP 8 and TP 16 (Table 2.26), where sizeable fragments of single vessels were present. The fresh condition of many of the sherds implies little exposure to attritional processes prior to the deposition of the Fen Clay.

Between four to eight individual vessels are represented. Where identifiable, these may be classified as Rusticated Beaker (three or more vessels in Fabric 2), Food Vessel or Food Vessel Urn (one or two vessels in Fabric 1), and possibly Grooved Ware (one vessel in Fabric 1).

Potentially being the earliest of this group, the sherd of putative Grooved Ware from TP 8 comprises a flattened and slightly expanded rim from a bowl- or tub-shaped vessel (Fig. 2.22:3). This is decorated externally with coarse multiple grooved horizontal lines.

Nineteen of the 21 sherds of Rusticated Beaker came from TP 8. The majority belong to a single large-diameter vessel with a simple rounded rim, decorated with all-over multiple horizontal finger-pinched ('plastic') cordons (Fig. 2.22:7; cf. Bamford 1982, fig. 38l). A second Beaker is represented by a large wall sherd decorated with multiple horizontal bands of twisted cord below which are multiple vertical lines of fingernail impressions (Fig. 2.22:6; cf. Bamford 1982, fig. 38d). Fragments of a third vessel include two base-angles and five wall sherds; all were weathered, with two displaying traces of thick twisted cord impressions. Further sherds from [1407] and [1415] may come these or additional vessels. That from the former is a weathered wall sherd with traces of fingernail or pinched decoration. The sherd from [1415] was heavily weathered and was identified as Beaker on fabric alone.

Three sherds of Food Vessel were recovered from TP 16. One of these is a portion of rim and neck from a large-diameter vessel, the rim profile being oblique to the vessel wall, squared, and internally and externally expanded (Fig. 2.22:5). It was decorated on the internal bevel and on the outer edge of the rim with thick twisted cord chevrons. Fragments from the same

tradition (Herne 1988). Locally, the sherds find parallel amongst vessels recovered from the fills of two large tree-throw pits at Barleycroft Farm, Needingworth (Evans *et al.* 1999; Evans & Knight 2001), and slightly further afield with pottery from the Early Neolithic house at Fengate, Peterborough (Pryor 1974).

The accepted early fourth millennium cal. BC date range for bowls of this sort would suggest broad contemporaneity with activity accompanying the construction and primary use of the long barrow, though the possibility of their relating to an episode of pre-monument occupation cannot be ruled out (see Chapter 3 below concerning the occurrence of comparable material within the barrow's mound).

*Late Neolithic–Early Bronze Age*
The remaining sherds, totalling 27 (369 g), are of Late Neolithic–Early Bronze Age date. Their distribution

or a second vessel include two sherds with horizontal cordons, one comprising part of the wall and possibly shoulder of a bowl decorated with bands of vertical twisted cord impressions between horizontal cordons (Fig. 2.22:4). Two base-angles from TP 1 are too small and weathered to be identifiable, though the fabric (1) suggests they also belong to Food Vessels.

Given the range of Late Neolithic–Early Bronze Age ceramic styles present, and their divergent distribution, it is likely that the material was generated by more than one episode of occupation/activity, potentially several events spread over two or three centuries. Assuming it is correctly identified, the single sherd of Grooved Ware would most probably belong in the mid third millennium cal. BC. A ridged Food Vessel from Spong Hill, Norfolk, is associated with a late third millennium cal. BC radiocarbon determination (2470–2040 cal. BC, BM-1532, 3810±70 BP: Healy 1988, 18); and the date range for Rusticated Beaker probably spans the late third–early second millennia cal. BC (Kinnes *et al.* 1991). Akin to the situation for the Early Neolithic, context may best be sought in a process of mobile, 'shifting', small-scale settlement, with periodic returns to favoured locales.

#### Fabric descriptions

1: Hard fabric with moderate FLINT, moderate fine SAND, and common small to medium GROG. Oxidized. Late Neolithic–Early Bronze Age.

2: Moderate to hard with fine to coarse SAND, and common small to medium GROG. Oxidized. Early Bronze Age.

3: Medium to hard fabric with moderate to common SAND, and common to abundant small FLINT. Oxidized exterior and reduced interior. Earlier Neolithic.

4: Hard fabric with abundant small FLINT. Reduced. Earlier Neolithic.

## Discussion

Common to many of the region's larger lithic scatter sites (see e.g. Edmonds *et al.* 1999), the terrace, and particularly its southern edge, clearly saw a palimpsest of activity. Within the confines of the dyke-side cuttings, and further demonstrated by the test pitting, three episodes of activity are attested to:

1) Later Mesolithic;

2) Early Neolithic;

3) Later Neolithic/Early Bronze Age.

This long-term usage of the terrace and the cumulative character of its assemblages should not detract from the terrace-edge site's extraordinary densities, as they are by far and away the highest encountered within the project and are only comparable with those of the Cracknell Farm scatter (see Chapter 4).

The indisputable recovery of earlier Bronze Age pottery from beneath the Fen Clay was the cause of some consternation. This material was substantially later than what had previously been accepted as the Late Neolithic dating of the marine incursion. This anticipation was largely framed in relation to Clark and Godwin's earlier Peacock's Farm investigations (see inset above; Clark *et al.* 1935; Clark & Godwin 1962), and in a search for 'operational' parallels (i.e. site genealogy) we were conscious of the dyke-side cuttings' resonance with that site. There was a sense of frustration; if only we could dig deep enough south across the line of the Backdrove we would also be able to generate sections of comparable elegance to Peacock's Farm in which that site's Mesolithic and Neolithic assemblages separated in the deep off-terrace peat sequences. However, almost concurrently, Cardiff's (re-)investigations at Peacock's Farm demonstrated just how minor and localized its Neolithic components seem to have been, and the vast majority of the material they recovered was attributable to the Late Mesolithic (Smith *et al.* 1989). Sampling that site in test-pit transects, their report suggests densities comparable to that at the Foulmire edge: 33.5 flints per metre-square. As part of that project an earlier Neolithic scatter on the nearby Letter F Farm site was also tested using a comparable methodology. The evidence there suggests densities in the range of only 8.7 flints per metre. (In their report artefact densities are not detailed and concentrations are not highlighted; the figures arrived at here are 'raw' and simply involve dividing the total number of worked flints by metre-squares excavated.) Based on this, in relation to the Foulmire investigations (and also the 'buried' ground surface fieldwalking trials at Barleycroft: Evans *et al.* 1999), it could be proposed that earlier Neolithic flint 'spreads' generally occur at lower densities than Mesolithic occupations. However, this would be to ignore more concentrated or sustained Neolithic occupations, with the vast high-density scatter at Honey Hill, Ramsey (Site 13) being a moot case in point (Edmonds *et al.* 1999). This knoll-top scatter, extending over *c*. 1 ha, was investigated in the course of the Fenland Management Project in 1992. Essentially of Early Neolithic attribution, fieldwalking demonstrated 'core' densities (over 700 sq. m) of 100–253 worked flints per 10 m collection unit. The metre test-pitting densities were equally high (0–96) with an overall mean of 27 pieces. This, however, excludes five sieved test pits (5-mm mesh) whose values ranged from 11–198 pieces (87 mean), and their inclusion raises the site's mean to 37 struck flints per metre. The high-density Early Neolithic scatter at Cracknell Farm on the northern margin of the Upper Delphs terrace is discussed in Chapter 4 below.

In the knowledge that the long barrow literally looms in the background of the dyke-side cuttings, is the Foulmire terrace to be considered in any way 'special'? Within the context of the project, parallels can only be drawn with the investigations on the Hermitage Farm terrace to the southwest, the results of which are fully outlined in Volume 2 (Chapter 2). At first glance the quantity of worked flint recovered from the Foulmire test pits seems substantially greater: 8.6 as opposed to 3.4 average densities (range 0–38 vs 0–8). However, to be truly comparable the Foulmire densities must be factored down by four to account for their greater sample size (2 × 2.00 m vs metre-square). By this the densities become broadly equivalent, with Foulmire having a mean of only 2.15 pieces per metre. The Foulmire values are, if anything, more sporadic and worked flint occurred in only 66 per cent of the test pits compared to 91 per cent representation on the Hermitage Farm terrace. What of the pottery? Including Grooved Ware, Food Vessel and Rusticated Beaker, Foulmire seems to include a high proportion of decorated later Neolithic–Early Bronze Age wares. Admittedly, sherds of Middle Neolithic Ebbsfleet ware and later Neolithic Beaker were recovered from the Hermitage Farm barrow excavations themselves (with Collared Urn associated with that monument's interments), but no 'early' pottery was recovered from the test pitting on that terrace. This negative test-pit recovery pattern is common and the frequency of the Foulmire pottery of this period does appear out of the ordinary. The question of whether it relates in any way to the presence of the long barrow must largely be left until the relevant chapter. However, one possibility is that rising marsh levels at this time led to a general concentration of activity on the upper flanks of the ('deep fen') riverside terraces. Yet that three round barrows were also sited on the Foulmire terrace would indicate that its crown was still 'dry' until the first centuries of the second millennium BC, they presumably being of Early Bronze Age attribution (see Volume 2, Chapter 2). While brackish waters may have eventually lapped up to their perimeter, no instances are known of barrow construction within saturated 'in-marsh' conditions in the region. (Coring in the Borough Fen barrow field near Peterborough also demonstrated a similar relationship between marine clays and round barrows: D. Hall pers. comm.)

The discovery of what is a 'new' Mesolithic site across the southern side of this terrace is itself of major significance. Due, in part, to the depth of cover, but also their sheer paucity, few sites of this period were identified during the Fenland Project (Hall & Coles 1994; Dawson 2000). This negative recovery pattern has, moreover, been further confirmed by subsequent fieldwork within the region. Within the broader environs, despite extensive recent development-led initiatives, the only site of any consequence has been on the northern margins of Cottenham (Mortimer 2000; Conneller forthcoming). Such sites do, indeed, seem to be rare.

The scale of the Foulmire terrace's Early Neolithic settlement activity is an issue that will be further pursued in relationship to the long barrow excavation *per se* (Chapter 3). Nevertheless, of the dyke-side investigation it is worth reviewing just how much material of this attribution was forthcoming. Including 22 sherds of plain bowl pottery, serrated blades, a leaf-shaped arrowhead and a fragment of a polished axe (and possibly other evidence of contemporary axe manufacture), this is relatively substantial. The ultimate question here is whether there is evidence of pre-barrow Neolithic occupation or if 'all' need be tied into a single narrative of the monument's origins.

Featuring in ensuing arguments relating to activity preceding the long barrow, the distribution of this material is relevant. Apart from the one-off recovery of 20 sherds of later Neolithic/earlier Bronze pottery from TP 8 (including a possible sherd of Grooved Ware and sherds from three different Rusticated Beakers), the vast majority of the material came from the southern flank of the terrace. Particularly important is the distribution of the earlier Neolithic ceramics, for the only other occurrence apart from the main cuttings was in TP 16, beside the dyke opposite Cutting A. Certainly there is no evidence of deposition within the immediate area of the long barrow.

Of course, post-depositional processes could well have contributed to the restricted distribution of earlier Neolithic material. It may be the case that it extended further up the terrace slope, but has been scraped away and redeposited during the cutting of turf for the construction of the long mound. A degree of support for this interpretation can be found in the distribution of the flint as a whole (the vast majority of it apparently of later Mesolithic date) as it essentially mirrors that of the Neolithic pottery. It could be argued that the two phases of occupation simply shared the same location along the southern terrace edge. However, the fact that the barrow mound included significant quantities of later Mesolithic flintwork, obviously derived from wider ground surface deposits, indicates truncation and redeposition of an adjacent spread(s). It can only be presumed that the extent of any earlier Neolithic activity may also have thus been effected and originally continued further up the terrace edge. (Some 60 sherds of Neolithic plain bowl pottery were recovered from the mound; the source of this material will be a topic returned to below.) While instances are known of long barrows occurring against/upon a background of Mesolithic pre-barrow Neolithic activity (e.g. Hazleton North: Saville 1990), based on these arguments, and the early date of forest clearance attested to by the Ouse roddon core (4470–4000 cal. BC; 5420±100 BP; Q-2814; see Peglar above), it may also be the case that some degree of blade-based Early Neolithic flintwork has been subsumed within the general later Mesolithic attribution of the lithic assemblage as a whole (see Chapters 3 & 4 for further discussion).

Burnt flint or 'pot-boiler' mounds such as was found in Cutting A are a common feature of the region's archaeology, and occur in marked distributions around the southern and eastern fen-edge (e.g Hall & Coles 1994, 58–64, fig. 39; Healy 1996). Often associated with Beaker material and clearly involving processing activities requiring water, the Foulmire example surely relates to the final phase of the terrace-edge's usage (i.e. presupposing higher water levels/marsh proximity). There has been much speculation as to the function of such features, ranging from the by-products of saunas to cooking and pot

temper (see e.g. Saville 1981c for overview). Given its limited excavation, the Foulmire mound does not particularly advance their interpretation.

What is interesting in the case of the Foulmire Fen example is its proximity to the long barrow. Instances are known in which burnt flint mounds have a mortuary association (e.g. Feltwell Anchor: Crowson 2000) and, given the selective character of their matrix (i.e. visual impact), their potential role as cairns (perhaps interacting with barrows as landscape markers) has been postulated (Edmonds et al. 1999). Nevertheless, there seems no reason to consider the Foulmire 'mound' anything other than domestic. As such, this suggests that some 1500–2000 years after the long barrow's construction, there may have been little sense of the terrace as any kind of exclusively ritual landscape. Yet, as marked by the secondary interments within its mound and, too, the adjacent round barrows on the terrace, it was certainly still a significant place. Alluding to Ingold's introductory quotation, this is reminiscent of another great painting by Bruegel, *The Fall of Icarus*, where in the background the 'mythological' plummets into the sea unnoticed by a labouring ploughman (see Fig. 6.1). The 'grand' and the mundane co-exist shoulder-to-shoulder; over time the Foulmire landscape similarly appears to have seen the interplay of the sacred and everyday, and was never one thing alone.

# Chapter 3

# The Long Barrow: Transforming Wood (and Bodies)

Local farmers remember the 'emergence' of the long barrow between the wars and said that it had increased in size since then as the peat has shrunk around it. It can be seen from Figures 2.8 & 3.1 that the higher and broader 'front' end of the barrow is towards the north-northeast and the barrow is aligned on a south-southwest/north-northeast axis. Long barrows in Britain and Europe are often found to be systematically oriented (e.g. Hodder 1984; Kinnes 1992). The most common direction faced by the wider entrance end is towards the east or southeast, and a similar orientation is found for Early Neolithic long-houses in central Europe.

The explanation usually given for the general orientation of these Neolithic constructions is that it protected their entrances from the prevailing west/northwest winds. Yet do we really believe that this was the prime determinant of the orientation of long barrows? To apply such arguments in a regional context is almost to hark back to themes of Fenland folklore and its near-obsession that the fall and lie of trees requires explanation. (As Godwin notes, its fallen trees do, however, tend to lie with their crowns to the northeast, this pattern probably being the result of the mean direction of southwesterly gales: 1978, 35.) Although potentially reflecting upon the resolution of culture in nature, our concern must rather be with the local expression of broader monumental traditions, and the issue of the barrow's orientation will be further discussed below.

From the pollen evidence it appears that the barrow was built towards the end of a period of clearance and agricultural activity (see Peglar, Chapter 2 p. 26). Oak had come to dominate the uncleared areas of dense forest. A similar picture is obtained from the more specific evidence of the soils beneath the barrow mound (see French below); a forested area had been cleared and seen cultivation. (The issue of the extent of 'contemporary' pre-Barrow Neolithic occupation has already been touched upon and will be further addressed below.)

The 'clearance' context of the monument is significant and questions relating to wood are paramount within this chapter as the timber of the barrow's mortuary chamber was uniquely preserved.

Involving great megalith-like bulks of oak, and dating to the first half of the fourth millennium BC, it constitutes one of the world's oldest timber 'buildings'. The basic trapezoidal form of the long mound may well distantly reference continental longhouses, and the arrangement of its many parts certainly involved structural components. Yet a crucial issue is whether we are dealing with a free-standing building phase at all, as opposed to what was essentially a closed monumental 'architecture' in which earthen construction was always integral and the role of 'great' wood was central. In this regard a series of transformations lie at the heart of this monument: trees into timber, the working of human bodies (i.e. intentional defleshing) and, eventually, the alteration of the mound itself (prompted by the decay, firing and collapse of timber elements) so it became another 'thing', another type of monument. Variously involving sequences of elaboration and/or stripping away, the crux issue is to attempt to define the point of transformation and metamorphosis into 'another thing'.

This emphasis on *process* challenges both a concern with formal architectural precepts (see Evans 2000d concerning the historiography of megalithic 'first architectures') and any sense of the monument as a 'tomb', focusing only upon the burial chamber as a closed event and on reading its embedded 'messages'. Certainly these associations are important, but equally so are the sequences of its many workings, the implied organization of labour and the cumulative character of its construction, and also the barrow's long-term 'place' associations within the cultural landscape (to the point that its mound effectively became an fen-fast island).

## The long mound: a diffuse matrix

It is often difficult to decide whether the results of an excavation should be presented by feature, trench or phase. There are many ways of organizing information, with some involving a higher level of synthesis than others. For example, to present the site immediately phase by phase would involve a relatively high level of abstraction and would limit the ability of the reader to evaluate the conclusions that have been reached.

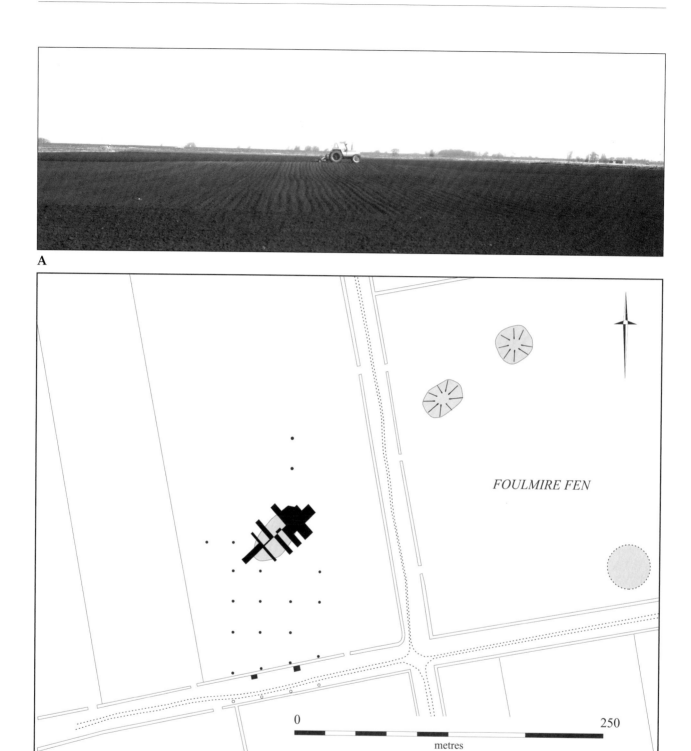

**A**

**B**

**Figure 3.1.** *Top, Foulmire Fen 1984, with tractor poised on the crown of the unexcavated long barrow. (Photograph C. Evans.) Below, trench location.*

Here, at least initially, the data will be treated by area and feature.

We are accustomed to reading monument sequences as a series of 'grand-scale' events. Often a product of the more summary recording procedures of earlier antiquarian efforts (i.e. an 'after the fact' record), this does not seem to be the case with this barrow. Its remarkable preservation does not necessarily ensure greater clarity, as the survival of its structural components equally implies the recovery of its above-ground 'mulch' of construction/destruction debris — a diffuse matrix. Yet herein lies a dilemma of interpretation. Involving a distinct kind of monumental architecture, the challenge the barrow's sequence poses is to make it 'work' as *a standing structure* and, given this, only so much ambiguity can be tolerated. The problem is how to deal with the data in a thoroughly contextual manner, but without simultaneously entertaining a series of over-complex alternative interpretations. In other words, informed by practice (historiography) and 'building sense', the possibilities are not open-ended.

We approached the monument tentatively. Although the contour map seemed fairly conclusive (Figs. 2.8 & 3.3), doubts had been expressed whether the long mound might not be a linked pair of round barrows and, at that time, few were convinced that a long barrow could exist in such low wet conditions. In any case we were uncertain whether our funding sources would be able to support an extended and expensive excavation. We also knew that the site would be difficult to dig. Experience with the Delphs' round barrows (see Volume 2, Chapter 2) and with the soil conditions in general had shown that the scale of leaching and discolouration was considerable. Given the complexity of long barrow construction sequences that had been demonstrated elsewhere in the country, would it be possible to discern details in leached Fenland soils?

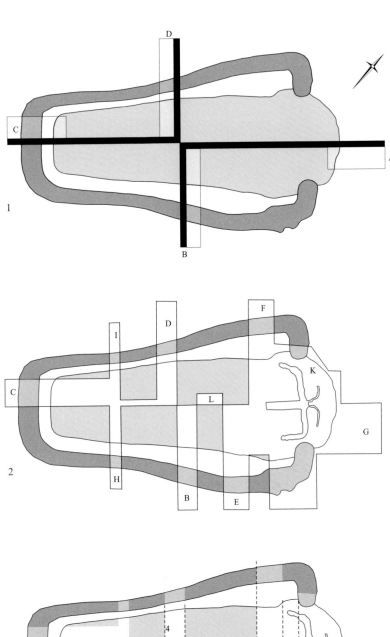

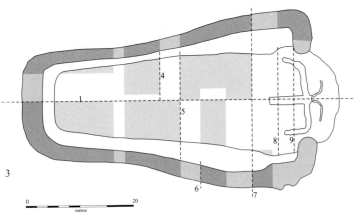

**Figure 3.2.** *Area and sequence of excavation (1 & 2); 3) section location.*

Following the terrace-side investigations described in Chapter 2, in 1985 the decision was taken to excavate axially staggered, metre-wide cross-transects across the profile of the barrow (Fig. 3.2). These were dug by hand

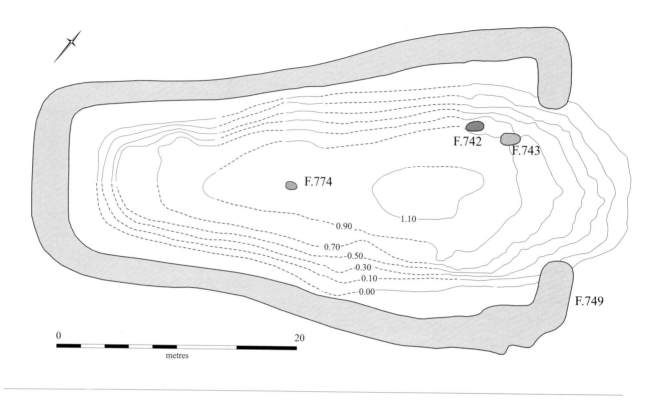

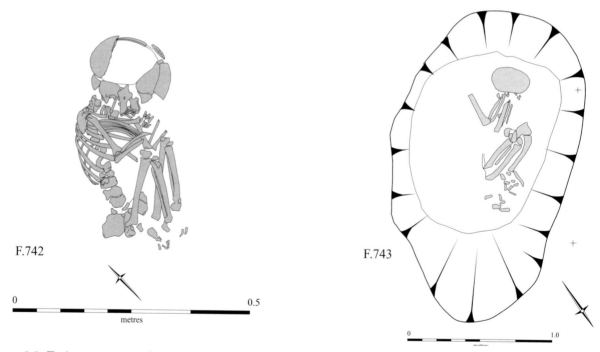

**Figure 3.3.** *Top) contour map of stripped long barrow mound surface showing mound-intrusive features; below) details of the inhumations.*

across the top of the mound (with wider cuttings off of its sides to expose its surrounding ditch) with the sole aim of demonstrating that this was, in fact, a long barrow. Thereafter progressing with the trial excavations, two trenches were dug (B & D) towards the centre of the mound. These were excavated in summer 1985 on either side of the central axis of the mound in order to obtain a complete cross-section. The specific aims were to obtain structural evidence of the monument's construction in what was hoped would be a relatively simple part of the mound, and to provide dating evidence that it was indeed of Neolithic date. The trenches were excavated by hand in 10-cm spits except where features, cuts or layers could be followed with ease. It often proved easier to dig in plan in these difficult soils and to reconstruct features and layers from the plan and section drawings. All deposits were at least partially dry sieved.

Before embarking on an account of the deposits of the mound it is necessary to explain the terms used to describe the barrow's main components. The mound itself was surrounded by a slight revetment 'trough' (F.762), on the outside of which were set banks (F.733 & F.734). Surrounding the barrow was a ditch (F.749, F.767–770; hereafter F.749). The northeastern end of the mound was revetted by a timber façade consisting of a line of substantial posts set into a construction trench (F.712 & F.713). Behind this was a wooden mortuary structure (F.750) surrounded by a ring-bank (F.725/726) which formed part of the mound. The mortuary structure had three axial posts, the proximal (F.707), medial (F.706) and distal (F.705), which divided the mortuary structure into back and front sections or sub-chambers. In the proximal section was found a turf mound (F.737). In front of the façade was a gravel forecourt (F.720) and a fore-structure consisting of a hornwork entrance-way (F.716–719; hereafter F.716), the latter revetting fore-banks on either side (F.746/747). Set above these and across the hornwork entrance was a 'façade-bank' (F.736); as will be outlined below, the status of this feature is extremely problematic.

A

B

**Figure 3.4.** *The mound: A) looking southeast across unexcavated 'front'; B) looking northeast across the pattern of the trenching. (Photographs G. Owen.)*

and which can therefore be described here in general terms (see e.g. Figs. 3.5 & 3.6).

*Mound weathering*: Deposits of sand silts and gravels (e.g. [2506] in F.766) were found above the gravel banks that flanked the sides of the mound. They appeared to be weathered or washed out from it and its banks. Most of these weathering deposits occurred beneath or contemporary with the earliest deposits of reed swamp (e.g.

### Post-mound deposits and features
Before reaching the mound and its surrounding ditch, a series of deposits were encountered within Trenches B and D which were later found elsewhere on the site

71

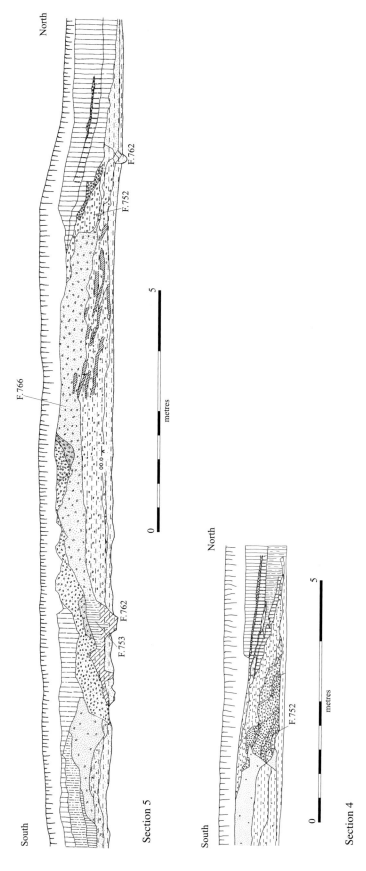

**Figure 3.5.** *Cross-sections through mound (Sections 4 & 5).*

[2507]). A later phase of weathering occurred above the reed swamp, but below the woody peat, and was only traced at the central rear of the long mound.

*The reed swamp*: An 'A'-horizon of fibrous peat sealed the sides and ditches of the long mound and was traced into the surrounding fields (the 'lower peat'). It consisted of a dark grey-green organic silt with visible organic material. This was generally 0.05–0.20 m thick but deepened to 0.50–0.60 m over the long barrow ditch. The surface of the peat lay at 0.00–0.05 m OD, but beside the barrow it rose to 0.50–0.80 m OD. The barrow's crown would have projected 0.40 m above the peat at the east end (at its surviving height) and up to 0.30 m above it in the west.

*The alluvium*: The onset of the Fen Clay was represented by a thin layer of alluvial clay which occurred discontinuously between the fibrous peat and woody peat layers surrounding the barrow. Consisting of a light grey clay, it lay as a thin band (0.05 m thick) over the reed swamp in the long barrow ditch and as a patchy layer (up to 0.13 m thick) across the exterior ground surface; its surface lay at 0.00–0.40 m OD. (The maximum height of this deposit corresponds with its level as found in the more recent excavations on the Sutton Site 1 'island' north of the Bedford Level, where it lay 0.50 m deep: Last 1997.)

*The woody peat*: A thick layer of woody peat, representing the latest surviving phase of peat formation, sealed the sides and ditches of the long barrow above the alluvium and reed swamp. Extending across the exterior ground surface, this deposit had been partly destroyed by agricultural activity with its decay being represented by the ploughsoil. The woody peat has also been subject to shrinkage as the result of drainage. As it survived at the time of excavation, it abutted the crown of the long barrow and it is clear, therefore, that it originally submerged the long mound.

*Modern disturbance*: Ploughmarks were found crossing the surface of the mound on the orientation of the modern field boundary and the gravel brought up from the mound was visible in the ploughsoil above it prior to excavation. A post-medieval drainage ditch crossed Trenches E and F and modern disturbances were dug within Trenches B and D. Because of the earlier submergence of the barrow, all this activity was recent and of limited impact. Deep ploughing had only just begun to bite into the top of the mound and most of its surface remained as it was at the onset of peat growth.

*Mound surface features*: After the barrow's closure the monument continued as a place of burial and two inhumations where found dug into the top of the mound (Fig. 3.3). These and other 'late' burials cannot of course be easily dated since they could have occurred at any time after the construction of the mound, all being unaccompanied by artefacts. However, the fills of the burial and other pits did not contain peaty deposits so they must have been dug prior to the submergence of the mound by the upper woody peat. It may also be relevant that round barrows in the area have proven to have Iron Age

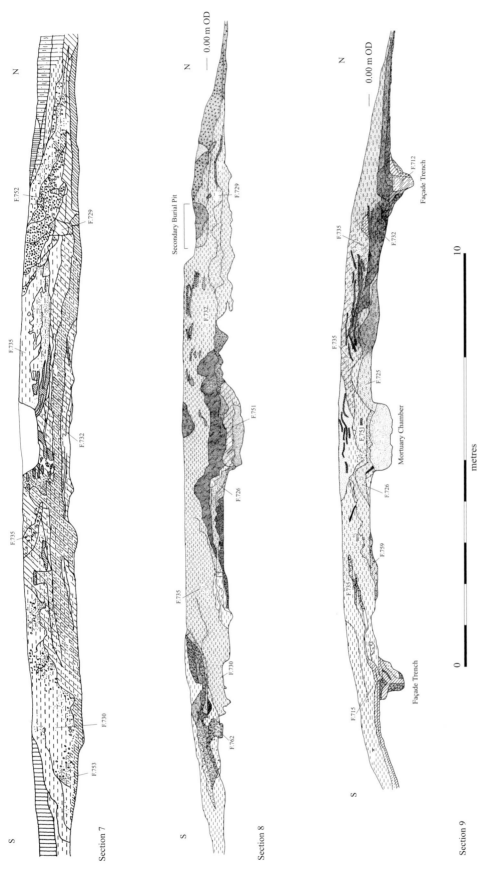

**Figure 3.6.** *Cross-sections through mound; Sections 7–9.*

features dug into their surfaces (see Volume 2, Chapters 2 & 3).

Burial pit [2921] contained the skeleton of an adult (F.743: Fig. 3.3). The pit was oval in plan and oriented on the main axis of the barrow. It had steep sides and an almost flat base, 0.40 m deep. The upper fill is consistent with the gravel capping the surface of the mound, suggesting that this was intact and uneroded when the burial was made. This and the fact that the burial respects the orientation of the mound (as well as its function) might indicate that the interment took place not long after the construction of the mound. A lower lens of grey sandy loam in the fill may have derived from decayed turf; the inhumation was crouched (Skeleton 2; see Lee below).

Burial pit [2902] contained an infant inhumation and was again oriented on the main axis of the long mound (F.742: Fig. 3.3). It had a flattish base and a surviving depth of 0.55 m. As with the F.743 burial, the upper fills of the pit were most likely derived from the gravel capping, and so the same arguments about dating apply. The crouched burial (Skeleton 1) was partially covered by turves.

A further pit (F.774), not used for burial but lined with pointed stakes, was cut into the surface of the mound in Trench D (Fig. 3.3). The pit had vertical sides in its lower half but a conical mouth, and survived to a depth of 1.3 m. The fill consisted of layers of gravels, sands and silts with clay towards the base. There were also deposits of twigs and other organic materials. Set vertically around its sides were 25 stakes which were generally 0.05–0.10 m in diameter and up to 0.65 m long, A relatively 'late' date is indicated for this feature by the very survival of the wood and the fact that the stakes appeared trimmed by a metal axe (M. Taylor pers. comm.).

Direct parallels for such wood-lined pits have been found on later Bronze Age sites in the region. That at West Fen Row was associated with burnt flint and interpreted as relating to cooking (Martin 1988). A more recent example from a terrace-edge settlement on the Ouse floodplain at Barleycroft Farm seemed, similarly to the long barrow feature, to contain an organic mulch, which it was thought pertained to tanning (it was clamp-sealed: Evans & Knight 1997; 2000). As indicated by the project's environmental studies, the crown of the mound would have stood proud (and relatively 'dry') above the surrounding marshes until the first millennium BC and, in this context, the presence of this feature speaks of later 'visitation'. This was apparently accompanied by only minimum deposition; only two definite post-Early Neolithic sherds were recovered, one probably the base of a later Bronze Age urn from the upper façade-bank, the other a grog-tempered sherd from Trench B (see Knight below). However, as detailed by Legge below, some of the animal remains associated with the barrow's weathering and the peat horizons (e.g. pike bones) could relate to the re-use of the mound (as an 'island'). As will be argued in Volume 2 in relationship to the round barrows, the crowns of earlier burial mounds appear to have been re-used, probably as short-lived procurement 'stations' for marshland resources.

*Trenches B & D*

These trenches allowed the basic structure of the mound to be investigated. It was surfaced with sandy gravels, generally 0.10 m thick but up to 0.40 m thick in hollows in the surface of the underlying deposits (Figs. 3.2 & 3.5). This layer survived better at the edges of the mound. Below the capping along the edges of the mound, thicker deposits of sand and gravel mixed with layers of loam were found to be 'banked' against its sides, though these deposits could not easily be distinguished from the slipped capping.

Below the gravel capping were found three main layers of silt and turf (F.766, the long mound *per se*).

Generally these deposits shared the same well-defined vertical/steep faces on the outer edges of the mound. This coincided with small linear features cutting the subsoil and filled with bank material. These were 0.10–0.20 m deep and 0.20 m wide and probably held timber revetments (F.762); the gravel 'banks' may also have helped to support the revetment (F.752 & F.753). The gravel capping and banks had slipped over the top of the revetment trench. Another interpretation is that the banks and capping sealed the trench and were later than the revetment. There is no evidence that a free-standing timber enclosure occurred prior to the building of the mound and, wherever observed, the revetment trenches seemed contemporary with the mound. The revetment was contemporary with or later than the façade and mortuary structure, and the latter could not have stood without a surrounding bank or mound (see below). It is unlikely, therefore, that the revetment stood before the mound and, in any case, the revetment trench is rather slight to have held timbers without the aid of the mound and banks.

While digging Trenches B & D we were aware that, although the overall sequences of deposits in the two trenches were similar, the nature of the deposits and the finds densities differed. The northern side of the barrow (Trench D) had slightly sandier layers and individual turves could more easily be seen. In addition, the density of flints to the north seemed higher (Fig. 3.57).

Can we be more precise about the soil that was used to build the mound and where it came from? Samples of the mound make-up were subjected to micromorphological analysis. French (below) suggests that considerable quantities of soil material for the mound were scraped up from the immediate surroundings. Evidence from the flint artefacts in the mound itself (see Middleton below) shows conclusively that the soil and turves had been taken from the area around the barrow. The capping gravels and surrounding bank gravels were derived from the deeper digging of the surrounding ditch.

*The east end of the mound (Trenches E, F, G, K & L)*
Trenches E & F were excavated in the summer of 1986 specifically to obtain a second cross-section of the mound and a further 10 m of the longitudinal section (Fig. 3.2). They were excavated by hand in a series of 5–10 cm deep spits. Trench G, a rectangular extension east of Trench E and to the south of the longitudinal axis of the long mound, was excavated in the autumn of that year. The trench was designed to complete the longitudinal section of the eastern half of the mound, to add a further cross-section (with Trench F) and to enable a substantial area of the mound to be

excavated, to clarify further the nature and date of its construction. A large portion of the ditch was also to be investigated.

A narrow slot trench was also dug against the northern east–west edge of Trench G over the eastern end of the barrow in order to assess whether a mortuary structure existed. In the western end of the trench the soil peeled off onto a glistening black surface. This was wood, and it appeared to be substantial (Fig. 3.7). Other pieces soon began appearing further to the west in the trench and it quickly became clear that the barrow's timber mortuary structure survived. This was the cause of much excitement and many official 'visitations' soon ensued. Given both the rarity and fragility of this finding (it being feared that the excavations to date had already altered the stability of the conditions which had allowed the wood to survive), under the auspices of the Fenland Committee English Heritage agreed to provide funding for the site's full excavation. This allowed the fieldwork to continue throughout the winter of 1986–7, which required erecting a shelter over the timber structure (Fig. 3.15). Despite snow, fen winds and low temperatures, it was possible to keep pumps going continuously through into the following summer and autumn, and to provide heat when necessary.

The excavation of the mortuary chamber (and its allied structures) will be discussed below. Its discovery meant that the whole of the eastern end of the mound had to be excavated, as well as Trench C. Trench K, a rectangular extension east of Trench F and north of the central east–west axis of the long mound, was excavated in the autumn, winter and spring of 1986–7. The 2 m swathe north of the central longitudinal axis was excavated in autumn 1986, together with the Trench G excavation, by 5–10 cm spits. Only once the mound was better understood could it be excavated by phase.

A gravel capping was again found in Trenches E, F, G & K, together with gravel banks and the revetment on the north and south edges of the mound (Fig. 3.6). The upper soil and turf deposits again showed evidence of a difference between the areas north and south of the central east–west axis: north of that line and in the infill above the mortuary structure turf lines could clearly be seen, while to the south the structure of the deposit was less well defined. There were again vague dumping lines, but no indication of any internal partition of the mound.

In order to appreciate the barrow mound's broader dynamics two other components must be mentioned at this time (Figs. 3.13 & 3.16). The first is the façade-front bank (F.736 et al.). The details of its construction will described below. Suffice it to state that this was substantial; 12.5 m long and 4 m wide, it

**A**

**B**

**Figure 3.7.** *A) Trench E/G showing the first exposure of preserved mortuary chamber wood; B) detail of timber. (Photograph P. Reeves.)*

stood 0.90 m above the contemporary ground surface. Possibly interrelated with the hornwork structure-retained fore-banks (F.746 & F.747), there is ambiguity as to whether it should be counted as an elaboration of the barrow's various front structures (i.e. those allied with the mortuary chamber) or as a remodelling of the barrow itself; if, indeed, a constructed feature

**Figure 3.9.** *Trench L north section showing east/west mound interface. (Photograph G. Owen.)*

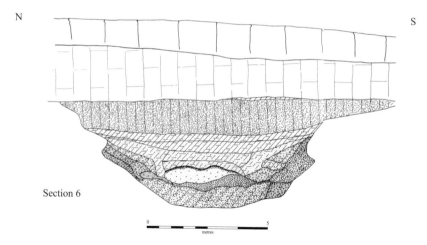

Section 6

0        5
metres

**Figure 3.10.** *Section across Ditch F.749 (Section 6).*

accompanied the construction of the mortuary chamber, an articulated red deer leg was found deposited on top of the western end of the ring-bank (see Legge below).

Finally, while really not so much an area of excavation as a slip-trench, Trench L was only rapidly dug to complete the longitudinal section through the length of the barrow (Fig. 3.2). (Unfortunately, no finds were recovered from this cutting and this severely compromises the barrow's artefact distributions.) From the bedding of the mound deposits immediately to the east, it was anticipated that some manner of division between a primary eastern mound (F.732) and its western 'long' extension might be distinguished at this point. This was, indeed, found to be the case: the edge of the primary mound was marked by a minor revetment trench (F.731) 0.20–0.40 m wide and 0.40 m deep; albeit discontinuous, this feature was thereafter traced in Trenches E & G.

*The western end of the mound (Trench C)*
Trench C was opened in the autumn of 1986 in order to recover the remaining length of the longitudinal section and to test whether the ditch circled the western end of the mound (Fig. 3.2). Two further trenches were excavated north and south of the central longitudinal axis 7 m west of Trench D. These were machine-excavated to the mound surface and were designed to obtain a profile of the west end of the mound; they were 2 m wide.

The sequence of deposits was as described in the earlier discussion of Trenches B & D. The only difficulty concerns the existence of a revetment. The excavation results, particularly the sections, left some leeway concerning whether one could be distinguished at this end (Fig. 3.8). Any such revetment would certainly have to have been slighter here than in other parts of the mound.

*The barrow ditch*
Trenches B & D–F were designed to sample 4–5 m lengths of the barrow's surrounding ditch

at all, as opposed to a collapse phenomenon. The other feature is the horseshoe-shaped ring-bank in which the mortuary structure was set and which opened eastward (F.725/726). This was 1.30–1.40 m wide and 0.50–0.60 m high, and generally consisted of upcast clay silts. At points immediately exterior to this feature, the source of its fabric could be distinguished as it was ringed by slight scoops or troughs. At 1.50–2.00 m wide and only 0.10–0.20 m deep, these evidently also resulted in the truncation of the pre-barrow surface deposits. Attesting to the fact that some degree of ritual activity

(F.749, F.767–F.770:Figs. 3.2 & 3.10). However, owing to the high water-table and difficulties of drainage, we were only able to excavate short lengths of it by hand, principally to retrieve sections. In Trench G, a longer (8 m) portion of the ditch was excavated and important dating evidence was obtained as well as a better understanding of the ditch's plan and fills (Fig. 3.11). Its excavation in Trench G meant that we could predict the position of and excavate the northern butt of the ditch in Trench K. The ditch was shown to surround the west end of the mound in Trench C.

The ditch proper lay within a wide truncation hollow, 5–8 m across and 0.40 m deep below the surface of the gravel terrace (although this 'truncation' may have been the result of erosion of the ground surface). The truncation, whatever its cause, began 1–2 m beyond the edge of the mound. The ditch itself was 2–3 m wide at the front of the barrow, but was up to 4 m across at the tail of the mound. Its base lay 1.40–1.65 m below the ground surface. The ditch's depth was uniform and was a deep 'basin-shape' in section with a concave base.

The ditch's fill sequence consisted of three naturally occurring deposits. All features with near-vertical sides cut into gravel terracing are prone to rapid erosion as the loose bonding of the sand and gravel matrix gives way under gravitational pull, especially when ground water is flowing through and undercutting the sands and gravels in their sides. The result is aggradation of the ditch's sides which can fill the profile by upwards of two-thirds in less than a year.

**A**

**B**

**Figure 3.11.** *The surrounding ditch (F.749): A) northwest terminal (note marl in lower profile); B) southeastern corner 'in flow'. (Photographs G. Owen & P. Shand.)*

The primary fills of the ditch consisted of two deposits (Figs. 3.10 & 3.11), the first of which had been produced in the way just described. Along the inner sides of the ditch were found deposits of grey-brown sand silts and gravel. The deposit filled the space between the ditch sides and the central marl 'platform'. This second primary fill developed at the same time as the sides of the ditch were being filled with gravel slip, and it prevented these deposits from extending completely across the ditch. The marl consisted of a whitish yellow-grey deposit filling the centre of the ditch. It often had near-vertical edges; appearing like a 'platform' in plan, when seen in section it was akin to a volcanic plume. A calcareous material deposited in spring-like conditions, there is little doubt that the marl was a waterborne, spring-created phenomenon attributable to the early history of the ditch (C. French pers. comm.); thin lines of reed and other organic material within the deposit represent phases of standstill in the rising marl.

The secondary upper fills of the ditch consisted of dark brown sandy clay. The dominant clay element was probably waterborne, while the continued degradation of the ditch sides may account for some of the sand and gravel fill.

A small pit, 0.40 m wide and 0.35 m deep, was recut into the marl in the northeast portion of the ditch. Filled with sandy clay silts, it appeared to be associated with the base of an upright pointed stake set within the pit. However, it is possible that the stake had been driven from a higher level at a late stage and it could potentially relate to the pit F.774, later Bronze Age usage. (It was not filled with peaty loam and, therefore, was unlikely to be of post-medieval attribution.)

Few finds were made in the ditch and no direct evidence for more than one phase of its cutting was found. The onset of the formation of the central marl deposit must have been swift because there are few traces of gravel slips beneath it. Indeed, the primary fills of the ditch provide strong evidence that the groundwater was already relatively high at the time of construction of the monument.

*Micromorphological analysis*
by C.A.I. FRENCH
Sixteen samples were analyzed in thin section using the standard methods of Murphy (1986) and descriptions of Bullock *et al.* (1985b). The buried soil preserved beneath the long mound was sampled at two loci. Profile A consists of four contiguous samples (8–11) taken from the *c.* 23-cm-thick soil profile beneath the east mound ([3391]). This soil was believed by the excavators to be relatively free of disturbance caused by the various phases of construction at the site, and in particular the construction of the wooden mortuary structure. Profile B consists of four contiguous samples (4–7) from top to bottom through the *c.* 25-cm-thick soil profile in the southeast quadrant.

Two further profiles through the buried soil associated with the mortuary chamber were examined. Profile C (Sample 12 & 13) was located beneath the floor of the mortuary structure (at 3.8 EW / 2.5–2.7 NS); and Profile D (Samples 14 & 15) beneath the façade of the mortuary structure (at 9.4 EW / 1.6–1.8 NS). A final profile (E; Sample 16) was taken at the interface of the

buried soil and the roof timber (at IC3). In addition, individual samples were taken of the make-up of the second long mound or west mound (F.766; Sample 1), the primary ovate mound or east mound (F.735; Sample 3), as well as the interface between the two (Sample 2).

*The buried soil*
*Profile A:* This buried soil profile is represented by an apedal, partially homogeneous, slightly disturbed soil fabric. The soil texture ranges from a loamy sand to a sandy clay loam, generally becoming slightly finer with depth; very fine quartz, silt and clay predominate. Although there is some illuviated clay present, as rare to occasional laminated and non-laminated dusty clay coatings of quartz grains and within the groundmass, they are insufficient to provide much insight into the history of the soil's development. The fabric is relatively organic and has been biologically reworked. It contains much amorphous organic matter, a few flecks of charcoal and wood fragments, as well as a few pseudomorphs of former plant tissues. The soil has also been subject to ferruginization and the deposition of calcium carbonate. These characteristics suggest that the soil fabric is representative of lower 'B'- or 'Bw'-Horizon material.

There have been several phases of water movement affecting this soil. Initially, some of the clay fraction (the non-laminated dusty clay) has been slaked due to hydromorphism. Second, there has been some iron movement and redeposition, due to alternating wet and dry conditions, probably as a result of a fluctuating local groundwater table, but it is impossible to date the inception of this process. Third, calcium carbonate crystals act as partial void infills, and comprise *c.* 10–75% of the total groundmass and void space, their abundance increasing dramatically with soil depth. This too is a consequence of hydromorphism and the drying out of base-rich soil water, which is probably a result of the general process of the drainage of the fen. Much of this micritic fabric also became impregnated with iron, again due to the fluctuating ground water table.

There are signs that the soil has suffered some disturbance. First, the soil fabric is not fully homogenized and exhibits poorly sorted, clumpy zones of fabric. Second, the rare to occasional presence of laminated and non-laminated dusty clay coatings of voids and channels suggest some limited soil disturbance. In one case, a pore is completely infilled with successive lenses of non-laminated and laminated dusty clay which are suggestive of either one major event or several inwashes of fines caused by successive phases of soil disturbance. It is generally believed that the illuviation of dusty clay coatings relates to forest disturbance in general (Courty & Fedoroff 1982; Scaife & Macphail 1983; Slager & van de Wetering 1977). Third, there are very rare fragments of laminated and non-laminated clay incorporated within the groundmass which are probably relics of former Bt or argillic horizon soil material (see below). Fourth, there are rare void infills of a foreign fabric, ferruginized very fine sand and silt. Fifth, fine amorphous organic matter is rarely associated with non-laminated impure clay coatings, giving it a dirty appearance. None of these features suggest more than slight disturbance of the buried soil, most probably associated with the building of the long barrow. As only the Bw horizon survives, the 'A'-horizon and turf must have been removed as a part of the construction of the mortuary structure and later mounds.

*Profile B:* This buried soil profile is an apedal, partially heterogeneous, slightly disturbed and leached loamy sand to sandy loam. Although very fine sand, silt and clay predominate, and increase slightly with depth, the fabric is fractionally more coarse than the soil in Profile A, with much medium sand.

The extant buried soil at this sample locus contains an abundance of illuvial clay. There are two main types of clay coating present in abundance, and another three types present in minor amounts. First, micro-laminated limpid clay, or alternating thin laminae of fine and speckled fine clay, occur rarely as partial infills of voids in the groundmass. This type of clay illuviation is indicative of former woodland conditions (Macphail 1986; 1987). Second, there are rare to occasional laminated dusty coatings of the voids and the groundmass, composed of alternating thick laminae of the same textured clay containing micro-contrasted or impure clay, which are suggestive of successive phases of tree clearance (Courty & Fedoroff 1982; Fedoroff 1968; Macphail 1986; Slager & van de Wetering 1977). Both these types of clay illuviation undoubtedly occurred before the construction of the mortuary structure/long barrow. The pollen analysis (see Peglar, above) provides strong corroborative evidence of former lime/oak woodland that was in decline after c. 4300 cal. BC (c. 5400 BP), and coincident with the first weeds and cereals indicative of human activity in the area. Third, many non-laminated dusty or impure clay coatings, containing numerous contrasting particles of fine silt size, occur in the groundmass, and rarely as partial void infills. This type of clay coating is especially indicative of soil disturbance (Jongerius 1970). In addition to this third type of coating, two other types of clay coating were observed which are also indicative of soil disturbance: rare to occasional non-laminated dusty/dirty coatings of the whole fabric, including the sand grains, groundmass and voids, as well as rare laminated dusty/dirty coatings occurring as partial void infills. The dirty aspect to these coatings is a result of the secondary incorporation of much fine organic matter and/or comminuted charcoal. Their combined presence is indicative of relatively severe and deep disturbance of the soil. The illuviation of these clays must have occurred whilst the area remained as dry land, both pre-burial and before the post-burial hydromorphic regime.

The abundance and variety of clay coatings indicate that this is a lower Bt or argillic horizon of an argillic brown earth soil (Avery 1980; McKeague 1983), despite the frequency of fine amorphous organic matter throughout the groundmass. This soil horizon becomes more well developed with depth.

Argillic brown earths are believed to have developed under a forest canopy. Leaf leachate mobilizes fine clay mainly in the Eb or eluvial horizon, and soil water translocates it down the profile into the illuvial or Bt (argillic) horizon which becomes enriched with clay (Duchaufour 1982; Fedoroff 1982; Fisher 1982). Development of such argillic horizons is strongly associated in temperate climates with the Atlantic/Sub-Boreal period (Bridges 1978; Macphail 1987; Weir et al. 1971). Argillic horizons in deeper soils, for example at the Mesolithic site of Selmeston in Sussex (Scaife & Macphail 1983) and Balksbury Iron Age camp (Macphail 1985a), are characterized by structural units and voids with clay coatings. These coatings comprise a first phase of fine limpid clay to micro-laminated clay, succeeded by increasingly coarse, dusty clay phases. This type of sequence, as evident here beneath the long barrow, is interpreted as a result of clay translocation under virgin woodland being followed by the translocation of impure clay under increasingly unstable conditions through forest clearance/disturbance and cultivation practises (Macphail 1986; Macphail et al. 1987; Slager & van de Wetering 1977). Similar types of clay coating are also found in the make-up of the later long mound (see below).

Both the fabrics of the buried soil and the make-up of the mound are characterized by very fine amorphous organic matter and finely comminuted charcoal, as are most of the dusty clay coatings. Some of the charcoal may possibly originate from the initial clearance of the area, but much of it may also result from activities associated with the construction and possible 'firing' of the mortuary structure and the construction of the successive mounds. Nevertheless, some of this fine organic matter may have

resulted from limited tillage of the soil after clearance and prior to the construction of the barrow. There is some corroboration from the pollen analysis for this with the occurrence of small quantities of cereal pollen and various weeds associated with human activity occurring at c. 4300 cal. BC (c. 5400 BP) or at about the same period as the observed decline in elm, that is prior to the construction of the barrow.

The relatively large amounts of coarse, impure or dusty clay coatings, often with included fine charcoal, may suggest either trampling and/or tillage, as suggested at Hazelton (Macphail 1985b). Certainly the mechanical damage caused by tillage and trampling makes the soil susceptible to slaking by rain/soil water. Unlike lessivage (fine clay illuviation under forest), not just fine clay but all of the fine fraction may be mobilized, including all sizes of silt and clay-sized material, plus fragments of organic matter and charcoal (Jongerius 1970; 1983; Romans & Robertson 1983; Macphail et al. 1987). But if the soil had suffered much trampling, a concentrated zone of slaked fines could be expected to have formed in the upper part of the surviving soil profile. As this is not the case, and the fines, comminuted charcoal and fine organic matter are found throughout the buried soils at several locations, there may have been some limited pre-burial tillage, but the absence of intermixed soil material from different soil horizons and the lack of characteristic small, sub-rounded aggregates with slaking crusts suggests that this is just a very disturbed and biologically mixed soil.

Almost half of the total groundmass has been subject to leaching, and the consequent removal of much of the fines content of the soil. This is particularly noticeable towards the base of the soil where there are greater and lesser densities of textural pedofeatures. It is most probable that this event occurred after the construction and use of the long barrow, and is probably mainly the result of the hydromorphic effects of a fluctuating groundwater table. There is every possibility that this occurred in the half millennium or so immediately after the construction of the long barrow, and was associated with the increase in the abundance of sedges observed in the pollen analysis (c. 3250–2500 cal. BC; 4500–4000 BP).

*Profile C:* This c. 20-cm-thick buried soil profile is represented by an apedal, homogeneous, sandy loam to sandy clay loam. The upper 10 cm is a sandy loam which is dominated by very fine quartz and smaller amounts of medium and fine quartz, silt and clay; and the lower 10 cm is a sandy clay loam with approximately equal proportions of medium and very fine quartz, silt and clay.

The amount of illuvial clay present increases dramatically with depth, especially in the lower half of the profile. The very rare micro-laminated limpid clay found in the groundmass of the lower part of the profile is indicative of former woodland conditions (Macphail 1986; 1987). There is also rare laminated dusty clay within the groundmass which is suggestive of tree clearance (Courty & Fedoroff 1982). As in Profile B, the illuviation of these types of clay could only have occurred prior to the building of the mortuary structure. In addition, there is abundant non-laminated dusty clay throughout the fabric. Its presence is indicative of considerable soil disturbance, which could have resulted from either soil truncation and/or the associated construction of the mortuary structure.

On the other hand, the organic content of the soil declines with depth, and consists mainly of small amounts of very fine amorphous organic matter, very few fragments of plant tissue and flecks of fine charcoal, as well as a few pseudomorphs of plant tissue. In addition, there have been minor amounts of calcium carbonate and iron movement and redeposition in the voids and groundmass due to hydromorphism.

In general, this buried soil profile resembles the soil Profiles A, B and D. Thus the soil profile comprises a 'B'- or 'Bw'-Horizon overlying a 'Bt'- or argillic horizon.

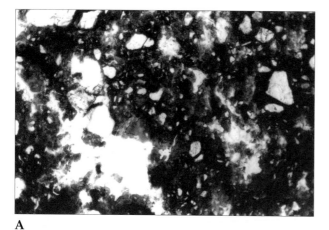

**A**

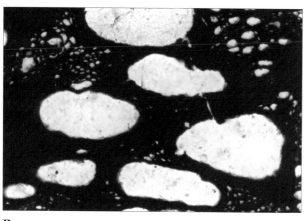

**B**

**Figure 3.12.** *Soil micromorphology: A) Sample 2, mound interface (sesquioxide impregnated; Bt/PPL/2 mm); B) Sample 16, roof timber and illuviated fines (PPL/2 mm).*

*Profile D:* The *c.* 20-cm-thick buried soil profile preserved beneath the façade area in front of the mortuary chamber is generally similar in its micromorphological features to Profile C beneath the chamber itself (see above).

*Profile E:* One of the lifted, complete sections of the roof of the wooden mortuary structure with the soil beneath (IC8) was thin sectioned and revealed a *c.* 8-cm-thick section through the oak roof timber (Fig. 3.12:B). The soil both above and below this roof timber is similar in composition. It is a relatively dense, apedal, heterogeneous mixture of two similar fabrics. Fabric 1 is a sandy (clay) loam which is dominated by more or less equal proportions of very fine quartz, silt and clay, which contains less organic matter (than Fabric 2) and is not impregnated with amorphous sesquioxides. Fabric 2 exhibits a similar soil texture, but contains very fine amorphous organic matter and is impregnated with amorphous sesquioxides.

Both fabrics contain abundant illuviated clay, including rare micro-laminated limpid clay, occasional to many laminated dusty clay and many to abundant non-laminated dusty clay in the groundmass and voids. They are indicative of argillic 'Bt'-Horizon material, as discussed for Profiles A–D (see above). This heterogeneous mixture of argillic horizon material within the mortuary structure probably results from the collapse of the structure under the weight of the overlying mound which contained much Bt horizon material, rather than the deliberate backfilling of the chamber after its use.

The presence of non-laminated dusty clay lining many of the cells of the oak roof timber suggests that soil disturbance occurred, probably associated with the remodelling of the overlying mound and later fluctuating groundwater levels.

**The mounds**
*The east mound* (F.732): In the field, the east mound (or the primary ovate mound) appeared to have been constructed of recognizable turves and soil. The micromorphological analysis of the soil in between the turves revealed a sandy clay loam with very abundant (*c.* 20–25%) illuvial clay coatings throughout the fabric.

The abundance and variety of these coatings are indicative of argillic or Bt horizon material, similar to that found below the long barrow in Profiles A and B (see above). The characteristics evident in this soil material give a good impression of the nature of the surrounding pre-barrow soil. There are at least three phases of pedogenesis evident. First, there is occasional, well-oriented limpid clay within the groundmass and voids, indicative of the illuviation of fine clay beneath stable forested conditions (Fisher 1982; Macphail 1986; 1987), and the formation of an argillic horizon (as described above; Avery 1980; McKeague 1983). Second, there are occasional laminated dusty clay coatings of both the groundmass and voids which are indicative of tree clearance (Courty & Fedoroff 1982; Macphail 1986; Macphail *et al.* 1987). Third, there are a variety of many other illuvial clay coatings, primarily non-laminated dusty coatings acting as partial void infills, rarely exhibiting laminations with the limpid and laminated dusty clay. Together, these latter illuvial clays are indicative of soil disturbance, most likely associated with clearance activities (Courty & Fedoroff 1982; Macphail 1986; Macphail *et al.* 1987). Some may also result from the disturbance caused by man in the act of scraping up the soil with which to construct the successive barrow mounds. This may have also been responsible for the sideways tipping of many of the coatings.

As in the surviving buried soil beneath the mounds, the mound fabric is very dirty in appearance, largely due to the abundance of fine organic matter and charcoal. This is probably due to the disturbance, and the incorporation of organic material, along with the pre-existing surface horizons used in the construction of the mounds.

Also, this former soil/mound material has been subject to similar hydromorphic effects as the underlying buried soil. Zones of the groundmass tend to be more or less depleted of textural coatings, and about a quarter of the fabric is impregnated with sesquioxides.

*The west mound* (F.766): The soil between the turves which together comprise the western long mound displays similar characteristics to the eastern mound's argillic soil horizon material described above, although it is a slightly more coarse-textured sandy loam. This reinforces the view that the pre-barrow soil was a well-developed argillic brown earth, which formed under stable, relatively dry, wooded conditions. Moreover, the incorporation of soil from the lower horizons in the barrow mounds indicates that considerable quantities of earth must have been stripped from the area surrounding the barrow, and that most of the former topsoil must have been kept for some other unknown purpose.

**East/west mound interface**
The interface between the two mounds was sampled to investigate the possible nature of the surface of the east or first ovate mound. Unexpectedly, it was composed of a similar sandy loam soil fabric to both mounds, and in particular exhibited traces of the original Bt or argillic soil material (Fig. 3.12.A). The more poorly sorted nature of this soil compared to the Bt soil material in the mounds above and below may be accounted for by disturbance of the mound's surface. Nevertheless, there was much organic matter, mainly in the form of ferruginized pseudomorphs of former roots and stems, which sug-

gests the presence of a former rooting zone and the establishment of vegetation on the surface of the first long mound. Indeed, *c.* 50–75% of the whole soil fabric exhibits strong ferro-manganiferous replacement of organic matter and pseudomorphic root replacement. This possibly indicates turf development on the surface of the mound, which by implication entails a time gap of a minimum of a few years before the construction of the second, long mound.

The combination of the *in situ* vegetation and the underlying turves within the eastern primary mound must have caused considerable impedance to the localized drainage. Also, compaction of this former surface by trampling and the deposition of the second or western long mound material may have led to further impedance of subsequent water movement at this surface and the formation of iron/manganese pans. These are believed to be a consequence of long and well-sealed burial, and relate to a change in soil redox through the anaerobic decomposition of organic matter (Bloomfield 1951; Duchaufour 1982). The soil watertable rises to within *c.* 4–5 cm of the old land surface after burial and a pan layer forms there.

In conclusion, the following points should be stressed:

1) The pre-mound soil in the vicinity of the long barrow was a well-developed argillic brown earth, which exhibited former forest development and clearance. Similar soil material was found incorporated within the turf and soil make-up of the east and west long mounds.

2) The buried soil beneath the mounds and the mortuary structure is a truncated argillic brown earth with only the lower B/Bt horizon surviving. It is slightly less well developed than the Bt material incorporated in the long mounds, but also exhibits features of former forest development and clearance. The pollen evidence provides a complementary picture of the pre-barrow environment. In general, the effects of Neolithic woodland clearance on the micro-fabric of soils are not often well recognized because of the general lack of survival of shallow Neolithic soils (Macphail 1986), and the obscuring effects of later land-use practices on deeper soils.

3) This soil, beneath the mounds in particular, has suffered considerable disturbance, some due to initial clearance activities and probably also the coincident soil truncation and the construction of the mortuary structure and the subsequent mounds.

4) The occurrence of relatively large amounts of finely comminuted organic matter and charcoal in the groundmass and dusty clay coatings are also indicative of biological mixing and soil disturbance. It is possible that clearance and limited tillage activities are responsible. Nevertheless, the soil fabrics are not sufficiently heterogeneous to suggest prolonged tillage, and the pollen record provides only slight indications of cultivation in the vicinity of the site.

5) The buried soil fabric exhibits hydromorphic effects, in particular relatively severe leaching which led to depletion zones in the groundmass of the soil. This was probably a consequence of a locally fluctuating groundwater table after building the barrow. There is also some deposition of calcium carbonate, probably as a result of the recent drying out of the base-rich fen.

6) Both the mounds are composed of turves (visible in section) and soil. The soil is generally 'Bt' or argillic horizon material in the eastern ovate mound, and a mixture of lower 'B'- and 'Bt'-horizon material in the western long mound. Also, this soil displays the same general soil characteristics as the buried soil. The general implication is that considerable quantities of soil material for the mounds was scraped up from the immediate surroundings. Another implication is that the material comprising the upper soil horizons was used either elsewhere in the mound (in an area not sampled), or somewhere else altogether.

7) The interface between the east and west mounds is characterized by much rooting and sesquioxide impregnation, probably resulting from a combination of compaction and trampling.

*Mound dynamics and layout*
Before proceeding to describe in detail the structural elements of the barrow's northeastern front, it is appropriate that stock should be taken of the monument's main earthwork components (Fig. 3.13). Accounting for the weathering of the barrow's flanks (1–4.00 m wide swathe, generally 2–2.50 m), the mound was of trapezoidal form and consisted of a turf core sealed by upcast gravels and clay silts. Variously redeposited and weathered into the front façade-bank (see below) and the slips that flank the mound, upwards of 50 per cent of the mound's bulk has been displaced. This suggests that its original profile was considerably more impressive with its front probably standing as much as 2.00 m high (see Fig. 3.14).

The revetment of the long mound would seem to have been straightforward and involved only a series of 'simple' structural components. The F.762 trough, probably holding no more than a wattle fence-line, supported the inner edge of the soil-/turf-stack banks, which confined successive dumps of soil and ditch upcast between them. Given that no real evidence of these works was found along the southwestern 'back end' of the mound, it may well have been the case that the revetment was limited to the barrow's long sides alone.

Revetted behind its northeastern façade (F.712/ F.713: Fig. 3.16), the mound's front was 14 m wide

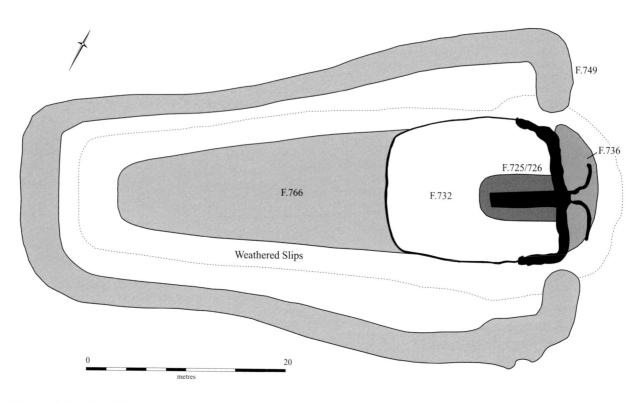

F.749

F.736

F.725/726

F.766

F.732

Weathered Slips

0                    20
metres

**Figure 3.13.** *Mound dynamics: the phasing sequence of primary and secondary barrow mounds (and also the façade-bank).*

(there surviving 0.90 m high) and, narrowing to a rounded western tail (there *c.* 0.75 m high and narrowing to 6.00 m in width), was 44.5 m long. The surrounding ditch generally respected its plan layout, with the terminals of its northeastern front (having a 15-m-wide entrance gap) being directly aligned with the façade trench (Fig. 3.13). Having a rather uncomfortable relationship, there was only a *c.* 1.00 m gap between the in-turned ditch terminals and the façade-supported mound at that point. Otherwise, the berm between the ditch and the barrow mound proper varied from 3.50–7.00 m, but generally was *c.* 5.00 m across (the greatest interval being along the southern side and the western tail-end).

The bulk of the mound (as opposed to the structural details of its northeastern components) had its own complications in terms of its original form and subsequent elaboration. Initially, the primary mound (F.732) consisted of a more ovate trapezoid (17 m long; also revetted by the front façade and 14 m wide) that was only subsequently extended into its long form (F.766), the division between the two builds being apparent in the east–west section of Trench L and distinguished in soil micromorphology (see French above). There is no direct evidence for the ditching of its original form, and the mound largely consisted of turf and grey-brown clay silt.

Locally it was capped by gravel, but this could have occurred during the monument's later expansion, and no quantity of gravel was found within its matrix as such. Nevertheless, in its ultimate plan the ditch kinked southwestwards beyond the end of the primary eastern mound and this could suggest that it originally had been flanked by more minor ditches (these could not have extended around the western end of the ovate mound).

Discussed in detail below, the possible addition of the façade-front bank (F.736) further 'closed' the barrow and rounded the front of the mound (Fig. 3.13). Radically changing the plan layout of the barrow, the implications of this development will be returned to below. Unlike the 'anticipatory' relationship between the ovate and long mounds, it will be argued that this altering of its front potentially constituted a redesign or transformation of the monument.

Yet there are difficulties in weighing the status of the 'embanked' deposits before the barrow's façade. This reflects what are a series of complications relating to the front end of the monument and the profile of the mounds. Firstly, as can be appreciated by comparing the plans of Figures 3.2 & 3.3, as it survived the mound was not actually highest at or just behind the façade but rather a quarter of the way along the mound's length (immediately west of the mortuary structure).

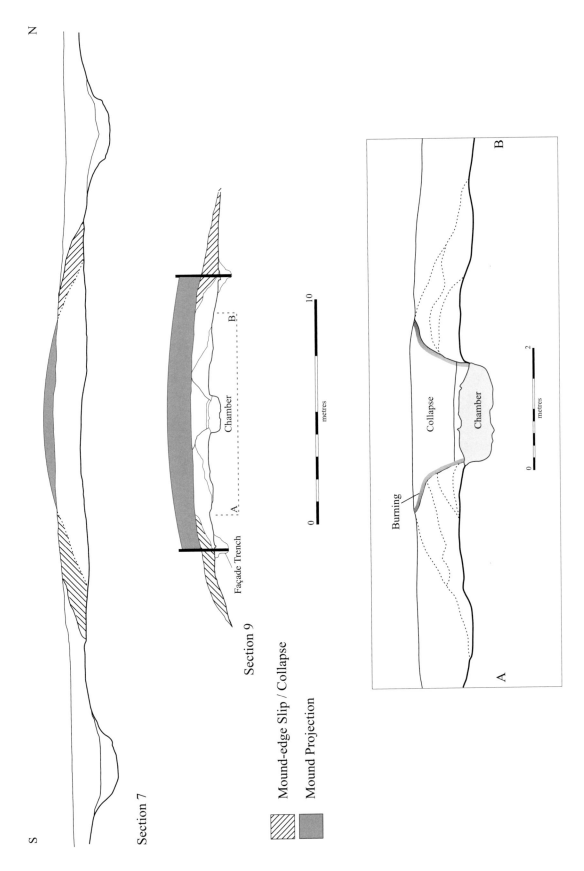

**Figure 3.14.** *Reconstructed barrow profiles: Sections 7 & 9, with detail of chamber below.*

A

B

**Figure 3.15.** *The facade trench (F.12/13; A); B) with packing fills still* in situ. *(Photograph G. Owen.)*

had been reworked into what was, in effect, a round barrow. However, for reasons that are outlined below, this does not seem a valid interpretation. Rather the key point of the mound's kinking at that point (where its side bows and the front begins to round) is that it occurs immediately beside the end of the façade's northern arm. This suggests that the rounding of the barrow's front relates, at least in part, to the collapse of the façade's timber revetment.

The distribution of artefact categories within the mound(s) will be addressed later in the chapter. However, in clear demonstration that the erection of the mound did not mark the cessation of depositional activity and that the mortuary chamber was not the only ritual focus, at this time it warrants notice that 'significant' bone deposits occurred elsewhere within the monument. Aside from the two secondary graves described above, (adult) human bone was recovered from three other locations (Fig. 3.64; see Lee below, *Addendum*). This includes a tibia mid-shaft from the northern terminal of the surrounding ditch (F.749; [3080] <27531>), a skull fragment from its southern terminal ([3045] <27557>) and fragments of a humerus from the mound's sandy slips in Trench E ([2883] <27847>). As will be detailed by Legge, 'placed' articulated animal bone deposits also occurred within the mounds, the most obvious being a red deer fore-limb from the F.725/726 ring-bank (Fig. 3.64).

### The front-end structures

Having considered the monument's basic two-phased mound sequence, the structural components of its northern front can now be addressed. The interrelationship between these elements was complex and their interpretation is not without a measure of ambiguity. In this context it would be misleading to simply present a structural succession (the site as so many 'building blocks' alone) and before establishing the barrow's phasing the sequence of its destruction and firing will require review (see *Burning and collapse sequence* below).

From that point its profile sloped down gradually to the northeast with no interruption above the façade. Given the structural configuration of the latter and its allied components, 'something' has clearly caused this to happen. Secondly, the rounded plan of the mound's northeastern end warrants scrutiny, especially the marked kink in its northern aspect adjacent to the ditch terminal (see e.g. Fig. 3.2). Given this, and in knowledge of the secondary inhumations within the mound proper (and the barrow's long-term land-scape/terrace associations; i.e. the barrow cemetery), the possibility must be considered that its front end

**Table 3.1.** *Post-pit data.*

| | Post pit | Length (cm) | Breadth (cm) | Depth (cm) |
|---|---|---|---|---|
| F.712 | [3702] | 61 | 53 | 68 |
| | [3701] | 70 | 53 | 85 |
| | [3718] | 73 | 64 | 74 |
| | [3719] | 82 | 55 | 81 |
| | [3736] | 111 | 67 | 96 |
| | [3737] | 141 | 71 | 104 |
| | [3738] | 73 | 50 | 76 |
| | [3739] | 60 | 50 | 75 |
| | [3740] | 54 | 47 | 75 |
| F.713 | [3707] | 100 | 68 | 66 |
| | [3706] | 81 | 60 | 65 |
| | [3705] | 76 | 61 | 67 |
| | [3704] | 76 | 74 | 75 |
| | [3703] | 120 | 86 | 108 |
| | [3708] | 115 | 72 | 60 |
| | [3709] | 80 | 54 | 87 |
| | [3710] | 106 | 55 | 85 |

**Table 3.2.** *Post-pipe data.*

| | Post pipe | Length (cm) | Breadth (cm) | Depth (cm) |
|---|---|---|---|---|
| F.714 | [3686] | 50 | 10 | 45 |
| | [3699] | 62 | 45 | 55 |
| | [3452] | 70 | 25 | 50 |
| | [3453] | 75 | 25 | 64 |
| | [3454] | 58 | 22 | 58 |
| | [3455] | 63 | 30 | 67 |
| | [3457] | 40 | 20 | 59 |
| F.714 | [3458] | 60 | 25 | 68 |
| | [3459] | 60 | 25 | 45 |
| F.715 | [3183] | 55 | 30 | 10 |
| | [3683] | 60 | 25 | 85 |
| | [3700] | 65 | 20 | 85 |

## The façade and forecourt

As many long barrows in Britain have concentrations of activities in the forecourt areas, the front of the barrow was approached with special care. Excavated between January and August 1987, the mound's longitudinal section was maintained (Figs. 3.2 & 3.8; Section 1) and further sections through the façade area were produced at 2 m and 4 m intervals north and south of this line. The resulting baulks at the first of these were wet sieved. Further sections were taken through the façade (F.712 & F.713) and forecourt trenches (F.716 & F.717), with two baulks from each wet sieved (Fig. 3.16).

It quickly became apparent that the mound's front emphasized barriers and entrances. On the one hand, the façade impressively faces forward, warding and blocking off. On the other hand, the fore-structure channelled people into the mortuary structure. These two functions of barrier and entrance are, of course, mutually exclusive and one of the main problems we were left with was that there seemed to be no clearly 'active' entrance into the barrow. Rather, there was an *entranceway* (the fore-structure) which led to a *barrier* (the façade). Perhaps the two functions were not contemporary. We have, for example, already seen that the façade-bank later blocked off the forecourt entranceway. Perhaps the façade, at least at the point of the mortuary chamber's entrance, post-dated the fore-structure. The evidence will therefore have to be scrutinized in order to see whether the mortuary structure, façade and fore-structure were all contemporary.

*The façade trench:* This was made up of northern (F.712) and southern lengths (F.713: Fig. 3.16). Its front was 12 m long (north–south), 0.8–1.4 m wide and 0.2–0.5 m deep. The return arms were 4 m long, 0.6–1.02 m wide and 0.2–0.4 m deep. The trench tended to be steep sided with a fairly flat base. The northern and southern lengths were found to cut the fill of the proximal post pit of the mortuary structure.

*The façade trench and posts:* 17 pits (9 in the northern trench and 8 in the southern) were cut through the base of the façade trench (F.714 & F.715: Figs. 3.16 & 3.17). These were circular to sub-rectangular in plan and were oriented along the façade trench. The post pits, generally cut off-centre towards the outer edges of the façade trench, were 0.54–1.41 m long, 0.47–0.80 m wide and 0.60–1.80 m deep below the ground surface (Table 3.1).

Evidence for the structure associated with the façade trench and pits consisted of post pipes defined either by carbonized oak deposits or by 'replacement' soil (see below). The charcoal and post pipes defined a series of vertical posts 0.40–0.75 m by 0.20–0.30 m, usually with a single post per pit but in some cases apparently two, and further posts were also present between post pits. This evidence might be taken to indicate more than one phase of façade construction.

Traces of nine posts survived in the north arm of the façade, with three found in the southern length in addition to the proximal posts. This would suggest at least 11 posts in each arm of the façade and more than 24 posts in the façade as a whole (Fig. 3.16). The façade was traced to a maximum depth of –0.54 m OD and to a minimum height of 0.40 m OD, suggesting timbers at least 0.94 m long projecting at least 0.60 m above the ground surface (Table 3.2). The post pipes were oval to semi-circular in plan with the flatter face of the 'D'-shaped timber often towards the inside of the mound, although this did not always appear to be the case. The post pipes appear to have been distorted during the removal of the uprights since the angles were not vertical in section. At both the butts of the northern and southern arms of the façade trench posts had been set at right angles to the rest suggesting that they had functioned as end posts. The façade posts were set closely together as the post pipe fills formed a continuous band in the façade trench.

The fills of the façade trenches and post pits could not be differentiated. They consisted of a mixed sand, gravel and clay-silt deposit, perhaps suggesting backfill. The packing filled the outer edges of the façade trench and formed a well-defined vertical edge against the post pipes. The façade post voids were filled with a dark

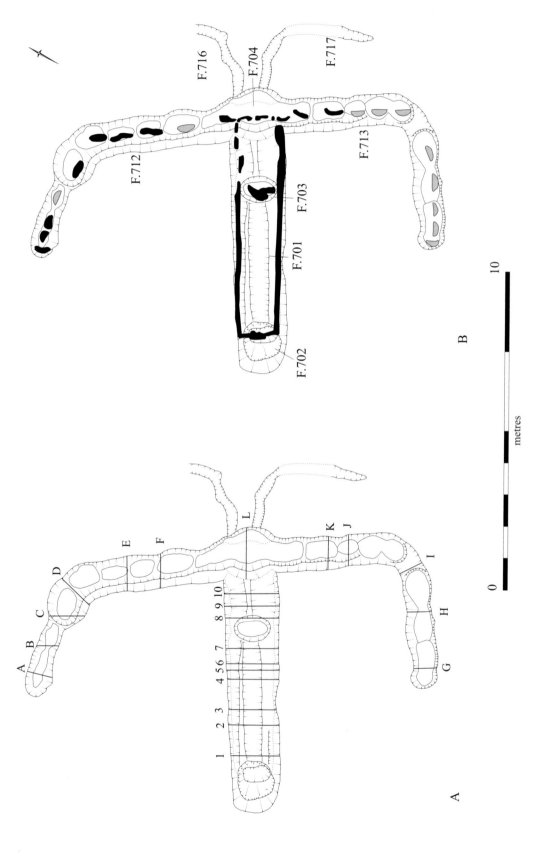

**Figure 3.16.** *Mortuary chamber, façade and fore-structure: A) section location; B) Major timber elements (black) and cut features.*

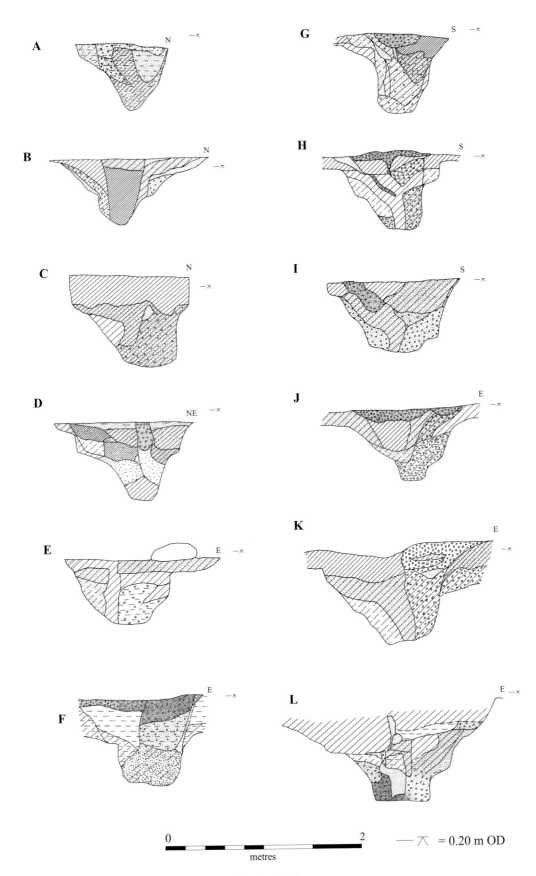

**Figure 3.17.** *Façade trench sections (see Fig. 3.16:A for location).*

grey, sometimes red-brown sandy clay-silt. The fill formed a continuous linear band in the surface of the façade trench, only reducing to individual post-pipes 0.45 m below the ground surface.

The evidence from the façade is thus ambiguous. On the one hand, the fact that the deeper post pits do not correlate precisely with the numbers and positioning of the posts in the façade strongly indicates two phases of construction, with an earlier façade of deeper and fewer post pits replaced by a façade trench containing a greater number of uprights. This would fit well with the evidence already mentioned that the façade trench cuts into the fill of the proximal post pits of the mortuary structure (F. 704). There is also evidence for more than one setting of timbers in the proximal post pit.

*The forecourt* (F.720): The forecourt had a linear western edge where it abutted the post pipes of the façade and a convex eastern edge running east, its overall plan being semi-circular (Fig. 3.28). This sand and gravel spread was generally 0.02–0.05 m thick, but in the façade trench beside the façade it was up to 0.30 m deep. Across its western half/third this deposit was continuous and 'robust', but to the east it became patchy, weathered and often contained less gravel; its survival was, at least in part, clearly determined by the covering of the barrow's collapse and weathered slips.

Although it was difficult to appreciate in its full detail, along the western foot of the façade the forecourt surface appear to seal slight upcast banks. Up to 0.15 m high, these consisted of brown-grey sandy clay silt and presumably represents upcast derived from the digging of the façade trench and its postholes. However, the fact that these deposits did not extend across the area of the entrance into the mound's chamber (i.e. between the fore-structure's arms; see below) would suggest a sense of planning and anticipation.

*The fore-structure and fore-banks:* The trenches of the fore-structure (F.716 & F.717) had a hornwork plan, leaving a 2-m-wide entranceway in front of the proximal posts of the mortuary structure (Fig. 3.16). The sides were steep and the bases narrow and flat, being up to 0.35 m below the ground surface. Their fills consisted of two deposits of sandy clay silts. The upper contained occasional oak fragments, together with pieces of the red and yellow stone, that were also found in the façade trench and in the proximal part of the mortuary structure (see below). The upper fill was deeper where there was evidence of post pipes, but both deposits may have consisted largely of infill since no clear packing deposits could be identified. The post pipes suggested round posts, 0.10–0.30 m in diameter, set 0.40–0.80 m apart (Fig. 3.28). These must have supported a further vertical element, probably bark or wattle panels.

The fore-structure trenches appeared to have cut both the fill of the proximal pit of the mortuary structure and the forecourt paving, though some ambiguity as to whether it may have had a predecessor immediately pre-dating the laying of the gravel surface must exist.

Apart from obviously acting to funnel access into the chamber, the main purpose of the fore-structure would seem to have been the revetment of banks along the foot of the façade. There, the fore-banks (F.746 & F.747) were 4.20–0.40 m long, 1.00–2.20 m wide and *c.* 0.30–0.40 m high (Fig. 3.28). They consisted of basal layers of grey silt capped by gravels that were also sealed by further dark grey silt horizons with extensive traces of burning. Inasmuch as their crests lay along the their central axis (north–south), from where their profiles sloped down to the west, they did not seem to have reinforced or further supported the façade timbers. Rather they seem a 'design element', their matrix probably deriving from upcast generated during the digging of the inturned terminals of the surrounding ditch. In fact, given their plan configuration and location, they may well have appeared almost as an inverted continuation of the ditch's terminals.

A wooden sheet, 2–4 cm thick, measuring 1.25 × 0.50 m, lay across the southern terminal of the northern bank ([3500]/[3132], *et al.*: see plan, Fig. 3.24), its long axis and grain running north–south. There would be two possible explanations for its occurrence. It might represent one of the panels of the fore-structure revetment. Yet this would imply that its revetment screen stood 1.25 m high, which seems much too great given the size of the supporting posts, and upwards of 0.50 m would be a more reasonable estimate. The alternative would be to have this sheet derive from some other structural element; possibly either the roof of a porch-like cover over the 'funnel' of the fore-structure or, more likely, a doorway blocking that could be inset to hinder access into the mortuary chamber. Apart from this piece and two other identifiable planks resting on the bank, part of a roundwood post was found in the same position.

The evidence from the eastern end of the mound provides a clear impression of the importance of the front which is emphasized by the gravel forecourt and the substantial façade. The evidence also indicates that one of the crucial functions of the front area was to define an elaborate entrance into the chamber. Yet that entranceway seemed blocked off by the façade and by the proximal posts of the mortuary structure. Taken at face value any attempt to argue that the entranceway and the barriers to entrance are not contemporary are frustrated by the stratigraphical evidence. The gravel surface of the forecourt was found to abut both the fore-structure trenches and the post pipes of the façade. While both the façade and fore-structure trenches cut the fill of the proximal posts of the mortuary structure, the gravel forecourt also abutted the proximal posts. Thus, at least theoretically, there could have been an earlier phase containing the proximal post and façade post pits. However, as mentioned, the original proximal post of the mortuary structure appears to have been removed and replaced by façade timbers. The crux point in terms of access (and blockage) into the monument's front is therefore how high the axial posts stood; could the structure have been penetrated?

Ultimately it was the restriction of entrance that prevailed, with the façade-bank (F.736) being built across the forecourt and fore-structure (Figs. 3.13 & 3.29). The top of the bank was associated with the burning of oak timbers. It could be argued that its construction, the pulling out of some of the façade posts, the dismantling of the fore-structure and the burning of the posts were all closely related events. Indeed, it might be claimed that the planks and roundwood found on the upper surfaces of the façade-bank were the dismantled and burnt remains of the façade and fore-structure. Yet this could be countered by the fact that the fore-structure was clearly dismantled, its trenches infilled and the façade-bank built before the burning occurred. There is a clear stratigraphical gap between the fore-

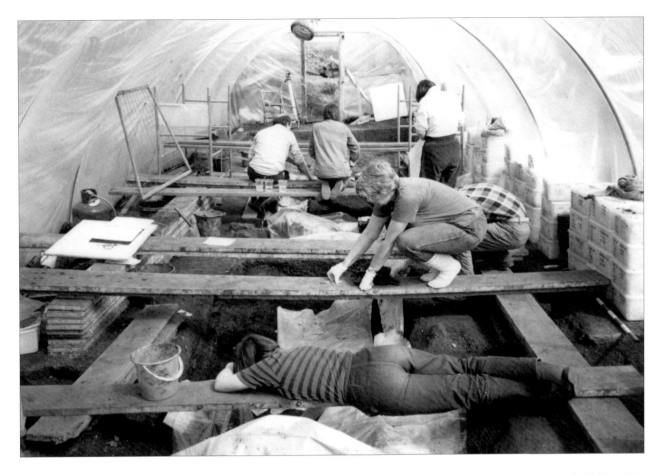

**Figure 3.18.** *Lifting of the mortuary chamber roof timbers (notice polythene lifting boxes, left). (Photograph P. Shand.)*

structure and the horizon of burning on top of the façade-bank. This intermediate phase implies that there were multiple phases of use and destruction (see *Collapse and burning sequence* below).

*The mortuary structure*
The upper deposits of the mortuary chamber were revealed between December 1986 and January 1987 and the wooden structure was excavated between then and August of that year. Usually suspended on planks above the timbers, the excavation was painstaking and was undertaken with trowels and wooden tongue depressors (Fig. 3.18). Most of the fills were wet sieved (the exception being the turf mound) and 10 per cent of each deposit was also processed through a flotation machine. In the case of the turf mound (see below), 50 per cent of the deposit was floated and none was wet sieved. Almost all the wooden elements were lifted for later examination. The lower timber in the distal fill of the mortuary structure was an exception; only one section was lifted with the rest being excavated by hand where it lay in direct relation to the human bone. Generally the lifting methods used would have

disturbed these vital deposits of human bone and, accordingly, a local grid was oriented over the structure to simplify the lifting process (Fig. 3.19). Sections across the structure were established on these grid lines. A central baulk was maintained on the x axis at 6.0 m, roughly on the mid point of the mortuary structure, to retrieve a complete section for recording and reference. To the east of the baulk the turf deposits were quadranted to establish a lateral and longitudinal section. To the west of the baulk lateral and longitudinal sections were built up by drawing layer profiles and adding the sections through the timbers. The timbers at all levels were recorded in section at 0.50 m intervals during the lifting process (Figs. 3.16, 3.22 & 3.23).

Lifting all the wood involved considerable effort. The wood was only partially preserved and the form of most of it depended on the surrounding soil matrix. It was not possible to handle and lift individual timbers; they had to be removed carefully with some of the surrounding soil still adhering. This slow process was justified, partly by the unique nature of the find and also the difficulty of identifying individual

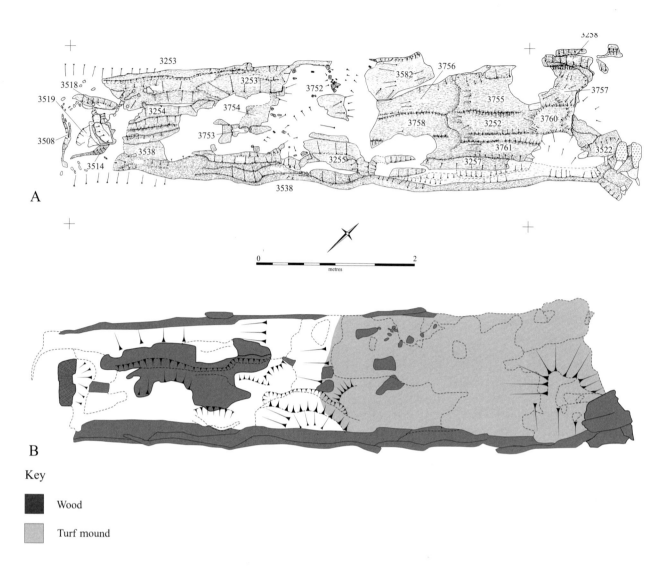

**Figure 3.19.** *Mortuary structure: roof timbers (A), with chamber 'infill' deposits below (including turf Mound; B).*

timbers in the field. Since many of these elements were eroded and smeared, one plank often merged imperceptibly into another. Full information concerning the wood and about the construction of the chamber could only be obtained under controlled laboratory conditions. The value of this exercise is clear in the reports by Ruth Morgan, where analysis of the lifted pieces and dendrochronological studies are outlined. Indeed, detailed description of the individual planks is left to that report. Nevertheless, careful descriptions of the wood were made in the field and are retained in the site's archive.

The interior of the mortuary structure was filled with successive layers of soil and wood chips and pieces of planking, probably derived from the walls and roof of the structure. Within this matrix, the following major components were identified:

*The upper planks* (F.727 & F.728): It was immediately apparent on uncovering the mortuary structure that what were assumed to be the roofing planks were higher and more complete at the eastern end of the structure (F.728: Fig. 3.19). Here, too, they had clear evidence of longitudinal ridges resulting from erosion either side of radial rays. The difference between the proximal (front) and distal (back) part of the mortuary structure therefore emerged early. The upper pieces of oak lying on the infill deposits can best be described in two groups: an eastern (proximal) group east of $X = 6.0$ m (F.728) and a distal group to the west of this line (F.727).

The eastern proximal group was dominated by two (or possibly a single broken) planks in the centre of the mortuary structure running east of $X = 6.0$ m above the medial post towards the proximal end of the structure. These planks, [3758]–[3761] and [3755]–[3757], were similar to the lower floor planks in the distal chamber in their central position, size and preservation, and roughly horizontal aspect. The timbers did not seem to represent either walls or floor planks and so may be assumed to have functioned as the roof. The two (or one) planks had been pressed and distorted over the underlying turf mound. To the west they dipped down behind the medial post.

There were also minor groupings of oak fragments to the north and south of the two main planks. These could not be assigned a function with any certainty and could equally have derived from roof, walls or from timbers of unknown function.

The western distal group of upper planks consisted of a southern and a northern group. The former probably derived from the southern wall of the distal sub-chamber. The planks were often irregular in shape. Some rested directly on the remains of the southern wall (see below), while others lay dipping on localized deposits of clay silt that appeared to have slumped from the southern banks or mound dumps. These sloping planks, partly resting on slumped soil, are most likely from the distal chamber wall. The planks in the northern group had the same characteristics and are again probably collapsed walling.

Various other distal upper planks cannot be assigned to these groups. There were also more than seven pieces of oak planking lying on top of the remains of the distal post and against its edge. Probably the result of the roof's collapse, the group was very fragmentary and many of the larger pieces were bedded vertically around the post.

*The mortuary structure walls* (F.723 & F.724): Along the edges of the mortuary structure trench was a mass of fragmentary and distorted oak planking. In some sections (Figs. 3.22 & 3.23) it could be determined that the oak was set on edge against the side of the mortuary structure trench within the wall slots (see below). It was clear in other cases that further fragmentary timbers had collapsed against these wall timbers. It appeared possible that the vast accumulation of wooden debris had all derived from single massive oak wall planks.

The wall timbers could more easily be identified in the distal sub-chamber. We shall see below that side 'wall slots' at the base of the walls only occurred in this distal area. These data could be read to argue that only the rear chamber was walled. Support, ambiguous and uncertain, could come from the mortuary structure banks along the outside of the walls. These upcast deposits appeared to have a division in line with the medial post. It is possible that the banks originally only surrounded the distal chamber. However, the evidence is partly contradictory here as the banks also appeared to continue to the façade, and if the proximal chamber was not walled it is difficult to see why the proximal sub-chamber did not contain soil from the surrounding mound. In any case some indication of walling is seen in the sections across the proximal sub-chamber. This may simply be a matter of consecutive phased construction, perhaps dictated by the lengths of the planks

*Deposits within the chamber* (F.750): The deposits in the distal chamber consisted of a primary and secondary deposit separated by two

**Figure 3.20.** *Mortuary structure roof: A) exposure of roof timbers; B) showing the polysulphide rubber mould coating. (Photographs G. Owen.)*

large planks (Figs. 3.19, 3.22 & 3.23). The primary soil deposit was localized to the distal sub-chamber and it was in this that the human remains were found. Although several lenses were described, the soil is best viewed as a single horizon. Found west of $X = 5.0$ m, the deposit was 0.10–0.22 m thick and consisted of brown-black organic silt with oak fragments (10–60%) which were finer and less

**Figure 3.21.** *Detail of the roof timber showing 'ridging' (cm scale). (Photograph G. Owen.)*

the mound with soil separately dumped in between. The latter generally consisted of sand silts with some clay and gravel components. On both sides of the medial post ash occurred in the lowest layer. In the proximal chamber the ash layer was associated with roundwood and displaced timbers. In the distal chamber similar associations included in addition a lens of oak charcoal. In the distal sub-chamber two levels of ash and charcoal could be identified at the base of the mound.

Few human bones were found beneath the turf mound. While the western edge of the mound overlapped the eastern distribution of the bones, no bones are found in the eastern section of the distal sub-chamber. Similarly no human bones were found in the proximal sub-chamber and it is as if the burnt mound was positioned to avoid the burials in the distal sub-chamber and its insertion may have involved some pushing back of the bodies.

*Roundwood on the mortuary structure floor*: As already noted, generally small pieces of roundwood were found on the floors of both the sub-chambers as well as on the timbers lying in the proximal sub-chamber. The pieces were usually irregular brushwood; 24 pieces were recovered in the proximal sub-chamber, while six were found in the distal sub-chamber below the turf mound. The pieces were 0.05–0.25 m long and were up to 0.07 m thick (see Morgan below).

*Timbers on the mortuary structure floor*: Beneath the turf mound were found the remains of three post-like 'D'-shaped timbers lying on the wooden floor of the mortuary structure (Fig. 3.24). The first ([3643]) was immediately west of the medial post while the other two were on the southern floor plank of the proximal sub-chamber. [3643] lay with its flat face uppermost. 1.1 m long and 0.62 m by 0.25 m, it lay beside the medial post and was similar to it in form and size. It seemed likely that it was originally part of the medial post and that it represented a stage in the potential dismantling of the mortuary structure. The two timbers in the proximal sub-chamber ([3642] & [3645]) were ovoid in plan and roughly 'D'-shaped in cross-section. Laying with their flat faces uppermost, these were 0.13 m and 0.18 m thick respectively, and were of a shape and size that suggested they could have derived from the proximal posts or façade posts. Certainly they are substantial and, although perhaps suggesting that they derive from the medial and proximal uprights, the key issue is whether their upper portions could have been cut down and thus 'dismantled'. If these massive timbers had, effectively, seasoned *in situ* it is most unlikely that by contemporary axe technology they could have been so cut off. Therefore the status of these important timbers and the entire question of whether the timber could, in fact, have been dismantled as opposed just undergoing collapse will be further discussed below.

Of clear significance is the stratigraphical position of these large timbers on the floors of the mortuary structure. The turf mound was placed over them and the 'stump' of the medial post.

*Axial pits and posts:* Perhaps the clearest evidence that the mortuary structure was divided spatially into a front and back area is provided by the three axial pits and post settings which form the proximal and distal sub-chambers (Figs. 3.16 & 3.24). Each of the three large pits contained one or more split oak posts which survived partly intact. The distal and proximal pits were 7 m apart and defined a linear zone 1.5 m wide which was subdivided by the medial post into a western 4.5-m-long sub-zone and an eastern 2-m-long sub-zone.

numerous towards its base. Along the north and south walls a 0.10–0.30 m thick deposit contained more than 70% large oak fragments in a loamy clay silt matrix. The deposit appeared heaped against the walls and is most probably part of the collapse of the walls. Beside the distal post was found a 0.10 m thick deposit of silt with 70% oak fragments, and the increase in oak content was thought to represent decay from the post.

Immediately above the primary soil deposit, to the centre-west of the distal sub-chamber, we came across two planks, [3540] and [3541], dipping slightly into what was recognized as a central trough. Above these the secondary soil deposit occurred in the distal sub-chamber. This also overlay part of the western edge of the burnt turf mound. To the south a southern extension reached east to the medial post. The deposit consisted of brown-grey sandy clay silt with up to 30% 1–6 cm³ oak fragments. Along the southern edge of the distal sub-chamber at this level deposits again occurred that appeared to be the result of slumping from the banks or mound dumps around the mortuary structure.

*The turf mound* (F.737): Set within the proximal sub-chamber and overlapping into the eastern portion of the distal sub-chamber was a small burnt turf mound (Fig. 3.19). At its highest level this was sub-rectangular in plan having straight edges to the north, south and east where it abutted the walls and proximal posts of the mortuary structure; to the west it was slightly convex. The mound was laid in the eastern half of the mortuary structure as far east as the proximal posts and as far west as X = 4.80 m. It thus gives clear evidence that the front of the mortuary structure was treated differently from the back. Abutting and covering the medial post, the mound was 4.6 m long (east–west) and 1.3–1.5 m wide (north–south). At the highest it was 0.50–0.60 m thick, but west of the medial post it tapered to less than 0.10 m. It also tapered to the east, being 0.30–0.50 m thick where it abutted the proximal posts.

In both sub-chambers the turf mound consisted of four layers of turf and soil, the uppermost ([3203]/[3204]) being a single 'unified' deposit which sealed the medial post. Each appeared to be burnt with burnt flints occurring in alternate horizons. The deposits were often scorched to an orange colour. In detail, it appeared that the turves with soil attached had been placed upside-down on

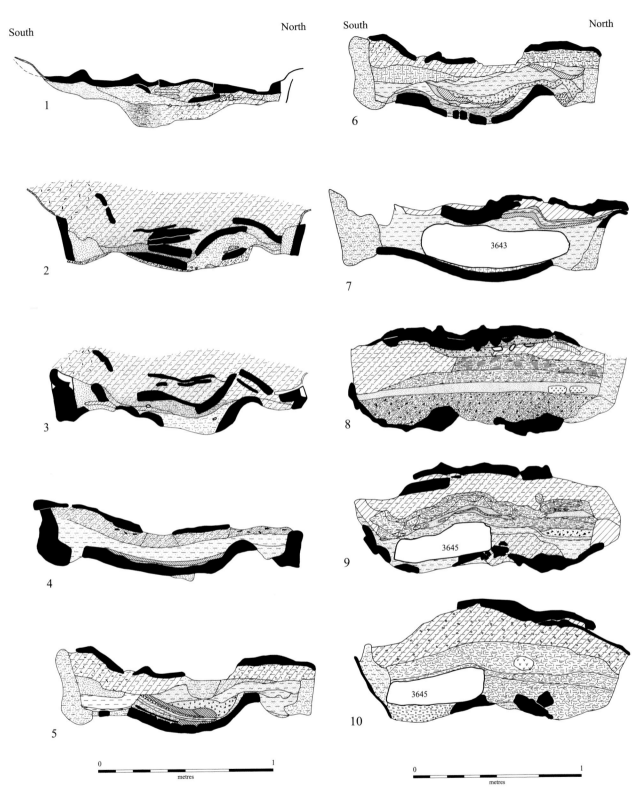

**Figure 3.22.** *Mortuary structure cross-sections (1–5; see Figure 3.16:A for location).*

**Figure 3.23.** *Mortuary structure cross-sections (6–10; see Figure 3.16:A for location).*

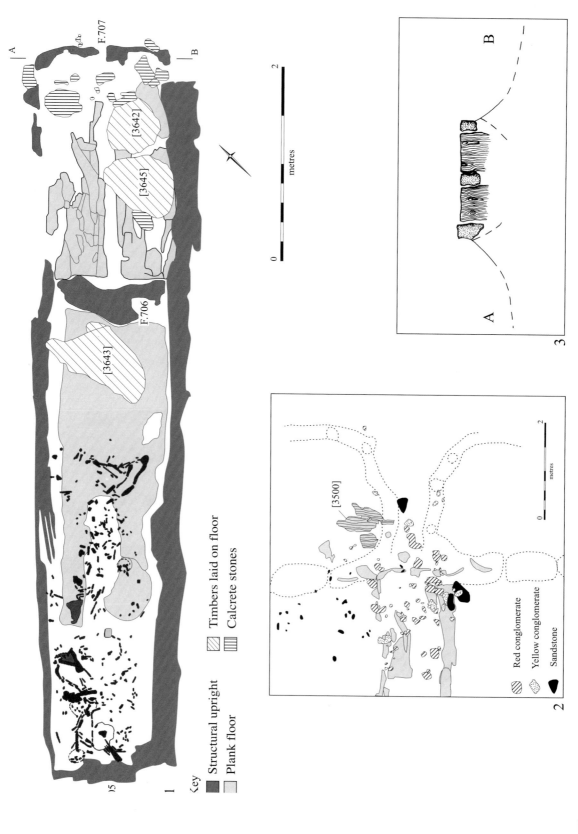

**Figure 3.24.** *The mortuary structure: 1) floor plan with human bone shown blackened; 2) distribution of stones (by type and colour) in area of the entranceway; 3) sketch section showing stone packing of F.707 proximal posthole/façade timbers.*

The distal post pit (F.702) consisted of two construction features (Figs. 3.8 & 3.16). An outer shallower cut was sub-circular in plan and formed the western terminal of the mortuary structure trench. The cut was up to 1.95 m in diameter and its basin-shaped floor was 0.60 m below the ground surface. The packing fill was composed of sand and gravel clay silts. The inner cut was sub-rectangular in plan, set at 90° to the main mortuary structure axis. The pit was 1.17 × 0.70 m and its flat base was 0.80 m below the ground surface. The central fill consisted of an inner zone of clay silts with fibrous silt and wood fragments which may indicate a decayed or replaced post, and an outer zone of sand silts with gravel. This outer zone filled the lower part of the outer packing pit and part of the inner post pit.

Three posts were set in the distal post pit. A large rectangular post, 0.54 × 0.25 m and 0.90 m high ([3509]/[3693]), was set centrally. Its lower 17 cm were reduced to a fibrous silt. The southern and northern posts were aligned, along with the central post, at right angles to the main axis of the mortuary structure and they filled the northern and southern quarters of the inner post pit (all F.705). The evidence for two post pits plus three posts within one post pit could be taken to suggest more than one phase of post setting of the distal posts. However, the fills of the post pits would not support this interpretation (Fig. 3.8); rather they suggest a single act of post setting.

The medial post pit consisted of a single cut (F.703), sub-rectangular in plan and oriented at right angles to the main mortuary structure axis. The steep-sided and flat-based pit was 1.05–0.28 m long (north–south), 0.5–0.88 m wide (east–west) and 0.75 m deep beneath the ground surface (Figs. 3.8 & 3.16). The fill consisted of five horizons of sandy organic silts locally containing concentrations of oak fragments. The medial post had its flat face towards the east (F.706). 1.18 m long (north–south) and 0.38 m wide, it was up to 0.70 m high (0.50 m above the ground surface); the lower 0.10–0.20 m of the post had decayed to a fibrous silt.

The proximal post pit (F.704) consisted of two construction features and contained the remains of two oak posts (F.707). The outer shallower cut was circular in plan, was up to 1.9 m in diameter and was 0.5 m deep. Only the west and east sides survived as the north and south sides had been cut away by the façade trenches. The deeper inner cut was sub-rectangular in plan; 1.2–1.3 m long (north–south) by 0.55–0.90 m wide, its flat base lying 0.80 m below the ground surface (Figs. 3.8 & 3.16). The central fill consisted of grey-brown clay silt and it held the reduced remains of the posts. In section to the east, there was an outer edge against the outer packing fill which may have represented an earlier cut (Fig. 3.8). Alternatively, the edge may have been formed by the decay of the posts. The packing, which filled the outer post pit, and part of the inner pit consisted of sandy gravel. The two oak posts ([3684] & [3685]) were of 'D'-shaped plan, the flat face of the northern one facing west and the face of the southern one to the east.

There is no clear evidence of recutting in the fills of the post pits. The lower parts of the posts, away from the burning in the mortuary chamber, had not survived well and soil had slumped into the voids which they left. Therefore, it would be a mistake

**Figure 3.25.** *The mortuary chamber from the distal end. (Photograph G. Owen.)*

to interpret some of the vertical edges in the sections across the post pit fills as recuts (Fig. 3.8), and the outer and inner cuts of the proximal and distal post pits are best seen as 'constructional events'. This being said, there is strong evidence that the proximal posts are a secondary setting within the main post pit. They are by far and away the most minor of the three axial settings and seem completely disproportionate to the size of the post pit. Rather, as is apparent in Figure 3.16, they seem to relate to the façade line.

*The mortuary structure trench* (F.701): The area between the distal and proximal post was found to have been truncated as a series of slots and trenches either side of the medial post to create a trough 0.25–0.35 m below the ground surface level (Fig. 3.16). The 7-m-long and 1.9-m-wide 'trench' removed the upper parts of the packing fills of the distal and proximal pits, and appeared to incorporate these into the general plan.

The below-ground trench consisted of a distal and proximal zone, divided by the medial pit. The area between the distal and medial pits consisted of three linear cuts. The central trough was 0.52–0.65 m wide (north–south) and was cut 0.20–0.30 m below the

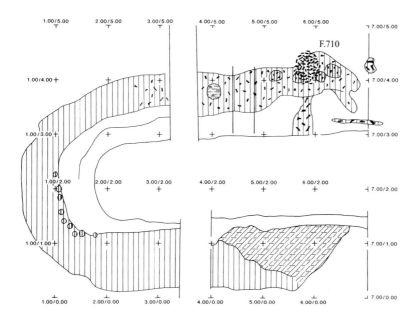

**Figure 3.27.** *Phase I pre-mortuary structure deposits and features (as sealed by F. 725/726 ring-bank).*

ground surface. It ran between the medial and distal posts and had a smaller trough on each side. These flanking troughs contained the bases of the walls of the mortuary structure and functioned as wall slots. Both the northern and southern slots were 0.09–0.40 m wide and 0.25–0.30 m deep. The central trough had no obvious function. The mortuary structure floor was placed across its top (Figs. 3.22 & 3.23).

The proximal zone of the trench into which the mortuary structure was set consisted of two linear cuts (Fig. 3.16). Each ran from the proximal to the medial posts with a central spine between. The slots were 0.15–0.40 m wide and bottomed 0.30–0.35 m below ground surface level.

*The mortuary structure floor* (F.708 & F.709): On the 'floors' of the proximal and distal chambers created by the axial posts and by the sunken troughs were placed planks which formed the mortuary structure floor (Figs. 3.22–3.24 & 3.26). The underlying troughs had produced an uneven surface. While the distal 1.4 m of this surface was left as bare earth, the rest of the sunken chamber was floored with oak planks which closely fitted the available space; the planks gradually sank down into the underlying troughs mirroring their undulating surface.

The placing of the floor planks again shows that the proximal and distal sub-chambers were treated differently. In the distal sub-chamber the eastern two-thirds of the floor was covered by a single massive oak plank ([3692]). This was generally rectangular in plan with linear and parallel northern and southern sides. At its eastern end the plank had been cut to produce a concave hollow that allowed it to fit closely against the curved face of the medial post. The western edge of the plank only existed along the sides of the central trough. The missing central area of the western part of this plank did not appear to have been cut and it seems likely that the timber was here lost through rotting. The plank was 2.5–2.7 m long, 0.98–1.20 m wide and 0.04–0.08 m thick. A number of linear cracks ran along its length (east–west) which seem to have been caused by the slumping of the plank into the central trough. Small rectangular planks ([3693] & [3694]) were found at the western end of the main plank.

A small squared oak timber 0.12 m long, 0.08 m wide and 0.09 m high rested in the centre of the trough at $X = 4.0$ m in the position of an upright. The oak planks just described ([3692]–[3694]) ended at this point and the area to the west was unfloored. Small pieces of roundwood filled the gap between the planks and the small 'upright'. It appears that the $X = 4.0$ m line represented a division of the distal chamber and that the small 'upright' helped to mark this division. Given its size and lack of bedding in a posthole, it certainly could not have represented a significant upright.

We shall see later that in fact the distal sub-chamber can be divided into three areas along its linear axis: an eastern floored area without human remains, and the central floored area and a unfloored western portion, both covered with human bones. The surface of this western third of the distal sub-chamber consisted of a bare earth floor of whitish-yellow clay-silt on which the bones had been laid. In the central trough the underlying natural gravels were usually visible. (Where the oak flooring lay on the trough it lay directly on the gravel.)

The flooring in the proximal sub-chamber was quite different from that in the distal sub-chamber. It consisted of two oak planks running east–west ([3689] & [3690]). They were not well preserved and were difficult to trace east of $X = 8.8$ m. They were 0.52–0.57 m wide and 0.02–0.12 m thick. The western edges of the planks were carefully dressed so as to fit snugly against the medial post.

The distal and proximal flooring was cut against and was clearly contemporary with the medial post. Yet we have seen that the distal sub-floor troughs cut into the fill of the distal posts. The axial posts/troughs/flooring sequence must therefore have been immediate as parts of one constructional event. The only scope for a longer sequence of phases of construction in the mortuary structure concerns the possibility of more than one phase of axial post alignment. Such evidence may relate to the phases of construction that were suggested for the façade.

*Features below the mortuary structure banks:* The evidence of burning on the sides of the F.725/726 ring-bank surrounding the mortuary structure makes it clear that the wooden mortuary structure was clearly contemporary with this upcast bank. The only way in which the walls of the mortuary structure could have stood vertically would have been by pinning them between the axial posts and the surrounding bank. Thus any features found surrounding the mortuary structure, but below the embankment, must be earlier than the mortuary structure. As we have seen, the mortuary structure trench was dug down into the earth and so earlier features in this area would have been gouged out. Only on/in the surrounding surfaces would earlier strata survive.

An arc of small post-holes was revealed 1.2 m west of the distal post of the mortuary structure and 0.40–0.50 m north and south of the mortuary structure walls (Fig. 3.27). Though difficult to see, these appeared to represent a series of post pipes (0.08–0.20 m in diameter) spaced at 0.05–0.20 m intervals, the interval between them increasing towards the east. The setting of posts appeared to have been 'U'-shaped in plan with the arms facing east, 2.3 m apart; the southern arm had been destroyed by the later cutting of the mortuary structure trench. There is some evidence to suggest that the post setting was partly standing when the mortuary structure was being constructed as a ridge of upcast from the mortuary structure trench had formed against the inside edge of the posts. Alternatively, as discussed below (see **Construction methods and materials**), it is conceivable that these related to the revetment of the mortuary chamber.

A shallow (0.20–0.25 m below the Neolithic ground surface) linear feature 5 m long and 0.50–0.60 m wide followed the northern arm of the post setting and was closely associated with it. The fill of this feature was a mixture of soil and oak charcoal and in one discreet area the charcoal was associated with burnt human bone (F.710: Fig. 3.27 and see Dodwell below). Further minor features of similar depth to the linear feature and also containing oak charcoal fragments were found to the north and near the mortuary structure trench which cut through one of them. 1.10 m to the northeast lay a second spread of oak charcoal and burnt bone, F.711, in a shallow irregular pit cut into the clay natural (Fig. 3.30). The pit was aligned northeast–southwest, measuring 1.30 × 0.60 m and c. 0.08 m deep.

Reported upon by R. Darrah, the oak charcoal from the F.710 horizon ([3399]) was up to 40 mm square and 5 mm thick. It had natural splits along the radial longitudinal sections (RLS) where both medullary rays and spring vessels were visible. Almost all the transverse surfaces were clean breaks at right angles to the RLS as would have occurred after either charring in fires or anaerobic decay. One piece had an angled surface which may have been cut. All the pieces came from slow-grown oaks with even growth rates. The fastest grown of these pieces had average annual ring widths of 2 mm per year, over approximately 20 years, and the slowest grown piece had an average annual ring width of 7 mm over almost 50 years. One piece had both pith and central rings of less than 1 mm annual ring width, but all the other pieces came from parts of the trunk where the rays when observed in transverse sections were parallel, suggesting large slow-grown trees. The medullary rays were long and thin (less than 0.5 mm thick) suggesting unstressed growth. All the indications were that the charcoal was from large oak trees which had grown evenly in either poor conditions or more likely in dense woodland. The charcoal would have been produced from the burning of large pieces of oak timber probably from several trees because of the different growth rates.

N. Dodwell has reported upon the two discrete spreads of primary context burnt bone. Though the majority of the fragments are unidentifiable, human bone was positively identified in [3192]. No bones are duplicated and whether they are human or animal they only represent part of the individual. The material was bulk-sieved using a 1-mm mesh.

F.711 [3192] (0–0.31 m OD): Unidentifiable burnt fragments and fragments of the posterior vertebral body and the left pedical (either cervical or upper thoracic). Of white and blue/black colour; the largest piece is 26 mm (7 g):
1) Vertebral articulating facet, fragments of glenoid cavity and fragment of orbit and possibly a fragment of proximal tibia; the largest fragment is 21 mm. Aside from unidentifiable fragments, all those pieces identified are probably human (4 g);
2) Unidentifiable fragment of shaft, 11 mm long (<1 g);
3) Unidentifiable fragments/crumbs; the largest is 5 mm (<1 g);
4) Unidentifiable inefficiently burnt (blue/black colour) fragments; the largest is 13 mm (<1 g).

F.710 [3399] (5.60/4.00; 0.37 m OD):
1) Unidentifiable burnt fragments/crumbs (mix of white and blue/black bone); the largest is 13 mm long (1 g);
2) Unidentifiable poorly fired fragments/crumbs; the largest is 10 mm (<1 g);
3) The majority of fragments are unidentifiable. They include a blackened, inefficiently fired ?human acromion (part of scapula), 36 mm long; if human then this would be adult sized. There is also a vertebral articulating facet that could be cervical or animal; total weight is 3 g.

Even if the status of the arc of posts is uncertain, the associated bank-sealed deposits (including the burnt human bone) provides the only unambiguous indication of a phase of funerary activity before the mortuary structure, as evidence for an earlier phase for the distal and proximal posts is unclear. The more complex pit cuttings and fills in the proximal and distal pits in comparison with the medial pit might be taken to indicate that proximal and distal posts initially existed on their own (see Morgan below). Together with the arc of posts they attest to an early phase of mortuary activities which was largely removed by the digging of the sunken mortuary structure trench.

The oak charcoal 'chips' would be open to two modes of interpretation. Either they directly relate to the cremation activity or they reflect the burnt remnants of woodworking; the latter is held to be the more likely.

*Burning and collapse sequence*

As is apparent in the longitudinal section (Fig. 3.8), there was a major 'disruption' within the barrow's strata immediately above the wooden structure. 1.20(+) m deep, this 'faulting' cannot have been the result of down-cutting or 'infilling' (as otherwise the top of the chamber would have to have been open to the elements), but rather *collapse*. This is readily appreciated by the fact that the structure's roof timbers continue to bed horizontally for 0.60 m above and west beyond its distal post, whereas immediately inside the chamber the same roof pieces lay 0.40 m lower. This drop in stratigraphy was obviously the result of the collapse of the wooden chamber. The use of timber in non-megalithic long barrows implies that this phenomenon (wood invariably eventually weakens and decays) should theoretically be commonplace. However, it seems not to have been distinguished before.

Apart from the implications of the evidence of collapse, another pressing issue relates to just how many episodes of firing the site's sequence attests to. As outlined below, the wooden mortuary chamber was itself intentionally set alight as part of the monument's closure. The upper surfaces of its surrounding ring-bank appeared reddened and scorched especially around the eastern edge of the mortuary structure. The scorching occurred 4.8 m west of the façade and the burning was up to 1.4 m wide above the edges of the mortuary structure (Fig. 3.14). A particular area of burning occurred on the edge of the south bank just west of the façade. There deposit [3029] consisted of three lenses (0.17 m thick): first, fragments of oak 0.10–0.20 m long and 0.10 m wide on the mound surface, second a layer of charcoal 1.9 m long and 1.2 m wide above it, and third an upper layer of light grey wood ash.

In the main, this evidence seems quite straightforward, as in the course of burning the chamber the surrounding matrix could well have been affected and

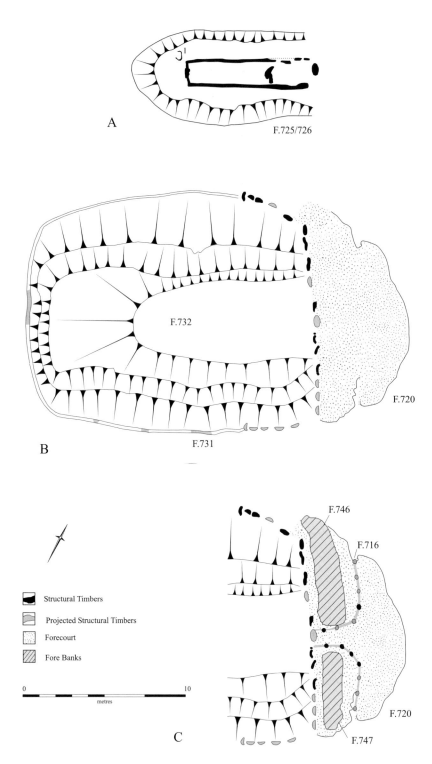

as in the surviving surface of the barrow's mound. This appeared to be continuous with that on the lower ring-bank and was found to extend onto the bank east of the façade (F.746 & F.747). The key source of ambiguity in this regard is whether the burning on the façade-bank was directly linked to the firing of the chamber as a single event or if two or more distinct phases of burning were evident.

In this context, the evidence of the putative 'façade-bank' (F.736) is particularly relevant, as its upper deposits consisted of large burnt timbers within a matrix of charred oak fragments and scorched soil and gravel (Fig. 3.29). This formed a continuous band across the summit and faces of the bank running parallel to the façade. Consisting of a grey sandy silt (up to 2 m wide and 0.05–0.15 m thick), concentrations of charcoal were greatest in a central area 1 m south and 3 m north of the central east–west axis. Overall the deposit was linear but slightly curved in plan with the north and south ends turning towards the west. The deposit was generally confined to the area in front of the façade, but was found to encroach on the façade at some points. The latter's uprights were clearly destroyed at this time as the post pipe of one of its posts was traced at this level. Several large pieces of intensely burnt oak timber survived in this layer; these may well have derived from the dismantled façade.

Below this horizon a layer of soil covered the F.746/747 fore-banks, extending them 0.30–0.50 m to the east and west, and also across the entranceway gap between them. 0.10–0.15 m thick, this appeared to have formed a continuous band parallel to the façade above the façade-bank. Consisting of a grey-yellow/buff-brown (sometimes

**Figure 3.28.** *Phase II features and Phase III.2 forecourt elements: A) mortuary structure and surround ring-bank (II.1); B) the primary ovate mound with façade and forecourt (II.2); C) primary mound with addition of fore-structure revetting the fore-banks (III.2).*

some of the barrow's turves may have even ignited. However, as indicated on Figures 3.14 & 3.29, the problem is that traces of burning also occurred as high reddened) sand loam, did this deposit in effect form a second façade-bank above the lower burnt horizon upon the fore-banks?

The real question here relates to what degree the F.736 embankment was, in fact, a constructed feature, as opposed to just reflecting the collapse of mound deposits revetted by the façade timbers, whether due to dismantling and/or decay. Certainly the latter collapse-related approach would better account for the series of interbedded burnt horizons apparent in these deposits.

Although not without ambiguity in its details, based on the evidence two modes of interpretation seem possible:

1) The firing of the chamber somehow caused the turves of the barrow themselves to ignite and led to the burning of its upper front end components. As will be further explored below (see **How the structure worked**), this would really only be feasible if the front end of the structure stood much higher than the back, and if the primary mound there provided only little soil cover: in which case there could have only been one firing, the burnt deposits later being raked down onto the façade-bank.

2) The chamber's firing was a distinct and localized (and controlled) event; a second firing, largely involving the façade timbers, occurred after the collapse of the chamber and the 'faulting' of the mound above.

Perhaps accompanied by some down-cutting to expose/loosen the façade timber, the latter would explain the fact that the burning bedded down into the 'infill' profile above the chamber and it seems the more likely proposition. Subsequent grooming of the front end of the collapsed mound and the raking down of scorched deposits (sealing (again) the chamber's entrance and effectively resulting in the 'façade-bank') would account for what appeared to be the latter's evidence of multiple burning episodes.

*Phasing summary: enfolding structures*
No matter how well preserved it is, there are genuine points of ambiguity concerning the interpretation of the barrow's sequence. This largely involves the interrelationship of its various 'fore-' components or 'allied structures', the collapse of the mortuary chamber (and the ensuing disruption of the overlying stratigraphy) and the number of burnt closing horizons that the sequence attests to. To some extent the attitude adopted towards the phasing structure is

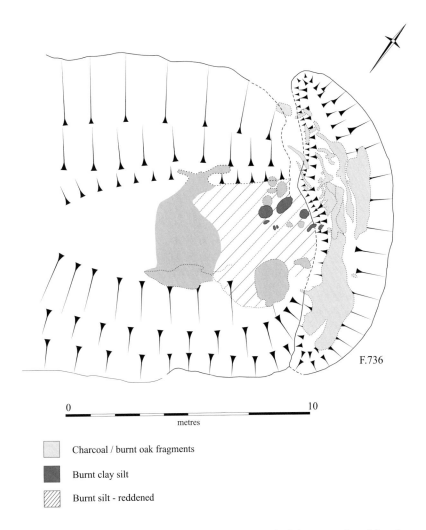

Charcoal / burnt oak fragments

Burnt clay silt

Burnt silt - reddened

**Figure 3.29.** *Burning associated with the east end of the mound and façade-bank.*

'hard-edged', and more complex sequences could be envisaged (e.g. further sub-divisions of the primary mound's construction). The strata have been phased in the belief that this exercise must also be informed by operational/construction principles (e.g. the collapse/decay of timbers) and should not be overly waylaid by the indistinct 'mulch' of the mound's diffuse fabric.

As is outlined below, the most singularly problematic aspect is the scale of the Phase I activities. It certainly involved cremation activity sealed and truncated by Phase II features; the issue is to what degree this occurred framed by an 'open' timber setting (i.e. non-mounded: Fig. 3.30). It is conceivable that all of the timber features assigned to that phase instead related to II.1 construction. However, the crux of this structure's existence relates to the evidence that the façade was extended and locally reset, and also

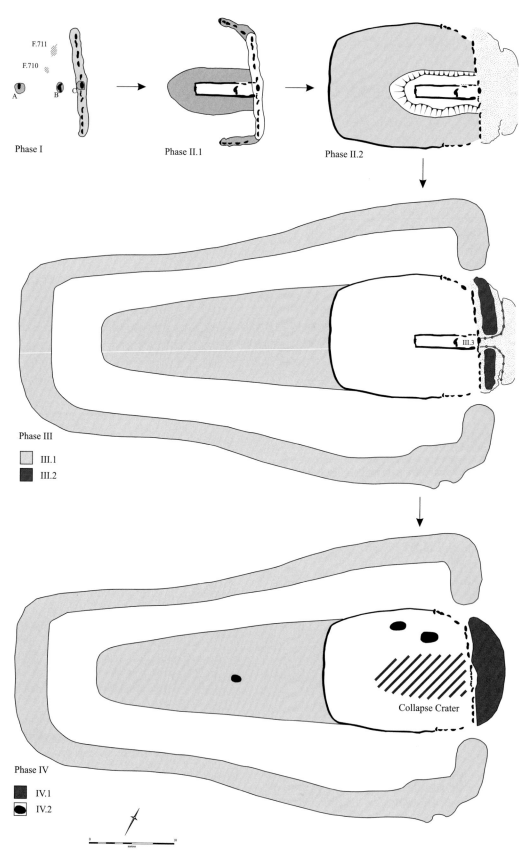

**Figure 3.30.** *Phasing sequence.*

the sheer scale of the three axial timbers and their packing pits (the latter being truncated by the II.1 mortuary chamber's trough). This admittedly involves a functionalist argument, as it seems inconceivable that such great baulks of wood were deployed to have stood only 0.40 m high above the mortuary chamber's floor. They must, therefore, have been cut down at some time. In the knowledge that seasoned oak cannot have been so trimmed, this must have occurred early in the sequence (and equally not when the chamber was roofed). Therefore, having to cut the posts when they were still green implies that as an independent timber structure the Phase I construction was short-lived, probably no more than a few months and perhaps even as little as a week.

Relating to this, there would seem to be no grounds by which to assign the F.763 trough any function other than the demarcation/revetment of the long mound's flanking banks. In short, there would be no evidence of a 'long' mortuary enclosure preceding the construction of the barrow. This is based on two factors: it mirrors the form of the long mound (and the primary ovate mound would intervene within their succession) and, apart from the Phase I features at the northeastern end, there was no direct evidence of ritual activity found beneath the bulk of the long mound.

What is described below is essentially the construction/usage sequence for the barrow proper (Fig. 3.30). Theoretically, the evidence of the site's pre-barrow occupation warrants phase-assignation. Yet this material was entirely found in residual context (i.e. struck flint redeposited within the mound deposits) and no associated features were recovered. Therefore, whilst this background settlement presence is fully acknowledged and its status is discussed at length below, it is here not enumerated or formally entitled as such.

*Phase I: The open mortuary structure*
This was marked by the erection of the axial 'totem pole-like' posts. Thereafter the northeastern line of the façade timbers were set as a free-standing screen incorporating the most easterly of the 'great' posts (and cutting its packing fills). Two cremation spreads (F.710 & F.711) were deposited behind the northern length of the façade screen.

*Phase II: The mortuary chamber and primary barrow*
This phase essentially describes a construction *sequence*; its subdivision only really relates to the mounds' sequence (ring-bank to primary barrow).
*II.1:* As is clear from the soil analyses, the turf was removed from the area. The truncation of the axial posts was followed by the upcasting of the F.725/726 ring-bank and the construction of the wooden mortuary chamber.
*II.2:* This saw the eastward extension of the façade front, followed by the construction of the primary ovate barrow. It is presumed that the laying of the forecourt gravels (F.720) would have occurred

immediately thereafter. However, without an obvious 'deep' quarry-source, this surface may not have been laid until Phase III.1. There then followed the usage of the chamber for interment, and human bones were placed in the distal sub-chamber.

*Phase III: The long monument*
*III.1:* This saw the western extension of the barrow with the construction of the F.766 long mound and the digging of the surrounding ditch (F.749). The development of a turf horizon on the Phase II barrow (as sealed by the Phase III mound; see French above) denotes 'time' and that the construction phases of the barrow mounds could not have fallen immediately upon each other. In other words, there clearly was an interruption in the construction sequence between Phases II and III.
*III.2:* The erection of the hornwork fore-structure (F.716–719) revetting the fore-banks (F.746/747) at the foot of the façade. Evidence of forecourt rituals and deposition is evidenced by the restricted distribution of pottery vessels in the funnel-like gap it delineated before the chamber's entrance. Here assigned as a separate 'action' to the III.1 long mound/ditch construction, there is no necessary reason that there was any substantial interval between them. In fact, the inturned terminals of the III.1 ditch are the most likely source for the fore-bank upcast.
*III.3:* The closure of the chamber as attested by the extraction of the proximal post (F.707) and its replacement by façade timbers, thereby blocking access. It is presumed that the insertion of the turf mound into the chamber and the firing of the structure would have immediately preceded this.

*Phase IV: Collapse, disuse and 'loss'*
*IV.1:* This was marked by the collapse of the mortuary chamber. This gave rise to the 'grooming' and infilling of the resultant hollow and the creation of the façade-front bank (F.736); the surviving façade posts appear variously to have been removed and/or burnt.
*IV.2:* Burials within the top of the mound (F.743 & F.744); pitting within the ditch and on the mound (F.774).
*IV.3:* Erosion of the mound, together with final infilling of the ditch and the growth of peat, which finally submerged the mound.

As expressed in this 'hard-line' manner, when the mortuary chamber was closed becomes, in effect, the hinge point of the sequence. Here a functional logic has been applied in the presumption that the III.2 fore-structure components actually 'worked' and facilitated/funnelled access into the chamber, as indeed did also the arrangement of the III.1 ditch-flanked front focus ritual 'action' towards the entrance. If espousing a purely symbolic logic, it could be argued that the Phase III components all occurred 'after the fact' and related to post-mound closure ritual activity in the forecourt space. This is simply a matter of interpretative approach, and there would be no ready means to resolve this issue.

There is much that remains to be added to this broad phasing sequence. For example, the evidence from the human bones and pottery and flint needs to be incorporated; any further detailing of the sequence can only be attempted once these additional categories of information have been brought to bear.

<table>
<tr><td>

**Köln-Lindenthal: long barrows and longhouses**
by J. Last

The publication of a major site like Haddenham provides an opportunity to consider its broader intellectual context. And at the start of a new century, we may care to wonder which was the most influential Neolithic site of that just past? From this side of the Channel one might think of great monuments like Stonehenge, but for its contemporary impact and continuing resonances I believe a strong case can be made for the excavation that took place at the Lindenthal site in Köln (Cologne), Germany, under the principal direction of Werner Buttler, in the early 1930s (Buttler & Haberey 1936).

The Köln-Lindenthal excavations were literally ground-breaking: they represented the first truly open-area investigation of a Neolithic settlement (over 35,000 sq. m), and as a consequence the characteristic post-built *Linearbandkeramik* (LBK) longhouses were exposed more clearly than on any previous site — exposed, but not recognized. For Köln-Lindenthal, standing on the cusp between antiquarian and modern archaeology, still inherited some of the misunderstandings which bedevilled earlier work, not least the assumption that prehistoric folk lived in pits. Lindenthal marks the beginning of the end for the prehistoric pit-dwelling, however, and the start of an interest in longhouses that also has great significance for how we interpret long barrows like Haddenham.

Historical contexts, even intellectual ones, have political dimensions too, and it is hard now to look objectively on German archaeology of the 1930s. But there is little of the Third Reich to be discerned among the pits and postholes of Neolithic Lindenthal. Indeed, the excavation's 'brilliant results' were lauded in Britain (Clark 1936) and the publication praised as 'impressive testimony . . . to the enlightened patriotism of the State' by the Marxist Gordon Childe (1936). The impact on contemporary British archaeology, with its emphasis on section cutting, was striking. Both Clark and Childe used their reviews to argue the case for projects of similar scope in Britain. But the nature of the archaeology impressed as much as its scale, the implication being that if British archaeologists looked in the right places, they too would find similar structures. In the meantime, Piggott wrote that, despite the lack of evidence for domestic structures, there was 'no reason to suppose that the southern English Neolithic was so immeasurably inferior to . . . Köln-Lindenthal with its timber houses, barns and granaries' (Piggott 1954, 26).

Piggott's turn of phrase is interesting, for Lindenthal, like other LBK settlements, did not contain 'timber houses, barns and granaries', but houses (which may include granaries) that had previously been misinterpreted as barns. German archaeology had, since the end of the nineteenth century, considered Neolithic pits to be dwellings, an interpretive position that reflects on many aspects of the discipline: the generally small scale of exposures prior to Köln-Lindenthal; the difficulty

</td><td>

archaeologists had in recognizing postholes; naive approaches to both natural and 'cultural' site-formation processes; and a tendency to ethnocentric and crude evolutionary thinking about prehistoric domestic life. When intercutting pits packed with material culture were found alongside posthole structures with no associated floors, it was natural to interpret the former as dwellings (so-called *Kurvenkomplexbauten*) and the latter as raised barns or granaries.

The same preconceptions operated in Britain. Curwen's famous picture of the squalid nature of life in 'the dank hollow of a wind-swept, half-silted ditch' at Neolithic Whitehawk Camp was later castigated by Piggott (1954, 26–8), but Piggott himself, in reporting excavations of a long barrow on Thickthorn Down, had made similar assumptions that material culture, especially what we would now recognize as 'structured deposition', provided direct evidence of occupation: 'Before any silting had taken place in the ditch, it had evidently been used as a shelter for flintknappers, "nests" of flakes being found on the bottom in six places' (Drew & Piggott 1936, 82). Thus, in an era of pit-dwellings, the ditches of long barrows and causewayed camps also became the habitations of our Neolithic forebears.

It is no coincidence that the pit-dwelling idea was largely laid to rest in Britain by Gerhard Bersu, who even before the War had realized that the Iron Age pits at Little Woodbury were simply 'filled with rubbish which was not the product of their occupation as any form of dwelling' (Bersu 1938, 310; see Evans 1989a). Bersu, a refugee from the Nazis, was perhaps the best field archaeologist of his generation, and had already recognized Neolithic post-built structures on the Goldberg in Württemberg (Bersu 1936); he was also the teacher of Werner Buttler. Meanwhile in Germany, the demolition of the pit-dwelling theory, facilitated by the results from Köln-Lindenthal, was left to Oscar Paret (1942), who argued that the so-called *Wohngruben* must have been borrow pits necessary to provide sufficient daub for the posthole structures so strikingly revealed there, which were simply the dry-land equivalents of the well-known timber *Pfahlbauten* from the Alpine lake villages.

With the pit-dwelling theory laid to rest by 1950, the cultural implications of the Neolithic longhouses of Köln-Lindenthal could be studied. It was perhaps Childe (1949) who first noted in print 'as a topical appendix' the similarities between houses and tombs, in this case the late Lengyel houses of central Poland and long barrows in the same region. He further stated that 'northern long barrows could well be regarded as durable imitations of the external appearance of a Danubian 1 longhouse' (Childe 1957, 238–9). This was highly significant at a time when long barrows were often connected with a megalithic tradition thought to be of Atlantic and ultimately Mediterranean origin.

Subsequently, Ian Hodder (1984; 1990; 1994) has revived this issue in terms of the operation of long-term symbolic principles (*domus* and *agrios*) in the Neolithic. He outlined several points of formal similarity between northwest European long mounds of the

</td></tr>
</table>

## Construction methods and materials

Having provided a 'skeletal' phasing sequence of the barrow's development, we must now consider the construction and arrangement of its structural elements. Given the monument's remarkable preservation, this accordingly focuses upon its timber elements. However, stones and 'earth' (i.e. turf and clay) were also involved. With the properties of the mound(s)

itself already discussed above, we are here concerned with the 'architecture' of the barrow's northeastern front. It is a matter of trying to reconstruct and envisage its standing components as distinct from how they were eventually deployed to 'close' the monument. Only once this framework has been established will the details of it as a 'container' for the dead be addressed. Thereafter, following discussion of the dynamics of its closure, and the presentation and

early fourth millennium BC and the central European longhouse tradition which, as radiocarbon dating now shows, began some 1500 years earlier. While Hodder, like Childe, focused mainly on the late Lengyel/TRB interface in Poland, Sherratt (1990) has also considered the influence of post-LBK (Villeneuve-Saint-Germain and Cerny) settlement in the Paris Basin. Others looked more generally at the question of why the longhouse form might have been reworked in funerary architecture; Bradley (1998a, 44–5), for instance, has suggested that the persistence of abandoned LBK longhouses as visible mounds, shown by the lack of intercutting of houses of different phases on many sites, might have led to them being associated with the deceased.

However, the most notable feature of mid fifth-millennium houses in both central Poland and western France is how different they are from the classic rectangular, posthole structures revealed at Köln-Lindenthal: sites such as Haut-Mée, with a structure of extreme trapezoidal form (Cassen *et al.* 1998), or Brzesc Kujawski, where the houses had trench foundations, lacked internal posts and, unlike the earlier sites discussed by Bradley, were frequently rebuilt on the spot (Grygiel 1986). So while we can perhaps trace the formal inspiration of the long mounds, these structures also show the degree to which the longhouse idea had already been reworked over large areas of time and space (along with changes in pottery styles, settlement structure, burial rites, etc.).

An acknowledgement of the great variability in 'Danubian' cultures over the long term leads one to question whether such

formal comparison actually enhances our understanding of either houses or tombs, e.g. asking why longhouses disappear towards the end of the fifth millennium. Similarly, the complexity of British long barrows is increasingly being recognized, with many altered or elongated over time, and others where the mounds cover previously free-standing mortuary structures, these internal or original forms bearing little resemblance to longhouses anyway. The need first to unpick the constructional history of these monuments might then lead us to consider the different ways linearity was expressed within the indigenous Neolithic monument tradition (long mounds, long mortuary enclosures, cursuses, etc.) before looking further afield for inspirations or parallels.

Given the variety and complexity of linear monuments in the British Neolithic, it seems odd that the few large post-built structures which have been found (e.g. Balbridie, Lismore Fields, White Horse Stone, Yarnton) are still usually interpreted as houses, since they are often associated with distinctive material culture or environmental assemblages (Thomas 1999, 25) and fit uneasily with the majority of Neolithic settlements that primarily comprise groups of pits (see Garrow below). One might suggest they are more plausibly understood as ceremonial or monumental structures, akin to Haddenham, than dwellings like those at Köln-Lindenthal. But perhaps it is simply that, 70 years after those excavations gave British prehistorians such an inferiority complex, we are still trying to find the missing longhouses . . .

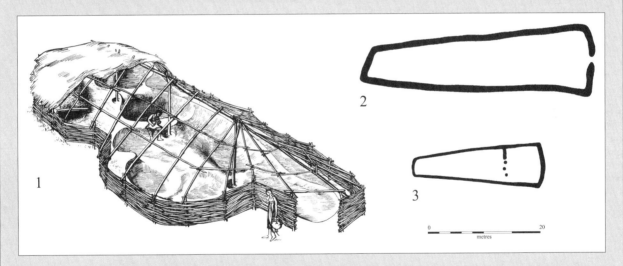

**Figure 3.31**. *1) Reconstruction of Köln-Lindenthal 'long pit-dwelling' (not to scale; Buttler & Haberey 1936, fig. 30); 2) Fussell's Lodge mortuary enclosure (after Ashbee 1966; Kinnes 1992, fig. 2.4.3); later Neolithic longhouse, Brzesc Kujawski, Poland (after Last 1996, fig. 3.4).*

distribution of its artefact categories, the monument can be considered with a sense of totality: in effect as 'process' or 'project'.

Before presenting the detailed studies of the mortuary structure it is necessary to summarize of our in-the-field understanding of its timbers. On excavation, the remains could be categorized into three main groups. First, there were obvious structural elements that appeared to be in position and were more or less

complete; the lower parts of the axial posts and timber flooring could be included in this group. Second, there were large timber elements, massive planks and lengths of post, which were most likely part of the mortuary structure but which were incomplete and not in their original positions. On the floor of the structure three post-like timbers were found ([3642], [3643] & [3645]) and many pieces of planking were present in the fill. These timbers were interpreted on site as parts of the axial posts, walls and roof of the structure. Third, there were layers of material that could be associated with the mortuary structure but which were in a decayed form. In this group can be included the lenses of oak chips within the mortuary structure and the areas where timber impressions were found but where the wood had decayed.

Any interpretation of the mortuary structure must weigh this evidence carefully; while all the evidence must be considered, it is difficult to avoid working from the better preserved evidence:

1) The best-preserved elements consisted of the axial posts and timber flooring of the mortuary structure. Associated with these were their accompanying constructional features (the postholes and the mortuary structure trench). Together the archaeological evidence suggested an oak-floored structure sunk 0.30 m below ground surface. At either end were massive posts, with a further post set one-third of the way along.

The sizes of the post pits and the posts themselves suggested that huge split oaks were used and that these were positioned in deep sockets. While implying that the posts may have been tall or would have supported a heavy superstructure, this presumes that they could have been truncated/cut: as discussed below, this is unlikely to have been possible once the wood had hardened through seasoning.

On its own, the evidence of the size of the posts and that the sides of the mortuary structure had not collapsed strongly suggested the presence of walls and a roof. As for the flooring, this had been cut to fit around the medial post. These planks could not therefore have come from any other part of the mortuary structure. They must be *in situ* elements.

2) The three large timbers placed on the mortuary structure floor appeared roughly 'D'-shaped in section and were interpreted as pieces of the axial posts. One lay beside the medial post and was similar to it in dimensions ([3643]). The two others were in the proximal sub-chamber and were similar in size to the proximal posts (though the evidence suggest that the front post had been replaced by façade-related timbers).

The rest of the timber consisted of various large and small sections of thick planks found in the fill of the mortuary structure. Two major patterns were observed:

i) Towards the centre of the structure, very wide planks up to 1 m wide and 2–3 m long were found. These tended to lie horizontally and appeared well preserved. They were interpreted as roof timbers because of their size, central horizontal position and because the eastern plank or planks overlay the medial post.

ii) At the sides of the structure, several layers of planks less than 0.5 m wide. These appeared to be quite long, but had numerous breaks along their length. The planks bedded at angles between 45° and vertical. The lowest pieces at the edge of the mortuary structure trench appeared to be set on edge and were interpreted as the side walls. The poor condition and bedding angles suggested that the timbers had collapsed from the walls above the level of the ground surface. Some had slumped in adhering to clods of earth.

3) The layers of chips of oak and the few pieces of decayed wood were less significant for interpretative processes. They suggest that the timbers had been partly broken down and that survival was uneven. The densities of small wood fragments increased as the layers approached surviving timbers. This was particularly true of the distal and medial posts and the side walls.

Taken together the evidence suggested that the mortuary structure was walled and roofed. The posts survived up to a height of 0.40 m above the ground surface level, with traces of wood chips (directly linked to the walls) found as high as 0.80 m above that level. As the surrounding mound survived 1.20 m above the ground surface, the structure's walls could thus have been 1.50 m high above the base of the mortuary chamber's trench. No joinery was found and it was assumed that the structure was held up without these techniques. As the best-preserved planks were in excess of 1 m wide it was possible to envisage the sides as consisting of planks pinned between the axial posts and the surrounding mound. The roof could have been composed of similar massive planks.

In their studies below, both Morgan and Darrah (informed by the original phasing sequence) approach the data from the face-value 'box-like' setting of the collapsed structure. Of necessity these are here included unrevised in the light of the final interpretative reconstruction presented below (see **How the structure worked**). Only recognized following long post-excavation musing, the primary difference is over the issues of whether the axial uprights were, in fact, ever load-bearing and when they were dismantled.

### Structural timbers and roundwood
by R. MORGAN, with a contribution by J. PRICE

The preservation of extensive areas of the wooden mortuary chamber enabled new technology to be applied to its removal for detailed study under controlled conditions. Traditional methods of handling waterlogged wood could not be used owing to its fragility. Nevertheless in spite of the problems, an intensive tree-ring study has been possible and has added detailed information to supplement the existing archaeological evidence.

The study of the wood had three major aims, which were defined by questions raised during excavation and immediate post-excavation work:

1) The wood had clearly been very compressed and distorted by the surrounding deposits, and the limits of each timber could not be defined on site. It was therefore crucial to determine the boundaries of the timbers in order to estimate the original size and age of the trees used, and in doing so examine the methods of woodworking employed to create the planks. The plank sections and sizes could then enable detailed reconstructions to be suggested, with important implications for the form of other wooden mortuary chambers where little has survived (see also Darrah below).

2) Tree-ring patterns of the planks and posts could be compared to indicate the relationship between individual timbers. Planks split from the same tree should demonstrate very similar pat-

terns of growth; the degree of similarity may suggest the number of trees used. Tree-ring patterns are the only means available of ascertaining the contemporaneity of elements of the structure and assist in the interpretation of phases of construction and demolition.

3) The correlated tree-ring patterns could form the basis of an average chronology representing tree growth in the centuries prior to the chamber's construction. The chronology would then be available for possible absolute dating by comparison with existing reference chronologies (in which each ring has been assigned a calendar year), based on the principle that trees growing over the same period of time will exhibit similar fluctuations in ring-width. If dendrochronological dating was not successful, the tree-ring related wood could be used for intensive radiocarbon dating, and 'wiggle-matching' with the calibration curve. Either technique could fix the chamber's construction date to within decades.

Relating primarily to issues of chronology, the latter two of these issues are considered later in this chapter (see *Tree-ring results* below).

*Methodology: sampling the wood sections*

The wood of the roof and floor was lifted by conservation staff John Price and Mary Macqueen of the Ancient Monuments Laboratory, HBMC, and their methods are summarized below. Sampling and study of the wood was carried out in a store in Sheffield, and the laboratory analysis in the Dendrochronology Laboratory and the Department of Archaeology & Prehistory, University of Sheffield.

Conservation summary
by J. PRICE

A

B

**Figure 3.32.** *Lifting the mortuary structure timbers: A) the roof blocks in polythene boxes and the wooden crates containing the entire cross-sections of the chamber floor (left side) were housed in a cool warehouse in Sheffield, beneath polythene tents with humidifiers; B) cross-section of the floor plank and wall timbers of the distal sub-chamber, viewed from above. From the left is the south wall [3723], small plank [3694] with [3692] below and the north wall [3722]. The wood shows as black against the light brown clays and gravels below; above the wood is the expanding foam which filled any spaces in the crate and enabled such fragile material to be lifted and moved without breakage. The cross-section at this point is 1.6 m wide and 0.45 m at its maximum height. (Photographs F. Jolley.)*

The Conservation Section of the Ancient Monuments Laboratory was instructed in late 1986 to provide maximum field support for the barrow excavations. After some preliminary work, this started in January 1987 and ended in the autumn of that year when investigations were completed. It was, of course, not known exactly what was to be discovered, but two main decisions were made: firstly, to undertake complete moulds of the uncovered timber structure and, secondly, to lift the very fragile remains of both roof and floor surfaces for further dendrochronological specialist investigation.

Work began with snow on the site, continued after a break in very hot summer conditions and finished in the worst floods for 40 years, providing a complete spectrum of weather conditions. Several hundred sections were successfully lifted, making the project the largest of its type attempted in the UK.

Because of the initial low temperatures, around 0°C, and high humidities, a polyurethane moulding material was used and four large moulds made, an aqueous polyethylene glycol solution being used as a separating agent. The roof section, cut into many small blocks, was packed into 'Giant Storer' sealable polyethylene boxes, whilst much of the floor section was cut into 10 large blocks weighing from 2–400 kg and boxed in polyurethane and plywood containers built *in situ*. The base was cut by specially

105

A

B

**Figure 3.33.** *Mortuary structure. Sampling the timbers: A) a slice cut from the northern wall timber [3722] (Block 6/1B) while encased in foam (its protection enabled the sampling to take place without damage); B) cut cross-section of floor planks and walls timber supported by foam, tissue, metal plates and bandage. (Photographs F. Jolley.)*

The roof sections

The wood which was thought to form the roof of the chamber had to be lifted to give access to the contents of the chamber, but was too fragile to remove as entire planks. It was thus decided to cut the wood into around 250 blocks, each on average 200 mm square, with supporting layers of soil deposits beneath. Each block was given a letter and number code along the structure. The roof was lifted in three 'phases', labelled I to III, I being the proximal roof, II being the upper distal and III the lower distal roof. Each section across the roof was thus made up of seven or eight blocks. There were some 40 cross-sections in all, giving a continuous record of the planks making up the roof layer. The task was then to reconstruct these sections in order to define the boundaries of the planks and their cross-sections.

The blocks were transported to Sheffield in sealed plastic boxes. For further study, a slice approximately 50 mm thick was then removed by bandaging one end of the block and cutting with a sharp knife through the wood and soil. Orientation of the blocks was defined by a label in a particular corner, and had to be carefully maintained in order to place each block correctly in relation to its neighbour. The cut slices were then sealed in polythene bags and deep-frozen. The remainder of the blocks were returned to the plastic boxes for longer-term storage and experimental work on conservation techniques.

Floor timbers and posts

The medial ([3687]) and distal ([3696]) posts were encased in polyurethane foam, lifted whole and packed in wooden crates. The floor and wall timbers were treated variously. Some areas were cut into square blocks, as used for the roof, and encased in foam. In other portions, complete cross-sections across floor and walls were cut, packed in foam, crated and lifted. All the boxes and crates were transported to Sheffield in March 1988, where they were covered with polythene tents and kept stable with the use of humidifiers.

Again it was necessary to cut thinner sections for further analysis, and some time was spent experimenting with methods of consolidating the wood sufficiently to cut with the minimum amount of damage. Portable freezing units, liquid nitrogen and dry ice were all tried, and have possibilities; after deep-freezing, one slice was cut using a reciprocating saw in the Metallurgy Department of the University of Sheffield. This very successfully cut a smooth slice only 20 mm thick, but the sample size is restricted by blade length, and the generated heat threatened to cause damage to the wood at the edges. In the end, no better method could be found than that used for the roof, that is, cutting the unfrozen slices with a sharp knife or similar. The very crumbly natural gravel deposits beneath the wood caused the most difficulty, by impeding the cutting and giving little support.

The large crates containing complete sections of the floor and walls were opened, and the foam was cut away. There were

made strengthened sharpened steel plates 170 cm wide and 5 cm thick. Three plates of depths up to 76 cm were used and were slowly inserted using three horizontal hydraulic rams. Further assistance was given later at Sheffield in unpacking and sampling for dendrochronology.

The project tested the ingenuity and stamina of the team but helped in the establishment of improved lifting techniques and a realization that this site set a 'benchmark' in the retrieval of very fragile remains in adverse weather conditions (see Price & Macqueen 1988; Price 1992 for fuller details).

seven of these (omitting 5/4 and 5/7, and 7/M reserved for the British Museum), each containing sections of two wall timbers and one or two floor planks. Each individual timber was sectioned by one of three methods: sawing, cutting with a sharp knife, or by pushing a metal plate under the wood using hydraulic jacks. As the slice was loosened, a metal plate was pushed underneath for support, and vertical cuts were made with a knife and plate. The section, around 100 mm thick, could then be eased away from the main block. Immediate bandaging, labelling with Dymo tape, wrapping and freezing caused the minimum of damage, and has created a permanent frozen record of the chamber's section at approximately 0.5 m intervals.

Parts of the floor were cut into smaller blocks which were easier to handle. The most successful slices were obtained from timbers completely encased in foam; where their orientation was known cuts could be made through both foam and wood, giving the slices excellent support. This applied particularly to the wall timbers: the proximal south wall timber [3575] (Block 7/A), the distal south wall timber [3723] (Block 6/2) and distal north wall timber [3722] (Block 6/1): and to the distal post [3696].

If the orientation of the wood within the foam was not known, the foam had to be cut away and could not be used for support. These samples include Blocks 5/9 to 5/29 from the distal sub-chamber floor plank [3692] and wall timbers [3722] and [3723] (excluding Blocks 5/25 and 5/27 reserved for the British Museum, and Block 5/10 undergoing X-ray analysis), Blocks 7/B to 7/K from the proximal sub-chamber floor planks ([3689] & [3690]) and Blocks 8/1 to 8/5 from the proximal posts ([3683], [3684] & [3685]). The loss of the supporting foam and the movement involved in cutting it off meant some damage to already vulnerable pieces, such as the wall sections (e.g. 5/12) or the proximal posts (8/1–5, although little wood survived in these). The small blocks from the floor resembled those from the roof, and were similarly treated by bandaging and cutting with a sharp knife.

The three horizontal timbers (displaced posts?; [3642], [3645] & [3643]), lying on the chamber floor, had been encased in plaster of paris and foam; one quarter of [3642] and [3645] had been removed on site to examine their sections, and the remainder was lifted on metal plates. Cross-sections were cut across them for further study, despite severe cracking. Timber [3643] was sliced vertically on site into five sections, which were examined whole.

Recording procedures

The condition of the wood was such that only deep-freezing consolidated it sufficiently for further analysis, and despite its fragile state, it survived remarkably well. Chemical tests

**Figure 3.34.** *Mortuary structure timbers: A) close-up view of the cleaned roof block I W1, showing the north edge of plank [3582] (at X = 6.5 m) and the top of the north wall timber [3722] coming up to meet it. The fragile and disorganized state of the wood can be seen, as can the direction of the tree-rings (photograph F. Jolley); B) the micro-structure of oak wood (*Quercus spp.*), showing the large spring vessels and dense summer wood which together form the annual ring. The abrupt start to the year's growth (a straight line to the left of the spring vessels) indicates the direction of growth, from left to right: this was important when trying to decide the relationship between parts of the planks. Note also the wide rays running across the rings: their direction can often be determined by the location of cracks in the wood. (Photograph C. Salisbury.)*

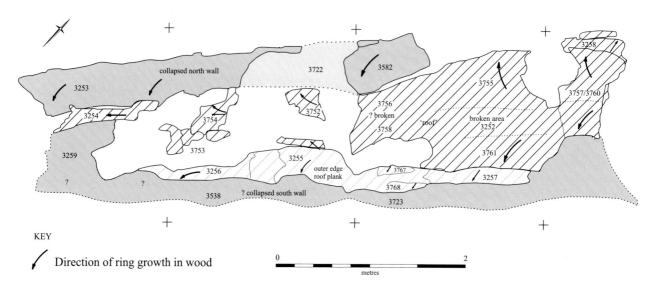

KEY

⟋ Direction of ring growth in wood

0 ⟋ 2
metres

**Figure 3.35.** *The mortuary structure roof and wall timbers.*

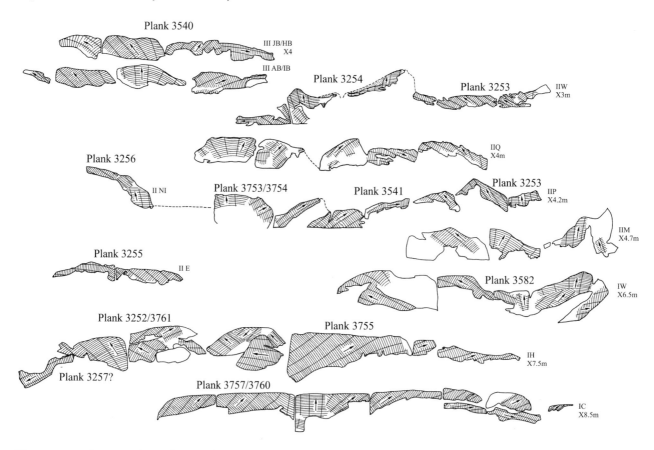

**Figure 3.36.** *Cross-sections of the roof.*

and SEM examination (Caple & Murray below; 1989) have shown the complete carbonization of the wood and the extent of the fissures and mineralization. Compression, erosion and waterlogging had all contributed to the deterioration as well as the survival of the wood. Owing to the coarse nature of the natural gravels beneath the chamber, decay had commenced from beneath, and little remained of the bases of the main posts. Standard dendro-chronological techniques were adopted for the frozen slices. Each sample was held firm in a vice and its transverse surface cleaned with a Stanley surform plane (its blades needing constant replacement owing to rapid wear by the underlying stony soil deposits). Most sections withstood such handling two or three times before being fully recorded; a few, especially the wall timbers, were too fragile for more than one cleaning.

The cleaned slices were allowed to defrost for some time, to clear the white surface and remove the ice from the wood structure. Each cross-section was then accurately drawn (actual size), with the location of soil and wood and details of the wood structure being recorded. All the timber was oak (*Quercus* spp.), a ring-porous wood; each year's growth consists of a line of very large vessels formed in May to carry sap to the developing buds, and a zone of dense supporting cells formed in June–September (Jane 1970; Morris & Perring 1974). Thus each ring is clearly defined even to the naked eye. The direction of growth can be determined by an abrupt edge to the vessels at the start of each year's growth, enabling the orientation of the planks to be determined. Running at right angles to the rings are thick rays, along which the wood splits naturally from pith to bark.

On the drawings, the direction and curvature of the growth rings and rays were marked to indicate the location of the wood in the original tree; for example, very curved rings from near the tree's heart or slightly curved rings from the outer parts. The direction of growth was marked by an arrow, and its determination proved very useful when linking drawings together. Where possible, the approximate number of rings present in each block was noted, with the aim of estimating the total number of rings in each plank, and thus the original tree's minimum age. The original diameter of the trees could also be estimated from the overall dimensions of the timbers. The age, size, general growth rate, straightness of grain and presence or absence of knots give a good indication of the quality of timber being felled and of the original woodland conditions in which it grew.

*Interpretation of timber cross-sections*

Roof sections

The precise drawings of each roof section were joined together as far as possible (as in Fig. 3.36) to give a series of plank sections at regular intervals of around 0.3 m. It must be noted here that the size estimates must remain approximate, and the interpretations tentative, owing to the error margins introduced by the lifting methods of the roof timbers, and their fragile condition. Generally, wood loss and erosion will have resulted in underestimates.

There were areas of severe damage (mostly original, but also caused during lifting and sampling), such as the south edge of plank [3758] at X = 6–7 m where wood fragments lay in all directions and reconstruction of the plank section was not possible. However, much of the wood survived analysis sufficiently well to give an impression of the plank sections, which could be checked in adjacent sections. Many of the plank sections revealed a soft black deposit, about 10 mm thick, beneath the wood (at the interface of the wood and underlying soil layers). Despite repeated cleaning, no wood structure could be determined, and this material is interpreted as a layer of decayed wood which may have unknowingly been removed from upper surfaces. It was not noted on the floor planks. Its interpretation does, however, influence the final conclusions concerning plank thickness.

The reconstructed sections have shown how the methods of conversion used to produce the roof planks (some of which are thought to be collapsed wall

timbers), the approximate age and size of the trees used, the extent of the planks, and where possible a record of their ring patterns (see below). A description of the form of the roof planks follows, starting at the east end, the façade, and ending over the distal post in the west. Plank numbers can be found in Figure 3.35; roof sections at regular intervals are illustrated in Figure 3.36.

Roof wood over the proximal sub-chamber at X = 8–8.5 m revealed cross-sections which were not easy to interpret; it could not be clearly determined whether one wide or two adjacent planks had formed the roof at this point. Two planks are shown in Figure 3.35. One [3760] was on the south side extending to around X = 8.3 m (in section I D; in I E, the ring direction changed). This was a tangential plank around 50 mm thick, and its rings faced towards the north, with the tree centre to the south. This ring direction continued to the north edge of the adjacent plank [3757], but in the centre was an interruption with the rings running across the plank (as they would near the centre of the tree) instead of at a 45° angle. It is thus unclear whether there is a very compressed break in the wood at this point (suggesting the presence of two planks), or whether one wide plank was split from a tree with some distortion of the ring pattern. Another possibility is incorrect orientation of several of the blocks.

Along the north edge beneath [3757] lay a plank only 10 mm thick, almost radial in section or with the rings sloping downwards at a 45° angle, and the tree centre uppermost to the south ([3258]). Around 0.6 m wide, the plank may be related to the group of small planks at the east end of the north wall ([3577]).

At around X = 8 m, between Phase I D & E, the wood direction changed. The growth rings, still at a 45° angle, faced towards the south with the tree centre to the north. This plank, [3761]/[3252], extended from the north edge of the hole at X = 8 m (I F3) to the south edge of the roof; there was no apparent distinction between the two parts of the plank which were given separate finds numbers. It had a width of around 0.58 m. The same ring direction continued through to about X = 7 m (I R). Further planking could be identified beneath, but no trace of [3759] was noted in the sections.

On the north side, from the edge of the hole at X = 7.8 m to at least X = 7 m, was a plank with rings at a 45° angle facing north, and the tree centre to the south ([3755]). This is in the opposite direction to the adjacent plank just described; it is estimated to be 0.6 m wide.

In size, section and ring direction, the two planks, [3761]/[3252] and [3755], could have formed two halves of one very wide tangential plank extending right across the roof, and split from across a large tree. The central break could have been a natural split, since tangential planks are prone to longitudinal splitting along the rays, or a wide plank could have been deliberately split and the two halves laid side by side. The various possibilities influence the interpretation of the form of the roof, whether flat or pitched. None of the wood sections indicate continuity across the centre of the plank, but breakage and distortion could have occurred under subsequent compression. Two blocks revealed a piece of wood almost triangular in section between the edges of the two half planks (at Y = 2.5 m), which may have some significance. It could either have fractured from the break in the planks or it could represent some sort of support for the roof.

The sections of both planks revealed an unusual and inexplicable feature. In the centre of the roof, the planks were around 0.12 m thick (e.g. in I G4, H4, I4 and R4); towards the edges of the roof, the plank thickness tapered to only around 0.03 m (Fig. 3.36). This shaping either occurred by chance on both undersides of the planks, perhaps through decay and erosion, or it was deliberately created by hewing down the planks before use (see Darrah below for further detail). This could have been done for reasons of weight reduction, or in an attempt to prevent longitudinal splitting near the centre. At around $X = 7$–$7.3$ m, these planks overlay or rested upon the medial post [3687].

On the surface of the southern plank [3761]/[3252], a number of pronounced ridges had been noted during excavation (Figs. 3.19 & 3.21). Owing to their upstanding nature, they were already in a fragile state when sampled, and suffered further during analysis. In Blocks II6 and G7, they appeared to be simply long slim pieces of wood resting on the surface, with the rings running across rather than at an angle; thus the vertical rays resisted erosion longer, and remained upstanding. The wood could be fragments broken from larger pieces, abraded subsequently perhaps by water action, and there is no apparent evidence of deliberate shaping. They could also have resulted from uncontrolled splitting (see Darrah below). Traces of a lower plank [3257] on the southern edge of the roof appeared in Blocks I E1/G9/H8. This was a radial plank with the rings running towards the south. The section is consistent with this plank being part of the same plank as [3256]/[3255]/[3768], along the southern flank of the roof.

The west end of plank [3755] (I S at $X = 7$ m) was quite damaged, as were all the subsequent Phase I roof sections from $X = 6$–$7$ m and $Y = 1.5$–$2.5$ m, making interpretation of the original plank forms impossible. Little can be said about the sections of planks labelled [3756] and [3758]; there were probably two layers of planking, the lower plank being tangential with rings at a 45° angle facing north, and the tree centre to the south. The upper plank appears to have had the same orientation in places (I T3, U4, V5), and was around 0.05 m thick.

At around $X = 7$ m on the north side, a change of ring direction and a very thin plank edge (less than 10 mm) indicated the start of another plank [3582]. This was a half tangential plank around 0.9 × 0.5 m in size. It had wide growth rings which faced to the south, with the tree centre to the north, thus opposite to most of the other roof material already described. It is suggested below that this plank is a continuation of [3253], on the basis of alignment, form of the cross-section and wide average ring-width. Furthermore, it abutted the north wall timber [3722], and there is a probable tree-ring link (described below) suggesting that this plank [3582]/[3253] may be the upper half of the north wall plank which collapsed over to lie alongside the roof planks. A small piece of wood at the northwest corner of [3582] (in Blocks I Y1/Z1) revealed rings running in the opposite direction; it may continue through the isolated piece (II E3) at $X = 5.7$ m, $Y = 3$ m. Otherwise, no wood survived on the north side between $X = 5$ m and $X = 6$ m. A number of small planks, all with consistent ring direction and sections, extended along the southern edge of the roof over the distal sub-chamber. The series starts (in Block II A2 at $X = 6.5$ m) with plank [3768], through plank [3255] (in Blocks II C1–I1 at $X = 5$–$6$ m), and plank [3256] (in Blocks II K1–Q1 at $X = 3.5$–$5.3$ m). All sections were almost radial, from the very outermost edges of a tangential plank, with rings running towards the south and the tree centre to the north (Fig. 3.36). The sections of plank were 0.1–0.33 m wide and around 0.03 m thick. Close tree-ring similarities (described below) indicate almost certainly that this was a continuous plank almost 3 m long. Movement of the surrounding deposits had caused the plank, especially at $X = 4$–$5$ m, to lie at a sharp angle with its higher edge to the south, and compression had folded the plank over the underlying deposits (especially clear in Block II N1 at $X = 4.2$ m: Fig. 3.36). Judging by its section and ring direction, this plank probably represents the outer edge of a roof plank; it also has tree-ring links with the posts and floor plank of the distal sub-chamber.

Alongside [3255] and to the north, at $X = 5$–$5.5$ m, was a small plank about 0.13 m wide and 0.03 m thick, with radial section and rings facing north (seen in Blocks II F2 and G3 at $X = 5.5$ m). No sections of [3528] were examined. Its position suggested it could have formed the collapsed upper edge of the south wall timber [3723].

In the large central empty area of $X = 5$–$6$ m, a patch of wood proved to be a tangential plank around 0.2 m wide and 0.04 m thick ([3752]). Its rings faced north and tree centre to the south (seen in Blocks II G1 and H1); in this it was consistent with the fragment alongside, [3255], of which it may be a continuation. Embedded in the concave upper surface of Blocks II G1 and H1 was an orange fine-textured deposit containing white flecks, possibly resulting from precipitation during subsequent gleying processes (French pers. comm.). It is noted since it occurred only here and on the surface of plank [3254] to the west, in line with [3752] at $c$. $Y = 2.5$ m.

Wood was again preserved from $X = 4.8$ m on the north side, with a half tangential plank [3253]. The tree centre lay downwards near the north edge of the roof, and the rings ran in a southerly direction as far as $Y = 2.5$ m (Fig. 3.36). The plank was up to 0.4 m wide and 0.03–0.04 m thick. Its growth rings were unusually wide. The plank had been pushed up to lie at an angle, the higher edge to the south. Cross-section and ring direction suggest that the plank continued without interruption to the distal post at $X = 2.5$ m, and probably extended across [3582] to almost $X = 7$ m, creating a plank over 4 m long. Its section, with the tree centre over the north chamber wall, and tree-ring links, suggest that it represents the upper half of the north wall [3722] which collapsed over. The east end at $X = 7$ m corresponds with the east end of [3722], and with the end of the south wall. At the extreme northeast corner of [3251] at $X = 5$–$5.5$ m was a slim plank about 0.08 m thick and 0.1 m wide, with vertical rays. It was noted in Blocks II L3/M5/N5, but its full extent cannot be determined since Blocks II O7 and Q5 are missing. The plank could be part of [3253].

The central roof area over the distal chamber contained only fragmentary pieces of wood. A probable half tangential plank [3754] at $X = 4$–$4.5$ m was also wide-ringed and possibly around 0.3 m wide. The tree centre lay beneath, and the rings faced up and to the north (Fig. 3.36). In Blocks II O4 and P8/P9, a lower plank sloped up to the surface. This was also wide-ringed and radial in section, with rings running in the same direction as [3754]. It may represent the top of lower plank [3540], and there is a tree-ring link between a section of [3540] and this plank (in Blocks II P8/Q8 and III JB); no sections of [3541] were examined.

Beneath [3754], between $X = 3.5$–$4.5$ m, was another tangential plank with a width of 0.6–0.7 m and a thickness of 0.04–0.05 m ([3540]: Figs. 3.19 & 3.23). Again the tree's heart was beneath and central (at $Y = 2.2$ m), and the wide rings faced up and to the north. The shallow curve of the rings indicated some distance (perhaps 0.2 m) from the pith of the tree itself. Useful long ring series were measured on outer parts of the plank (on Blocks III HB and JB). The cross-section and central location of this plank suggests that it formed *in situ* roof material, reflecting the floor plank of the distal sub-chamber beneath, and corresponding to the tangential planking to the east ([3755] and [3252]). The form of this plank is one of the reasons for suggesting a flat roof for the chamber. The superimposed plank [3754], with the same cross-section, is less easy to explain.

Running alongside [3251], from $X = 2.7$ m to $X = 3.5$ m, was a tangential plank around 0.3 m wide and only 0.01–0.04 m thick ([3254]: Fig. 3.36). It had been split from outer parts of the tree, and was a tangential plank from the outer trunk with vertical rays, the only plank of this type noted in the structure. The rings faced upwards and the tree centre was below. Much of this plank (in Blocks II U3/V3/W3/X3) was covered in the calcite deposit already noted on the surface of [3752]. Plank [3254] had been compressed into a concave section and its north edge was pushed up and over [3253]. To the south of [3254] was an area of very broken fragments representing the remains of plank [3259]. Generally the pieces were horizontal radial fragments, but rings ran in both directions so the plank's orientation was not clear.

Initially the condition of the roof wood led to some doubt as to whether any information could be derived from its study. However, by piecing together the details from over 240 sections, it has been possible to make many observations about the original nature of the planks, their size, sections and relationships. Some of the wood, particularly over the proximal sub-chamber (X = 6–8 m) and the central lower area over the distal sub-chamber ([3540]), appears to represent original roof material, in that the planks are consistent in cross-section and orientation, and they also reflect the floor planks beneath. They appear to have been deliberately made and placed in position, whether during use of the chamber or during the phase of destruction or both.

It cannot be confirmed whether one wide plank or two narrower planks covered the proximal sub-chamber; the possible roof wood over the distal sub-chamber ([3540] with its curved inner rings central) tends to suggest one wide plank. Thus the roof could either have been flat, the planking being supported on the posts, or ridged in some way which subsequently collapsed. Some of the smaller planks over the distal sub-chamber have the appearance of pieces of varied origin, tossed in to create some form of covering during the phase of destruction of the chamber. The planking down the north and south edges of the distal area (X = 2.5–7 m) almost certainly originated as the collapsed upper halves of the wall planks, both of which terminated around X = 7 m. The wood here loosely termed 'roof' wood thus had a variety of origins, and its present form probably bears little resemblance to the original covering of the chamber during use, if one existed.

All the planking consisted of full or half tangential planks, with the rings facing upwards and the tree centre beneath, carefully corresponding with the wall and floor planks; the heart of the tree faced into the chamber on every timber. The estimated widths of the planks as reconstructed suggest an original tree diameter of at least 1.2 m (for example, the half plank [3755] in Blocks I H1–4 is 0.6 m wide: Fig. 3.36), and with allowances for missing inner wood and outer sapwood, may have reached 1.5 m. Approximate ring counts indicate a tree age exceeding 300 years. These figures for size and age are almost identical to those for the floor planks and posts (see below).

## Posts

A small post [3595] was found on the surface of the lower façade-bank F.736, close to the proximal posts. It was not *in situ*, but is thought to have formed part of the post and plank funnel-shaped entrance. The post consisted of a split half-trunk 0.26 m in diameter.

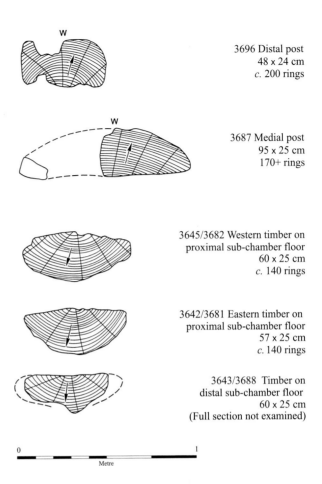

3696 Distal post
48 × 24 cm
*c.* 200 rings

3687 Medial post
95 × 25 cm
170+ rings

3645/3682 Western timber on
proximal sub-chamber floor
60 × 25 cm
*c.* 140 rings

3642/3681 Eastern timber on
proximal sub-chamber floor
57 × 25 cm
*c.* 140 rings

3643/3688 Timber on
distal sub-chamber floor
60 × 25 cm
(Full section not examined)

**Figure 3.37.** *Sketch drawings of the cross-sections of the posts and horizontal timbers.*

With 80 growth rings and no sapwood, the original tree must have been over 100 years old.

Little remained of the proximal posts [3684] and [3685] when examined in the laboratory; only thin radial fragments up to 130 × 30 mm in section adhered to the soil surface when the protective foam was cut away from Blocks 8/1 to 8/5. The posts are recorded on site as being around 0.6 m wide and 0.2 m deep, with the heart of the tree facing towards the west, into the chamber.

The medial post [3687] (Fig. 3.37) was a split half trunk, split again along its inner face (from which a tangential plank of similar section to the floor and roof planking could have originated). The post's width of 1.18 m indicates an original tree diameter of up to 1.5 m, with allowance for missing sapwood. The fragile condition and vertical position of the post led to some collapse on site, and the entire section would probably not have survived examination. The radial segments into which it split were more suitable for tree-ring measurement, and enabled reconstructions of the tree section and ring pattern. The combined ring series totalled 170 years (see below), and indicate a tree age of 200–300 years. The heart of the tree faced east into the proximal sub-chamber.

The distal post [3696] was oriented the same way, the tree's heart facing to the east. The post had the same cross-section as [3687], but had lost its northern and southern edges, either through decay or deliberate trimming (the resulting gaps were filled with other pieces of timber which were not examined in this study). This left the post with a more rectangular section, 0.6 m wide and 0.25 m deep (Fig. 3.37). The original tree diameter is less easy to estimate due to this loss of wood. Ring series totalling 180 years were recorded, suggesting an original tree age of well over 200 years.

With average ring widths of around 1.1 mm, and a steady yet sensitive growth pattern (i.e. ring-width variation), the tree(s) which provided the posts was growing steadily in high forest, with little cause for wide variations in growth rate.

Horizontal timbers: displaced posts?
Three large pieces of oak wood lay on the floor of the chamber. Two oval timbers rested on the southern floor plank [3690] in the proximal sub-chamber; [3642/81] at $X = 9$ m was $0.55 \times 0.53$ m in size, and [3645/82] at $X = 8$–8.5 m was slightly larger at $0.76 \times 0.56$ m. The third piece [3643/88] lay on the floor of the distal sub-chamber, and was $1.05 \times 0.6$ m in size. All three pieces had cross-sections similar to that of the medial post, of a tree split and split again (Fig. 3.37), and all had been carefully laid with the tree centre facing upwards.

Around 130 rings were recorded on [3642] and [3645]. Their overall pattern was unusual compared to other timbers in the chamber, in having wide inner rings followed by a 50-year period of very erratic fluctuations in width, from extremely narrow to very wide rings. The close correspondence of this pattern in both timbers almost certainly indicates an origin in the same tree, one which suffered a series of severe setbacks in growth in its last few decades. These periods of senescence indicate much reduced cambial activity which could have had a number of causes, such as waterlogging of the soil, severe insect attack on the foliage (Varley 1978), frost damage (Baillie 1989), or extensive cutting back (pollarding) of the crown (Bridge 1983). Each time the tree gradually recovered and was capable of very fast growth (wide rings).

On the evidence of location, size and cross-section, and by analogy with the possible link of timber [3643/88] with medial post [3687] (described below), it is suggested that these two pieces of wood may have once formed the tops of the two proximal posts [3684] and [3685]. These could have been

removed, trimmed to shape and carefully placed on the floor during the process of dismantling the chamber. Since the proximal posts no longer survive, this possibility cannot be checked. Alternatively, the two timbers (and [3694]) could have originated from another context.

Timber [3643/88] had just over 100 rings, and its possible association with post [3687] (suspected during excavation by its shape and position) has been demonstrated by corresponding tree-ring patterns. Its addition to the top of the medial post would give the post a minimum height of about 1.7 m, or 1.1 m above natural ground surface. It seems unlikely that the top of the post could have fallen naturally in this way, even if weakened by charring, thus leading to the conclusion that it was deliberately removed and laid on the floor during the phase of dismantling.

Floor planks
The proximal sub-chamber was floored with two planks, both up to 0.5 m wide (Fig. 3.24). The northern plank [3689] was around 0.1 m thick, and the southern plank [3690] was thinner at 0.05 m. Both were recorded in five or six cross-sections (in Blocks 7/B to 7/L), the last section being at $X = 7.7$ m. The edge abutting the medial post in Block 7/M was not examined. The northern plank [3689] was extremely wide-ringed, with about 50 rings around 5 mm wide; such fast growth suggested an origin near the heart of the tree. The thick and heavy plank had been laid with the centre of the tree uppermost and to the north; the rings lay at a 45° angle to the plank surface. The southern plank [3690] was almost radial in section, with wide inner rings which became narrower; about 100 rings could be counted although the surface of the plank was in poor condition. The plank was laid with the tree centre to the south; it was thus in the opposite direction to plank [3689], and there is no possibility of the sub-chamber being floored with one wide plank which subsequently split into two along its length. [3690] could have been split from the same tree as [3689], but from further out on the tree's radius (there are no tree-ring links between the two). The distal sub-chamber was floored with one massive tangential plank [3692] (Figs. 3.24 & 3.26), which was 0.98–1.2 m wide and up to 3.1 m long. This was recorded in ten cross-sections from around 25 blocks (from 5/1 to 5/28: Figs. 3.22 & 3.23). The eastern end of the plank had been carefully shaped to fit the outer curve of medial post [3687]; this area (in Blocks 5/25 and 5/27) has been reserved for possible conservation. The western end of the plank had inexplicably disappeared, or never existed; a hollow about 1 m deep (at $X = 4$–5 m) left two arms projecting towards the back

of the chamber. The northern arm was around 0.25 m wide, and lay at a steep angle with the higher edge to the north. During excavation this wood was thought to represent a separate plank ([3693]), but there is no evidence from the cross-sections or the tree-ring links that a small plank was laid on top of [3692] at this point, as on the southern arm. The northern arm is thus treated as part of [3692] in this report.

The southern arm of [3692] was of similar width to the northern arm at its eastern end, but widened to around 0.3 m towards the west end. Superimposed on it, and clearly visible in the cross-sections by differing ring orientation, was a small plank ([3694]). This piece was 0.45 m long and 0.23 m wide. Unusually the tree centre faced downwards, and the rings were wide with a sudden change to narrow and variable. The ring pattern conforms to that of the two timbers on the proximal sub-chamber floor, [3642] and [3645], suggesting almost certainly an origin in the same tree. It also suggests that the small plank was deliberately laid on the floor during the same dismantling phase as the large timbers. The main floor plank, [3692], was compressed in cross-section into a concave shape about 0.1–0.15 m deep. This is unlikely to be due to deliberate shaping or hollowing out of the wood, but to subsequent settlement and compression. Wide longitudinal grooves and cracks along the length of the plank suggest that the chamber was exposed sufficiently long for shrinkage and cracking along the vertical rays, erosion by waterborne deposits and compression. Such warping of the plank section would also have opened a gap between the plank and the chamber walls. Decay and erosion had caused a hole in the plank on the southern edge at $X = 5.7–6$ m, where it was only around 20 mm thick.

Generally the plank was around 50 mm thick, with a tendency for the southern edge to be thinner than the northern (although removal of the original surfaces through decay and erosion may have reduced the thickness). The centre of the plank (probably some 0.15–0.2 m from the pith of the tree) was central to the chamber. The heart of the tree faced inwards. At its outer edges, the plank was almost radial in section. Ring-widths declined from wide to narrow and uniform, averaging 1 mm or less in width, and approximate counts give an estimated tree age of 350–400 years (over 300 rings could be counted on Block 5/8B at $X = 5.4$ m). Allowing for missing sapwood and inner wood, tree diameter is estimated to have reached 1.5 m.

## Wall timbers

Wall timbers remained to a height of about 0.35 m along the entire south wall of both sub-chambers, and to a height of about 0.2 m along the north wall of the distal sub-chamber. The north wall of the proximal sub-chamber was present only near the proximal post ([3685]), surviving as four plank fragments, leaving a gap of around 1 m. It was not clear during excavation whether one continuous plank extended along the entire structure, or whether several planks had been used. In addition, the relationship of the planking which lay immediately above the wall timbers needed to be clarified. The detailed cross-sections and tree-ring patterns (though few could be recorded from these timbers) have been invaluable in the interpretation of the wall construction. Excavation records suggested the presence of more than one plank along each wall. The north wall was numbered [3722] along the distal sub-chamber, a plank 5.2 m long, and the small group of planks at the east end were [3577]. The south wall consisted of [3723], 5.1 m long, and [3575], a group of planks along the proximal sub-chamber wall. The cross-sections were unclear as the planks appeared to have slumped; dimensions given refer to the actual width and thickness of slumped wood and soil, and not to the original plank thickness. Their condition was poor owing to their high surfaces, exposed and vulnerable both before and during excavation.

The wall timbers from $X = 2.5–4$ m and $X = 7.5–9.5$ m were lifted whole (in Blocks 6/1, 6/2 and 7A); the remainder were sectioned as part of the complete cross-sections (such as Block 5/8) or as small individual sections (such as 5/17). Section 5/10 (at $X = 5.8–6.5$ m), showing evidence of a possible joint or knot in the south wall, has not been examined here.

*Distal south wall* ([3723]): A total of 11 records of this timber were made at 0.3–0.9 m intervals. Records are sparse to the east of $X = 5.8$ m, owing to the absence of Block 5/10, and problems in sectioning 5/23. The vulnerable upper edges of the plank had suffered from decay and desiccation, and were very fragile, but in most sections the overall direction of the wood elements could be distinguished.

A series of sketch sections of [3723] are shown in Figure 3.38. At the west end, it demonstrated a roughly rectangular section 0.13 × 0.28 m in size at $X = 2.5$ m (in Block 6/2C), becoming 0.19 m square at $X = 3.2$ m (in Block 6/2B), and then developing its characteristic cross-section of a vertical south face with a height of about 0.28 m, a thin top about 0.1 m across and a thick base about 0.25 m wide. The direction of the rings and rays showed that the timber had originally been a tangential plank, with the rings facing outwards and the tree centre to the inside of the chamber (Fig. 3.38). The wood, through waterlogging and compression, had gradually folded and slumped downwards, while the upper edge of the plank may have collapsed inwards as plank [3538] among the roof timber. The remaining upper edge of the south wall plank had folded over soil deposits still embedded in the wood section (for example in Block 5/5A at $X = 5$ m: Fig. 3.38). In each section, the rings run vertically down the south face, and the rays run horizontally. At the upper and lower edges of the plank, the rings curve round to a 45° angle. Original plank thickness is difficult to estimate since there is much compressed debris on the inner face of the sections. By $X = 5.5$ m

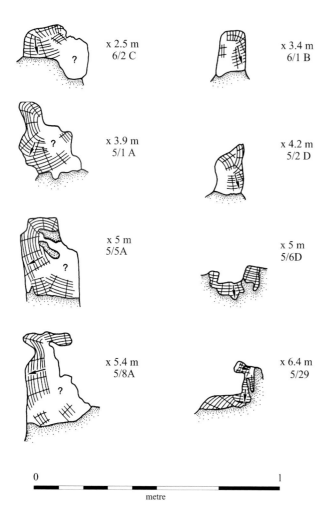

x 2.5 m
6/2 C

x 3.4 m
6/1 B

x 3.9 m
5/1 A

x 4.2 m
5/2 D

x 5 m
5/5A

x 5 m
5/6D

x 5.4 m
5/8A

x 6.4 m
5/29

0                                                    1

metre

**Figure 3.38.** *Sketch drawings of [3722] and [3723] wall timbers.*

the wall height had increased to about 0.35 m (in Blocks 5/8A and 5/12); at X = 6.5 m (in Block 5/23) the section differed, but was not well preserved. A central area of wood, a lower fragment and a thin radial piece on the surface were all that remained of the presumably decayed eastern end of the plank, which was thought to terminate just east of the medial post [3687]. No wood was then examined until X = 7.9 m, leaving a gap of over 1 m. No sections of the south wall survived sufficiently well for ring-width measurement, so there were no records of its pattern to associate it with other timbers in the relative dating framework.

*South wall of proximal sub-chamber* ([3575]): Seven sections of this area from X = 7–7.9 m (in Blocks 7A and 7L) were examined. The intensive study was necessitated by the indeterminate nature of the first three sections; further samples were then taken. The section at X = 7.7 m (in Block 7L) revealed a very thin almost radial plank 0.22 × 0.03 m, lying at a steep angle lining the inner curve of the chamber wall. At its base lay two or more pieces of roundwood. By X = 8 m (in section 7A West), this was a tangential wide-ringed piece. At X = 8.5 m (in 7A mid), possibly five superimposed planks were found, the upper sloping piece a radial, a tangential beneath, then a further tangential and two small radial pieces, one with very wide and one with very narrow rings. The variety of ring direction and width enabled each to be clearly distinguished, and suggests

they were not broken parts of the same plank. Each had a layer of soil between. At the east end of the wall at X = 9.3 m (in Block 7A east), a single radial horizontal plank lay on the surface.

In order to determine the original length of these planks, the sections between were also examined. They suggested that the planks were only short fragments, perhaps broken pieces used to line the earthen bank of the proximal sub-chamber wall.

*North wall of distal sub-chamber* ([3722]): This was recorded 14 times along its length of 5.2 m, at 0.1–0.6 m intervals. It extended from the distal post to X = 7 m. At the west end (in Block 6/1D, fig. 3.38), the timber was slight, around 0.07 m square; it was of radial section with rings running downwards. By X = 4 m (in Block 5/1D), it had reached 0.15 m square, with rings running downwards on the north face and horizontally at the base. As with the south wall, the plank gave the appearance of having been folded over under pressure. As always the rings ran outwards, with the tree centre facing into the chamber. There was a possible discontinuity at X = 4.5–5 m, where there was a split in the plank; the subsequent sections (Fig. 3.38) show probably two adjacent radial pieces with the rings heading downwards. By X = 6–6.5 m, the plank had taken on an 'L'-shaped section, the north vertical edge around 0.15 m high consisting of a folded radial plank with rings heading out and down, and the base a tangential piece about 0.15 m wide with rings probably in a northerly direction. The wood in this area was poorly preserved and thin, and may be displaced broken remnants of the wall plank.

One of the wall sections (at X = 5 m in Block 5/6D) provided two short ring patterns, one of which has been linked with plank [3582]/[3253] along the northern edge of the roof; their relative positions and similar cross-sections tend to confirm that they were halves of the same collapsed plank. [3582]/[3253] would have formed the centre and upper edge of the plank, and [3722] the lower edge. No wood survived, if it ever existed, along the north wall from X = 7.5 to X = 8.5 m.

*North wall of proximal sub-chamber* ([3577]): This group of small planks was examined only within the context of proximal post [3685], with which they were lifted as a group (in Block 8/1). At least two pieces were small radial planks with wide growth rings, one lying horizontally and the other vertically with a neat vertical edge butting the post. One of the plank fragments provided a short ring series which appears to link with the relative dating framework for the distal sub-chamber wood. Both walls of the distal sub-chamber thus appear to have been uniformly constructed of long tangential planks, probably with the same tangential cross-sections as the floor and roof planks, extending from the flanks of the distal post to just east of the medial post, a total length of about 5 m. Presumably they were kept from falling in by the support of the posts and from falling back by the earthen bank behind, since their foundation slots were very shallow. It is difficult to calculate the original height of the walls owing to the degree of slumping, but by adding the width of the collapsed wall tops to the height of the surviving 'unfolded' walls, an approximate estimate has been made. The south wall [3723] is given a minimum height of 0.75–1 m (0.3 m of [3538] and 0.45–0.6 m of [3723]), and the north wall [3722] must have been at least 0.65 m high (0.5 m of [3253]/[3582] and 0.15 m of [3722]).

The wall structure of the proximal sub-chamber differed, in that the earthen bank at this point was simply lined with small plank fragments; it is possible, although unlikely in view of the very variable ring widths and directions, that these represent the folded remnants of more substantial planking.

## Roundwood

A quantity of roundwood was found scattered on the floor of both sub-chambers. The tree-ring study did not include a systematic collection and examination of roundwood, the pieces described here being found among the sampled timber sections as well as a few collected during excavation. The non-oak species were identified at the Ancient Monuments Laboratory, HBMC, by Jacqui Watson; many were too degraded to give precise identifications. In the proximal sub-chamber, an oak stem 100 mm in diameter and 21 years old lay on floor plank [3689] (at around $X = 8$ m in Blocks 7G and 7J). Another oak stem 65 mm across and 18 years old lay just south of plank [3690] close to the south wall plank [3575] at $X = 8$ m (in Block 7L B), near a four-year-old twig 20 mm in diameter of alder or hazel (*Alnus/Corylus*). Other roundwood from the distal sub-chamber included two split charcoal fragments of alder/hazel and willow/poplar (*Salix/ Populus*) from [3189] ($X = 3.84$ m; $Y = 2.06$ m), and two halved stems 13 mm in diameter and 10 years old of alder/hazel and willow/poplar came from [3337] ($X = 4.5–5$ m; $Y = 2–2.5$ m).

Just north of proximal post [3685] was an oak twig 15 mm in diameter. Among the roof planking was a twig of willow/poplar, 8 years old and 8 mm in diameter. At $X = 6.5$ m on the south wall plank [3721] (in Block 5/23A) was a twig 6 mm in diameter, which was too degraded to identify.

The samples examined and the excavated evidence suggest the presence of a quantity of round-wood of all sizes from twigs to substantial stems, lying on and around the chamber floor. The likely purpose of this roundwood was as fuel.

*Conversion method and tree size*

Almost all the wood sections examined had been tangentially split from the tree, that is with the rings parallel or at an angle to the plank's width. The more usual method of radial splitting exploits oak's natural tendency to split along the rays, but gives a product limited in width to the radius of the tree, whereas a tangential plank can extend across the entire diameter. Tangential splitting is less easy to accomplish and relies on careful choice of location to start the split, critical to the eventual uniformity in thickness of the whole plank (see Darrah below for a full description).

The main disadvantage of tangential planks in use is their tendency to split lengthwise down the rays, as in floor plank [3692]. Any pressure on one wide plank would soon result in it splitting into two half planks (which should be easily identifiable as such by their identical ring pattern). It is possible that the tapering from thick to thin of the roof planking [3755]/[3252] was a deliberate attempt to prevent such splitting; however, such a cross-section could not be achieved through controlled splitting.

The timber in the distal sub-chamber was remarkably uniform in both cross-section and dimensions, as well as being consistently oriented with the tree's heart facing into the chamber and the original bark surface to the outside. This uniformity must have had practical reasons, such as to avoid detrimental warping of the planks.

It has been estimated from plank size and approximate ring counts that trees up to 1.5 m in diameter and 300–400 years old were felled for the posts and floor plank, and perhaps 200 years old for the horizontal timbers. The timber was very straight-grained and knot-free, indicating a long clean bole with no side branches. Only one or two trees with boles of 5 m or more would have sufficed to provide all the planks and posts, and tree-ring correlations suggest a common origin for some of the timbers (see below), but clearly more trees were involved judging by the variations in ring patterns and widths. Conversion of the timber is dealt with further by Darrah below.

No examples of the pith of the tree were found on any timber, and it must have been deliberately removed. Experimental work on tangential splitting revealed the necessity of splitting out the centre of the tree because of overgrown side branches (see Darrah below). Wide inner rings occurred on planks [3694] (in Block 5/1B), [3689] (in Blocks 7G–L) and [3692] (in Block 5/28), and in displaced posts [3642] and [3645]. By their curvature, these wide rings could be shown to lie close to the pith, perhaps within 0.15–0.2 m. By contrast, very narrow outermost rings were found at the edges of [3692] (e.g. in Block 5/32), and on posts [3687] and [3696], but it is now impossible to determine how much outer wood has been lost in trimming and decay. No trace of outer sapwood was seen, but is unlikely to have survived the severe conditions suffered by the timbers. Sapwood varies in width but on average is 30–50 mm, with an estimated range of 10–55 years (Hillam *et al.* 1987).

The amount and variability in the annual growth rate suggested that the trees had grown in relatively congenial conditions, apart from the stress demonstrated by the [3642]/[3645]/[3694] tree. Oak woodland probably clothed the slopes and margins of the river floodplain; had it grown closer to the river, the growth rate may have been faster and less sensitive. The straight grain and absence of knots suggests initial rapid growth in high woodland (which would create a tall bole), where competition for light would draw the trees upward.

*Conclusions*

The unique preservation of the mortuary chamber in the Haddenham barrow has led to the first detailed

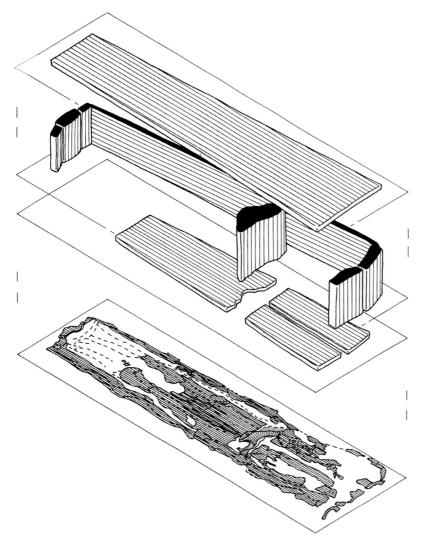

sections led to the conclusion that several very large and aged oaks had been felled; they probably reached 1.5 m in diameter and 300–400 years old, of a size and quality rarely seen today. The straight grain and knot-free trunks testify to initial rapid growth in woodland, probably on dry slopes in the area. The trunks were expertly split in half and halved again, to give both tangential planks and huge posts, discarding the inner and outer wood. Since the chamber was used, extensive processes of decay and erosion have removed any original surfaces and traces of woodworking techniques, such as adze or axe marks.

The distal sub-chamber was floored, and probably walled and roofed, with tangential planks about 1 m wide; at either end stood large split posts. The proximal sub-chamber differed in being floored with two smaller planks of varying cross-section, and the walls were lined with small plank fragments. On the floors lay several horizontal timbers. The two oval pieces on the proximal sub-chamber floor may have formed the tops of the decayed proximal posts; they came from the same tree as a small plank on the distal sub-chamber floor. A large timber just west of the medial post probably once formed the top of the post. All these timbers give the appearance of having been carefully removed and laid on the floor during a phase of dismantling of the structure. The wood of the roof was found to be a combination of probably original tangential planking, of collapsed wall planking and of plank fragments filling spaces. The original form of the roof cannot be determined with certainty; it could either have been a flat roof of one or two large tangential planks supported by the main posts, or a ridged roof which subsequently collapsed. The evidence favours the first theory.

All the timber of the distal sub-chamber was carefully oriented with the centre of the tree facing into the chamber and the outer surfaces facing outwards. This chamber would have taken the form of a box about 1 m square, with or without a lid initially, and

**Figure 3.39.** *Reconstruction of the mortuary chamber: in this reconstruction, it is assumed that the trunk was 1.5 m diameter and the wall timbers were all 0.1 m thick, and that the medial and distal posts were outer tangential splits of section CT. All wall, roof and floor timbers of the distal chamber would come from one inner tangential split of section DT (see Fig. 3.41:2). The proximal chamber could have been made from one inner tangential split of section DT. The two proximal posts were from a smaller diameter tree.*

technological and chronological record being made of oak wood from such a structure. The experience of handling waterlogged and carbonized wood in such a delicate condition has been extremely valuable, and encourages further sampling of similar material in the future.

The wooden roof, floor, walls and posts were lifted in around 340 sections, each supported by the surrounding soil deposits. Little by little, the cross-sections of the chamber at regular intervals have been reconstructed. The drawings and frozen cross-sections remain as a permanent archive. The form of the cross-

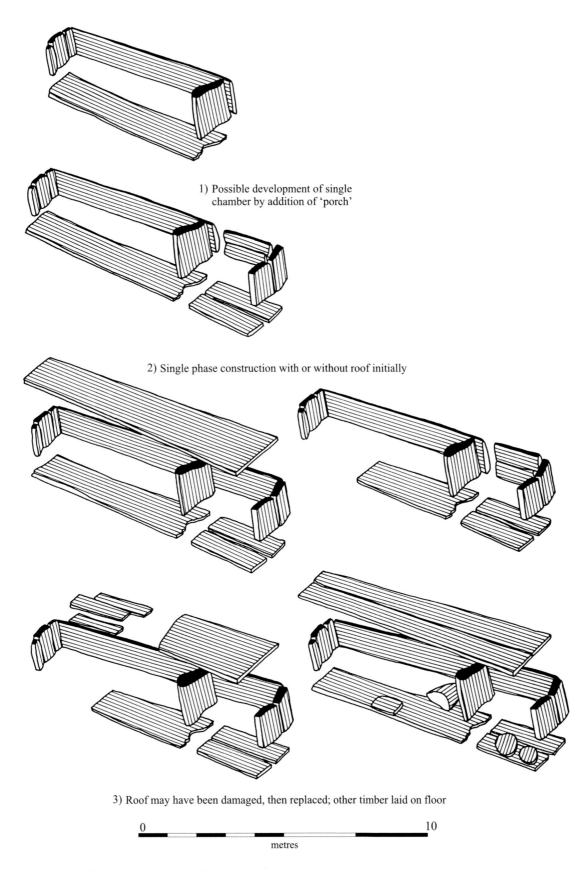

1) Possible development of single
chamber by addition of 'porch'

2) Single phase construction with or without roof initially

3) Roof may have been damaged, then replaced; other timber laid on floor

0 _____ 10

metres

**Figure 3.40.** *Possible reconstructions of the mortuary chamber.*

without any means of jointing or pegs to connect the timbers; the earthen outer banks and the posts must have provided support on both sides.

## Wood technology
by R. DARRAH

The timbers surviving from the mortuary chamber are remarkable for their large size, and planks at least 1.2 m wide were used in the construction. Morgan has built up a picture of these from their fragmented parts by carefully recording their sections, growth rates and the directions of their rays. Here her evidence will be used to consider the production of these timbers from the original trees and to explore what this might tell us about the trees used in the construction of the long barrow.

### Tangential splitting and radial split oak timber
The process of splitting involves a tree trunk being split along its length, initially into two equal halves. These may subsequently be converted into either planks with radial cross-sections, or tangential cross-sections. The process in radial splitting is that the wedges are hammered into the side of the tree along the line of a plane of radii, causing the wood to split open along the medullary rays which form natural radial planes of weakness and produce planks which are triangular in cross-section (Fig. 3.41:1). In tangential splitting the split is started across the end of the tree, by hammering in a number of wedges. Once started the split is held open by applying further wedges into sides of the tree, slowly forcing the split down the length of the timber. To control the direction of the split care has to be taken that the piece is being split into two equally bendable halves so that the split runs straight down the timber. This means that the thickness of the timbers and position of the splits are defined in a trunk of known diameter, unless timber is first hewn off the outside of the tree (Fig. 3.42:1). The timbers that are produced will be parallel-sided.

The two main differences in the timber produced by these types of splitting are that in tangential split planks the full width of the tree may be produced, whereas with radial splitting the planks are always less than half its diameter. Also there will be a difference in grain direction between the two types of split timber (Figs. 3.41:1 & 3.41:2). Although most timber can be split, the presence of knots, side branches, spiral or twisted grain, and stress within the timber make splitting difficult to control, with the end product being twisted and hard to use. Tangential splitting is of its nature more difficult to control than radial splitting and in practice the only timber which may be split into parallel planks in a controlled way is straight-grained without knots, side branches or stress.

### Evidence that the mortuary chamber timbers were split
The two types of splitting define the thickness and positions of long planks in a trunk, so that it may be possible to see whether surviving timbers from the barrow chamber are the correct sections to have been produced by tangential or radial splitting. We can also consider whether the surviving timber is of a high enough quality to have produced planks split in a controlled way. The timbers surviving in the barrow's chambers are either heavily rotted or have been partially burnt. Morgan mentions that on some there is a layer of dark amorphous wood surrounding the surviving structurally sound timber. Therefore, unfortunately, little can be said about the original surfaces and the ways that these timbers were originally finished, except for the following points:

1. the floor plank ([3692]) was carefully shaped to fit round the curved edge of the medial post, even following an indentation in it;
2. some of the planks were much thinner at their outside edges than in their centres;
3. one of the roof timbers has a ridged surface ([3252]/[3761]).

It is only the latter ridged surface that may be directly associated with splitting, but although splitting may produce this type of surface, the same effect can be caused by rotting. This type of ridged surface is seen in modern oak where there has been uncontrolled splitting, as would occur during windblow. Although it may be the case that the Haddenham barrow builders made use of such a split surface, it cannot be used here to demonstrate that the timbers were being split into shape in a controlled way. Thus, there is no surface evidence that the timbers were converted by splitting. However, both the annual rings and the direction of the grain of the timber have survived, enabling its quality to be assessed and the sizes, thickness, and the positions in the trunk from which some of the planks came to be determined. This evidence can give us clues as to what techniques may have been used to convert this timber.

The fact that series of annual rings have survived has enabled Morgan to undertake the mammoth task of piecing together these blocks of rings confirming that they were originally wide oak planks, many of which were tangential cross-sections (not necessarily tangentially split) similar to the main floor plank of the distal chamber ([3692]). This oak floor plank has survived as a single timber 3.5 m long by 1.2 m wide and 0.1 m thick.

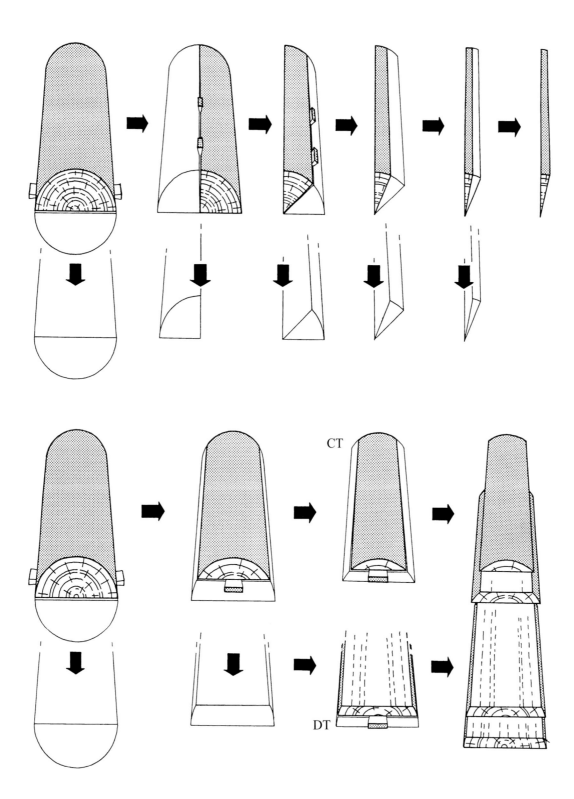

**Figure 3.41.** *The process of splitting wood. Top series) Radial splitting: the sections of timber which would be produced by the technique of radial splitting. In this process the wedges are hammered into the outside of the trunk, and the split follows natural planes of weakness. Bottom series) Tangential splitting: the sections of timber produced by the technique of tangential splitting. In this process, the wedges are hammered into the end of the trunk to start the split across natural planes of weakness. Once the split has started the wedges are hammered into the sides of the trunk to force the split along the trunk: CT is an outer tangential split, DT is an inner tangential split.*

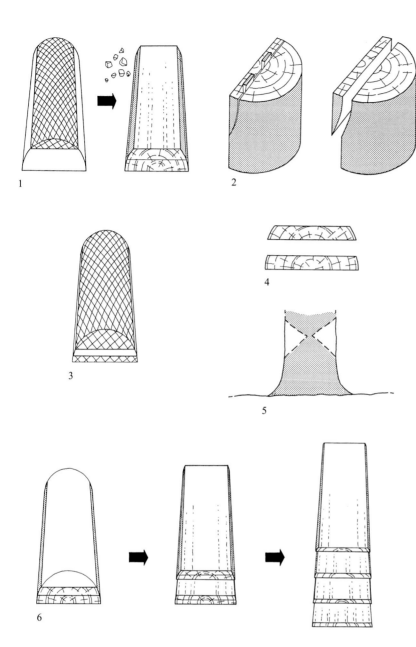

As the least damaged/most complete timber which has a tangential cross-section stretching across the width of a trunk, this timber may have been produced in a variety of ways:

1. by hewing from the solid out of half a trunk (Fig. 3.42:3);
2. by burning to shape out of half a trunk;
3. sawing;
4. by splitting to shape in a controlled way;
5. by a combination of splitting off small chunks and hewing.

It is convenient to look at how the tangential floor plank [3692] could have been produced using these various techniques. This 0.1-m-thick, parallel-sided oak timber spanned the width of the tree, with its inside edge between 0.1 m and 0.15 m from the centre of the tree. To produce this timber from a trunk split in half *c.* 2.5 cubic metres of timber would have to be removed, leaving a finished plank of *c.* 0.4 cubic metres. If the plank had been hewn to shape from the solid 2.9 cubic metres timber, three tons of unseasoned oak would have had to have been chipped away. If the tree took 90 man-hours to fell, hewing away the timber might be expected to take a similar time.

If the three tons of timber had been burnt away, a very large amount of firewood would have been required to heat the oak so

**Figure 3.42.** *The process of splitting wood. 1) Changing the spacing of the splits: when the hatched section has been hewn away, the timber is split up into two equally bendable pieces, but their width will be different from the widths produced from the original section. 2) Uncontrolled splitting: when an attempt is made to split a thin section off the edge of thick timber the split will run out; if the length of timber to be split is short this technique may be used. From experience, it is expected that a thin split of 0.1 m on a timber of 0.5 m will run out if the timber were longer than 0.5 m. 3) Removing timber by hewing and burning: the parts of the timber to be removed by hewing or burning are marked by cross-hatching. In producing a 0.1-m-thick plank from a 1.5-m-diameter trunk approximately 0.8 m³ would have to be removed for each metre of trunk length. 4) The cross-section of a tangential oak plank (showing the direction of the medullary rays). If the plank spans the full width of the tree, the rays are at right angles to the split surfaces at the centre of the plank, and almost parallel to the split surfaces at the approach to the edges. 5) The buttressing at the base of an oak trunk. The spread of an oak tree at its base would make felling at the base exceptionally difficult. The dotted line suggests the position which would take least effort, although a platform would have to be built at that height. With a tree of 1.5 m diameter approximately one cubic metre of timber would be removed in felling with axes. 6) Conversion of an inner tangential split into four planks: this section would be split in half across its width then in half again across its width.*

that it burnt. Although it is not impossible to burn freshly felled oak, it tends to char, and the charred wood insulates the remaining timber from burning so that large oak timbers are not easily consumed by fires. The builders of the Hillsborough dugout canoe found it impossible to burn the oak wood even with white heat produced by bellows (Seaby 1989). It is therefore unlikely that the barrow timbers were burnt to shape.

There are no saw marks surviving from the Neolithic period, although both axe marks and split surfaces survive. Although it is not impossible that the timbers were cut with some form of saw, no evidence of such a technique has yet been discovered.

In controlled splitting timber is split into a series of pieces with specific cross-sections. The floor timber has the typical cross-section of a plank which had been tangentially split. Its position in the trunk would fit with it being the second split out from the centre of the tree, if eight tangential planks had been produced from half a trunk. The cross-section of this plank would not be compatible with radial splitting as it spans the tree. The straightness of grain of the timber used, and the lack of knots found in the sections taken through the timber by Morgan, both point to the timber being of a quality which could be tangentially split into planks.

Each plank split to size would take three to four man hours to produce and would have had smooth surfaces without any further work. In my experience tangential splitting would involve far less effort than the other suggested techniques of conversion. Perhaps the best evidence for tangential splitting is from the medial post [3687] that has a cross-section identical with an outer tangential split (Fig. 3.41:2). If this timber had been produced by hewing, then 950 kg of wood would have been removed in producing a timber of 660 kg, which would have been narrower than that which would have been produced had the outer part been hewn away and the inner part left, in which case far less wood would have been removed.

A single tree of 1.5 m size if tangentially split could have produced all of the wide timbers used in the structure except for the two proximal posts [3684] and [3685], which came from one or more smaller trees. Tangential splitting alone would not have produced the thinning of the outer edges of the roof planks. The flat split surfaces would have had to be reworked to produce this thinning probably by hewing or splitting and hewing to thin the timber. This secondary working would have enabled any irregularities or twists in the timber to be removed. There is contemporary evidence for the use of the technique of tangential splitting in the Sweet Trackway of the Somerset levels.

Even the roof timbers where the central part is too damaged to determine the plank's distance from the centre of the tree, can be seen from the outer parts of the planks to be tangential sections some distance from the centre of the tree. Even if the side wall timber [3723] and roof timbers were originally thicker than 0.1 m, then they would still fit into the range of sections which could be split.

There is the possibility that all these timbers came from the same tree.

Tangential splitting would explain the process by which most of the timbers could have been produced with speed and efficiency, but there is no conclusive evidence that this technique was used.

Producing the planks by a combination of splitting and hewing without producing a stack of planks, but wasting the remainder of the timber, would have been faster than hewing but would have taken a similar amount of time to controlled splitting.

### Non-tangential section timbers

The process of tangential splitting is one by which timber is converted according to a set pattern. Although short lengths of under one metre may be split up in any way, longer trunks can only be split first into halves, then each half into halves and so on. Several timbers have cross-sections which do not conform to this pattern. Examples are timbers [3681] and [3682], which although not central have only 0.1 m missing to the centre, and are 0.25 m thick. If these were originally part of long timbers then the missing central part must have been removed by some other means than splitting (e.g. rotting or hewing; Fig. 3.42:2). Although the majority of timbers would fit into the cross-sections which could be produced by tangential splitting, there are some sections which could not have been split in this controlled way. If these timbers were produced by some more arduous technique, it is possible that all the timbers could have been produced in that way.

### Timber size

The widest surviving timber is the floor plank ([3692]) with a width of 1.2 m. From the convergence of the medullary rays and the curve of the annual rings Morgan suggests that the inside surface of this plank came from 0.1 m to 0.15 m of the centre of the tree, indicating a minimum diameter at that point on the trunk of 1.35 m.

The medial post [3687] was 1.18 m wide, and its inner surface was considerably further out from the centre of the tree. This timber appears to be an outer tangential split. As the surviving timber is more than 0.37 m thick its inner surface must have been at least 0.35 m from the centre of the tree (if it were split in the same way as the Minsmere timber; see below), which is consistent with the curve of the annual rings and convergence of the medullary rays. This would give a diameter at this cross-section of the trunk of 1.5 m. In estimating the minimum diameter of the timbers it has been assumed that there was no drying of the wood, as the damp conditions of the mound interior would have prevented this. However, had timber been allowed to dry before the structure was built then the original tree diameter must have been greater, a minimum of 1.6 m.

The longest timber surviving intact is the wall timber ([3722]), which is 5.2 m long. If this was originally as wide as the other wide timbers, it would have come from a length of trunk 5.2 m long by 1.5 m wide at its bottom end. As a clean grown oak trunk it would taper over its length; the diameter at the top end of this 5.2 m length would have been approximately 1.25 m. The timber maximum length would have remained unchanged on drying at 5.2 m.

*Source and selection of oak timber*
Soil evidence from around the barrow suggests that it was an area which had changed from woodland to open country in the period before the barrow was built. This open land would not have produced the straight-grained branch-free trunks which could have been converted into the wide planks required for the construction of the mortuary chamber. Such trees would only grow in shaded woodland, which encouraged the trunks to grow tall, straight, and quickly lose their lower branches. Open land produces fast-grown oaks with short trunks and many large side branches. There is no evidence of a change in growth rate that might indicate that this tree was a relict of the previous woodland which had grown faster in the recent more open conditions. The timber used had the regular slow, even growth of a tree or trees which had grown in high forest.

Contemporary pollen and floral remains in the fens collected from within nine miles of the barrow indicate that there was mixed deciduous woodland in which oak trees may have represented 30 per cent of the timber trees. Oak would have stood alongside lime, wych elm and ash, the other large timber trees. Bog oaks which are contemporary with the barrow, and which grew in the surrounding area, often survive with trunk lengths in excess of 10 m, suggesting that the woodland was similar to modern high forest, with stands of slow-grown trees with trunks 10–15 m tall. There is some indication that the trunk lengths

may have grown longer than those found in modern high forest; Rackham (1980) records a bog oak with a 27-m trunk.

The Neolithic builders would have been looking for timber which was straight-grained and free from side branches with diameters up to 1.5 m and straight trunks of up to 5.2 m after felling. The existing woodland would provide a large number of trees of several species with trunk lengths in excess of 10 m, but of these only ash, oak, lime, willow and wych elm would be likely to grow to the desired diameter of 1.5 m. Although lime, ash, willow and wych elm can be split, they are more difficult to split than oak. There is evidence for them all being used as split timber in the Neolithic.

This means that the barrow builders did not select oak as the only species available, but for some other reason or reasons. Though the impetus to select oak may have had ritual connotations, there would also be a number of practical reasons for its selection for the mortuary chamber. Oak is probably the easiest timber to split in a controlled way and this is particularly important in tangential splitting. Lime, ash, willow and wych elm also do not resist rot as well as oak.

The tree which was selected would have been one of the giants of the forest, although evidence for the use of even larger trees has survived from prehistoric boats. If the structure was intended to last for several generations, then oak would be the only tree which could both be split easily and would resist rot well. The frequent use of oak planks in the Sweet Track in Somerset, which is almost contemporary, suggests an easy familiarity with the techniques of radial and tangential splitting, and either an abundance of or preference for that species.

*Labour estimates*
The figures and estimates in the following section are presented to give an idea of the time involved in the preparation of the timbers and are gleaned from personal experience, except where otherwise stated. Although the time taken to complete a specific task may be recorded in an experiment, there are a large number of variables which cannot easily be quantified. For example the process of converting a short 2.5-m length of trunk, of 1.35-m diameter, into the equivalent of 28 tangential planks took nine days of 5.5 hours each in winter (see below). In summer the process of splitting up the tree would have taken less time, but high undergrowth in the work area would have to be cleared. This simple factor would have increased the overall length of time that the conversion took. In felling a tree the height, weight,

and motivation of the axe-user would be important factors in the length of time taken for the felling.

Felling

The largest trunk used would have had to have been at least 1.5 m diameter at 1.2 m above ground level. This is the height at which the regular width of the trunk begins. From there downwards, in a tree of this diameter the trunk quickly widens so that at the top of root buttresses (c. 0.9 m above the ground) it would be c. 1.9 m diameter and at ground level it would be c. 2.5 m diameter (Fig. 3.42:5). Cutting the tree at the base would both increase the work of felling and make splitting the wood more difficult. In the author's experience the timber from the buttresses and base of the trunk is exceptionally hard, and difficult to split down the grain. To minimize the amount of wood removed in felling and the work involved, it would have been necessary to fell the tree above the buttressing with the base of the cut at c. 1.2 m above the ground.

Surviving Neolithic stumps suggest that trees were felled by chipping all the way around the trunk, although this makes it difficult to control the direction the tree will fall in. Far less timber would have been removed if the tree had been felled by hewing from two sides towards a diameter. This also allows the wood left along the diameter to act as a hinge, which helps make the tree fall at right angles to the line of the hinge, controlling the direction of fall of the tree. Even so, a cubic metre of timber would have to be removed in felling a tree of this size (Fig. 3.42:5).

This direction of fall would be important when felling a tree in a dense woodland, as a tree falling in the wrong direction could get lodged against other trees and have been impossible to move. A felling cut would leave either a curved or sloping face across the end of any timber. No such facets survive from the Haddenham timbers. The medial post, the most likely contender, has a flat base.

It may have been possible to have burnt the tree down. However ethnographic references for this practice do not come from oak, which in my opinion is difficult to burn, as the surface protects the remaining wood from burning. This is confirmed in the reconstruction of the Hillsborough logboat (Seaby 1989). Even if the tree could have been burnt down, the burnt surfaces would have had to have been cleaned, since partly dried burnt timber would tend to have cracks which would make controlled splitting much more difficult.

As there is no contemporary evidence for the amount of time that such a large oak tree would take to be felled, I have made use of the following information provided by Phil Harding, who has felled a number of oak and birch trees with stone axes. The largest, a birch tree 0.4 m diameter, was felled in 1 hour 58 minutes with about 6800 blows from a Group VI axe. (The axe was 142 mm long, 31 mm thick with an edge length of 71 mm and an edge angle of 80°. It was hafted with an ash handle 0.65 m long and had a total weight of 1.14 kg. It is clear from the surviving felled surfaces, and the photographs of felling, that the final felling cuts were at 90° to each other.)

To extrapolate from the felling of a birch tree of 0.4 m to the felling of an oak tree 1.5 m diameter, the following assumptions have been made:
1. that oak and birch behave similarly when hit with a stone axe when the wood is green;
2. that the felling cut would be the same shape on the larger tree;
3. the process of felling would involve chipping all of the wood out, not splitting it;
4. that the volume of timber removed from the birch during felling could be calculated by assuming that the part of the trunk in which the felling cut was made was a cylinder, and that the wood that remained after felling was two truncated cones, so that by subtracting the volume of the truncated cones from the volume of the cylinder the quantity of wood removed by the stone axe in the two-hour felling period could be calculated.

Using these data, the time taken to fell the larger tree could be calculated from the volume of timber which would have to be removed (1.25 cubic metres of timber would have been removed in 150 hours by one axe-user):

0.53 m is the diameter of the inner circle, produced when the timber fell

Radius of the inner circle = $0.53 / 2 \times 3.142 = 0.084$ m

Height of the small cone ($h$) = radius of the small cone ($r$)

Volume of the small cone = $1/3 \times 3.142 \times r \times r \times h = 0.00062$ m$^3$

Height of the cylinder = $(2 \times$ height of the large cone $(H)) - (2 \times$ height of the small cone $h) = (2 \times 0.191) - (2 \times 0.084) = 0.214$ m

Volume of the cylinder = $3.142 \times 0.191 \times 0.191 \times 0.214 = 0.0245$ m$^3$

Volume of the large cone = $0.33 \times 3.142 \times 0.191 \times 0.191 \times 0.191 = 0.00438$ m$^3$

Volume of the large cone – small cone = $0.003759$

Volume of the wood removed in felling = Volume of the cylinder $- 2 \times$ (volume of the large cone – small cone) = $0.0245 - 2 \times (0.00438 - 0.000621) = 0.01698$ m$^3$

**Table 3.3.** *The volumes and weights of the timbers used in the mortuary chamber calculated from their original sizes (assuming green oak weighs 1073 kg/m³).*

| Timber | Section | Length (m) | Width (m) | Thickness (m) | Volume (m³) | Weight (kg) |
|---|---|---|---|---|---|---|
| Trunk | AT | 10 | 1.5 | 1.5 | 17.67 | 18,960 |
| ¹/₂ trunk | BT | 5.2 | 1.5 | 0.75 | 4.595 | 4930 |
| Floor plank | KT | 3.5 | 1.2 | 0.1 | 0.42 | 451 |
| Medial post | CT | 1.7 | 1.18 | 0.4 | 0.7 | 751 |
| Wall plank | JT | 5.2 | 1.2 | 0.1 | 0.624 | 670 |
| Roof plank | LT | 5.2 | 1.2 | 0.1 | 0.624 | 670 |
| Proximal wall timbers | JT | 2.4 | 1.2 | 0.1 | 0.288 | 309 |
| Proximal floor timbers | KT halved | 2.4 | 0.5 | 0.1 | 0.12 | 129 |
| Proximal roof timbers | LT | 2.4 | 1.2 | 0.1 | 0.288 | 309 |
| Proximal posts | BT | 1.7 | 0.8 | 0.4 | 0.85 | 912 |

*Felling the 1.5-m-diameter tree*

Assumption that the tree would fall when the remaining diameter was reduced to 0.3 m

Small cone = $0.333 \times 3.142 \times 0.15 \times 0.15 \times 0.15 = 0.00353475$

Large cone = $0.333 \times 3.142 \times 0.75 \times 0.75 \times 0.75000 = 0.4414$

Height of cylinder = 1.2 m

Volume of cylinder = $3.142 \times 0.75 \times 0.75 \times 1.20000 = 2.12085$

Volume of the wood removed in felling = volume of the cylinder $- 2 \times (0.437865) = 2.12085 - 0.875730 = 1.245120$

$1.245120/0.01698 = 73.328622$ number of hours to fell large tree $= 2 \times 73.329 =$ approximately 150 hours.

## Converting and shaping

Having felled the straight-grained branch-free trunk 10 m long, the crown would need to be removed (at a point where the diameter would still be over 1 m). The tree would probably have been converted on site as oak is much easier to split when green, and it would be easier to move the split timber than the whole tree.

The tree would first be split down its length into two equal halves. This would take one man-day plus the time taken to make 50 wooden wedges which would be damaged in use. The easiest strategy would then be to cut the timber to the required lengths. It could thereafter be split tangentially to the required thickness. Each tangential split, 5.2 m long, would take three to four hours to complete. The final timber thickness (0.1 m) could be produced by splitting the inner tangential section of the trunk into four tangential pieces using the technique as detailed below. Each of these planks would be more than 1.2 m wide and more or less parallel-faced. Timbers produced by splitting will never be exactly parallel-faced due to imperfections in the grain and inaccuracy in the splitting technique. There is evidence from Morgan's studies for variation in the thickness of the timbers, which would not be explained if the planks were perfect tangential splits; for instance the roof timbers are thinner at their outer edges. Although I have split timbers that have run out of true producing a thin edge, this process was uncontrollable and could not be deliberately used to produced the effect found in the roof timbers. I would suggest that tangentially split timbers should be considered to be regular in their cross-section, so that the thickest surviving part of the timber should be considered to be the original thickness of the plank. Any subsequent changes in the thickness should be assumed to be due to shaping by hewing or fire or to decay. This further shaping could not have been created by radial splitting of pieces to thin the timbers as the thinning had been done at an angle to the medullary rays, whereas if radial splitting had been used the thinning would run parallel to the ray.

## Transporting the timber

As thick sections of oak timber take years to dry, the timber would probably have been moved unseasoned. At 1073 kg per cubic metre, the density of unseasoned oak timber is greater than water. It could not therefore have been floated, even if water were available, and would have to have been moved overland.

A small number of people could easily have moved the heaviest timber using rollers on rails. Unless rollers are placed on rails they dig into the soft woodland soils. I have moved timbers weighing 200 kg with ease on my own using this technique and have moved a 2000 kg timber with the help of one other person. Alternatively, a large number of people could have carried a timber on poles. The heaviest timber that has survived is the medial post whose two parts combined form a timber 1.7 m long × 1.18 m wide × 0.37 m thick, which would have weighed 660 kg. The wall timber [3722], 5.2 m long × 1.2 m high × 0.1 m thick, originally also weighed 660 kg (Table 3.3). Moving these timbers would present no problem to an 'enthusiastic' group of people.

*Volume of timber and the significance of the number of trees*

In this section a number of issues will be considered: the volume of timber necessary to construct the burial chamber, the potential of tangential splitting to produce the timbers needed, the minimum number of trees actually used in the structure itself, and the reasons for any discrepancies between the minimum number of trees necessary to construct the structure and the actual number made use of in the burial chamber. The simplest possible structure with the minimum number of pieces is assumed. However, the argument here is not affected if some of the timbers assumed to be single were actually in several pieces, as the volume would still be the same.

The volume of timber

The structure survives in a fragmented and compressed form with many of its timbers dissociated from their original positions. As such, it has been described in detail by Morgan. Despite this unpromising material it is clear that the original structure was a double chamber, with wooden floor, walls and roof all made from wide oak planks.

In its simplest form the structure was a box 7.6 m long × 1.2 m high × 1.5 m wide, with the proximal posts 0.8 m diameter, the medial post (1.2 m wide and 0.37 m thick) dividing the box into two 'rooms' 2.4 m from the entrance, and the distal posts marking the rear of the back chamber 4.5 m behind the medial post (Fig. 3.39). The back chamber was floored with a 1.2 m wide oak plank (0.1 m thick), but the front chamber had two narrow planks laid side by side, and between 0.3 and 0.5 m wide, flooring it. The walls of the distal chamber, 1.2 m high and 5.2 m long, were each a single plank stretching from the row of posts at the distal end to 0.25 m in front of the medial post. The walls of the proximal chamber may have been similar but do not survive. The whole structure was, in its simplest form, covered by either one or two wide tangential planks laid end to end.

In the 'theoretical' structure the four planks making the side walls, roof and floor of the distal chamber and the distal and medial posts could all be made from half of one 5.2 m length of an oak tree 1.5 m in diameter, if the planks were each 0.1 m thick.

The proximal chamber could easily have been made from the other half of the same length of trunk. As with the floor plank of the distal chamber and the medial post, the timbers making up the floor of the proximal chamber could have been split to the full width of the tree; however advantage was not taken of this wide timber. Morgan has pointed out that the timbers were carefully oriented within the structure so that the heart side faced inwards, so that we must assume that the structure was not haphazard. The medial post definitely came from a tree of 1.5 m diameter which with its slow, even growth rate and straight grain would be unlikely to have had a usable trunk of less than 10 m in length, which means that the structure could easily have been built from half the usable trunk of one tree.

Although it cannot be proved that the timber used to build this structure came from one tree, the dimensions of the larger timbers and their similar growth rates suggest one main source. If these large timbers were produced from one length of a halved trunk, then the cross-section of surviving timbers should fit together to make up this trunk. It should be possible to look at these surviving cross-sections of the timbers and see whether they fit this interpretation. Unfortunately the central parts of the cross-sections rarely survived well enough for their exact position in the trunk to be determined. However, the direction of the medullary rays near the outside edge of planks clearly indicate that timbers [3256], [3252], [3540], [3541], [3754] and [3755] came from further out in the trunk than the floor timber [3692].

Number of trees used

Morgan's master chronology (Fig. 3.69) shows the dendrochronological relationships between timbers in the structure, which can be cross-matched (see below). Unfortunately $t$ values which compare the statistical similarity between the variation in the growth rate of the timbers cannot confirm with certainty that the timbers came from the same tree, although high $t$ values suggest a strong probability that the timbers came from the same tree. Timber within a trunk may vary in its growth rate, but high-quality timber which could be split in a controlled way would be expected to have a straight grain and even growth rate throughout the parts of the trunk which were used, except that there may be a slight decrease in the ring width up the length of the trunk timbers. If the growth rates of the timbers from the master chronology are graphed together so that the rates of growth can be compared it can be seen that a number of them have growth rates of the same gradient (Fig. 3.43). So even if these timbers cannot be proved to have come from the same trees,

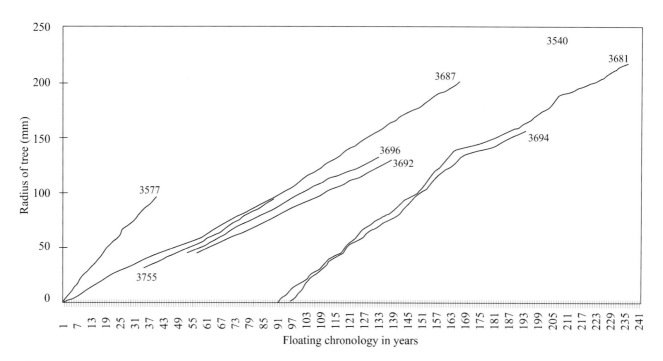

**Figure 3.43**. *Graph of tree-growth rates.*

it can be said that they came from trees which were growing at the same rate at the same time. This is a remarkable coincidence as the chance of there being a large number of trees which eventually reached very large diameters growing at the same rates at the same time is very low. This strongly suggests that this group of timbers ([3687], [3696], [3755], [3692] and [3540]) represents the wood from one tree, from which the major components of the structure were formed.

It is also clear that some of the timbers found in the structure were growing in a different way and cannot have come from the same tree as the rest, as can be seen from the erratic growth rate of the horizontal timbers [3645/82], [3642/81] and [3694]. The faster growth of the north wall timber ([3577]) can clearly be seen from Figure 3.43 and this timber could not have come from the same trunk. The other timbers which may have come from a different source from the main large tree are the floor timbers of the proximal chamber. It is clear from their size and cross-section that they differ from the wide tangential timbers used in the remainder of the structure.

Significance of the number of trees used in the structure
Parts of at least four trees have survived in the Haddenham barrow:
1. the erratically grown timber resting on the floor of the distal chamber;
2. the 1.5-m-diameter tree used for the medial post,

distal post and probably a number of other timbers in the distal chamber;
3. the faster grown timber from the proximal chamber;
4. the smaller diameter trees used in the façade.
If the timber had been tangentially split then the whole structure could have been made from half of one 10 m length of 1.5 m diameter trunk. It would have been possible to waste half of this trunk and still make the whole structure from one tree. Therefore, the presence of more than one tree in the structure suggests either the use of another less efficient technique than tangential splitting, or the intentional inclusion of more than one trunk in the structure.

*Conclusions*
1. It appears that the timbers used in the construction of the Haddenham were produced by tangential splitting. The evidence for this is as follows:
   i) The timbers used are correct in growth rate and cross-section to have been tangentially split.
   ii) The effort and the quantity of timber needed for other techniques would have been much greater than with tangential splitting.
   iii) Surface features: Unfortunately no surface features survived which could be identified as clearly the product of splitting. However, thinning at the outside edges of some planks indicates some surface finishing. This implies that the structure was of carefully finished timber and not a 'rough and ready' structure.

2. All of the evidence suggests that almost all of the timbers came from one very large, evenly grown and straight-grained oak tree. Some timber from at least three other trees was incorporated into the structure.

3. Oak trees of this size and growth rate would be expected to grow in high forest.

4. One half of a 10 m oak trunk 1.5 m diameter could have been split into all the timbers needed for the structure in 40 hours excluding felling times.

## The Minsmere experiment: converting a large-diameter oak tree
### by R. Darrah

The oak trunks used in the mortuary chamber had a diameter of 1.5 m and trunk lengths of 5.2 m, a size of timber now rarely available. To explore the feasibility of splitting up a trunk of similar dimensions, advantage was taken of a tree with a diameter of 1.2 m and a useable trunk length of 2.5 m which had blown over in the hurricane of October 1987. It was a straight-grained timber which was ideal for splitting into planks. The details of the process of splitting the tree both tangentially and radially are recorded below. The aim was not to replicate exactly the Neolithic technology, but to demonstrate the feasibility of the process and the quality of the product that could be produced, and also to get some idea of the time involved in converting the tree.

*The experiment*
An initial inspection of the trunk and bark suggested that the quality of the timber was good enough for splitting, as the bark often indicates the straightness of the grain of the underlying timber (Fig. 3.44:A). This was confirmed by cutting through the bark revealing the ends of the medullary rays, which ran straight up the trunk indicating the direction that splits would follow. Being a wind-blown tree some damage had occurred on one side and it was not possible to view the bark on the underside of the tree for hidden knots, as it was buried in the ground. Scars on the bark indicated that there was one large overgrown knot on the top side of the tree. The hidden underside proved to have some knots in it as well, as was discovered on splitting up the tree.

The trunk was cut free from both the root-plate and the crown using a chainsaw, producing a straight butt 2.5 m long and with a bottom diameter of 1.35 m and a top diameter of 1.2 m, which had grown evenly throughout its 200-year life. Unfortunately, further damage was done to the trunk on cutting off the root plate, leaving a ragged ridged split tangentially along the bottom side of the trunk (Fig. 3.45). This meant that the controlled tangential splitting had to be restricted to the top side of the trunk. The length of trunk was carefully examined for other damage; the growth pattern was checked to ensure that it was regular and that the pith was central to the tree, then the line of the first split was decided.

The process of converting the trunk into planks began by cleaning the bark off the sides of the trunk along the line of the intended split which coincided with the horizontal diameter at the base of the trunk. Seasoned oak wedges were then hammered into each side of the trunk close to the bottom end in line with this diameter. When the splits from opposite sides which could be seen spreading across the end of the trunk had joined at the centre of the tree, further wedges were hammered in on both sides of the trunk at the leading edge of the split. This forced the split to run along the length of the trunk in the plane of weakness which coincides with the medullary rays. As the split opened up, large wedges were forced into the open ends of the split both to

hold it open and help support the weight of the upper side of the trunk. When the trunk had been split down its length the top half of the trunk was then slid off onto bearers ready for the first true tangential split.

A large number of seasoned oak wedges were required to split the trunk in half. These varied in size; the smallest starting wedges were 0.15 m long × 0.05 m wide × 0.015 m thick tapering to a knife edge, and the largest wedges were 0.5 m long × 0.15 m wide × 0.12 m thick. Each of these wedges took between five and ten minutes to make. Although wooden wedges may be used on their own to split up trees of this size, a large number of wooden wedges get broken, so that some metal wedges were used in this experiment solely to save the time involved in making the wooden wedges. Wooden wedges are more effective in some circumstances and have to be used in starting splits in the end grain, and where the wood is under extreme pressure, as under these conditions metal wedges will bounce out of the wood when hammered in.

Splitting the trunk into two halves, and moving the top half, took two men four hours; over 25 oak wedges were broken during this split. The split-off upper side of the tree weighed 1.5 tons, but was easily slid onto wooden bearers at the edge of the bottom side by two men using levers.

The line of the first tangential split was selected across the end grain of the top side of the trunk, so that the timber would be split into two equally bendable pieces. This made the upper section slightly thicker at the centre than the lower piece. This line was selected, since if one half bends more than the other half, the split will run off its intended course and produce a plank tapering in thickness over its length. A series of very small seasoned oak wedges less than 10 mm thick were hammered in along this line (Fig. 3.44: C). Once the split had opened up across the full width of the timber the fine starting wedges were replaced by slightly larger wedges in the end-grain. The sides of the trunk had been cleaned of bark so that the direction of splitting could be followed. When the crack had opened up for 0.6 m along the sides, wedges were driven into these side splits, encouraging them to run further along the trunk. This process was continued until the end of the trunk was reached.

Due to inexperience, the selection of the initial line of the split was not quite right, resulting in the split moving up from one end of the trunk to the other. Insufficent allowance had been made for effect of the weight of the upper part of this exceptionally heavy timber restraining the bottom half of the timber from bending; this initial split should have been slightly lower. The split did not twist, except where it ran around a large hidden knot, and was straight and parallel to the line that began the split.

The split produced two planks, the lower one an inner tangential split with two flat surfaces, and the upper one an outer tangential split with one flat and one curved surface. The plank with the two flat surfaces was slightly thicker at the crown end; the upper plank correspondingly tapered slightly towards the top end.

This first tangential split took four hours. In the process of completing it, 32 small seasoned oak wedges were broken. As each took several minutes to make using a steel draw knife, the wedges would have taken at least as long to make as the time taken to split the timber.

Unfortunately, because of the large knot it was impossible to split these two timbers into flat thin tangential planks to the full width of the tree, so that subsequent splits were as follows. Both the outer and inner tangential planks (0.39 m and 0.35 m thick) already produced were split radially along their lengths, into two equal halves (Splits 3 & 4). The knot-free sections were then split tangentially. At each stage the line of the split was chosen so that the timber was split into two equally bendable pieces so that the split ran straight. In the sixth split, on a 0.19 m thick piece, the split began to run out when it was half way

**Figure 3.44.** *The Minsmere experiment: A) the fallen trunk; B & C) inserting the wedges of the first split; D) reassembled tangentially split planks; E) detail showing grain and rays of split planks. (Photographs G. Owen & R. Darrah.)*

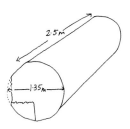

A split across the side where a branch had broken off about 20 years ago. The split underneath the trunk was caused when the trunk was cut off from the root plate.

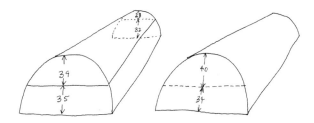

A) The line across the trunk which was chosen for the second split, this split moved up as it ran along the trunk.
B) The dotted line is the suggested line that should have been chosen for the split to run straight along the trunk.

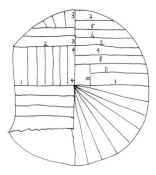

Section of the trunk showing the lines of the splits, the first eleven splits have been numbered.

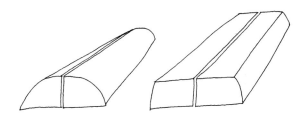

The line of the radial splits on the inner and outer tangential splits.

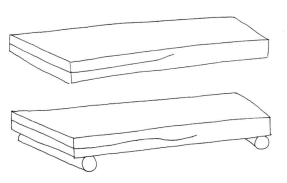

Bending a timber to control a split.
A. The split has begun to move up from its intended line in the centre of the timber.
B. The timber is turned over, placed on bearers and bent downwards in the middle, as the split is continued it is forced to return to the centre line.

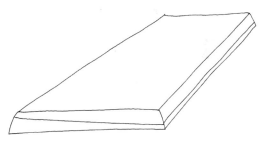

Splitting at an angle across a length of timber may be possible if this timber were bent in a controlled way. A split may run out to produce this section.

A chevron split would be impossible to control.

**Figure 3.45.** *The Minsmere experiment. Sketch drawings of trunk-splitting sequence.*

along the timber. This was corrected by turning the timber over, and bending the timber with three people standing on it whilst continuing to split.

Before Split 11 was made the central part of the tree was split away, as it was full of knots from the early growth of the tree. If this timber had been the full width of the tree, it would

have been impossible to have controlled the split this close to the centre of the tree because of these knots.

The quarter tree which was straight-grained was converted into eight tangential planks; of those the outer plank was almost all sapwood, but the remaining seven were all straight tangential planks, each 0.1 m thick. These eminently usable planks varied in width from 0.5 m to 0.6 m and were all 2.5 m long. Each of these planks took an hour to make. The remainder of the tree was split up either radially or tangentially into wide planks. The whole tree produced over 30 square metres of usable planks.

One tangentially split plank already had a crack along the medullary rays at right angles to the intended line of the next tangential split. Although this crack ran for half a metre down the length of the timber, the tangential split was made across it without the original crack spreading.

Not all the planks split from the tree were perfectly parallel sides. The fifth split up from the bottom was started from the far end and did not run parallel to the other surfaces. It exhibited the same degree of irregularity as most of the timbers.

From the experience of splitting this tree, and other timbers, I suspect that it is impossible to control splits on wide timbers where the split begins to move away from the centre line towards the top or bottom of the plank. When a split runs off its intended course, the direction of the split is very difficult to correct. When this happened in the case of Split 6, the timber had to be turned over, supported on bearers at each end, and bent by three people standing near the centre of the timber.

*Discussion*
In the conversion of the Minsmere timber, the large knot on the upper side of the timber and the existing damage on the lower half of the tree meant that it was not possible to demonstrate the process of splitting the tangential planks to the full width of the timber. However, although only the two original planks the full width of the tree were produced, it should be assumed that production of the whole set of full-width planks would have required techniques identical to those used. Each split would probably have taken as long as the first full tangential split.

It is clear, from the care required in selecting the positions of the splits, that the thickness and position of the splits in the cross-section of a trunk of known diameter are defined, if the process of splitting is to be controlled. In the first tangential split across the upper side of the trunk, the selected position for the split was not quite right. It was made slightly high and moved upward during the course of the split. It was then possible on continuing the split to bring it back to the middle of the plank edge. In one tangential split it was possible to control the split, bringing it back to centre after it had wandered off true, by applying force. It may just be possible to control a split running at an angle across a knot-free length of timber, as long as a large number of people are available to bend the timber. However, I would suggest that it would be impossible to control a chevron split as seen in the roof timbers of the Foulmire barrow. As a general rule I feel it may be assumed that where long lengths of oak have been split across the medullary rays, the sides of the split piece would have been intended to be parallel, and that any deviation from parallel was a mistake or due to the surface being removed later by other means such as splitting or hewing. However, it is quite possible that Neolithic people with 1000 years of experience behind them may have acquired techniques for splitting odd shapes that have now been lost.

The experimental tangential splitting shows the remarkable flatness of the surfaces and straightness of the splits, even after the split has moved through 2.5 m of trunk. This is only true where the timber is free from knots, and this type of splitting only really works in knot-free timber.

Where straight-grained, unstressed, knot-free timber is available, tangential splitting is a fast and efficient way of producing wide planks with a smooth surface finish. Made entirely with seasoned wooden wedges, the conversion of the whole tree into approximately 30 sq. m of usable planks took 50 man-hours (Fig. 3.44:D).

The modern experiment of tangential splitting probably differs from the prehistoric technique in two respects. Firstly,

the Minsmere oak was only 200 years old, with an even growth rate. Prehistoric trees of the same size from high forest may have been twice as old with half the growth rate, which may change the properties of the timber. The author has noted changes in the way oak from a single tree splits as the growth rate changes. Generally, the faster-grown wood is less brittle and easier to split. Thus the Foulmire barrow oak may have been harder to split true. Secondly, the Minsmere tree was cut across with a chain saw, leaving a flat surface on which it would be easier to choose the perfect position for a split than with axe-cut timber.

In the Minsmere trunk, it was necessary to split out the knotty timber from the centre of the tree, as the uneven early growth made it impossible to split the timber with the section into two planks the full width of the tree. The Minsmere tree grew in open conditions, but it is probable that a tree growing in high forest, like that presumably used at Foulmire, would have lost its side branches earlier, resulting in a much less knotty centre.

## Burning of the chamber

Why the wood of the mortuary chamber survived has not so far been raised. One possibility is water-logging. The evidence from the barrow's ditches indicates that they quickly held water and we know from the pollen core that the area was gradually becoming wetter. However, there are late Neolithic artefacts adjacent to the long barrow beneath the Fen Clay, and so it seems likely that the locality was at least seasonally dry at ground surface for many hundreds of years after the construction of the mortuary building. Indeed, we have seen that the lower portions of the axial posts, well protected from any burning, have not survived well. These lowest elements of the mortuary structure would be expected to have survived if waterlogging was the key factor. Certainly wetness contributed to the survival of the wood; during the excavations it was clear that once exposed to air, much of the wood quickly turned to a fine dust, and it had to be continually sprayed with water. But wetness was not the dominant factor in the original survival of the wood.

Also relevant to the survival of the timbers was heavy mineralization due to the leaching of iron salts through the mound. Even when exposed to air some of the timber seemed quite stable. But the main reason for the survival of the wood seemed to be that it had been burnt, as was evident from the scorched earth in and around the chamber and from the fire-cracked flint. Away from the burning (for example at the bottom of the axial posts) the wood did not survive well and it was best preserved in association with the burnt turf mound.

However, an immediate problem arises. If the wood had indeed been burnt, why had the whole building not been reduced to ashes in the conflagration? Somehow the fire must have been controlled or (perhaps accidentally) smothered. Perhaps, indeed, there were many small and controlled fires. Clearly needed were studies of the wood which would explore the temperatures reached and the nature of the firing process. The second of the following two studies was designed specifically to answer these questions. The first was undertaken in order to contribute to the conservation of the wood, but it had results which were relevant to an understanding of the charring process.

*Charred structural timbers*
by C. CAPLE & W. MURRAY

Initial examination of samples of wood taken from throughout the mortuary chamber, using reflected light microscopy, confirmed that charring had taken place. Much of the cellular structure of the wood is still visible but it is preserved as a skeleton of black charred cell wall material, the cell contents having been lost during the charring episode. Characteristic features of charred materials visible under the light microscope are their distorted, shrunken structures and glassy, highly reflective, brittle fracture.

The combustion of organic materials is a complex process which can have two main forms. Pyrolysis involves the thermal degradation of organic materials in the absence of oxygen to produce volatile compounds and a residue of char. Oxidation involves the reaction of those products with oxygen in the atmosphere to produce CO, $CO_2$ and mineral ash. In order to establish the degree of combustion of the mortuary structure a range of studies was undertaken.

SEM (scanning electron microscopy) was used in order to examine the wood and compare it with samples of charred modern oak. ESR spectrometry was applied in the hope of understanding the maximum temperature and duration of heating (cf. Griffiths below). Light element analyses, X-ray fluorescence analyses, atomic absorption spectrometry and X-ray diffraction studies were also carried out. The results are reported in full in the report held in the archive, and only a brief summary of the results concerning the charring is provided here.

From the work done on the conditions necessary to create a char, there can be reasonable certainty that the massive timbers of this structure were set alight, but starved of oxygen, and underwent pyrolysis rather than combustion. The temperature reached in the pyrolysis of the chamber has been suggested by Griffiths below, using ESR data from the flint in the chamber, as being approximately 450–600°C. The very tentative ESR data for the char suggests a lower temperature of 200°C. Stronger evidence of the

temperature of pyrolysis is provided by the results from the light element determination. This suggested that a temperature of 300–400°C would have been most likely to create the C/O, H/O ratios which were noted. Information on the charring temperature is also provided by the visual evidence derived from SEM examination. This revealed a regular microstructure throughout much of the char which is indicative of a 'long slow' combustion process at a relatively low temperature. Within the cell structure, however, there was no evidence of a middle lamella remaining. This is usually attributed to the complete conversion of the cellulose to char, thus suggesting a temperature of more than 300°C had been reached in the pyrolysis process. Further detailed experimentation, particularly on slow charring of material, will be needed to provide comparative data for ESR analysis before any conclusion can be reached on the actual temperature of charring.

The char itself is a pyropolymer, as confirmed by light element analysis. The extent of conversion to polymeric carbon could not be tested, as no cellulose or lignin analysis was carried out. Charring at a temperature of 300–400°C over a long period would probably see the complete conversion of cellulose to pyropolymer, either by direct heat decomposition or radical path pyrolysis. Not all the lignin in the wood need have been converted at these lower temperatures and some traces of it may still be present in the char.

Details of the highest levels of microstructure of pyropolymers are uncertain. The nature of the porosity of the material, for instance, can produce variable results. It does appear that both the nature of the wood, its condition and the heating regime it underwent all affect the nature of the final material. In general terms, however, there should be a relatively high degree of porosity in a material which has been heated in the 300–500°C range, and the Haddenham char appears unlikely to have been heated at the higher temperatures, which see the loss of porosity and chemical surface reactivity associated with pyrocarbon formation. It also appears likely that the tarry materials normally residual within a low temperature char, will have been removed by the effects of years of groundwater, thus increasing the porosity of the material. The deposition of salts from the same groundwater will, however, have subsequently considerably reduced the porosity of the material. The nature of the salts reflects the level and composition of the partially soluble salts in the groundwater in the long barrow area. The 'active' effect of the charcoal in attracting the salts as compared with the surrounding soil, and the nature of the bonding of the salts to the char surface, have not been investigated.

In more general terms the microstructure of the char accurately reproduces that of the wood. The lack of distortion in the microstructure perhaps indicates that the wood was in a good, relatively dry condition when pyrolysed. Traces of what appear to be old or original fungal hyphae may, however, suggest that the wood was just starting to undergo fungal attack (i.e. it was not newly felled when charred). In some areas the microstructure is poor. Cell walls appear to have distorted and coalesced. This characteristic has been noted with charred samples of Dichrostachys which had been soaked in water. Clearly comparative evidence documenting the effects of water and pressure on pyrolysed microstructures are required in order to determine the reasons for the coalescing of cell walls upon pyrolysis.

The possibility exists of the timbers being wet when burnt. The consuming of the heat energy necessary to vaporize the water from the sodden timber may have resulted in pyrolysis rather than combustion. However, the degree of regularity of the char microstructure favours the explanation of restricted oxygen supply. Though this can be achieved in a number of ways, a covering of earth or turf over the timber prior to firing is perhaps the most likely explanation.

### Heated flint fragments
by D. GRIFFITHS

A number of burnt flint fragments were recovered during the excavation. As it was suspected that the barrow had been burnt, these fragments were analyzed with the aim of looking for evidence that might corroborate or disprove this suspicion. It was also of interest to discover the degree of heating (if any) for each fragment in the hope of learning more about the extent of any burning episodes.

Many types of analysis have been investigated for their potential for determining the thermal history of materials. In the case of flint, changes in colour, in the lustre of fracture surfaces formed after heating, in strength and in microscopic appearance have been reported. Changes in X-ray diffraction patterns, thermoluminescence glow curves and differential thermal analysis curves have also been said to be diagnostic of past heating in flint. These indicators all have limitations and generally require reference material of the same type and provenance as the possibly heated material. Because of the limitations of existing techniques it has been considered worthwhile to investigate the use of electron spin resonance (ESR) spectroscopy in detecting and quantifying the past heating of flint. This report is the first to apply this

technique to the investigation of the heating of flint on an archaeological site (the full report is held in the project archive).

The results presented here are based on detailed study of flint from the prehistoric mines at Grimes Graves, Norfolk. No inconsistencies have yet emerged in comparing its results to those obtained from laboratory heating of numerous other flint samples from Britain, France and the Middle East (Griffiths *et al.* 1982; 1986). As a first approximation, the degree to which a sample of flint has been heated in the past can be estimated from the presence or absence of certain features such as the perinaphthenyl or carbon radical signals and the overall appearance of the spectrum. This approach was chosen in the present work in order to allow a survey of a range of flint fragments from various parts of the site to be conducted.

It may be noted that the above paragraph refers to the degree to which a flint sample has been heated rather than simply the temperature to which it has been heated. This is because the ESR spectra monitor the extent to which certain reactions and changes in the flint structure have taken place. Generally speaking one might reach a given situation either by a long duration of heating at a low temperature or by a shorter duration at a higher temperature. The results obtained for the Haddenham material assumed a 30-minute duration of heating. Given this duration, the estimates of temperature are probably accurate to within +50°C or better in the range 250–450°C. If the archaeological heating event was in fact considerably longer than 30 minutes the actual temperatures attained would be slightly lower.

In conclusion, all the 29 flint samples examined had been subjected to considerable heat consistent with having been in a fire. The temperatures obtained ranged from 275°C to 600°C. There is no suggestion that these temperatures might be the result of 'heat treatment' intended to improve the flaking qualities of the flint: the temperatures involved are nearly all too high. A spatial plotting of the studied flints indicated two patterns (Fig. 3.46):

i.   The temperatures attained by pieces (four samples) from the forecourt are all distinctly lower (275–375°C) than those from the mortuary structure (14 samples giving a range 450–600°C). To a lesser extent, lower values were also found for the façade-bank. This evidence seems consistent with a hypothesis that the flint was *in situ* at the time of a burning centred on the mortuary structure and mound.

ii.  In the mortuary structure there was a cooler patch at $X = 6.5–9.0$ m. This area at the back of

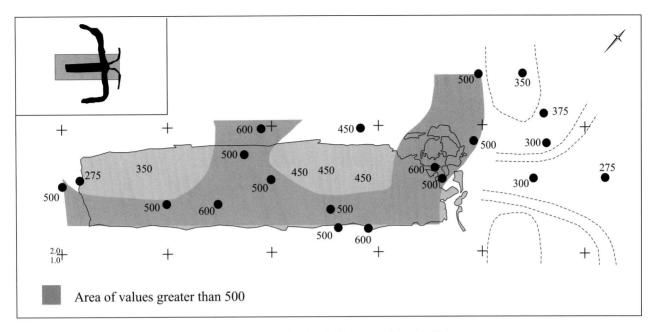

**Figure 3.46.** *Distribution of ESR spectroscopy results for the heating of struck flint.*

the chamber reached temperatures of only 450°C. This evidence is consistent with the evidence from the burnt mound that the fire was centred in the proximal area.

### Calcrete stone firing
by D. ATKINSON

A block of consolidated red gravel (calcrete stone) was investigated in an attempt to understand its thermal history. This was sampled for routine thermal demagnetization and also for the determination of some basic rock magnetic properties. The block was composed predominantly of small pieces of flint in a soft matrix of red silt and sand. Sub-sampling was difficult because of the irregular combination of hard and soft material. Sampling was intended to be a simple traverse from A (the red surface) to B (the browner surface) but the samples became scattered about A–B because of the irregular nature of the material. Six samples were cut for thermal demagnetization; two of these were 'dry cut' cubes, the remainder being one-inch cylinders cut using a standard palaeomagnetic drill. The uneven surface of the block did not allow accurate relative orientation of the samples although rough orientation was obtained. Absolute orientation was impossible because *in situ* orientation was unknown.

*Thermal demagnetization and rock magnetism:* Thermal demagnetization is a standard palaeo / archaeomagnetic technique for resolving the magnetization of natural materials such as rock, brick and sediment into their constituent magnetic vector components (these different components can arise in many ways). Stepwise thermal demagnetization involves heating a sample to successively higher temperatures

in a magnetic field-free space, with the magnetization of the sample being measured after each heating step. This treatment progressively removes lower temperature parts of the magnetization. This leaves for most palaeo / archaeomagnetic work a magnetic vector which is hoped to be representative of the ancient geomagnetic field.

Thermal demagnetization is useful in the present context because it can show up any differences in the magnetic components that make up the magnetization of the different samples. For example, when a sample is formed it usually acquires a magnetization in the direction of the ambient magnetic field (i.e. a primary magnetization). Under thermal demagnetization this primary magnetization is gradually removed at temperatures from room temperature up to the Curie temperature of the magnetic mineral concerned (i.e. the temperature at which the spontaneous magnetization of the mineral is destroyed). However if at a later time the sample was heated, for example to 400°C, then part of the primary magnetization (that which would be demagnetized between room temperature and approximately 400°C) would become magnetized on cooling in the direction of the ambient magnetic field at the time of heating. Thus the magnetization of such a sample when thermally demagnetized would consist of a component between room temperature and 400°C with one direction and the remains of the primary component between 400°C and the Curie temperature with another direction. So the basis for determining the thermal history of a sample is the identification of temperature components with different directions of magnetization.

All six samples were thermally treated. The natural remnant magnetization (NRM) of each sample was measured prior to heating. The NRM intensities are listed in Table 3.4. The result of thermal demagnetization up to 300°C shows that all of the samples have only a single component (within the experimental errors). Two examples of the demagnetization behaviour using orthogonal vector projections with the North component plotted against the East component of magnetization and the East component plotted against the vertical component of magnetization show that the magnetizations of samples are stable (i.e. repeatable on remeasurement) at each temperature step up to 300°C. The direction of this component of magnetization is similar between samples. At 350°C, the next step, the magnetizations of all the samples become unstable and have larger magnetizations than previously.

**Table 3.4.** *NRM intensities of consolidated red gravel.*

| Sample code | NRM intensity $(10^{-5}\ Am^2kg^{-1})$ | Comments |
|---|---|---|
| CII.1A | 1.32 | Cube. Red surface |
| CII.6A | 0.93 | Cube. Red surface |
| CII.2A | 1.72 | Core. Brown surface |
| CII.3A | 1.01 | Core. Brown surface |
| CII.4A | 1.70 | Core. Brown surface |
| CII.5A | 1.00 | Core. Brown surface |

A thermomagnetic investigation on powdered sister samples which were heated in air in a Curie balance revealed the cause of the unstable magnetization. Thermomagnetic curves were obtained by heating the sample in the presence of an intense magnetic field (0.5T), the curves represent the change with temperature of the near saturation magnetization of the samples. For a mineral which does not chemically alter the curve is usually convex, and the cooling curve retraces the heating curve showing the reversibility of the magnetization.

In the present study the thermomagnetic behaviour is variable but all of the samples show massive chemical alteration which produces a magnetically soft (multidomain) mineral, probably magnetite (further evidence for this is provided by hysteresis measurements before and after heating). This alteration is observed as a peak on the heating curve of the thermomagnetic run (as more magnetic material is produced) which commences at temperatures between 270°C and 370°C with the peak for most samples commencing around 300°C.

This investigation aimed to determine whether the block has been heated and, if so, to elucidate any variation of heating across the block. A systematic variation of NRM intensity can be indicative of differences in magnetization. No such variation is observed from A to B and what differences there are seem relatively small, these probably being due to variable amounts of the non-magnetic flint in the samples. Thermal demagnetization up to 300°C showed that all samples have only a single stable component. The direction of this component is similar between samples. Above 300°C the production of new magnetic material occurs; this is magnetically soft and contributes an unstable component to the magnetization of all samples. This new unstable component prevents any further information about the original magnetization being obtained from thermal demagnetization.

The production of new magnetic material indicates the presence of a thermally unstable material. The presence of this material suggests that the block has not been heated significantly above 300–350°C. However, it may be that the unstable material was produced chemically after the block was laid down in antiquity.

In conclusion, the similarity between samples during demagnetization up to 300°C indicates no differences due to heating for different regions of the block. Above 300°C an unstable mineral phase breaks down. If this phase was present in antiquity it is highly unlikely that it would survive heating to around 350°C or above without breaking down to some extent. Therefore it can be concluded that if the block was heated it was not heated above 350°C. However this study cannot discern whether the block has or has not been heated up to less than that temperature.

### Calcrete stones
with L. Webley

Eighty-one pieces (141 kg) of calcrete stone were recovered in association with the long barrow, and appear to have been used in the monument (Fig. 3.24). Calcrete is a concretion of sand and gravel cemented with iron oxides and hydroxides, which naturally occurs in sand/gravel deposits (Limbrey 1975). The stone could either have been obtained from the excavation of the ditch surrounding the barrow, or quarried from elsewhere in the vicinity. Many of the pieces comprise roughly oblong blocks, although the soft stone has clearly suffered considerably from breakage, so that there is wide variation in block size. Twenty-five of the pieces had crumbled to small fragments and were not measured. Of the remainder, their length ranges from 4–36 cm, width from 2–26 cm and thickness from 1–14 cm; average dimensions are 14 × 10 × 5 cm. Twelve large blocks survive to more than 20 cm long. If tessellated perfectly, the surviving blocks would cover an area of just over 1 sq. m; the estimated total area being *c.* 1.40 m (including unmeasured pieces based on weight).

The only other known prehistoric usage of such calcrete slabs in the region is the later Bronze Age 'cist' cremation burials inserted into the Deeping St Nicholas barrow, south Lincolnshire (French 1994, 39–40). Prone to disintegration, such fragile 'stone' would have had little load-bearing capacity.

A striking feature of many of the blocks is their vivid colours, and within the barrow they occurred in yellow, red and black. Though in at least one instance yellow and red were represented on a single block, the pieces can be divided up according to predominant colour. Red stones form just over half of the total, with the remainder roughly equally divided between yellow and black (Table 3.5). The red and yellow stones are significantly larger on average than the black stones, with none of the latter measuring longer than 16 cm.

Though the colour of the blocks could suggest their potential use as some manner of decorative capping, the distribution shows this not to be the case (Fig. 3.24). The vast majority occurred within the proximal sub-chamber and the area of the forecourt (with a marked concentration in the fills of the mortuary structure's proximal pit), with only a few pieces scattered along the line of the façade and façade-bank. The red and black stones almost exclusively occur within the proximal sub-chamber, with the yellow in the 'fore' area, thus indicating that their colouring may have been affected by burning.

Given the stones' dispersion it is difficult to account for their function and certainly they did not constitute a continuous surface. As indicated in Figure 3.24, during the careful excavation of the proximal post pit (F.707) stones were found set on end between and beside the two façade-replacement posts relating to the final blocking of the chamber. Although not without some element of doubt, given this and their distribution (and that the closed entrance was obviously an important feature) it seem probable that here the stones framed these two timbers up through the entire height of the façade.

## Burnt clay
with M. KNIGHT

Ten burnt clay fragments were recovered from the interior of the mortuary chamber. Generally with a pale grey to buff orange sandy clay fabric, these had clods of soil adhering to them (i.e. inseparable/ingrained). Most of the fragments were small, though there were some larger 'fist-sized' pieces, two of which have distinct structural impression (Fig. 3.47). These are roughly pyramid-shaped (8 × 8 × 6 cm) and both pieces hold roundwood impressions. The remaining surfaces consist of either moulded or pressed faces, the latter suggesting that they had been applied against soil. Although the firing of the two lumps appears to have been accidental, the consistent shape of the fragments attests to roundwood structural components.

*Fragment A*: 440 g of pale buff/mottled orange sandy clay with sparse small gravel inclusions. The surface of the flat 'base' is obscured by a clump of unburnt soil. The roundwood impression has a diameter of about 3.5 cm and has the imprint of bark (?alder). The top of the lump is lipped around the wood and the remaining faces are smeared and irregular and contain probable finger impressions.

*Fragment B*: 269 g of pale grey sandy clay with sparse to common small gravel inclusions. The 'base' is uneven and stony as if it once rested on a soil interface. The roundwood impression has a diameter of 2.9 cm and has left a clear imprint of its bark. With the exception of one face the remaining surfaces are rough and irregular and may be broken. The surviving surface is slightly concave and may have been pressed against a piece of flat wood, although there are no clear grain or bark impressions.

These are intriguing pieces, as they indicate the structural use of roundwood such as was found on the floor

**Table 3.5.** *Weight of stones. Averages are mean followed by median in brackets.*

|  | No. | Total weight (kg) | Weight range (kg) | Average weight (kg) |
|---|---|---|---|---|
| Yellow stones | 19 | 45.9 | 0.143–10.500 | 2.415 *(0.922)* |
| Black stones | 18 | 6.9 | 0.035–2.000 | 0.385 *(0.347)* |
| Red stones | 44 | 87.9 | 0.019–9.500 | 1.999 *(0.537)* |
| **Total** | **81** | **140.8** | **0.019–10.500** | **1.738** |

of the mortuary chamber and their recovery within its fill suggests an association. The clay appears to have been variously pressed against faces of soil and timber, both upon larger flat elements (?planks) and roundwood stakes or wattles; though the main impressions suggest that the roundwood was impressed into the clay. The most likely possibility is that they relate to a roundwood 'pinning' of the walls of the chamber that was effectively 'fixed' by clay applied upon the planks and pressed against the flanking mounds behind. It is this which causes us to re-appraise the status of the Phase I stakeholes found ringing the chamber's main trough (Fig. 3.27). Instead of being the traces of an independent pre-chamber structure, those probably marked the base of roundwood stakes driven in to hold the chamber's planks, and at least some of the roundwood found within the chamber may attest to the extraction of this revetment when the upper wall planks were dismantled. (This revised interpretation of the Phase I stakes would not, however, deny the existence of the other pre-chamber structural elements and ritual activity, to which the bank-sealed burnt spread with burnt human bone still attests; just that it was not associated with a freestanding roundwood-stake structure.)

## Overview discussion: how the structure worked
with M. TAYLOR

There is very little Neolithic timber or wood-working debris surviving for comparison. When considering prehistoric timber working as a whole, however, it becomes apparent that there are a number of constraints and considerations which may have affected techniques. Wood-workers in the Neolithic and Bronze Age appear to have had access to the fine, tall, straight forest-grown oaks which are particularly suitable for high-quality splitting. The trunks of the great forest oak trees, if radially split, produce unwieldy baulks of wood with a triangular section. These can be further split to square them up, but the wastage is

135

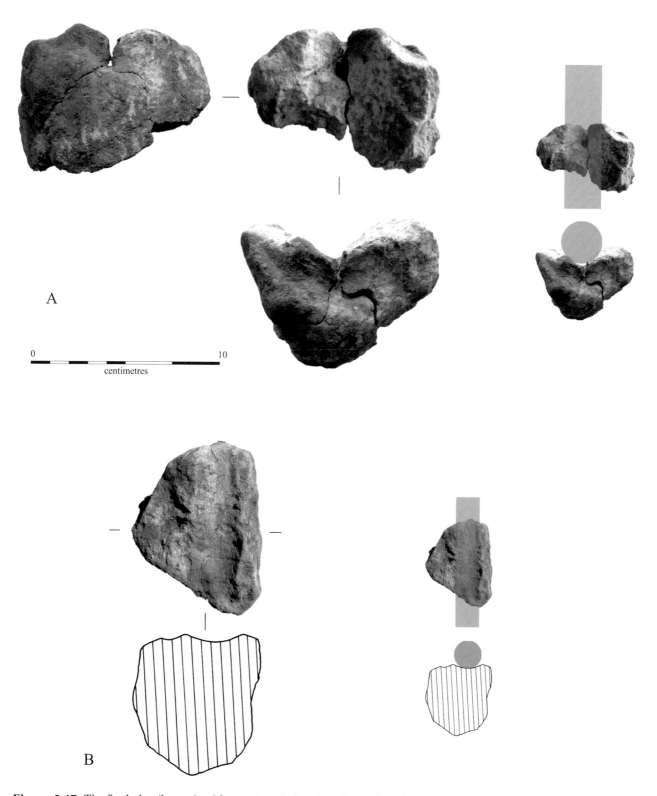

**Figure 3.47.** *The fired-clay 'lumps', with grey tone indication of roundwood pieces.*

high. The tangential splitting of huge trees produces thick 'boards', which lend themselves to monumental architecture. Examples of this kind of timber, but of a much later date, were found at Flag Fen (Taylor 2001, figs. 6.38 & 6.39). These great boards were split out of huge trees with straight grain and no knots or blemishes. This quality of tree was available to the Neolithic wood-workers. Boards of this quality could easily be produce by them, as the splitting is best done when the tree is fresh or 'green' and the splitting wedges are made of seasoned oak. Timbers B63 and BXX from Flag Fen were both tangentially split from trees which must have been well over 1.5 metres in diameter. One of these boards was 3.00 m long, 0.60 m wide and 0.70 m thick.

It may be that very large trees were reserved for monumental building or it may be that large trees can be easily split down to produce timber of 'monumental quality'. This kind of timber was not used for domestic structures. If it had been, there would be more evidence surviving of Neolithic and Early Bronze Age houses. Radial splitting of smaller trunks produces smaller, easier to handle planks which are very serviceable, especially for domestic use,

The qualities of stone axes and their behaviour in use impose considerable constraints on the woodworker. All the indications are, for example, that hewing would be much more difficult with stone axes than with metal. There are problems for the experimental woodworker attempting to replicate Neolithic work, as quite different techniques have to be employed to get the best out of the stone tools (Jørgensen 1985, 33). Neolithic timbers from Etton (Taylor 1998, 147–8) and the Sweet Track (Coles & Coles 1986, fig. 10) show that Neolithic woodworkers were sophisticated and capable of working to a very high standard, but very little is known of techniques actually used. The technique of felling may possibly have been quite different from that used with metal tools (Jørgensen 1985). Debris of a distinctively Neolithic type were recovered from the ditch of the long barrow at Stanwick (Healy & Harding forthcoming) from working in situ and it may be significant here that the axe used to work the timber was also incorporated into the mound. Splitting timber with wooden wedges would be the same using stone or metal tools, but all these techniques leave distinctive evidence in the woodchips.

Recent work has begun to extend ideas on the symbolism of trees in anthropology (Rival 1998). The use of the 'big tree' in the construction of the timber circle at Holme-next-the-Sea shows that there can be a high level of complexity in what might appear initially to be a simple structure. This monument, partly because it was built in one episode and not later modified, preserves remarkable insights into the status of an individual tree. Firstly, timbers derived from the central tree trunk, which was inverted, were only found in the panel opposite the entrance and not in the side arcs. This suggests that the tree itself had a specific status, especially as these timbers were not of particularly high quality. Another unexpected aspect

to the construction which points towards the status of the tree, rather than individual timbers, is that almost all the timbers in the circle were set with the bark to the outside and the split surfaces to the inside of the circle. Thus from a distance the circle might have resembled a large tree trunk, and being inside the circle might resemble being inside a tree.

The availability of large oaks, and the ease of splitting, would make oak the first choice for a monumental structure such as the long barrow. Oak heartwood is extremely resistant to decay and would therefore be a particularly good choice for an earth-bound structure. It is also the best load-bearing timber for a structure where the roof planks have to be self-supporting as well as taking the weight of the overburden of the mound.

There is increasing evidence from prehistoric sites, admittedly largely from the Bronze Age, that much more woodworking was done on site than may previously have been thought. Most of the wood from Etton was debris (73.81%), with virtually no finished artefacts (0.37%) or timber (0.04%). The timber circle at Holme-next-the-Sea was constructed from 56 timbers and there was no evidence from the excavation for leaves, twigs etc. The trees felled for the structure may have had the crowns and smaller side branches trimmed off, but some work was done in situ. Four hundred and twenty-two pieces of bark and wood-working debris were accidentally incorporated into the monument, largely dragged into the bedding trench when the vertical timbers were erected (Brennand & Taylor in press). Much of the debris was interpreted as deriving from the splitting of the large trunk, which, with the carefully cut tow-holes on the central timber, adds to the likelihood that the central tree was brought to site in large sections and subsequently split down. The 'tow-holes' on large timbers have been seen in the Somerset Levels (Coles et al. 1983), Flag Fen (Taylor 2001, 204–8) and in the Trent Valley (Garton et al. 2001). The examples from the latter site are cut through entire tree trunks.

Having considered the constraints and differences between working wood with stone and metal, it is interesting to look at the structure in the barrow at Haddenham. It is important to make two observations. The first is that the main proximal post appears to have been replaced with different timbers which are more like those of the façade. The second is that oak heartwood can only be worked whilst 'green' using bronze or stone tools (Pryor & Darrah pers. comm.). The time taken for oak to season varies considerably depending upon the storage conditions, and will be faster, for example, in hot dry environments. If the wood is buried in cool, damp conditions the process will be slowed down but not halted. This means that quite quickly the upper portions of the massive axial posts could not have been modified or trimmed down using the available technology. The effect of this is that timber [3643], although it is probably derived from the same tree as the adjacent medial post, cannot be an 'off-cut' from later modification. As these timbers are split along the grain and stood on end, it is also not possible that timber [3643] has sheared off another post, or snapped. Ancient oak heartwood from timbers of this quality retains a great deal of tensile strength for hundreds of years. It must be considered likely, therefore, that timber [3643] is the original proximal post, which, when it was replaced during the extension of the façade line across the front of the chamber, was 'buried' in the chamber. The timber could not be discarded because, although superfluous in the new structure, it retained its importance and 'power' and needed to be treated with appropriate respect.

This, together with the evidence for serious vertical collapse in the structure, suggests that the axial posts could not have been load-bearing. They may, instead, have separated and defined various areas within the structure and, effectively, acted as kerbs. The gap between the tops of the timbers and the roof can be seen in Figure 3.8, where there is some 0.10 m thickness of soil between the top of the distal timber and the roof. (This would probably have been twice as thick originally, as the soil/turf must have undergone considerable compression.)

This leaves the problem of how the roof might have been supported. There is the ring bank (F.725/726), which with the evidence of the cross-sections along the structure (Fig. 3.6) makes it most likely that the roof was planked and rested on top of the encircling bank and above the wall planks. This would mean that the side walls, which would have been held in place by both the floor timbers and the axial 'kerbs', were effectively revetments. The upper edges could have been braced, and held in tension, by struts (possibly of roundwood) which might also have helped stop the roof from sagging.

What this therefore describes is a remarkably simple plank-lined (and supported) 'passage chamber' (Fig. 3.48). Taking, as a minimum, that the roof stood 0.80 m above the ground surface (1.00–1.10 m to the floor level), and from the evidence of Figure 3.8 that it was 0.60 m high at its back/distal end (presuming a 50% soil compression factor), this would mean that there was respectively 0.80 m and 0.90 m clearance above the top of the medial and original proximal 'post kerbs'.

Providing a means of ready access along the length of the passage chamber, in its very simplicity

this reconstruction makes sense of much of the structure's otherwise 'uncomfortable' attributes. It means, on the one hand, that the massive weight of the roof timbers would not have had to be lifted in order to gain entry into the chamber (given that the façade blocking of the front was secondary). It would equally account for the ribbing of the upper surface of the roof timber. Darrah (above) speculated that this might have been the result of hewing, but in fact a similar effect has been observed on large oak timbers at Flag Fen. The large 'monumental' oak timbers referred to above had, at Flag Fen, been placed as part of a walkway directly onto wet or damp mud. This had resulted in the establishment of wet rot (Pryor 2001a, 160). The timbers looked perfect on their upper sides but when turned over were heavily ribbed, with the rotten remnants of the decayed wood still *in situ*. In the case of a wooden structure built under an earth mound, the upper side of the roof timbers would have been in close contact with the soil and this is where the wet rot could become established. The charred underside, being exposed to the 'air' of the open chamber, would have been less susceptible to rot which thrives in constantly damp conditions. The ribbed effect simply reflects the difference in resistance to the rot between the oak's medullary rays and the wood between.

This means, therefore, that the mortuary structure was never a free-standing 'building', but a passage chamber, with the strength of the structure depending on the earthen components such as the encircling banks. Within the simplicity of this reconstruction two further points require explanation. Firstly, the chamber would originally have been open at the front and this would accommodate and complement the screen-like façade hornwork (F.716–F.719) which would have funnelled and framed the inward access. However, whether the passage chamber was always 'open' is questionable. It could be the case that the hornwork structure was relatively light (i.e. posts supporting no more than wattle panels) and that the large timber lying on the side of the northern hornwork fore-structure (Fig. 3.24) actually had a door-like function which could otherwise blocked passage into the chamber.

The other major issue lies in symbolism of the tree. Although it was never clearly established which way the timbers were aligned, it seems likely, given the chamber's slightly trapezoidal plan (tapering to the southwest), that this taper coincided with the taper of the original trunk. There is also evidence that the timbers were arranged with the sapwood to the outside and the heartwood to the inside. If we accept the importance of the tree as a symbol, then we must also consider the possibility that the chamber at Haddenham was constructed from one great tree,

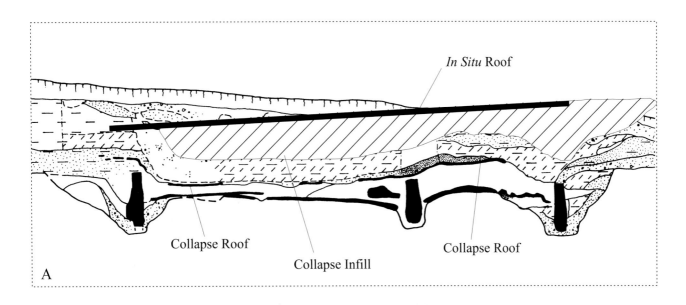

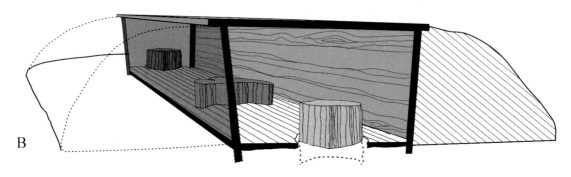

**Figure 3.48.** *The mortuary chamber reconstructed: A) detail of longitudinal section (Fig. 3.8) showing proposed original position of roof; B) the chamber's entrance as seen from the east (note roof carried on F.725/726 ring-bank and the stub/kerb-like situation of axial posts).*

or that the components were arranged to represent a great tree. As the chamber lies in a trough, it is possible that this was the result of first dragging the trunk to its final resting place and then working it down *in situ*. The key to whether this happened would have lain in the woodworking debris, but only five woodchips survive from the excavations. All were in poor condition, but four of them were clearly radial woodchips of oak heartwood, the classic debris from splitting timber. If this is accepted as a feasible interpretation, then the relationship of the passage chamber and the tree trunk are even more direct, the tree itself being an integral part of the primary structure and, effectively revered. (NB This interpretation would either presuppose that the wood had been dragged into place prior to the insertion of the axial posts, and therefore its trough[s] could not truncate their backfill, or that the posts had been removed and reset with the Phase II construction. Alternatively, the central trough[s] may have been an

intentional construction feature [II.1] and relate to the draining off of the bodily fluids of the interred.)

As discussed further in the final chapter discussion, this interpretation brings a structural dualism to the monument's basic arrangement. Whereas its trapezoidal plan may distantly evoke Continental long houses, this has little direct relevance, given the flimsy character of most 'native' domestic structures (see Last's inset and Chapter 4 below). The structure of the chamber was that of an earth-fast passage within the mound. When entering into the passage one may also have been passing into the tree. It is with exactly this kind of seemingly arbitrary juxtaposition of cultural associations or structuring 'values' that relevant ethnography abounds.

Concerning the destruction and ensuing preservation of the chamber, Atkinson's tentative conclusion that the calcrete block was not heated above 300–350°C corresponds with the results obtained by Caple and

Murray for the wood. Considering the higher range of temperatures suggested by Griffiths from the study of the burnt flint, it should be noted that a 30-minute fire was assumed. Since the evidence suggests a long slow burn, his estimates should be lowered. Overall, it can be concluded that whatever the precise temperatures reached (probably in the 300–350°C range), they were low and controlled and the burning took place over a long period and was starved of oxygen because of an earth covering. The fire was centred in the proximal area of the mortuary chamber and lower temperatures were reached at the back of the chamber.

The low temperatures and the starving of oxygen could have occurred by accident. It seems more likely, however, that the burning was intentionally controlled. There is no sign that at any stage a raging high-temperature fire had caught hold. Indeed, everything suggests planning and control. The cutting and careful laying down of the upright timbers and the building up of the turf mound with soil placed over burning turves all suggest that the aim was not to reduce the chamber to ashes, not to destroy, but to burn slowly.

**Burial dynamics: the interred**

Having established the barrow's phasing and structural framework, its *raison d'être*, the dead, can now be addressed. Unlike most individual interments where once buried the dead are left undisturbed, this is often not the case in mass Neolithic burials. Therefore, the monument's human remains do not just relate to issues of population, but are also relevant concerning access into the chamber and the 'processing' of the dead and its relationship to identity (i.e. individual vs group). To this end, Lee's analysis of the bone is followed by studies of its distribution and also the results of the phosphate surveys, the latter being particularly relevant to skeletal representation and any possible shifting of the human remains within the chamber.

*Human skeletal remains*
by F. Lee, with a contribution by J. Wakely
The excavations produced over 2848 fragments of human bone. The pieces were carefully excavated and drawn *in situ* at a scale of 1:5 and each was given an individual number. Before lifting, the bones were examined for any evidence of articulation and the angle of bedding and orientation was noted. The surrounding deposits were subsequently wet sieved through a 3-mm mesh, ensuring that accidental loss during excavation was kept to a minimum, although some bone may have been removed during the sampling of the wooden roof.

Eleven entries were made for each bone, recording the bone type, individual bone number, number of fragments, side of the body, relative age and sex, state of preservation, colour, type and stage of weathering, and type of post-mortem fracture. Finally, any joins between fragments were noted, along with the skeleton to which the bone belonged.

**Catalogue** (Figs. 3.26:A & 3.50)

The dentition is given in the following manner:

Permanent Dentition

|  | *Right* | | *Left* | |
|---|---|---|---|---|
| **Upper Jaw** | 8 7 6 5 4 3 2 1 | | 1 2 3 4 5 6 7 8 | |
| **Lower Jaw** | 8 7 6 5 4 3 2 1 | | 1 2 3 4 5 6 7 8 | |

Deciduous Dentition

|  | | *Right* | | *Left* |
|---|---|---|---|---|
| **Upper Jaw** | e d c b a | | a b c d e | |
| **Lower Jaw** | e d c b a | | a b c d e | |

X  loss before death (antemortem)
/  loss after death (post-mortem)
–  jaw missing
C  caries
A  abscess
U  unerupted
O  erupting
NP  not present
R  root only
(after Brothwell 1981)

**SKELETON A**
Male: adult
*Bone preservation*: Poor: the body is well represented but very fragmentary. The left lower leg, lower spinal column pelvic girdle are absent.
*Body position*: Extended burial with the arms lying by the side of the body. The legs appear to be contracted but this may be as a result of movement.
*Dentition*:

```
                R              R          R
         6      3              4          8
      8 7 6 / / /       -  3 4 5 6 7 8
      R R R                R R R R   R
```

*Pathology*:
Trauma: Colles fracture, well healed, to distal end of L. ulna.
Degenerative: Incipient osteoarthrosis to R. acromio-clavicular joint.
Osteochrondritis dissecans: Small lesion to L. navicular.

**SKELETON B**
Sex unknown, but the long bones are gracile in appearance: adult
*Bone preservation*: Poor: the legs, lower trunk and arms are represented, the upper part of the body absent. There is considerable impregnation of the bone by iron salts and deterioration of the bone through crushing and mineralization.
*Body position*: The legs appear to be tightly contracted and slumped into the pit for the western post. Alternatively this may represent a cleared burial, or burial pushed to one side to make room for another. However, the bones are still in their correct anatomical order.

*Pathology*:
Degenerative: Pitting to the proximal articular surface of the L. ulna. Ridge of bone to the distal articular surface of the L. and R. humeri, between the trochlea and capitulum. Lipping to the articular surface of R. patella.

### SKELETON C
Adult
*Bone preservation*: Poor: left leg and right lower leg long bones only.
*Body position*: The left leg appears to be still in articulation or in an anatomical position. This may be part of Skeleton F.

### SKELETON D
Child, aged 2–4 years
*Bone preservation*: Poor: the body is incomplete with a very high degree of fragmentation to the skull. The arms and lower legs are conspicuously absent. The skull is white in colour in comparison to the rest of the body which is better preserved and black in colour.
*Body position*: The body is contained in a single area and probably represents a discrete inhumation. The preservation of the body defies an observation on its articulation.
*Dentition*:

```
 U         U            U
 6         3            2
 6               a   a   /   d   e   6
 U               R   R   3   R   R   U
```

### SKELETON E
?Male: adult (middle)
*Bone preservation*: The bone is light in colour, the long bones cracked and warped with evidence for compression. The upper part of the body is not well represented and scattered including fragments of the right arm, left hand, skull and upper spinal column.
*Body position*: The body is a crouched inhumation visible in the contracted legs at the front of the burial deposit. The upper body has slipped into the central, east–west trough where there is considerable movement. Fragments of the skull are still extant.
*Dentition*:

```
           R           R          R
   6       3           3   4   6   8
           3       1           7
```

Enamel hypoplasia to the mandibular canine.
*Pathology*:
General health: Harris line to R. tibia.
Enthesopathy: L. fibula flange bone to proximal end of shaft.

### SKELETON F
Male: adult
*Bone preservation*: Fair/Poor: Fragmentary skull, left arm and area of elbow of right elbow.
*Body position*: The skull, upper cervical vertebrae and left arm are still in articulation. The rest of the body is absent or may be part of Skeleton C.
*Dentition*:

```
    A      R   R
    /   /  6   5   /   /   /
   NP  7  6   5   4   3   /   /     /   /   3
       R   R   R   R                   R
```

Periodontal disease to the incisor region.
*Pathology*:
Degenerative: Exostosis to the anterior aspect of the odontoid facet. Osteophytic lipping to the distal articular surface with some new bone encroaching onto the articular surface.
*Other features*: R. humerus: numerous small cut marks to the anterior aspect of the distal end of the shaft and to the medial aspect immediately above the medial epicondyle. There is no evidence for any

bone reaction, and these were almost certainly inflicted post-mortem but in antiquity (see Wakely below).

### *Mound burials*

### SKELETON 1 (F.742; Fig. 3.3)
Infant aged 18 months–2 years±8 months
*Bone preservation*: Fair: the body is complete and relatively well preserved.
*Body position*: Crouched inhumation, oriented west–east with the head turned towards the north. The body was located in a pile of turves immediately beneath the gravel capping of the final mound.
*Dentition*:

```
 U  O   O                    O     O  U
 6  e   d   c   b   a     a   b   c   d   e   6
 6  e   d   c   b   a     a   b   c   d   e   6
 U  O                              O  O  O  U
```

### SKELETON 2 (F.743; Fig. 3.3)
?Male: adult
*Bone preservation*: Poor: only the more robust bones of the body survive, namely the long bones and the skull; the vertebral column, the feet and hands are only present as a soil stain. The long bones which are present are completely covered by a concretion, formed of iron panning and sand.
*Body position*: Crouched inhumation, located in the main mound construction.

## Number of individuals

The human skeletal remains were excavated from two discrete contexts, from the burial chamber and from contexts within the mound proper. A minimum total of seven individuals are present: a minimum of five individuals from the mortuary structure and a further two inhumations from the mound.

The minimum number of individuals was estimated by counting the number of occasions in which each type of bone was encountered (see Table 3.6). The fragmentary nature of the assemblage and the degree of movement within the wooden chamber resulted in a strong possibility that a single bone might appear in more than one context. To overcome this, an attempt was made to reconstruct the bones and rearticulate individual bodies, thereby producing a more realistic estimate.

From the contexts external to the main chamber an adult and an infant aged 18 months to two years were recovered. Within the burial chamber a minimum number of four adults and a child aged between two and four years were present; a more precise age for the adults proved impossible due to the highly fragmentary state of the assemblage.

From the limited material available for sexing it was determined that at least two individuals were male. Skull F had a prominent nuchal crest, and pronounced supraorbital ridges. The mastoid processes of the skulls of Skeletons A and F were noted to be large and the posterior root of the zygomatic processes extended beyond the external auditory meatus and were

**Table 3.6.** *Proportional representation of different bones of the body from the skeletal remains in the mortuary structure. The bracketed figures reflect the numbers minus the child skeleton.*

| Bone | No. | No. of expected occasions | % of expectation |
|---|---|---|---|
| Femora | 10 | 10 | 100 |
| Fibula | 9 | 10 | 90 |
| Skull | 4 | 5 | 80+ |
| Tibiae | 8 | 10 | 80 |
| Ulnae | 8 | 10 | 80 |
| Thoracic | 47 | 60 | 78.3 |
| Scapulae | 7 | 10 | 70 |
| Patellae | 7 | 10 | 70 |
| Humeri | 7 | 10 | 70 |
| Sacrum | 3–4 | 5 | 60 |
| Innominate | 6 | 10 | 60 |
| Cervical | 20 | 35 | 57 |
| M. Tarsals | 28 | 50 (40) | 56 (70) |
| Radii | 5 | 10 | 50 |
| Tarsals | 34 | 70 (56) | 48.6 (60.7) |
| Lumbar | 12 | 25 | 48 |
| Clavicle | 4 | 10 | 40 |
| Ribs | 43 | 120 | 35.8 |
| M. Carpals | 15 | 50 (40) | 30 (37.5) |
| Carpals | 17 | 80 (64) | 21.3 (26.6) |
| Phalanges (feet) | 30 | 140 (112) | 21.4 (27) |
| Manubrium | 1 | 5 | 20 |
| Sternum | 1 | 5 | 20 |
| Phalanges (hand) | 23 | 140 (112) | 16.4 (20.5) |

**Table 3.7a.** *Permanent dentition.*

| | Mandible | | | | | | | | Maxilla | | | | | | | | |
|---|---|---|---|---|---|---|---|---|---|---|---|---|---|---|---|---|---|
| Tooth position | 8 | 7 | 6 | 5 | 4 | 3 | 2 | 1 | 1 | 2 | 3 | 4 | 5 | 6 | 7 | 8 | |
| No. of teeth | 3 | 5 | 5 | 3 | 2 | 5 | | 1 | 1 | | 2 | | 2 | 3 | 2 | 1 | Fully erupted |
| | | | | | 4 | | | | | | | | | | 3 | | Unerupted |

**Table 3.7b.** *Deciduous dentition.*

| | | | | | | | | | | |
|---|---|---|---|---|---|---|---|---|---|---|
| Tooth position | e | d | c | b | a | a | b | c | d | e |
| No. of teeth | 3 | 3 | 3 | 2 | 2 | 2 | 2 | 2 | 2 | 2 |

human bone studies as anthropological markers and may be determined by both genetic and environmental conditions.

Dental pathology
A total of 68 teeth were examined; 44 permanent teeth of which nine were unerupted, and 24 deciduous teeth from two children (Table 3.7). The teeth were badly weathered and in most instances only the roots and dentine remain, the enamel crown of the tooth having shattered.

In Skeleton F, an adult male, there is evidence for an apical abscess at the position of the right maxillary 2nd and 3rd molars. This is a localized area of infection resulting in the development of pus with local bone destruction. It may be a secondary effect of dental caries or result from infection through the pulped cavity as a result of extreme attrition. In advanced cases, as here, the pus bursts through the bone and drains into the soft tissue of the gums.

In the same individual (F) the right mandibular 3rd molar has failed to develop. This is not an uncommon occurrence; the absence of the 3rd molar may occur in as much as 20 per cent of the sample (Banks 1934).

Palaeopathology
The study of diseases in past populations is important in providing information on the health of the individual and the population as a whole. Pathological changes in bone result from an imbalance in bone formation and resorption. Most diseases affect the soft tissue only and consequently do not induce bone change. In this assemblage the pathology rarely can be related to the individual.

Skeleton A, an adult male, has a fracture of the distal end of the shaft of the left ulna. The break is well healed and occurred some considerable time before death. The shaft is very slightly misaligned resulting in some slight shortening of the bone. Fractures of the lower end of the radius and ulna, the Colles fracture, are common throughout life. They are almost always the result of accidental injury in which the individual falls onto an outstretched hand.

A single lumbar vertebra exhibits a pit or small depression of the centre of the intervertebral surface. This is a Schmorls node, a lesion which arises during childhood and adolescence, the result of the intervertebral disc protruding into the adjacent vertebral body.

well defined. These are characteristics attributed to the male. Sexing was only attempted for the adults as the definitive traits used in sexing skeletal remains are not present until the onset of puberty. Consequently the reliability of sexing immature individuals is questionable.

Proportional representation
Morphological variations within the sample were impossible to establish from the limited measurements available from the assemblage. Nor were there sufficient opportunities available for the scoring of non-metrical traits in the skeleton. These are used in

Skeleton E, an adult, exhibits an arrested growth line at the distal end of the shaft of the right tibia. These are marks of increased mineral density caused by temporary arrested growth in childhood. In the same skeleton there is an enamel hypoplastic line of the crown of the right lateral incisor. This defect occurs during the enamel production. The defect is visible macroscopically as lines or pits on the surface of the tooth. Both arrested growth lines and enamel hypoplasia represent minor metabolic disorders manifest in osseous change, resulting from disturbances in the developmental stage of the skeleton. They may be due to a variety of causes including nutritional deprivation, disease and parasitic infection.

Most of the pathological conditions recorded were the result of degenerative disease. The degenerative arthritic diseases of the body may result, in part, from continued or successive trauma of a mild nature sustained over a period of years. They reflect everyday wear and tear on the body which is inseparable from a normal but vigorous life and consequently appear to be closely associated with advancing age. In archaeological material, degenerative changes consist of two conditions, vertebral osteophytosis and disc degeneration, and osteoarthrosis. These are separate entities and their aetiology is distinct (Manchester 1983, 65).

Three vertebral bodies from a single individual exhibit intervertebral osteochondrosis. The manifestations range from slight pitting of the vertebral body to complete destruction of the vertebral body plate with perforations and cyst formation. This condition is closely associated with vertebral osteophytosis, and results from pathological changes of the intervertebral disc, most probably a feature of age.

Osteoarthrosis or degenerative joint disease is a common disorder of the diathrodial joints. The features present in bone are associated with the destruction of the articular hyaline cartilage. Eburnation or bone polishing, osteophytic remodelling around the joint margins and porosity of the bone surface by subarticular cysts are all features of osteoarthrosis. The main clinical symptomatic effect on the individual is pain, loss of function of the joint and stiffness. The inferior apophyseal joints of two thoracic vertebrae exhibit eburnation of the marginal aspect of the joints. Skeleton E has osteoarthrosis of the right vertebral facet of the first thoracic vertebra. The odontoid facet of the atlas of an adult is severely affected, the articular surface has been completely destroyed and is highly eburnated. Associated with this is the growing and extension of the articular surface by new bone formation.

An adult male (A) has early degenerative change of the right acromio-clavicular joint visible as pitting and new bone deposition at the joint surfaces.

Skeleton B has incipient degenerative change of the left elbow joint visible in new bone at the margins of the articular surface of the ulna and humerus.

Skeleton F, an adult male, has osteophytic lipping of the distal articular surface of the left ulna thereby extending the articular surface.

Early degenerative change was also present as new bone at the right temporo-mandibular joint of an adult, to the head of a 1st metatarsal and to the sesamoid bone of the 1st metatarsal.

The left navicular bone of Skeleton A has a localized disorder of the talar joint surface, present as a shallow pit in the articular surface. This is the result of osteochrondritis dissecans in which an area of subchondral bone becomes avascular and necrotic separating to form a loose body in the joint (Adams 1981). The disease occurs in adolescents and young adults and is more common in males. The precise cause is unknown although impaired blood supply to the affected area has been suggested. There may be some susceptibility to the disease, and a familial occurrence has been observed (Ortner & Putschar 1985, 242). Trauma and mechanical stress have also been suggested as possible causes (Wells 1974).

Burial rite

The human bone comes from within the wooden structure and from the mound itself. The burials from the mound were both crouched inhumations; they are discrete burials and represent isolated instances (Fig. 3.3).

During the excavation a certain amount of articulation and patterning of the bone was noted from within the mortuary chamber. Subsequent post-excavation work confirmed and furthered our understanding of the relationship between identified bone types. From this study six distinct areas of articulation were found, representing a minimum of five individuals (Fig. 3.50).

At the western end of the structure, lying on the floor of the chamber was a fragmentary but well represented skeleton of an adult male, Skeleton A (Fig. 3.50). The body was aligned northeast–southwest with the head to the southeast. During the excavation of the skeleton the left femoral head was noted to be in its correct anatomical position, lying in the acetabulum of the left innominate. Elements of the vertebral column, and the distal end of the left tibia and tarsals, were also recorded as being in articulation. The upper part of the body, although fragmentary, can be seen to show

**Figure 3.49.** *Looking west along the mortuary chamber with human bone* in situ. *(Photograph G. Owen.)*

that the bones were in their correct position (Fig. 3.50 combined with the observations made on site). The arms were lying by the side of the body while the legs appeared to be flexed, the left leg uppermost, suggesting that the body was lying on its right side.

The remains of the upper body of a second individual (F), an adult male, lay directly over the trunk of Skeleton A (Fig. 3.50). The body is represented by a complete but fragmentary skull, lower jaw, upper cervical vertebrae, left arm and possibly the distal end of the right humerus (Bone no. 360). The left humeral head and the glenoid cavity of the scapula were recorded, on site, as being in articulation. The position of the atlas and axis immediately beneath the base of the compressed skull indicates that they too were almost certainly in articulation with the occipital condyles of the skull. Finally, the position of the ulna and radius of the forearm lying side by side, with the proximal articular surfaces located close to the distal end of the humerus, suggests that the left arm was complete. While the right arm was incomplete and not in articulation, the size and general appearance suggested that it was from the same individual. The head was to the north of the rest of the upper body, although the orientation of the individual is questionable.

To the southern aspect of the western end of the mortuary structure were the remains of the lower trunk, arms and legs of a third individual, Skeleton B (Fig. 3.50). The legs were in their correct anatomical position with the patellae located at the distal end of the femora and proximal end of the tibiae, and the tarsals and metatarsals at the distal end of the tibiae and fibulae. However, the degree of flexion between the femur and tibia, which lay parallel to each other, would have been impossible in life. The orientation and bedding of the bone suggests that there was some slipping and movement within the depression caused by the western axial post.

A child aged 2–4 years, Skeleton D (Fig. 3.50), was located on the northwest side of the structure, lying on one of the horizontal wooden planks. The body was badly fragmented and disturbed; however, elements of the vertebral column appeared to be in articulation and the ribs lay in an organized anatomical arrangement. The fragmentary remains of this child were all contained in a small localized area, suggesting that this was a discrete burial and was at least partially, and more probably fully, articulated.

Lying on the wooden floor to the front of the burial area were the articulated lower legs of an adult, Skeleton E (Fig. 3.50). The legs were in a crouched position with the body lying on its right side and oriented southwest–northeast with the head to the southwest. From the limits of the wooden floor the

body was disturbed and incomplete. To the west of the legs lay the remains of a fragmentary skull which was in the correct position for the head of the same individual. Other components of the body were to be found within the trough or depression which ran centrally through the mortuary structure from southwest to northeast.

Finally, and the most questionable example of articulation, is the position of the femur, patella and tibia of Skeleton C (Fig. 3.50). The bones lay in their correct anatomical position with the patella located close to the proximal end of the tibia and distal end of the femur. However, the bones were particularly badly compressed and fractured.

Preservation

The preservation of the human bone from the long barrow is poor with the exception of the infant burial in the mound external to the mortuary structure. The other crouched inhumation within the mound was extremely poorly preserved, only the long bones being identifiable, the bones of the hands, feet and vertebral column only visible as a soil stain. Those bones which had survived to fossilization were difficult to identify other than by their position as the surface of the bones was covered in a thick concretion, a mixture of sand cemented by iron salts resulting from iron panning. This made only limited observations on the bone possible.

Within the mortuary structure, the bones were poorly preserved with a high degree of post-mortem fragmentation. Wherever possible some attempt at reconstruction was made, although this was more to obtain an accurate estimate of the minimum number of individuals than to look at the problems of preservation.

The bone appears to have been heavily mineralized prior to fossilization and this may account for much of its inherent fragility. Some 2848 fragments were recovered from the bone deposits within the mortuary structure. Only 38 bones representing 1.3 per cent of the entire assemblage were complete. These were all small bones of the hands and feet, including carpals, tarsals, metacarpals and phalanges, although a single clavicle was also complete. 79 per cent of the total bone assemblage from within the structure was under 50 mm in size, 19 per cent was between 50–100 mm, and only 2 per cent of the fragments were larger than 100 mm (Table 3.8). The articular ends of the bones were rarely present and had been subjected to erosion exposing the trabeccular bone. A large percentage of the assemblage consisted of small unidentifiable fragments.

The type and angle of post-mortem fracture was recorded for every bone fragment. Many of the bones

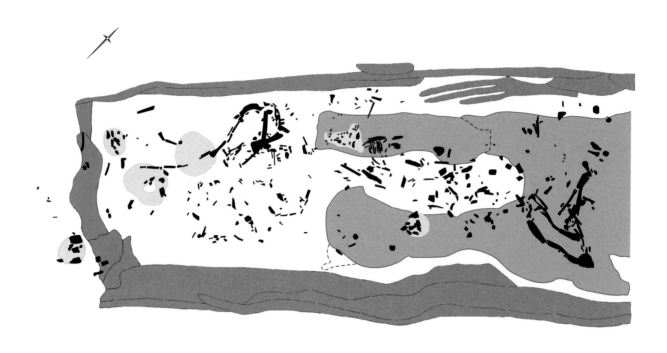

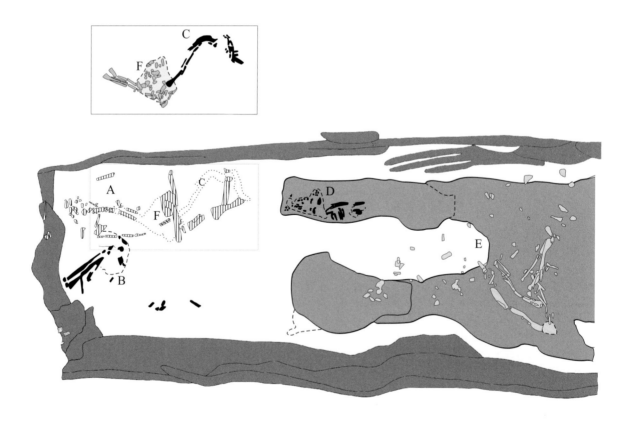

**Figure 3.50**. *Mortuary structure human bone deposits. Top, distribution of bone; below, interpretation of body position.*

Table 3.8. *Size and relative proportions of bone fragments.*

| Size | No. | % |
|---|---|---|
| 10 mm | 18 | |
| 20 mm | 145 | |
| 30 mm | 114 | |
| 40 mm | 64 | |
| | | 78.7 |
| 50 mm | 39 | |
| 60 mm | 17 | |
| 70 mm | 17 | |
| 80 mm | 7 | |
| 90 mm | 2 | |
| | | 19.4 |
| 100 mm | 1 | |
| 110 mm | 3 | |
| 120 mm | 3 | |
| 130 mm | 1 | |
| 140 mm | | |
| 150 mm | 2 | |
| | | 2.1 |

Table 3.9. *Type and percentage of post-mortem fractures.*

| Postmortem fracture | No. | % |
|---|---|---|
| Linear / longitudinal | 117 | 38 |
| Transverse | 156 | 50.5 |
| Curved | 17 | 5.5 |
| Cracked | 4 | 1.3 |
| Oblique | 13 | 4.2 |

Table 3.10. *Percentages of bone in particular colour categories.*

| Bone colour | % |
|---|---|
| Black | 75.5 |
| Red / Brown | 5.4 |
| Orange | 2.7 |
| Light blue / violet | 2.7 |
| Grey | 7.1 |
| White / cream | 8.3 |

Skeleton A must have been earlier as the skull and pectoral girdle of Skeleton F lay directly over it (Fig. 3.50).

The colour of the bone within the mortuary deposits ranged from black through to white including a progression of colours through brown-grey, light blue / violet, cream and light grey, with some bones exhibiting a range of colours. 75 per cent of the assemblage was in the black category with only 18 per cent in the light grey-white; 8.3 per cent were white (Table 3.10).

The degree of movement of bone within the chamber is visible in Figure 3.55, shown by joins between fragments of the same bone. The movement is predominantly along the east–west axis of the structure and fits well within the confines of the wooden structure (see *Human bone distributions* below).

fractured on lifting; however, it was almost impossible to separate these from the other fractures and they were included in the final impression. 88 per cent fall into the transverse and longitudinal category, while only 4.2 per cent were oblique fractures (Table 3.9).

Proportional representation of different bones of the body from the skeletal remains in the mortuary structure was estimated by recording the number of occasions in which individual types of bones were represented and then by expressing this as a percentage of the predicted number calculated from the minimum number of individuals (Table 3.6). The femora alone are present on 100 per cent of occasions, although the tibiae, fibulae, ulnae and skull are all well represented (80 per cent of occasions). Indeed, the long bones are represented in every individual with the exception of the child Skeleton D. The vertebrae are less well represented, although surprisingly the cervical vertebrae are well represented, in particular the atlas and axis (80 per cent). In general, the vertebrae more often than not were present as fragments of the neural arch, which survives better than the more fragile vertebral body. The bones which were least often present are the smaller bones of the hands and feet and the flat bones, the ribs and innominate.

Evidence, from the human remains, for chronological use of the monument comes firstly from the two inhumations in the mound which must have been interred during the mound construction. Secondly, the only evidence for chronological deposition in the chamber comes from the deposition of burials A and F.

Other marks
A single bone produced cut marks which have been examined by Dr Jennifer Wakely of the Department of Anatomy, University of Leicester, and is reported upon by her below. There is no evidence for gnawing of the bones by animals.

The specimen consists of the distal end of the right humerus of a small adult individual (Skeleton F; Bone no. 360). The bone is deeply stained black and this colouration has penetrated throughout the compact and cancellous parts of the bone. Additionally patches of a crumbly orange deposit are present on the bone surface. X-ray microanalysis of these deposits in the scanning electron microscope shows the presence of high concentrations of iron (Fig. 3.53).

Cut marks are present on the anterior, medial and posterior aspects of the bone in the areas of attachment of the brachialis muscle anteriorly and the medial head of the triceps posteriorly and medially (Fig. 3.51). There are six strong and two faint cut marks confined to the anterior surface of the bone. The deeper cuts form intersecting pairs. Four cuts, two forming a pair, extend from the anterior to the medial side. Five short cut marks are confined to the medial border of the bone and 15 cuts extend from the medial to the posterior aspect. The cut surfaces are of the same black colour as the rest of the bone, and in places contain the orange iron-rich deposits. The similarity argues against their having been recently inflicted.

A latex replica was made of the medial and posterior aspects of the bone from which a resin cast was prepared for examination in the scanning electron microscope (Shipman & Rose 1983; Andrews & Cook 1985; Wakely & Wenham 1988). The poorer preservation of the anterior aspect prevented the use of this method for that part, which was viewed only in a binocular dissecting microscope.

The microscopial features of the bone surface are blurred to some extent by weathering but nevertheless the following characteristics are common to all the cuts:
1. A straight or almost straight course over the bone surface (Fig. 3.51);
2. Sharply defined boundaries (Fig. 3.51);
3. One or both extremities, usually the most posterior, sharply pointed (Fig. 3.51:C);

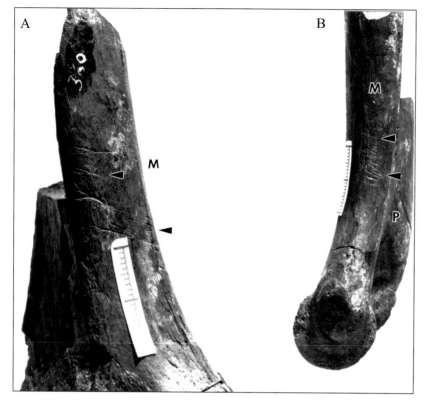

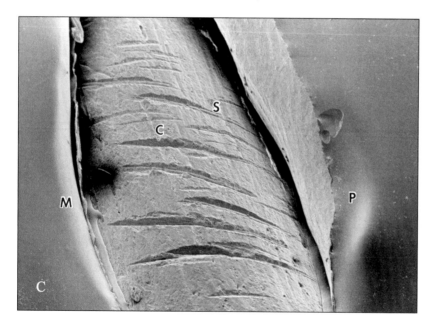

**Figure 3.51.** *The anterior (A) and medial and posterior (B) aspects of the Skeleton F humerus showing cut marks (arrowed; scale in cm). C) Low-powered scanning electron micrograph showing a group of cut marks on the medial to posterior aspects of the bone: M = medial; P = posterior; C = chattered surface; S = smoother surface.*

4. A marked directionality, either anterior to medial or medial to posterior in many cuts, with one end 'chattered' and the other smooth, with fine longitudinal parallel striations on the walls of the cut (Figs. 3.51 & 3.52);

5. A slightly asymmetrical 'U'-shaped profile (Fig. 3.52:B).

Similar features are characteristic of the marks produced by the impact of stone on bone in a number of experimental studies and were also recorded in observations of natural skeletal decay (Shipman & Rose 1983; Andrews & Cook 1985; Brommage & Boyde 1984; Cook 1986b). Their clear definition and the presence of fine striations within the main cut mark points to the cuts having been made recently after death while substantial amounts of organic matrix remained in the bone structure (Brothwell 1971). They bear a particularly close resemblance to cuts made with a slicing action (Shipman & Rose 1983).

It is important but not always easy to distinguish between cut marks occurring naturally as the bone is scraped by stones in the burial environment and cut marks inflicted deliberately by human activity using stone implements in the course of funeral rituals or other behaviour involving manipulation of the dead. Straightforward examination of the marks themselves may not always give an unequivocal answer, but circumstantial evidence may assist in arriving at a reasonable conclusion.

On the bone in question the cut marks are noticeably grouped in the attachment areas of brachialis and the medial head of the triceps and not found elsewhere. This clustering, together with the directionality in their gross and fine structure, is unlikely to have been produced by random and undirected rubbing against stones but is suggestive of purposeful human activity. Chatter marks, in particular, are typical of cuts made with stone tools (Olsen & Shipman 1988). If we accept this, the next question concerns the meaning of the marks. Comparative studies are a useful aid in interpreting their significance.

A two-stage burial rite involving excarnation of the body and separate burial of the bones with or without selection and sorting is widespread in Neolithic Europe (Atkinson 1965; Ucko 1969; Grinsell 1975; Burl 1981; Jacobsen & Cullen 1981; Hedges 1983; Gilks 1989) and in many parts of the world even in recent times (Ucko 1969; Tainter 1978; Burl 1981; Bloch & Parry 1982; Henderson 1988). The ritual may involve only exposure to the weather and to scavenging animals to reduce the body naturally to a skeleton, or it may involve deliberate cleaning of partly skeletonized bodies by cutting or scraping away soft tissue such as muscles and ligaments. Patterning of cut marks and their grouping in areas of muscle and ligamentous attachment is suggestive of this practice (Cook 1991; Olsen & Shipman 1988) whether the bones are human or animal.

De Laet (1958) described a collection of disarticulated bones from a Neolithic burial at Furfooz, Belgium, of which at least 50 show cut marks. He interpreted this finding as evidence of excarnation by deliberate removal of soft tissue. Fulcheri *et al.* (1986) illustrate a specimen from Ponte Paolina, Sicily, consisting of the distal end of a humerus with grouped cut marks in the same area of muscle attachment as on the bone from Haddenham. They, too, regard the marks as evidence of this practice.

A variety of marked human bones dating from the glacial period were found at Gough's Cave, Somerset (Cook 1986a; 1991). Ullrich (1982) and Russell (1987) have also observed patterned cut marks on various bones, including humeri and including their anterior and postero-medial borders from Palaeolithic sites in Europe. Deliberate dismemberment of the body, whether in a burial rite or from other purposes, is seen by these authors as the most likely explanation for the presence and clustering of cut marks on such bones.

Similarities between examples like these and the bones examined in the present study suggest that it, too, has been subject to intentional defleshing involving removal of the brachialis and triceps muscles from their attachments to the bone. Both of these muscles take origin from the humerus by means of many short tendon fibres that bind the deep surface of the muscle to the bone over a broad area of attachment. Removing the muscle requires many short slicing cuts to undercut the muscle and peel it away from the bone (Fig. 3.54). This would inevitably scrape the bone surface if one were attempting to clean off the muscle as completely as possible, especially with the relatively thick and serrated blade of a stone implement.

At present the available evidence does not permit any further speculation on the treatment of this bone, beyond the conclusion that the cuts were probably inflicted during removal of the brachialis and triceps muscles of the arm from their bony origins, and this may have been part of the funeral ritual practised by the people using the barrow.

## Interpretation

*Selective processes:* One of the most fundamental questions to be asked of any burial monument concerns the selective process for burial. The human bone assemblage within the mortuary structure at Foulmire Fen does little to further our understanding of the processes. Only two of the four adults could be positively sexed; both were male. A common feature of many Neolithic collective burials is the under-representation of women. In this context it does not reflect selective processes for burial, so much as the problems inherent in sexing skeletal remains, compounded by the fragmentary and incomplete nature of the deposits. The determination of sex is dependent upon the differences in robustness between the sexes and the adaptation of the female for childbirth.

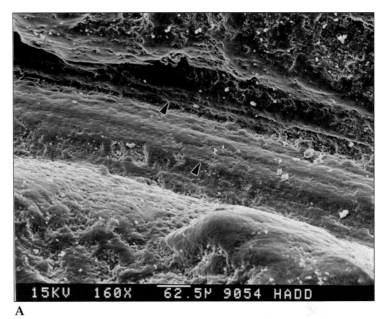

A

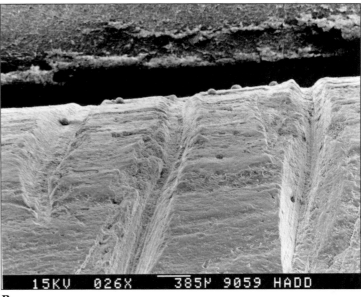

B

**Figure 3.52.** *A) Scanning electron micrograph showing the fine parallel striations on the wall of a cut mark (arrowed). B) Scanning electron micrograph to show the shape of the cut marks in profile, also the presence of parallel striations on their walls.*

In fragmentary assemblages the more pronounced features will be more positively scored than the less pronounced; consequently the females will have a tendency to be more frequently placed in the unsexed category. At Haddenham none of the adults could be identified as female. However, Skeleton B was noted to be more gracile in appearance than the other skeletons and a tentative suggestion is that this individual may represent a woman.

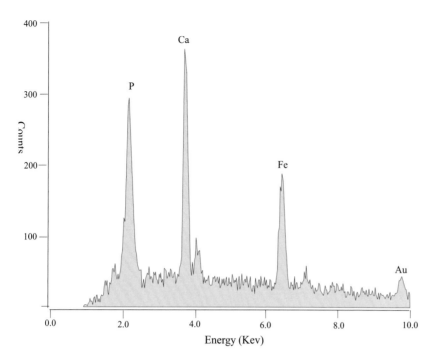

**Figure 3.53.** *Spectrum obtained by X-ray microanalysis of the orange deposits on the humerus, showing high concentrations of iron (Fe) in addition to the calcium (Ca) and phosphorus (P) expected from bone and the gold (Au) from the coating applied during processing for the scanning electron microscope.*

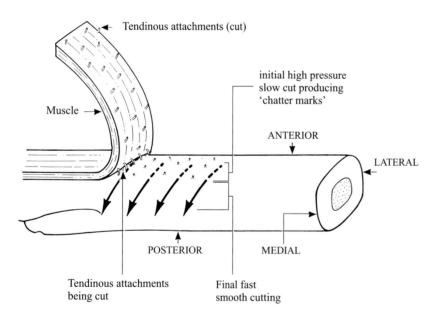

**Figure 3.54.** *Illustration of the manner in which the brachialis and triceps muscles may be peeled away from their humeral attachments.*

The mortality curve for the population buried in the long barrow is no more informative. Four of the individuals are adult, but the degree of fragmentation resulted in it only being possible to place them in a very

broad age category. The fifth skeleton from the mortuary structure is that of a young child. In prehistoric and pre-industrial communities, the literature on infant mortality indicates that 32–50 per cent of individuals died before reaching adulthood with about 11 per cent of deaths sustained within the first year of life (Hassan 1973; see also Zubrow, Volume 2, Chapter 6). The under-representation of juveniles and the absence of neonatal and infant bones in the Haddenham long barrow requires some explanation. The first possibility is that the absence of infant burials reflects cultural practices excluding the burial of the very young. Alternatively, the more fragile bones of infants and young children would have been unlikely to survive to fossilization given the degree of post-mortem fragmentation and weathering visible in the extant bone assemblage.

*Arrangement of the bone deposits:* The arrangement of the bone is funda-mental to the interpretation of burial rite. The two crouched inhumations within the mound proper were iso-lated occurrences. Secondary burials within earthen long barrows are not uncommon; the most frequent local-ity for these burials is either within the mound or dug into the ditch silts. They are all single graves and may be either extended or crouched, only rarely containing any grave goods (Ashbee 1984).

The evidence for articulation within the mortuary structure argues for the disposal of the body whilst still in articulation (Skeletons A, D & E), with some evidence for subse-quent rearrangement (Skeleton B & F). Movement of the bones is visible in the arrangement of the lower half of the body of Skeleton B, resulting either from the bones slipping into the depression caused by the axial post, or as a result of a previously articulated inhu-mation being pushed to one side to make room for a later burial. The upper body of Skeleton of F may also represent the remnants of a partially cleared burial.

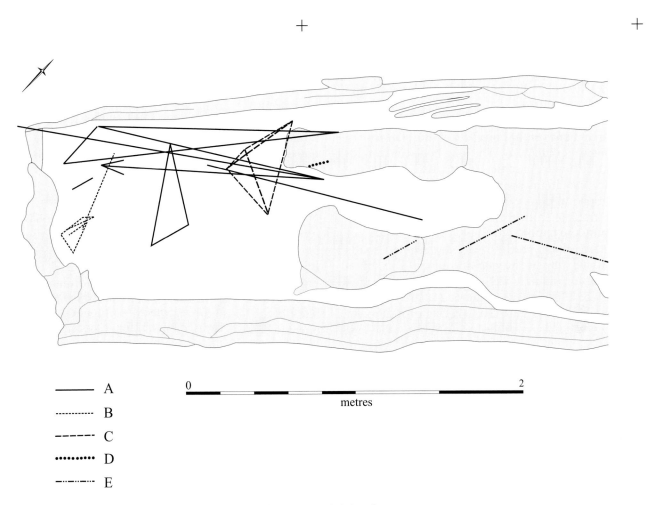

|   |   |
|---|---|
| ——— | A |
| ------------ | B |
| – – – – – | C |
| •••••••••• | D |
| –··–··–··– | E |

**Figure 3.55.** *The displacement of human bone showing conjoining fragments.*

Movement within the mortuary structure also can be seen in the concentration of disarticulated bone in the centre of the mortuary structure along the east–west axis. This corresponds with the observations on the bedding and orientation of the bone, which appears to show that the bone has slipped into a trough, or depression, between the two horizontal planks on either side of the wooden structure (see below). Figure 3.55 shows the movement of bone, plotting the position of bones from adjoining fragments and for individual skeletons where applicable. The solid line represents the position of the wood within the mortuary structure, again showing the maximum movement to be within the confines of the wood.

*Taphonomy:* The survival of bone to fossilization is dependent upon soil conditions and the rate of the destructive processes. At Haddenham all of the material had been subjected to a high degree of postmortem fragmentation. The bone is mineralized, the result of impregnation by iron salts, and there is some

iron panning surrounding the bone, particularly of the adult skeleton within the mound itself (Skeleton 2). The effect of both heavy mineral impregnation and waterlogging as well as the effect of water movement within the monument has yet to be established. It is, however, possible that erosion and degradation of the more fragile bones of the body and those bones where the cancellous tissue had been exposed may have resulted in total bone destruction, and in some instances account for their absence.

*Proportional representation:* The reasons for the disparity in the relative numbers of different bones of the body are numerous. Their absence may be due to loss prior to secondary burial in the tomb. This had been used by Chesterman and Hedges to support the theory of excarnation in the disarticulated and disorganized bone deposits in the chambered tomb of Isbister, Orkney (in Hedges 1983). At Haddenham the burial deposits are by no means disorganized and it seems unlikely, given the degree of articulation, that the bodies were exposed prior to burial. The absence of many of the bones must therefore reflect either intentional cultural selection of specific bones, and their subsequent removal from the mortuary structure, or be accounted for by differential preservation and loss during excavation.

To some extent the proportional representation of different bones of the body reflects the character of the bone itself (Table 3.6). The long bones or weight-supporting bones are conical in structure, with dense compact bone in the shaft and cancellous or spongy bone at the articular ends. The shaft is therefore less vulnerable to fracture and weathering, as can be seen by the femora which are present on 100 per cent of occasions, and the well-represented shafts of the tibiae, fibulae, humeri and ulnae. The spinal column is surprisingly well represented; more often than not only fragments of the neural arch survive. The vertebral body, which has a higher proportion of spongy bone, is more prone to weathering. The best illustration of this is given by the odontoid peg and facet of the atlas and axis which were present on 80 per cent of occasions. Again, these are areas of the vertebra with a high ratio of dense cortical bone and little cancellous tissue.

The flat bones are less well represented. They are composed of thin layers of compact bone enclosing variable amounts of cancellous tissue, and are consequently more susceptible to taphonomic processes. The manubrium and sternum are rarely present while the scapula is reasonably well represented, although only the glenoid cavity and fragments of the acromion process and axillary border survive, areas of the bone designed for strength. The innominate is present in 60 per cent of cases but was very poorly preserved, and in at least two instances the bone was only possible to identify because of its position (Skeletons A & B).

The greatest disparity is in the smaller bones of the hands and feet. At Haddenham they are under-represented but still are not uncommon findings. If the child burial is discounted, the percentage increases to the figure given in brackets in Table 3.6, and is not too dissimilar to the proportional representation of other bones of the body. Moreover, in inhumation cemetery excavations where excavation conditions and the preservation of the body are good, the smaller bones of the hands and feet are still frequently overlooked.

*Post-mortem fracture:* The condition of the bone and the activities which lead to their breakage may be implicated in the type of post-mortem fracture. At Haddenham, the pattern of breakage was predominantly longitudinal and transverse. These are breaks commonly found in dry bone, where the organic and fat content is reduced. They are produced by lateral pressure, which would be consistent with damage inflicted during the collapse of the monument and from the weight of the mound. Some damage may also have occurred during access to the chamber. Oblique and spiral fractures, on the other hand, occur predominantly in new bone. They result from bending or twisting actions, although spiral fractures may also be the product of trampling. Very few of these fractures were present within the assemblage (Table 3.8).

*Burning:* The human bone assemblage at Haddenham was closely studied for evidence of burning, recording bone colour, patterns of bone cracking and shrinkage. In cremation studies bone colour has been used as an indication of the temperature at which burning took place, with a progression of colour from the blue-black of the least burnt to the buff-white of the most burnt (Ubelaker 1974). Other studies have suggested that the amount of oxygen is also important in the determination of colour, with low-temperature colours resulting from a lack of free circulation of air (Parker 1985). Colour may also be indicative of the state of the body, a certain amount of body fat aids combustion and in modern-day cremations the initial input of heat is only maintained until the body fats are alight (McKinley 1989).

The pattern of bone cracking in cremated bone studies has been used to establish whether the bone was burnt in a fleshed or defleshed state. Baby (1954) noted that in fleshed cremations transverse curved fracture lines, irregular longitudinal splitting and some warping and splintering occur, while in defleshed bone superficial checking, fine and deep longitudinal fractures and no warping are more common. Bone shrinkage is also a significant element in cremation deposits. Again this is a feature of temperature; below a critical temperature level shrinkage may not occur.

The material from Haddenham shows evidence for only moderate burning. The legs of Skeleton E are light in colour exhibiting irregular longitudinal splitting and some warping and deformation of the bone. These features are consistent with high temperature burning in a fleshed or partially fleshed state. The majority of the deposits (75 per cent) on the other hand are black in colour, with no warping or bone shrinkage and transverse and longitudinal cracks. These features are more in keeping with either scorching or low temperature burning with breakage or fractures to defleshed bone. The enamel of the teeth in cremated deposits tends to shatter, as the enamel structure is rigid and does not allow for expansion of the molecules, exposing the underlying dentine.

The majority of the teeth have lost their enamel, however in at least two instances the crowns survive. The unerupted tooth crowns of the child, Skeleton D, also survive, presumably because they were protected by their position within the jaw.

One explanation for the condition of the bone might be that the burning of the mortuary structure was the final act before closure, with the majority of the bodies in a skeletal or defleshed state. The exception is Skeleton E, which may represent a late burial. The general colour of the bone indicates that the burning temperature was low or the flow of oxygen restricted. Alternatively, the bone may simply have taken up the stain from the underlying blackened and waterlogged timbers before it became mineralized, although this explanation does not account for the lighter colours and the twisting and warping of the long bones of Skeleton E. (NB Lying immediately beside the turf mound Skeleton E would have been exposed to the most intense temperatures: Figs. 3.19 & 3.24 & 3.50.)

*Cut marks and gnawing*: The absence of gnawing marks on the bone is significant in two respects. The gnawing of bones has been used in some studies to support the argument that the bodies were exposed in a position accessible to scavenging animals prior to burial in the monument. Secondly, their absence supports the archaeologists' interpretation that the wooden structure was not open for any length of time. The cut marks to the distal end of the humerus have been discussed above (J. Wakely).

## Conclusion

A total of seven individuals were buried at the Haddenham long barrow. A minimum of five of these were interred in the mortuary structure, and a further two individuals were buried in the barrow mound. There is no evidence for exposure of the bodies whether through weathering or gnawing of the long bones. The patterning within the burial chamber shows that the bodies were placed in the chamber whilst still in articulation and some may have been later pushed to one side to make way for later burials. The presence of cut marks to the right humerus of one suggests that there may have been some form of ritual which involved the removal of soft tissue from the bones.

### Addendum

Originally attributed as animal bone, four pieces of adult human bone (and a tooth) were omitted from the above analysis. Identified by N. Dodwell, these are:

1. [3080] <27531>: Refitting fragments of a tibia midshaft (82 mm length) from the northern terminal of the surrounding ditch (F.749: Fig. 3.64);
2. [3045] <27557>: Skull fragments from southern terminal of surrounding ditch (F.749: Fig. 3.64);
3. [2883] <27847>: Refitting fragments of the distal half of left humerus (138 mm; the extreme distal end is missing) from the mound in Trench E (Fig. 3.64);
4. [3720] <28065>: A left 3rd metatarsal (unburnt) from the fill of the medial mortuary structure post pit (F.706);
5. [3443] <28069>: A fragment of a parietal bone (skull), measuring *c.* 25 × 19 mm and a ?3rd maxillary molar was recovered from the fill of the distal post pit (F.705), into which it had presumable slipped. Two of the roots of the tooth are broken off and while the occlusal surface of the crown is intact, other aspects appear to have eroded away. Both elements are black in colour.

### Human bone distributions
with P. SHAND

If the bones had indeed been moved, however slightly, an effect should be visible in the spatial sorting of bone sizes and in the orientation and bedding of the bones. Full analyses of such patterning were carried out, whose results are summarized here (Fig. 3.55):

*Bone bedding*: The angle at which the human bone rested was recorded *in situ*. The bones were allocated by eye to general categories such as horizontal, less than 15° and more than 15°. Only the bone recorded *in situ* could be used (i.e. not the bone recovered by sieving) and only 268 pieces were sufficently large to suggest a clear bedding angle.

In general there is a high proportion of bone at fairly steep angles: 60% was at angles less than 15°, 27% was less than 30° and 17% was angled at greater than 30°. The proportion of bone at steeper angles tended to be greater on the sides of the chamber. It was observed in the field that much of the skeletal material lay on the sides of the central trough, the edges of which dipped 15–30° towards the central axis of the mortuary structure. If the bone was originally laid on the sides of the central trough it is not surprising that a high proportion of the bone in this area is steeply bedded.

There was also an increase in sharply bedded bone east of $X = 4.0$ m, which was particularly marked east of $X = 5.0$ m. The burials at this point were closer to the central trough than they were west of $X = 4.0$ m, and they were laid on the oak floor rather than directly on the ground. While the floor would originally have been flat, when it slumped into the trough the bones would have tended to dip towards the centre. It is probably this effect which has made the bedding more steeply angled towards the east.

A high proportion of steeply bedded bone was also found west of $X = 3.0$ m. The reason for this again lies in the micro-topography. The bone is here slipping down into the hollow above the distal post pit.

*Bone orientation*: The *in situ* larger bones were categorized by eye into general categories of orientation (four categories were used). 181 pieces were recorded in this way; the data in each instance was also compared with the bedding angle to produce an orientation of bedding.

Along the north edge of the mortuary structure 54% of the bone dipped to the south, along the southern edge 61% dipped towards the north and in the central trough 50% dipped north or south. This pattern is clearly the result of the slight slumping of the bones into the central trough. A high percentage of bone also dipped west at $X = 4.5$–5.5 m. This may be connected to the collapse of the oak floor

**Table 3.11.** *Summary of phosphate results.*

| Survey | No. samples | Mean | St. dev. | Min. | Max. |
|--------|-------------|------|----------|------|------|
| 1 | 159 | 55 | 27 | 19 | 170 |
| 2 | 68 | 194 | 112 | 37 | 360 |
| 3 | 78 | 200 | 125 | 18 | 380 |
| 4 | 231 | 42 | 15 | 13 | 94 |
| 5 | 20 | 16 | 6 | 9 | 36 |

here and it may suggest that the floor slumped to the west first; most of the bone west of $X = 3.0$ m bedded west where it slumped into the top of the distal post pit.

*Bone size*: All the human bones recovered from the mortuary structure were measured either *in situ* or after sieving. A difficulty with interpreting size-based spatial distributions is that bones from smaller individuals (such as a child) will not be distinguished in the statistics from highly fragmented larger bones. Certainly some of the localizations of small bone encountered correspond with the child burial in the mortuary structure. However, a general trend emerged for larger bone to occur in the central trough. It may well be the case that the bone survived better in the trough because the bones at the sides endured the full weight of the timbers and mound directly upon them. Finally, very small bone was found west of $X = 2.5$ m. We have already seen that the bone here was dipping into the top of the distal post pit. It has also been noted in the bone report that the bone here was relatively disarticulated and re-arranged. These factors may have contributed to its fragmented nature.

In summary, much of the patterning of the bone sizes, bedding and orientation is the result of slight movement into the central trough and into the top of the distal post pit. There is little evidence of any deliberate sorting of the bone fragments beyond that already identified. The overall evidence supports the view that little disturbance of the bones took place and that access and activities were relatively restricted within the chamber.

*Phosphate surveys*
by D. GURNEY
Five areas were sampled, with samples being taken on a 20-cm grid. The samples received were extremely wet and clayey, and considerable care had to be taken to ensure that there was no contamination of each sample by the last when pre-treating. After being air-dried for several weeks, the samples were crushed and passed through a 1.4-mm mesh to provide a sample of 1+ g for analysis. The method of analysis used is based on the molybdenum blue method of Murphy & Riley (1962; for details and references see Gurney 1985). The sample areas were:

*Survey 1*: Samples were taken from an area just outside (to the south of) the proximal posts, along the line of the façade trench. Samples were also taken north of the proximal chamber, inside the line of the façade trench and along the line of the façade-bank.

*Survey 2*: Burial chamber, upper sampling level. From the fine black organic silt at the top of the layer [3337]/[3339] — the main burial deposits. Along the north and south edges of the chamber, traces of the oak floor were beginning to appear. Approximately 5–10 cm above the sampling horizon of Survey 3.

*Survey 3*: Burial chamber; lower sampling level. At the base of layer [3337]/[3339] after removal of the main bone deposit. In places, the sandy clay subsoil was showing, and also the oak floor. Approximately 5–10 cm below the sampling horizon of Survey 2.

*Survey 4*: Samples were taken from the gravel pavement or forecourt, over an area to the south of the proximal posts just outside the façade trench.

*Survey 5*: Samples were taken from the eastern (proximal) chamber of the mortuary structure, between the medial and proximal posts. The sampled horizon was the floor level, a sandy clay subsoil and a black organic silt where this occasionally adhered to wood. No human bone was found in this area, and the survey was undertaken as a control.

*Survey 1*: The results here are generally higher than values from the forecourt (Survey 4), and are markedly higher than the values from the proximal chamber (Survey 5). The highest values in Survey 1 are fairly well scattered, but immediately east (outside) the proximal posts, values are consistently low across a 1-m-wide strip in front of the posts. On either side of this strip, slightly higher values occur, mixed with lower values, and this more so to the south than to the north. While values from the 'low' strip are higher than results from the proximal chamber, the strip is low in comparison with the rest of the façade/forecourt area, suggesting that the phosphate results define some feature related to the point of access to the mortuary structure. This could have been, for example, a 'clean' pathway across the forecourt area.

*Surveys 2/3* (Fig. 3.56): These surveys of the burial deposits in the distal chamber are considered together; the results suggest a number of enhanced areas within the burial chamber. The most marked feature of the phosphate distribution is the apparent division of the chamber, both transversely and longitudinally, this being particularly clear at the west end of the chamber in Survey 2 (Fig. 3.56). A transverse division (dividing the chamber into east and west sub-chambers) is defined by low phosphate values along grid E3.60 and E3.80, and a longitudinal division is defined by low values along grid N2.40. This suggested patterning is less well-defined in the lower Survey 3, while in the eastern half of the chamber the results of both surveys suggest that the higher results are more centred within the chamber, and no low values divide the chamber into north and south area of enhancement. The relationship between areas of enhancement and the burials defined in the chamber is considered below.

*Survey 4*: The results show no consistent or apparently meaningful patterning, and the highest results are well scattered: the mean value of 42 mg, and the highest value is only 94 mg. There do not appear to be any areas of significant enhancement on the forecourt.

*Survey 5*: The results are consistently low, the highest value being only 36 mg, and the mean value 16 mg. These are the lowest values encountered, and are lower than the results from outside the mortuary structure (Surveys 1 & 4). The results from Survey 5 (the proximal chamber) contrast dramatically with those from the distal chamber (Surveys 2 & 3), the medial post dividing these two areas. It seems certain that the proximal chamber never contained burials, and on the basis of the phosphate evidence, one might suggest, tentatively, that the proximal chamber was kept scrupulously clean.

The burial chamber

As noted above, the results from the burial chamber (especially Survey 2) suggest division of the chamber, both longitudinally and transversely. This is best seen in a simple plot of high values from both surveys (Fig. 3.56.III), and this can be compared to the plan of bone in the burial chamber. On Figure 3.56 the skulls and the probable outlines of the body areas (where known) are indicated by grey tone. In the western half of the chamber, west of grid E3.5, there are two groups of high values, both aligned east to west. The north group of five high values coincides with burial group A/F/C — three adult inhumations. The high results here come from east of each skull, and just north of the bone scatter

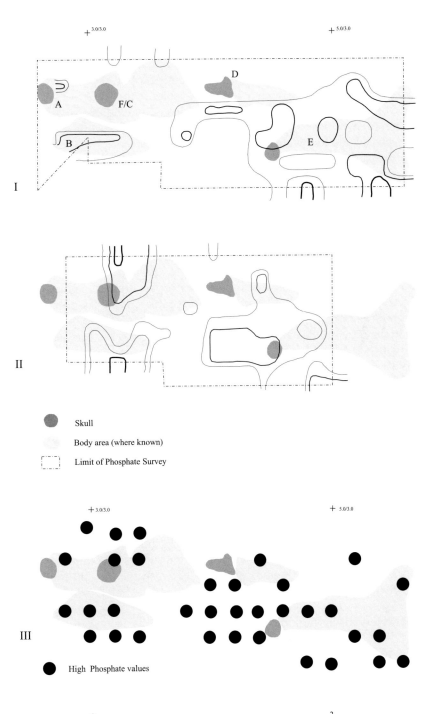

**Figure 3.56.** *Phosphate survey: I) Survey 2 (A–F indicates skeleton location); II) Survey 3; III) combined phosphate values.*

from the eastern of the inhumations. This might suggest some movement, the burials perhaps originally being positioned a little closer to the north edge of the chamber. The southern group of six high values is associated with Skeleton B, with high phosphate values extending to the south of the bone scatter, again suggesting some movement of the bones towards the central depression. In the western half of the distal sub-chamber, the phosphate results are therefore consistent with the observed bone distribution, with (most probably) pairs of inhumations aligned east to west on either side of the chamber.

In the eastern half of the chamber, east of grid E3.5, the distribution of high values presents a less coherent pattern. This may be largely due to undefined processes of disturbance or movement in this part of the chamber. There are three or four high values in the area of the child inhumation D, and perhaps as many as ten high values associated with adult inhumation E. One isolated high value north of E and towards the northeast corner of the survey area appears to relate to a small group of five or so bones. There are two further areas with high values: 1) a group of seven high results west of the skull E and south of infant D; and 2) two high values south of E; neither group can be related to observed bone deposits.

In summary, at least some high phosphate values can be directly equated with all the defined burial groups in the distal sub-chamber, especially bone groups A/F/C, B, D, and E. Corpses rank very high as a source of phosphates, especially the skeleton (Bakkevig 1980, table 1). Hammond cites figures of 600–800 g P for a body, mostly in the skeleton (1983, 47), and Johnson gives the figure of 630 g P for a 70 kg male, 80 per cent of which is the skeleton (1954–56, 203). It is not, therefore, surprising that these relatively undisturbed burials have generated areas of significant phosphate enhancement in the burial chamber.

Beyond the burial chamber, the proximal chamber produced extremely low results, and this was clearly not used for burials or any other activities which might generate a phosphate enhancement. It may have been kept clean. There is some patterning of results in the forecourt area, particularly immediately in front of the mortuary structure. This might suggest a 'clean' path across the forecourt area between the hornwork of the fore-structure.

## Overview discussion: burial contexts

The evidence from the human bones, difficult as it is, lends support to the idea of a long controlled or low temperature burning of the chamber with higher temperatures associated with the burnt turf mound (Skeleton E). But this burning was only one aspect of a complex burial ritual.

The human remains would seem to suggest that the use of the chamber was relatively short-lived. There are not large numbers of disarticulated bones resulting from a long period of disposal and reordering. There are no gnawing marks or indications of weathering which would suggest that the chamber or the bones were open or exposed for a significant length of time. There is, however, more than one phase of burial. There is some evidence of the pushing

aside of earlier bones, and Skeleton F was placed over Skeleton A. Much of the localized movement and angle of the bones is the result of slumping into the central trough (see also below), but certain bones had moved 1.5–2.0 m on a linear axis (Fig. 3.55) which cannot be similarly explained. It seems likely that while some of the bones at the back of the chamber were defleshed at the time of burning, the body (E) towards the front remained partly fleshed. Certainly one bone from the mortuary structure, probably associated with Skeleton F, had been cut with a sharp flint tool soon after death in order to remove the tissue.

The phosphate surveys generally complement these interpretations and the bone data. Whilst confirming that there may have been some limited shifting of bodies, the results indicate that interment was indeed restricted to the distal sub-chamber and there is no evidence to suggest that further bodies were ever set into the chamber only to be later removed (or substantial parts thereof, see below).

In this context the recovery of the metatarsal from the fill of the medial post pit (Addendum No. 4) is potentially telling, as otherwise no human bone occurred this far east within the chamber. Whilst possibly attesting to the further movement of bodies, that it was unburnt (i.e. protected from the firing of the chamber) could even suggest that it derives from Phase I pre-chamber activities.

The overall evidence suggests that the chamber was used for burial on more than one occasion. The specific burial rite included placing at least partly articulated and fleshed bodies in the chamber. The dry bones of earlier burials were pushed aside for later burials. In at least one case the flesh was removed by cutting. (It has recently been recognized that there is evidence of dismemberment with lithic implements amongst the human remains at the chambered tombs at Coldrum in Kent and Eyford, Gloucestershire (Wysocki & Whittle 2000, 595); cut and scraping marks have also been identified on both the articulated and disarticulated remains of 23 individuals from a total population of c. 75 at Hambledon Hill; McKinley, in Mercer & Healy forthcoming.)

Similarly, the spatial structuring of the bones is of interest despite the poor survival conditions. Most obviously the bones are placed at the back of the mortuary chamber. In addition, the skeletons which are most likely to have been rearranged (B and F) are at the back of the distal chamber, whereas Skeleton E, towards the front, may represent a relatively late burial which was fleshed or only partially defleshed at the time of burning. Early burials may, therefore, have been placed at the back of the chamber and only later burials placed towards the front. Alternatively, bodies may have been gradually set towards the back as they became increasingly defleshed. That all the bodies seem to lie with their heads to the west emphasizes the importance or dominance of the innermost end of the mortuary chamber.

Certainly the evidence that tissue was, at least in part, stripped from one of the interred, and that probably the last body inserted into the chamber, implies a sense of 'scheduling' in relationship to the firing of the chamber anticipating its closure. It suggests that this transformational process could only occur upon decomposed corpses, once the signs of individual identity were eradicated. In order to achieve this, the *appearance* of decomposition could clearly be hastened with the stripping of flesh. Many explanations could be proposed for what prompted the barrow's schedule of closure; why the chamber had to be burnt then (and by extension subsequently sealed). Whilst these could range from the dying out of a family line to the enactment of a long-term ritual cycle, its actual cause cannot be known.

We need also to consider the deposition of human bone outside of the chamber. These 'secondary interments' fall into two categories: the later inhumations within the mound itself and 'loose' human bone found at three localities (Fig. 3.64). Both are of particular interest as they question the too-ready demarcation of 'closed' and 'open/active' monument phases. The recovery of the loose individual human bones could suggest two sources for this material. The humerus from the back side of the primary mound in Trench E could well have been removed from the chamber. Greater ambiguity exists as to where the skull and tibia fragments in the ditch terminals derive from. Their location suggests 'active' respect of the monument. Yet, occurring within the ditch (assigned to Phase III and the probable closure of the chamber) unless curated this suggests that it would not have come from the chamber's interments. As further discussed in Chapter 5 (and as possibly comparable to the occurrence of human bone in the circuit of the causewayed enclosure), 'tokens' of deceased individuals may still have been brought to the monument after the sealing of the chamber. This would indicate that the monument remained a place of 'active ritual' after its formal closure.

The secondary inhumations are unaccompanied by artefacts and therefore can not be directly dated. Given their location in the upper portion of the northern aspect of the mound's front, it is conceivable that they related to the primary Phase II mound and could, theoretically, have been inserted while the chamber was still in use (Figs. 3.3 & 3.30). If so, they could reflect upon who was excluded from burial within the chamber; perhaps a child and adult from another lineage. Far more likely, however, is that they relate to when the chamber was closed and the long mound established. In this case the question then becomes, given their location relative to the mound, whether they are of subsequent Neolithic attribution and represent a continuity of burial practices (i.e. familial). The alternative, in the light of their position on the monument's high front and its rounding with the addition of the façade-bank (from which a second-millennium BC sherd was recovered), is that they relate to Bronze Age interment and are what initiated the construction of the neighbouring round barrow group. With the mound then much denuded by weathering, did the monument effectively serve as a surrogate round barrow?

## Artefact studies: grave goods

Reported in detail below according to their respective artefact categories, few finds within the chamber could in any way be classed as either grave goods or personal ornaments, and this paucity is typical of interment of this period in general. Two leaf-shaped arrowheads were found within the chamber, both being burnt. One was recovered in the fill of the proximal post pit, and the other lay sufficiently south of Skeleton D that neither can be said to be directly associated with any one individual. (Note that the status of the two other arrowheads and reworked axe found in close proximity, but not on the chamber floor *per se*, is considered in the Overview below.) As discussed by Middleton, it is interesting, given the chamber's survival conditions, that these showed no signs of hafting, which could suggest that they were deposited as valued objects in their own right (i.e. rather than 'arrows'). Not including their presence as the cause of death, leaf-shaped arrowheads have been documented in six other long barrow mortuary associations (Kinnes 1992, 109–10; though see also Wysocki & Whittle 2000 concerning their representation and the possibility of unidentified flesh wounds).

A unique find in a mortuary context, the wooden pin pieces found in the fill of the distal post pit (presuming that these/it had slipped into that position from the chamber's floor) may have pinned a garment, in which case it could indicate that the dead were clothed.

Though pottery vessels (and what 'stuffs' they contained) were evidently placed as offerings at the mound's forecourt and its entrance, pottery did not feature within the chamber itself. Otherwise, the only other find which may have directly accompanied the dead was the articulated hind limb of a dog found on the floor of the proximal sub-chamber (see Legge below).

### Pottery
by M. KNIGHT, after P. SHAND

The assemblage comprises 219 sherds weighing 1412 g (mean sherd weight 6.4 g). The material as a whole consists of small abraded fragments, and includes extremely friable pieces some of which were recorded *in situ*. With the exception of fragments belonging to a near-complete vessel located within a façade post-pipe, the majority of the sherds measured between 10–50 mm in size. Overall the assemblage is earlier Neolithic in character and includes fine carinated Grimston-type bowl forms (Herne 1988), heavier plain bowl forms and fragments from at least three decorated Mildenhall vessels (Longworth, in Clark *et al.* 1960). Two grog-tempered sherds represent possible later Neolithic/Early Bronze Age forms.

*Fabrics*
Four main fabric types have been identified, two of which are common with the terrace-side cuttings assemblage (Fabrics 2 & 3; see Pollard & Johnston above). Further sub-division could be applied to the series, but given the poorly sorted nature of these early fabrics it was considered appropriate to 'lump' some variants together. Surface treatment consists of wiped and slightly burnished external surfaces and includes fine mechanical slips.

Developing upon Pollard & Johnston's series, the newly identified fabrics are:

5: Medium hard fabric with poorly sorted, white-grey medium-sized angular QUARTZ and rare medium FLINT. Earlier Neolithic (majority fabric).
6: Medium hard fabric with frequent medium-sized VOIDS (lost organic/calcite filler?). Earlier Neolithic (Grimston-type bowl).

*Forms*
The bulk of the assemblage consists of small, plain body sherds, although a limited number of feature sherds (36 in total) were also identified and these have been assigned to vessels. Three vessels in particular stood out: a near complete Grimston-type bowl (P1: Fig. 3.58), fragments of a decorated Mildenhall bowl (P2: Fig. 3.58), and the rim of a fine plain bowl (P4: Fig. 3.58); these have been used as templates for the reconstruction of the rest of the assemblage. The Grimston vessel is distinguished by its flaring neck, fine carinated form and corky fabric, whereas the Mildenhall vessel has an externally expanded rim

and upright neck, has a burnished finish which is decorated with incised lines, and is quartz tempered. The plain bowl has a rolled rim and, like the Grimston bowl, a flaring neck, but its fabric is the same as the Mildenhall pot.

Decoration
Decoration is restricted to the Mildenhall fragments. It consists of incised lines (P2) or impressed dots (P3 & P5). The incised decoration is simple diagonal lines occurring on the rim and internal and external surfaces of the neck. The dots on P3 are shallow and rounded and are arranged in closely spaced rows around the shoulder. This design is consistent with vessels found at the type-site Hurst Fen (Clark *et al.* 1960). The dots on P5 are made with a sharp, narrow point which cuts deep into the sherd's surface and are arranged in evenly spaced horizontal rows. That the decoration appears to 'cross' the shoulder onto the neck zone is unusual, as normally Mildenhall decoration changes between the three main parts of the pot (rim, neck and shoulder).

Vessels
The Grimston-type bowl P1 (Fabric 6; Sherds 132–246; Fig. 3.58) is a fine carinated vessel with a slightly rolled rim and flaring neck. It is decorated internally with a 7-cm-deep band of narrow, vertical fluting but otherwise is plain with a smoothed finish. The rim measures 30 cm in diameter and the waist 28 cm. The estimated height of the vessel is 16 cm.

The decorated Mildenhall bowl P2 (Fabric 5; Sherds 2, 7–8, 10, 12, 15, 19–22, 24, 253–254: Fig. 3.58) has an 'angular' externally thickened rim and an upright neck which is broken above the shoulder line. The decoration comprises diagonal incised lines both along the top of the rim and on the internal and external faces of the neck. All of the sherds share the same distinctive burnished finish. Importantly, Sherds 7 and 10 refit.

P3 Decorated Mildenhall bowl (Fabric 5; Sherd 9; Fig. 3.58): A single sherd containing multiple dot impressions represents this vessel. It is difficult to ascertain the exact orientation of this fragment but it is likely to be a shoulder piece containing at least five rows of dots above a single vertical line of dots. This piece could belong to P2.

P4 Plain bowl (Fabric 5; Sherd 66; Fig. 3.58): One sherd represents this vessel: a plain, fine flaring neck sherd with a rolled rim. Two other sherds of similar thickness and surface appearance could also belong to this vessel (Sherds 89 and 125).

P5 Decorated Mildenhall bowl (Fabric 5; Sherd 55; Fig. 3.59): One sherd represents this vessel: a 'shoulder' fragment decorated with horizontal rows of small impressed dots (spaced approximately 10 mm apart). This vessel is slightly unusual in that, unlike normal

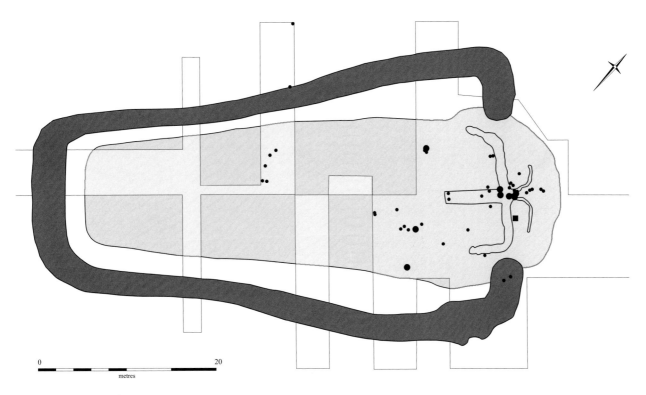

0                      20

metres

- •     Single sherd
- ●     Multiple sherds
- ■     Complete vessel

0                      20

metres

- •     1 flint
- •     2 - 4

**Figure 3.57**. *Artefact distributions. Top, pottery; below, struck flint.*

159

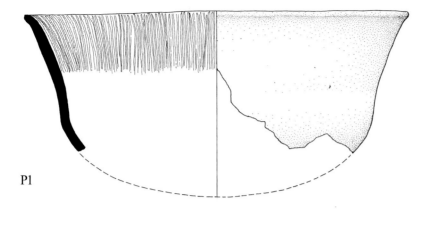

P1

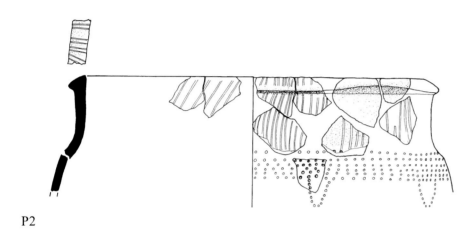

P2

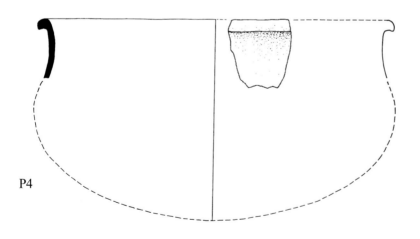

P4

decorated Mildenhall bowls, the decoration is not interrupted at the line of the shoulder.

P6 Plain Bowl (Fabric 5; Sherd 119; Fig. 3.59): One sherd represents this vessel: a small, simple out-turned rim belonging to a plain upright neck.

P7 Plain Bowl (Fabric 5; Sherd 117; Fig. 3.59): A single, out-turned rim fragment.

P8 Early Bronze Age Urn? (Fabric 2; Sherd 40; Fig. 3.59): A single base angle with pinched fingertip impressions (from the façade-bank).

P9 Decorated Mildenhall bowl (Fabric 5; Sherd 67): A single 'angular' externally thickened rim. This fragment bears a strong resemblance to the rim fragments from P2.

Three further feature sherds include two small plain neck fragments (Sherds 121 and 265) and a plain shoulder fragment (Sherd 82). If these are seen as representative of single vessels then the minimum number present is 12. A single abraded, grog-tempered piece (Sherd 124) stands out as being different and probably Late Neolithic/Early Bronze Age, this being located in the pre-mound land surface in Trench B.

*Context*
The distribution of vessels and sherds is plotted on Figures 3.57 & 3.60. The Grimston bowl P1 was found complete close to the outside edge of a post-pipe belonging to the main façade trench F.15 and, as such, it can be seen as being an early deposit associated with a primary structure. Meanwhile, the Mildenhall vessel P2 survived as fragments immediately outside

**Figure 3.58.** *Pottery. Grimston (P1), Mildenhall (decorated; P2 & P3) and Plain Bowl (P4) vessels.*

the blocked entrance of the main chamber and within the restricted space of the external 'hornwork', and can therefore be seen as being deposited later in the sequence. The survival of P1 as a complete vessel was dependent on its location, up against the main façade but away from the main access to the chamber. In contrast, P2 was located within the narrow 'route' of the fore-structure hornwork where it could have been subject to repeated trampling (hence its fragmented nature). The chronological and contextual separation of the two types is reminiscent of a similar pattern recorded at the nearby site of Barleycroft Farm, where fragments of plain Grimston-type bowls were found in tree-throw features whereas decorated Mildenhall sherds were exclusive to circular pit features (see Chapter 4 below; Evans *et al.* 1999). Both sets of features were located within the same area, but radiocarbon dates suggest that they were in use at separate times, albeit by a short period, with the tree throws being the earliest (tree throw, 3790–3630 cal. BC, OxA-8110, 4920±40 BP; Mildenhall pit, 3780–3380 cal. BC, OxA-8108; 4820±45 BP).

*Discussion*

The major part of the assemblage is represented by small abraded pieces but at least 12 vessels have been identified, and these can be separated into four main types: Grimston bowl (P1); Plain Bowl (P4, P6 & P7); Decorated Mildenhall (P2, P3, P5 & P9); Early Bronze Age Urn (P8). The Grimston Bowl P1 was deposited whole and belongs to the earliest phase of construction. Although all of the plain bowl vessels share the same fabric as the decorated Mildenhall fragments, at least one of these vessels (P4) has strong affinities with the Grimston tradition. The general contextual separation between the plain and decorated vessels is significant in that the plain sherds occur either side of the chamber blocking whereas the decorated sherds (P2 & P3) only occur immediately outside of it. Otherwise, the majority of the material is abraded and located within the primary and secondary mounds and must be viewed as redeposited. That it was in secondary context suggests that 'occupation' deposits had been disturbed in order to construct the mounds.

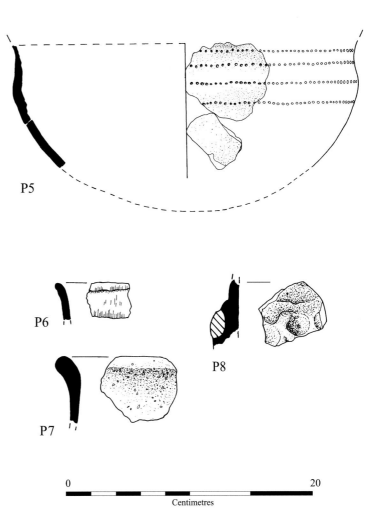

**Figure 3.59.** *Pottery. Mildenhall (decorated; P5), Plain Bowl (P6 & P7) vessels; P8, Bronze Age base angle.*

**The struck flint**
by H.R. MIDDLETON

The assemblage, comprising 501 pieces, can be divided into two approximate groups: firstly, residual material incorporated into the mound and banks from the surrounding land surface, and secondly material contemporary with the monument itself. These two groups could not be readily distinguished at the single artefact level and could only be so by typology of individual implements. The general technological traits of the assemblage were compared and contrasted with the discrete Late Mesolithic material from the neighbouring Foulmire Fen site (Chapter 2) in order to distinguish a date for the majority of the material.

Although the data presented here is broken down by broad structural phase/component group-

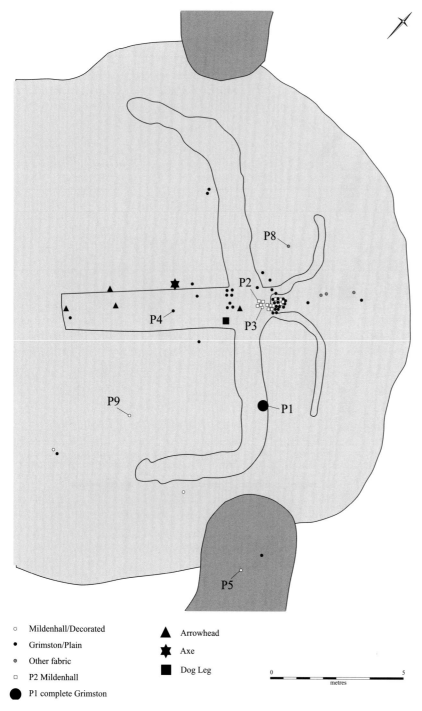

Group C: Above-chamber collapse/'infill' and façade-bank (93)

Group D: The barrow mounds and surrounding ditch (289)

Group E: Mound weathering, surface features and ploughsoil (53)

*Condition (Table 3.13)*

The large majority of the material exhibited fresh and unabraded edges with 7.7 per cent having signs of post-depositional alteration, consisting of small removals on fragile edges. No pieces had extensive edge damage, either by removals or rounding. The degree of abrasion did not vary by group, although the small amount of material in the buried soil was all in a fresh condition.

Similarly the degree of patination varied little, although Groups B and C had slightly lower proportions of unpatinated material. This proved no guide to the date of individual artefacts with both some Late Mesolithic (e.g. Fig. 3.61:21) and Neolithic artefacts (Fig. 3.61:1) being unpatinated. This must reflect small scale changes in the mineral composition of the ground water both in the monument itself and the former contexts of the residual material.

The number of burnt pieces averaged 7.4 per cent of the group totals with the only slight outlier being Group A where this figure was 11.5 per cent. This reflects the burning of material within the mortuary chamber during its destruction.

*Raw material*

On 77.1% of pieces the cortex was thin (0–2 mm thick) and abraded, being characteristic of gravel-derived flint (Gibbard 1986). The flint was of good quality, with only 1.8% of pieces being of sufficiently poor quality to affect the method of flaking. Only five pieces (1%) were made of medium-grained flint, the remainder being fine grained.

The variety of colours reflects that of the gravel source, with the majority (57.4%) being black in colour. The remainder varied between light grey and dark

Legend:
○ Mildenhall/Decorated
● Grimston/Plain
◉ Other fabric
▢ P2 Mildenhall
● P1 complete Grimston

▲ Arrowhead
★ Axe
■ Dog Leg

0 ────── 5
metres

**Figure 3.60.** *Distribution of pottery and other key artefacts within the area of mortuary structure and forecourt.*

ings, the results will be skewed towards Group C as it contained over half of the whole assemblage (number in brackets indicates number of flints by group):

Group A: The buried soil (11)

Group B: The mortuary chamber and forecourt (56)

**Table 3.12.** *Foulmire Fen long barrow: flint typology (by group).*

| Type | A No. | A % | B No. | B % | C No. | C % | D No. | D % | E No. | E % | Site total No. | Site total % |
|---|---|---|---|---|---|---|---|---|---|---|---|---|
| Waste flakes | 8 | 88.9 | 50 | 96.2 | 83 | 96.5 | 254 | 94.5 | 47 | 97.9 | 442 | 95.5 |
| IWW | 0 | 0 | 0 | 0 | 0 | 0 | 4 | 1.5 | 0 | 0 | 4 | 0.9 |
| Cores | 1 | 11.1 | 2 | 3.8 | 3 | 3.5 | 9 | 3.4 | 1 | 2.1 | 16 | 3.4 |
| Micro-burins | 0 | 0 | 0 | 0 | 0 | 0 | 1 | 0.6 | 0 | 0 | 1 | 0.2 |
| **Total** | **9** | **100** | **52** | **100** | **86** | **100** | **268** | **100** | **48** | **100** | **463** | **100** |
| Utilized flakes | 1 | 50 | 2 | 50 | 1 | 16.7 | 7 | 33.3 | 4 | 80 | 15 | 39.5 |
| Retouched flakes | 0 | 0 | 0 | 0 | 1 | 16.7 | 2 | 9.5 | 0 | 0 | 3 | 7.9 |
| Scrapers | 1 | 50 | 0 | 0 | 0 | 0 | 3 | 14.3 | 0 | 0 | 4 | 10.5 |
| Knives | 0 | 0 | 0 | 0 | 0 | 0 | 3 | 14.3 | 0 | 0 | 3 | 7.9 |
| Denticulates | 0 | 0 | 0 | 0 | 0 | 0 | 1 | 4.8 | 0 | 0 | 1 | 2.6 |
| Leaf arrowheads | 0 | 0 | 2 | 50 | 1 | 16.7 | 1 | 4.8 | 0 | 0 | 4 | 10.5 |
| Axes | 0 | 0 | 0 | 0 | 0 | 0 | 1 | 4.8 | 0 | 0 | 1 | 2.6 |
| Piercer | 0 | 0 | 0 | 0 | 0 | 0 | 1 | 4.8 | 0 | 0 | 1 | 2.6 |
| Microliths | 0 | 0 | 0 | 0 | 2 | 33.3 | 2 | 9.5 | 1 | 20 | 5 | 13.2 |
| Burin | 0 | 0 | 0 | 0 | 1 | 16.7 | 0 | 0 | 0 | 0 | 1 | 2.6 |
| **Total** | **2** | **100** | **4** | **100** | **6** | **100** | **21** | **100** | **5** | **100** | **38** | **100** |
| Assemblages total | 11 | | 56 | | 92 | | 289 | | 53 | | 501 | |
| Implement:by-product ratio | 1:4.5 | | 1:13 | | 1:14.3 | | 1:12.8 | | 1:9.6 | | 1:12.1 | |

**Table 3.13.** *Foulmire Fen long barrow: flint condition.*

| Group | A No. | A % | B No. | B % | C No. | C % | D No. | D % | E No. | E % | Site total No. | Site total % |
|---|---|---|---|---|---|---|---|---|---|---|---|---|
| *Condition* | | | | | | | | | | | | |
| Abraded | 0 | 0 | 3 | 5.4 | 10 | 10.9 | 14 | 5.2 | 4 | 9.3 | 31 | 6.2 |
| Fresh | 11 | 100 | 53 | 94.6 | 82 | 89.1 | 275 | 94.8 | 49 | 90.7 | 470 | 93.8 |
| **Total** | **11** | **100** | **56** | **100** | **92** | **100** | **289** | **100** | **53** | **100** | **501** | **100** |
| *Degree of patination* | | | | | | | | | | | | |
| Unpatinated | 9 | 81.8 | 40 | 80 | 52 | 60.5 | 187 | 68 | 39 | 76.5 | 327 | 69.1 |
| Partially | 1 | 9.1 | 7 | 14 | 19 | 22.1 | 36 | 13.1 | 4 | 7.8 | 67 | 14.2 |
| Completely | 1 | 9.1 | 3 | 6 | 15 | 17.4 | 52 | 18.9 | 8 | 15.7 | 79 | 16.7 |
| **Total** | **11** | **100** | **50** | **100** | **86** | **100** | **275** | **100** | **51** | **100** | **473** | **100** |
| No. Burnt | 0 | 0 | 6 | 11.5 | 8 | 8.7 | 21 | 7.3 | 2 | 3.8 | 37 | 7.4 |

brown with the latter representing 14.6% of the assemblage.

No material from other flint sources, notably chalk, the Breckland and till deposits was present. This contrasts with the situation in the southeastern fens in the Late Mesolithic and Early Neolithic, where a variety of sources appear to have been used (Healy 1991), particularly sources from till on the floor of the fens covered by later deposits. This may suggest that the gravel terraces of the Cam and Ouse rivers (Hodge & Seale 1966; Seale 1975a,b) were the most accessible sources.

*Technology (Tables 3.14–3.16)*
Although the assemblage was undoubtedly mixed

in terms of typology (Table 3.12), the technological data suggests a relatively homogeneous assemblage with a number of points of similarity with the adjacent terrace-side Mesolithic site. Data from the earlier Neolithic Etton causewayed enclosure are also relevant (Fig. 3.62; Middleton, in Pryor 1998). In the following discussion the assemblage will be considered to be discrete and largely Late Mesolithic in date except where noted in the text. The terminology used in the following discussion follows that of Cotterell & Kamminga (1987). All figures are a percentage of all unretouched flakes where data was recorded.

Although no hammer stones were present within the assemblage, an examination of the flaking at-

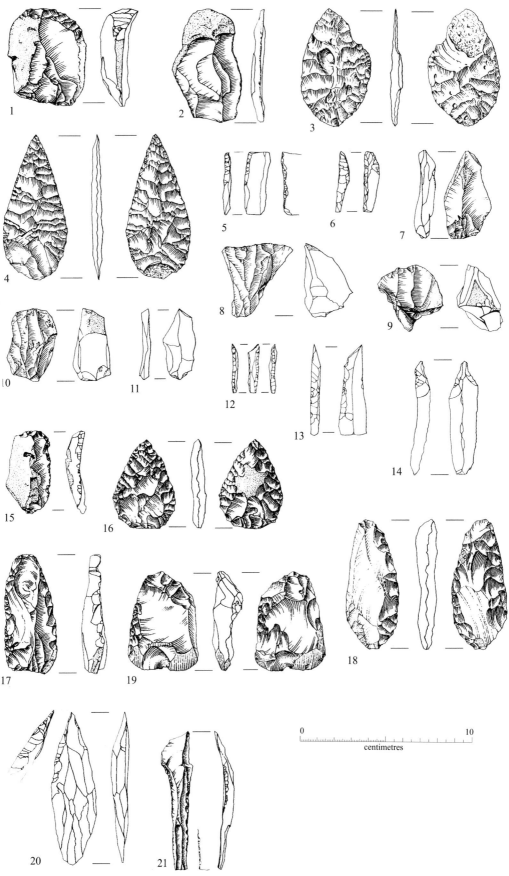

**Figure 3.61.** *(left) Foulmire Fen long barrow struck flint.*

1) *Buried soil: end scraper, RA 70°, wt 44.2 g, <16055> flint no. 72, 1951/6785.*

2) *Chamber floor: utilized flake (class A), wt 15.8 g, <27966> flint no. 499, 2.73/2.18.*

3) *Chamber floor: leaf arrowhead, wt 1.4 g, <27962> flint no. 490, 3.95/2.37.*

4) *Chamber floor: leaf arrowhead, wt 2.1 g, flint no. 533, 8.85/2.76.*

5) *Primary mound: obliquely blunted point with ancillary retouch, wt 0.1 g, <27753> flint no. 331, 1974.02/6983.55.*

6) *Mortuary structure deposits: edge-blunted point with ancillary retouch, wt 0.2 g, <27935> flint no. 514, 2.25/2.76.*

7) *Primary mound: burin, wt 10.8 g, <27515> flint no. 456, 1982.27/6781.8.*

8) *Mound (East): core type B1, wt 24.9 g, <27634> flint no. 223, 1974.15/6780.0.*

9) *Mound (West Upper): core type A2, wt 24.4 g, <16006> flint no. 23, 1985/6802.*

10) *Mound (West Lower): core type A2, wt 25.5 g, <27852> flint no. 202, 1949.4/6772.45.*

11) *Mound (East): micro-burin, wt 0.4 g, <27765> flint no. 346, 1973.32/6783.37.*

12) *Mound (West Lower): scalene triangle, wt 0.1 g, <16294> flint no. 181, 1964.6/6776.77.*

13) *Mound (East): edge-blunted point, wt 0.5 g, <27629> flint no. 211, 1973.71/6783.45.*

14) *Mound (East): piercer, wt 0.8 g, <27812> flint no. 393, 1979/6773.3.*

15) *Mound (West Upper): end scraper, wt 11.7 g, RA 80°, <16251> flint no. 93, 1970.8/ 6778.4.*

16) *Mound (East): leaf arrowhead, wt 2.2 g, <27969> flint no. 217; 1976.2/6732.39.*

17) *Enclosing ditch: flake knife, wt 26 g, <16051> flint no. 84, 1979.65/6771.97.*

18) *Mound (East): flake knife, wt 26.2 g, <27568> flint no. 423; 1974.81/6786.6.*

19) *Mound (East): polished flint axe fragment, wt 36 g, <27543> flint no. 433, 1978.31/6784.81.*

20) *Mound slip (East): obliquely blunted point, wt 2.3 g, <27502> flint no. 419, 1986.79/6789.35.*

21) *Mound slip (West): utilized flake (Class A), wt 5.8 g, <16005> flint no. 24, 1977.45/6770.98.*

tributes of the unretouched flakes reveals the majority (85.9 per cent) to possess hertzian cones of percussion suggestive of the use of hard hammers. The remainder had bending fractures which may have been created either by the use of soft hammers or by corticaled flint pebbles.

The lack of soft hammer-struck material has also been documented in other areas of the fens, including the western fen-edge, and in other gravel flint-based assemblages such as that from Irthlingborough, Northamptonshire (Humble pers. comm.). This contrasts with the widespread use of soft hammers in the Late Mesolithic of the southeastern fens (Healy 1991) and the Thames basin (Holgate 1988, 54). This may reflect the dependence upon relatively small nodules of raw material and a commensurate need to adopt knapping strategies to conserve raw material. This would have precluded elaborate core preparation necessary for the use of soft hammers.

An examination of the amount of cortex on the unretouched flakes suggests that all stages of the knapping sequence were present (Table 3.15). The lack of cortical material in the buried soil (Group A) and in Group B deposits is probably a reflection of the small sample present. The comparisons with the terrace-side assemblage and the Etton enclosure reveal very similar patterns (Fig. 3.62), suggesting that these proportions are consistent with the gravel-based technology. Although the relatively high proportions of non-cortical material may suggest the import of semi-worked flint nodules. This contrasts with the slightly lower proportions of non-cortical material from the sites containing predominantly Mesolithic material from the Norfolk Fen Survey where the complete knapping sequence was undertaken (Healy 1991).

The overall quality of the flaking sequence is attested by a number of technological traits apparent in the unretouched flakes: the dominance of feather terminations (91.1%); the lack of cortical platforms (3.5%), side-struck (3.8%) and bashed pieces (0.8%); and the small number of hinge terminations (8.3%). Faceted platforms were only present in small numbers (2%).

The waste flakes were divided in to groups based upon their position in the knapping sequence (full details are presented in the Chapter 2 terrace-edge assemblage; Table 2.8). All stages of the core reduction sequence were present and comparisons with the terrace-side assemblage and the Etton causewayed enclosure (Fig. 3.62) reveal very close comparisons with the former, bearing this out. The small number of preparation flakes, combined with the cortical data, may be a further suggestion of the import of partially worked flint nodules. Further experimental work needs to be done to establish a precise relationship between these stages for a gravel flint-based technology.

Core rejuvenation was by means of the creation of striking platforms at right angles to the existing one, producing characteristic core recovery flakes. No core tablets were recovered.

**Table 3.14.** *Foulmire Fen long barrow: unretouched flake technology.*

| Group | A No. | A % | B No. | B % | C No. | C % | D No. | D % | E No. | E % | Site total No. | Site total % |
|---|---|---|---|---|---|---|---|---|---|---|---|---|
| *Initiation* | | | | | | | | | | | | |
| Hertzian | 4 | 80 | 15 | 88.2 | 31 | 96.9 | 99 | 83.2 | 22 | 84.6 | 171 | 85.9 |
| Bending | 1 | 20 | 2 | 11.8 | 1 | 3.1 | 20 | 16.8 | 4 | 15.4 | 28 | 14.1 |
| **Total** | **5** | **100** | **17** | **100** | **32** | **100** | **119** | **100** | **26** | **100** | **199** | **100** |
| *Termination* | | | | | | | | | | | | |
| Feather | 2 | 50 | 9 | 100 | 29 | 85.3 | 106 | 96.4 | 19 | 82.6 | 165 | 91.7 |
| Hinge | 2 | 50 | 0 | 0 | 5 | 14.7 | 4 | 3.6 | 4 | 17.4 | 15 | 8.3 |
| **Total** | **4** | **100** | **9** | **100** | **34** | **100** | **110** | **100** | **23** | **100** | **180** | **100** |
| *Platform preparation* | | | | | | | | | | | | |
| Plain | 5 | 100 | 16 | 94.1 | 31 | 96.9 | 112 | 93.4 | 25 | 96.2 | 189 | 94.5 |
| Facetted | 0 | 0 | 0 | 0 | 0 | 0 | 4 | 3.3 | 0 | 0 | 4 | 2 |
| Cortical | 0 | 0 | 1 | 5.9 | 1 | 3.1 | 4 | 3.3 | 1 | 3.8 | 7 | 3.5 |
| **Total** | **5** | **100** | **17** | **100** | **32** | **100** | **120** | **100** | **26** | **100** | **200** | **100** |
| *Striking* | | | | | | | | | | | | |
| End | 7 | 100 | 19 | 95 | 44 | 93.6 | 151 | 96.8 | 30 | 90.9 | 251 | 95.4 |
| Side | 0 | 0 | 1 | 5 | 3 | 6.4 | 4 | 2.6 | 2 | 6.1 | 10 | 3.8 |
| Bashed | 0 | 0 | 0 | 0 | 0 | 0 | 1 | 0.6 | 1 | 3 | 2 | 0.8 |
| **Total** | **7** | **100** | **20** | **100** | **47** | **100** | **156** | **100** | **33** | **100** | **263** | **100** |

**Table 3.15.** *Foulmire Fen long barrow: unretouched flake cortex (all unretouched flakes).*

| Group | A No. | A % | B No. | B % | C No. | C % | D No. | D % | E No. | E % | Site total No. | Site total % |
|---|---|---|---|---|---|---|---|---|---|---|---|---|
| *% cortex* | | | | | | | | | | | | |
| 0 | 6 | 85.7 | 13 | 65 | 32 | 64 | 107 | 63.7 | 21 | 60 | 179 | 63.9 |
| 0–25 | 0 | 0 | 5 | 25 | 12 | 24 | 42 | 25 | 4 | 11.4 | 63 | 22.5 |
| 26–50 | 0 | 0 | 2 | 10 | 5 | 10 | 14 | 8.3 | 5 | 14.3 | 26 | 9.3 |
| 51–75 | 1 | 14.3 | 0 | 0 | 1 | 2 | 3 | 1.8 | 4 | 11.4 | 9 | 3.2 |
| 75–100 | 0 | 0 | 0 | 0 | 0 | 0 | 1 | 0.6 | 0 | 0 | 1 | 0.4 |
| 100 | 0 | 0 | 0 | 0 | 0 | 0 | 1 | 0.6 | 1 | 2.9 | 2 | 0.7 |
| **Total** | **7** | **100** | **20** | **100** | **50** | **100** | **168** | **100** | **35** | **100** | **280** | **100** |

**Table 3.16.** *Foulmire Fen long barrow: waste flake typology.*

| Group | A No. | A % | B No. | B % | C No. | C % | D No. | D % | E No. | E % | Site total No. | Site total % |
|---|---|---|---|---|---|---|---|---|---|---|---|---|
| Unretouched flakes | 7 | 87.5 | 20 | 40 | 50 | 60.2 | 168 | 66.1 | 34 | 72.3 | 279 | 63.1 |
| Dressing chips | 0 | 0 | 16 | 32 | 19 | 22.9 | 54 | 21.3 | 4 | 8.5 | 93 | 21 |
| Trimming flakes | 1 | 12.5 | 9 | 18 | 5 | 6 | 11 | 4.3 | 6 | 12.8 | 32 | 7.2 |
| Preparation flakes | 0 | 0 | 5 | 10 | 5 | 6 | 11 | 4.3 | 3 | 6.4 | 24 | 5.4 |
| Thinning flakes | 0 | 0 | 0 | 0 | 1 | 1.3 | 1 | 0.4 | 0 | 0 | 2 | 0.4 |
| Core recovery Flakes | 0 | 0 | 0 | 0 | 3 | 3.6 | 9 | 3.6 | 0 | 0 | 12 | 2.7 |
| **Total** | **8** | **100** | **50** | **100** | **83** | **100** | **254** | **100** | **47** | **100** | **442** | **100** |

Implement production is attested by the occurrence of a single micro-burin from the Group C deposits. Several of the dressing chips may be derived from the retouching or resharpening of implements, although this cannot be demonstrated.

The core typology reveals that the assemblage can be divided into two parts (Table 3.17). The first group, comprising the Group C deposits, contained one- and two-platformed examples, 67 per cent of which had blade scars. The second group, being made

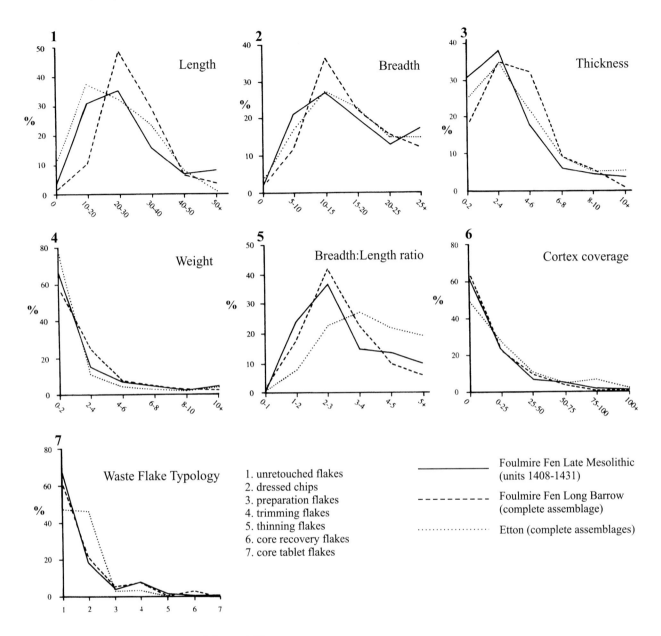

**Figure 3.62.** *Comparative waste flake variables.*

up of the remaining phases, had either multi-platform or unclassified examples. This latter type usually had no discernible platforms. Of the second group, only one (14.2 per cent) had any blade scars. This may suggest that the Phase 3 material may have contained a greater proportion of Late Mesolithic material given the association of material of this date with blade cores (Ford 1987, table 2; Holgate 1988, 54–9).

The mean core weight of 20.2 g accords with other Fenland gravel-based assemblages from both the Late Mesolithic such as Bedlam Hill (Middleton, in French & Pryor 1993) and the earlier Neolithic, such as Etton (Middleton, in Pryor 1998). This suggests a common discard behaviour once the cores had been

reduced to a certain threshold beyond which no usable flakes could be removed. This is further supported by the data on surviving cortex where 75 per cent of all the cores had a 25 per cent covering or less. This suggests that the cores were worked to exhaustion, with no partially flaked material being discarded.

*Metrical attributes*
In order to determine chronological and technological attributes within the material the complete unretouched flakes were measured according to the method outlined by Saville (1980a). The data is presented in Tables 3.18–3.22. In order to place this data within a chronological framework comparisons

**Table 3.17.** *Foulmire Fen long barrow: core typology.*

| Group | A | B | C | D | E | Site total |
|---|---|---|---|---|---|---|
| *Type* | | | | | | |
| A2 | 0 | 0 | 0 | 4 | 0 | 4 |
| B1 | 0 | 0 | 0 | 1 | 0 | 1 |
| B3 | 0 | 0 | 0 | 2 | 0 | 2 |
| E | 0 | 1 | 1 | 0 | 0 | 2 |
| Unclass. | 1 | 0 | 2 | 0 | 1 | 4 |
| Fragment | 0 | 1 | 0 | 2 | 0 | 3 |
| **Total** | **1** | **2** | **3** | **9** | **1** | **16** |

with the terrace-side assemblage (Late Mesolithic) and the Etton causewayed enclosure (Middle Neolithic) are illustrated in Figure 3.62. Although the number of pieces is small in all groups except Group C, the data do suggest that, in terms of waste flake form, the assemblage was largely homogeneous.

The largest number of flakes were 20–30 mm long, 10–15 mm broad, 2–4 mm thick and weighed between 0–2 g. These data contrast with those from the terrace-edge cuttings where a greater range of material was present. This is particularly noticeable in terms of lengths and breadths, where it does appear

**Table 3.18.** *Foulmire Fen long barrow: waste flake lengths (all complete unretouched flakes).*

| Group | A | | B | | C | | D | | E | | Site total | |
|---|---|---|---|---|---|---|---|---|---|---|---|---|
| | No. | % | No. | % | No. | % | No. | % | No. | % | No. | % |
| *Length (mm)* | | | | | | | | | | | | |
| 0–10 | 0 | 0 | 0 | 0 | 0 | 0 | 1 | 1.1 | 1 | 5.6 | 2 | 1.4 |
| 10–20 | 1 | 20 | 2 | 25 | 0 | 0 | 9 | 10.2 | 3 | 16.6 | 15 | 10.7 |
| 20–30 | 3 | 60 | 3 | 37.5 | 15 | 71.4 | 41 | 46.6 | 6 | 33.3 | 68 | 48.6 |
| 30–40 | 1 | 20 | 1 | 12.5 | 3 | 14.3 | 30 | 34.1 | 6 | 33.3 | 41 | 29.3 |
| 40–50 | 0 | 0 | 2 | 25 | 1 | 4.8 | 5 | 5.7 | 1 | 5.6 | 9 | 6.4 |
| 50+ | 0 | 0 | 0 | 0 | 2 | 9.5 | 2 | 2.3 | 1 | 5.6 | 5 | 3.6 |
| **Total** | **5** | **100** | **8** | **100** | **21** | **100** | **88** | **100** | **18** | **100** | **140** | **100** |

**Table 3.19.** *Foulmire Fen long barrow: waste flake breadths (all complete unretouched flakes).*

| Group | A | | B | | C | | D | | E | | Site total | |
|---|---|---|---|---|---|---|---|---|---|---|---|---|
| | No. | % | No. | % | No. | % | No. | % | No. | % | No. | % |
| *Breadth (mm)* | | | | | | | | | | | | |
| 0–5 | 1 | 20 | 0 | 0 | 0 | 0 | 1 | 1.1 | 0 | 0 | 2 | 1.4 |
| 5–10 | 1 | 20 | 1 | 12.5 | 2 | 9.5 | 12 | 13.6 | 1 | 5.6 | 17 | 12.2 |
| 10–15 | 0 | 0 | 1 | 12.5 | 10 | 47.6 | 35 | 39.8 | 5 | 27.8 | 51 | 36.4 |
| 15–20 | 1 | 20 | 2 | 25 | 4 | 19.1 | 17 | 19.3 | 7 | 38.8 | 31 | 22.1 |
| 20–25 | 2 | 40 | 3 | 37.5 | 2 | 9.5 | 13 | 14.8 | 2 | 11.1 | 22 | 15.7 |
| 25+ | 0 | 0 | 1 | 12.5 | 3 | 14.3 | 10 | 11.4 | 3 | 16.7 | 17 | 12.2 |
| **Total** | **5** | **100** | **8** | **100** | **21** | **100** | **88** | **100** | **18** | **100** | **140** | **100** |

**Table 3.20.** *Foulmire Fen long barrow: waste flake thicknesses (all complete unretouched flakes).*

| Group | A | | B | | C | | D | | E | | Site total | |
|---|---|---|---|---|---|---|---|---|---|---|---|---|
| | No. | % | No. | % | No. | % | No. | % | No. | % | No. | % |
| *Thickness (mm)* | | | | | | | | | | | | |
| 0–2 | 2 | 40 | 0 | 0 | 3 | 14.3 | 17 | 19.3 | 2 | 11.1 | 24 | 17.1 |
| 2–4 | 1 | 20 | 2 | 25 | 9 | 42.9 | 30 | 34.2 | 7 | 38.9 | 49 | 35 |
| 4–6 | 2 | 40 | 5 | 62.5 | 7 | 33.3 | 26 | 29.5 | 5 | 27.8 | 45 | 32.2 |
| 6–8 | 0 | 0 | 1 | 12.5 | 2 | 9.5 | 8 | 9.1 | 2 | 11.1 | 13 | 9.3 |
| 8–10 | 0 | 0 | 0 | 0 | 0 | 0 | 6 | 6.8 | 2 | 11.1 | 8 | 5.7 |
| 10+ | 0 | 0 | 0 | 0 | 0 | 0 | 1 | 1.1 | 0 | 0 | 1 | 0.7 |
| **Total** | **5** | **100** | **8** | **100** | **21** | **100** | **88** | **100** | **18** | **100** | **140** | **100** |

**Table 3.21.** *Foulmire Fen long barrow: waste flake weights (all complete unretouched flakes).*

| Group | A | | B | | C | | D | | E | | Site total | |
|---|---|---|---|---|---|---|---|---|---|---|---|---|
| | No. | % | No. | % | No. | % | No. | % | No. | % | No. | % |
| *Length (mm)* | | | | | | | | | | | | |
| 0–2 | 3 | 60 | 4 | 50 | 11 | 52.3 | 53 | 60.2 | 10 | 55.5 | 81 | 57.9 |
| 2–4 | 2 | 40 | 3 | 37.5 | 8 | 38.2 | 19 | 21.6 | 3 | 16.6 | 35 | 25 |
| 4–6 | 0 | 0 | 0 | 0 | 2 | 9.5 | 8 | 9.1 | 1 | 5.6 | 11 | 7.9 |
| 6–8 | 0 | 0 | 1 | 12.5 | 0 | 0 | 4 | 4.6 | 1 | 5.6 | 6 | 4.3 |
| 8–10 | 0 | 0 | 0 | 0 | 0 | 0 | 3 | 3.4 | 1 | 5.6 | 4 | 2.8 |
| 10+ | 0 | 0 | 0 | 0 | 0 | 0 | 1 | 1.1 | 2 | 11.1 | 3 | 2.1 |
| **Total** | 5 | 100 | 8 | 100 | 21 | 100 | 88 | 100 | 18 | 100 | 140 | 100 |

**Table 3.22.** *Foulmire Fen long barrow: breadth:length ratios (complete unretouched flakes; figures in brackets include broken blades as % of all unretouched flakes).*

| Group | A | | B | | C | | D | | E | | Site total | |
|---|---|---|---|---|---|---|---|---|---|---|---|---|
| | No. | % | No. | % | No. | % | No. | % | No. | % | No. | % |
| *Ratios (n:5)* | | | | | | | | | | | | |
| 0–1 | 1 | 20 | 0 | 0 | 0 | 0 | 1 | 1.2 | 0 | 0 | 2 | 1.5 |
| 1–2 | 1 | 20 | 2 | 25 | 4 | 21.1 | 14 | 16.5 | 3 | 18.7 | 24 | 18 |
| 2–3 | 1 | 20 | 1 | 12.5 | 10 | 52.6 | 39 | 45.9 | 5 | 31.3 | 56 | 42.1 |
| 3–4 | 2 | 40 | 2 | 25 | 3 | 15.7 | 19 | 22.3 | 4 | 25 | 30 | 22.6 |
| 4–5 | 0 | 0 | 2 | 25 | 1 | 5.3 | 8 | 9.4 | 2 | 12.5 | 13 | 9.8 |
| 5+ | 0 | 0 | 1 | 12.5 | 1 | 5.3 | 4 | 4.7 | 2 | 12.5 | 8 | 6 |
| **Total** | 5 | 100 | 8 | 100 | 19 | 100 | 85 | 100 | 16 | 100 | 133 | 100 |
| % Blades | | 40 | | 25 | | 21.1 | | 17.7 | | 18.7 | | 19.5 |
| | | (57.1) | | (50) | | (48) | | (30.9) | | (29.4) | | (35.8) |
| % Flakes | | 60 | | 62.5 | | 73.6 | | 77.6 | | 68.8 | | 74.5 |
| % Broad flakes | | 0 | | 12.5 | | 5.3 | | 4.7 | | 12.5 | | 6 |
| % All unretouched flakes with blade scars | | 71.4 | | 50 | | 62 | | 45.8 | | 41.2 | | 49.1 |

as if flakes 20–30 mm long and 10–15 mm broad were selected. Similarly there are more thicker and heavier flakes than from the other two sites. This may suggest that larger flakes were selected for use on site or, more likely given the waste flake typology given above, that the smaller material was not present due to the redeposited nature of most of the material.

The metrical data fit with other gravel-based assemblages such as that from Staines (Healey & Robertson-Mackay 1987, table 15) and Padholme Road, Fengate (Pryor 1978, tables 1–3) but contrast with the larger, later Neolithic and Bronze Age assemblages such as those from the March/Manea area (Middleton 1990).

The breadth:length data indicate that the assemblage as a whole contained 19.5% blades, 74.5% flakes and 6% broad flakes. The number of blades rises to 35.8% when broken examples are considered. Where differentiation occurs between the phases, principally the high proportion of blades in the buried soil and

Groups A and B, is a reflection of their low numbers. These data place the material within other local Late Mesolithic assemblages, such as Guys Farm and Bedlam Hill (Middleton, in French & Pryor 1993), and contrast with material from other periods, principally in the relatively large number of blades and the small number of broad flakes (summarized by Ford 1987, tables 2–4). Given the chronological nature of changes in waste flake shape (Ford 1987; Pitts & Jacobi 1979), the similarity between the long barrow and terrace-side assemblages suggests that the bulk of both date to the same period. The marked divergence from the earlier Neolithic assemblage from Etton further substantiates this point.

The technological data do suggest that core reduction was aimed, at least partially, at the production of blades, some of which were later made into microliths and points. It is likely, given the small number of other implements, that many of the unretouched blades were used in their raw state. However, insufficient use-wear analysis has been undertaken on these artefacts for this question to be resolved (*vide* Dumont 1987).

*Discussion*

This part of the report will concern, in turn, broad groupings of material from the monument's various components (the overall typology is given in Table 3.12):

*The buried soil:* The buried soil under the monument produced a small assemblage. The only implements were a single utilized flake and a scraper (Fig. 3.61.1). All of this material had fresh edges and was largely unpatinated (Table 3.13). Although the bulk of the material was undateable, a number of factors suggest that it may have been associated with the initial construction of the monument. Firstly, there was no evidence for *in situ* knapping, in the form of dressing chips. Secondly, the two implements, particularly the scraper (Fig. 3.61:1) displayed substantial macroscopic edge damage, consistent with heavy use. Lastly, the high implement:by-product ratio (Table 3.12) compared to the other phases indicates that this assemblage may not have been the products of *in situ* knapping and may have been brought in for a specific purpose.

These data may suggest that these artefacts were used in the initial construction of the monument, possibly for the final trimming of the timbers in the mortuary structure. The redeposited Neolithic artefacts from the other phases of the monument, particularly Phase 5, may also be associated with this activity. Their provenance may suggest that some of this was carried out away from the immediate vicinity of the site. This is further suggested by the lack of substantial axe debris, particularly flakes fractured off the tip during use (Olausson 1983) and larger woodworking implements if these can in fact be recognized as such (Saville 1980b, 22). A similar situation has been noted from a Bronze Age context at Irthlingborough, where high-power microwear studies have established the use of unretouched and retouched flakes for the final trimming of a coffin *in situ* (R. Grace pers. comm.).

*The mortuary chamber and forecourt:* The material derived from three principal contexts: the banks around the mortuary chamber, the chamber itself and the forecourt. The bulk of it derived from the mortuary structure banks and primary 'core' mound and differed from the buried soil material in containing all stages of the core reduction sequence (Table 3.16). Although it is difficult to be specific concerning such a small amount of material, the overall high proportion of blades (Table 3.22) coupled with its overall technological similarity to the material from Groups B and C, would suggest a Late Mesolithic date for most of this material. This must have derived from the scraping up of soil from the surrounding area to form the banks and so incorporating residual material. It is likely that the isolated waste flakes from the forecourt area were similarly derived.

This material contrasts with the few artefacts from the chamber, most significant of which were the two burnt leaf arrowheads (Figs. 3.61:3 & 3.61:4). The burnt tip of a leaf arrowhead from the chamber filling (unillustrated) may also originally have been associated with the Group A material. It is likely that the arrowheads were placed in the chamber in a fresh condition and were burnt in the subsequent firing of the chamber.

The overall quality of their manufacture (particularly Fig. 3.61:4) and their direct association with the skeletal material suggests that they were grave goods placed to accompany the bodies in the tomb. The fact that no traces of hafting were found would, given the quality of preservation in the remainder of the chamber, suggest that the arrowheads were placed in the chamber as found, rather than losing their hafts through post-depositional actions. Further,

that they were both burnt suggests that they were 'outside' bodies when the chamber was fired (i.e. not embedded within the flesh of the dead). These data suggest that the pieces were placed in the chamber, presumably as grave goods. Leaf-shaped arrowheads have a consistent association with the chambers of long mounds (e.g. Thurnam 1869; Ashbee 1984, appendix 8; Lynch 1969). However, given the disturbance of long barrow deposits both during their main use, and in subsequent periods, there are no good parallels for definite deposition in the manner recovered here (*vide* Ashbee 1984, xxxv).

The only other artefact associated with the burials was a burnt utilized flake which, by its condition and position, would suggest a similar depositional situation to the arrowheads. It is difficult to determine whether this would have been a grave good or accidentally incorporated during the interment of the burials. The form of the piece, when compared with the standard of workmanship of the arrowheads, would suggest that it was an incidental inclusion, possibly from the buried soil, within the chamber deposits. The remaining material from the chamber comprised two, presumably residual, waste flakes within the filling of the proximal and distal pits.

It may be that the whole of the structure was cleaned of flint, given the lack of material directly associated with the construction of the chamber and forecourt coupled with the fact that the bulk of the assemblage came from the earthworks where it would have been hidden from view. This process would have left just the artefacts in the chamber visible.

*Chamber collapse/infill and façade-bank:* Both the technological and typological data suggest this to be a discrete assemblage, with the bulk of it dating to the Late Mesolithic. This is supported by the occurrence of microliths of Late Mesolithic type (Figs. 3.61:5 & 3.61:6) and a single burin (Fig. 3.61:7). It is likely that this material derived from the old land surface which was scraped up to form the earthworks. The presence of residual material within the filling of the chamber suggests that it was also filled in with topsoil. The single leaf arrowhead fragment from the mortuary structure deposits (unillustrated) is likely to be associated with the reworking of the Group B deposits from the floor of the chamber.

*The barrow mounds and surrounding ditch:* The large majority of the whole assemblage (57.7%) derived from this phase, with the bulk of it coming from the final mound with a smaller amount from the west mound revetment and a single piece (Fig. 3.61:17) from the second phase of the enclosing ditch. The technology and typology again suggest that most of the assemblage can be assigned to the Late Mesolithic, and derived from the processes described for the mortuary chamber and forecourt material above. This includes the relatively high number of both blades (Table 3.22) and blade cores and the occurrence of microliths (Figs. 3.61:12 & 3.61:13), a piercer (Fig. 3.61:14) and a single micro-burin (Fig. 3.61:11) which can all be paralleled at the neighbouring Late Mesolithic site (Chapter 2).

However, there are indicators within the typology suggesting a Neolithic presence within this assemblage, such as the reworked polished axe fragment (Fig. 3.61:19), leaf arrowhead (Fig. 3.61:16), denticulate (unillustrated), knives (Figs. 3.61:17 & 3.61:18) and scrapers (Fig. 3.61:15). This material may have derived either from the surrounding ground surface, or be the product of activities associated with the mound. The lack of patterning, both horizontally (Fig. 3.57) and vertically indicates that the Mesolithic and Neolithic material was well mixed when incorporated within the mound, suggesting that both derived from the old land surface. This may have been associated with the initial construction of the monument (see above).

The distribution of flints within the mound shows discrete concentrations of material particularly on the northwestern side (Fig. 3.57). This may suggest that the flint, both Mesolithic and Neolithic, derived from settlements in that area. However, the lack of material on the southeastern side is noteworthy considering the presence of the neighbouring Mesolithic site (which also produced a small amount of Neolithic material). This indicates that there might not be a straightforward relationship between the position of the material in the mound and its source in the surrounding landscape. The lack of flintwork from the ditch, coupled with the lack of material from the surface of the mound, suggests that no knapping was undertaken at the site subsequent to the construction of the mound and surrounding ditch.

*Mound weathering, surface features and plough-soil*: All of this material probably derived from the main barrow mound through erosion, ploughing and the digging of features. Although the assemblage is small, the technological and typological data suggests that it is similar to the mound assemblage itself. The paucity of later material suggests that there was no further flint working in the vicinity of the monument after its final phase.

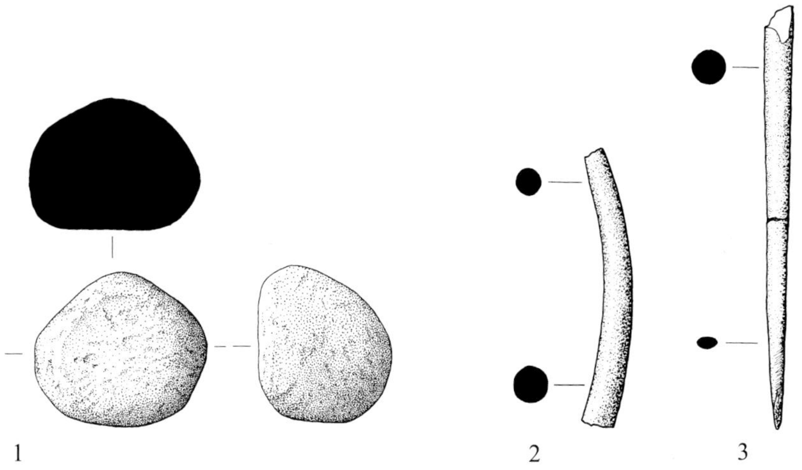

**Figure 3.63.** *Other finds: 1) rounded cobble, possible quern rubber; 2 & 3) yew wood pin fragments.*

## Other finds

### Stone
Aside from calcrete stone discussed above, two pieces of stone warrant mention:

[2966] <27783>: A rounded cobble (?flint) with one flat, smoothed surface (5.5 × 5.0 × 4.5 cm); possibly a quern rubber (Fig. 3.63:1); from Phase III long mound in Trench E.

[2995] <27613>: A small piece of slate occurred within the upper primary barrow deposits ('barrow infill'). However, given the rarity of slate within Neolithic contexts in southern Britain, in all likelihood this must have been intrusive.

### Wooden pin fragments
by J. POLLARD, with P. MURPHY

From [3443], the fill of the distal post pit, came six fragments of wooden pin that refit to form two sections (Figs. 3.63:2 & 3.63:3). Both sections are made from a fine-grained roundwood. The wood is heavily mineralized and stained black, initially leading to its identification as jet. As a result it had already been conserved and consolidated when it was viewed by Dr P. Murphy and therefore it was only possible to examine the fractured transverse sections. He reported that it was made from a young stem of a maximum diameter of *c.* 8 mm. It had been trimmed more on one side of the stem than the other, so that the pith is now eccentric. It is a coniferous wood, with relatively thick-walled tracheids, and in the sections available for examination no resin canals are visible. These features suggest that it is probably of yew (*Taxus* sp.).

All the fragments may be part of one pin, though the two sections are here described separately. The larger section is from the body and point of an elongated pin. It has a surviving length of 73 mm and maximum diameter of 5 mm. The shaft has a round cross-section, flattening towards the proximal (pointed) end. In profile, the pin narrows gently over 35 mm to form the point. A very fine surface finish with a high polish has removed traces of all but one or two shaping facets. The smaller section (46 mm in length, 5.5 mm in diameter) is from the medial section of the same or a second pin, again with a round cross-section. It has suffered from slight distortion and the surface is more poorly preserved.

If both fragments derive from the same pin, it would have had an overall length in excess of 120 mm. Speculatively, the survival of such fragile organic objects may in part have been aided by the surface treatment afforded during the final stages of production, producing a dense and largely impermeable finish, resulting in the high polish seen on the larger pin fragment.

The pin(s) is of a long-lived Neolithic type, found in both wood and bone. Immediate parallels are provided by four wooden examples from the early fourth-millennium BC Sweet Track, in the Somerset Levels (Coles *et al.* 1973, 284–5). These elongated 'conical' pins had been formed by cutting, shaving and smoothing long splinters of yew, and then providing them with gently curved longitudinal profiles through steaming and bending. Later Neolithic skewer-pins of bone are of the same basic form (Piggott 1954, figs. 62–3), a number coming from cremation and individual inhumation burials, as at Dorchester-on-Thames, Oxfordshire (Atkinson *et al.* 1951, 72), Duggleby Howe, Yorkshire (Kinnes *et al.* 1983), and Stonehenge (Cleal *et al.* 1995, 409–10). The function of such pins is potentially varied, ranging from clothes and/or bag fasteners to hair and nose pins (Coles *et al.* 1973, 285). Their use as weaving pins can probably be discounted because of the absence of evidence for textile production during the period. Later Neolithic examples have specific associations with individual burials (Atkinson *et al.* 1951, 142–4), and by extension with personal adornment and self-fashioning. The contexts of the early fourth-millennium BC examples from Haddenham and the Sweet Track have less to do with individual identity, at least directly, and more to do with projects that signified collective endeavour (a long barrow and trackway respectively). However, this is simply a reflection of depositional circumstance, and the use of the pins as personal dress fittings or body adornments can be reasonably inferred.

## Animal remains
by A.J. LEGGE

The animal bones from the long barrow are generally in a poorer state of preservation than the causewayed enclosure, their condition varying from fair in the mound itself to eroded and concreted from the buried soil and ditch fills. Several instances are found within the barrow structure where bones were deposited in articulation. Because of this, they are described below by context, in chronological order of deposition.

Buried soil
Fox: upper canine, right
Roe deer: distal metatarsal shaft, left
Cattle size: shaft of large limb bone, very eroded pelvis fragment

*Mortuary structure*
Floor
Canid: fragmentary hind limb, including head and shaft of femur, metatarsals III & IV and four other metatarsal fragments, four phalanx 1, four phalanx 2. The femur is burnt, as are the metatarsals at their proximal ends. The distal phalanges are partly calcined by burning. The specimens articulate, and were very probably deposited at least partly articulated. From the size of the bones, they are probably from the dog *Canis familiaris*.
Cattle: proximal rib fragment
Other: small fragments of skull and tooth enamel; identification not possible
Medial pit (F.706)
Cattle: distal radius/ulna, very crushed, right
Turf mound (F.737)
Cattle: phalanx 2, fused, large specimen (gnawed distal)
Red deer: diaphysis of left humerus, juvenile (eroded, referred)
Ring-bank (F.725/726)
Cattle: proximal metacarpal shaft, right (gnawed)
Red deer: complete front limb, comprising scapula, humerus, radius, ulna, carpals and metacarpal. The humerus is unfused proximal and probably distal. Proximal ulna and distal radius unfused. The limb bones are missing below the unfused metacarpal. The bones of the limb are cemented in a tightly flexed position and the bones were certainly deposited in articulation, probably with the meat upon them.

Barrow mounds
Primary eastern (F.732)
Pig: shaft of left humerus, infantile metatarsals III & IV, juvenile

fragment of innominate shaft of femur, left, infantile shaft of tibia, right, juvenile metacarpal III, unfused, right femur, left, fused distal (broken in excavation) radius, right, unfused distal (large)
Cattle: molar fragments proximal radius (eroded — referred)
Other: mandible fragment, water vole *Arvicola terrestris*

Collapse/'infill' over mortuary structure
Pig: cervical vertebrae (3); fused proximal, unfused distal proximal and distal tibia, unfused, left proximal ulna and part of proximal radius, juvenile, right (probably deposited in articulation)
Cattle: fragment of proximal femur shaft (eroded — referred); radius shaft, right, very eroded
Toad: part skeletons of three individuals; probably *Bufo bufo*

Western long mound (F.766)
Red deer: distal metacarpal, left?, fused; poor preservation
Red deer: distal metacarpal, fused, left; poor preservation

'Mounds'
Fox: metacarpal IV, right metapodial fragment
Pig: proximal scapula, right, infantile radius and ulna, left, infantile radius, left, infantile innominate, right, infantile astragalus, calcaneum, navicular, cuboid, infantile — articulate fibula, infantile mandible, left, new-born (unworn dp4)
Roe deer: edentate infantile mandible, right, referred to this species (possibly caprine)
Red deer: distal metapodial with 2 phalanx 1, unfused, 1 phalanx 2, unfused, 2 phalanx 3; poorly preserved and concreted together in articulation, left astragalus, concreted, large (probably not part of specimen above) proximal metacarpal, right, poorly preserved.
Cattle: distal shaft of radius, right, eroded shaft fragment of ulna, right, eroded vertebra fragments upper M2, right, young adult molar fragments
Pike: operculum and other skull fragments; all probably *Esox lucius*
Toad: part skeletons, 3–4 individuals; probably *Bufo bufo*

Weathering slips and peat
Roe deer: metatarsal shaft, right, juvenile
Pig: radius, infantile, very poorly preserved — referred ulna, infantile, poorly preserved
Cattle: shaft of femur, left fragments of horn core (2), phalanx 2, fused
Caprine or roe deer: proximal shaft, tibia, right
Bird: proximal right coracoid; referred to the mallard *Anas playrhynchos*
Caprine: proximal right scapula, fused, poor preservation

*Ditch fill* (F. 749)
Caprine: distal shaft or metacarpal — probably *Ovis*, distal tibia, fused, left
Caprine or roe deer: femur, shaft fragment
Pig: shaft of tibia, left, fused distal shaft of tibia, right, unfused (large)
Cattle: proximal scapula, fused, right proximal femur, fused, right shaft of proximal tibia, right distal tibia, fused, left, plus six shaft fragments, two parts frontal bone or skull, with skinning (?) cuts rib fragment mandible, left, P2–P4, young adult

*Stake-lined pit* (F. 74)
Pig: mandible fragment, edentate, infantile
Caprine or roe deer: proximal tibia, unfused, left proximal metacarpal, right
Cattle: mandible, right, P3–M2, young adult; poor preservation
Water vole: mandible fragment

Ploughsoil
Canid: ramus and condyle of juvenile mandible, right, poorly preserved — referred

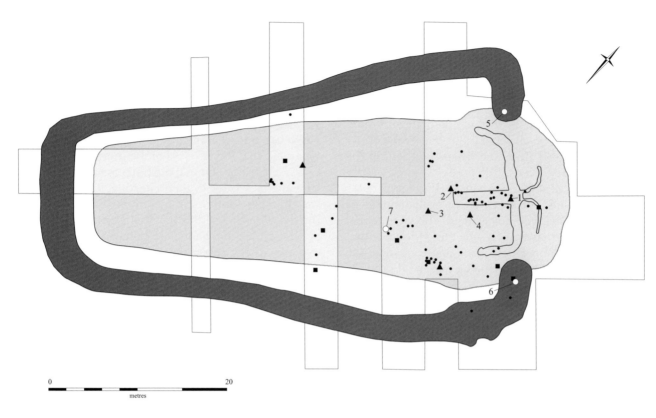

**Figure 3.64.** *Distribution of articulated animal bone deposit and 'loose' human bone. Animal: 1) dog's leg in chamber; 2) deer's leg in/on ring-bank (F.725/726); 3 & 4) pig deposits. Human: 5) tibia in northern ditch terminal; 6) skull fragment in south ditch terminal; 7) humerus in back side of Phase II mound.*

Red deer: complete metacarpal, fused, left proximal metatarsal and shaft, left frontal bone of skull and pedicels; antlers shed? Poor preservation phalanx 2, fused vertebra T4, fused proximal — poor preservation (referred)
Caprine: metatarsal shaft, left

*Articulated bones*

Three instances were found where limbs or part limbs of mammals had been buried in different parts of the barrow structure when in articulation (Fig. 3.64). These are:

1. Mortuary structure floor: dog hind limb (Fig. 3.60)

2. Mound: red deer lower front limb

3. Ring-bank: red deer front limb (Fig. 3.28).

Other groups of associated bones suggest further such deposits, but poor preservation and disturbance make this less certain. These are:

4. 'Infill' over mortuary structure: juvenile pig bones. Among

these are a radius and an ulna, bones closely articulated in life but not fusing together in this species.

5. Primary mound: bones of probably two infantile/juvenile pigs; differences in size suggest two individuals

6. Mound: associated pig bones

7. Mound slip: pig radius and ulna.

*The faunal assemblage*

The fauna from the barrow is difficult to quantify as a good deal of the bone is found in articulated groups, and most is rather poorly preserved. However, it is possible to see that the fauna is a good deal more diverse than that of the causewayed enclosure, and that more wild animal bones were found. Red deer bones were found in some quantity, along with those of the roe. The fact that the roe deer is identified from the most obvious bones (usually metapodials) suggests that other poorly preserved specimens in the 'caprine or roe deer' group belong to the latter species.

173

Certain finds of wild cattle, *Bos primigenius*, are rare. Comparison of the measurements given below with those published by Grigson (1965) and Degerbøl & Fredskild (1970) show that most of the cattle fall within the range of bone measurements known for Neolithic domestic cattle. Perhaps the single exception is the phalanx 2 from the turf mound of the mortuary structure, which on all dimensions falls at the upper limit for Neolithic domestic males, and within the range of *Bos primigenius*.

The finds of amphibian bones in the mound raises certain questions. The specimens are all identified as the common toad *Bufo bufo* which is known to tunnel deeply for hibernation. It seems quite probable that these rather well preserved small bones are intrusive into the mound rather than being preserved from the Neolithic, bearing in mind the hostile burial conditions for even large bones. The finds of a mallard bone and pike bones in the mound may represent quite recent intrusions.

*Bone measurements*
Measurements have been taken where possible, following von den Dreisch (1976). The symbol (E) indicates that the bone measurement is estimated where the bone has suffered slight damage at that point.

**Cattle**
P scapula R LG = 57.7  Bg = 49.7  GLP = 69.5  SLC = 53.4
D tibia L Bd = 60.4  Dd = 44.4
phalanx 2  GLPe = 50.0  Bp = 37.3  Sd = 28.8

**Pig**
radius R GL (ex unfused articulation) = 137.3+18 mm (articulation measured from recent wild specimen) = 155 mm (E). Recent wild GL = 150.2 mm

## Pollen and plant remains

During the course of the excavation S. Peglar examined a number of both pollen and bulk samples for plant remains; the results proved entirely negative. Nevertheless, 40 flotation samples were eventually sorted and examined (variously by M. Hastie, G. Jones and K. Roberts). Apart from a single very small glume base from [3196] (*Triticum* sp.), no cereals whatsoever were otherwise present and only common weed seeds were identified. The latter includes *Chenopodium* sp. (goose foot), *Fallopia convolvulus* (black bindweed), *Rumex crispus* (curled dock), Polygonaceae indet., *Vicia/Lathyrus* (vetch/wild pea), *Rubus fruticosus* agg. (bramble) and Asteraceae indet. (daisy family). Beyond this, charred hazelnuts were recovered from [3182] and [3044]; no grain or plant impressions were apparent on any of the pottery.

Generally the monument's plant remains indicate no more than that the barrow stood in open 'scrubby' ground, and the evidence as a whole suggests that plant remains (particularly cereals) played little or no role in the barrow's rituals.

## Overview discussion: depositional practices and finds distributions

However remarkably preserved, it has been demonstrated that the survival of the mortuary chamber was not 'perfect' and that the timbers had undergone fungal attack prior to their charring. Therefore, had the chamber's interior, for example, been shallowly incised with 'megalithic art' this is unlikely to have survived (deeply channelled patterns should, however, have been apparent: see Evans 1989b). The one artefact whose recovery allows us to assess in any way the 'missing' as regard organic material culture is the yew pin from the distal post pit. The recovery of this fine piece alone allows us to question why the leaf-shaped arrowheads were without their hafts or the absence, for example, of wooden bowls. Of course, in this context and given the character of Neolithic mass interment practices as regards individual identity, a prime concern is whether the dead were buried clothed. Unfortunately the evidence is ambiguous. On the one hand, no trace of any textile was identified, and clothing might have been expected to have otherwise kept bundles of quasi-articulated/defleshed human bone together in the light of the displacement of individual pieces. Yet, if presuming that the purpose of the yew pin was primarily to hold together clothes (vs e.g. hair), then this presupposes that the dead were dressed.

Although impossible to associate directly with an individual interment, it is only the one leaf-shaped arrowhead and the yew pin that could in any way be classed as grave goods, and the latter is, in fact, probably better thought of as a personal ornament. Whilst the paucity of accompanying grave goods is surely telling of the generic status of the individual at that time (and the deconstruction of identity through mass interment), the 'experience' of the chamber as a ritual space is also relevant. As will be further explored in the chapter's Concluding Discussion, the reeking 'charnel house' environment of its interior would simply have made it an unlikely vehicle of public display and grave goods clearly did not significantly feature in its rituals.

In contrast, as is evident in the pottery plotting (Fig. 3.60), the chamber's eastern entrance was clearly the main venue for placed deposition. The other leaf-shaped arrowhead in the upper fills of the proximal pit may have occurred in a similar capacity, as indeed may also the articulated limb of a dog set in the mouth of the chamber. Based on the distribution of Pot 2 it would seem that it was probably complete vessels that were set at the chamber's entrance. These may have held offerings of food and/or drink for the *en masse* 'generic' ancestors or, alternatively, have been deliberately broken there so that the pot itself was 'sacrificed'.

It is difficult to establish the phasing of these offerings. On the one hand, if the pots were set there whole then this would have made it awkward to gain access to the chamber and, therefore, it would be logical to assign them to the Phase III.3 'closure'. Yet, on the other hand, they do seem effectively confined within the hornwork-funnel of the fore-structure and this suggests chamber-contemporary activity (Phase III.1). Here it is relevant that a complete Grimston Ware vessel (P1: Figs. 3.58 & 3.60), probably a Phase I deposit and certainly occurring no later than Phase II, was set at the foot of the façade *c.* 3.00 m south of the entrance so as to not impede access and thereby incur its breakage.

As discussed by Knight above, whether or not the monument's usage actually spanned a transition between Grimston/plain bowls and decorated Mildenhall vessels, it is surely relevant that only the former wares occurred within the chamber itself. Apart from the presence of one sherd within the southern side of the primary mound (P9) (that may have been 'introduced' through the secondary expansion of the mound), the decorated wares all occur exterior to the Phase II mound and the chamber, and therefore their deposition is probably best assigned to the Phase III 'closure' activities and 'exterior' rituals. Here the recovery of the decorated P5 sherd from the southern ditch terminal is particularly relevant. Occurring beside a human skull fragment (Figs. 3.60 & 3.64), it suggests an intentional association deposit and that in Phase II it was not just the sealed chamber entrance but the entire eastern front of the barrow that was considered an 'active' ritual venue.

As previously mentioned, the occurrence of a base sherd from a later Bronze Age urn in the IV.1 façade-bank, which subsequently sealed the funnel entranceway of the hornwork (and the pot cluster), is intriguing. Whilst possibly suggesting that the remodelling of the front of the monument was a substantially later event (Early Bronze Age?) and related to round barrow construction in the area, without further collaborative dating evidence (e.g. no later flintwork was identified) this cannot be demonstrated.

Although animal bone occurred only in low numbers, the relative proportion of the species represented has been calculated (by C. Swaysland; Table 3.23). The faunal assemblage is interesting on a number of counts, primarily for its frequency of wild animals, specifically red and roe deer which together represent 25 per cent (MNI; 21.7% NISP).

It may be relevant that the only articulated animal bone group found within the mortuary chamber was the hind limb of a dog. If associating it with the leaf-shaped arrowheads, then arguments could be mounted concerning the possible representation of hunting activities, and this could be furthered by the recovery of an articulated red deer limb from the F.725/726 ring-bank. Yet the relatively high numbers of pig, especially when compared to the causewayed enclosure (see Legge, Chapter 5), could equally attest to a forest-based economy such as is more commonly found on later Neolithic sites, particularly Grooved Ware occupations (e.g. Grigson 1982). Again, it is noteworthy that of the four bone groups listed by Legge as possibly representing other articulated deposits, all of these are pig (including juvenile groups within the primary mound), and no articulated cattle offerings were identified. However, rather than being directly representative of economy *per se*, taste and structured cultural choice may have determined this. Admittedly producing only a very small assemblage, no pig whatsoever was forthcoming from the adjacent terrace-side investigations (see Legge, Chapter 2).

As indicated in Table 3.24, what is equally noteworthy is just how much of the monument's animal bone was articulated. Accounting for a third of the assemblage (and again in contrast to the causewayed enclosure), this must essentially reflect placed offerings of meat. It is surely relevant that, apart from the dog leg, all of these deposits occurred within the mound *per se* and appear to have been placed as construction-related rituals. Unlike the pot at the chamber's entrance, these would have been inaccessible to scavengers (i.e. 'hidden') and this suggests that a certain degree of pragmatism underlay these rites. (Of course, had articulated cuts featured in the forecourt offerings then these might have been entirely removed by animals. However, few bones occurred within this swathe, and that the phosphate levels were low there would equally indicate that meat was not amongst the placed goods/stuffs.)

As noted above, the occurrence of bird and fish bone within the mound deposits may reflect its later usage (Bronze/Iron Age) as an in-fen 'stand'.

As is apparent in the distribution plot (Fig. 3.57), the bulk of the flint assemblage clearly occurred within the area of the eastern primary mound, and its edge, especially along the southern side, can actually be distinguished by this plotting. This is attributable to a number of factors, including activity associated with the 'function' of the barrow itself, as well as

**Table 3.23.** *Major species relative proportions, MNI calculated by context.*

| Species | NISP | NISP % | MNI | MNI % |
|---|---|---|---|---|
| Cattle | 35 | 33.0 | 10 | 35.7 |
| Caprine | 2 | 1.9 | 1 | 3.6 |
| Pig | 31 | 29.2 | 9 | 32.1 |
| Roe deer | 2 | 1.9 | 2 | 7.1 |
| Red deer | 21 | 19.8 | 5 | 17.9 |
| Canid (dog?) | 15 | 14.2 | 1 | 3.6 |

**Table 3.24.** *Major species proportion of MNI deposited in articulation.*

| Species | Total MNI | No. disarticulated | No. articulated | % articulated |
|---|---|---|---|---|
| Cattle | 10 | 10 | 0 | 0 |
| Canid (dog) | 1 | 0 | 1 | 100 |
| Pig | 9 | 3 | 6 | 66.6 |
| Caprine | 1 | 1 | 0 | 0 |
| Roe Deer | 2 | 2 | 0 | 0 |
| Red Deer | 5 | 3 | 2 | 40 |
| **Total** | **28** | **19** | **9** | **32.1** |

the weathering of material redeposited within the mound's make-up.

Yet are we, in fact, seeing a 'lithic site' redeposited within the bulk of the barrow's mound(s)? Taking the figures 'raw', the *c.* 500 flints recovered from *c.* 3750 sq. m of turf (or at least non-ditch derived upcast soils) that has been estimated to have gone into the mound's construction overall represents a density of only 1.3 pieces per metre square. Even if we double this figures in recompense for the proportion of the mound actually excavated, it still does not approach 'site' densities as opposed to 'background' distributions (see Chapter 4 below for discussion of site density 'thresholds'). Within the area of the primary barrow alone (F.732), the density of struck flint was only 1.7 per metre square (0–15 range).

Two distinct concentrations of material were nevertheless apparent; one in the northwestern quarter of the primary mound (A), with the other in the core of the secondary long mound in Trench B. Unfortunately the non-recovery of finds from Trench L compromises their analysis, as it is impossible to determine whether these conjoin and represent a continuous higher-density swathe limited to the north half of the mound or, indeed, two distinct concentrations. Here it is presumed that the two were discrete. The eastern cluster (A) was by far the more dense and flint occurred at a mean density of 5.8 pieces per metre square (1–15 range) as opposed to the Trench B scatter (2.8 per metre square mean; 0–6 range). Whereas the former contained both Mesolithic and Neolithic types, in contrast to Cluster B in which Neolithic plain bowl pottery also occurred, ceramics did not feature in Cluster A and it may, therefore, have been largely of Mesolithic origin. Evidently at least in part of Neolithic date, the Cluster B material would be attributable to two explanations; it must either represent traces of a pre-barrow occupation or relate to activities contemporary with the usage of the 'open' Phase II mound and/or its construction (i.e. camping by the labour force). Whilst the densities of both of these flint clusters are greater than that of the terrace's test pits at 2.15 per metre (3.25 exclud-

ing nil values: see Chapter 2 above), the in-mound cluster values should be reduced by a factor of a half to two-thirds in recompense for the multiple turf/buried soil horizons that contributed to their per metre density.

As was the case with the terrace-side scatter (see Chapter 2 above), there is a real problem in the designation of the barrow's flint assemblage. It has essentially been described as being of later Mesolithic date with a minor earlier Neolithic component. Yet in recent years the degree of overlap between these two lithic technologies has been highlighted (e.g. Edmonds *et al.* 1999). In the case of the barrow's assemblage, leaving aside pieces directly associated with the Neolithic chamber itself, less than two per cent of the assemblage is attributable by type to either of these periods (four each of distinctly Mesolithic and earlier Neolithic date). This, and the sheer quantity of plain bowl sherds present in the barrow (and also in the terrace-side cuttings), raises the issue of to what degree the flint assemblage should either be considered 'transitional' and/or attest to both substantive Mesolithic and Neolithic activity.

Finally, we need to consider what other pieces of the barrow's assemblage were recovered in direct association with the chamber, but cannot be formally assigned as grave goods. The reworked polished axe (Figs. 3.61:19 & 3.60) was found on the interior edge of the chamber's ring-bank along its northern side and must have been placed there, probably following the working of the structural timbers. Aside from the leaf-shaped arrowhead recovered from the fill of the proximal post pit (and that in the distal sub-chamber), two others were found in the mound 'infill'/collapse immediately behind and above the timbers of the distal sub-chamber (Fig. 3.60). Taking the total number of arrowheads associated with the chamber up to four, given that comparable pieces were not found anywhere else within the mound the occurrence of the latter cannot be co-incidental and they also must have been thus 'placed'.

## Dating evidence

Eight radiocarbon dates were initially submitted (HAR-9171-78: Table 1.1). Of these, the two bracketing the series seemed obviously unacceptable: taken from the primary F.710 wood debris from under the mortuary structure's banks, the HAR-9171 date of 3620–3340 cal. BC (HAR-9171; 4660±50 BP) seems one to three centuries too late; whereas HAR-9178 (4950–4450 cal. BC; 5770±140 BP), from the secondary inhumation (F.742) in the top of the barrow mound, must be one to two millennia too early. (In a further effort to date the IV.2 inhumations, in 2003 bone from the other burial, F.743, was submitted to Beta Analytic for analysis, but unfortunately proved to have insufficient collagen.) Otherwise, apart from HAR-9173, the dates from the timber structure showed strong concordance and all fell between c. 3900–3600 cal. BC. Fortunately greater resolution of the dating was forthcoming through Morgan's study of the timbers' tree-rings, for which five further radiocarbon dates were obtained (UB3167-71: Table 1.1).

### Tree-ring results
by R. Morgan

The aims of the tree-ring study were to demonstrate links between the timbers to provide an internal relative dating framework, and as a result to produce a site master chronology for the purposes of absolute dating. The condition of the wood and the method of conversion did not initially suggest that attempts to measure and cross-match tree-ring patterns would be successful. However, ring patterns were recorded on some fragments lifted during excavation, and many of them could be correlated (Figs. 3.65–3.68), encouraging further work on the reasonable assumption that many samples would have originated in the same timber or tree. Ring patterns were measured wherever possible; despite many failures, the cross-matching procedure has produced valuable results. Shorter series have been extended by averaging several overlapping sections from the same timber, and these in turn have enabled further series to be fitted into place. The methods of tree-ring study are outlined in greater detail below.

Tree-ring dating is based on the principle that two trees growing over the same period of time will exhibit similar fluctuations in the widths of their annual rings; a record of the growth pattern of each timber can thus be used to demonstrate their relationship in time. Where upwards of about 25 growth rings could be determined, without cracks or interruptions, the exact ring-widths of the Haddenham timbers were measured. Size posed no problem in the smaller slices from roof blocks, but one or two of the larger floor sections were too thick and heavy for the equipment used for measuring rings, and the rings were measured manually using a ×10 Beck magnifying lens. Most sections were recorded using the standard equipment of a binocular microscope, with a Bannister incremental measuring machine linked to an Apple II microcomputer, using software written by Dr J.R. Pilcher of Belfast. (Further details can be found in Baillie 1982; Hillam 1985; Morgan 1988.) Oak rings were measured along one radius, from the start of one line of early wood vessels to the start of the next. The Haddenham sections were particularly difficult owing to the 45° angle of the rings and rays to the plank surface; this necessitated regular re-alignment of the wood in order to follow a new radius. Where a pronounced pattern of wide and narrow rings was present, this movement caused no problem, but could be a source of error in samples with very uniform ring-widths. Added to this, the cracking and compression of the wood had clearly caused interruptions to the tree-ring record, and some attempts at measurement had to be abandoned. Prior to measurement, each group of five rings was marked using typewriter correction fluid, and this process sometimes revealed inconsistencies of growth pattern on either side of an invisible crack. Such series would be unreliable; it is suspected that some of the failures in cross-matching were due to this problem of cracks going unrecognized.

Cross-matching was aided by the CROS progam (Baillie & Pilcher 1973) with modifications (Okasha 1987), used both on the Apple II and mainframe Prime computers. The length of ring series and overlap is taken into account in the calculation of Student's $t$ values, which may be significant to 95 per cent confidence limits when over 3.5. All possible matches must be checked back by visual overlays of the plotted graphs, and must be replicated by being internally consistent.

A number of short ring series were measured on the Haddenham wood, the theory being that many could be broken fragments from the same planks and may therefore show clear cross-matching. However, this possibility would also rely on the presence of several longer series to link the short ones together. The minimum ring series length of 50 years applies to samples of split wood submitted for absolute dating. It has been shown that short ring series of 30+ years can be useful in tree-ring dating (Hillam et al. 1987; Mills 1988), and roundwood with bark surface is particularly suited to the establishment of relative dating frameworks (Morgan 1988; Hillam 1985; Bartholin 1978) and even absolute dating (Hillam 1987).

It would be particularly useful to be able to define precisely which of the mortuary chamber timbers originated in the same trees on the basis of the degree of similarity of their ring patterns. It is usually assumed that correlations of, for example, $t = 10$ or higher suggest a common origin. The only study of within- and between-tree variation in living oaks (Milsom 1979) suggests little difference in the ring patterns within one tree and between different trees growing in the same woodland; average correlations of 0.577–0.756 were found between trees, and 0.553–0.753 within individual trees. On the basis of level of $t$ value, visual appearance of the tree-ring match, and information on the wood such as location, size and cross-section, it can be suggested that two timbers came from the same tree, but this can never be definitely proved.

### The floor timber and posts

The floor planks and posts provided a total of 74 measured tree-ring series, up to 116 years in length. The 74 series (listed in Tables 3.25 & 3.26) represented four posts, four floor planks, the north wall timber, the three large horizontal timbers and 15 isolated fragments perhaps broken from the timbers in the distal sub-chamber. The sources of the tree-ring series are illustrated in Figure 3.69.

177

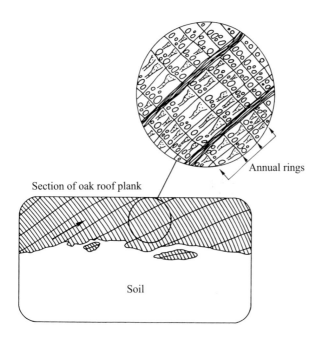

Figure 3.65. *Schematic cross-section of a block from the roof.*

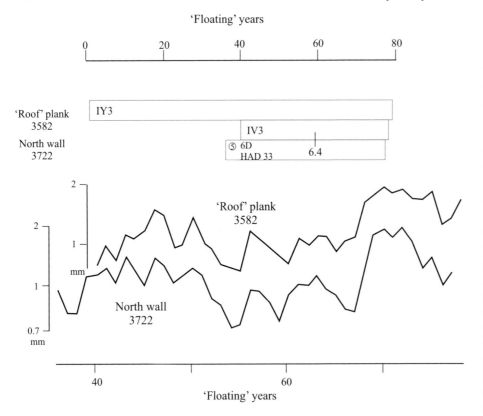

**Figure 3.66.** *Corresponding tree-ring patterns.*

procedures and duplication of ring patterns where possible. Many of the short series could not of course be matched with certainty.

A number of the ring series were duplicate sets of measurements on fragments of wood known to be from the same timber; this was often necessary because of fragmentation during lifting or sampling. It was also useful to extend and confirm the pattern in cases of cracking or other difficulties. For example, medial post [3687] was measured along nine radii; the ring series of each radius could be correlated over 170 years and averaged to give a much more secure record. Horizontal timbers [3642] and [3645] were measured eight and four times respectively, and linked together into series of 133–134 years. The degree of correspondence ($t$ value) between the individuals (shown in matrices accompanying each bar diagram) leaves no doubt that the patterns have been correctly recorded. The averaged 170-year series from the medial post [3687] became the centre of the cross-matching process, and its time scale remained the same throughout the study (i.e. year 1–170 of the relative framework), although the last 20 rings represented by only one sample have been omitted from the master chronology. The first correlation appeared with the horizontal timber [3643] which lay just to the west on the floor of the distal sub-chamber; its ring pattern corresponded with that of the medial post ($t = 6.3$). Given the location, cross-section and size of [3643], supported by the tree-ring correlation, it is possible that [3643] represents the top of post [3687], apparently carefully removed and laid on the floor during dismantling. It is impossible to prove whether two timbers came from the same tree, as $t$ values can be equally high between adjacent trees as within the same tree (Milsom 1979), but the combination of evidence here suggests that it may be so. The ring series from distal post [3696] then proved to correlate with the pattern from [3687] and [3643] ($t = 7.9$ and 4.4 respectively). This post too could have

During the course of this study, there was an awareness of the short length of many of the ring series, which led to more intensive cross-matching

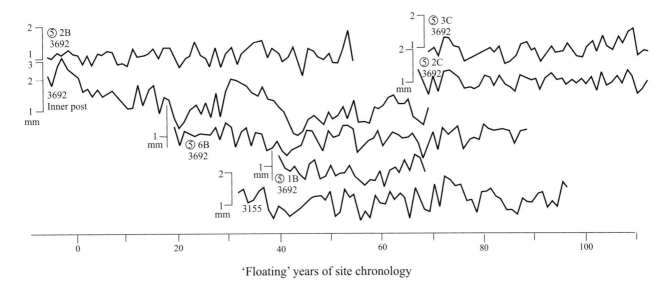

'Floating' years of site chronology

**Figure 3.67.** *Corresponding tree-ring patterns.*

been cut from the same tree or an adjacent tree in the same woodland. The *t* values show a better match between [3687] and [3696] than between [3643] and the other two. This group of timbers demonstrated a steady growth rate of about 1.1 mm per year.

The rings of both [3643] and [3696] were measured in two parts, and in each case there was an earlier series of about 100 years which could not be matched at this stage. There was known to be little time lapse between the two sections measured on post [3696], but the series from [3643] was based on a separate piece of wood of unknown relationship (except to say that it was earlier).

The next stage was to combine multiple series from several other timbers. A total of 18 series were measured from different parts of the distal sub-chamber floor plank [3692], of varying lengths between 30 and 112 years (Table 3.26; the location of each series is shown in Fig. 3.69). Linking these together proved to be the most difficult process of the study for various reasons. The large size and estimated 300 rings in this plank meant that many shorter series did not overlap with each other. Also, the rings were quite narrow and uniform at the edges of the plank, giving little pattern, so that overlaps were less likely to be revealed by reasonable t values or good visual correlations. Two groups of curves were assembled from the [3692] sections. One consisted of

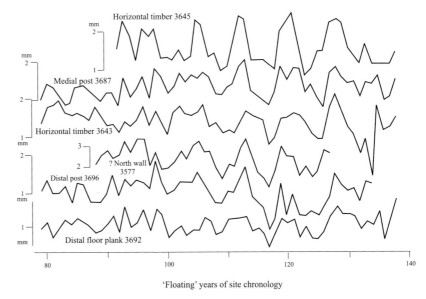

'Floating' years of site chronology

**Figure 3.68.** *Tree-ring patterns from [3692], etc.*

five individuals and spanned 146 years ([3692/1]), and a second spanned 83 years and included four individuals ([3692/2]). From the relative positions of each set of measurements, it was known that the longer curve [3692/1] preceded the shorter [3692/2]. Initially a tentative link was established with [3692/2] added on to the end of [3692/1], but with an overlap of only 22 years ($t = 3.1$). Despite the short overlap, this position was consistent with other data sets, and with the order of ring pattern groups measured on the same piece of plank (e.g. in Block 5/2C, the approximate relationship of tree-ring sequence HAD31 to HAD31A was known).

**Table 3.25.** *Details of the tree–ring series from floor, posts and roof of the chamber.*

| Timber no. | Function | No. of rings | Series included | Relative time span | Average ring-width mm. |
|---|---|---|---|---|---|
| 3255/3256 | south roof edge | (76) | 4 | (78–153) | 1.26 |
| 3540 | roof over distal sub-chamber | 104 | 3 | 114–217 | 1.38 |
| ?3577 | north proximal wall? | 40 | 1 | 88–127 | 2.36 |
| 3595 | forecourt post | 86 | 5 | – | 1.66 |
| 3642/81 | horizontal timber on proximal sub-chamber floor | 134 | 8 | 110–243 | 1.54 |
| 3645/82 | horizontal timber on proximal sub-chamber floor | 133 | 4 | 92–224 | 1.45 |
| 3687 | medial post | 170 | 8 | 1–170 | 1.15 |
| 3643/88 | horizontal timber on distal sub-chamber floor | 111+82 | 2 | 36–146 | 1.21 |
| 3689 | northern floor plank, proximal sub-chamber | – | – | – | est.3–5 |
| 3690 | southern floor plank, proximal sub-chamber | 87 | 2 | – | 1.61 |
| 3692 | floor plank, distal sub-chamber/1 | 146 | 6 | ?–67–78 | 0.95 |
| 3692 | floor plank, distal sub-chamber/2 | 83 | 4 | 57–139 | 1.02 |
| 3694 | small plank on distal floor | 101 | 2 | 97–197 | 1.5 |
| 3696 | distal post | 100+82 | 1 | 53–134 | 1.07 |
| 3722 | north distal wall | 42+48 | – | – | 0.78/1.11 |
| 3755 | roof over proximal sub-chamber | 57 | 3 | 35–91 | 1.14 |

Further comparisons then went on to reveal a correlation of curve [3692/2] with the [3687]/[3643]/[3696] chronology in years 57–139 ($t$ = 7.8). If the short overlap with [3692/1] was correct, this would suggest an end date of arbitrary year 78 for [3692/1]. No significant $t$ value was found at this point with the [3687] group; however, [3692/1] was also linked with a ring series from a wood fragment from context [3155] (found at the west end of the distal sub-chamber, perhaps broken from a timber), which may cross-match with [3687] at this point ($t$ = 3), and with the earlier series from post [3696]. The ring series from roof plank [3755] also links the group together. This rather involved series of correlations has left the [3692/2] group definitely linked with the overall post chronology, and the earlier [3692/1] group, apparently in position and internally consistent (but with few and rather short overlaps), extending the post chronology back by a further 67 years, but only represented by two ring series before year –6. The relative dating framework has therefore been left as before, and the [3692/1] individuals are not included in the master bar diagram since their positions cannot be confirmed with certainty. There were a further eight measured tree-ring series from floor plank [3692]. A probable match occurred of a series from the southeast edge (in Block 5/32) in years 14–113 of the [3687] group ($t$ = 5), showing in particular the distinctive signature of alternating wide and narrow rings in arbitrary years 90–100. This left seven series from plank [3692] unmatched, all short and less sensitive and thus of low potential for cross-dating. Horizontal timbers [3642] and [3645], as already mentioned, were thoroughly

examined and gave average curves of 134 and 133 rings respectively; the two patterns were extremely similar ($t$ = 9.4 between the average patterns for each), with clear visual cross-matching in the inner series of wide uniform rings which suddenly changed to very erratic growth rates (zones of wide rings of up to 5 mm, separated by several years of very slow growth of less than 1 mm with gradual recovery). It is thus very likely that these two timbers were split from the same tree and could even be two halves of the same section. In the averaging process used to create masters, the first 18 rings of [3645] and the last 23 rings of [3642] have been omitted, since they are represented by single samples and are thus unreplicated.

At a later stage, an 88 year series from the small tangential plank [3694] (which lay on the south arm of distal floor plank [3692] — Fig. 3.69) was also linked to this group ($t$ = 11.4 with [3642]) by the same erratic growth rate. These were the only timbers in the chamber to exhibit such variability, and it subsequently became clear that their ring pattern extended further towards the present than did those for the posts and floor planks. There were a number of isolated ring series. Rings were measured on the north wall of the distal sub-chamber [3722] (in Block 5/6D); one of the two measured series correlated with the ring pattern of roof plank [3582] ($t$ = 6.4), and suggested that plank [3582] was the collapsed upper half of the wall plank.

Another series, probably from the north wall plank fragment [3577] (at the northeast corner adjacent to the proximal post [3685]) gave a correlation with the [3687] group in years 88–127 ($t$ = 5.6), but its short length of 40 years reduces its validity to some extent.

**Table 3.26.** *List of tree-ring records from floor and post timbers and isolated finds; context and timber numbers can be found in Figures 3.19, 3.22–3.24, 3.35 & 3.36.*

| Context/ Timber no. | Lifting phase + Block no. | Dendro no. | No. rings | Relative time span |
|---|---|---|---|---|
| *Isolated finds* | | Had | | |
| 3155/A | | 1 | 66 | 21–86 |
| 3155/7 | | 2 | 50 | (MEAN1) |
| 3531/14 | | 3 | 47 | – |
| 3659/11 | | 4 | 49 | (MEAN1) |
| /18 | | 5 | 70 | (MEAN1) |
| 3155/11A | | 6 | 60+ | (MEAN1) |
| 3155/2 | | 7 | 42 | – |
| 3155/12 | | 8 | 69 | (MEAN1) |
| 3189/17 | | 9 | 26 | – |
| 3155/8 | | 10 | 35 | (MEAN1) |
| 3155/8A | | 11 | 37 | (MEAN1) |
| 3155/10 | | 12 | 60 | – |
| /9 | | 13 | 61 | – |
| 3189/16 | | 14 | 36 | – |
| 3189/15 | | 15 | 39 | – |
| *Horizontal timbers* | | | | |
| 3681/3642 | 4 | 19 | A 56 | |
| | | | B 31 | |
| | | | C 79 | |
| | | | D 21 (134) | |
| | | | E 64 111 | 110–220 |
| | | | F 30 | |
| | | | G 33 | |
| | | | H 40 | |
| 3682/3645 | 4 | 19 A(43)25 | | |
| | | | B 115 | |
| | | | C 76 (133) | |
| | | | D 38 115 | 110–224 |
| 3688/3643 | 4 | 20 | A 111 | 36–146 |
| | | | B 83 | 59–141 |
| | | | TOP 82 | |
| *Posts* | | | | |
| 3595 (forecourt) (II K10) | | 16 | 86 | |
| 3687 medial | 5/24 | 20 | A52\ | |
| | | | A1 50 | |
| | | | B 75 | |
| | | | D1 62 | |
| | | | D2 78 | |
| | | | D3 79 (170) | |
| | | | D4 51 150 | 1–150 |
| | | | E74 | |
| | | | F(87) 67 | |
| | | | G53 | |
| *Posts* (cont.) | | | | |
| 3696 distal | 4 | 20 | 100 | ?–38–61 |
| | | | A 82 | 53–134 |
| 3696 area | | 18 | 40 | 76–115 |
| *Façade area* | | | | |
| ?3577 | 8/1E | 25 | 40 | 88–127 |
| | 8/2 | 26 | 36 | |
| *North wall* | | | | |
| 3722 | 5/6D | 33 | D 42 | |
| | | | D1 48 | |
| *Floor planks* | | | | |
| 3690 south proximal | 7/F | 22 | 87 | |
| | 7/I | 22 | 31 | |
| 3692 distal | 5/2B | 17 | 112 | ?–67–44 |
| | 5/2C | 31 | 36 | 19–54 |
| | | | A 59 | 57–115 |
| | | | B 48 | |
| | 5/3C | 34 | 81 | 59–139 |
| | 5/6B | 32 | 70 | 9–78 |
| | | | A 35 | 78–112 |
| | 5/13 | 28 | 46 | 11–56 |
| | 5/16 | 30 | 30 | 29–58 |
| | | | A 35 | |
| | | | B 31 | |
| | 5/19 | 23 | 70 | –6–61 |
| | 5/21 | 29 | 50 | |
| | | | A 36 50 | |
| | 5/26 | 35 | 35 | 81–115 |
| | 5/28 | 36 | 72 | |
| | 5/30 | 27 | 43 | |
| | 5/32 | 21 | 100 | ?14–113 |
| 3694 | 5/1B–2B | | (101)88 | 110–197 |
| *'Roof' planks* | | | | |
| 3255/ 3256 | II C1/P1/N1/E1 | | (76) | (78–153) |
| 3540 | IIIJB/IIQ8/IIP8 | | 104 | 114–217 |
| 3582 | I Y3/V3 | | 40+ | |
| 3755 | I I3/R2 | | 57 | 35–91 |
| 3760 | I A1/C1 | | 70 | |

It is the only possibly linked tree-ring pattern from the proximal sub-chamber. The other measured series from this area came from the southern floor plank [3690], a series of 87 rings which could not be matched with any other material from the entire chamber. The lack of correspondence adds to the increasing volume of evidence for a slightly different date for the proximal sub-chamber.

Ring series were also measured on 15 isolated fragments of oak from the area just east of and above the distal post ([3696]) from contexts [3155], [3189] (the primary fill of the distal sub-chamber), [3531] and [3659]. Details are given in Table 3.26. These could be fragments broken from the post or roof planks in the area. Seven of the fragments revealed corresponding ring series and were averaged into a 69 year sequence, but this could not be linked further into the dating framework. There could be two explanations for this lack of cross-matching: either they come from the existing timbers but pre- or post-date the series already

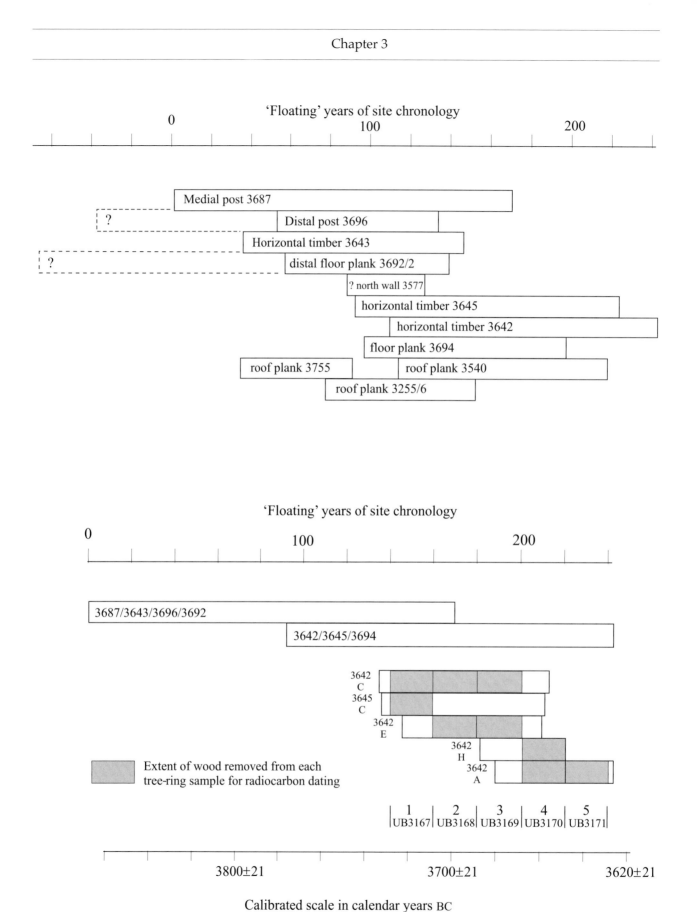

**Figure 3.69.** *Floating site chronology (above), with radiocarbon calibration (below).*

established, or they originated in other timber such as firewood or later roof planking.

The final ring series came from post [3595] associated with forecourt deposits; the 86 rings could not be correlated with any other series, and this suggests that the post is earlier or later than the chamber complex. Its pattern did show a correlation of 5.1 with the Irish long chronology (Brown *et al.* 1986) approximately spanning the century 3800–3700 BC, but the dating cannot be confirmed at the relative position with the other timbers' growth patterns. The fact that this is a single curve of relatively short length reduces the likelihood of secure dating.

Having established the composite and individual curves for each timber and some of the obvious links between them, the final stage was to check and confirm all the correlations, using extensive computer comparisons and visual checks. The major result of this work was the establishment of the link between the [3687] group and the [3642]/[3645]/[3694] group, the latter extending the chronology by a further 73 years; the 78 year overlap gave a *t* value of 5.59 (reduced to 4.5 in the shortened masters). The chronology was thus lengthened to 243 years, represented by 32 individual ring series from seven major structural timbers all within the distal sub-chamber (with the exception of [3577]). The final version of the chronology omits the last 23 rings (which are represented by only one sample of [3642]), giving a final length of 220 years.

The degree of correspondence between each curve combined with the methods of conversion suggested the presence of two or more trees. The [3642]/[3645]/[3694] ring series start not far from the pith (with around 0.1 m or perhaps 30–40 inner rings missing); the pith of the [3687] group must have been formed several decades earlier. This suggests that at least two trees are represented, one younger than the other; the time lapse is rather large to suggest an origin higher up the bole of the same tree (where the pith is formed several years later than at the base). It was noted that the terminal rings of the [3687] group coincided with the very sudden fall in ring-width in timbers [3642]/[3645]. In arbitrary year 171, ring-widths dropped from an average of over 2 mm to an average of 0.5 mm, and took some 40 years to gradually recover. Again in year 214, a fall of similar magnitude took place, with gradual recovery. These very sudden periods of extreme stress caused such slow growth that almost no dense summer wood was formed; this zone of continuous early wood vessels could have formed a line of weakness in the timber and led to fractures at this point, resulting in the termination of the wood around year 170.

This earlier end year for [3687] gives an impression on the bar diagram (Fig. 3.69) that the [3687] group may have come from a tree (or trees) felled some decades earlier than the [3642] group. It is impossible in the absence of sapwood to prove or disprove this possible varied felling date. The addition of sapwood to the [3687] group would extend its ring series to at least arbitrary year 200. If a felling date of around this time was proposed, it would suggest that the posts and floor were put in place at least 80 years or so before the horizontal timbers were placed on the floor. There is some archaeological evidence for such a lengthy duration of use of the chamber (e.g. in the evidence for early activity and different phases of posts), and it might also be supposed that timber [3643] was placed on the chamber floor in a period of dismantling which could be considered contemporary with the deposition of [3642], [3645] and [3694]. It is quite likely that a certain amount of wood (only a few centimetres if the rings are narrow) has been lost through decay or trimmed from the timber of the [3687] group (given the possible weakness just described) which would bring its felling dates in line with the [3642] group. In addition, the ring record for the medial post [3687] was based on fragments, and the main section may have contained later rings which went unrecorded, thus allowing for some of the time lapse. As a result of the tree-ring correlations, it can be concluded that the floor and posts at least (little can be said about the relationship of the walls) of the distal sub-chamber formed part of a homogeneous structure, built of timber made specifically for the purpose. It is suggested that only one or two large oak trees were split to provide the planks and posts. Another tree was used (possibly for the proximal posts) to produce the large horizontal timbers on the proximal sub-chamber floor and a small plank on the distal sub-chamber floor, laid during a phase of dismantling. Any variations in felling date cannot be determined in the absence of outer sapwood. The wood of the proximal sub-chamber differs in character and shows little correlation in tree-ring pattern: this evidence combined with stratigraphical detail suggests that the lining of the proximal sub-chamber may have been a later addition, or perhaps made use of timber from other sources.

The roof timber

A major aim was to determine the character of the roof by attempting to assess the nature of the planking and its relationship to the floor planks and posts beneath. It was hoped that even short ring series could be correlated into groups originating in the same plank without much difficulty. However, with the realization that the estimated age of the trees was over 300 years, the chances of overlapping and matching series of 30–40 rings became much lower.

A total of 55 ring series up to 88 years in length were measured on a possible 13 planks; the largest number of records were made on planks [3755], [3760], [3258], [3582], [3252], [3256] and [3255]. Most ring series were in the 30–40 year range. In a number of examples, several apparently overlapping sets of measurements were made in the hope of extending the patterns and some of these could be linked together; these multiple series of measurements were often necessary because of the 45° angle of the rings to the plank surface, so that a radius could be followed only a short distance before needing to cross several rays, a possible source of error. In other cases, confirmation of the pattern came from corresponding series from adjacent blocks. Much time was spent attempting to match these short series, with the aid of a Sheffield computer program CROST-ALL (Crone 1988, modified by Okasha 1987), which produces a matrix showing the highest correlation between every pair of curves. Mills (1988) has demonstrated the potential value of a new approach to the cross-matching of short series, using a program called CROS-TWENTY; this compares overlapping 20-ring blocks of data, and increases the chances of finding correct matches in series of 50+ years. Those curves in the 30–40 year group indicated as many spurious as correct correlations.

The same conclusion had to be reached about most of the short series from the roof timber: the correct position of match could not be isolated from several possible positions. A number of groups were established, providing small mean curves for further comparison. One pair from the southeast corner of plank [3760] (in adjacent Blocks I A1 and C1) matched with a $t$ value of 4.7. Another group followed plank [3255]/[3256] (in Blocks II N1, C1, E1 and P1); their patterns were very similar, indicating their common origin, but a group of narrow rings in the central area meant that a final average ring pattern could not be resolved with certainty. Further comparisons were made using the individuals. A group of three series from the centre of plank [3755] (in Blocks I I3 and R2 at $X = 7.3$ m just east of the medial post over the proximal sub-chamber) could be correlated over a span of 57 years.

Links between ring patterns from Blocks I Y3 and V3 provided a record for plank [3582], over the northeast corner of the distal sub-chamber. A further correlation was found with the north distal wall timber [3722] (in Block 5/6D at $X = 5$ m); this tends to confirm the suspected origin of [3582] as collapsed wall planking.

The final identifiable group represented plank [3540], the lower level plank over the centre of the distal sub-chamber roof. One long series (from Block III JB) and two shorter series (II Q8 and P8) were linked into a 104-year sequence. Several probable correlations of these curves with the established chronology for the floor and posts suggests some contemporaneity of parts of the roof wood. This had already been surmised from the size, orientation and sections of some of the planks (such as [3755]/[3252] and [3540]). Links were found with the tree-ring patterns from plank [3755] (Blocks I I/R) and wood from context [3155] (possible roof collapse fragments within the chamber deposits) and the plank [3692/1] group (Fig. 3.36). The suggested date span for the [3755] group of arbitrary years 35–91 could be confirmed by clear similarities with individual and mean curves ($t = 6.4$ with [3692/1]; $t = 5.3$ with [3692/2]). Another possible match of the rings of plank [3760] (Blocks I A1/C1) with [3692/1] ($t = 4.1$) in arbitrary years –8–61 is a further link between roof and floor wood. However, this whole early group based on [3692/1] is not as firmly placed as the main floor plank, post and horizontal timber complex. The second group to be correlated was from planks [3255/3256] (Blocks II C1–P1) with the overall chronology in years 78–153 (possible mean $t = 6$, II N1 $t = 5.5$ and II E1 $t = 4.5$ with [3696]). This plank, judging by its cross-section and the direction of growth of the rings, probably represents the outer edge of a tangential roof plank.

The third link was between the pattern for plank [3540] (III JB,II Q8 and P8) and the main chronology in years 114–217 ($t = 5.2$).

These links are sufficient to show that parts of the roof at least were from trees felled around the time of construction of the distal sub-chamber. The lack of evidence from other planks does not necessarily indicate a different date, but perhaps simply a lack of overlap or little evidence of a unique match of these short series. The impression given by the roof wood is one of a combination of the remnants of original wide tangential planks ([3540], [3755]/[3252]) split and laid to reflect the floor plank [3692] below, of collapsed wall planking ([3538], [3253]) and of plank remnants placed in gaps ([3254]). In view of the evident decay and loss of outer wood, there is no relative dating information in the cross-matching of the roof and floor wood; if the trees for the roof planking had been felled 10 or 20 years later than the trees for the posts and floor planks, this short time lapse could not be determined from the tree-ring record. The correlations therefore cannot prove a common felling year, but only a general contemporaneity.

Calendar and radiocarbon dating

The radiocarbon dates obtained on material submitted during excavation indicate a calibrated (Pearson *et al.* 1986) date range of approximately 4000–3500 cal. BC, giving some guide as to the time span of the 220-year master chronology from the planks and posts of the distal sub-chamber. Comparisons were made between this chronology and existing dated reference chronologies of this period. However, it was anticipated that the fact that the chronology was represented by only a few trees might be detrimental to its chances of absolute dating; the averaging process of a large number of trees removes any single tree idiosyncrasies, and maximizes the climatic signal inherent in the growth pattern. The failure to date some prehistoric chronologies is thought to be due to this problem of lack of representation.

There is also limited reference material spanning the fourth millennium BC. A long chronology back to 5289 BC and before has been established on bog oaks in Northern Ireland (Brown *et al.* 1986), complemented by several chronologies for regions of West Germany from bog and river gravel oaks (Leuschner & Delorme 1986; Pilcher *et al.* 1984; Becker 1983). All these are based on oaks growing on peat bogs or river floodplains and killed by natural events, and these effects on their growth patterns must be taken into consideration; by contrast, the Haddenham oaks were probably growing on dry slopes, and were felled and thus preserved by human intervention. In Belfast, the construction of a continuous English chronology has been under way, using a large assemblage of oaks from Lancashire bogs which gave a chronology starting in 3198 BC, but with a group of earlier trees spanning 3601–3109 BC, and Fenland bog oaks collected by Godwin and now dated to the period 3196–1681 BC (Baillie & Brown 1988). Good correlation of the Fenland material with the Irish chronology gave encouragement for the possible dating of the Haddenham material with Ireland, although the first radiocarbon dates made it clear that the mortuary chamber must date earlier in the fourth millennium BC than the first submerged bog oaks of the fens.

Apart from these assemblages, the only other material dating to the fourth millennium BC is the now dated chronology of 438 years based on archaeological timbers from the Sweet trackway in the Somerset Levels, submerged forest oaks from the Somerset shore, and river gravel oaks from the river Trent (Morgan *et al.* 1987; Morgan 1988). On radiocarbon evidence, this master chronology spans approximately 4200–3750 cal. BC (Baillie & Pilcher 1988); the recent absolute dating has confirmed the suspected end date of 3807 BC for the Sweet track, and the whole

chronology is now known to span 4202–3779 BC (Hillam *et al.* 1990). With the assistance of the Belfast team, comparisons were made of the Haddenham chronology with much of this unpublished data. No significant *t* values emerged from computer runs with the long reference chronologies nor with the Lancashire or Fenland material (which is probably too recent, judging by the Haddenham radiocarbon dates). Computer testing was extended by running overlapping 50- and 100-year sections of the chronologies together, to determine if there were shorter periods of clearer cross-matching. The only possible position was a tentative overlap of about 100 years (*t* = 4.76) beyond the end of the Sweet track group, and the suggested date span would be consistent with the existing calibrated radiocarbon dates, giving a calendar date of *c.* 3600 BC or after for the end of the Haddenham chronology.

Since the mortuary chamber was clearly built at a time which has so far produced few other wooden archaeological structures, and thus dendrochronological material, an alternative method of dating was sought. In certain circumstances, radiocarbon dating has the potential to provide an end date in calendar years almost as precise as a tree-ring date, especially in cases where no sapwood survives. The technique of 'wiggle-matching' is designed to reproduce the fluctuations or 'wiggles' in the calibration curve over a century or more (Pearson *et al.* 1986; Pearson 1986), through the radiocarbon dating of a series of samples of known relative age. In reproducing the fluctuations in the level of radiocarbon over a short period of time, the dated series can pinpoint a much more precise end year for a floating tree-ring chronology by much reducing the standard deviation (through both high-precision dating and 'wiggle-matching') compared to a standard radiocarbon date. Although the time lapse between the end year of the chronology and the felling date of the trees cannot be determined (owing to the loss of outer wood), some knowledge of the source of the wood relative to time of construction is a great improvement on the random collection of samples for single radiocarbon dates. Since the trees' age is known to exceed 300 years, the use of a wood sample from near the centre of the tree for a single radiocarbon date could already introduce a dating error of several centuries.

The calibrated series of dates fix the final phases of the chamber's life much more clearly than the spread of single dates already obtained for the timbers, based on wood from unknown positions within these aged trees. The result of 4950±70 BP (HAR-9175) from wood of floor plank [3692] is consistent with the results presented here; other dates are not. A series of radiocarbon samples were cut from selected rings and submitted to the Belfast Radiocarbon Dating laboratory, which specializes in high-precision dating. Five wood samples were cut from the rings of horizontal timbers [3642] and [3645] (the only timbers which could provide sufficient material), each spanning consecutive groups of 20 years; they thus represent the final 100 years of the arbitrary tree-ring scale (Fig. 3.69; Table 1.1).

The radiocarbon dates were calculated to lie between 4874 and 4947 BP within one standard deviation of ±20 years (Table 1.1). The pattern shown by the series of dates was readily matched against two calibrations (Fig. 3.70), one as published (Pearson *et al.* 1986), and a more recent unpublished version still being checked, which will result in around a 20 year shift in the published dates (Pearson pers. comm.). The end result of the 'wiggle-matching' was a date of 3631±22 cal. BC or 3625±20 cal. BC (with confidence limits of 72% and 80% respectively) for year 240 of the 243-year chronology. The two dates can be averaged to 3628±21 cal. BC, or a date span of 3649–3607 cal. BC (at one standard deviation) for the end of the chronology. Since no sapwood was traced, an allowance of at least 10–55 years must be added (Hillam *et al.* 1987), and there is in addition an unknown amount of missing heartwood. Felling could then have taken place after 3618–3573±21 cal. BC, or 3639/3594–3597/3552 cal. BC if the sapwood estimate is added to the date span. The dating suggests that in all likelihood the tree(s) used for the horizontal timbers was felled around 3600–3550 cal. BC, and that the chamber may have been constructed at the same time or shortly after.

The use of wood for dating from the two horizontal timbers on the proximal chamber floor was necessitated by the insufficient quantities available from other sources of wood in the chamber. Despite the possibility that these timbers represented a destruction phase and not the main construction phase of the chamber, their relationship in time to the main structural timbers ([3687], [3692] & [3696]) is known through their tree-ring patterns; thus the radiocarbon dates can also be made relevant to the construction phase. The tree(s) which supplied the horizontal timbers [3642] and [3645], and the small plank [3694], may have been felled a little later (but only decades) than the tree(s) used for the floor plank and posts. If the two horizontal timbers were once the tops of the proximal posts, then the calibrated dates may refer to the construction of the proximal sub-chamber and perhaps the façade. In a wider context, the dates place the chamber roughly half way through the time span of long barrow construction, suggested by single uncalibrated radiocarbon dates (e.g. Piggott 1973, 36); all the dates obtained hitherto have been single dates

from unknown parts of the tree and with high standard deviations, and therefore cannot be considered at all precise. There cannot be any doubt that the prior establishment of a tree-ring chronology to provide a related set of radiocarbon samples is a much more precise means of dating structures than an equivalent number of single and unrelated dates.

Conclusions

The tree-ring correlations in particular were more successful than had been expected, given the condition of the wood. Some 130 records of the tree-ring pattern of the timber were made, and many were linked together to form a representative series for each timber. The complexities of cross-matching these ring patterns are described in this report, but can be simply summarized. Similarities in ring pattern clearly linked the major timbers of the distal sub-chamber together: the medial and distal posts, the floor plank and the large timber lying on the floor. Another linked group formed by the two oval timbers and a small plank from the distal sub-chamber floor overlapped the post group to give a final master chronology of 220 years. This curve represents several trees, eight timbers and 28 individual tree-ring series.

An earlier group of tree-ring patterns are less certainly correlated, but could extend the master chronology back by over 60 years. There were also several links with the roof planking, suggesting that some of the roof was contemporary with the other chamber components.

There is virtually no tree-ring link with the timber of the proximal sub-chamber, and its varying form may suggest it was a later addition. Nor could a match be found with a possible forecourt post.

The loss of outer wood and the vital sapwood meant that no precise relative dating information could be derived from the end years of the timbers. Time lapses of decades could have occurred between parts of the construction and these would not be identifiable in the tree-ring record.

The end result of the tree-ring correlations, a master chronology of 220 years, was then used in attempts to define the calendar date span of the growth of the trees. As already mentioned, the dating of the end year of the chronology would only provide a *terminus post quem* date for the construction of the chamber. A calibrated date range of *c.* 4000–3500 cal. BC for the various phases of the site suggested the probable location of the chronology, but comparisons with dated reference chronologies have so far failed to reveal any certain correlations. This is probably due to the few trees represented by the Haddenham chronology and to their different original growth environment, both of which could affect the overall ring pattern. As an alternative, a series of five radiocarbon samples based on tree-ring groups from 20 year intervals were submitted for dating, and gave a calibrated date of 3628±21 cal. BC (with confidence limits of about 80 per cent) for near the end year (arbitrary year 240) of the chronology. In the absence of sapwood and unknown amounts of heartwood, the felling date probably lies some time after 3618–3573 cal. BC, using the 10–55 year sapwood band (Hillam *et al.* 1987), and gives some indication of the dating of the final phase of activity in the mortuary chamber.

## Overview discussion: timing events

Given the tree-ring correlations between the chamber's timbers, by normative archaeological logic the dating of the monument is essentially a matter of pegging an 'event'. To this extent the 3600 cal. BC attribution based on the Belfast radiocarbon samples generally seems a reasonable 'fixing' of the timbers' felling. That it is later than the majority of the other radiocarbon assays can presumably be credited to the fact that it must have been the heartwood rather than the outer sapwood that registered, and by this and the size/age of the timbers involved, a 3600 cal. BC date could directly coincide with three of the original samples (HAR-9172, HAR-9174 & HAR-9175).

This attribution would furthermore be generally appropriate to what comparative local dates are available for the monument's material culture. At the Barleycroft Paddocks site a date of 3780–3630 cal. BC (OxA-8110; 4020±40 BP) was achieved for a Grimston Ware/plain bowl-associated tree-throw assemblage, and a date of 3780–3380 cal. BC (OxA-8108; 4820±40 BP) was obtained for a Mildenhall Ware pit group (Evans *et al.* 1999). The barrow's 3600 cal. BC date would be slightly too late to support the idea that its sequence marks the change between these two pottery traditions, but then it would be naive to think that such a short-lived sequence would actually bridge the 'moment' of their transition, and surely some of degree of overlap of these types must have been involved.

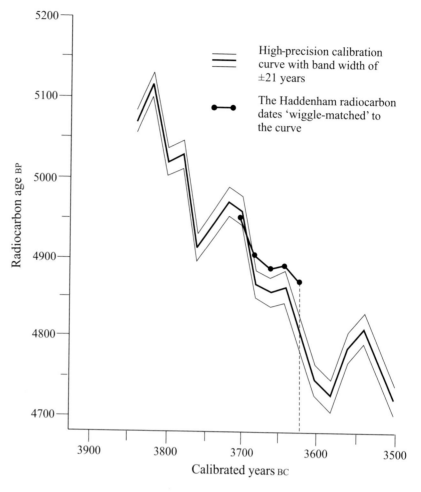

**Figure 3.70.** *'Wiggle-matching' of site chronology with radiocarbon calibration curve.*

Having provided a felling 'event date' can we estimate what kind of interval the barrow's active usage involved? In other words, where in the sequence the passage of time was expressed? On the one hand, the fact that oak wood chips, presumably related to the *in situ* working of wood, were found to directly overlie the southern ring-bank sealed cremation suggests that the interval between Phases I and II was brief. Otherwise, a build-up of soil and a greater wood decay might have been expected to have occurred. On the other hand, the development of a turf line between the Phase II and III mounds, the ovate and long barrows, attests to time. This would correlate to the fact that the chamber's wood appears to have undergone fungal attack prior to charring.

In relationship to the sequence of Phase II/III activities, the issue equally arises as to whether the firing of the chamber was directly responsible for its collapse. While in all likelihood this weakened it, that *c.* 10 cm of soil had filtered into the chamber (and off the turf mound) to seal the skeletons and to

**A central Betsimisaraka tomb in eastern Madagascar**
by M. Parker Pearson

In the region around Foulepointe, a former eighteenth–nineteenth-century slaving port on the east coast of Madagascar, the Betsimisaraka people ('the many inseparables') participate in a cult of the ancestors, in their own expression of this island-wide tradition of respect for the spirits of the dead. In much of this flat and low-lying coastal zone of tropical rainforest there is no naturally occurring stone, ordinarily the medium of ancestral remembrance. Consequently these communal tombs are constructed out of timber. They are located in the vicinity of the village, sometimes by the side of the road and in other circumstances deep in the forest. Each tomb is communal, containing the remains of as many as a hundred individuals. Traditionally these mortuary houses were built for the leading families of the area. The tomb is constructed by digging a large rectangular trench on an east–west axis, about 3–5 m wide by 5–10 m long, into the sandy soil and lining its sides and base with very thick planks so that the corpses will never come into contact with the ground. The dead are buried singly within the trench, shrouded only in a *lamba* (shawl), their heads facing towards the north, and the trench is then covered over with 10–15 large and roughly hewn timbers of the *nato* tree (*Labramia bojeri*). These are removed and then put back each time a new corpse comes to join the ancestors. Sometimes a tomb will have a pair of trenches side by side, one for men and boys and the other for women and girls. Each tomb is shaded from the sun underneath a hangar, roofed with corrugated iron or reeds and supported on many uprights. There may also be tree-trunk coffins placed under the hangar, each containing the corpse of those rich individuals who wished to be buried separately.

Like everywhere in Madagascar, funerals are important events when hundreds attend, cattle are sacrificed and observances are made to the ancestors. Ceremonies are also held at the tomb when the blessing of the ancestors is required or when a run of bad luck needs to be resolved. Unlike elsewhere in Madagascar, including the neighbouring Betsimisaraka to the north, there is no *famadihana* ('turning the dead') at which the bones are exhumed. Instead, gifts of *lamba*, rum and food are made during the *famadihana* season in September. At the east end of the tomb, the direction of the ancestors, small offerings of food and bottles of rum accompany some of the clothing, hats and personal items of the individual dead. Many Betsimisaraka, being Christian, also visit the tomb on All Saints' Day to light candles, clear the tomb area and repair the structure. At a traditional funeral the corpse is washed and wrapped in a white *lamba* or shroud, secured by seven wrappings. The bamboo which contained the water is broken. Mourners' tears are accompanied by small gifts, money or rice given to the bereaved family. The family provide food and drink for the long string of ceremonies over several days and nights; singing, playing discordant music, and playing games such as 'fighting the steer' before sacrificing it. Fires are lit outside around the village and the nights are spent in games and drinking. Formerly the deceased remained exposed, suspended in the house so that the liquids of putrefaction might drain into the hollow trunk of a *ravinala* palm. The liquid was then transferred to a pot and buried away from the village where a stone (*vatolahy*) or wooden *vatolahy* would be erected as a place for sacrifices and prayers.

On the day of burial, the family place the corpse by the door and file round it six times, the women untying their hair. Four men carry the corpse — sometimes in a *ravinala* coffin — on a bier, followed by the crowd. The procession to the tomb is long and circuitous, commencing with several laps around the village and punctuated by frequent stops and dancing. At the grave, the timbers are moved aside and the corpses already in residence are moved and packed to one side if necessary. Before the tomb is closed up, the seven wrappings are cut and the corpse is put in the grave covered only by its shroud. The head of the family takes a branch and hits the ground, asking the dead who have changed skin that, if the deceased died from sorcery, they will cause the death of those responsible before it withers. If, on the contrary, the deceased lived the time destined then they must bring good luck to the mourners. The branch is then abandoned on the tomb. The head of the family then pays the gravediggers, to remove the taboo which has affected all who have come in contact with the corpse. The pollution is finally lifted when mourners wash themselves back at the village and burn the house or outhouse where the death occurred (it is always a good idea to move the dying to a spot which can be burnt at little cost).

Betsimisaraka burial practices are diverse. To the north of Foulepointe the dead are buried in shallow graves, their bones being exhumed and placed in above-ground wooden boxes, sometimes with the bones of the men in a box to the north and those of women in the box to the south. Further inland, where the coastal plain meets the rock massif which runs the length of Madagascar, the exhumed bones are placed in caves, rock shel-

bed between the floor and the collapsed roof would 'mark' time and that the structure only fell sometime thereafter. The interval between the III.1 closure and extension of the barrow and its III.2 collapse-induced remodelling might span anywhere from a decade to a century.

Having established these dating principles, the question then becomes, how long was the II.2 chamber actively used as a place of burial? Here the interred provide a sense of measure. Of the five bodies identified, given their relative state of articulation and displacement we know that one at least was 'secondary' and that the appearance of its decomposition was 'hurried' by the stripping of its flesh. A short chronology could therefore only span upwards of 20–40 years.

This would have the four other bodies all interred at roughly the same time (perhaps over a decade), a 20- to 30-year period of decomposition before the last body was inserted, shortly followed by the chamber's firing and closure. If the four original bodies were put in sequentially, with each having a period to decompose, then a longer interval of approximately 80–100 years could be proposed.

Based on these figures and the temporal indicators of the phasing sequence, the barrow's 'active' usage, Phases I to III (?and IV.1), might have been as short as 50 years' duration and could span the period of 3600–3550 cal. BC. However, weighing the evidence, a somewhat longer chronology of at least a century seems more probable and, based on parallels to other

ters and crevices. In the hilly area to the south, Betsimisaraka tombs have small rectangular stone walls, and in the coastal areas are surrounded by palisades of hardwood.

Ancestors continue to inhabit the world of the living. Traditionally they are considered to become reborn as *babakoto* ('father's son'), the largest of the lemurs known as *Indri indri*, whose haunting calls once echoed throughout the eastern rainforests. Europeans used to kill these transformed ancestors and their numbers have also dwindled through loss of habitat. Contact with the ancestors is made at the tombs or at the wooden *jiro* post, set up on level ground nearby. Ancestral shrines (*fisokina*) of forked posts are also set up within villages for sacrifices and other ceremonies. The ancestors are one of four sets of entities which may be found in most parts of Madagascar:

*Zanahary* (the creator), *Andriamanitra* (God — a recent Christian concept), the *razana* (the ancestors), and other invisible spirits such as *Vazimba* (the original inhabitants of Madagascar), *kalanoro* and *zazavavy-ndrano* — spirits of the forests and waters. Spirit possession is a feature of life in Madagascar and the living may be possessed by the spirit of an ancestor as well as by the other supernatural forces. Additionally, spirits inhabit the trees, the hills, the grass, the earth and the animals — all is sacred. Before breaking the ground for use as a rice paddy, prayers to the spirits are necessary for permission to be given. For groups that practice *tavy* (slash-and-burn agriculture), like the Betsimisaraka, the spirits' permission is required before forest clearance begins. The summits of hills are, however, never cleared and these remain as domains of those spirits.

**Figure 3.71.** *A present-day Betsimisaraka timber mortuary house, Foulepointe region, Madagascar.*

sites (and even with some doubt of the precise fixing of the dendrochronological sequence), the monument's usage would seem most appropriately assigned to *c.* 3700–3500 cal. BC.

This, however, would not necessarily encompass the dates of the secondary inhumations within the mound proper. Whilst possibly of Neolithic attribution and relating to the reworking of the mound's front, they could alternatively be of earlier Bronze Age attribution (lacking any manner of grave goods, two attempts to absolutely date them failed). If of Bronze Age date they would presumably have related to the establishment of the round barrow cemetery

on this terrace, with the higher front of the long barrow perhaps substituting as a 'round' mound. (As discussed, the possibility that the rounding of the barrow's front actually reflects a Bronze Age remodelling of the mound's northeastern end into a round barrow has been fully considered. However, this has been rejected on the basis that only one find of this date was recovered (a single grog-tempered sherd from an urn) from the upper façade-bank. Albeit attractive in the light of arguments of long-term usage, the evidence would not support this interpretation and the sherd is instead assigned to subsequent 'incidental' activity.)

**Concluding discussion: transformation and passage**

The argument that Neolithic long barrows resonate and evoke the plans of contemporary longhouses is well rehearsed (see Last above; e.g. Sherratt 1990; Hodder 1994). Certainly when viewed in the context of the regional and national corpora in which the Haddenham barrow features (Kinnes 1992; Jones 1998) its trapezoidal arrangement is striking and it appears to more closely reference longhouse form than any other barrow in Britain. Yet, as outlined below, its internal organization and operation had little direct relationship to house architecture (and the 'domestic sphere' generally). This gives rise to a series of contradictions between its plan-form and content. These are telling of the character of ritual and domestic contexts, and they enable us to explore the nature of metaphor and the role of reference/experience in the constitution of a monumental architecture. However, before addressing issues relating to the barrow itself, it is appropriate that the evidence of the terrace's preceding land-use is first reviewed.

*Pre-barrow occupation*
As detailed by Middleton, the flint assemblages from the barrow and terrace-side cuttings share the same basic characteristics, as both seemingly include later Mesolithic and earlier Neolithic components. Their occurrence raises a number of issues, which we will consider in turn. Firstly, do they represent one or more sites? Although certainty is impossible, the latter proposition seems the more likely. Based on the estimated area of de-turfing required for the barrow's construction (*c.* 3750 sq. m; see below), this would not extend as far as the southern terrace-edge scatter. What is more, the majority of the flint redeposited within the barrow was in the northern half of its mound(s). Whilst not necessarily deriving from a site on that side, presupposing that the turf cutting symmetrically ringed the monument, this would be the more feasible option. This, therefore, implies that the terrace-side scatter was essentially discrete, with the finds redeposited within the mound probably attesting to another occupation focus north of the barrow. (In hindsight, our test pitting programme should obviously have been far more extensive.)

Having established this, the question then arises: what was the character (and chronology) of this occupation? Given the evidence of axe manufacture within the terrace-side cuttings, it is likely that some element of its usage related to the construction of the barrow, perhaps the work gang's (and their attendants') campsite. If so, what of the earlier Neolithic presence as represented by the finds within

the bulk of the mound? Again, it is conceivable that these reflect either construction-related occupation and/or ritual activity associated with Phase I/II of the barrow's sequence. This, however, seems unlikely, given the unequivocal evidence of pre-barrow Neolithic activity within the Foulmire environs. The Ouse palaeochannel pollen core attests to clearance and arable production (4470–4000 cal. BC; 5240±100 BP; Q2814) more than 500 years before its construction (see Peglar, Chapter 2), and soil micromorphology points to pre-barrow arable activity (i.e. ploughing; see French above). In the light of this, it is most likely that at least some of this plain bowl-associated material related to pre-barrow Early Neolithic occupation.

The issue thereafter becomes the interrelationship of the later Mesolithic and earlier Neolithic components of both of these assemblages: did both foci each see occupation from these two periods? It has to be suspected that the answer is no, and rather we are seeing later fifth- and/or earlier fourth-millennium BC occupation having both Mesolithic and Neolithic attributes: in short, mixed or 'transitional' assemblages. Unfortunately as neither site produced contexts appropriate to date these assemblages absolutely, this matter cannot be resolved. However, since the time of the barrow's excavation hard-edged typological distinctions between the two periods have been eroded (e.g. Edmonds *et al.* 1999). Given the scant Neolithic settlement record prior to the 3700–3500 BC 'monument' horizon (and possibly also the advent of pit-type settlements; see Chapter 4 below), few definite sites of this period have been identified: it stands as a problem that we can only 'think ourselves' into. Nevertheless, in the light of Foulmire's early clearance date and the nature of the sites' flint assemblages, we may well be seeing evidence of 'transitional' occupation on this island and certainly it would warrant further investigation and study.

*A monumental architecture*
Organized around principles of axial linearity, crosscut by the imposing front of its façade works, the long barrow's is an entirely monumental architecture, and it is therefore appropriate that its 'design' procedures and construction stages are reviewed:

*Phase I*: The monument's linear axis established by the main post settings; set behind the façade screen were two cremation deposits.

*Phase II*: In the first instance this saw the reinforcement of the monument's linear axis with the construction of the mortuary chamber that was ringed by the ring-bank behind the façade screen (II.1). Thereafter, the primary ovate mound was constructed encircling the ring-bank and mortuary chamber (II.2).

*Phase III*: This saw the elongation of the barrow's mound, and the ditch concentrically surrounding the whole (III.1). The latter's inturned terminals reinforced the monument's northeastern façade front, that was still further emphasized by the addition of the fore-structure-revetted fore-banks (III.2). Ritual offerings continued to be made in front of the chamber between the hornwork-like funnelled-entranceway of these works. III.3 marked the replacement of the proximal kerb/post with façade timbers and the closure of the chamber.

*Phase IV*: This saw the collapse of the mound above the chamber and the possible grooming/rounding of the monument's front (IV.1). Thereafter, construction of the barrow *per se* ceased; the insertion of the secondary inhumations within the mound and the pitting in its top are thought to have occurred subsequently (IV.2).

As is clear from the size of the Phase I timbers, it was a matter of 'grand-scale' construction and clearly its end (the *long* barrow) was intended from the outset. The site's sequence (at least until Phase IV) essentially marks a series of construction events. Admittedly the turf growth on the primary Phase II mound attests to 'interruption', but given the scale of the primary façade (and axial posts), at no point in its building does it seem possible that it could have become any other than the long mound it became (i.e. an ovate barrow alone, though see below).

The barrow's layout unequivocally vindicates the concept of mortuary 'linear zones' (Kinnes 1975; 1979, 59–61; 1992, 85–6). With its 'design' organized in relationship to a linear orientation and a trapezoidal format, the key principle behind its construction was 'crescentric symmetry'. This can be read in the manner in which the Phase I ring-bank encompassed the chamber and was itself (at least behind the axis of the façade screen) encircled by the primary ovate barrow. Phase III saw a comparable elaboration: the elongation of the barrow with the entire mound concentrically ringed and enclosed by the surrounding ditch. As indicated on Figure 3.72 the sequence therefore describes a four-fold series of successive 'encirclements': the ring-bank around the mortuary chamber (1); the Phase II ovate mound about the ring-bank (2), with the final form of the Phase III long mound concentri-

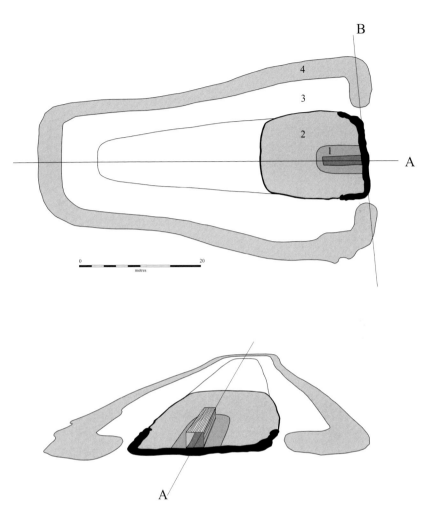

**Figure 3.72** *Crescentric design. Top, construction 'encirclements' (1–4) and main axes of orientation (A & B); below, isometric projection.*

cally ringed by the surrounding ditch and the 'berm swathe' between the mound and ditch (3 & 4). In its layout there is a sense of 'enfolding' design structures, with the absolute primacy of the façade-line being maintained throughout (at least until the Phase IV.1 'grooming' when the layout of the barrow was radically altered). What is equally apparent on that figure is that the line of the façade (B) was actually somewhat oblique to the monument's central east–west axis (A). Despite the formality of its arrangement, the barrow's 'geometry' was not perfect. However, as can be seen in the isometric projection it is unlikely that such a subtle design 'fault' would have been appreciable.

The barrow was clearly a finished work. Its mound(s) appears to have been contoured so that once turf developed on the secondary 'long' extension (Phase III.1) no seam or disjunction would have been readily appreciable between it and the primary ovate mound. In short, the monument's various upcast components would have all been masked by the overall bulk of the final barrow. Similarly, though the surrounding ditch may have originally been dug in a lobate pit-manner comparable, for example, to the causewayed enclosure, its circuit was eventually groomed to be complete and uninterrupted (apart, of course, from its northeastern entranceway). The end result, the achieving of the Phase III works, was a unified construction.

Perhaps the most telling characteristic of the barrow as a distinctly monumental architecture (with little reference to immediately contemporary domestic structures) is that earthen components were integral to the Phase II timber mortuary 'structure'; it could not have stood without the support of the surrounding ring-bank. That the wooden structure was not a free-standing building, but a matter of a timber chamber, provides a sense of contradiction and almost irony in relationship to the Continental longhouse-referencing of the barrow's trapezoidal arrangement. Whether consciously or not, distantly echoing a 'formal' house-type the long mound effectively took this model and radically changed it into a '*passage* into the ground'.

The use of bulk timbers within the chamber clearly evokes megalithic 'slab-style' building techniques (see Daniel concerning 'megaxylic' construction; 1950) and, without evidence of joinery, this was not a particularly sophisticated timber technology. Yet the chamber's construction also involved stone, round-wood and clay/earth. It does not just seem a matter of directly translating stone building techniques to wood, but rather a shared grammar of mass construction. The use of timber in the barrow also reflects upon the appreciation of process and the perception of time and the duration of monuments. The survival of barrow mounds and the evocative stone settings of henges and chamber tombs conveys a conscious sense of enduring landscape statements: things built for posterity (e.g. Bradley 1993a, 5). But the use of wood, prone as it is to decay, in the majority of lowland constructions of this type could suggest otherwise. Did they know that façade/henge posts would eventually rot and chambers collapse? Daily exposed to rotting fallen trees, it has to be expected that Neolithic communities understood their decay. Therefore, if the use of bulk timber within monuments related to concepts of endurance, then posterity would have been only a matter of centuries rather than 'forever'.

The employment of timber (as opposed to stone) in this capacity would equally involve a different relationship to transformational processes. Upon burning stone will soot and blacken, but wood will char and ignite, and thereby more directly change. The moot point, given a logic of ritual transformation (and perhaps having distinct parallels with the burning of bodies), is that firing may have conceptually turned wood into 'something else'.

*Passage/screening — experience/rarefaction*
Cramped and confined, the chamber would not have been easily negotiated by the living. Access would have demanded crouching down; upon entering, one person alone would have entirely blocked daylight into its back portions. It would have been only the proximal sub-chamber and, particularly, its threshold that would have had any potential *appreciable* ritual display.

Whilst not wishing to evoke a sense of nineteenth/early twentieth-century 'hygienic' concerns, smell would surely have been a major component of the chamber. Eventually the stench of decomposing bodies would become almost over-powering, whereas earlier in its usage the chamber would be pervaded by the acidic tang of newly worked oak (the product of the wood's tannic acids and known to be a pre-servative). Unlike stone, eventually the timber would absorb the 'smell of the dead'. By any normative standards this would not have been a space to linger in and its sensory impact may well have been part of the transformational experience.

No matter how organic was the 'matrix' of the chamber and primary mound (e.g. the wood-chip 'mulch'), the monument was nevertheless a rarefied context. In all probability the below-floor trough was intended to drain bodily fluids, just as its firing marked a cleansing of the bones and effectively a drying. This sense of a 'special' context distinct from the everyday was equally expressed in the monument's depositional practices. Almost no evidence of its constructional techniques/tools were left *in situ*; that no antler picks were recovered and only a single reworked axe fragment was found suggests that the site was 'tidied' following construction. (Antler was recovered beyond its circuit in the terrace-side section and a worked piece was found in Test Pit 2; extensive evidence of axe manufacture was also found in the terrace-edge cuttings: see Chapter 2.)

Similar concerns are reflected in the location of its placed deposits. The inclusion of articulated animal cuts within the primary mound's sequence indicates that episodes of construction were marked by ritual. Yet, equally, that meat was only really set within the bulk of the mound itself (where its decay would go un-noticed and it would not be susceptible to scavengers) suggest aspirations towards 'cleanliness', and this is further demonstrated by the low phosphate values across the forecourt entrance. Finally, there is also the distinct character of these deposits. With its frequency of deer and pig, the ritual 'economy' was evidently not that of the everyday. At least in the case of the deer, this potentially correlates with the inclusion of the arrowheads (and the chamber's dog burial) and suggests an emphasis on 'woodland life' as opposed the daily 'cattle economy' (e.g. Thomas 1999, 26–8, fig. 2.5). In fact, taken at face-value the monument's representation could suggest a quasi-Mesolithic lifestyle. Its emphasis on hunting would seem at odds with the evidence of, for example, the causewayed enclosure and contemporary settlement sites. It is as if the world portrayed within the long barrow reflects a marginality beyond the domesticated core of the Neolithic and, potentially, it references an older way of life. This constitutes still another significant contradiction within the monument's expression. However much its plan might echo the form of Continental longhouses, its operation seems to be infused with a near-Mesolithic hunting ethos.

Beyond this, the idea of *passage*, and with the implication of rites and transformation, lies at the core of the monument's organizational structures: a sense of linear progression. The living would have approached the barrow, funnelled to its entrance by the hornwork of the fore-structure. Only a select few would have attended the dead and transgressed the chamber's entrance, its threshold marking the monument's nexus. The chamber itself would have been a place of visible corporeal transformation: the dead went in and, through time, shed their individuality and became generic ancestors to be deployed by and drawn upon by the living.

Echoing the transformation of the body (in one instance involving the stripping of flesh from a 'late' skeleton to accord to the schedule of closure) there would have been a parallel with wood (resonating with the span and development of human life) and the cutting of turf may have also involved similar associations. This sense of transformational process is not, of course, antithetical to house-derived models of human development (see e.g. Tilley 1996, 238–41, fig. 5.15; Parker Pearson & Richards 1994). Nevertheless, the sense of the chamber as effectively a closed tunnel-like space would rather emphasis a sense of (in-ground) *passage* as opposed to *dwelling*. It was not a house of the dead: they were not set there to dwell in a corporeal afterlife, but to become something else.

Here the schedule of the chamber's closure may be relevant. We cannot know what the interrelationship was between the interred population; certainly they seem a 'mixed' group. As outlined by Kinnes (1992, 98–101, table 2:5.2), the majority of the interments within long barrows consist of 'mass' groups, variously fragmentary, disarticulated or cremato-

ria-related remains involving up to 54 individuals. Complete skeletons, as would seem to be the case at Haddenham, are in the minority and, with few exceptions, these do not accompany 'mass' deposits. Of the 19 known instances of complete interments, 17 (90 per cent) consists of three individuals or fewer; single cases are documented of four- and five-individual groups. Equally, there is only one example of a complete child's burial (Nutbane: Morgan 1959). Though more common in mass deposits, their frequency in those contexts is still under-represented in relationship to pre-modern mortality rates.

The number of interments within the Haddenham chamber (four plus a 'secondary' laid atop) nevertheless appears to complement the available space. Its 'operation' does not seem a matter of creating a charnel house packed full of bone, but of filling the available floor space of the chamber (subject to shifting with the insertion of the turf mound). The timing of the chamber's closure may not have related to the total representation of any one kin group sub-set, but simply the interment of a sufficient number of dead so that the mound could become a empowered place of ancestors: *a landscape pivot* rather than the receptacle of all of one population sub-group.

Whilst admitting the in-mound deposition of animal cuts and 'activity' along the back side of the Phase II ovate mound (in marked contrast to its Phase III extension), it is telling of the monument's unified organization that the northeastern façade (and specifically its entrance) remained the focus of ritual activity. The 'front', with the dead behind (be it the Phase I cremations or the Phase II chamber's interments), was maintained throughout, with the screened 'backspace' being accessible until the Phase III closure. Even thereafter the front-space seems to have hosted ritual activities. This suggests that though the arrangement of the Phase I structure differed greatly from the Phase II/III barrow, its context and operation was, effectively, comparable. If accepting this, then it may not have only been the *passage* of the deceased, but also the *façaded screening* of their attendants that may have been paramount: who could approach and handle the dead and, thereby, command ritual authority. (The addition of the hornwork fore-structure, a more slight, fence-like setting, would have 'softened' the appearance of the façade while emphasizing the chamber's entrance and contributing to the theatricality of the façade/forecourt space.)

*Authority and the measure of labour*
One means by which to evaluate further the sequence of the barrow's construction lies in the estimation of labour involved. This can only ever provide a 'rule-of-

thumb' measure; it cannot gauge the diverse modes of the organization of labour, nor what might have been the ritualized stages or symbolic character of the project of building itself. Nevertheless, such accounting does offer a framework by which to evaluate just what the barrow's erection entailed. In attempting this the size of the working gang must, of course, be postulated. In this case presuming the involvement of a lineage group, a figure of 10 adults out of a total population of *c.* 20–30 is proposed (it being presumed that other members would been allocated to food gathering/preparation and watching children or stock, etc.).

To start, the bulk of the mound in its entirety represents *c.* 875 cubic metres of soil. The ditch circuit would have had a capacity of *c.* 375 cubic metres. Working from Startin's (1982) figures, the latter could have been quarried by a gang of 10 in 18.4–27.6 days, it being estimated that they could have dug between 13.6 and 20.4 cubic metres per day. There is, of course, a discrepancy of 500 cubic metres between what the mound entailed and the ditch would have generated. Assuming that this would have largely consisted of turf, and that each turf was *c.* 0.20 m thick, then this volume could have been cut from an area of 2500 sq. m. Yet this figure cannot be used raw, as when set within the mound the turves eventually would have undergone compression. Equally, through cutting and transportation the root mat would have lost much of its adhering soil. Here a figure of 50 per cent loss/collapse has been assumed, which would increase the area of de-turfing to *c.* 3750 sq. m (equivalent of 50 × 75 m). Presuming that an individual could cut turf at a rate of *c.* 12.5–25 sq. m per day, then a 10-strong gang could have stripped this swathe in between 15 and 30 days. Adding these figures to the ditch-quarrying, the barrow thus required 33.4–57.6 days of gang labour. What these estimates do not, though, include is the transportation of the soil and the building of the mound itself. This could have increased these figures by a factor of 50–100 per cent, leaving us with a range of 50.1–86.4 days. Approximately two to three months' work or *c.* 4000–6900 person-hours, this is comparable, for example, to Startin & Bradley's (1981) estimate for Fussell's Lodge.

Even with the many caveats already applied to these estimates, these figures are probably still too low as they take no account of 'breaks' (periods of conversation, days of rest and ritual activity) and they involve assumptions of 'work discipline'. Nevertheless, it does imply that it is conceivable that the mound and ditch could have been built in one season. Yet, what would then become an issue is how long this 'community' could sustain itself at this locale, especially given

the loss of the workforce dedicated to construction. Would, for example, food stuffs have had to have been brought in? This drain on resources could have been offset by the phased construction of the monument. By progressing through the same series of calculations, the primary mound (if not involving any ditched component, but only soil stripping and turf stacking) could have been built in 12.15–32.4 days by the same group, reducing the construction time need for the main phase of the barrow by a quarter to a third. The remainder of the main mound may itself have been built over two or three annual seasons. Therefore, the consecutive construction of the 'collective' mounds (and the ditch) could have involved upwards of a month's work (and sustained 'gathering') *per annum* over three to four years.

This estimated labour involved in the barrow's construction is insightful on a number of accounts. Not least is the demonstration that it could have been built by quite a small group. Equally significant is that its labour compares, for example, with that of more renowned Wessex barrows. Just because it was located within an extreme lowland situation (and its timbers survived) there is nothing particularly environmentally specific in its construction; it was not some manner of debased version of more 'classic' upland barrows.

Finally, in reflecting upon the barrow as a planned (and completed) project, is the co-ordination of labour. A sense of intention and authority are apparent throughout; it can only be presumed that this was an extension of the ritual authority involved with who could approach and manipulate the dead and, as it were, transgress the façade-screen. The fact that the sequence was initiated by interments (i.e. the Phase I cremations) may have been a statement to that effect: ritual consecration preceding the construction of the main body of the mound(s) and the operation of the barrow.

*Orientation and structural parallels*

At the time of the Haddenham barrow's excavation there were only early pre-war barrow-excavations to draw upon from within the region: West Rudham, Norfolk (Hogg 1940), Therfield Heath, Royston, Herts. (Phillips 1935) and the Giants' Hills, Lincolnshire barrows (Phillips 1936; Evans & Simpson 1986). Subsequently, there have been two major long barrow excavations within Eastern England; at Raunds, Northants. (Healy & Harding forthcoming) and, much near at hand on the upper reaches of the Ouse, at Eynesbury, Cambs. (Ellis forthcoming). Whilst providing much needed regional context, unfortunately in the case of the latter its mound did not survive to any appreciable degree and, equally lacking evidence of any mortuary chamber or structures, its relevance is thereby limited. (At Raunds the mound survived 0.60 m high, within the tail of which was a limestone slab cist containing fragments of human long bone dated to the fourth millennium; Healy & Harding forthcoming and Healy pers. comm.)

The evidence of pre-chamber, Phase I cremation-related activity at Haddenham would have few regional parallels. At Therfield Heath a 'heap' of calcined human bones was found and two 'cists'/axial pits contained ashes (Phillips 1935). At West Rudham the mortuary house appeared to have been burnt and a patch of reddened sand and gravel was reported as a 'platform cremation' (Hogg 1940). As opposed to 'crematoria' (that is the burning of the interred through the firing of the chamber which is held to be a classic feature of northern sites, e.g. Willerby Wold and Garton Slack) the occurrence of pyre-burnt bone is much less common and has only been documented at Street House, Slewcairn and Lochhill (Kinnes 1992, 84–5, 101), cremation only becoming commonplace during the later Neolithic (Kinnes 1979). Whilst superficially the occurrence of the Phase I cremations otherwise seems at odds with the barrow's interments, in terms of a purely ritual logic its mortuary practices 'enfold' upon each other: *the 'active' monument was both initiated and closed with the burning of bodies.*

In Figure 3.73 the Haddenham barrow is shown centrally with the neighbouring long barrows respectively arranged by cardinal direction. What is immediately obvious is their degree of variability. This extends to both their orientations, which range from east–west (Swaffham Prior and Therfield Heath; 7 & 8), southeast–northwest (Giants' Hills 2 and Roughton; 4 & 6), northeast–southwest (Haddenham and Raunds; 1 & 3) and north-northeast–south-southwest (Eynesbury and West Rudham; 2 & 5), and their plans. The latter encompasses the teardrop-shaped ovoid of the Royston barrow (8) and also the elongated trapezoid plan of the Giants' Hill barrow (4). In the main, however, two main types can be distinguished: elongated ovals (Eynesbury, West Rudham, Roughton and Swaffham Prior; 2, 5–7) (of which the Royston 'teardrop' could be considered a variant) and rectangular/trapezoidal plans (Haddenham, Raunds and Giants' Hills 2; 1, 3 & 4). Whereas examples of the ovoid-type plan barrows occur on all alignments but the northeast–southwest, barrows of the latter grouping only occur on that axis, and return southwest–northeast orientations.

The northeast–southwest alignment of the Haddenham barrow is somewhat usual, as the majority of the long barrows in Kinnes's Midlands group (and throughout Britain in general; 1992, fig. 2.2.10)

are oriented east-southeast. Aside from the Raunds long barrow (Healy & Harding forthcoming), locally it shares this alignment with the 'hugely' monumental trapezoidal enclosure and its post array at Rectory Farm, Godmanchester (McAvoy 2000), both dating to the first half of the fourth millennium BC (Fig. 3.74); and other examples are discussed below. Whilst perhaps suggestive of a distinct Early Neolithic alignment, the orientation of the Haddenham barrow within the immediate environs can only be appreciated when other factors are brought to bear. This will be attempted in the final chapter.

The barrow's 'open' ditched layout, interrupted along its northeastern front, is also unique for the region, where otherwise completely ditched ovoid barrows or long mortuary enclosures dominate (the Raunds barrow having only flanking ditches along its long axis: Healy & Harding forthcoming). It is only in southwest Wessex (Kinnes Group A4: Kinnes 1992) that ditched 'U'-plan long barrows otherwise occur (Type B: Kinnes 1992). However the latter group is not truly comparable to the Haddenham barrow as none have the inturned 'front' ditch terminals and their mounds are generally of more ovate form.

Of the long barrows excavated in Eastern England, at least four others are known to have timber façade settings. This would include the Giants' Hills, Lincs. barrows with out-turned terminals (Kinnes 1992, figs. 1D.19 & 1D.20); of modest scale, that at Eynesbury only ran straight across its north-northeastern front without any return arms. Having in-turned terminals, the façade trench of the Raunds barrow provides the closest parallels with the Haddenham setting (Healy & Harding forthcoming). This was a primary feature and was later superseded by a more minor palisade trench that continued around its front and along its two long sides. Further afield, Nutbane similarly had a sub-rectangular in-turned façade setting (Fig. 3.76.3; Morgan 1959); whereas comparable to the Giant's Hill barrows, out-turned more hornwork-like façade trenches are common in the north (Raisthorpe, East Heslerton, Kemp How, Willerby Wold and Street House; Kinnes 1992, fig. 1D.21–1D.22 & 1D.27). Haddenham's antennae-like fore-structure is entirely without direct parallel, with only vague similarities to, for example, the out-turned southern terminals of Pitt Rivers' Wor Barrow palisade trench (Fig. 3.76.2; Pitt Rivers 1898). Yet its fore-structure trenches are only *c.* 0.35 m deep, and comparable features may have been destroyed through ploughing on less well-preserved sites.

As indicated in Table 3.27, the size of the Haddenham chamber accords well with those from other long barrows. There are also a number of

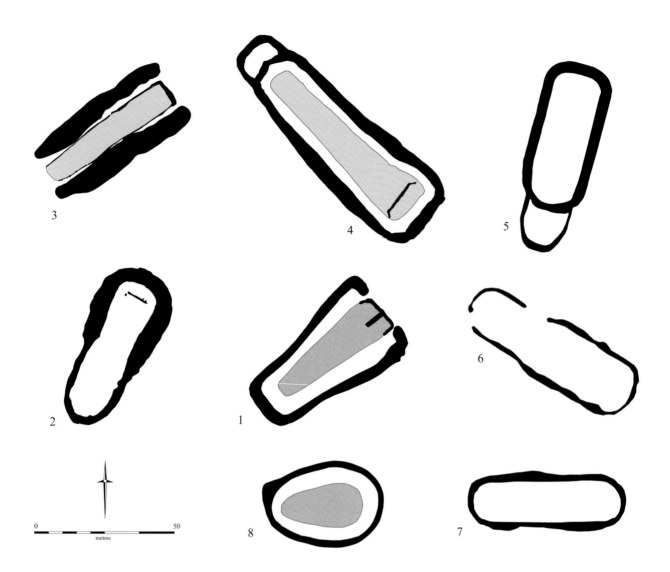

**Figure 3.73.** *A regional barrow corpus. 1) Haddenham Phase III barrow; 2) Eynesbury, Cambs. (Ellis forthcoming); 3) Raunds, Northants (Healy & Harding forthcoming); 4) Giants' Hills No. 2, Lincs. (Phillips 1936); 5) West Rudham, Norfolk (Hogg 1940); 6) Roughton, Norfolk (Oswald et al. 2001, fig. 6.7); 7) Swaffham Prior, Cambs. (Shell 2002, fig. 8b–e and pers. comm.); 8) Therfield Heath, Royston, Herts. (Phillips 1935).*

instances in which the chamber is sub-divided into two by upright posts bracketed by proximal and distal post settings (Figs. 3.76.4 & 3.76.5; Lochhill and Street House, also Dalladies 2) and elsewhere similar arrangements are determined by the situation of major pits along the chambers' axis (Fussell's Lodge and Willerby Wold). At both Wor Barrow and Nutbane the embanked chambers (and the interred) were bracketed by large pits; in the latter the eastern pit contained a post and two other large post pits were arranged on the chamber's eastern side.

It could be argued that the primary eastern mound of the Haddenham barrow has affinities with ovoid barrow forms such as Radley or Maxey

(Fig. 3.75; Bradley *et al.* 1984; Pryor *et al.* 1985). However, this would not seem valid given the later attribution of these sites and that they involved single inhumations (with a successive interment at Radley). Complementing the final layout of their mounds, these moreover were set central to their plan and these barrows were without linear mortuary chambers. The primary mound at Haddenham would rather directly anticipate the 'long form' of the final mound and only mark a stage (albeit following interruption) in its construction sequence.

Yet there is one site that potentially challenges this interpretation, the main Orton Meadow barrow (OLB 2) near Peterborough. Unfortunately it is unpublished (though see Brown 1983 for summary; Mackreth *et al.* forthcoming) and, including two successive linear zone interments, its sequence is extremely complicated. Indeed there is issue whether its Neolithic phases should be accredited as constituting a very small long barrow or relate to an ovoid barrow form. Nevertheless, involving distinct parallels with Haddenham's sequence, its salient features warrant summary. The primary monument, a northeast–southwest oriented oval mound (10.50 × 6.50 m) upcast from two opposing crescentic ditches, sealed a 1.50 × 7.00 m linear zone (Fig. 3.74:6.A); the latter being defined on one side by a burnt wooden fence and, on the other, by limestone slab settings. A limestone upright marked its southwestern end and its northeastern aspect had a possible wooden façade. Three complete Grimston-style bowls had been set inverted close to the southwestern upright; within the burial trough were the remains of two adults, an adolescent/young adult and two children.

Following recutting of the ditches and the insertion of a crouched burial a second linear zone was established along the northeastern flank of the first phase mound (Fig. 3.74:6.B). Extending over 2.00 × 8.00 m, this was bracketed by two axial postholes that held either large stone slabs or planks (the remains of a woman had been placed in one) and interred within these were the remains of eight individuals. Somewhat reminiscent of Haddenham's hornwork structure, two divergent troughs extended from the northeastern setting. These were succeeded by a stone façade and a paving was laid along the central alignment; a stone cairn was later built over the chamber's northeastern end (its situation being suggestive of the calcrete stones scattered through Haddenham's proximal sub-chamber and forecourt). Certainly there can be no doubt that, in at least this phase, the monument was oriented northeastwards. Thereafter followed earlier Bronze Age usage involving further burials and, apparently, the construction of a 'round' barrow; the latter being enclosed by a ovoid-shaped ditch (23.5 × 28.5 m internally) that had a causeway along the south-central axis of its northeastern aspect.

Complications of sequence and issues of detail aside, the monument's linear interment zones display very strong parallels with the Haddenham Phase II.1 structure. Whilst it could be argued that this erodes arguments that Haddenham's 'long monumentality' was not necessarily intended from the outset (i.e. it could potentially have remained as an ovate barrow alone), the greater scale and formality of its façade and the very fact that the Orton barrow saw two successive linear zones would suggest that at some stage in its sequence the latter became a very different type of monument.

**Table 3.27.** *Comparative mortuary chamber dimensions and sub-divisions.*

| Site | Length (m) | Width (m) | No. of sub-divisions |
|---|---|---|---|
| Haddenham | 7.5 | 1.7 | 2 |
| Street House | 6 | 1 | 2 |
| Dalladies (2) | 7 | 2.2 | 2 |
| Lochhill | 5.5 | 0.9 | 2 |
| Fussell's Lodge | 6 | 1.4 | 2 |
| Wor Barrow | 2.5+ | 0.9 | – |
| Waylands Smithy | 4.9 | 1.15 | – |
| Nutbane | 4 | 2.5 | – |

The Orton Meadow barrow would also have affinities to other earlier Neolithic round barrow-associated mortuary structures found along the River Nene, the Aldwincle Site 1 barrow and the Grendon Ring-ditch C. The Grendon monument involved a 'D-'shaped mortuary structure with a 'C'-plan ditch configuration closed by a straight façade trench whose post had been burnt (Fig. 3.74.4; Gibson & McCormick 1985). Although distinct mortuary deposits did not survive, human remains were recovered from at least two of the complex's earlier Neolithic features (listed in the animal bone section of fiche M8; F. Healy pers comm.). Grendon's mortuary structure complemented (and anticipated) the plan of its ring-ditch/round barrow monument; the same was not true of Aldwincle, where the interrelationship between the sub-rectangular trench-defined mortuary enclosure and the surrounding ditches was very 'uncomfortable' (Fig. 3.74.5). Amid the many postholes within its interior were at least two large axial post pairings, though human interments (two adult males) only survived in association with one of these (F.21/22; Jackson 1976; see also Kinnes 1979, fig. 11.1 for interpretative sequence and also Coles & Simpson 1965 for a comparable large post-pit arrangement associated with a Neolithic round barrow at Pitnacree, Perthshire).

All three of these complexes share a northeastward orientation and to this could also be added the Fengate mortuary house (Fig. 3.74:7). Not only do these small Nene Valley monuments further confirm that this was a significant earlier Neolithic alignment (and also emphasize the importance of riverine 'groupings'; see Chapters 5 & 6 below), but their scale could help explain the paucity of long barrows throughout much of the region. Associated with round/ovoid barrows, or in the case of the Fengate 'house' without any manner of mound at all, there evidently was a much greater diversity of earlier Neolithic mortuary practices than is often acknowledged. Indeed, the arrangement at Orton Meadows erodes any easy distinc-

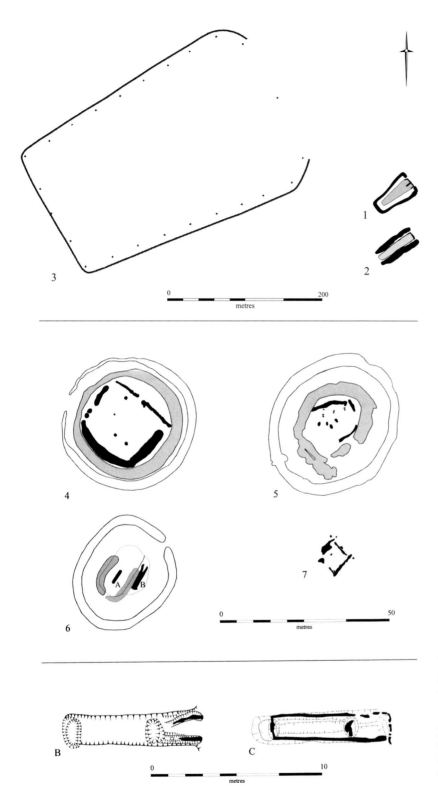

tion between ovoid and long barrow types. Although sharing comparable structural elements (e.g. façades and large paired post/linear settings), these did not necessarily anticipate long barrow construction and it can only be suspected that (unlike long barrows *per se*) these will continue to be discovered in some frequency.

Although there are clear structural parallels for the general layout of the Haddenham barrow's mortuary chamber, no other Neolithic barrow has been found with a comparable degree of preservation. While some of the woodworking debris (largely oak) found in the Raunds barrow ditch may have related to the construction of its timber façade, the presence of coppice rods and stools could derive from other activities (a large sheet of lime bark possibly reflecting bast fibre processing; Taylor in Healy & Harding forthcoming). Certainly the power and impact of 'great' trees is similarly manifest in the Holme-next-the-Sea, Norfolk timber circle (Pryor 2001b). Admittedly a monument of quite different character and date (an Early Bronze Age henge), the bulk of the evocatively inverted trunk in its centre further tells of the symbolic qualities of trees in prehistory — again, in this instance, oak. Equally reminiscent of the arrangement of the long barrow's timbers, in that henge's split-oak post circle (closely set to screen its interior) all the posts had their heartwood set inward, as if its participants were themselves inside a / *the* tree.

A comparable sense of the *surround* of timbers is amongst the Haddenham chamber's most remarkable qualities. Box-like, it was even floored in timber and the dead

**Figure 3.74.** *A northeastern axis: 1) Haddenham, Phase II barrow; 2) Raunds barrow (Healy & Harding forthcoming); 3) The Rectory Farm, Godmanchester complex (McAvoy 2000); 4) Grendon Ring-ditch C (Gibson & McCormick 1985); 5) Aldwincle Site 1 barrow (Jackson 1976); Orton Meadows, Peterborough (OLB 2; Mackreth* et al. *forthcoming) with A and B indicting linear mortuary zones (note enlargement of secondary 'chamber' below compared to the Foulmire Fen 'passage'); 7) Fengate, Padholme Farm Funerary House (Pryor 1974; 1988).*

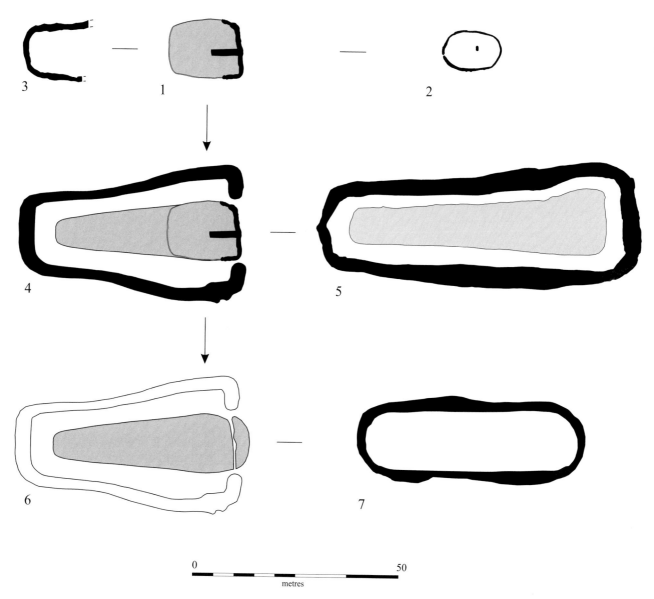

**Figure 3.75.** *Barrow affinities. 1) Haddenham, Phase II ovate mound; 2) Maxey oval barrow (Pryor & French 1985); 3) the 'Barford U' (Loveday 1989); 4) Haddenham, the Phase III trapezoid; 5) Giants' Hills No. 2 (with rear extension omitted; Phillips 1936); 6) Haddenham, the elongated rounded mound (Phase III.2); 7) Swaffham Pryor (Shell 2002, fig. 8b–e and pers. comm.) (NB: not shown to north).*

lay on its planks. This is not unique, and decayed traces of wooden flooring have been identified at other long barrows (e.g. Dalladies 2, Lochhill and Street House: Kinnes 1992, fig. 2.4.1) and megalithic tombs are often paved. The Haddenham chamber was akin to a coffin and, in reference to arguments concerning the 'sacred' nature of the earth *per se*, the dead evidently did not lie on the ground. From this it could be inferred that formal burial may have had quite a different series of symbolic associations than the deposition of human skulls and other 'loose' bodily parts in the ditches of causewayed enclosures

(see Chapter 5 below) or, subsequently, in the long barrow's mound and ditch terminals. By the same measure, the occurrence of human remains in the ditch of the Eynesbury long barrow also must attest to comparable practices. Apparently of Middle Neolithic date and completely ditch-enclosed (with a heavily enlarged perimeter around its north/ northeastern front; Fig. 3.73.2: Ellis forthcoming), it suggests that without ready access to the barrow itself (or, at least, the façade-front for rituals), in compensation depositional rites may have been transferred to its ditch; the inclusion of loose human

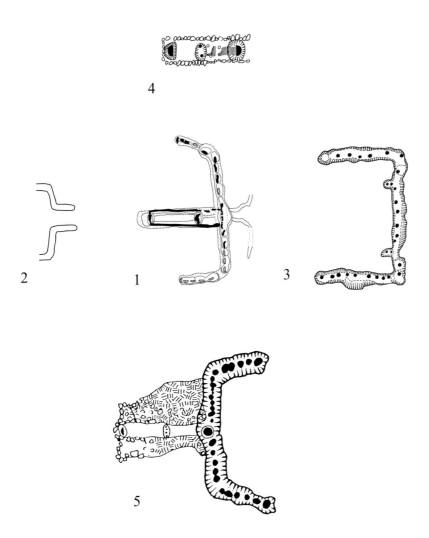

**Figure 3.76.** *Structural parallels: 1) Haddenham; 2) Wor Barrow (forestructure: Pitt Rivers 1898); 3) Nutbane (façade: Morgan 1959); 4) Lochill (chamber; Masters 1973); 5) Street House (façade and chamber: Vyner 1984) (all figures after Kinnes 1992).*

upon the sense of the barrow as a rarefied context, the berm between the mound and the ditch was a singularly 'empty' ground or divide and, effectively unapproachable, nothing appears to have occurred there (i.e. no placed deposition).

However much the monument may seem to be an integrated 'design project' up to the completion of the Phase III works (the closed façade, and the addition of the long mound and its surrounding ditch), thereafter happenstance intervened with the collapse of the chamber. How long after the closure and completion of the mound this occurred cannot be established; nevertheless it appears to have led to the grooming of the fallen mound in Phase IV.1. The collapse of the chamber must rank as a major mishap. Creating a substantial crater in the front of the mound, this was unforeseen and, in effect, an accident.

It is relevant to the lingering role of the monuments that, despite its closure, efforts were still directed towards the barrow's repair. Yet what is particularly interesting is that grooming of the mound in the wake of the chamber's collapse appears to have led to a remodelling of its front. Relating to the dismantling and firing of the façade timbers, this marked the end of the mound as a place of active deposition (apart, of course, from the insertion of the IV.2 burials).

remains implying a marked transformation of the rites of interment.

*Closure and historical aftermath*
Unlike, for example, the open character of the mass-group/gathering enclosures (e.g. causewayed enclosures), one of the key elements that distinguishes the monumentality of funerary constructions is their *closure*. Much of the lure of 'the tomb' derives from the sense of sealing off the dead in a buried 'timeless room'. Upon its closure the mound would effectively have been inaccessible. Individuals could, of course, have clambered over the façade or negotiated the narrow interval between the ditch terminals and the façade/mound corners, but effectively it would have amounted to 'dead space'. Further reflecting

The reworking and rounding of the monument's front arguably amounted to its transformation into another 'type'. Its plan then became closer to elongated, more ovoid barrow forms, which generally seem of somewhat later, Middle/Late Neolithic date. By no means is it being suggested that the Haddenham barrow actually documents *the* transition between two long barrow 'types' or that any kind of strict typological distinction is possible (as opposed to propensity). Nevertheless, it is surely pertinent that if more trapezoidal and straight-fronted mounds distantly related to Continental longhouse precursors, only through time would this new monument-specific form have emerged (i.e. the elongated oval; Fig. 3.75).

Whilst not seeking recourse in any kind of mechanistic environmental determinism (and it could be argued that the rounding of the monument's front actually began with the addition of the III.2 fore-structure works), here it is relevant to question the role that sequence and 'nature' (i.e. weathering and erosion) may have played in such developments. Compare the 'as surviving' plans of the Foulmire barrow with the more cigar-shaped oval outline of the Sutton 11 barrow (cf. Figs. 2.6 & 2.7 and 3.2 & 3.3). In knowledge of the collapse/remodelling of the front end of the former, can we be sure that they were not both long barrows of the same basic 'type'? The outward collapse of the façade revetments of trapezoidal or straight-fronted barrows would inevitably result in more ovoid mounds, which may themselves have inspired subsequent barrow/long mortuary enclosure forms. As such, this would be telling of the resolution of culture or building/monument traditions in nature, and the continual interplay between them concerning matters of intention, 'matrix' and possibility.

Thereafter, the Foulmire Fen barrow itself seem to have attracted a diverse range of activities. On the one hand, there are the round barrows immediately to the east. Possibly in an effort to establish landscape ancestry, the northern 'pair' (Site 7) were clearly aligned upon the long barrow (even if their orientation was not precise and also related to broader landscape factors; see Fig. 3.1 and Chapter 6). Yet equally important is the sense of this as a domestic locale; both the evidence of the terrace-side burnt flint mound (Chapter 2) and, too, the stake-lined pit dug into the crown of the barrow. The latter arguably attests to later Bronze Age usage, at which time the bulk of its mound may well have served as a fen-fast 'station' and effectively as a small raised island for marshland procurement activities (thereby marking still another change in context). Similar activities were also evidenced on the round barrows on the riverside terraces adjacent to the Upper Delphs (see Volume 2, Chapters 2 & 3). This suggests that, much denuded, the long barrow was not then accredited any unique status. It was simply a convenient raised mound amid the wet.

To some extent contradiction and irony underlie the long barrow's sequence. As a 'working' standing structure, it has a *de facto* hard-edge phasing structure that itself attests to time and action as it became 'different things'. As will be outlined in Chapter 5, this very much contrasts with the causewayed enclosure. In this case, within its unified construction the barrow saw a series of distinct transformations: from an *open-screen timber setting* (Phase I) to an *ovate mound* (II.1) to a *trapezoidal barrow* (III.1) to a *long oval form* (III.2/IV.1) and, finally, to a fen-surrounded *island* (IV.3). All this took place, at least until the final manifestation, whilst maintaining its integrity as a monument. As has been argued, in its Phase III 'grooming' (and possible maintenance), the barrow effectively denied time and masked or subsumed change as its elaborations enfolded upon themselves. Of course, looming behind these various changes in context sits the most radical transformation of all — not the working of the bodies and trees — rather how a trapezoidal longhouse model was, in effect, reworked and altered into being a *passage into the ground*. The character of these many transformations, each effectively statements, generally speaks of both the intentionality and endurance of monuments.

# Chapter 4

# The Delphs Terraces

In this chapter the focus shifts to the Delphs terraces and it effectively sets the scene for the causewayed enclosure's excavations. Here issues of sampling (and the limitations thereof) begin to feature. Following discussion of the immediate area's environmental sequence and topography, the results of the project's sampling procedures are outlined: first across the crown of the Upper Delphs and then the adjoining lower terraces. (The western Hermitage Farm Terrace investigations are only summarily presented as they are reported in Volume 2 with the excavation of the round barrow there; Chapter 2.) Thereafter, in reference to these results and anticipating issues relevant to the causewayed enclosure, the vexed theme or 'problem' of earlier Neolithic settlement is reviewed.

By way of introduction (and in the context of the volume's 'woodland' concerns), it should be stressed that despite numerous attempts we failed to obtain any pollen record of the immediate area's pre-Bronze Age landscape. Based on the Ouse channel core (see Peglar, Chapter 2 above) and in the light of environmental analyses of comparable 'monument' landscapes of the period, while a woodland clearance setting is presumed it has not been documented. This is particularly unfortunate for it is precisely this (relatively) 'dry' lowland land use that is such a challenge to envisage, and we should not approach the Neolithic landscape with knowledge of the later Fen Clay 'marine datum' in mind. Yes, the landscape was very low and surely would have had locally deep marshy pools. However, the fact that the Ouse channel core suggests a rise of groundwater level at just below –3.67 m OD, bracketed between the dates for the woodland clearance at c. –4.25 m OD (4470–4000 cal. BC; 5420±100 BP; Q2814) and the onset of marine flooding at c. –3.25 m OD (2870–2140 cal. BC; 3950±95 BP; Q2813), does not necessarily imply any contemporary landscape-wide inundation above c. –1.00 to 0.00 m OD.

## Landscape prospection

In this section of the text the project's sampling procedures will be overviewed. This involves three different categories of investigations. The first is that undertaken primarily for environmental purposes.

This not only includes Cardiff's transect programme, but also various coring and test-pit sampling whose main aim was the mapping of the buried landscape. The second is the test pitting undertaken across the main Upper Delphs fields. Aside from palaeo-topographic reconstruction, its primary purpose was to provide large-scale distribution data, both artefactual and chemical (phosphate and magnetic susceptibility). Finally, there are the additional sampling 'fields' scattered throughout the Delphs, where further test pitting occurred when the opportunity arose. The division between these is not strict and, as for example on the Hermitage Farm terrace, environmental and artefact sampling procedures overlapped.

As will be apparent, there are gaping holes in our understanding of the Delphs' topography. The challenge of 'capturing' an entire landscape and its sequence (if such a thing is ever possible) proved to be beyond our resources. Nevertheless, these investigations provide context for the main Delphs excavations and raise key questions concerning the definition for sites from 'background' landscape activity.

### Stratigraphy and pollen
by E. CLOUTMAN

The organic deposits in the vicinity of the Delphs terraces were investigated by taking borings along three transects (A, B & C: Fig. 4.1). A series of individual boreholes was made to define the Fen Clay margins and organic deposits bordering the main excavation areas. Pollen diagrams were constructed to provide the vegetational historical background (Haddenham Site 900/50; the results from Foulmire Fen Cutting A are presented in Chapter 2 above).

The majority of the transects were constructed by taking borings with a Hiller peat borer. Several borings were made with a Russian sampler to allow a more detailed analysis of the deposits. Samples for pollen analysis were removed from the field in 15 × 15 cm monolith boxes. These were sub-sampled for pollen analysis in the laboratory. The relative pollen diagrams are based on total land plant pollen excluding floating aquatics and spores. A count of 500 pollen grains was attempted for each sample. Where this was not

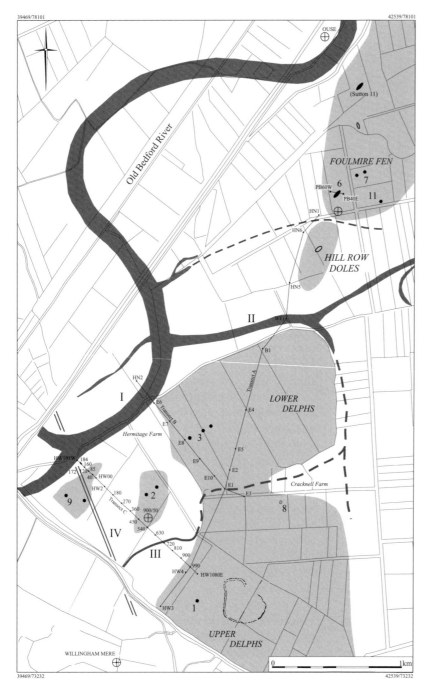

peat except in Transect C where a fine detritus mud containing shell fragments was present (Boreholes HW172W–HW195W). The latter lies in a deep channel and probably marks an ancient water course.

As outlined in Chapter 2, there is a reedy transition from the lower 'peat' to Fen Clay where the latter is present. The Fen Clay covers most of the area investigated to the north of the A1123. It forms a band about 50 cm to 100 cm thick and aggrades to about 0 m OD. The clay's margin is obscured in many places by a roddon which runs along the line of the A1123, but it was positively identified to the south of this road in Transects B and C; the margin was located in Transect C where the sub-surface contours descend steeply. Much of the remaining area investigated lies at or above the 0 m OD sub-surface contour and this horizon is absent. It is possible, however, that the basal clayey sands that are present in Transect A (E5, E2, E1), Transect B (E8) and Transect C (HW85W–HW450E) may be contemporaneous with the top of the Fen Clay. In other places the basal gravels are overlain by a clayey sand, the latter often containing wood remains. This deposit is particularly interesting along Transect C (HW450E–HW990E).

The upper 'peat' deposits were in many cases too badly oxidized to identify their content, but in general they consisted of a reedy organic mud above the areas of Fen Clay, while above the clayey sands a discontinuous layer of fen carr peat was present (shown hatched in Fig. 4.2). The discontinuity of this peat may indicate discrete areas of fen carr but is more likely due to subsequent erosion. The upper organic muds often have a high silt content which suggests episodes of flooding. This suggestion is supported by the presence of an aquatic calcareous mud in Borehole E4.

A pollen monolith was taken from a gravel terrace in the Lower Delphs gravel ridge covered by about 1 m of organic deposit (Haddenham 900/50). The basal

**Figure 4.1.** *The Delphs Terraces: transect locations, terrace islands (grey toned) and palaeochannels systems (I–III; IV indicates line of the Car Dyke).*

possible due to poor preservation or a lack of pollen, the total sum is shown alongside the sample in the pollen diagrams.

The sections constructed from the transects can be seen in Figure 4.2. The typical Fenland tripartite sequence of upper 'peat', Fen Clay and lower 'peat' is present in all. In general the lower 'peat', which overlies the basal sands and gravels consists of wood

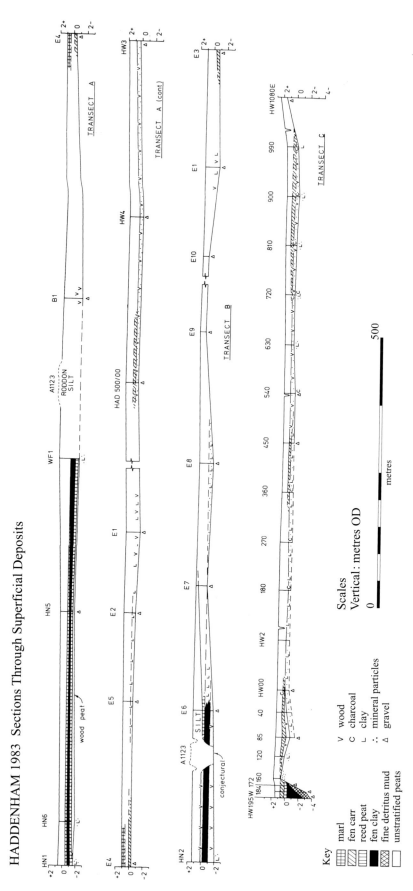

**Figure 4.2.** *The Delphs Terraces: transect sections.*

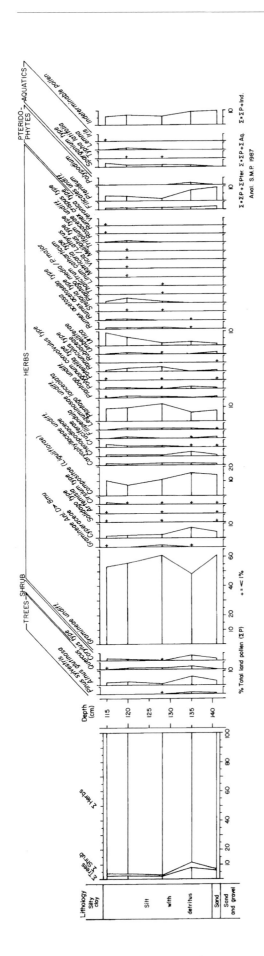

**Figure 4.3.** *The Delphs Terraces: pollen sequence (900/50).*

50 cm of organic deposit was sampled and about 15 cm of the mineral substrate. The monolith was sited about 400 m away from the present wetland margin adjacent to the causewayed enclosure (Fig. 4.1).

| Altitude | Stratigraphy |
|---|---|
| 0.80–0.65 m OD | greyish clay/silt containing many *Salix* leaves |
| 0.65–0.60 m OD | layer of wood |
| 0.60–0.34 m OD | organic mud with occasional reeds and containing a large piece of charcoal |
| 0.34–0.18 m OD | grey clay/silt becoming stony at the base with large pieces of charcoal and occasional pieces of wood |

The diagram (Fig. 4.3) has been divided into the following pollen assemblage zones:

*h4* Gramineae: *Sparganium/Typha*: Cyperaceae
*h3* *Salix*: *Alnus*: Presence of cereals and ruderals
*h2* *Salix*: *Alnus*: Umbelliferae: *Sparganium/Typha*
*h1* *Alnus*: Gramineae: *Sparganium/Typha*: Umbelliferae

Their vegetational interpretation being:

*h4* Fen, subject to flooding with nearby willow
*h3* Willow carr locally: evidence of farming
*h2* Willow carr
*h1* Alder carr: evidence of farming.

The interpretation is based on the pollen analyses and the stratigraphy:

*Phase h1 (0.24–0.30 m OD):* The site appears to have been relatively dry at the beginning of Phase h1 and the radiocarbon date of 2040–1680 cal. BC (3510±70 BP; CAR-725C fine particulate fraction) suggests a Bronze Age date from the basal gravels. Charcoal from the same sample gave a slightly later date of 1530–1130 cal. BC (3100±80 BP; CAR-725A). The relatively high *Alnus* pollen values suggest that the drier areas of Fen probably supported alder carr. The presence of cereal pollen and weeds associated with agriculture as *Artemisia* (Mugwort) and Chenopodiaceae (Goosefoot family) suggest that the dry-land areas were being utilized for arable farming, while the presence of *Plantago lanceolata* and *Pteridium* (bracken) are probably indicative of grazing.

*Phase h2 (0.30–0.46 m OD):* The site lithology changes from gravel to a grey clay/silt and then to organic mud containing reeds. This sequence probably indicates a rise in water level. The silt/organic mud boundary was dated to 1260–830 cal. BC (2830±70 BP; CAR-770) which falls in with the Late Bronze Age. The pollen evidence suggests that willow became the dominant fen shrub, possibly occupying areas formerly colonized by alder. Again, this may have been a response to a rising water level. The continuing *Plantago lanceolata* and *Pteridium* curves suggest that grazing was still taking place. Above 0.44 m OD, however, these cease and there is a dramatic rise in the *Sparganium/Typha* (Bur-reed/Bulrush) curves and fall in the *Salix* curve. Further, two pollen grains of *Nuphar* (Yellow Water-lily) were present, indicating open water at the site or close by. This most likely represents a flooding episode and would explain the marked decrease in willow, though there is no stratigraphic evidence in support of this view.

*Phase h3 (0.46–0.64 m OD):* The *Salix* curve recovers and the Umbelliferae curve declines. There is a rise in the disturbance indicator curves Chenopodiaceae and particularly *Artemisia*. The

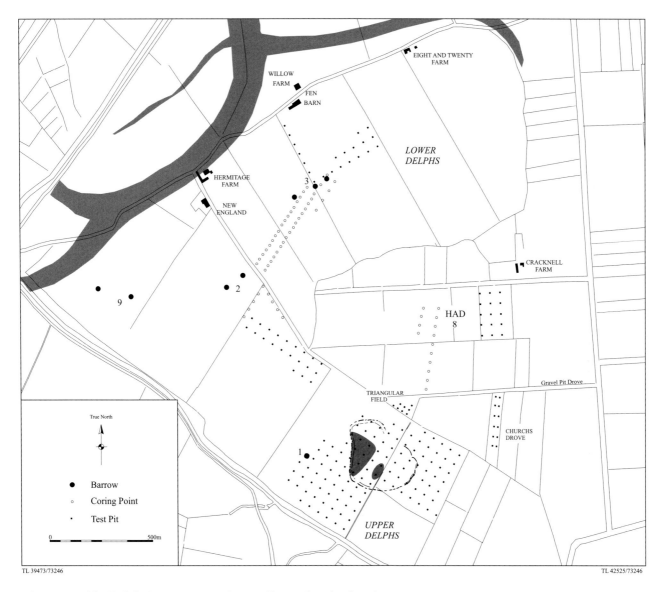

**Figure 4.4.** *The Delphs Terraces: test-pit sampling and coring locations.*

*Plantago*, *Pteridium*, and later *Rumex* curves rise and cereals are present above 0.52 m OD. These agricultural practices can probably be attributed to the Iron Age as the end of the Phase (0.46 m OD) is dated to 400–40 cal. BC (2180±70 BP; CAR-771). The wetlands would have been under willow carr.

*Phase h4* (0.64–0.76 m OD): The pollen curves of *Salix* (willow) and *Alnus* (alder) fall and there is a rise in the curves of Gramineae (grasses), *Sparganium/Typha*, and Cyperaceae (sedges). There is a lithological change from an organic mud to a wood layer (0.58–0.63 m OD) and above this a greyish clay/silt which suggests a flooding episode. The silt was full of *Salix* leaves. The evidence suggests that willow was growing at the location early in the phase, while the leaves were almost certainly washed into the later deposits from sites nearby. The increase in grasses, sedges and Bur-reed/Bulrush probably indicates that open fen was replacing willow carr. The deposition rate suggests this occurred during the Roman period. The deposition also suggests that the Upper Delphs ridge to the south was peat-free until at least the Roman times.

*A subtle topography*

Through the test pitting programme undertaken across the main Upper Delphs fields (see below) the 'lie' of the terrace was firmly established. Generally its surface beds between 2.00–2.50 m OD, though it drops to *c.* 1.80 m OD along the northeastern margin of the area (Figs. 4.1 & 4.5). There is a subtle rise, and a slight spur runs east–west across the western field where the gravels rise above the 2.40 m OD level and 'peaks' at 2.70–2.80 m OD. Much greater uncertainty exists concerning the topography of the terrace's lower skirtland. Although the swathe north of the causewayed enclosure was not surveyed in detail, there the terrace's gravels seem generally to bed between 1–2.00 m OD. As outlined below, adjacent to Cracknell

**Figure 4.5.** *The Upper Delphs: sub-surface topography and test-pit locations (note area above 2.50 m OD indicated in grey tone).*

Farm their 'edge' was exposed and the ground surface sloped down to the north to *c.* 0.10–0.20 m, where it was overlain by Fen Clay (Fig. 4.12).

The Cardiff transect running northwest from the Upper Delphs ('C') indicates that the terrace ends abruptly along the edge of the field and it drops down by 1.80 m between HW1080E and 990 (Fig. 4.1). As confirmed by test pitting across the next field, there no basal gravels occur along it until the northwestern boundary, and they 'emerge' again in the transect between points 450 and 540. This must correspond with the southern end of the island on which the two Haddenham Site 2 barrows are located. Thereafter no basal gravels are apparent over Transect C for 450 m, and they appear again between points HW00 and 85. Their occurrence at this point must mark the northern end of the terrace island on which the Haddenham

Site 9 barrows lie. While it is conceivable that a spur of this rise may run northeastwards to conjoin the Site 2 island, this seems unlikely given their delineation (and fieldwork southwest of the Old West River in Over Fen opposite indicates a similarly fractured 'islanded' topography). Whether this Haddenham Site 9 terrace extends as far south as and beyond the river was not determined.

The basal geology rises again at the extreme northwestern end of Transect C (at point 160). This may effectively mark some manner of riverside levee (top at *c.* 0.70 m OD), for the last three coring points of the transect clearly struck the main Ouse palaeochannel (including the southeastward limits of the Fen Clay within its fill sequence).

East of the Earith/Haddenham road (A1123) the other two Cardiff transects (A & B) indicated quite a different basal strata, as gravels were struck throughout their length. These generally lie quite low at between –0.30 m OD and –1.00 m OD; the location of the coring positions along Transect B gives little indication of the Hermitage Farm terrace rise, on which the line of the three Haddenham Site 3 barrows are located. The results of the sampling relating to this terrace are fully described in Volume 2 (Chapter 2), the surface of its gravels peaking between *c.* 0.50–1.00 m OD. Unlike the southern two terraces (HAD Sites 2 & 9 locations), here the barrows were not sited on an 'island' *per se*, but rather a 'rise'. The low basal gravels here continue southeastwards to conjoin with the Upper Delphs, even if during the course of the Bronze Age this rise eventually became isolated as a discrete marsh-surround island (see Cloutman's comments above concerning whether the sandy clays found across this area may be contemporaneous with the Fen Clay). The southern limit of this terrace (showing that it was indeed separate from the Site 2 island to the south) was determined through our coring programme.

Cardiff's Transect B, southeastwards of the Hermitage Farm terrace, indicates a gravel elevation between points E9 and E10 which may indicate still another 'rise'.

Project-specific environmental sampling was undertaken in 1983 at two locales (Fig. 4.4). The first was across the low ground immediately west of the Upper Delphs and the main fields north of the river. This involved the machine-excavation of 23 test pits (generally 2 × 2.00 m) on a 50-m grid. 1.10–1.85 m deep, although the basal 'geology' could not be achieved in all due to high water levels, these basically confirmed Cardiff's Transect C sequence. The Oxford clay natural bedded between –0.50 to +0.90 m OD; no terrace gravels were present and the profile was without any buried soil, hence artefact sampling was not possible. In addition, coring also occurred in

A

B

**Figure 4.6.** *The Lower Delphs river systems: 1) late palaeochannel course extending north from Old West River; 2 & 3) line of Car Dyke canal (note the marked kink in the course of the river at this point); 4) HAD 2 round barrows (CUCAP Rc8-HB 281 & Rc8-37).*

the northwestern corner of field, which successfully delineated the edge of the Site 2 terrace island.

The second sampling location was north of Upper Delph Drove in the area of the Haddenham

**Table 4.1.** *Upper Delphs flint typology (based on whole assemblage).*

| Type | HAD III/IV | | HAD V/VI | | HAD VII | | Cracknell Farm | | Sampling squares | | Church's Drove | | Hermitage Barrow | |
|---|---|---|---|---|---|---|---|---|---|---|---|---|---|---|
| | No. | % | No. | % | No. | % | No. | % | No. | % | No. | % | No. | % |
| Waste flakes | 467 | 91.6 | 509 | 93.9 | 91 | 89.2 | 226 | 93.4 | 231 | 86.8 | 40 | 100.0 | 36 | 94.7 |
| I.W.W. | 18 | 3.5 | 14 | 2.6 | 1 | 1.0 | 9 | 3.7 | 14 | 5.3 | 0 | 0.0 | 0 | 0.0 |
| Cores | 21 | 4.1 | 18 | 3.3 | 9 | 8.8 | 6 | 2.5 | 20 | 7.1 | 0 | 0.0 | 2 | 5.3 |
| Micro-burins | 4 | 0.8 | 1 | 0.2 | 1 | 1.0 | 1 | 0.4 | 1 | 0.4 | 0 | 0.0 | 0 | 0.0 |
| **Sub-total** | **510** | **100** | **542** | **100** | **102** | **100** | **242** | **100** | **266** | **100** | **40** | **100** | **38** | **100** |
| Utilized flakes | 12 | 18.8 | 48 | 37.2 | 11 | 33.3 | 4 | 22.2 | 2 | 12.5 | 1 | 25.0 | 2 | 40.0 |
| Retouched flakes | 16 | 25.0 | 28 | 21.7 | 3 | 9.1 | 4 | 22.2 | 3 | 18.8 | 2 | 50.0 | 1 | 20.0 |
| Serrated flakes | 1 | 1.6 | 1 | 0.8 | 1 | 3.0 | 1 | 5.6 | 2 | 12.5 | 0 | 0.0 | 0 | 1.0 |
| Edge blunted flake | 0 | 0.0 | 2 | 1.6 | 0 | 0.0 | 0 | 0.0 | 0 | 0.0 | 0 | 0.0 | 0 | 0.0 |
| Scrapers | 13 | 20.3 | 13 | 10.1 | 10 | 30.3 | 2 | 11.1 | 2 | 12.5 | 1 | 25.0 | 1 | 20.0 |
| Fabricators | 1 | 1.6 | 1 | 0.8 | 0 | 0.0 | 0 | 0.0 | 0 | 0.0 | 0 | 0.0 | 0 | 1.0 |
| Knives | 3 | 4.7 | 4 | 3.1 | 2 | 6.1 | 0 | 5.6 | 1 | 6.3 | 0 | 0.0 | 1 | 20.0 |
| Knife (polished) | 0 | 0.0 | 0 | 0.0 | 0 | 0.0 | 0 | 0.0 | 0 | 0.0 | 0 | 0.0 | 0 | 0.0 |
| Leaf arrowbeads | 1 | 1.6 | 2 | 1.6 | 0 | 0.0 | 1 | 5.6 | 0 | 0.0 | 0 | 0.0 | 0 | 0.0 |
| Transverse arrowhead | 3 | 4.7 | 0 | 0.0 | 0 | 0.0 | 0 | 0.0 | 0 | 0.0 | 0 | 0.0 | 0 | 0.0 |
| Barbed & tanged arrowhead | 0 | 0.0 | 0 | 0.0 | 0 | 0.0 | 0 | 0.0 | 1 | 6.3 | 0 | 0.0 | 0 | 0.0 |
| Flint axes | 0 | 0.0 | 3 | 2.3 | 0 | 0.0 | 1 | 5.6 | 0 | 0.0 | 0 | 0.0 | 0 | 0.0 |
| Piercer | 2 | 3.1 | 8 | 6.2 | 1 | 3.0 | 2 | 11.0 | 2 | 12.5 | 0 | 0.0 | 0 | 0.0 |
| Notched | 7 | 10.9 | 7 | 5.4 | 3 | 9.1 | 1 | 5.6 | 0 | 0.0 | 0 | 0.0 | 0 | 0.0 |
| Microliths | 2 | 3.1 | 1 | 0.8 | 0 | 0.0 | 1 | 5.6 | 1 | 6.3 | 0 | 0.0 | 0 | 0.0 |
| Burin | 3 | 4.7 | 4 | 3.1 | 1 | 3.0 | 0 | 0.0 | 0 | 0.0 | 0 | 0.0 | 0 | 0.0 |
| Truncated flake | 0 | 0.0 | 5 | 3.9 | 0 | 0.0 | 0 | 0.0 | 2 | 12.5 | 0 | 0.0 | 0 | 0.0 |
| Denticulate | 0 | 0.0 | 2 | 1.6 | 1 | 3.0 | 0 | 0.0 | 0 | 0.0 | 0 | 0.0 | 0 | 0.0 |
| **Sub-total** | **64** | **100** | **129** | **100** | **33** | **100** | **18** | **100** | **16** | **100** | **4** | **100** | **5** | **100** |
| **Assemblage total** | **574** | | **671** | | **135** | | **260** | | **282** | | **44** | | **43** | |
| Implement:by-product ratio | 1:8.0 | | 1:4.2 | | 1:3.1 | | 1:13.4 | | 1:16.6 | | 1:10 | | 1:7.6 | |

Site 3 barrows: the Hermitage Farm terrace. In the field immediately south of the A1123 (and Willow Hall Farm) this involved the excavation of test pits on a 50-m interval; six extended in a line along the southwestern dyke-side so as to primarily define the side of the terrace's rise, and a further 15 were dug across its crown. In the case of the latter buried soil was found to survive beneath the upper peat to a depth of 0.05–0.15 m and this was duly sampled. Ranging from 1–6 pieces per metre square, struck flint was recovered from all but one of the points in which this horizon was present. The sampling revealed that the crest of the terrace carries 0.60 m soil cover, whereas along the north edge of the field the sequence is *c.* 1.30 m deep.

Augmented by six machine-dug test pits, two coring transects (25 m interval) were also undertaken along the southern side of this terrace down to the northern side of Upper Delph Drove. In these the southern side of the gravel terrace was distinguished 140–230 m north of the drove. There is a *c.* 120-m-wide gap between the northern end of the Site 2 terrace and, bedding upon an Oxford clay basal strata, there organic deposits lie up to 1.65 m deep.

The distinction of what seems to have been Fen Clay in the course of the Cracknell Farm investigations would push the southern boundary of this 'Fenland datum' further than has been plotted (Waller 1994, fig. 5.19). This is not particularly surprising given that no coring occurred across the northeastern side of the Delphs during the Fenland Survey and the Foulmire Fen investigations established that this marine clay 'escaped' or extended beyond the main Ouse palaeochannel in that direction (i.e. penetrated the backwater system). Equally, the distinction of Fen Clay within the Ouse palaeochannel in the northeastern end of Cardiff's Transect C would mark the most westerly indication of this horizon. Although clearly requiring further environmental study to document the extreme distribution of these clays, what this indicates is that the marine flooding divided around the Delphs, continuing up the main Ouse palaeochannel to the west and southeastwards along what was probably a second channel skirting the north side of the Delphs.

**Table 4.2.** *Upper Delphs flint condition (based on whole assemblage).*

| | HAD III/IV | | HAD V/VI | | HAD VII | | Cracknell Farm | | Sampling squares | | Church's Drove | | Hermitage Barrow | |
|---|---|---|---|---|---|---|---|---|---|---|---|---|---|---|
| | No. | % | No. | % | No. | % | No. | % | No. | % | No. | % | No. | % |
| *Condition* | | | | | | | | | | | | | | |
| Abraded | 110 | 26.1 | 202 | 30.4 | 36 | 26.7 | 79 | 32.6 | 69 | 24.5 | 16 | 59.3 | 12 | 27.9 |
| Fresh | 424 | 73.9 | 463 | 69.6 | 99 | 73.3 | 163 | 67.4 | 213 | 71.5 | 11 | 40.7 | 31 | 72.1 |
| **Total** | **574** | **100** | **665** | **100** | **135** | **100** | **242** | **100** | **282** | **100** | **27** | **100** | **43** | **100** |
| *Degree of patination* | | | | | | | | | | | | | | |
| Unpatinated | 501 | 87.3 | 583 | 88.7 | 115 | 85.8 | 218 | 90.1 | 243 | 100.0 | 38 | 95.0 | 35 | 81.4 |
| Partially | 59 | 10.3 | 68 | 10.4 | 19 | 14.2 | 22 | 9.1 | 0 | 0.0 | 2 | 5.0 | 8 | 18.6 |
| Completely | 14 | 2.4 | 6 | 0.9 | 0 | 0.0 | 2 | 0.8 | 0 | 0.0 | 0 | 0.0 | 0 | 0.0 |
| **Total** | **574** | **100** | **657** | **100** | **134** | **100** | **242** | **100** | **243** | **100** | **40** | **100** | **43** | **100** |
| *Breakage* | | | | | | | | | | | | | | |
| Complete | 359 | 62.7 | 399 | 60.0 | 87 | 64.4 | 117 | 48.3 | 179 | 63.5 | 15 | 37.5 | 18 | 41.9 |
| Broken proximal end | 74 | 12.9 | 105 | 15.8 | 15 | 11.1 | 37 | 15.3 | 32 | 11.3 | 10 | 25.0 | 10 | 23.3 |
| Broken distal end | 72 | 12.6 | 88 | 13.2 | 19 | 14.1 | 40 | 16.5 | 28 | 9.9 | 2 | 5.0 | 7 | 16.3 |
| Broken both ends | 68 | 11.9 | 73 | 11.0 | 14 | 10.4 | 48 | 19.8 | 43 | 15.2 | 13 | 32.5 | 8 | 18.6 |
| **Total** | **573** | **100** | **665** | **100** | **135** | **100** | **242** | **100** | **282** | **100** | **40** | **100** | **43** | **100** |
| *Burning* | | | | | | | | | | | | | | |
| No. burnt (worked) | 13 | 72.2 | 21 | 9.1 | 6 | 60.0 | 13 | 92.9 | 9 | 6.3 | 7 | 100.0 | 0 | 0.0 |
| No. burnt (cores) | 0 | 0.0 | 0 | 0.0 | 1 | 10.0 | 1 | 7.1 | 0 | 0.0 | 0 | 0.0 | 0 | 0.0 |
| No. burnt (implement) | 1 | 5.6 | 1 | 0.4 | 2 | 20.0 | 0 | 0.0 | 0 | 0.0 | 0 | 0.0 | 0 | 0.0 |
| No. burnt (unworked) | 4 | 22.2 | 208 | 90.4 | 1 | 10.0 | 0 | 0.0 | 133 | 93.7 | 0 | 0.0 | 0 | 0.0 |
| **Total** | **18** | **100** | **230** | **100** | **10** | **100** | **14** | **100** | **142** | **100** | **7** | **100** | **0** | **100** |
| % Burnt flint | | 3.1 | | 26.2 | | 7.4 | | 5.4 | | 34.2 | | 15.9 | | 0.0 |

(Fen Clay has yet to be encountered in the Over Fen investigations: Seale 1980, fig. 1 shows it extending upstream above Earith.)

As they are indicated on the research area maps (after the 'official' Fenland Survey plotting), the main palaeochannels of the Ouse have been established from aerial photographs and by plotting the courses of upstanding roddons. (Roddons are the remnant of silt-filled palaeochannels which do not undergo the same degree of organic collapse as the surrounding peat.) With its base lying at −4.00 m OD, there can be little doubt that the channel struck at the western end of Cardiff's Transect C was the same as the main Ouse palaeochannel cored north of the long barrow (see Peglar, Chapter 3 above; Fig. 4.1:I). (Where cored by Seale southeast of Ramsey, the Ouse's palaeochannel was there found to be some 240 m across and 8 m deep: 1980, figs. 1 & 3.) Given the ancient river's plotted course along the western side of the Lower Delphs it is interesting that the two boreholes at the end of Transect B failed to locate it (HN2 & E6). In the schematic section of the transect (Fig. 4.2) the conjectured position of the river is based solely on the rise of the A1123 roddon and not the channel *per se*. Given that Fen Clay was present in both of these

coring locations (and that in Transect C this marine horizon did not extend east of the river), it does seem likely that its course actually ran immediately to the west of the A1123 between boreholes E6 and E7. *De facto* formed only within peat (and being made 'proud' by its ensuing collapse), the roddon route probably marks a somewhat later channel (i.e. post-Bronze Age).

The same is also equally true of the subsidiary channel that has been plotted as running northeast from the main course (Fig. 4.1.II), and from which an arm branches southward around the end of the Lower Delphs. Visible on aerial photographs, again no trace of this was apparent in Cardiff's Transect A, borehole WF1, which should have struck its centre, and it probably should be identified with the A1123 roddon silts just to the west. Despite that no Fen Clay was found south of that borehole (possibly due to underlying 'geological' rise), it may be the case that this subsidiary course was somewhat, or at least in part, of a later date. (The occurrence of Fen Clay at Cracknell Farm suggests that an early channel must skirt the northeastern edge of the Delphs.)

The later attribution of Channel II is based on what appears to be a southeastern length of the same

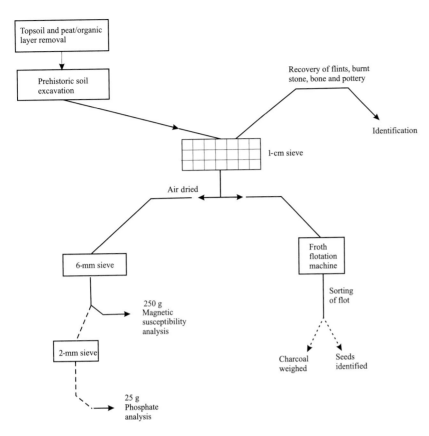

**Figure 4.7.** *Test-pit processing stages.*

Figs. 4.1:IV & 4.6:2). There can be no doubt that this diagonal marks the line of the Roman Car Dyke. Only vaguely correlated with the line of the Old West River west of Cottenham (e.g. Bromwich, in Phillips 1970), the exact route of the canal in the immediate landscape was previously unknown (and especially how it 'dog-legged' northwestwards to join with the Colne Fen, Somersham length).

The implications of this discovery will be fully discussed in the context of the area's Roman landscape (Volume 2, Chapter 8). At this time what is important is that the canal's recognition provides a 'datum' for this Delphs' palaeochannel, as it can not be coincidental that it strikes the river at the point of its Car Dyke alignment. The river's flow can only have then been westwards and, therefore, the palaeochannel must have discharged northwards and related to the Late/post-Roman disuse and abandonment of the canal system.

channel in the low grounds west of the Upper Delphs (Fig. 4.1:III). On aerial photographs that palaeochannel can clearly be seen running southwest–northeast across the lower central portion of the field up to the Upper Delph Drove (e.g. CUCAP RC8-HB: Fig. 4.6). (Although plotted somewhat further east along the western side of the upper Delphs, the tongue of alluvium shown on Godwin's FRT map of the area, TL 47SW, must also correlate with this channel.) Not marked on the Fenland Survey maps, its potential was only really appreciated in the final stages of post-excavation when trying to establish the northern skirtland of the Delphs. The crucial issue must then be what was the direction and date of the channel's discharge, for its southern end clearly conjoins with the Old West River. Given this relationship the palaeochannel may well have been quite recent. However, on scrutinizing aerial photographs, particularly CUCAP RC8 EC-37, it became apparent that a major linear cropmark runs diagonally across the two western fields south of New England Farm (adjacent to Site 9) to meet the river at the point of its junction with this palaeochannel (and where the Old West kinks sympathetically to the alignment of the linear:

*The Upper Delphs grid*
The project was, to some degree, an off-shoot of the then on-going Fenland Survey, a region-wide field-walking programme. Accordingly, during the 1981 season surface collection was attempted over an area of 1.5 ha across the eastern perimeter of the causewayed enclosure where ploughing was clearly beginning to reach the buried soils. Pick-up was by 0.25-ha unit and, ranging from 0–10 pieces of struck flint and 0–4 burnt flints, the densities were low. The worked flint only averaged 3.7 pieces per 50 sq. m, this representing the equivalent of 0.25 pieces per 10 sq. m (cf. densities on contemporary Fenland sites in Evans 1993 and Edmonds *et al.* 1999). The four collection units falling within the area of the 1982 excavations only averaged 4.5 pieces per 0.25 ha, as compared to an average buried soil density there of 1.5 pieces of struck flint per metre (0–7 range; see Chapter 5 below) or the equivalent of 150 pieces per 10 sq. m (3750 pieces per 0.25 ha). Owing to this low level of surface-to-buried soil representation and the fact that this was the area of greatest intensity of plough damage within the Upper Delphs fields (i.e. in most areas arable activity does not effect the buried soil), the decision was made to discontinue surface collection and, instead, concentrate on buried soil test pitting.

Supervised by O. Bone and T. Whitelaw (on whose results this account is based), the test-pitting programme was undertaken across the main fields between 1981 and 1983. It was found that the excavation of 1-m squares on a 50-m grid was sufficient to allow spatial variation in artefact density to be observed (Fig. 4.4). Closer spacing and larger sample squares would have been desirable, but had to be offset against the time-consuming effort of digging down to reach the prehistoric soil and sampling it intensively. Topsoil and peat were removed, often with the aid of a mechanical digger. All the buried soil within the square metre was then excavated and sieved by hand through a 5-mm mesh. Soil samples were collected in buckets under the sieves for processing in the flotation machine, and smaller samples were taken for air drying for magnetic susceptibility and phosphate analysis. The flots from the flotation machine were sorted, the charcoal weighed and the seeds identified (see Fig. 4.7 for procedure of processing).

Struck flint occurred in 73 of the 111 test pits (66 per cent) and, ranging from 0–8 pieces, had a mean of 1.8 per metre (2.8 excluding nil values). In Figure 4.8, excluding 1–2 occurrence(-only) localized 'highs' around the southwestern and northeastern margins of the grid, three higher value 'spreads' are apparent. Defined by values of three or more flints per metre, each of these have high value 'cores' with consistent densities of five or more pieces:

A) Extending across an area of 3.6 ha south from HAD VIII and the western interior of the causewayed enclosure, this has an 8100 sq. m core at its northern end (restricted to within the interior of the causewayed enclosure) wherein the mean density was 6.4 pieces.

B) This runs irregularly across the central-southeastern interior of the causewayed enclosure for 1.3 ha; there is a very localized two-test pit high value core.

C) Continuing across only 5302 sq. m, this lies southwest of the HAD III/IV complex and could represent an extension of Spread A; it has two test-pit core zones.

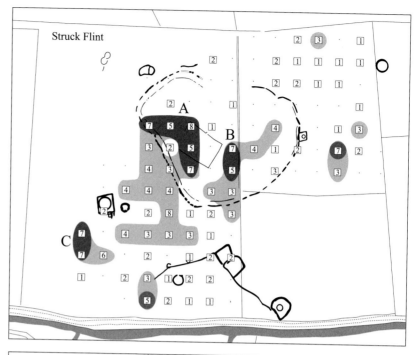

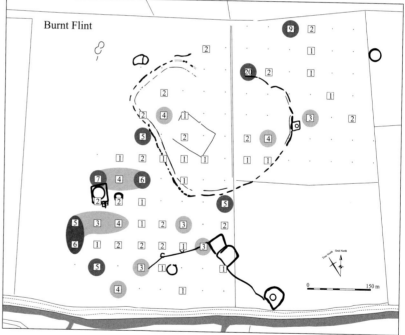

**Figure 4.8.** *Upper Delphs. Test-pit distributions: top) struck flint (A–C indicate main 'spreads'); below) burnt flint.*

Ranging from 0–20 pieces per metre (2.9 mean excluding nil values), burnt flint occurred in 53 of the test pits (47.7 per cent: Fig. 4.8). Apart from two three-/four-test pits highs (≥3 pieces) flanking the northern and southern sides of HAD III/IV, there were no consistent spreads and 'highs' only registered as

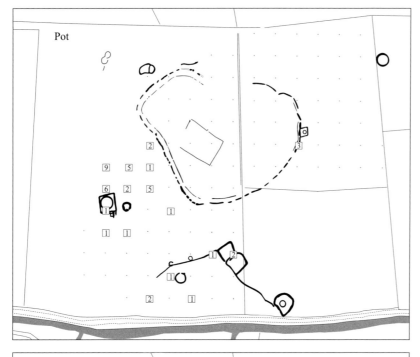

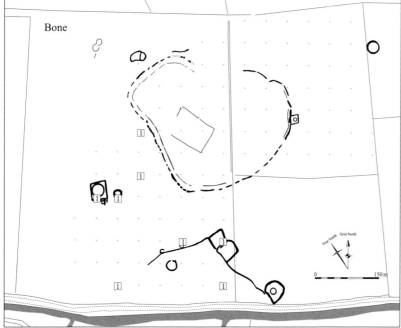

**Figure 4.9.** *Upper Delphs. test-pit distributions: top) pottery; below) bone.*

a range of 0–9 sherds per metre (2.6 mean excluding nil values), its distribution is restricted to the western exterior of the causewayed enclosure extending south to HAD III/IV (Fig. 4.9). It occurs again, however, in the vicinity of the HAD VI compound and its attendant field system (HAD VII; the area of the other Iron Age enclosures, HAD V & IX, was not sampled in this manner).

Bone has a similarly limited distribution as the pottery, its frequency however is so low (only 7.2 per cent of the test pits) as to be without statistical validity (Fig. 4.9).

The results of the chemical sampling (phosphate and magnetic susceptibility) are also discussed in Volume 2 (Chapter 2). In both instances higher values occur exterior to the causewayed enclosure, but these also extend across its perimeter to suggest that these traces essentially relate to post-Neolithic land-use (i.e. the enclosure was no longer a significant earthwork 'divide'). Again, in both cases high values occur within the area of the HAD III/IV complex; phosphate alone registers 'high' in the vicinity of the HAD VI compound (Fig. 4.10).

At this point in the text the only finds category from the sampling that warrants discussion is the distribution of the struck flint. The main spread (A) is essentially confined to the crest of the terrace spur and largely falls above the 2.50 m OD level, with all the high value spreads otherwise occurring above 2.00 m OD (Fig. 4.8). Against this, given the westward 'pull' of all the other finds categories beyond the line of the causewayed enclosure, it is noteworthy that the high value 'cores' of Spreads A and B both lie within the central swathe of the enclosure. Although in the case of Spread A this also correlates with the area of HAD VIII, this nevertheless suggests that these distributions relate to the causewayed enclosure. Part of the reason why these two highs seem so marked is by immediate contrast, as the northern third of the Neolithic interior appears essentially devoid of lithic material. The implications

dispersed single-test pit occurrences. This being said, although isolated occurrences, it is potentially interesting that the highest single values (20 and 9 pieces) both fall in the northeastern quarter of the area beyond the perimeter of the causewayed enclosure.

Largely of Iron Age attribution, the distribution of pottery is appropriately discussed in Volume 2. Occurring in only 15.3 per cent of the test pits, with

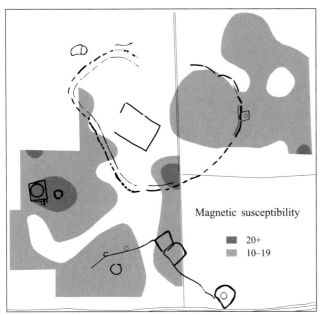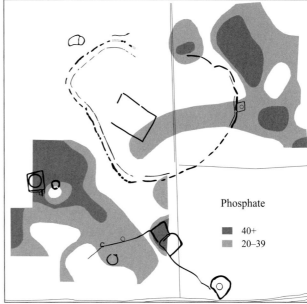

**Figure 4.10.** *Upper Delphs: magnetic susceptibility and phosphate distributions.*

of this will only become apparent in the context of the enclosure's excavation (Chapter 5).

### The lithic assemblage
by H.R. MIDDLETON

Reflective of the broad area (and the site/'landscape' range) from which the test pit material derives, overall the quality of flaking was poorer than the causewayed enclosure itself (Tables 4.3 & 4.4; see Chapter 5 below). 91% had hertzian cones of percussion indicating hard hammer striking; 43% had feather terminations and 40% had hinge fractures. 62% had non-cortical platforms; 47% were side-struck and less than 22% had faceted platforms. Most platforms were 0–10 mm long, 0–2 mm wide and were struck at an angle of 100–110° (73% were struck at 90–120°).

All stages of the core-reduction sequence were present (Tables 4.7–4.9). 92% of the flakes had less than 25% cortex on their dorsal surface, while 3% had more than 50%. 9% of non-retouched flakes were 100% cortical and 16% of waste flakes were preparation flakes, suggesting a high degree of initial core working. The presence of 9 core-reduction flakes, 11 thinning flakes and 20 (8%) cores suggest all stages of flaking and high levels of core discard. While there is no direct evidence for implement production, the 14 dressing chips and core-reduction evidence suggest at least the production of flakes. The cores were generally small; 60% were under 20 g in weight and were well flaked as 40% had less than 25% cortex. However, 35% had more than 50% cortex suggesting the discard of little used or poor-quality material.

This supports the evidence for initial and later phases of core work.

Most of the waste flakes were 10–30 mm long, 15–20 mm wide, 2–6 mm thick and 0–2 g in weight (47% were over 2 g in weight: Tables 4.5 & 4.6). These measurements generally suggest shorter and thicker flakes than those found at the causewayed enclosure itself. The breadth/length ratios show that 5% were blades, 58% were flakes and 36% were broad flakes. (With the addition of broken blades, the percentage rises to 10%, and 12% of flakes had blade scars on their dorsal surface.)

Most of the cores had no platforms or were keeled (Table 4.9). More than 50% of cores had broad flake scars and very few had blade scars.

Generally the raw material was of a quality comparable to the later material in the causewayed enclosure, but the quality of flaking was rather poor. The metrical analysis indicates a high percentage of broad flakes but also a minor blade component. However the cores were largely without platforms and of broad flake varieties. Three retouched flakes (19%) were the most common implements, with two (10%) each of utilized flakes, short scrapers, serrated blades and piercers also being recovered; a single barbed and tanged arrowhead and a flake knife were also found. The implements generally suggest a late date, and with the evidence for poor flaking possibly attesting to Early Bronze Age activity. However, an earlier Neolithic component is also present.

Perhaps not surprisingly given the exent of the area from this material derives, there is strong evidence

Table 4.3. *Upper Delphs unretouched flake technology (based on complete waste flakes).*

| Technology | HAD III/IV | | HAD V/VI | | HAD VII | | Cracknell Farm | | Sampling squares | | Church's Drove | | Hermitage Barrow | |
|---|---|---|---|---|---|---|---|---|---|---|---|---|---|---|
| | No. | % | No. | % | No. | % | No. | % | No. | % | No. | % | No. | % |
| *Initiation* | | | | | | | | | | | | | | |
| Hertzian | 253 | 91.0 | 252 | 94.7 | 51 | 92.7 | 86 | 94.5 | 123 | 91.1 | 13 | 100.0 | 13 | 86.7 |
| Bending | 25 | 9.0 | 14 | 5.3 | 4 | 7.9 | 5 | 5.5 | 12 | 8.9 | 0 | 0.0 | 2 | 13.3 |
| **Total** | **278** | **100** | **266** | **100** | **55** | **100** | **91** | **100** | **135** | **100** | **13** | **100** | **15** | **100** |
| *Termination* | | | | | | | | | | | | | | |
| Feather | 146 | 52.0 | 135 | 49.8 | 33 | 58.9 | 58 | 63.7 | 60 | 44.4 | 10 | 71.4 | 9 | 60.0 |
| Hinge | 103 | 36.7 | 97 | 35.8 | 12 | 21.4 | 27 | 29.7 | 52 | 38.5 | 2 | 14.3 | 4 | 26.7 |
| Plunging | 7 | 2.5 | 14 | 5.2 | 2 | 3.6 | 1 | 1.1 | 3 | 2.2 | 1 | 7.1 | 2 | 13.3 |
| Stepped | 25 | 8.9 | 25 | 9.2 | 9 | 16.1 | 5 | 5.5 | 20 | 14.8 | 1 | 7.1 | 0 | 0.0 |
| **Total** | **281** | **100** | **271** | **100** | **56** | **100** | **91** | **100** | **135** | **100** | **14** | **100** | **15** | **100** |
| *Platform preparation* | | | | | | | | | | | | | | |
| Plain | 241 | 86.7 | 210 | 78.9 | 44 | 80.0 | 67 | 73.6 | 98 | 72.6 | 10 | 76.9 | 9 | 60.0 |
| Facetted | 33 | 11.9 | 29 | 10.9 | 5 | 9.1 | 15 | 16.5 | 26 | 19.3 | 2 | 15.4 | 2 | 13.3 |
| Abraded | 4 | 1.4 | 27 | 10.2 | 6 | 10.9 | 9 | 9.9 | 11 | 8.1 | 1 | 7.7 | 4 | 26.7 |
| **Total** | **278** | **100** | **266** | **100** | **55** | **100** | **91** | **100** | **135** | **100** | **13** | **100** | **15** | **100** |
| *Platform cortex* | | | | | | | | | | | | | | |
| Complete | 61 | 22.0 | 62 | 23.4 | 9 | 16.4 | 9 | 9.9 | 35 | 21.1 | 0 | 0.0 | 3 | 20.0 |
| Partial | 28 | 10.1 | 29 | 10.9 | 5 | 9.1 | 9 | 9.9 | 22 | 16.4 | 0 | 0.0 | 2 | 13.3 |
| Absent | 188 | 67.9 | 174 | 65.7 | 41 | 74.5 | 73 | 80.2 | 77 | 57.5 | 13 | 100.0 | 10 | 66.7 |
| **Total** | **277** | **100** | **265** | **100** | **55** | **100** | **91** | **100** | **134** | **100** | **13** | **100** | **15** | **100** |
| *Striking* | | | | | | | | | | | | | | |
| Side | 153 | 54.8 | 120 | 43.5 | 25 | 45.5 | 23 | 25.3 | 70 | 51.1 | 4 | 28.6 | 7 | 46.7 |
| End | 124 | 44.4 | 152 | 55.1 | 30 | 54.5 | 68 | 74.7 | 66 | 48.2 | 10 | 71.4 | 8 | 53.3 |
| Bashed | 2 | 0.7 | 4 | 1.4 | 0 | 0.0 | 0 | 0.0 | 1 | 0.7 | 0 | 0.0 | 0 | 0.0 |
| **Total** | **279** | **100** | **276** | **100** | **55** | **100** | **91** | **100** | **137** | **100** | **14** | **100** | **15** | **100** |

for intensive flint working from the initial preparation of cores through to discard, and this may have included implement production. The range of implements found was not extensive and there was a low implement:by-product ratio (1:17); 133 pieces of burnt unworked flint were also recovered from the sampling.

*Sampling fields*
In 1983, eight test pits were dug in the triangular field immediately northwest of the main fields (Fig. 4.4). With 0.50–0.70 m soil cover (including 0.15–0.45 m depth of buried soil), the terrace sloped down from 2.00–2.10 m OD to 1.80 m OD in the northwest. Struck flint was present in all of the test pits and, ranging from 1–23 pieces per metre with a mean of 6.5, it occurred in substantially higher densities than across the main grid.

When in 1987 a new field was established off of Gravel Pit Drove *c.* 400 m east of the causewayed enclosure (*Church's Drove*) the opportunity arose to excavate 12 further test pits (Fig. 4.4). Here the surface of the terrace gravels was found to slope down from *c.* 2.15 m OD in the south to *c.* 1.50 m OD in the north

(over 250 m length). Although burnt flint occurred at seven points scattered throughout the grid (range, 1–2 fragments), struck flint only occurred at either extreme of the field (four instances). With a range of 0–5 pieces, the latter had a mean of 0.8 pieces per metre (2.5 excluding nil values).

The lithic assemblage
by H.R. MIDDLETON
The quality of flaking in this assemblage was comparable with the better-quality flaking from the causewayed enclosure as well as with the Cracknell Farm scatter (see below; Tables 4.3 & 4.4). All the flakes had hertzian cones of percussion suggesting hard hammer striking; 71% had feather terminations and 14% had hinge fractures. All had non-cortical platforms and less than 29% were side-struck. 15% had faceted platforms. Most platforms were less than 5 mm long, were less than 2 mm wide and were struck at an angle of 100–110° (85% were struck at 90–110°).

Most flakes had less than 25% cortex but one flake had 50–75% cortex suggesting that primary

**Table 4.4.** *Upper Delphs platform characteristics (based on complete waste flakes).*

| Technology | HAD III/IV | | HAD V/VI | | HAD VII | | Cracknell Farm | | Sampling squares | | Church's Drove | | Hermitage Barrow | |
|---|---|---|---|---|---|---|---|---|---|---|---|---|---|---|
| | No. | % | No. | % | No. | % | No. | % | No. | % | No. | % | No. | % |
| *Platform length* (mm) | | | | | | | | | | | | | | |
| 0–5 | 77 | 27.9 | 92 | 34.6 | 21 | 38.2 | 41 | 45.1 | 35 | 27.1 | 6 | 46.2 | 5 | 33.3 |
| 5–10 | 90 | 32.6 | 83 | 31.2 | 17 | 30.9 | 32 | 35.2 | 48 | 37.2 | 1 | 7.7 | 6 | 40.0 |
| 10–15 | 58 | 21.0 | 51 | 19.2 | 5 | 9.1 | 13 | 14.3 | 26 | 20.2 | 2 | 15.4 | 1 | 6.7 |
| 15–20 | 22 | 8.0 | 18 | 6.8 | 6 | 10.9 | 2 | 2.2 | 15 | 11.6 | 2 | 15.4 | 2 | 13.3 |
| 20–25 | 16 | 5.8 | 10 | 3.8 | 4 | 7.3 | 2 | 2.2 | 3 | 2.3 | 2 | 15.4 | 1 | 6.7 |
| 25+ | 13 | 4.7 | 12 | 4.5 | 2 | 3.6 | 1 | 1.1 | 2 | 1.6 | 0 | 0.0 | 0 | 0.0 |
| **Total** | **276** | **100** | **266** | **100** | **55** | **100** | **91** | **100** | **129** | **100** | **13** | **100** | **15** | **100** |
| *Platform width* (mm) | | | | | | | | | | | | | | |
| 0–2 | 120 | 43.3 | 127 | 47.6 | 26 | 47.3 | 53 | 58.2 | 50 | 38.5 | 8 | 61.5 | 9 | 60.0 |
| 2–4 | 59 | 21.3 | 63 | 23.6 | 13 | 23.6 | 25 | 27.5 | 36 | 27.7 | 1 | 7.7 | 2 | 13.3 |
| 4–6 | 45 | 16.2 | 42 | 15.7 | 7 | 12.7 | 9 | 9.9 | 27 | 20.8 | 0 | 0.0 | 3 | 20.0 |
| 6–8 | 20 | 7.2 | 17 | 6.4 | 3 | 5.5 | 1 | 1.1 | 10 | 7.7 | 0 | 0.0 | 0 | 0.0 |
| 8–10 | 11 | 4.0 | 7 | 2.6 | 2 | 3.6 | 2 | 2.2 | 3 | 2.3 | 2 | 15.4 | 1 | 6.7 |
| 10+ | 22 | 7.9 | 11 | 4.1 | 4 | 7.3 | 1 | 1.1 | 4 | 3.1 | 2 | 15.4 | 0 | 0.0 |
| **Total** | **277** | **100** | **267** | **100** | **55** | **100** | **91** | **100** | **130** | **100** | **13** | **100** | **15** | **100** |
| *Platform angle* | | | | | | | | | | | | | | |
| –80 | 13 | 4.7 | 7 | 2.6 | 3 | 5.5 | 2 | 2.2 | 6 | 4.4 | 0 | 0.0 | 1 | 6.7 |
| 80–90 | 20 | 7.2 | 20 | 7.5 | 1 | 1.8 | 7 | 7.7 | 12 | 8.9 | 0 | 0.0 | 1 | 6.7 |
| 90–100 | 41 | 14.8 | 56 | 21.0 | 143 | 25.5 | 24 | 26.4 | 32 | 23.7 | 5 | 38.5 | 4 | 26.7 |
| 100–110 | 93 | 33.6 | 82 | 30.7 | 22 | 40.0 | 35 | 38.5 | 45 | 33.3 | 6 | 46.2 | 3 | 20.0 |
| 110–120 | 76 | 27.4 | 65 | 24.3 | 11 | 20.0 | 18 | 19.8 | 26 | 19.3 | 1 | 7.7 | 5 | 33.3 |
| 120–130 | 29 | 10.5 | 34 | 12.7 | 1 | 1.8 | 2 | 2.2 | 13 | 9.6 | 1 | 7.7 | 0 | 0.0 |
| 130+ | 5 | 1.8 | 3 | 1.1 | 3 | 5.5 | 3 | 3.3 | 1 | 0.7 | 0 | 0.0 | 1 | 6.7 |
| **Total** | **277** | **100** | **267** | **100** | **55** | **100** | **91** | **100** | **135** | **100** | **13** | **100** | **15** | **100** |

working of cores occurred elsewhere (Table 4.7–4.8). However, two preparation flakes, four core reduction flakes and a thinning flake were found together with a single dressing chip suggesting some flake production (unretouched flakes account for 77% of the waste flakes). Production was certainly at a low level and no cores were found, indicating that no discard of fully worked material occurred.

Most flakes were 10–20 mm long, 5–10 mm wide, 0–2 mm thick and 0–2 g in weight (43% were over 2 g in weight: Tables 4.5 & 4.6). This is comparable with the 'palisade', 'ditch' and 'pit' of causewayed enclosure. The breadth:length ratios show that 14% were blades, 71% were flakes and 14% were broad flakes. The number of blades rises to 23% if broken blades are included; 20% of flakes had blade scars on their dorsal surface.

The quality of the flint and the quality of the flaking was comparable to the earlier material from the causewayed enclosure. The metrical analysis shows that a high percentage of blades were present but that broad flakes also occurred. A utilized flake, two retouched flakes and a scraper were the only implements recovered and are not very helpful for dating purposes. The quality of the material and the metrical analysis would suggest an earlier Neolithic dating.

Evidence for the material's function is sparse. There is no evidence of initial core preparation, nor of the discard of fully worked cores. However there is some evidence for low levels of flaking. Most of the material was unretouched flakes with little cortex but there were very few implements; 18% of worked pieces were burnt.

*The Cracknell Farm scatter*
In the 1987 the decision was taken to investigate a field within the vicinity of Hall's Haddenham Site 8: the Cracknell Farm scatter. This is located *c.* 600 m northwest of the causewayed enclosure on a slight rise, which accounts for its distinction through fieldwalking (Figs. 4.4 & 4.11). In the first instance 15 test pits were excavated on a 50-m gird. Lying adjacent to the terrace's edge, the gravels were found to slope quite markedly from *c.* 2.00 m OD along the mid western side down to *c.* 1.20–0.30 m OD in the south and

**Table 4.5.** *Upper Delphs metric analysis (based on complete waste flakes).*

| | HAD III/IV | | HAD V/VI | | HAD VII | | Cracknell Farm | | Sampling squares | | Church's Drove | | Hermitage Barrow | |
|---|---|---|---|---|---|---|---|---|---|---|---|---|---|---|
| | No. | % | No. | % | No. | % | No. | % | No. | % | No. | % | No. | % |
| *Length* (mm) | | | | | | | | | | | | | | |
| 0–10 | 21 | 7.4 | 6 | 2.1 | 1 | 1.8 | 6 | 6.5 | 9 | 6.5 | 0 | 0.0 | 2 | 13.3 |
| 10–20 | 111 | 38.9 | 96 | 34.2 | 18 | 32.1 | 31 | 33.3 | 53 | 38.1 | 7 | 50.0 | 4 | 26.7 |
| 20–30 | 105 | 36.8 | 102 | 36.3 | 24 | 42.9 | 42 | 45.2 | 54 | 38.8 | 4 | 28.6 | 5 | 33.3 |
| 30–40 | 40 | 14.0 | 55 | 19.6 | 11 | 19.6 | 9 | 9.7 | 19 | 13.7 | 3 | 21.4 | 3 | 20.0 |
| 40–50 | 7 | 2.5 | 16 | 5.7 | 2 | 3.6 | 3 | 3.2 | 4 | 2.9 | 0 | 0.0 | 0 | 0.0 |
| 50+ | 1 | 0.4 | 6 | 2.1 | 0 | 0 | 2 | 2.2 | 0 | 0 | 0 | 0.0 | 1 | 6.7 |
| **Total** | **285** | **100** | **281** | **100** | **56** | **100** | **93** | **100** | **139** | **100** | **14** | **100** | **15** | **100** |
| *Breadth* (mm) | | | | | | | | | | | | | | |
| 0–5 | 5 | 1.8 | 1 | 0.4 | 0 | 0 | 3 | 3.2 | 1 | 0.7 | 0 | 0.0 | 0 | 0.0 |
| 5–10 | 28 | 9.8 | 16 | 5.7 | 3 | 5.4 | 21 | 22.6 | 8 | 5.8 | 5 | 35.7 | 0 | 0.0 |
| 10–15 | 53 | 18.6 | 62 | 22.1 | 8 | 14.3 | 31 | 33.3 | 35 | 25.2 | 3 | 21.4 | 6 | 40.0 |
| 15–20 | 68 | 23.9 | 63 | 22.4 | 18 | 32.1 | 19 | 20.4 | 35 | 25.2 | 2 | 14.3 | 3 | 20.0 |
| 20–25 | 48 | 16.8 | 50 | 17.8 | 9 | 16.1 | 15 | 16.1 | 30 | 21.6 | 2 | 14.3 | 3 | 20.0 |
| 25–30 | 44 | 15.4 | 38 | 13.5 | 11 | 19.6 | 2 | 2.2 | 20 | 14.4 | 1 | 7.1 | 1 | 6.7 |
| 30–35 | 19 | 6.7 | 27 | 9.6 | 4 | 7.1 | 1 | 1.1 | 7 | 5 | 0 | 0.0 | 1 | 6.7 |
| 35+ | 20 | 7.0 | 24 | 8.5 | 3 | 5.4 | 1 | 1.1 | 3 | 2.2 | 1 | 7.1 | 1 | 6.7 |
| **Total** | **285** | **100** | **281** | **100** | **56** | **100** | **93** | **100** | **139** | **100** | **14** | **100** | **15** | **100** |
| *Thickness* (mm) | | | | | | | | | | | | | | |
| 0–2 | 41 | 14.4 | 21 | 7.5 | 7 | 12.5 | 37 | 39.8 | 13 | 9.4 | 6 | 42.9 | 2 | 16.7 |
| 2–4 | 75 | 26.3 | 84 | 29.9 | 14 | 25.0 | 34 | 36.6 | 39 | 28.1 | 3 | 21.4 | 5 | 41.7 |
| 4–6 | 69 | 24.2 | 70 | 24.9 | 19 | 33.9 | 12 | 12.9 | 43 | 30.9 | 3 | 21.4 | 0 | 0.0 |
| 6–8 | 44 | 15.4 | 46 | 16.4 | 3 | 5.4 | 24 | 4.3 | 28 | 20.1 | 1 | 7.1 | 2 | 16.7 |
| 8–10 | 12 | 4.2 | 23 | 8.2 | 5 | 8.9 | 12 | 2.2 | 10 | 7.2 | 0 | 0.0 | 1 | 8.3 |
| I0–12 | 15 | 5.3 | 14 | 5.0 | 3 | 5.4 | 31 | 1.1 | 3 | 2.2 | 1 | 7.1 | 1 | 8.3 |
| 12+ | 29 | 10.2 | 23 | 8.2 | 5 | 8.9 | 3 | 3.2 | 3 | 2.2 | 0 | 0.0 | 1 | 8.3 |
| **Total** | **285** | **100** | **281** | **100** | **56** | **100** | **93** | **100** | **139** | **100** | **14** | **100** | **12** | **100** |
| *Weight* (g) | | | | | | | | | | | | | | |
| 0–2 | 137 | 48.1 | 121 | 43.1 | 25 | 44.6 | 62 | 66.7 | 74 | 53.2 | 8 | 57.1 | 8 | 53.3 |
| 2–4 | 58 | 20.4 | 70 | 24.9 | 15 | 26.8 | 21 | 22.6 | 34 | 24.5 | 2 | 14.3 | 3 | 20.0 |
| 4–6 | 32 | 11.2 | 31 | 11.0 | 6 | 10.7 | 3 | 3.2 | 17 | 12.2 | 3 | 21.4 | 2 | 13.3 |
| 6–8 | 18 | 6.3 | 21 | 7.5 | 3 | 5.4 | 1 | 1.1 | 6 | 4.3 | 0 | 0.0 | 1 | 6.7 |
| 8–10 | 7 | 2.5 | 13 | 4.6 | 1 | 1.8 | 0 | 0 | 3 | 2.2 | 1 | 7.1 | 1 | 6.7 |
| 10–12 | 12 | 4.2 | 5 | 1.8 | 3 | 5.4 | 2 | 2.2 | 1 | 0.7 | 0 | 0.0 | 0 | 0.0 |
| 12–14 | 5 | 1.8 | 4 | 1.4 | 0 | 0 | 2 | 2.2 | 2 | 1.4 | 0 | 0.0 | 0 | 0.0 |
| 14+ | 16 | 5.6 | 16 | 5.7 | 3 | 5.4 | 2 | 2.2 | 2 | 1.4 | 0 | 0.0 | 0 | 0.0 |
| **Total** | **285** | **100** | **281** | **100** | **56** | **100** | **93** | **100** | **139** | **100** | **14** | **100** | **15** | **100** |

*c.* 0.13–0.25 m OD in the northeast (Fig. 4.12). Generally the terrace was sealed by 0.30–0.45 m soil cover (with the buried soil being struck by the plough). Across the north/northeastern quarter of the field this deepened to 0.60–0.90 m depth and there Fen Clay appeared to be present in the basal profile (northernmost and lowermost line of test pits only).

It was later found that one of the test pits was not dug to a sufficient depth to have reached the buried soil and, accordingly, it is discounted from the site's tallies. Otherwise worked flint occurred in a range 0–21 pieces per metre with a mean of 5.1 (5.5 excluding a single nil value).

The southwestern quarter of the field was thereafter targeted for more intense investigation. Across an area of 400 sq. m the sample grid was reduced to a 10-m interval through the digging of eight further test pits; one other metre test pit was excavated, as was also a 2 × 2 m area (the buried soil from the latter being completely sieved). Present in all of these exposures, struck flint occurred within a range of 8–70 pieces, with a mean of 20 per metre (Fig. 4.12).

As this was the highest flint density encountered on the Delphs terraces, two areas (A & B) were then machine-exposed in order to investigate whether the scatter had accompanying features. Both *c.* 6 × 7 m in

**Table 4.6.** *Upper Delphs flake characterization (based on complete waste flakes).*

| | HAD III/IV | | HAD V/VI | | HAD VII | | Cracknell Farm | | Sampling squares | | Church's Drove | | Hermitage Barrow | |
|---|---|---|---|---|---|---|---|---|---|---|---|---|---|---|
| | No. | % | No. | % | No. | % | No. | % | No. | % | No. | % | No. | % |
| *Ratios* (n:5) | | | | | | | | | | | | | | |
| 0–1 | 1 | 0.4 | 2 | 0.7 | 0 | 0 | 1 | 1.1 | 1 | 0.7 | 0 | 0.0 | 0 | 0.0 |
| 1–2 | 8 | 2.9 | 17 | 6.0 | 2 | 3.6 | 13 | 14.0 | 4 | 2.9 | 2 | 14.3 | 0 | 0.0 |
| 2–3 | 38 | 13.8 | 50 | 17.8 | 12 | 21.4 | 31 | 33.3 | 19 | 13.7 | 4 | 28.6 | 3 | 20.0 |
| 3–4 | 57 | 20.7 | 51 | 18.1 | 11 | 19.6 | 24 | 25.8 | 24 | 17.3 | 5 | 35.7 | 5 | 33.3 |
| 4–5 | 48 | 17.5 | 52 | 18.5 | 8 | 14.3 | 13 | 14.0 | 34 | 24.5 | 1 | 7.1 | 1 | 6.7 |
| 5–6 | 43 | 15.6 | 44 | 15.7 | 6 | 10.7 | 3 | 3.2 | 24 | 17.3 | 1 | 7.1 | 2 | 13.3 |
| 6–7 | 29 | 10.5 | 24 | 8.5 | 8 | 14.3 | 2 | 2.2 | 18 | 12.9 | 0 | 0.0 | 1 | 6.7 |
| 7–8 | 19 | 6.9 | 18 | 6.4 | 3 | 5.4 | 1 | 1.1 | 6 | 4.3 | 0 | 0.0 | 2 | 13.3 |
| 8–9 | 17 | 6.2 | 10 | 3.6 | 3 | 5.4 | 1 | 1.1 | 5 | 3.6 | 0 | 0.0 | 1 | 6.7 |
| 9+ | 15 | 5.5 | 13 | 4.6 | 3 | 5.4 | 4 | 4.3 | 4 | 2.9 | 1 | 7.1 | 0 | 0.0 |
| **Total** | **275** | **100** | **281** | **100** | **56** | **100** | **93** | **100** | **139** | **100** | **14** | **100** | **15** | **100** |
| % Blades | 9 | 3.3 | 19 | 6.8 | 2 | 3.6 | 14 | 15.1 | 5 | 3.6 | 2 | 14.3 | 0 | 0.0 |
| % Flakes | 143 | 52.0 | 153 | 54.4 | 31 | 355.4 | 68 | 73.1 | 77 | 55.4 | 10 | 71.4 | 9 | 60.0 |
| % Broad flakes | 123 | 44.7 | 109 | 38.8 | 23 | 41.1 | 11 | 11.8 | 57 | 41.0 | 2 | 14.3 | 6 | 40.0 |
| % Flake - blade scars | 36 | 7.7 | 64 | 12.6 | 12 | 13.2 | 37 | 16.4 | 28 | 12.1 | 8 | 20.0 | 2 | 5.6 |
| % Blades + brk blades | 26 | 5.6 | 23 | 4.5 | 2 | 2.2 | 44 | 19.5 | 23 | 10.0 | 9 | 22.5 | 0 | 0.0 |
| *Possible use* | | | | | | | | | | | | | | |
| Cutting | 7 | 2.5 | 10 | 3.6 | 2 | 3.6 | 5 | 5.4 | 4 | 2.9 | 0 | 0.0 | 0 | 0.0 |
| Awls | 5 | 1.8 | 13 | 4.6 | 1 | 1.8 | 5 | 5.4 | 2 | 1.4 | 2 | 14.3 | 0 | 0.0 |
| Other | 263 | 95.6 | 258 | 91.8 | 53 | 94.6 | 83 | 89.2 | 133 | 95.7 | 12 | 85.7 | 15 | 100 |
| **Total** | **275** | **100** | **281** | **100** | **56** | **100** | **93** | **100** | **139** | **100** | **14** | **100** | **15** | **100** |

**Table 4.7.** *Upper Delphs flake cortex (based on complete waste flakes).*

| | HAD III/IV | | HAD V/VI | | HAD VII | | Cracknell Farm | | Sampling squares | | Church's Drove | | Hermitage Barrow | |
|---|---|---|---|---|---|---|---|---|---|---|---|---|---|---|
| Division | No. | % | No. | % | No. | % | No. | % | No. | % | No. | % | No. | % |
| *% Cortex* | | | | | | | | | | | | | | |
| 0 | 102 | 35.7 | 73 | 26.3 | 24 | 42.9 | 44 | 46.8 | 42 | 30.2 | 10 | 71.4 | 7 | 46.7 |
| 0–25 | 107 | 37.4 | 125 | 45.0 | 25 | 44.6 | 30 | 31.9 | 59 | 42.4 | 3 | 21.4 | 7 | 46.7 |
| 25–50 | 24 | 8.4 | 33 | 11.9 | 0 | 0.0 | 10 | 10.6 | 14 | 10.1 | 0 | 0.0 | 0 | 0.0 |
| 50–75 | 20 | 7.0 | 24 | 8.6 | 3 | 5.4 | 6 | 6.4 | 6 | 4.3 | 1 | 7.1 | 0 | 0.0 |
| 75–100 | 15 | 5.2 | 8 | 2.9 | 3 | 5.4 | 4 | 4.3 | 6 | 4.3 | 0 | 0.0 | 0 | 0.0 |
| 100 | 18 | 6.3 | 15 | 5.4 | 1 | 1.8 | 0 | 0.0 | 12 | 8.6 | 0 | 0.0 | 1 | 6.7 |
| **Total** | **286** | **100** | **278** | **100** | **56** | **100** | **94** | **100** | **139** | **100** | **14** | **100** | **15** | **100** |

**Table 4.8.** *Upper Delphs flake typology (based on all waste flakes).*

| | HAD III/IV | | HAD V/VI | | HAD VII | | Cracknell Farm | | Sampling squares | | Church's Drove | | Hermitage Barrow | |
|---|---|---|---|---|---|---|---|---|---|---|---|---|---|---|
| Type | No. | % | No. | % | No. | % | No. | % | No. | % | No. | % | No. | % |
| Unretouched flakes | 345 | 73.9 | 403 | 79.2 | 67 | 73.6 | 190 | 84.1 | 160 | 69.3 | 31 | 77.5 | 24 | 68.6 |
| Dressing chips | 46 | 9.9 | 28 | 5.5 | 5 | 5.5 | 13 | 5.8 | 14 | 6.1 | 1 | 2.5 | 3 | 8.6 |
| Trimming flakes | 2 | 0.4 | 1 | 0.2 | 0 | 0.0 | 1 | 0.4 | 0 | 0.0 | 0 | 0.0 | 1 | 2.9 |
| Preparation flakes | 45 | 9.6 | 31 | 6.1 | 10 | 11.0 | 11 | 4.9 | 37 | 16.0 | 3 | 7.S | 1 | 2.9 |
| Thinning flakes | 15 | 3.2 | 27 | 5.3 | 4 | 4.4 | 2 | 0.9 | 11 | 4.8 | 1 | 2.5 | 3 | 8.6 |
| Core-rejuvenation flakes | 14 | 3.0 | 19 | 3.7 | 5 | 5.5 | 9 | 4.0 | 9 | 3.9 | 4 | 10.0 | 3 | 8.6 |
| **Total** | **467** | **100** | **509** | **100** | **91** | **100** | **226** | **100** | **231** | **100** | **40** | **100** | **35** | **100** |

**Table 4.9.** *Upper Delphs core typology.*

| Type | HAD III/IV | | HAD V/VI | | HAD VII | | Cracknell Farm | | Sampling squares | | Church's Drove | | Hermitage Barrow | |
|---|---|---|---|---|---|---|---|---|---|---|---|---|---|---|
| | No. | % | No. | % | No. | % | No. | % | No. | % | No. | % | No. | % |
| *Clarke typology* | | | | | | | | | | | | | | |
| A1 | 1 | 4.8 | 0 | 0.0 | 0 | 0.0 | 0 | 0.0 | 0 | 0.0 | 0 | 0.0 | 0 | 0.0 |
| A2 | 9 | 42.9 | 1 | 5.6 | 3 | 33.3 | 2 | 33.3 | 1 | 5.0 | 0 | 0.0 | 0 | 0.0 |
| B1 | 0 | 0.0 | 0 | 0.0 | 0 | 0.0 | 0 | 0.0 | 1 | 5.0 | 0 | 0.0 | 0 | 0.0 |
| B2 | 1 | 4.8 | 1 | 5.6 | 0 | 0.0 | 1 | 16.7 | 1 | 5.0 | 0 | 0.0 | 0 | 0.0 |
| B3 | 0 | 0.0 | 2 | 11.1 | 3 | 33.3 | 1 | 16.7 | 2 | 10.0 | 0 | 0.0 | 0 | 0.0 |
| C | 0 | 0.0 | 0 | 0.0 | 0 | 0.0 | 1 | 16.7 | 1 | 5.0 | 0 | 0.0 | 0 | 0.0 |
| D | 5 | 28.8 | 4 | 22.2 | 0 | 0.0 | 0 | 0.0 | 4 | 20.0 | 0 | 0.0 | 1 | 50.0 |
| E | 2 | 9.5 | 0 | 0.0 | 1 | 11.1 | 0 | 0.0 | 1 | 5.0 | 0 | 0.0 | 0 | 0.0 |
| Damaged | 1 | 4.8 | 4 | 22.2 | 1 | 11.1 | 0 | 0.0 | 3 | 15.0 | 0 | 0.0 | 1 | 50.0 |
| Ill defined | 0 | 0.0 | 2 | 11.1 | 1 | 11.1 | 0 | 0.0 | 1 | 5.0 | 0 | 0.0 | 0 | 0.0 |
| Crude bashed pebble | 2 | 9.5 | 4 | 22.2 | 0 | 0.0 | 1 | 16.7 | 5 | 25.0 | 0 | 0.0 | 0 | 0.0 |
| **Total** | **21** | **100** | **18** | **100** | **9** | **100** | **6** | **100** | **20** | **100** | **0** | **0.0** | **2** | **100** |
| | | | | | | | | | | | | | | |
| *Ford typology* | | | | | | | | | | | | | | |
| Type 2 | 1 | 5.0 | 2 | 13.3 | 0 | 0.0 | 3 | 50.0 | 1 | 6.3 | 0 | 0.0 | 0 | 0.0 |
| Type 3 | 2 | 10.0 | 1 | 6.7 | 0 | 0.0 | 0 | 0.0 | 0 | 0.0 | 0 | 0.0 | 0 | 0.0 |
| Type 4 | 0 | 0.0 | 1 | 6.7 | 1 | 11.1 | 0 | 0.0 | 1 | 6.3 | 0 | 0.0 | 0 | 0.0 |
| Type 5 | 2 | 10.0 | 1 | 6.7 | 1 | 11.1 | 1 | 16.7 | 1 | 6.3 | 0 | 0.0 | 0 | 0.0 |
| Type 6 | 15 | 75.0 | 8 | 53.3 | 7 | 77.8 | 2 | 33.3 | 10 | 62.5 | 0 | 0.0 | 1 | 50.0 |
| Type 8 | 0 | 0.0 | 2 | 13.3 | 0 | 0.0 | 0 | 0.0 | 8 | 18.8 | 0 | 0.0 | 1 | 50.0 |
| **Total** | **20** | **100** | **15** | **100** | **9** | **100** | **6** | **100** | **16** | **100** | **0** | **0.0** | **2** | **100** |
| | | | | | | | | | | | | | | |
| *Core weight* (g) | | | | | | | | | | | | | | |
| 0–10 | 1 | 4.8 | 2 | 11.1 | 1 | 11.1 | 1 | 16.7 | 5 | 25.0 | 0 | 0.0 | 0 | 0.0 |
| 10–20 | 10 | 47.6 | 9 | 50.0 | 4 | 44.4 | 3 | 50.0 | 7 | 35.0 | 0 | 0.0 | 2 | 100 |
| 20–80 | 6 | 28.6 | 0 | 0.0 | 1 | 11.1 | 0 | 0.0 | 5 | 25.0 | 0 | 0.0 | 0 | 0.0 |
| 80–40 | 1 | 4.8 | 5 | 27.8 | 2 | 22.2 | 1 | 16.7 | 3 | 15.0 | 0 | 0.0 | 0 | 0.0 |
| 40–50 | 0 | 0.0 | 1 | 5.6 | 0 | 0.0 | 0 | 0.0 | 0 | 0.0 | 0 | 0.0 | 0 | 0.0 |
| 50+ | 3 | 14.3 | 1 | 5.6 | 1 | 11.1 | 1 | 16.7 | 0 | 0.0 | 0 | 0.0 | 0 | 0.0 |
| **Total** | **21** | **100** | **18** | **100** | **9** | **100** | **6** | **100** | **20** | **100** | **0** | **0.0** | **2** | **100** |
| | | | | | | | | | | | | | | |
| *% Cortex* | | | | | | | | | | | | | | |
| 0 | 1 | 4.8 | 2 | 11.1 | 0 | 0.0 | 1 | 16.7 | 2 | 10.0 | 0 | 0.0 | 0 | 0.0 |
| 0–25 | 7 | 33.3 | 8 | 44.4 | 2 | 22.2 | 2 | 33.3 | 6 | 30.0 | 0 | 0.0 | 2 | 100 |
| 25–50 | 4 | 19.0 | 6 | 33.3 | 5 | 55.6 | 0 | 0.0 | 5 | 25.0 | 0 | 0.0 | 0 | 0.0 |
| 50–75 | 6 | 28.6 | 2 | 11.1 | 1 | 11.1 | 3 | 50.0 | 6 | 30.0 | 0 | 0.0 | 0 | 0.0 |
| 75–100 | 3 | 14.3 | 0 | 0.0 | 1 | 11.1 | 0 | 0.0 | 1 | 5.0 | 0 | 0.0 | 0 | 0.0 |
| 100 | 0 | 0.0 | 0 | 0.0 | 0 | 0.0 | 0 | 0.0 | 0 | 0.0 | 0 | 0.0 | 0 | 0.0 |
| **Total** | **28** | **100** | **18** | **100** | **9** | **100** | **6** | **100** | **20** | **100** | **0** | **0.0** | **2** | **100** |

plan, no features were identified in Area B and, listed below, those found in A must be considered suspect:

F.502: possibly the base of either a small pit or large posthole filled with buried soil-derived sandy silts; 18 flints were present within its matrix.

F.504: A pit, *c.* 0.40 m in diameter and 0.20 m deep, with an irregular concave base. It was filled with reddish brown-grey sand-silt with occasional charcoal; nine burnt flints were recovered.

F.505: A small pit, 0.20 m in diameter and 0.20 m deep; *c.* 20 struck flints were recovered from its grey-brown sandy silt fill.

F.506: A 0.35-m diameter posthole (0.50 m deep) filled with grey-brown sandy silt with frequent charcoal; a gravel packing fill was evident around its sides.

A section was dug across an area of irregularly variegated gravel and silts (F.503). Despite the recovery of a pottery sherd, this must represent 'natural' disturbance.

Identified by C. Swaysland, the investigations only produced two pieces of bone. One was a fragment of a left femur from a sub-adult cow ([3752.X]); the other was an adult cattle tooth (upper right P3) with medium wear ([3750.B]). In an effort to date the site's occupation, in 2003 the femur was submitted for radiocarbon dating, producing a date of 1750–1510 cal. BC (3340±50 BP; Beta-180720): for whatever reason this is considered unacceptably late to attribute the site's main usage.

## Pottery
### by J. POLLARD

Six weathered sherds and crumbs in flint-, grog- and sand-tempered fabrics were recovered. With the exception of the grog-tempered sherd from [3750] (<28499>), which may be of later Neolithic–earlier Bronze Age date, all probably derive from Early Neolithic bowls.

[3750] <28499>: Weathered, small grog-tempered sherd; later Neolithic–Early Bronze Age

[3756] F.503 <28463>: Flint-tempered crumb; Early Neolithic

[3750] <28484>: Weathered, small sherd in reduced laminar fabric with flint; probably Early Neolithic

[3750] <28465>: Two weathered sherds in flint and sand-tempered fabric with reduced core and interior; oxidized exterior; Early Neolithic

[3750] <28464>: Weathered sherd as above.

## The lithic assemblage
### by H.R. MIDDLETON

The quality of flaking was good (Tables 4.3 & 4.4) and comparable to the higher-quality material from the causewayed enclosure. 99% had hertzian cones of percussion suggesting extensive use of hard hammers; 61% of flakes had feather terminations, while 32% had hinge fractures. 80% had non-cortical platforms and less than 22% were side-struck; 16% had facetted platforms. Most platforms were less than 10 mm long, less than 2 mm thick and were struck at 100–110° (90% were struck at angles between 90–120°).

No flakes were recovered with 100% cortex on the dorsal surface (77% had more than 50% cortex on the dorsal surface: Tables 4.7–4.9) and preparation flakes were only present in small numbers (5%). Though this may suggest that initial working of cores was done off-site, the presence of nine core reduction flakes, two thinning flakes, nine IWW, 13 dressing chips, six cores and a trimming flake indicate that the later stages of

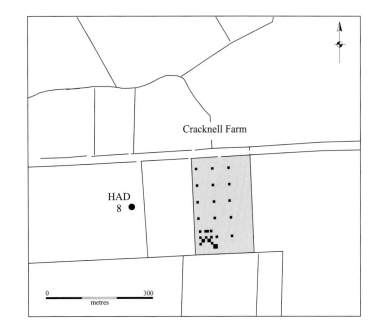

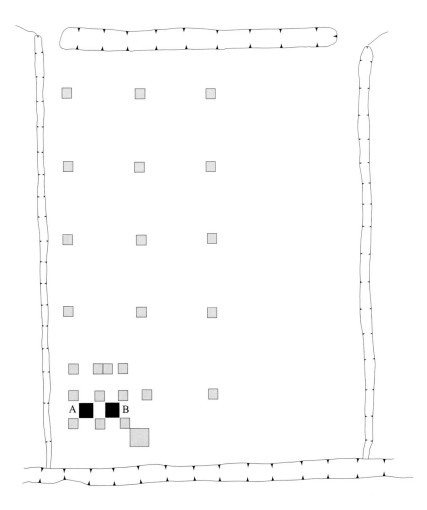

**Figure 4.11.** *The Cracknell Farm scatter: location and test-pit sampling plans.*

221

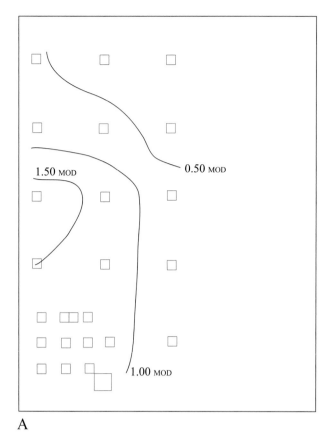
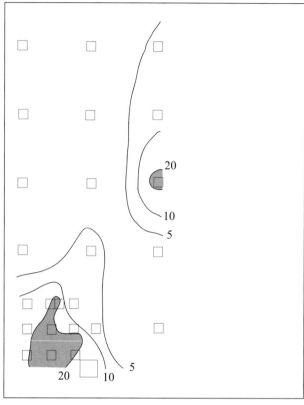

A

B

**Figure 4.12.** *The Cracknell Farm scatter: A) sub-surface contour; B) flint density.*

core reduction/discard and the production of flakes and implements took place. Of the cores recovered, most were under 20 g in weight and these generally had little cortex (under 25%), although half had more than 50% cortex. This would support the idea of on-site core working, but would suggest the discard of partially worked or poor-quality cores.

Most waste flakes were 20–30 mm long, 10–15 mm wide, 0–4 mm thick and 0–2 g in weight (33% were over 2 g in weight: Tables 4.5 & 4.6). These measurements are comparable with those from the causewayed enclosure but the flakes tend to be longer and thinner. The breadth: length ratios indicate that 14% were blades, 80% were flakes and 6% were broad flakes. When broken blades are included the total rises to 20%, with 16% of flakes having blade scars on their dorsal surfaces.

Of the six cores, two were Type A2, one was Type B2, another was a B3, one was C and another was on a crude bashed pebble (Table 4.9). Most had platforms; four had blade scars and two had broad flake scars.

The quality of the raw material and of the flaking was comparable to that of the earlier material from the causewayed enclosure. The metrical data shows that

a high percentage of blades were present, although a significant proportion of broad flakes also occurred. Most of the cores had platforms and a high percentage had blade scars. High percentages of utilized flakes (22%) and retouched flakes (22%) were found. A leaf-shaped arrowhead, a serrated flake, an axe fragment, a flake knife, a notched flake, two piercers and two scrapers were also recovered. As none of these were on broad flakes or suggested late forms, the material should be assigned an earlier Neolithic date.

As to function, there was no evidence to suggest that initial working of cores occurred on this site but all other stages of working, including implement production and core discard, are present in quantity. While there is a wide range of implements, the implement: by-product ratio was low (1:13); a small proportion of worked flints were burnt.

*Other lithic sites*
The two round barrows that were investigated within the course of the project are reported upon in Volume 2 (Chapter 2) and are only summarized here (see Figs. 1.7 & 4.13 for location):

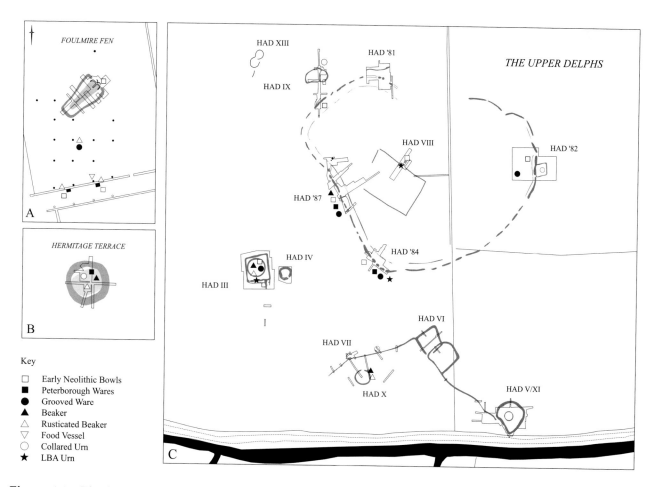

**Figure 4.13.** *The distribution of pre-Iron Age pottery types.*

*The Snow's Farm barrow* (HAD III/IV): Aside from a single sherd from an Early Neolithic Mildenhall bowl, pre-barrow activity was attested by a sealed Grooved Ware occupation spread. A 'primary' (?) cremation pyre was present on the northern side and 10 secondary cremations were recovered from the barrow's southern flank, with four of the latter deposited within Deverel-Rimbury urns.

Analyzed together with the material from the adjacent HAD IV Iron Age enclosure, the site's lithic assemblage was primarily of later Neolithic date and included scrapers, three transverse arrowheads, notched flakes, burins, piecers and a fabricator. However, as represented by a leaf-shaped arrowhead and a serrated flake, a distinctly earlier Neolithic component was also present. 21 cores were recovered, with all stages of core reduction attested to. (For the purposes of analysis the flint from the adjacent HAD IV Iron Age compound was included with the main barrow assemblage.)

Both plain and rusticated Beaker sherds were recovered from barrow contexts (one of the former possibly instead being from a Food Vessel). Several post-Deverel-Rimbury sherds were recovered from the mound's surface; the monument was later re-invested as a Romano-Celtic shrine.

*The Hermitage Farm barrow*: This had its origins in a small ovoid mound with an associated infant burial. Inserted into the side of this small monument was a cremation placed within a large Collared Urn with two accompanying vessels set inside it (one a small Collared Urn). Evidently a second 'primary' interment, the barrow was subsequently expanded into its round form and a single secondary cremation was set in a pit cut into its southern side.

One or possibly two sherds of Middle Neolithic pottery (one definitely Ebbsfleet ware) were recovered. Also found were sherds from at least four fine ware Beakers, and a rusticated Beaker sherd was also present. Aside from the main cremation group, a number of refitting sherds from another small Collared Urn were recovered; the monument's later re-use was attested by sherds from post-Deverel-Rimbury jars.

The site's lithics are essentially of Early Bronze Age attribution and include a flake knife and a scraper on a broken flake.

The excavation of the two sub-square Iron Age compounds, HAD V and VI, and the associated HAD VII field system extending west from the latter (and the contemporary HAD X 'circle'), are presented in Volume 2 (Chapters 5 & 6). Yet, as the lithic assemblages generated from them essentially have no direct relationship to their later phases of occupation, they are reported here below. This being said, a small pit (F.368) truncated by the HAD X circle contained 31 sherds from at least 9–12 fine and Rusticated Beakers. Located in some proximity to the Snows Farm barrow, this group is only discussed in detail within the second volume (Chapter 3).

The quantity of struck flint recovered from HAD V and VI might suggest that the Iron Age enclosures overlay an earlier 'lithic' site(s). This, however, does

**Table 4.10.** *Upper Delphs: raw material (based on whole assemblage).*

| Raw material | HAD III/IV | | HAD V/VI | | HAD VII | | Cracknell Farm | | Sampling squares | | Church's Drove | | Hermitage Barrow | |
|---|---|---|---|---|---|---|---|---|---|---|---|---|---|---|
| | No. | % | No. | % | No. | % | No. | % | No. | % | No. | % | No. | % |
| *Source* | | | | | | | | | | | | | | |
| Pebble | 261 | 80.4 | 278 | 67.5 | 44 | 62.0 | 68 | 63.0 | 131 | 78.9 | 7 | 58.1 | 13 | 72.2 |
| Abraded nodule | 64 | 19.6 | 123 | 29.9 | 25 | 35.2 | 39 | 36.1 | 34 | 20.5 | 5 | 41.7 | 5 | 17.8 |
| Unabraded nodule | 0 | 0.0 | 11 | 2.7 | 2 | 2.8 | 1 | 0.9 | 1 | 0.6 | 0 | 0.0 | 0 | 1.0 |
| **Total** | **327** | **100** | **412** | **100** | **71** | **100** | **108** | **100** | **166** | **100** | **12** | **100** | **18** | **100** |
| *Quality* | | | | | | | | | | | | | | |
| Good | 490 | 85.4 | 546 | 82.6 | 110 | 81.5 | 200 | 82.6 | 242 | 86.1 | 39 | 97.5 | 32 | 74.4 |
| Bad | 0 | 0.0 | 0 | 0.0 | 0 | 0.0 | 1 | 0.4 | 1 | 0.7 | 0 | 0.0 | 0 | 0.0 |
| Indifferent | 84 | 14.6 | 115 | 17.4 | 25 | 18.5 | 41 | 16.9 | 37 | 13.2 | 1 | 2.5 | 11 | 25.6 |
| **Total** | **574** | **100** | **661** | **100** | **135** | **100** | **242** | **100** | **281** | **100** | **40** | **100** | **43** | **100** |
| *Grain* | | | | | | | | | | | | | | |
| Fine | 478 | 83.3 | 551 | 81.7 | 112 | 83.0 | 210 | 86.8 | 244 | 86.8 | 39 | 97.5 | 38 | 88.4 |
| Medium | 96 | 16.7 | 108 | 16.3 | 23 | 17.0 | 32 | 13.2 | 37 | 13.2 | 1 | 2.5 | 5 | 11.6 |
| Coarse | 0 | 0.0 | 0 | 0.0 | 0 | 0.0 | 0 | 0.0 | 0 | 0.0 | 0 | 0.0 | 0 | 0.0 |
| **Total** | **574** | **100** | **661** | **100** | **135** | **100** | **242** | **100** | **281** | **100** | **40** | **100** | **43** | **100** |
| *Colour* | | | | | | | | | | | | | | |
| Dark grey/brown | 351 | 61.1 | 351 | 52.9 | 69 | 51.1 | 117 | 48.3 | 167 | 59.2 | 16 | 41.0 | 19 | 44.2 |
| Light grey | 57 | 9.9 | 46 | 6.9 | 21 | 15.6 | 22 | 9.1 | 26 | 9.2 | 7 | 17.9 | 5 | 11.6 |
| Light brown | 161 | 28.0 | 260 | 39.2 | 44 | 32.6 | 103 | 42.6 | 84 | 29.8 | 16 | 41.0 | 19 | 44.2 |
| White | 1 | 0.2 | 3 | 0.5 | 1 | 0.7 | 0 | 0.0 | 2 | 0.7 | 0 | 0.0 | 0 | 0.0 |
| Other | 4 | 0.7 | 4 | 0.6 | 0 | 0.0 | 0 | 0.0 | 3 | 1.1 | 0 | 0.0 | 0 | 0.0 |
| **Total** | **574** | **100** | **664** | **100** | **135** | **100** | **242** | **100** | **282** | **100** | **39** | **100** | **43** | **100** |

not seem to be the case. Rather it reflects how much of the compounds' surface deposits (and buried soil) was excavated by hand. In sieve-control metre transects, the density of flint at both was only found to range from 0–4 pieces. With site means of *c.* 0.6 pieces per metre, this indicates no more than generic 'background' densities.

The lithic assemblages
by H.R. MIDDLETON
*HAD V & VI:* The material from HAD V was of a quality comparable to the later material from the causewayed enclosure (Tables 4.3 & 4.4). 95% of flakes had hertzian cones of percussion indicative of hard hammer striking. 51% had feather terminations and 38% had hinge fractures. 65% had non-cortical platforms; 40% were side-struck and 10% had faceted platforms. The HAD VI material was of slightly poorer quality. Most of the platforms were 0–5 mm long, less than 2 mm wide and were struck at an angle between 100–110° (78% were struck between 90–120°).

All stages of the core-reduction sequence were present at HAD V (Tables 4.7–4.9). 29% of flakes had more than 25% cortex on their dorsal surface; 88% had less than 50% cortex on their dorsal surface, while 12% had more than 50%. More than 5% were primary flakes suggesting the initial working of raw material on site. The presence of 19 core reduction flakes and 22 thinning flakes together with 18 cores suggests the later stages of core reduction and flake production and the presence of 28 dressing chips and a thinning chip indicate that implement production took place on site. Though HAD VI lacked evidence for the later stages of core reduction and discard, it did contain a high percentage of prepara-

tion flakes, suggesting initial core preparation. Most cores from HAD V were under 20 g in weight and were well worked, but 40% were over 30 g in weight and 11% had more than 50% cortex. This confirms that initial working of cores occurred on this site as well as complete reduction and discard. The discard of little-worked cores may also suggest poor quality of raw material.

Most waste flakes were 20–30 mm long, 15–20 mm wide, 2–4 mm thick and 0–2 g in weight (57% were over 2 g in weight: Tables 4.5 & 4.6). These measurements are comparable with those from the causewayed enclosure but, like HAD III/V, tend to be longer and wider. The breadth:length ratios indicate that 7% of the flakes were blades, 55% were flakes and 38% were broad flakes. Blades and broken blades represent 5% of the assemblage and 13% of flakes had blade scars.

Of the 18 cores, four had platforms, four were keeled and 10 were crude, ill defined or damaged (Table 4.9). 53% had broad flake scars, 20% had blade scars with ratios over 5:2 and 13% had blade scars of ratios between 5:2 and 2:1, suggesting a mixed technology.

Though the quality of the raw material was rather poorer than that of the later material from the causewayed enclosure, the quality of the flaking was comparable. The site contained high proportions of broad flakes and most cores had broad flake scars, but a significant proportion of cores had blade scars and the site contained a few blades, suggesting a predominantly later Neolithic assemblage with an earlier Neolithic component. This is supported by an analysis of the implements: utilized flakes (37%), and retouched flakes (22%) predominate and significant proportions of each are on blades and on broad flakes. The same is true of the knives (3%). Of the scrapers, half are short end-scrapers and half are on broken flakes or are disc scrapers. Two leaf-shaped arrowheads, three polished axe fragments and a serrated flake were found. Piercers (6%), notched flakes (5%), burins (3%) and a fabricator (1%) were also recovered.

All stages of the core-reduction sequence were found. Initial preparation of cores, flaking, implement production and core discard are all present. There is a wide range of implements and a high implement:by-product ratio (1:4) that suggests a range of activities in addition to flint work. 229 pieces of burnt unworked flint were also recovered, but may relate to the Iron Age occupation.

*HAD VII:* The quality of flaking is comparable to the later material from the causewayed enclosure (Tables 4.3 & 4.4). 92% of flakes had hertzian cones of percussion, suggesting hard hammer striking. 62% had feather terminations and 18% had hinge fractures. Less than 79% had non-cortical platforms and 42% were side-struck; 8% had faceted platforms. Most of the platforms were short (less than 5 mm long), and thin (under 2 mm wide) and were struck at an angle of 100–110° (87% were struck at angles between 90–120°).

All stages of the core-reduction sequence were present (Tables 4.7–4.9). However only seven (12%) of unretouched flakes had more than 25% cortex on their dorsal surface (98% had less than 25% cortex on their dorsal surface while 2% had more than 50%). Ten preparation flakes, five core-reduction flakes, four thinning flakes and five dressing chips were present, but unretouched flakes dominated (74%). The quantity of core-reduction flakes, preparation flakes and thinning flakes suggests a significant element of core preparation and reduction. A high percentage of cores were found, suggesting the later stages of core reduction and discard were plentiful. It is possible that mainly pre-prepared cores were used here. While most cores were under 20 g in weight and had less than 50% cortex covering, two cores had more cortex and one core was over 50 g. This may suggest the use of some large material and the discard of partly-used material.

Most of the waste flakes were 20–30 m long, 15–20 mm wide and 4–6 mm thick and 0–2 g in weight (55% were over 0.2 g in weight: Tables 4.5 & 4.6). These measurements compare well with the causewayed enclosure but have a tendency to be wider and thicker. The breadth:length ratios show 5% are blades, 59% are flake and 36% are broad flakes. The number of blades rises to 6% if broken blades are included, and 13% of flakes had blade scars on their dorsal surface.

Nine cores were found: six had one-/two-platforms, one was keeled and the other two were damaged or ill defined (Table 4.9). Seven had broad flake scars and two had blade scars of length/breadth ratios between 5:2 and 2:1.

While the raw material was of a poorer quality than the material from the causewayed enclosure, the quality of flaking was comparable. The preponderance of broad flake scars on cores suggests a late dating but a small number of blades and blade cores were also found. The implements also suggest a mixed assemblage: seven of the utilized flakes were flakes or broad flakes, the two knives and three retouched flakes were flakes and broad flakes and the ten scrapers were short (two were under 20 mm long) and were of poor quality. However a serrated blade was also found and four of the utilized flakes were blades. Together this evidence is comparable to that from the 1981 and 1982 areas of the causewayed enclosure and suggests a predominantly Early Bronze Age dating with a more minor earlier Neolithic component.

The waste flake data suggest that preliminary working of cores was undertaken elsewhere, but flaking did occur on this site. However, the majority of unretouched flakes lacked cortex, which suggests that levels of production were low. The range of implements is wide and contains high proportions of utilized flakes (33%) and scrapers (30%) as well as retouched flakes (8%) and notched flakes (9%); two knives, a piercing tool and a burin were also found. The ratio of implements:by-products is high (1:3) and must suggest that the main site functions were of a general nature. A small proportion of the worked flints were burnt.

## Struck flint: an overview
by H.R. MIDDLETON

Aside from the causewayed enclosure, the various Upper Delphs investigations produced 1944 pieces of worked flint from the buried soil and features from sites dating from Bronze Age to Roman times. Only in the case of the excavated barrows can any of this material be considered to be in its original context, while the rest is residual. Flint artefacts were found dating from the Mesolithic to the Bronze Age, but most of the material dates from the Middle and later Neolithic, the flint from most sites being of mixed age.

### Condition
The majority of the material was in a fresh and unabraded condition (Table 4.2). The Church's Drove and Cracknell Farm scatters and the flint from the Iron Age sites HAD V and HAD VI were exceptions. In the case of the latter compounds this may best be explained by the extensive Iron Age activity on the site and the residual nature of the finds. As regards the flint scatters, it is best explained by modern agricultural activity.

The material from most of the sites showed a similar degree of patination, although the material from the flint scatters and test pits had less than 10 per cent of pieces patinated. A higher percentage of patinated pieces came from sites where material was excavated from cut features (e.g. 29 per cent were patinated from HAD VI where most finds came from the deep-cut ditches). Similarly, the overall proportion of complete finds was similar to the causewayed enclosure and where variation occurred it can generally be related to the degree to which the finds were protected by cut features (e.g. high proportions were broken from the flint scatters while low percentages were broken from HAD VI, IX and the HAD VIII Neolithic pit, the latter lying within the causewayed enclosure's interior).

### Dating
Small quantities of Mesolithic material, including microliths, edge-blunted blades, truncated blades, and micro-burins were recovered from many of the sites but were not in sufficient quantities to suggest that activity was other than light and dispersed:

| | |
|---|---|
| **HAD V** | Two edge-blunted blades, a microlith, five truncated blades, two denticulates |
| **HAD VII** | A micro-burin, a denticulate |
| **HAD III/ IV** | Two microliths, four micro-burins |
| **Cracknell Farm** | A microlith, a micro-burin |
| **Upper Delphs test pits** | A microlith, two truncated blades, a micro-burin. |

The Church's Drove and Cracknell Farm investigations produced almost exclusively Early Neolithic material; HAD III–V had mixed Early and Late Neolithic assemblages, though they were predominantly of later Neolithic attribution. HAD VII and the test pits contained only minor quantities of Early Neolithic material. They were essentially mixed Late Neolithic and Early Bronze Age assemblages, and both HAD VII and the Hermitage Farm barrow produced quantities of Early Bronze Age material.

*Discussion*

In terms of function, Church's Drove, HAD VIII and the Hermitage Farm barrow had little or no evidence of flint production and included few artefact types, but had high implement:by-product ratios. In the case of HAD VIII and the barrow this may be explained by their Early Bronze Age attribution. The Church's Drove material was of earlier Neolithic date and was unusual in having 18% of worked flint burnt. This may suggest that the 'site' had a special non-industrial function.

Most of the sites (HAD III/IV, V, the test pits and the Cracknell Farm scatter) had evidence for the general flaking of cores and core discard, although this was most intense at HAD III/IV and the test pits. Each of the sites had similar ranges of artefacts and similar implement:by-product ratios. Only the Cracknell Farm scatter lacked evidence for initial core working and implement production and it had a very low implement:by-product ratio. The test pits also had a low implement:by-product ratio. HAD V had a high implement:by-product ratio including three polished axe fragments. HAD III/IV had a high percentage of scrapers.

*Raw material exploitation*: As with the Mesolithic sites and the causewayed enclosure, on most corticated pieces the cortex was thin and abraded, typical of gravel flint. However, as also with the causewayed enclosure, some sites had an element with chalky unabraded cortex; HAD V, the test pits and the Cracknell Farm scatter included this material in small amounts.

Only Church's Drove had flint of a quality comparable to that of the earlier material from the causewayed enclosure. The Cracknell Farm scatter included material comparable with that from the later material from the enclosure, but at HAD III/IV, V and VII the material was of poorer quality. The cores from the latter sites (and the test pits) show that the discarded material tended to be large in comparison to the Mesolithic sites, with 40–50% weighing more than 20 g and with up to 40% of the cores having more than 50% cortical surfaces. Most of the cores from these sites

tended to have no platforms and were fairly crude. This would suggest a greater use of primary material on the later sites and a poorer working technique/raw material. The cores from Cracknell Farm were mainly platform varieties and as with HAD V cores tended to be smaller and more fully worked.

*Relationships*: The raw-material analysis suggests a general decline in the quality of the material and its working between the Mesolithic, Early Neolithic and later periods. This appears to be linked to a later tendency toward non-platform cores and high levels of discard.

The dating of the sites suggests that the Upper Delphs area was a focus of activity in the Middle and later Neolithic and to a lesser extent in the Early Bronze Age, and that often the same sites were being used in the Middle and later Neolithic. In the earlier Neolithic the western façade of the causewayed enclosure was clearly a focus and the HAD III/IV areas immediately to the west may have been closely associated with it, while the HAD V area may also have then been utilized. Earlier Neolithic activity also extended north towards the Long Barrow, as at Cracknell Farm and Church's Drove. However, in the earlier period, levels of deposition appear to have been relatively low.

The dates relating to the earlier Neolithic suggest dispersion and specialization of function. The primary ditch contexts of the enclosure, its palisade and the HAD VIII pit, as well as the Church's Drove 'site', all lack evidence for production and appear to contain special deposits. Inside the causewayed enclosure, however, a great deal of flint working took place, including the initial working of cores and implement production. The HAD III/IV and HAD V sites suggest similar functions, but at Cracknell Farm no initial core work took place.

The later Neolithic material occurs in greater quantities in the causewayed enclosure (see below), HAD III/IV and at HAD V and the test pits. This suggests the continued significance of the causewayed enclosure as a locale. In fact there then appears to have been a denser concentration of activity in this area. There is no evidence to suggest a continued emphasis on the western facade and rather the later material tends to be to the east of the causewayed enclosure. Neither is there evidence for special deposits at the site connected with this phase.

All the later Neolithic sites produced a similar range of material: all core-reduction phases are present and implement production is evident. There is a wide range of implement types and low implement: by-product ratios.

The Early Bronze Age activity relates to the two barrows and HAD VII, and is linked to a lack of production, few artefact types and high implement: by-product ratios.

## Distributions and settlement densities

Although in part anticipating the results of the excavation of the causewayed enclosure, Figure 4.13 schematically shows the distribution of pre-Iron Age pottery within the study area. If we add to this the evidence of the lithics, there seems little sense of distinct landscape 'zonation' with most chronological markers or types being present across the obvious topographic categories: the (palaeo-)riverside terraces/islands, the Upper Delphs and the latter's lower northern skirtland. A number of factors contribute to this picture of dispersed land use. The foremost is surely the limitation of the project's sampling. Its extent and intensity was inadequate to the landscape at hand and, concentrated on the Upper Delphs, was biased towards land above the level of 2.00 m OD. There was simply insufficient coverage below 1.00 m OD to model the loss of land during the later Neolithic and Bronze Ages owing to marine incursions, and also the depth at which Late Mesolithic and Early Neolithic occupation had earlier been possible. In this regard, only rarely can test-pit sampling generate the kind of nuanced early land-use/settlement mapping that is available through sustained fieldwalking from, for example, the Isleham and Soham environs (Brown, in Hall 1996; Edmonds *et al.* 1999, fig. 14) or the Wissey Embayment (Healy 1996).

The other main factors that influence this sense of dispersed land use are the concepts of 'taskscape' and lithic 'background'. Within the region the impact of the latter was first really developed by Pryor (1982; see also Evans 1993) and primarily relates to the widely cleared landscapes of the second millennium BC. In these 'open' lands people expediently used whatever flint was at hand; at most detaching off a flake or two to provide a useful sharp edge, employing it to the immediate task and thereafter directly discarding it. The outcome of such activity was widespread low density distributions of largely non-diagnostic material. The distribution of struck flint within the Upper Delphs test pits would generally seem largely to reflect such casual (and predominately Bronze Age) lithic 'fall out'.

First proposed by Ingold (1993) and developed by Edmonds and others (Edmonds *et al.* 1999), the idea of 'taskscape' largely pertains to pre-Middle/later Bronze Age land use. Prior to the establishment of more robust modes of obviously permanent settlement at that time, occupation would have required much daily off-site resource 'tasking' (i.e. hunting and food gathering). Water collection would have featured and the advent of formal wells in the second millennium BC clearly marks a major change in the character of settlement. Routinely going out into landscape would obviously have contributed to dispersed lithic patterning. (This sense of a mid second millennium BC 'sea-change' should not, however, be applied too rigorously and, as discussed in Volume 2, the area's Iron Age communities also regularly went out into the marshes and evidently utilized the crowns of fen-fast barrows as procurement 'stations'.)

Leaving aside the area's Neolithic monuments, generally the distribution of later Mesolithic and earlier Neolithic material would seem broadly comparable: dispersed throughout the area, though with evidence of somewhat more intense Neolithic activity. It is potentially telling that the two major occupation sites that can be assigned to these times, at Foulmire Fen and Cracknell Farm, were both situated on rises adjacent to backwater palaeochannels and these locales saw both Late Mesolithic *and* Early Neolithic usage. (Hall recovered Mesolithic material from the larger Cracknell Farm spread in the fields immediately southwest of our investigations: 1996, 61, 64).

Bearing in mind the restriction of the project's sampling, there does seem to have been a propensity for earlier Neolithic activity on the lower northern terrace below the main rise of the Upper Delphs (below 2.00 m OD and the causewayed enclosure). Against this, by the fact that later Neolithic material was not recovered from this area but rather seems concentrated on the higher ground of the Upper Delphs, it could be proposed that this represents a retreat in the face of rising water levels during the third millennium BC due to marine incursions north of the study area (see Waller 1994, figs. 5.18 & 5.19). Yet to advocate this a number of different strands of evidence would have to be ignored. Most significant is the recovery of later Neolithic–earlier Bronze Age material at just above sea level at Foulmire Fen. Similarly, the siting of the round barrows on that terrace at this same low level would complement the dates of Cardiff's 900/50 core which indicate that it was only really in the later Bronze Age that land below *c.* 1.00 m OD got wet.

Given this, over the course of the Neolithic land below 0 m OD would have become increasingly saturated, and this would have isolated and effectively 'islanded' areas of higher ground. Equally, cultural landscape associations, and particularly the lingering impact of the causewayed enclosure (i.e. a 'sense of place'), may itself have drawn later Neolithic activity to the Upper Delphs crown (above

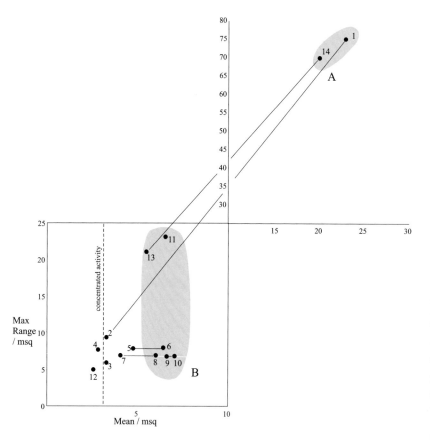

**Figure 4.14.** *Plot of site/area flint densities. Foulmire Fen: 1) mean cuttings density; 2) test pits. 3) Hermitage Farm Terrace test pits. Upper Delphs Fields: 4) main grid; 5) Spread A, with '6' its core densities; 7) Spread B, with '8' its core; 9) Spread C, with '10' its core. 11) Triangular Field test pits. 12) Church's Drove test pits. Cracknell Farm: 13) main test pits grid, with '14' its core (*NB *lines between linking points indicate interrelated sampling values).*

2.00 m OD). However, given the limitations of the project's sampling below that depth, the possibility of later Neolithic sites occurring lower than that level around the terrace's skirtland cannot be dismissed. This crucial issue will be further discussed in the concluding chapter.

There can, of course, be no strict thresholds for the definition of sites from lithic distributions alone, and a particular problem resides in the distinction of 'events' or one-off stays from sustained occupations. The extent of densities is also a factor. Restricted by the scale of the Upper Delphs sampling grid, in an effort to factor-out very localized high values 'spreads' have been defined by the occurrence of high densities over three consecutive test-pit points. This is potentially a major bias and, for example, an intensive occupation extending over an area of 45 m across would therefore only register as a single test-pit 'high'.

Although subject to caveats concerning multi-period usage/representation, what Table 4.11 and Figure 4.14 attest to is that major occupations, such as at Cracknell Farm and the Foulmire Fen cuttings, occur at densities of 15–20 and more flints per metre square. At the other end of the scale, the application of a figure of three or more flints as marking 'concentrated activity' based on the definition of the Upper Delphs spreads (A–C) would also directly correspond to the Ouse-side terrace densities: both the Hermitage Farm sampling and the Foulmire Fen test pits. The issue now requiring address is whether the 5/6+ flint 'core' densities within all three of the Upper Delphs spreads (and the Triangular Field) represents another threshold of medial usage/occupation. This can only be addressed in the context of the causewayed enclosure excavations presented in the ensuing chapter.

### Early Neolithic settlement: the problem
with a contribution by D. Garrow

In an effort to set the broader Haddenham landscape investigations in context, and before the causewayed enclosures results are presented, it is appropriate that the 'problem' of pre-later Bronze Age settlement, particularly earlier Neolithic occupation, is outlined. As discussed in Chapter 1, a gulf exists in our expectations between the scale of the period's monuments and the slight character of its settlement 'architecture'. The general paucity of substantial structures is no longer seen as merely as an archaeological invisibility, but as actual evidence for the impermanence of dwellings. Sustained rescue and research projects have consistently failed to recover definitive evidence for permanent or large-scale settlements, leading to the observation that '*the essence of the Neolithic seems to lie elsewhere*' (Whittle 1999, 59; emphasis added). As a consequence modes of settlement mobility, with varying degrees of permanence, have been explored. Pollard has suggested that 'the rhythm of occupation would have involved periodic clearance, settling down for a few years or so, followed by abandonment and movement to another locale' (2000, 364), but others have favoured a more fluid approach: 'short term camps for a handful of people; settlements occupied by an extended family; and places where families gathered, perhaps for a season, perhaps for a genera-tion or more' (Edmonds 1997, 104). It is, of course, the 'rhythm' of settlement and landscape movement that is crucial and what potential distinguishes these arguments from more established swidden-based modes of settlement shift. In short, is it a matter of annual quasi-nomadism or short-lived permanent settlements, however insubstantial their traces (see Rowley-Conwy 2003; 2004 for review)?

Certainly models of 'tethered' mobility or 'short-term sedentism' have become commonplace in studies of the British Neolithic (e.g. Whittle 1997). Their application does not so much arise from the determination of seasonality, but rather the paucity of 'robust' settlement remains (e.g. seemingly permanent buildings). Attractive though these may be given the evidence, the problem lies in what could cause this 'moving'. If estimating earlier Neolithic territorial ranges to fall within the area of hundreds of square kilometres or less (see Chapter 6), then in eastern England, aside potentially from lithic resources, there seems insufficient environmental variability to warrant this movement. In a forested landscape, especially as it seems that marine or marshland-spe-cific resources were not then significantly utilized, there are no determining factors to move from one locale to another. Times of social gathering, whether for funerary rites or festivals, would have demanded displacement, but otherwise the resources of one location would have been much the same as the next. There seems little sense of 'marginal' land, nor would population pressure have compelled seasonal utilization. While there is evidence to suggest that during the later Neolithic/Early Bronze Ages, at least locally, there would have been sufficient woodland clearance to necessitate limited journeying to forests for collection and hunting purposes, this would not have been true of the earlier Neolithic. The outcome of this must be either to question the validity of such residential mobility models or to see such movement as essentially relating to the maintenance of previous Mesolithic 'cycles' (i.e. hunting 'lifeways') into what was essentially a pastoralist regime.

Of course, in this capacity the bulky character of Neolithic material culture would itself have impeded extensive movement. It could be presumed that the period's large pottery vessels would have to have been disposed of and/or cached for portions of the year (see inset above).

Recent large landscape-scale investigations within the region have demonstrated that the dis-

**Table 4.11.** *Struck flint densities (\*indicates nil test-pit values excluded; \*\*indicates factored figure).*

| Area | Range (per m sq.) | Mean (per m sq.) |
|---|---|---|
| *Foulmire Fen* | | |
| Cutting A | 6–76 | 29.1(47.3\*\*) |
| Cutting B | 12–36 | 16.8 |
| Test Pits | 1–9.5 | 3.25\*\* |
| *Hermitage Farm Terrace* | 1–6 | 3.2\* |
| *Upper Delphs Fields* | | |
| Main grid | 1–8 | 2.8\* |
| Spread A | 3–8 | 4.7 |
| Core | 5–8 | 6.4 |
| Spread B | 3–7 | 4.1 |
| Core | 5–7 | 6 |
| Spread C | 6–7 | 6.6 |
| Core | 7–7 | 7 |
| *Triangular Field* | 1–23 | 6.5 |
| *Church's Drove* | 1–5 | 2.5\* |
| *Cracknell Farm* | | |
| Main grid | 1–21 | 5.5\* |
| Core | 8–70 | 20 |

persed traces of Early Neolithic settlement are not uncommon. Consisting of small lithic 'events' or iso-lated pit groups extending over *c.* 25–100 sq. m, these are found on both gravel and clay sub-soils and must essentially represent 'taskscape' activities and/or short-stay camps (e.g. Evans *et al.* 1999). Against this, Grahame Clark's two main Neolithic excavations in the region in many respects epitomize what may be distinct 'types' of more intense Neolithic occupation. On the one hand, there are lithic scatters in the manner of Peacocks Farm, and a number of such sites were identified in the course of the Fenland Survey (Hall & Coles 1994). Clark *et al.*'s Hurst Fen excavation would be representative of what may be the other mode of settlement: pit sites (Fig. 4.17). Discussed by Garrow below, these consist of extensive clusters of shallow pits whose matrix includes high densities of pottery and flint. The moot question in this context is whether these are two different types of occupation.

A number of Early Neolithic scatters were inves-tigated within the course of the Fenland Management Project (Crowson *et al.* 2000; Hall & Coles 1994) and, much in the manner of the Cracknell Farm site, these generally did not produce convincing feature associations. The most obvious case in point is the vast and extraordinarily dense scatter at Honey Hill, Ramsey (Site 13). There both geophysical survey and grid-based 'test station' trial trenching could not locate

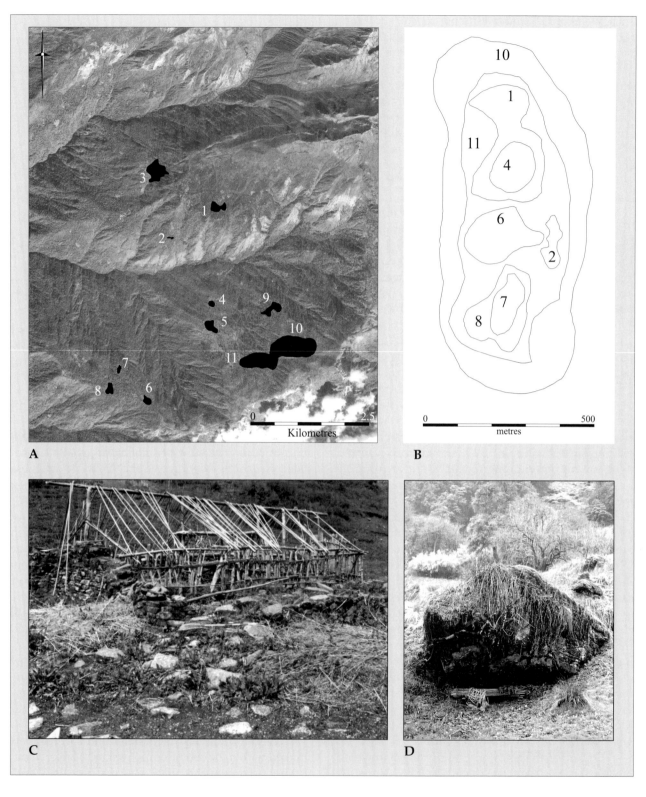

A

B

C

D

any accompanying features (Edmonds *et al.* 1999). In part, this may relate to the scale and techniques of excavation. As indicated in Figure 4.16 which shows the Barleycroft Paddocks excavation (Evans & Knight 2000), where unequivocal Early Neolithic settlement remains were discovered (both utilized tree throws and pit clusters; see below), the dispersed character of these sites demands large-scale exposure. Yet on that site, despite the quantity of material recovered from its cut features, it left little contemporary artefact trace

230

### Forest pastoralism: clearance and cachement

Modes of forest pastoralism is a theme that has received little attention in ethnographic literature. Quite by chance one of us spent a considerable part of the 1990s working on a series of highland sites just below the snow-line of the Nepalese Himalayas (c. 2500–3500 m OD: Evans 1999b). These heavily forested slopes are used by upland sheep- and buffalo-pastoralists for summer pastures. Historical sources and the frequency of obviously 'old' encampment sites indicate that these practices were much more widespread prior to the twentieth century (slash-and-burn arable is now impacting on the margins of the highlands: see Pignede 1993; Macfarlane 1976; Messerschmidt 1976). Admittedly a far cry from the Cambridgeshire Fenlands in which to find analogical sources, nevertheless in the context of this volume two points are of relevance. The first is the scale of the encampment clearing, which in this case is partially determined by the availability of suitably level ground. Plotted from satellite imagery, most range in size from 0.5–6 ha, though there are a few larger 'meadows' of 20–40 ha. Pastoralist compounds have been observed both arranged along only one side of clearings and, alternatively, dotted throughout the open ground. While partially dictated by the 'lie of the land', generally the clearances are of sub-ovoid plan with irregular 'nibbling' of their edges (though see the 'nipped' or bi-partite plan of Clearance 1).

The other point of potential relevance concerns 'caching'. The pastoralists construct a variety of low drystone wall compounds. These carry timber superstructures for the housing of herds and their attendants. The stonework is left standing throughout the year and, upon their seasonal occupation, to these are added split-bamboo thatch-covered roofs. When traversing the uplands one comes across pastoral caches, either under large rock overhangs or placed in the burnt-out interior of lightning-struck trees (see Evans 1999b concerning the local typologies of such rendered trucks). These will include the shelters' bamboo roof pieces and other equipment (e.g. ropes and ladders) that are only required in the uplands. Thus hidden, these items need not be taken up and down the mountain each year.

These forest-based activities impact on the survival of upland ruins; the clamp-pits of charcoal burners are found cut into sites, and pastoralists rob stone for the construction of their shelters (see Volume 2, Chapter 1 concerning the mis-application of transhumant modelling in Fenland archaeology).

**Figure 4.15** (left). *Forest pastoralism: A) Satellite image of the Annapurnas of central Nepal (northeast of Pokhara) with black areas indicating major woodland clearances that are plotted right (1–10; 'B'); C) 'buffalo-type' pastoralist shelter; D) equipment cache under rock overhang (photographs C. Evans).*

occupation refuse was intentionally 'tidied up' and backfilled into cut features. If so, this could indeed suggest that 'featureless' lithic scatters and pit-type Neolithic settlements may represent different modes of occupation. Whether this respectively reflects specialist/base-camp distinction (the latter feature-based occupations seeing more extensive pottery usage) and/or chronological factors has yet to be determined, as unfortunately open scatter sites invariably produce little material suitable for absolute dating. However, the seemingly mixed later Mesolithic/earlier Neolithic flint assemblages such as found at Cracknell Farm or Foulmire Fen (and the Soham scatters: see Edmonds et al. 1999) do not seem to occur in the pit sites. This could, therefore indicate that the pit 'occupations' were indeed a mid fourth millennium BC (and later) phenomenon and that the scatters probably relate to earlier, 'transitional' activity.

Slight traces of light structures were found in association with Barleycroft Paddocks' pits (Fig. 4.16) and there the possibility was raised that, akin to Mesolithic pit dwellings, up-turned tree-bowls (and their resultant crescent-shaped 'kick-up' hollows) were utilized to support tents or lean-to-type structures (Evans et al. 1999). In the course of the Cambridge Archaeological Unit's 1992–95 investigations at Fen Drayton, located four kilometres upstream from Over on the southern edge of the Ouse floodplain, two comparably small, stake- and post-built structures were recovered. These occurred adjacent to a cluster of intercut pits that produced earlier Neolithic flintwork, and elsewhere in the area other 'suggestive' pit and postholes groupings were identified (Wait 1992; Lucas & Wait 1996). From one of these pit clusters more than 50 sherds from both Peterborough Ware and earlier Neolithic bowls were recovered, with a minimum of nine vessels being represented (Mortimer 1995). Interestingly enough in the light of arguments concerning the role of the causewayed enclosure in lithic exchange (see Chapter 5 below), amongst the latter's assemblages were nine flakes from at least six different polished implements, both flint and fine-grained stone. (The evidence of Middle/later Neolithic activity at this locale is also relevant given that a possible cursus with an aligned mortuary enclosure is known immediately south of the quarry. As the most easterly downstream monument setting of this type on the Ouse, it will be further discussed in Chapter 6).

Otherwise, within the region and across southern Britain in general, more substantial post-built buildings (usually of sub-square shed-like plan) have only really been found on Middle/later Neolithic sites (e.g. Pryor 2001a, fig. 3.13), Pryor having re-interpreted the sub-

in the buried soil (Edmonds et al. 1999). Unfortunately, too few 'pit-type' sites have had accompanying surface deposits investigated in sufficient detail to provide comparative data. Nevertheless, based on the Barleycroft evidence, it may be the case that

**Figure 4.16.** *The Barleycroft Paddocks excavations (A): B) Mildenhall pit cluster; C & D) 'open' stakehole structures (after Evans & Knight 2001).*

rectangular wall-trench building at Padholme Road, Fengate as a funerary 'house' (2001a, 406; see Chapter 3 above). Given this and the bulk-timber construction of the Foulmire Fen mortuary chamber, it does seem remarkable that, while obviously familiar with wood-working techniques and living in a widely forested environment, Early Neolithic communities seem to have drawn so little upon wood for domestic construction (compare this to the terrace's Iron Age houses, built in a largely cleared landscape: Volume 2, Chapters 5 & 6). Surely this tells of the impermanent character of settlement itself and the situation of the 'home' (i.e. the/a house *vs.* the environment in general).

Below, Garrow reviews the recent evidence of earlier Neolithic pit settlements. The primary reason for its inclusion is that one feature of this type was found within the interior of the causewayed enclosures during the course of the HAD VIII excavations. Described in detail in the following chapter, in hindsight we should have investigated that area in much greater intensity as, in some respects, the interpretation of the monument hinges upon it.

*Pit settlements*
by D. GARROW

The issue of Neolithic 'settlement' in Britain and Ireland has long been an awkward one. In contrast to the picture in continental Europe, houses or other similar structures are conspicuous by their absence across large areas (with notable exceptions in Ireland and northern Scotland). Where buildings are found, they tend to be of slight construction, and few and far between in their distribution (Darvill 1996: Thomas 1996b). Over the last 15 years especially, however, it has been realized that even if *houses* may be absent in many areas, 'settlement' or perhaps more correctly evidence of occupation is not. Excavations have continually produced Neolithic pit features, sometimes in very large numbers. In many places across Britain it seems that pit sites, perhaps along with surface scatters, represent the closest thing we have to Neolithic settlement.

The pits under discussion are usually relatively small (less than a metre in diameter), circular or oval in plan, and bowl-shaped in profile, with rounded or flat bases. They normally contain a variety of cultural material, including pottery, worked and burnt flint and stone, animal and occasionally human bone, along with burnt organic material (including charcoal, charred hazelnuts and seeds); sometimes they are empty. The finds within pits can lie densely packed on their bases, but are more usually distributed throughout their fills, suggesting deposition within a soil matrix. Some artefacts appear to have

been selected specifically, whilst others seem to have found their way into pits as part of a general dump of cultural material collected from a midden (Pollard 2001; Thomas 1999). The number of pits on any given site varies enormously. Sometimes they occur singly or in pairs, within an otherwise archaeologically empty landscape; at the other extreme, hundreds may be found in a small area. This variability is also seen through time: sites appear to be largest in terms of pit numbers earlier on, during the fourth millennium. There is a suggestion that deposition acquires greater formality during the late Neolithic (Pollard 2001; Thomas 1999), and the tradition of placing material within pits is a long-lasting one, extending into the early Bronze Age and beyond.

Neolithic 'pit-dwellings', 'cooking holes', 'hearth sites' and other such features have been discussed at various times since the latter part of the nineteenth century (e.g. Pitt Rivers 1898; Wyman Abbot 1910; Warren *et al.* 1936). Perhaps *the* key turning point in terms of the way pits have been approached, however, came with the excavation of Hurst Fen (Clark *et al.* 1960). For the first time, a major site *containing pits alone* had been found. Through comparison with similar, basket-lined pits in Egypt, and presumably also influenced by understandings of the Iron Age, the excavators reached the conclusion that the features at Hurst Fen were best interpreted as storage pits (Clark *et al.* 1960, 211). The material within them was of secondary importance, seen as rubbish simply filling convenient hollows. The discovery of Hurst Fen sparked a discussion on the nature of Neolithic pits that was to continue for a number of years. C.H. Houlder widened the debate, in relation to his site at Hazard Hill in Devon, suggesting an array of other functional possibilities, including their use for food and water storage, as pot stands, cooking holes or quarries (Houlder 1963). Isobel Smith promptly dismissed his speculations, choosing to follow Clark *et al.* in viewing pits as grain storage facilities (Smith, in Field *et al.* 1964), and took the argument a stage further by relating the geographical distribution of pits to a proposed agrarian economy of lowland England. Interestingly in the light of recent discussions, she actually entertained the possibility that pits may have had a non-utilitarian function, but in the end concluded that 'they can reasonably be interpreted as connected with domestic rather than ritual activities' (Smith, in Field *et al.* 1964, 369). It is important to note the underlying assumption within these early discussions that pits were simply one aspect of *permanent* settlements, which would also have included (archaeologically invisible) houses and other structures.

Over the past 20 years or so, these arguments have become increasingly untenable, mostly as a

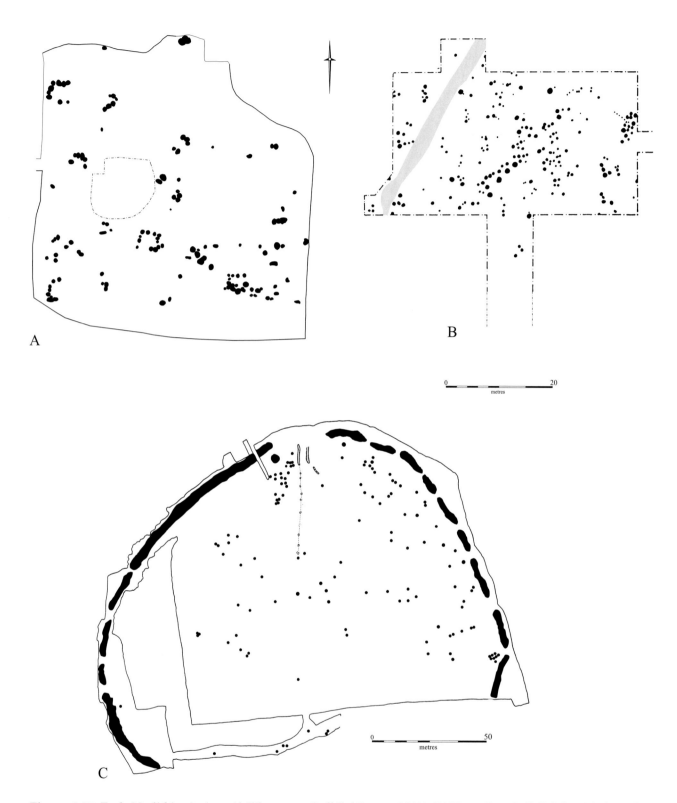

**Figure 4.17.** *Early Neolithic pit sites: A) Kilverstone, Suffolk (Garrow 2003); B) Hurst Fen, Suffolk (after Clark* et al. *1960); Etton causewayed enclosure (after Pryor 1998).*

consequence of new ways of understanding Neolithic 'settlement'. In recent years, Neolithic pits have come to be addressed in their own right, as well in the context of wider subjects such as settlement mobility (Edmonds 1999; Pollard 1999; 2000; 2001; 2002; Thomas 1996a; 1999). The argument that they were used for grain storage has been entirely dismissed, on practical grounds but also due to changing conceptualizations of Neolithic subsistence. While the possibility remains that pits may have had some other primary function, it is not a favoured interpretation. The cleanly sculpted shapes (even in soft sand) and homogeneous, often single fills of pits suggest that most were dug and backfilled almost immediately (Thomas 1999, 65). An appreciation of the fact that much of the material within pits represents more than just 'rubbish' (Thomas 1999, 65–8), along with an awareness that (structured) deposits, in many different contexts, were a fundamental part of life during the Neolithic in Britain, has allowed the possibility that they may have been dug *purely for the deposition of cultural material.*

## Current themes

Recent discussions concerning the nature of Neolithic pits have explored a number of aspects. These have taken place within the context of increased interest in Neolithic depositional practices as a whole, in causewayed enclosures, long barrows, henges and other places. The idea of 'structured deposition' (Richards & Thomas 1984) has been explored in relation to all of these contexts in recent years, and researchers have begun to move beyond the simple recognition of 'ritual' to say something much more meaningful. Whilst interpretations of pits can sometimes appear somewhat different, they should not necessarily be seen as incompatible. It seems that these features could play several different roles, and we must be cautious in expecting any single interpretation to fit the tremendous variability of pit-related practices (Pollard 2002). Current themes in the interpretation of pit sites can be divided into a number of closely related categories; these are explored below.

A predominant focus within much recent work has been the effect that pit-digging would have had in relation to the places where it was carried out: a pit 'would have been less conspicuous than a stone or earth monument, but would have had a similar effect in transforming the significance of a place' (Thomas 1999, 71). Bradley has discussed the ways in which 'altering the earth' through monument building may have been fundamental to a Neolithic way of life (1993a); pit sites have been situated within this context: *the creation of place*. It is generally understood that, through pits, people would have changed the nature of the space in which they dug them, *adding* to it both physically and metaphorically. By excavating pit features, and depositing artefacts within them, people created particular memories; these memories were situated in a particular location, and would thus qualitatively have altered perceptions of that place.

Most writers suggest that the construction of pits would have taken place at the *end* of relatively short-term visits to a particular location. Pollard has written that the act of abandoning a settlement 'was probably perceived as threatening to the social order and in need of mediation through ritual practice', arguing that 'pit deposits may have served to counter this' (1999, 89). Edmonds has suggested a crop-related metaphor: 'created as people left for a season, the filling of pits, like the planting of crops, offered the hope of renewal, regeneration and return' (1999, 29). A strong connection between pits and mobile/temporary occupation practices runs throughout these approaches. Such interpretations have only become a possibility since Neolithic settlement was seen to be impermanent. The desire to alter a place physically, to secrete material culture within it, and to create a memory of this practice, appears to have been intimately related to the fact that people had to *leave*.

Other interpretations have focused more specifically on the material culture deposited at these sites. The case that the contents of pits represent more than just 'rubbish' has most easily been made in relation to 'special' artefacts such as pristine tools, whole pots, human bones or articulated joints of meat (Thomas 1999, 65–8). However, where deposits containing broken pottery, flint-knapping waste and charred hazelnut shells (generally considered to be redeposited midden material) are concerned, the point must be made in more detail. It has been suggested for some time that Neolithic material culture was caught up in complex webs of meaning and association. Objects could come to stand for much more than their functional attributes, 'being redolent of the network of relationships between kin and others, places and agents in the landscape, and the roles and responsibilities of people, animals and things' (Pollard 2001, 323). Material culture, it is suggested, had come to signify many different aspects of life: a particular 'Neolithic' way of living; social and material relationships; the practices which had occurred in a particular place. In essence, then, it seems that while much of the material buried in pits was *in a certain sense* 'rubbish', it can also be seen as much more than that. Pits provided a medium through which people were able to focus on certain items of material culture, and thus by association on many aspects of life in general.

A final major theme that has been addressed in recent work is the performative and aesthetic aspect of pit deposition (Thomas 1999; Pollard 2001). Initial attempts to engage with widely-applicable, underlying ideologies behind these deposits proved largely unsuccessful. Recent work has instead begun to investigate the more esoteric aspects of deposition: 'while the practices concerned might constitute a recognisable tradition, they appear not to have been bound by a strict set of rules', but were instead 'improvised, in the context of local conditions' (Thomas 1999, 69), and Pollard has focused even more closely on pits' aesthetic aspects (2001, 315). Such approaches have begun to address the experiential or phenomenological side of pit deposits. The focus has been on particular acts of deposition, and the intimacy and creativity involved in placing certain items in a particular way within a small hole in the ground: what Thomas describes as 'creative play or *bricolage*' (1999, 80). The localized scale of the approach, within an extremely widespread and long-lived tradition, complements well the other more general levels of practice that have been explored elsewhere.

Wider contexts

In terms of discussions of the Neolithic as a whole, it is often reiterated that the deposition of material culture within pits was part of a much wider 'genealogy of deposition' (Thomas 1999), in many different archaeological contexts. It is certainly true that deposition at pit sites should be viewed as one part of a wider spectrum of practice. It is also important, however, to view them separately; as discussed above, pit sites (along with surface scatters) are for most of Britain the only *non*-monumental archaeology we have.

In this respect, it is useful to bring the discussion back to East Anglia. The lack of monuments in eastern England, particularly in comparison to 'classic' areas such as Wessex, has long been noted (e.g. Healy 1984). So much so, in fact, that Bradley, in his 1993 review of the prehistory of the region, asked rhetorically 'Where is East Anglia?'. Interestingly, this scarcity of monuments corresponds with an apparently high frequency of pit sites; most of the 'classic sites', including Hurst Fen, Clacton and Broome Heath (Clark *et al.* 1960; Longworth *et al.* 1971; Wainwright 1972) have been found within the region. Importantly, a number of recently excavated and/or published sites, mostly recovered within the context of developer-funded archaeology, have confirmed these impressions. The principal sites amongst these, along with other significant Earlier Neolithic pit sites in East Anglia, are detailed below.

*Hurst Fen, Suffolk* (NGR 57260 27675; Fig. 4.17:B; Clark *et al.* 1960): Hurst Fen was excavated by Clark, Higgs and Longworth as a research project with Cambridge University during the 1950s. Massive quantities of pottery and flint had been found within the topsoil and the excavation aimed, essentially, to recover what was presumed to be the Neolithic settlement associated with the scatter, including 'huts or houses'. In total, 200 earlier Neolithic 'Mildenhall' pits were found, along with a probably later ditch, but none of the expected structures. The full extent of the pits' distribution does

not appear to have been recovered, despite the fact that the main excavation area measured '150 by 100 feet'. Hurst Fen was one of the first non-monumental Neolithic sites to be excavated in East Anglia, and is perhaps the best known pit site of all.

*Broome Heath, Norfolk* (NGR 63440 29120; Wainwright 1972): Broome Heath was excavated between 1966 and 1971 in advance of the construction of an extension to school buildings; the project was funded by the Ministry of Public Building and Works/DoE. Excavations focused on a scheduled 'C'-shaped earthwork enclosure, and a large area (150 × 90 m) inside it. A total of 67 earlier Neolithic pits, as well as 36 pits containing burnt flint were recovered; 64% of the total weight of 'Grimston' pottery came from just two of the pits. The site provides a good comparison with Hurst Fen, and importantly, at the time of its excavation, added weight to the idea that there might be a number of very large pit sites in East Anglia.

*Spong Hill, Norfolk* (NGR 59810 31950; Healy 1988): Excavated as a DoE funded rescue excavation between 1972 and 1981, the primary focus of the project was a massive Early Saxon cemetery; a large number of prehistoric features were also recovered. In total, 122 pits were found across the extent of the site, along with a few amorphous 'spreads' containing Neolithic material. The vast majority (89) of the pits were earlier Neolithic in date, although a few later Neolithic and Early Bronze Age features were also present. The earlier Neolithic pits formed five distinct, spatially discrete groups of features (with some 'outliers'). Healy has suggested that each cluster may represent 'a distinct, short-lived, small-scale occupation', and that in total they may have spanned 'more than 500 years' (Healy 1988, 105). Spong Hill provides an interesting point of comparison with Hurst Fen, as whilst it shares strong similarities in terms of its date, the density of features and site morphology are quite different.

*Barleycroft Farm, Cambridgeshire* (NGR 53517 27227; Fig. 4.16; Evans & Knight 1997; 2001): Barleycroft Farm was excavated between 1994 and 1998 by the Cambridge Archaeological Unit in advance of gravel extraction. The size of the quarry ensured that the archaeology was approached on a very large scale. The prehistoric landscape uncovered included numerous Neolithic pits, as well as Bronze Age barrows, field systems, post alignments and settlements. The site detailed here, known specifically as Barleycroft Paddocks, produced a relatively dense cluster of earlier Neolithic pits, as well as other isolated later Neolithic and Early Bronze Age features and a later Bronze Age settlement. In total, 22 'Mildenhall' pits were recovered across the site, 18 of which were clustered within an area measuring 40 × 15 m. The pits contained sometimes large amounts of earlier Neolithic pottery, flint and hazelnuts, and in many cases appeared to have been dug in pairs. In addition, two 'tree throws' were recovered; these seemed to have been treated in a similar way to the pits and contained massive quantities of pottery and worked flint. The pits and tree throws at Barleycroft Paddocks, like those at Spong Hill, appear to have been produced during occasional, small-scale visits to a particular point in the Neolithic landscape.

*Etton, Cambridgeshire* (NGR 51383 30739; Fig. 4.17:C; Pryor 1998): Etton causewayed enclosure was excavated between 1981 and 1987, as a response to its imminent destruction by gravel quarrying; the project was funded by a variety of organizations, including the British Museum and the DoE/English Heritage. The site lies within an extremely dense prehistoric landscape, which includes the Maxey henge complex and cursus monument, as well as numerous ring-ditches and other enclosures, most of which have been identified through aerial photography. Approximately 80 per cent of the causewayed enclosure's interior, and slightly less of the segmented ditch, were excavated. Numerous artefacts were recorded within the ditch segments, many of which were interpreted as 'structured' or 'ritual' deposits. A large number of features were recovered within the interior of the monument, including pits, post-holes, ditches, etc. Amongst these, a total of 122 'small filled pits' were found (other similar features, which did not have distinctive shapes or artefact assemblages, were termed simply 'pits'). Many of these contained quantities of pottery, flint and other materials, and at times resembled the deposits excavated within the enclosure ditch. Most appeared to be earlier Neolithic in date, although a small number of later Neolithic and Early Bronze Age pits were also found. Etton is perhaps unique in allowing us an opportunity to investigate the relationship between an impressive monument and the large scatter of pits within it, all of which were excavated and recorded to modern standards.

*Maxey, Cambridgeshire* (NGR 51360 30700; Northants Archaeology 1998): Excavations are currently being undertaken at Maxey by Northamptonshire Archaeology, in advance of gravel extraction. The site lies immediately adjacent to the Etton causewayed enclosure, and has produced massive numbers (hundreds) of pits, similar to those within the monument; these appear to date from all phases within the Neolithic (I. Meadows pers. comm.). The site adds an extremely important extra dimension to the enclosure and the pits within it, and has changed dramatically our understanding of that particular prehistoric landscape.

*Kilverstone, Norfolk* (NGR 58840 28365; Fig. 4.17:A; Garrow 2002, 2003): Kilverstone was excavated between 2000 and 2002 by the Cambridge Archaeological Unit in advance of a housing development. In total, five separate excavation areas were investigated, producing significant archaeology from the Neolithic through to the post-medieval period. Areas A and E, separated by a gap of 150 m, produced a total of 224 earlier Neolithic pits (86 in Area A, 138 in Area E). These contained large quantities of Mildenhall pottery (and some Peterborough Ware), worked and burnt flint, quernstones, hazelnuts, etc. In both areas, spatially discrete clusters of pits could be discerned; the features within each cluster appear to have been closely related, often containing pottery from the same pot and re-fitting flints. Kilverstone is the largest earlier Neolithic pit site yet found in Britain. It represents a clear parallel for Hurst Fen, both in terms of the number of pits and the scale of deposition; importantly, due to its recent excavation, the site provides the vital contextual detail lacking from the earlier site.

# Chapter 5

# The Causewayed Enclosure: a Great Clearance

The chapter's sub-title, *a Great Clearance*, is appropriate on two accounts. On the one hand, it continues the volume's theme of Neolithic 'woodland life' and, more specifically, it refers to the notion that causewayed enclosures might have mimicked or at least resonated in relationship to forest clearances. The Neolithic experience of landscape may, in effect, have provided a basic model of 'openly bounded' and concentrically organized social space (see Evans 1988c; Whittle *et al.* 1999). Secondly, this entitlement is accurate in its reference to scale. The Upper Delphs causewayed enclosure is truly 'great' and, extending over 8.75 ha, it is one of largest monuments of this type known in Britain. It contrasts markedly with the other known Fenland-associated causewayed enclosures which are relatively small (Oswald *et al.* 2001, 72–5, fig. 4.23). As first identified from aerial photographs, it has two basic components: a main causewayed ditch circuit and an internal palisade which runs closely concentric to the ditch perimeter. Again, palisades are not a common feature of causewayed enclosures (see below) and its occurrence further distinguishes the Delphs enclosure.

Falling between 2.10 and 2.60 m OD, the enclosure is situated below the higher ground of the southwestern quarter of the Upper Delphs and straddles the spine of the terrace (Fig. 4.5). To some extent its topographic situation abets understanding of its irregular plan. Its straight western aspect was sited across the width of the ridge, whereas the awkward, almost heart-shaped line of its northern circuit followed the *c.* 2.10-m contour of the terrace on that side (the only aspect of the enclosure sensitive to contour). These two sides, which evidently determined the ultimate plan, were linked by the more circular arcs of southeastern and northwestern circuits; though the question of whether this plan was actually intended from the outset will have to be considered.

Issues relating to the layout of the enclosure and its affinities to other monuments of this type will all be duly discussed below. Here, however, from the outset it is the parameters of our knowledge that must be addressed. This is not a fine-grained archaeology in the manner of that of the long barrow. Although dug

over four separate summer campaigns (with the HAD VIII excavations also occurring within its interior; the HAD IX exposure was concurrent with the main HAD '87 excavation), this represents only a very small sample (Fig. 5.1). As detailed in Table 5.1 below, *c.* 230 m in length of the enclosure's causewayed perimeter was investigated in total. Representing a *c.* 20 per cent sample of its 1113-m-long perimeter, this can be considered adequate for the purposes of general characterization (compensating for half-sectioning, only 102 m of the ditch was excavated *per se*, a *c.* 9 per cent sample). The same, however, cannot be said of the enclosure's interior. Only *c.* 5 per cent of it was tested and this is insufficient to 'know' it. The vast majority of these interior exposures were, moreover, off the enclosure's perimeter and far too little of its central core was opened to satisfactorily determine its usage. Yet, as will be all too apparent below, we were probably over-ambitious to tackle the enclosure even in the manner we did, given the project's constrained resources. This is especially marked in relation to the site's environmental studies (see e.g. Jones below). All this implies that a degree of interpretative modesty is warranted when evaluating the results.

In contrast with the apparently 'unified construction' of the long barrow, the causewayed enclosure cannot have a site-wide phasing structure. Yes, propensities or trends in its development will be distinguished, but it is telling of its scale and 'openness' as a monumental project (and the degree

**Table 5.1.** *Areas of excavation (NB the area of the enclosure's interior does not include test pits or miscellaneous trenches).*

| Area/year | Total area (sq. m) | Length of perimeter (m) | Area of interior (sq. m) |
|---|---|---|---|
| 1981 | 1266 | 44 | 405 |
| 1982 | 2802 | 51 | 1253 |
| 1984 | 862 | 53 | 602 |
| 1987 | 1751 | 68 | 1439 |
| HAD VIII | 512 | – | 512 |
| HAD IX | 163 | 16 | 73.5 |
| **Total** | **7356** | **232** | **4284.5** |

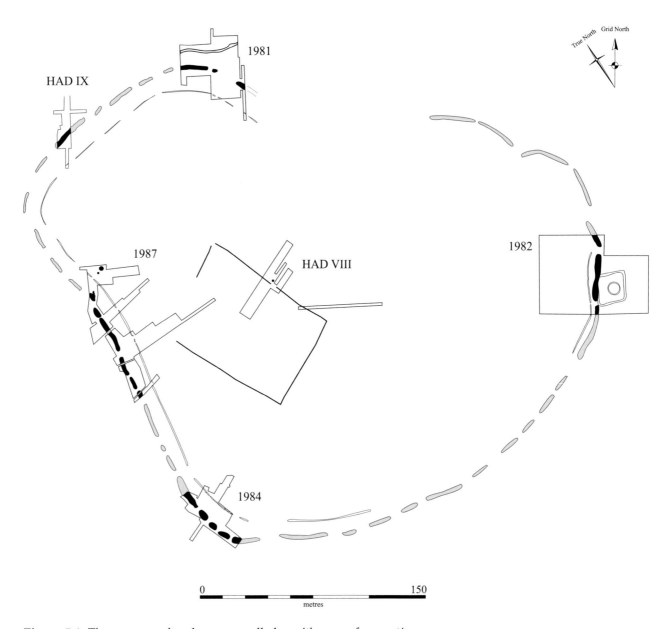

**Figure 5.1.** *The causewayed enclosure: overall plan with areas of excavation.*

of localized variability) that the imposition of a rigid phasing structure seems entirely inappropriate. This is also influenced by frameworks of knowledge and, more specifically, the limits of analogy. Despite considerable variability in their plans, construction and depositional sequences, there is greater assurance that we can 'know' the role of long barrows. Their practices are not necessarily more familiar; it is just that their prime function obviously related to the interment of the dead. This is not the case with causewayed enclosures. After much sustained investigation, as a monument type these multi-faceted enclosures still evade pigeon-holing and easy categorization. They were clearly not 'one thing' (e.g. Evans 1988b; Edmonds

1993; 1999; Bradley 1998b). Accordingly, issues of general methodological approach and how interpretation is achieved are highlighted to a greater extent than in any of the project's other investigations.

Beyond this, the Delphs enclosure also challenges established tenets of the interpretation of causewayed enclosures. Here context is relevant. The 1970s saw a spate of causewayed enclosure excavations in Eastern England, including Staines (Robertson-MacKay 1987), Briar Hill (Bamford 1985), Orsett (Hedges & Buckley 1978) and, locally, Great Wilbraham (see inset below). Of these, however, only Orsett had been published at the time of excavation. The Delphs fieldwork occurred, moreover, concurrently with Pryor's excavations at Etton (1998), and both were concerned with problems of buried soil strata and their distributions (though Etton's greater preservation and waterlogging was to give rise to a quite different focus). Of the excavations within the region, these very much occurred within an over-arching framework of 'Fenland archaeology' and assumed a wetland perspective (i.e. that the region then existed as a distinct cultural/environmental entity). While this has been subject to reappraisal (e.g. Evans 1987), it is nevertheless crucial that this research not just be viewed in the light of Wessex-derived models but appreciated in its own right. In contrast to modes of 'over-emphasized' interpretation, among the most remarkable aspect of the Delphs enclosure is its minimalism and particularly the paucity of finds. Given this, its sheer size and all that would have entailed, this has the potential to shift the focus to the act of the enclosure's construction itself rather than an uninterrupted legacy of its long-term use. The demonstration of this will require considerable modelling of the enclosure's patterns of deposition and its various populations.

## The enclosure's circuits: a hermeneutic circle

It is the 'hermeneutic circle' that frames the narrative of the enclosure's investigations and provides its dominant interpretative metaphor. Entirely unintentionally and largely determined by contingency, the site's excavations themselves describe 'a circle'. Beginning in 1981 in the north, thereafter they progressed clockwise around the enclosure's perimeter (Fig. 5.1). This was to the point that, in the course of backfilling on the last day of the final season the decision was taken to re-open a portion of the original 1981 trenches (Fig. 5.3). With the benefit of lengthy experience of the enclosure's archaeology and more informed expecta-

A

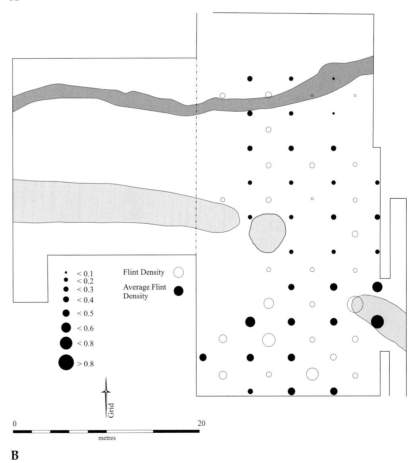

B

**Figure 5.2.** *HAD '81. A) Photograph looking north; note that the 'A'-horizon remains across the northern third of the site, whereas in the mid- and foreground the surface has been stripped down to the gravels. (Photograph G. Owen.) B) The distribution of flint in buried soil samples (1500 cc units).*

tions, this was to ensure that crucial data had not been missed (which indeed they had).

241

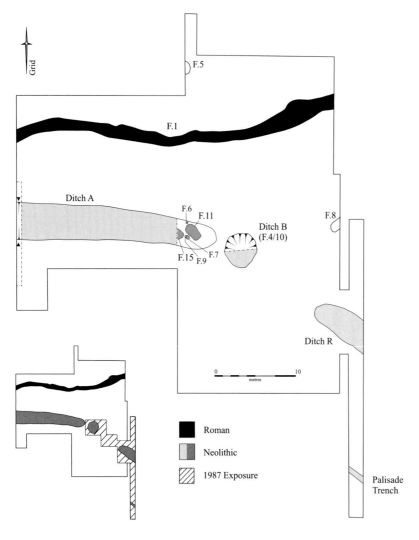

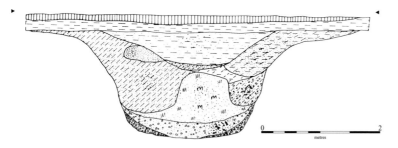

**Figure 5.3.** *HAD '81: top) feature plan (with inset showing '87 trench exposures); below) section across Ditch A.*

adjusting our theories accordingly. Data is situated as much as possible in terms of a general theory and, in other words, is *contextualized*. The notion of a hermeneutic is closely linked to that of context, giving meaning to a particular piece of data by embedding it more and more fully in its surrounding data. When a theory makes all the data 'fit', then we say that the data 'make sense'.

The main problem with the hermeneutic circle is that it is potentially vicious, in that arguments overtly or covertly assume what they are trying to prove. The data are not approached with blank minds and, as the paradox of hermeneutics claims (Scruton 1982), 'no interpretation is possible until interpretation has begun'. Context frames our definition of the archaeological context. It could be argued that we work in a closed circle which encompasses past and present. We 'read' the data by translating it into our own terms and construct the past in the present.

On the other hand, it can be argued that the hermeneutic circle is more properly described as a spiral, in that we never return to exactly the same spot as we move between theory and data. According to this view, the experience of data forces us to adjust our interpretations, or at least we can choose between alternative hypotheses (such as event and sequence perspectives). There is some degree of independence between past and present contexts: we learn as we 'read'.

Certainly, in approaching the causewayed enclosure we came with a vast background of theoretical knowledge. First, given its formal attributes as established from the aerial photographic plotting, is that it was, in fact, a monument of this type. Knowing that we were dealing with a causewayed enclosure, what then were the main pieces of interpretative 'baggage' that were brought with us? One was its implication for *sequence*, and the ensuing approach to fieldwork in its environs was underlain by the idea that the enclosure was central to a long-term

The concept of the hermeneutic circle has been thoroughly outlined (Hodder 1999a) and need not be rehearsed at length. Suffice it to state that, in our view, hermeneutics provides a far better description of what archaeologists actually do than any positivist hypothesis-testing procedure. Essentially we work back and forth between theory and data, showing that some theories account for more of the data than others, and

sequence of activities in the landscape. There was, in effect, a presumption that it connected to other sites such as the long barrow and the later round barrows, and also contemporary settlements. During the course of the fieldwork a debate developed as to whether, in fact, the enclosure itself was used and built in an accretionary manner over the long-term, or had been laid out as an *event*, planned from the outset as a major monument with major entrances, front and back spaces?

By far the largest piece of baggage with which we approached the enclosure was labelled 'ritual'. The literature on causewayed enclosures encouraged us to assume that, while some or all of these enclosures saw some occupation, stock management or defensive functions, they were also foci for rituals involving feasting and 'special' activities: variously 'placed' and 'structured' deposits (e.g. Richards & Thomas 1984; see below concerning ritual and 'play'). The definition of ritual is, of course, highly problematic. We must be wary of imposing universalizing expectations upon the data and understand that its 'signature' will differ by time and place. We must not then simply dump down our heavy ritual baggage on the past. Rather, we must open up the 'suitcase', examine its contents and 'dress the past' in appropriate ways, choosing the best theory for the particular data. Here the attempt is made to explore ritual and its definition through contextual differences.

We also came to the causewayed enclosure with assumptions concerning social evolution. It has become generally accepted that the Neolithic of Britain saw only a low level of political development character-ized by lineages which may have been emerging into chiefdoms. While the causewayed enclosure heralds this higher level of development, long barrows are understood to represent lineages. Within this general notion of a segmented, relatively decentralized society, much of the Neolithic data has been interpreted as attesting to small-group organization. For example, both the mounds of long barrows and the ditches of barrows and enclosures have been claimed to be built in sections, perhaps by 'work gangs'. So one of the expectations here was that variability would be found amongst the ditches, and evidence that individual lengths had been dug in smaller segments. The way we initially approached the ditches, for example by digging so as to leave longitudinal sections in 1982, was designed to pick up recutting along the ditch lengths. However appropriate this may have seemed to investigate 'segmentation' in its many guises, this procedure was gradually abandoned as it was realized that it obscured understanding of the full range of activities within the ditches.

More specifically, on the aerial photographs evidence of the varied, decentralized nature of the society which produced the causewayed enclosure seemed to be apparent. In some parts of the circuit an inner palisade was clearly visible. In other sections there was either no palisade or it was set well back from the ditches. Whereas for most of the enclosure a single ditch circuit could be seen, in the northwest zone two parallel ditches occurred as in the multiple circuits found at other enclosures in England. The 1981 excavations were thus located over the double-ditches so as to investigate this internal difference.

Other specific assumptions came from our evaluation of the site itself. For example, given its environmental setting there was an expectation of good preservation. After all, we were working in a fen-edge environment. Although the Upper Delphs island is relatively high it seemed reasonable to expect that the deeper ditch bottoms might contain waterlogged material. At that time we did not know the detailed environmental history of the area. In any case, field-walking over the western half of the enclosure had produced extremely low densities of material (see Chapter 4 above), which suggested peat and alluvial cover of the prehistoric land surface. Preliminary bor-ing through the ploughsoil had indicated that the peat coverage was thickest in the northwestern part of the site. The same conclusion was drawn from the aerial photographs. These showed a darker stain of thicker peat where the enclosure ditches sloped down the northwestern edge of the island. Thus another reason for the specific location of the 1981 excavations was to explore the enclosure in what was potentially its best-preserved sector.

We have explained the main baggage that was brought to the first season of excavation at the enclo-sure. Of course, there was much else, both general and specific, but we have defined the main themes. So that we did not simply take the themes of sequence, ritual, social evolution and so on for granted, we needed to remain sensitive to the particular contextual data. This involved digging the enclosure ditch by ditch and gradually building up an argument which accommodated both data and theory. One ditch on its own would tell little unless we were happy with fitting it immediately into our general schemes. But we can increase our understanding of the individual ditch length through its similarities and contrasts with other ditches in the 'whole' which makes up the enclosure. In other words, each ditch can be gradually placed into the context formed by all the ditches. The resultant 'whole' is not a given, but an interpretative construct built up from the parts. In relation to each ditch an interpretation is constructed which is then used for other ditches. These ditches force us to change the interpretation and so we have to re-interpret the first ditch, and so on. Thus moving back and forth, we work within the hermeneutic circle.

Yet, however powerful and potentially all-embracing is the hermeneutic circle as an interpretative metaphor, there comes a point of breaking the narrative strand: stopping the circle. It is in the nature of work itself that other metaphors arise and we need to be able to stand back and overview the 'whole' (such as is ever contingently possible) with greater detachment from the process of excavation and further informed by the results of subsequent research on other sites. This will occur in the **Context and enclosure** section below, only following presentation of the artefact and environmental specialist reports.

Prior to this, and in the light of the amassed data that immediately follows, two of the excavated features deserve special notice as they seem to 'speak' clearly (if entirely differently) amidst so much that is otherwise ambiguous. One is Ditch I in the 1984 area of excavation. Having an extraordinary series of recuts, a mounded 'ditchwork' and unequivocal evidence of 'placed' deposition, it undeniably attests to a ritual content and has distinct parallels with activities at the long barrow (see Edmonds, inset Chapter 6 below). The other feature was a finds-packed pit found in the course of the HAD VIII investigations (F. 534). Directly comparable to features on 'pit-type' settlements (see Chapter 4 above), its presence within the enclosure clearly tells of domestic usage. Cross-cutting issues of methodological finesse, the recovery of these two features testifies to the twin, often oscillating ritual/ domestic poles that have dominated traditions of causewayed enclosure research (see Evans 1988b; Oswald *et al.* 2001). Thus announced from the outset, in the case of the Delphs enclosure its interpretation cannot therefore be a matter of 'either/or', but must explore the character of their interrelationship.

*The enclosure ditches: the 1981 season*
The main area of excavation (Figs. 5.1–5.3) consisted of a north–south swathe across what appeared to be two parallel enclosure ditches on the aerial photograph and an east–west trench following the line of the two ditches. The methods were slow and careful, as it was expected that protected beneath the peat would be an undisturbed buried soil from which we wanted to gain maximum information. The alluvial ploughsoil and underlying thin peaty layer (the latter averaging 5–10 cm thick over the immediate site) were removed by machine to the lower portion of the peat. The stripping stopped much higher than in later years and was not allowed to bite into the buried soil horizon at all,

the interface between peat and the buried soil being removed by hand.

As the peat layer was removed the ditch was immediately visible as it snaked across the northern part of the excavated area. Clearly filled with peat deposits, the ditch (F.1) had a gravel upcast bank on either side but the southern was more substantial. This made sense because this larger bank was on the inner side of the enclosure. Other evidence too made sense. In the deepest part of the ditch there was a quantity of waterlogged wood, and above this a concentration of large animal bones. Skull, mandible, pelvis and scapula were the main body parts represented and there was very little pottery or flint associated. Surely this was clear evidence of a ritual 'placed' deposit.

One of the bones was a horse mandible. That was disturbing as domesticated horse was thought to have been introduced into Britain only at the end of the Neolithic. Could this be a late Neolithic enclosure? Several eminent Neolithic specialists visited the site during this period and pronounced their verdict. Yes, they could see that the ditch had shallower portions which represented the causeways. The deeper pit with wood and bone represented the butt end of a ditch. The data fit well with other causewayed enclosures where concentrations of finds have been claimed at the butt ends of ditches. Yes, the small undiagnostic sherd was probably late Neolithic, fitting in with all the flint artefacts found in the ditch fills.

Yet the aerial photograph showed two parallel ditches at this point in the enclosure's perimeter. Where was the other circuit? It simply could not be seen. This was especially surprising because we examined the buried soil horizon below the peat in the rest of the uncovered area very carefully. Hoe and trowel were used to clean off the peat to the top of the soil horizon and in the further removal of the buried soil (Fig. 5.2). The latter was excavated in approximately 2.5-cm spits and planning of suspected features occurred at each level. A range of techniques was used to enhance the visibility of features in the buried soil. These included covering and 'sweating' the site under plastic, having the local fire brigade spray the area with water, carefully cleaning both before and after wetting, and so on. Quantities of flint artefacts were discovered and features gradually began to appear, including possible pits and post-holes, but no other ditch.

Perhaps the aerial photographs had been misrectified or the position of the ditches incorrectly surveyed. Checked and double-checked, nothing seemed wrong. In frustration we decided to get the machine back to dig a deep slot trench at the western edge of the site, to the south of ditch F.1. Again, nothing.

Why could we not see the other ditch? A clue emerged towards the end of the season. At the northern edge of the site, after several spits of buried soil had been taken off, a hearth suddenly emerged (F.5). This must originally have been cut from the top of the buried soil and yet it was no longer visible on the surface. Other evidence began to point to a heavily leached and discoloured buried soil. Acidity tests by the Cambridge University Department of Geography showed that pH levels increased from 4 to 6 with increasing depth through the buried soil, largely due to leaching during peat formation and water coverage. Because of these relatively high acidity levels bone and pottery were rarely preserved in the buried soil and tops of the ditches. However preservation of such materials was substantially better in the lower ditch profiles where pH values varied between 6 and 7.

Something clearly was not right. Why was the F.1 ditch clearly visible on the surface of the buried soil, filled with peaty soil, while other prehistoric features had been heavily leached during their coverage by the peat? The features and the ditch must be of substantially different dates. In any case the 'causeways' in ditch F.1 simply did not exist. The ditch seemed to be continuous.

Another worrying feature of the excavations was that Feature 4/10 seemed to be enormous, while features such as 11 seemed to be dug into soil slightly different from the buried soil (see below). Few finds were made in these enigmatic features. Were they natural, and if not why had such large features not appeared on the aerial photographs? After all, they were considerably larger than ditch F.1. On the penultimate day of the scheduled excavation, re-examination of the machine-cut section at the west of the site showed what was, in comparison to the F.1 ditch, an enormous ditch. It had been difficult to see, being filled with gravel and lenses of clays and silts as in the surrounding Pleistocene gravels. And it was different and so much bigger than our train of thought, which had understood the shallow ditch F.1 to be the causewayed enclosure, had led us to expect. Yet this much more substantial ditch was more what was expected on the basis of other causewayed enclosures.

Suddenly everything made sense. The large ditch was the main causewayed ditch (here termed Ditch A), on the same alignment as the large feature (perhaps part of Ditch A) under Features 11, 15, etc. and on the same alignment as the large 'pit' F.4/10 (later called Ditch B). These causewayed ditches could not easily be seen in the surface of the buried soil because of the same leaching which had affected the hearth F.5. Ditch F.1 must have been cut through the buried soil at a much later date. Indeed, a radiocarbon date of

370 cal. BC–320 cal. AD (1990±120 BP; BM-2091R) was later obtained for it, and it was evidently of later Iron Age/early Roman attribution (see Volume 2, Chapter 6). The horse was thus explained, and the deposit of wood and large bones duly re-interpreted as butchering residue without ritual component.

The causewayed enclosure at this point did not after all have a double ditch. What could be recorded of the 'real' Neolithic 'inner' ditch (i.e. A & B) was achieved quickly, although in the short time available we were never able to understand it properly. For example, we were unable to pump out the water in the machine slot so that a full section could be drawn (Fig. 5.3 is an interpretation of the evidence recorded) and we could not remove all the buried soil between the slot and the Features 15, 11, etc. in order to discover whether a further causeway existed in this area (i.e. within Ditch A). The aerial photographic plots were not clear enough to allow resolution of this problem.

Ditch A, as seen in the machine slot, was 3.25 m across and 1.80 m deep below the top of the buried soil (Fig. 5.3). The primary fills consisted of sands and gravels which had been cut into in ways which at the time made little sense. Ditches had been dug along the inner edges of the primary ditch leaving an upstanding mound in the middle, although it was also possible that these recuts represented single ditches dug at different times. These recut ditches were themselves filled with sands and gravels. At a late stage the whole ditch was then recut down the central axis to produce a shallow ditch 0.75 m below the old ground surface. The top of the ditch contained silts on which a buried soil had formed and been leached continuous with the surrounding soil. No trace of a bank was found on either side.

To the east, the presumed butt end of Ditch A and F.4/10 (Ditch B) were only excavated to the bottom of the upper silt layers. These contained few finds but the Ditch A butt end (unlike B) did show evidence of further recutting and burning. Indeed, the careful treatment of the buried soil in the area showed that a series of pits and activities were concentrated in the butt end of the A ditch and did not occur in the substantial causeway to the east of F.4/10. None of the features in the top of the ditch butt-end were immediately visible on the surface of the buried soil which had formed over the ditch, except as slightly darker patches representing slumping and staining from the peat above.

Features 6, 7, 9, 11 and 15 attest to a set of activities involving burning in the butt end of Ditch A. Features 6, 7 and 9 were small post-holes, 0.05–0.20 m deep, containing charcoal and burnt stones. Feature 11 was a rectangular (1.25 m wide and 2.25 m long), steep-sided and flat-bottomed pit (0.50 m deep). The basal deposits consisted of redeposited clay gravels, but the upper layers consisted of sandy loams above and below a charcoal filled layer which produced samples of carbonized seeds (see Jones below). F.15 represented another recut in the top of the ditch butt although it ran out of the excavated area to the west. The eastern butt end of this feature (possibly a ditch) sloped up gradually, but elsewhere it was flat bottomed and steep sided (1.15 m wide and 0.60 m deep). The upper fill within this recut contained a large amount of charcoal and the lower silts contained a charcoal lens.

In summary, the 1981 causewayed ditches consisted of two (A & B) and possibly more (if A was itself causewayed) ditches. The primary fills of sand and gravels had been recut along both edges of Ditch A. A major recut was identified at the butt end of Ditch

**Figure 5.4.** *HAD '82. Photograph showing buried soil still* in situ *punctuated by the metre-square sampling grid. Note in the upper left hand corner the circle-in-the-square of the HAD II enclosure visible at this level, which the causewayed enclosure is not (photograph G. Owen).*

A, with evidence for later activities including burning, possible post-holes, further recuts and crops. There was no evidence for such activities in the clean upper fills of F.4/10 (Ditch B) and no evidence of activities in the causeway east of Ditch B. There was no evidence of a bank to the south of the ditch, nor seemingly of a palisade (see below).

The 1981 excavations provided a good example of how the hermeneutic circle is constructed. We started with certain assumptions which affected our initial understanding of the data but we gradually modified theory and data until they harmonized. Thus we had expected Neolithic ritual and found it in butchering residues in an Iron Age/Roman ditch. We had wanted variability and good preservation and had found double ditches at this point in the enclosure circuit and well-preserved wood in ditches. But the need for internal coherence in our arguments gradually forced us to correct our interpretations. Bits and pieces did not fit. These included later horse bones in what should have been earlier Neolithic ditches, and

the lack of convincing causeways in ditch F.1. It did not make sense that it was easily visible while other features were apparently sealed by the buried soil surface. Finally, an alternative hypothesis was found which made sense of the data. There was only one Neolithic causewayed enclosure ditch containing later recuts and covered by a leached soil; ditch F.1 was of later Iron Age/early Roman date. The hermeneutic circle had proved not to be vicious; we had been able critically to compare data and progress.

The revised hypothesis still allowed for variability since we had not found a palisade trench as was visible on the aerial photographs in other parts of the enclosure. And we had found an enormous causeway to the east of Ditch B. Variability was still a possibility but segmented digging of the ditches would have to be explored by complete excavation of ditch segments now that we knew how difficult they were to distinguish. The revised hypothesis also allowed for ritual. Although we had not found 'placed' deposits,

246

the fills of the ditches had produced very few artefacts. This may partly have been a matter of preservation but as far as the flint was concerned it implied that there were few flints in the surrounding soil when the ditches filled up. On the other hand, high flint densities were found in the late features cut into the butt end of the causewayed ditch. In addition, flints were found in the buried soil within the immediate area of the enclosure ranging from 0–3 per square metre. It was possible that these densities related to the final phase of activity in the top of the ditch and indicated a secondary, more intense occupation of an earlier, largely unoccupied monument.

As a result of the initial errors described above, we left the 1981 excavations without having understood the causewayed ditch very well. We did not understand the unusual double recut leaving a central 'rise' within the ditch, and the numerous later recuttings. Other portions of the circuit would clearly need to be excavated in order to put these initial findings in context, to identify those parts of the initial evidence which were salient, and to evaluate the still general expectations about variability and ritual.

*The 1982 season*
In 1982 we moved clockwise to the eastern side of the enclosure. Actually, at no point during the four seasons of excavation did we realize that we were digging in a circular manner. The choice of excavation was always dictated by contingency. For example, in that year we had developed cordial relations with a different farmer whose fields were under a cereal crop that would permit us five weeks of excavation in September and October. In addition, we had begun to wonder, given the enormous size of the enclosure and our inability ever to excavate more than a small portion of it, whether we should not concentrate on parts of the enclosure's perimeter that might be expected to yield most information. Partly on the basis of known enclosures, it was thought likely that concentrations of activities and rituals might occur at major entranceways into the enclosure. Thus our thinking was again strongly affected by the presumption of ritual. The notion of major entranceways would also have a major impact on the notion of variability. An argument was beginning to develop amongst ourselves. Was the enclosure built in a variable, segmented way, perhaps as a sequence of events, or was it planned as one event with an overall design, implying greater centralization of decision-making? What was the relation between part and whole? The presence of a major entranceway might provide some insight into these questions.

We were also influenced by the idea that the enclosure might have an effect on later settlement. On the aerial photographs a sub-square enclosure could be distinguished associated with the causewayed ditches at this point. What was their chronological relationship? In fact the square enclosure turned out to be of Romano-British attribution, containing a circular ditch of unknown function (see Volume 2, Chapter 8), recalling the later ditch outside the Neolithic enclosure during the 1981 season.

The 1982 area of excavation was situated on one of the higher points of the gravel island (Figs. 5.1 & 5.5) and during initial machine stripping of the site no peat horizon was found, although peat did occur within the fills of the later square enclosure. The site was machine-stripped twice during the course of excavation. The experience of 1981 had shown that we would not be able to discern Neolithic features in the surface of the buried soil; this did indeed prove to be the case in 1982, despite very careful cleaning and watering. However, we had also showed in 1981 that the buried soil contained finds distributions. Initially, therefore, the site was machine stripped to clear onto the top of this horizon, which was then carefully cleaned, artefacts collected and late features excavated. The buried soil was also sampled down to the underlying gravels by hand-excavating 1-m squares on a 5-m grid (Fig. 5.4). The area was then machined again by removing the buried soil down to the underlying gravels. In the 1982 site the causewayed ditches and palisade stood out clearly against the surrounding gravels. In contrast to 1981, it was thus possible to readily identify the ditches and excavate them 'properly'. The ditches were excavated by leaving, where possible, longitudinal sections in order to distinguish variability along their lengths (Figs. 5.5 & 5.6).

Three lengths of ditch were exposed: C to E from north to south. Owing to the instability of the surrounding Pleistocene gravels and subsequent slippage and collapse within their profiles, the original form of the ditches remained rather elusive. Effectively, little of their original shapes remained. Essentially, as they survived, the ditches were butt-ended in squared terminals with roughly straight and vertical sides. Generally, the sides of the ditches sloped quite steeply, at an angle of 45° or greater. There was no distinct nor uniform difference between the slopes of their interior and exterior sides; the bases were predominantly flat.

*Ditch C*
This ditch immediately looked 'odd' in relation to the other two (Fig. 5.5). In the first place, it had a rather different alignment, diverging from the enclosure's 'circle'. The aerial photographs at this juncture are not clear but they could be read to indicate a major realignment of the ditch circuit at this point. In the second place, the palisade did not continue inside it as it did along side Ditches D and E.

Otherwise, Ditch C was similar to the other ditches. It was 1.40 m deep below the buried soil and 4.0 m wide. The primary fills consisted of collapsed sands, clays and gravels from the sides of the ditches. At the ditch sides there were substantial 'blocks' of collapsed material (up to 0.50 m across) which may have resulted from undercutting by standing water in their profiles. There was

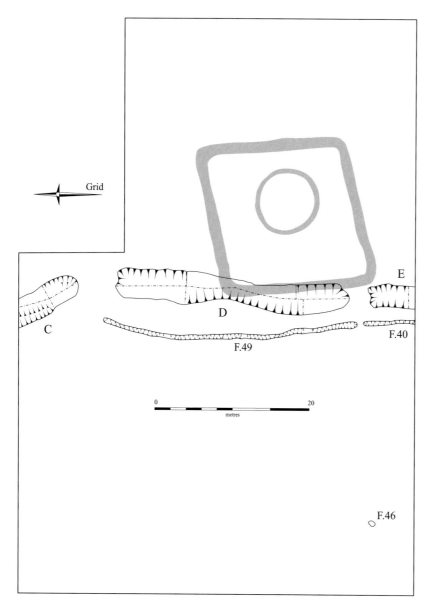

be some evidence for this process. During the secondary period of weathering, activities concentrated at the terminal.

*Ditch D*
This was excavated along its full length and proved to be complex (Figs. 5.5 & 5.7). It was 29.20 m long, 2.50–4.75 m wide and 1–1.75 m deep below the buried soil. There was a marked change in alignment in the middle of the ditch where it was found to bend and narrow. It was also substantially more shallow at this point, being only 1.0 m deep; the base sloped steeply to the north of the central rise and gently to the south.

In view of this 'division' of the ditch into two 'ends', it is interesting to note the patterning of finds in the fills. The primary fills were similar in nature to those in Ditch C. However a concentration of large pieces of bone occurred in the primary fills in the northern section of the central rise. Otherwise, there was again a low density of artefacts and no evidence of *in situ* burning.

The lower secondary fills also contained bone deposits associated with the central shallower and narrower section of the ditch. Immediately south of the narrowing was a dense spread of charcoal and calcined bone. From the sheer concentration of charcoal in these deposits, it appeared that burning had taken place within the ditch rather than the burnt material having been dumped into it, although it was impossible to say with any certainty as there was no evidence of *in situ* scorching as such. 0.10–0.20 m above this horizon was a second high concentration of charcoal. However, in this deposit there were no artefacts or burnt stone.

In summary, there was again no evidence of recutting that we could identify, but Ditch D differed from C in having concentrations of later activities which remained in its central portion rather than moving to its ends. The central area of dumping or burning was reused three times during the gradual filling up of the ditch.

**Figure 5.5.** *HAD '82: feature plan with the HAD II Romano-British enclosure indicated in grey tone outline.*

*Ditch E*
This continued south beyond the excavated area, but was found to be 2.80 m wide and 1.50 m deep below the buried soil (Fig. 5.5). The primary fills consisted of collapsed sands, clays, sandy loams and gravels from the sides of the ditches. There were no bone deposits, nor evidence of burning and only a few artefacts. The same was true of the secondary deposits which once again contained no recutting but also had little evidence of dumping or other activities.

no clustering in the low densities of cultural material and there was very little charcoal and no evidence of *in situ* burning.

The secondary fills consisted of loams and clays with a varying gravel component. The upper fill, a leached buried soil, was largely the product of weathering and erosion from the sides of the ditches and showed no evidence of recutting. At the southern terminal *in situ* burning had occurred and this included large charcoal fragments which may have been the remains of a substantial burnt post. The burnt deposit decreased towards the northern, main body of the ditch. Bedded immediately upon this burnt horizon was a deposit of silty clay in which was found a small cluster of worked flint, including a finely finished blade/knife.

In summary, Ditch C appeared to be relatively simple, with early deposits that had rapidly covered the base of the ditch. The Pleistocene gravels and sands were extremely unstable and the ditch sides would quickly have collapsed and there does seem to

Three ditches of the causewayed enclosure had been recovered, whose sequences seemed comparable to Ditch A. Ditches C, D and E all seemed similar to each other in general outline, with primary and secondary phases of fill and activity, and with burning associated with the secondary activities. Perhaps these phases recalled the primary and secondary recutting in Ditch A. The evidence was as yet too scanty to allow generalization, but the possibility was emerging that all the ditches had gone through similar phases of use.

On the other hand, the differences from Ditch A were marked. The 1982 ditches did not appear to contain obvious recuts (though it was suspected in the case of D). The variability was indeed considerable. The palisade accompanied Ditches D and E, but not C, the latter being also on a different alignment. Evidence of bone concentrations and burning were found at different places along the ditches (for example, in the centre of D) and were absent from E. There was no evidence of a major entranceway between Ditches C and D, although it remained possible that C (without its palisade), was not part of the circuit at all, but acted to channel movement into the interior of the enclosure. The other side of an entranceway may have been found by excavating farther to the north. Yet this seems unlikely given the similarity of this ditch to those to the south and given the lack of special activities associated with the northern butt end of Ditch D. The aerial photographs rather suggest that the circuit changed its course abruptly at this point as it did in the northwest corner (Fig. 5.1). The lack of a major entranceway undermined the notion of a unified plan and concentrated our attention once again on the variation and segmentation of activities around the enclosure. Indeed it was possible that the two deeper ends of Ditch D somehow indicated 'segmented activities' (Fig. 5.7) but we had no evidence of this as yet.

The densities of artefacts and activities in the ditches were low and there was little to suggest ritual deposits. All the evidence could be contained within a scenario of mundane dumping and burning. Overall, the evidence seemed relatively simple. Was this because relatively little had happened in this part of the site or had the evidence been missed? After all, 1981 had demonstrated the difficulties resulting from

A

B

**Figure 5.6.** *HAD '82: top) looking northeast across the line of the palisade and the causewayed perimeter (Ditches D & E) with the HAD II enclosure in the background; below) looking southwest, with the terminal of Ditch Segment C in the right foreground with the elongated middle ditch length (D) beyond and the palisade behind. (Photographs G. Owen.)*

inexperience of the site. Progress was certainly made in 1982, but had we really discovered all we might have? To make matters worse, the weather had been extremely dry during the September excavation and on the well-drained gravels the stratigraphy had been difficult to distinguish. Conversely, in the final week, when we were digging the lower levels of the ditches, the weather was remarkably wet and so too were these

A

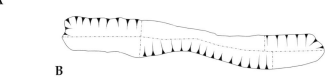

B

C

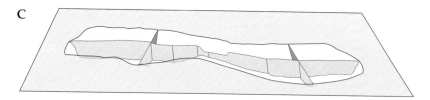

**Figure 5.7.** *HAD '82. A) Looking northwest with longitudinal section of Ditch Segment D truncated by circuit of HAD II enclosure. (Photograph G. Owen.) B & C) plan and isometric section of Ditch D.*

features of different dates, and also from the project's environmental studies (see HAD III & V; Volume 2).

The conclusion had also been reached that the resources spent in stripping the site twice were not offset by the information gained by the site-wide sampling of the buried soil. Leaching was severe and there was now evidence that the island had been under plough in the Iron Age. Artefact densities were low and only flint had survived well in the buried soil. It was decided, therefore, to machine the soil down to the underlying gravels in a single operation, although during the stripping the buried soil was first cleaned off in order to identify any later, peat-filled features. A sample transect of the buried soil was, however, left in order to address specific questions. In particular, could variation in densities of material be associated with the positions of the palisade and causewayed ditch?

The specific location of the 1984 excavations was again partly contingent on harvesting and planting regimes. We were allowed a window of five weeks in September and October. On the aerial photograph the palisade seemed to be set much farther back from the ditches than in the 1982 area of excavation (Figs. 5.1 & 5.10). Was this an example of variability around the enclosure, and in what other ways were the ditches here different from those in other parts of the enclosure? We also wanted to examine the relationship between the causewayed circuit and what appeared on the aerial photographs to be part of a larger field system associated with Iron Age enclosures. In the event, the part of this field system examined in 1984 proved to be a natural fault in the Pleistocene deposits (running across the site at Ditch H).

In 1984 the policy of obtaining longitudinal sections along the ditches was adhered to. In the cramped conditions of the longitudinal section of the narrow part of Ditch D it was realized that important information might be missed. We were more ready in 1984 to look for patterning across the full width of the ditches.

deposits. Despite these logistical problems, perhaps we had still to learn how to see recuts. The 'data' are part of the hermeneutic circle: we saw what we had the experience to see. Other sections of ditch would have to be excavated in order to evaluate fully the existence of recuts.

*The 1984 season*

The next time the causewayed enclosure could be excavated was in the late summer of 1984. By then three summers of fieldwork experience of the soils and conditions on the Delphs sites had been gleaned. We had, for example, come to realize that peat formation on the terrace was relatively late, and that all peat-filled ditches and features were later than the late Iron Age. This realization partly derived from excavating

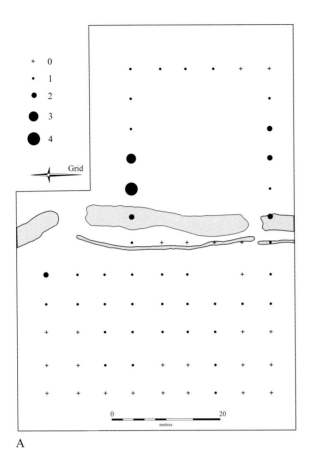

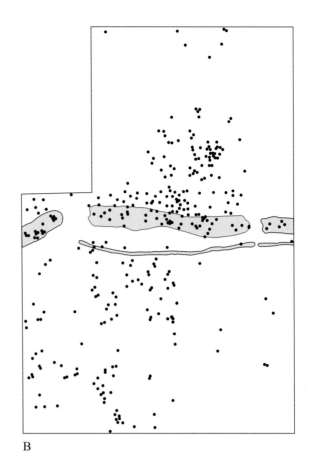

**Figure 5.8.** *HAD '82. Distribution of worked flint: A) metre square buried soil samples; B) surface finds and from cut features.*

*Ditch F*

At this point the surrounding subsoil consisted of interbedded fluvio-glacial deposits of clay, sand and marl. The lack of gravel here (and up to the natural fissure at Ditch H) meant that collapse during excavation was frequent and the distinction between the natural and the primary fills (always difficult) was here particularly intractable. Accordingly, for Ditches F to H dimensions must be approximate.

The southern end of Ditch F continued to the south beyond the excavated area (Fig. 5.10). The northern butt end was relatively square in plan but all the sides of the ditches sloped down at about 40° to an uneven flat base. The hollowing along the length of the base of Ditch F perhaps recalled the two deeper ends of Ditch D. The immediate problem was that the evidence could be interpreted in opposing ways. The uneven shape of the base of the ditch could simply be the result of the way in which the ditch was dug as one event and by one group. The unevenness would then simply be the result of informality in the digging process. Alternatively, the ditch could initially have been dug as different events, either by different 'gangs' at the same moment in time or by one group producing recuts at different moments. There was a range of possibilities from a simple single event to a more complex dual event to a sequence of events: the underlying issues being those of *variability* and *sequence*.

The ditch was *c.* 4.0 m wide and 1.1 m deep below the surface of the buried soil. The fills began with a general deposit of fine sand silt containing burnt flint. Above this were secondary fills of sandy silts and clays which appeared to show two recuts in the south and north of the ditch. These were associated with localized activity at

the northern end of the ditch. At the base of the fills was found a deposit on the northeast slope of the ditch, about 0.60 m by 0.80 m in extent, containing a high density of charcoal and three sherds. There was some evidence of a slot or other intrusion dug into the top of the secondary fills at the northernmost extremity of the ditch, but this was difficult to define.

The top of the ditch was filled with a material very similar to the buried soil horizon. It should be noted, however, that this upper horizon seemed to continue across the causeway and join up with the upper fill in Ditch G. Any such final ditch which ran the length of both the earlier Ditches F and G would only have been 0.60 m deep below the old ground surface and would have had sloping sides and a flat base.

In summary, Ditch F could be seen as having undergone up to four recutting events after the initial ditch had been dug. More parsimoniously, an event-led viewpoint would only have recutting when Ditches F and G were joined at a late stage, although there were likely candidates for two smaller ditches at one point in the life of the enclosure. There was evidence of burnt flint in the primary fill and charcoal and pottery at the base of the secondary fills. These localized traces of discard were concentrated at the northern butt end, adjacent to the causeway, although the overall distribution of finds in the ditch was concentrated in the middle of the excavated portion of the ditch away from the causeway. Overall, we were beginning to see, or thought we could see, more evidence of recutting and an extended sequence. Despite this greater complexity, some patterns seemed to hold, such as a major division into two phases of activity in the primary and secondary fills and a distinction in artefact patterning between the central and end portions of the ditches.

A

B

**Figure 5.9.** *HAD '84: A) looking south across causewayed enclosure perimeter (the northwestern extension of the site not yet opened; note that the intensity of the field background is a result of stubble burning); B) looking southeast with Ditch Segment I in lower right foreground and line of palisade left.*

*Ditch G*

This was 3 m wide, 8 m long and 1.25 m deep (Figs. 5.10 & 5.12). The sides sloped at about 45° all the way round the ditch and the base appeared flat in cross-section. However in longitudinal section the base had a 0.20 m high 'hump' about one third of the way along from the southern end. Thus two slight hollows were formed in the northern and southern ends of the ditch, as indeed had been found in Ditch D. This could represent two events (i.e. segmented work organization) or two phases of ditch cutting, and slight irregularities in the surface plan of this ditch could support this argument (Fig. 5.10). Yet there was no evidence at all in the fills of Ditch G for recutting. The primary fills occurred discontinuously around the edges of the ditch and consisted of layers of clay, sand and gravel, one of which contained faunal remains.

The secondary fills which covered the centre of the ditch consisted of sandy clays and silts which towards the top were very similar to the buried soil. Scattered along the ditch were small patches of charcoal in the lower parts of these secondary fills (as had also been found in Ditch F). The most substantial of these, 0.65 × 0.60 m and 0.10 m deep occurred exactly over the hump in the base of the ditch although separated from it by a 0.10-m-thick fill horizon. The patch consisted of charcoal within a sandy silt matrix and recalled the evidence from Ditch D.

As noted in the discussion of Ditch F the top fil of Ditches F and G were continuous and indicate a late recutting of the ditches to form a single shallow segment.

In summary, Ditch G seemed relatively simple, containing either one or two recuts and a relatively low density of finds. There is again evidence for the discard of burnt material towards the beginning of the secondary fills. The finds tend to concentrate at the northern end.

*Ditch H*

5.8 m long, 4.25 m wide and 1.6 m deep, at first sight the primary cut of this ditch seems simple, with sloping sides except at the northern end where the sides are nearly vertical (Figs. 5.10 & 5.12), and with a flat base. The southeastern edge of the primary cut was, however, extremely difficult to establish. The fills and ditch's sides appeared to interbed. In the end a machine cut was made deep into the adjacent deposits in order to attempt to clarify the situation. What became clear was that the glacial deposits at this point contained a gravel and shell marl which had washed into the ditch and hardened into a compact concretion. An early cut appears to have specifically quarried out the marl and a later cut in the northern part of the ditch which left a slight ridge against the marl and a small bump on the floor of the ditch.

The primary fills lined the lower sides and base of the ditch and consisted of gravel silts. Directly on these in the southeastern side of the ditch was a small area of charcoal. The secondary fills consisted of silts with varying amounts of gravel, sand and clay. It is possible to interpret the deposits as indicating two phases of recutting although the evidence is by no means conclusive. These recuts would have created ditches in the same location as the original ditch but slightly shorter and narrower and only 0.70 m and 0.90 m deep.

At the southern end of the ditch three possible post-holes were found dug into the uppermost secondary fills. One of these was very shallow and difficult to define, but the others were 0.30–0.35 m in diameter and 0.25–0.30 m in depth. These late features recall the post-holes and pit in the butt end of Ditch A.

In summary, in both the primary and secondary fills the main evidence of discard, pitting and post-holes occurred at the southern end of this ditch. Although there was only a very low density of finds, the southern end of the ditch is complicated and appears to have seen an early recut or ditch extension.

*Ditch I*

However complex Ditches F to H are thought to be, the move to Ditch I sees a undeniable rise in cuts, fills and deposits, and clearly it represents a long drawn-out and elaborate sequence of activities.

The ditch as a whole was 7.8 m long, 4.4 m wide and 1.6 m deep below the buried soil, although these dimensions are the result of numerous smaller-scale events (Figs. 5.10, 5.13–5.15). The ditch was relatively steep-sided and flat-based. However, it was initially dug so as to leave a ridge of natural gravel down its central axis. 0.32 m high and 0.70 m wide, this ridge of natural gravel sloped down gradually to the north leaving a gap between its northern end and the northern side of the ditch. The southern end, however, was abrupt and steep. This edge of the axial ridge may have been cut by a secondary extension of the ditch, slightly expanding it to the south. But is also possible that the axial ridge never extended to the south of the ditch as it had not extended to the north.

The ditch must originally have been dug in two linear halves, leaving a ridge along the central axis (F.138). This central ridge recalls the irregularities on the bases of the Ditches D and F to H, and it retained an importance throughout the life of the ditch. Above the axial ridge was a mound 0.60 m thick and 0.90 m wide. Its matrix consisted of very pure redeposited sands and gravels. It is possible that this deposit was originally built up over the axial ridge as a mound. However, the deposits were clearly horizontally banded and showed little indication of slumping on its sides. Therefore, while it seems most likely that the 'mound' material was originally part of a primary fill of the ditch that was otherwise (re)cut away, its intentional 'enmoundment' must remain a possibility.

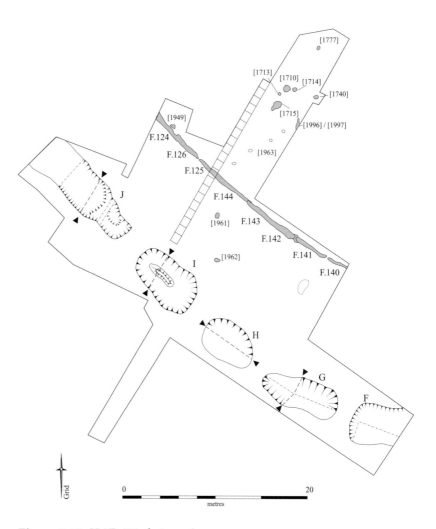

**Figure 5.10.** *HAD '84: feature plan.*

Nevertheless a mound was then produced immediately above the central ridge by recutting a ditch (F.137) around the inner sides of the earlier ditch, leaving the mound upstanding in the middle. This ovoid 'ring-ditch', averaging 1.5 m wide, flat-based and often cutting down to the base of the original ditch, had a sand and gravel primary fill. In the southern part of the ditch, a deposit of clay and gravel containing bone and charcoal was found bonded with a heavy iron concretion ([1747]). This deposit continued the line of the axial mound although with a slight break between them formed by the inner edge of the 'ring-ditch'. Several human cranial fragments were found in this deposit (see Dodwell below) and perhaps at this time the butt end of a Group VI polished axe was placed on the top of the main axial mound. There was evidence of the recutting of a small pit containing charcoal into the [1747] deposit.

A ditch had thus been created with a central mound which had been extended to reach the southern edge of the ditch (F.138). A 'U'-plan 'ring-ditch' was left running along the sides and the 'back' of the mound. This ditch was then filled with varied deposits of gravel and clay which were at times very clean and may have been placed intentionally. A small pit or post-hole ([1839]) was dug into the western part of the ditch before it was filled up to the height of the central mound.

The 'U'-shaped ditch had by now filled up so that the whole of Ditch I was a small shallow ditch (F.122) above what had been the central mound. Again, there must be some question whether this was simply a natural infill profile or an intentional recut. Nevertheless, the bottom of the flat-based F.122 'ditch' contained deposits that were sufficiently pure to argue that the deposits may have been dumped into the ditch. The northern end of the ditch was at this time redug twice (F.123 & F.121) in order to redefine the curved back end of the 'U'-shaped ditch. First a short shallow, square-ended ditch was dug in order to curve round the northern end of the earlier mound (F.123). The fill of this feature consisted of a clay silt in the middle of which was a 0.40-m-wide patch of soil containing charcoal, scorched pebbles and burnt animal bone. There was also human bone: two tibia shaft fragments, a fibula shaft and one navicular fragment. A larger kidney-shaped ditch (F.121) was then dug curving round in the northern part of the ditch and cutting into the northern edge of F.123 (Fig. 5.14). Once again this ditch redefined the northern end of the axial mound. 3.2 m long, 1.5 m wide and up to 0.80 m deep, this had steep sides and contained a clay silt with moderate charcoal inclusions.

Albeit somewhat ambiguous, there was evidence that the whole of Ditch I was again recut at this point, producing a shallow ditch (F.120) and, at the northern end, a shallow hollow ([1889]) was cut above the earlier features. Less equivocal, two small post-holes ([1923] & [1924]) were cut into the northwestern lip of the ditch and the base of the F.120 recut and the [1889] hollow were covered with a deposit of charcoal, burnt sandstone fragments, animal bone flint and pottery. Since the surrounding soil was not burnt

**Figure 5.11.** *HAD '84: looking northwest with Ditch Segment F in foreground, G & H in mid-field and I in background (northern extension not yet opened).*

In summary, Ditch I is indeed remarkable in its complexity. This was the first ditch segment for which it was possible to argue unequivocally for a ritual interpretation. Certainly Ditch I was 'odd' in various ways. The central ridge or mound was an odd thing to leave in the centre of a ditch and it was at a different angle from the smaller humps which had been found in the base of other ditches. Moreover, the ditch seemed 'special' in that it contained not only very complex recutting in comparison to the other ditches but also human bones and a polished axe. This assemblage, associated with the axial mound in the ditch and thus intentionally 'placed', suggested formalized behaviour related to burial. It was difficult to argue that the deposits were purely the result of refuse discarded from domestic or 'feasting' activities.

Also relevant to the ritual interpretation of the ditch are the parallels which can be drawn between the overall sequences of activities in the ditch and in the long barrow. First the two linear halves of the ditch were dug so that the central axis remained, as the long barrow was built respecting a central axis. The ditch was filled but then recut

this material must have been dumped. This material ([1871] in Fig. 5.15) was thickest at the northern end of the ditch where the deposit was divided by a lens of weathering suggesting that at least two phases of dumping had occurred. The deposit continued in a patchy manner over the entire length of the underlying axial mound. This final phase of burnt deposition was covered by weathered redeposited buried soil.

leaving a mound in the centre of the ditch. Deposits were then placed at the southern or southeastern end of the mound, filling the ditch at this point. As a result a 'U'-shaped ditch had been produced, for all the world like the 'U'-shaped ditch around the long barrow. Human bones were associated with both the ditch and the long barrow. A broken axe was placed on top of the mound in the ditch.

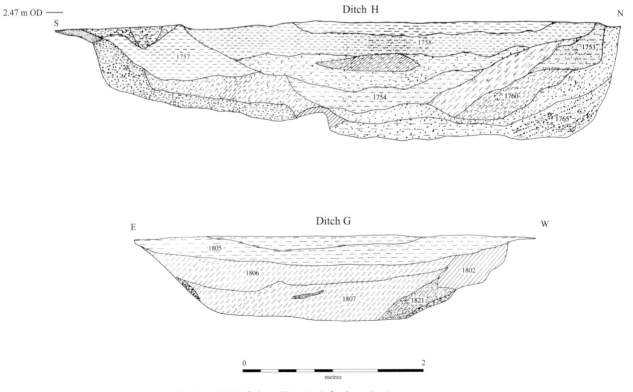

**Figure 5.12.** *HAD '84: sections, Ditches H & G (see Fig. 5.10 for location).*

The 'U' shaped ditch filled up but was recut twice at the northern end in order to redefine the axial mound. Burnt material was deposited in these recuts as it was in the fill which covered over the mound. The final fill of the ditch contained redeposited soil. These penultimate acts of burnt material which in effect 'close off' the use of the ditch and its central mound recall the 'crematoria' closing of the long barrow.

There are of course differences between Ditch I and the long barrow, particularly in the way in which artefacts were deposited and in their orientation. It may not be too fanciful to suggest, however, that the human bone deposit at the southeastern end of the ditch mound parallels the human bone deposit at the northeastern end of the long barrow mound. In both cases the opening in the 'U'-shaped ditch is associated with the human bone deposits. In both cases the mound is higher with a steeper 'front' at the eastern end.

*Ditch J*

Moving across what appeared to be a narrow but was earlier a wide causeway, lay a long section of ditch (J). This was again the focus of intense activities. The ditch continued northwards out of the excavated area but was at least 15 m long, 4 m wide and 1.5 m deep (Figs. 5.10, 5.14 & 5.15).

The sides of the initial ditch were fairly steep and the base rounded to flat. Only a very small area of the base at its southernmost end was excavated and so it is not possible to say whether the ditch had axial ridges as in the Ditches F to I to the south. Almost immediately primary weathering slips of sands, gravels and clays had formed along the sides of the ditches and a thin weathering of fine sand had covered the base, the ditch becoming filled to half its depth with a pure and uniform deposit. Flat-topped, this material was a compacted light yellow to mid brown sand within a pale grey to white shell marl. It was initially thought that this was an intentionally packed marl platform around which ditches had later been cut. However, excavations at the long barrow discovered identical deposits in the ditch which were the result of water movement (see Chapter 3). We have already seen in Ditch H that marl deposits existed within the adjacent glacial deposits and it is entirely likely that localized springs brought clay deposits containing fossil shell material into Ditch J.

The apparent ditches which filled the gap between the marl deposit and the sides of the ditches, superficially so similar to the ring and 'U' ditches around the mound in Ditch I, were entirely natural in Ditch J. They clearly undercut the marl deposit and, as at the long barrow, they represented the primary slips of sands, clays and gravels at the sides of Ditch J. Perhaps the wetness of the ditch at an early stage discouraged the intensity of primary activities noted in Ditch I.

The marl and primary fills around the edge of the ditch had created a flat platform covering the bottom of a shallow ditch

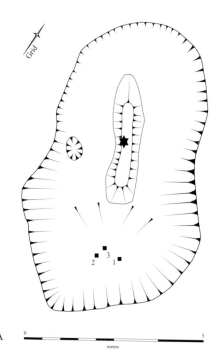

A

B

**Figure 5.13.** *HAD '84. Ditch I. A) plan showing low 'ditchwork' mound in base (1–3 indicate human skull fragments, with the position of the axe starred); B) south-facing section; note gravel ridge/mound in central base. (Photograph C. Evans.)*

(Fig. 5.15). The top of the marl deposit and parts of the top of the primary fills were covered by a thin (0.04-m-thick) horizontal layer of sandy clay ([1909]) which towards the centre of the platform contained frequent charcoal and burnt bone. Whether additional fills occurred in the ditch at this point in time is unclear, but the ditch was perhaps recut (F.131) to the top of [1909] on the platform and certainly the ditch was now extended to the south by 4.4 m to narrow the causeway between Ditches I and J. This ditch extension

**A**

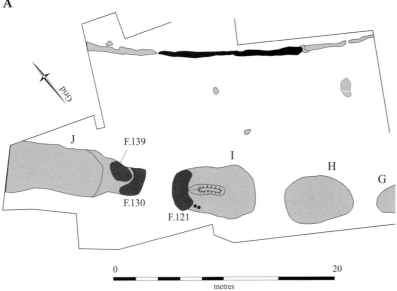

**B**

**Figure 5.14.** *HAD '84. A) F.121/123 re-cutting of northeastern terminal of Ditch I. (Photograph C. Evans.) B) Plan shows 'late' recuts in Ditch I & J, and burnt portion of palisade (blackened).*

tomed ditch (F.131). The whole length of the ditch except the southern 1 m may then have been recut as a shallow (0.30–0.50 m deep below the base of the buried soil) ditch with sloping sides and 'V'-shaped base (F.129). Alternatively, it is conceivable that this 'ditch' simply represents a stage in the natural infill of ditch F.131. Whatever the case, a large pit (F.139) was dug into the southern end of the ditch soon after weathering of the sides had begun (Fig. 5.14). This oval pit was 0.50 m deep and flat based and reformed the butt end of ditch F.129. It contained sandy silts. This activity at the butt end of the ditch was extended by the digging of a shallow (0.30 m deep) hollow to fill the entire butt end of ditch F.131. This redefinition (F.130) of the southern butt end of Ditch J recalled the kidney-shaped recuts in the northern end of Ditch I (Fig. 5.14). However, the base of the hollow (F.130) in Ditch J contained two concave hollows divided by a gravel ridge and each about 0.50 m in diameter. These hollows may originally have contained a pair of posts at the butt end of Ditch J, which were later dismantled. The fill of the overall hollow was mixed and perhaps disturbed. Elsewhere along ditch F.129 dumping of material with a high charcoal density occurred as the ditch filled up through natural weathering. Such deposition was most notable in the northernmost part of the excavated section of the ditch.

In a final phase of activity on the now largely infilled ditch, a small post-hole was dug in the northern end of the excavated portion with traces of a burnt post and packing ([1856]) and two small post-holes ([1863]) occurred in the eastern lip of the butt end of the Ditch F.129. Most of the activity, however, was again concentrated on the butt end of the overall ditch adjacent to the causeway. The butt end was again redefined by a series of hollows and post-holes above both F.139 and F.130. This new area of activity (F.127) was irregular and only 0.15 m deep. The eight small (on average 0.30 m in diameter and 0.10 m deep) post-holes did not form an identifiable pattern. The overall hollowed area fitted against the centre of the butt end of Ditch J. It is of course possible that similar features originally existed on the adjacent causeway and in adjacent areas of the enclosure but that shallow features only survived in the slumped ditch deposits. Nevertheless, within the excavated length of the ditch, these late features were concentrated at the butt end.

In summary, Ditch J continued the evidence of a long sequence of activities found in Ditch I. Not only were these two ditches distinctive in the amount of activity which occurred in them, but the sequences of activity had an overall similarity. Soon after the gap between them had been narrowed, the focus of activities in each of the ditches shifted to the butt ends on either side of the causeway. Clearly in the latter part of the period of the use of the ditches the entranceway had come to take on a special significance. This entrance-related activity was not evident earlier on.

Little is known of the earliest phase of digging of the ditch since only a small portion of it was excavated to its base. However, the initial fills seem to be relatively straightforward and naturally

was 2.8 m wide and 0.40 m deep below the base of the buried soil. The base of this extension was flat and was at the same level as the top of the flat marl platform in the earlier ditch to the south.

A series of various 'hollows' (potentially slots and post-holes up to 0.45 m deep) were though to have been 'cut' into the top of the marl platform (see Evans 1988a, fig. 7.2). However, it is clear that their identification was influenced by the recovery of the unequivocally mounded 'ditchwork' in Ditch I and the knowledge that there were 'constructions' within the ditches themselves. Yet, in hindsight and with greater experience of the geological marls both in the HAD '87 area and at the long barrow, the Ditch J 'cut' features were all probably just solution hollows and were without structural intent.

Various weathering deposits consisting of sands and silts with variable gravel content then occurred in the extended flat-bot-

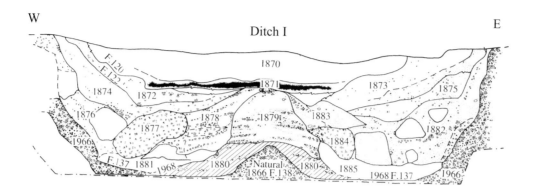

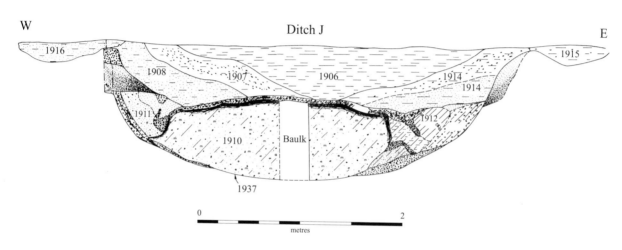

**Figure 5.15.** *HAD '84: sections, Ditches I & J (see Fig. 5.10 for location).*

produced. At this stage, therefore, Ditch J differed from the mound-producing activities in Ditch I. However, at about the same time as the ditch was extended to the south in order to narrow the causeway, a complex series of pits was placed in the flat bottom of the ditch away from the butt end. These had no counterpart in Ditch I unless they related to the cutting of the 'ring-ditch' and deposition of bones around the axial mound.

It was in the latest phases of activity in Ditch J that the entrance became the focus of activities. In both ditches the butt end was redefined several times by the digging of kidney-shaped ditches and in both cases larger areas of charcoal were found dumped along the ditch as a whole. Ditch J saw a final phase of activity associated with its butt end in which a series of post-holes and hollows was dug (F.127).

We began to think that we had missed a lot of evidence in earlier years on the enclosure ditches. Greater familiarity with the difficult and leached soils allowed us to find more evidence of recutting in 1984. Relaxation of the policy of maintaining longitudinal sections had allowed for further understanding of the ditches more as wholes. As a result 'event' and 'sequence' viewpoints developed, which were argued out on a daily basis on the site. Was the irregularity in the cutting of the ditches the result of different 'work gangs' or sequences of different events? Should fill horizons be interpreted as recuts? The resolution of these problems was not always clear-cut, but at least we were now raising the questions.

The notion of variability was now becoming a central issue. On the one hand, the variation in the activities in the ditches was marked. Ditches I and J were much more complex than those adjacent to the south (F, G & H). Also, there was variation through time in that Ditches F and G were joined into one at a late stage, and the early large gap between I and J was later narrowed. On the other hand, the gap between Ditches I and J could be interpreted as a major entranceway into the enclosure. In this case, the complex deposits in Ditches I and J related to activities associated with entering the enclosure as a whole. The existence of one or a few entrances would imply an overall plan

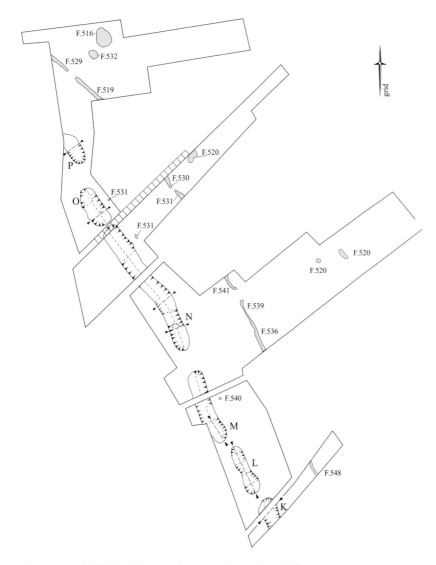

**Figure 5.16.** *HAD '87: area of excavation and main features.*

There were less 'placed' deposits in the upper fills, but recutting was often complex, involving pits and post-holes.

Finds seemed either to be concentrated in the central part of the ditches, sometimes associated with the central mounds or humps, or to be found near the terminals. A pattern sometimes occurred whereby an earlier emphasis on the central part of the ditch was replaced by a shift to the terminals (Ditches D, I & J). This sequence was supported by the evidence of later recutting of the terminals in Ditches I and J.

*The 1987 season*
In the years between 1984 and 1987 we debated whether there was an overall plan to the enclosure, a 'façade front' and back space (see *Design principles* below). On the one hand it seemed possible to point to all the variability that had been found and to the apparently random variation in length of ditch as one moved around the circuit. The palisade was either absent (1981 season) close to the ditches (1982 season) or distant from them (1984 season). On the other hand, regularities in the way the ditches were dug and used over time had been discerned. Perhaps part of the circuit should be excavated where a major entrance seemed most likely on the aerial photographs.

Ditches K to P were excavated in the late summer of 1987, often in severe weather conditions involving storms and a high water table. (Work had to continue for two weeks after the renowned October gales of that year when the site (and the fen) was completely flooded; see Figure 5.17. This required sandbagging portions of the site and simply blasting the water away using the largest pump that was locally available.) The aims were to investigate a part of the enclosure circuit where an inward bend of the ditches appeared to define a wider causeway and a possible major entrance (Figs. 5.1 & 5.16), although as usual much depended on the availability of the field between crops. Our strategy continued to be influenced by the idea that there may have been major entrances into the enclosure. The location of the 1987 excavations in our last season therefore left large

to the site and therefore draw attention to the whole rather than to segmentation and variability. Indeed some aspects of the layout of the enclosure could be argued to support the notion of an overall plan with major entranceways (Evans 1988a).

Other aspects of the data were beginning to suggest a pattern. There certainly seemed to be many similarities between the ditches found in all the seasons of excavation, not only in terms of widths and depths but also of the sequences of activities within them. In general terms the primary cutting of the ditches seemed to consistently involve a separation of deeper ends from a higher middle. The primary deposits represented a quick filling of the ditches, sometimes associated with special (e.g. Ditch I) or dumped (e.g. Ditch D) deposits. The secondary fills often began with traces of burning, and there was generally more burning in these upper layers.

parts of the circuit (particularly in the southeast and the northeast of the enclosure) uninvestigated. A concern with this issue also meant that we concentrated again on the perimeter of the enclosure rather than on large areas of the interior, although resources were found to excavate limited parts of the area within the enclosure (see HAD VIII below).

Nevertheless, the search for major entrances was combined with a decision to excavate as large a section of the perimeter as was possible within the season's constraints. Six ditch segments (K to P) were dug across a considerable area (Fig. 5.16). The aim was to obtain a further idea of the variability between ditches within a localized part of the perimeter. If another extensive length of ditches was uncovered, what type of variability might be found?

Speed was of the essence given our resources. It had come to be realized that we needed to dig a large sample of ditches and uncover extensive areas of the interior of the enclosure. So it was decided to begin, as in 1984, by removing the buried soil by machine, leaving a transect of the buried soil for hand-excavation and sieving (see below). The technique was, however, altered in the ditches. Since fills had in any case proved difficult to follow in plan even in 1984, it was decided to excavate the ditches in 10-cm or 20-cm artificial spits unless clear structures and layers could be followed. This allowed us to dig quickly and yet retain control over artefact location and stratigraphy where it was possible to follow. Plans were made of

A

B

**Figure 5.17.** *HAD '87: the aftermath of the October gales, after which the excavations continued for a further two weeks. Note, concerning the material culture of excavation (and its 'genealogies'), that the Department of Archaeology's site huts shown below are the same that feature in Figure 5.43 (see also Grahame Clark's* Prehistory at Cambridge and Beyond *of 1989, fig. 34).*

the surface of each spit and levelled so that they could be related in post-excavation analysis to the sections. By retaining longitudinal and frequent cross-sections, a close hold could be maintained on the recuts within the ditch fills.

*Ditch K*

Entering the southern part of the excavated area, and its southern butt end was not uncovered (Fig. 5.16). However, at the southern end of the ditch the fills were found to be sloping upwards as if

towards the butt end. It was therefore assumed that the edge of excavation did not lie far from its southern extremity.

The ditch may have been 6.4 m long. It was 3.2 m wide and 1.90 m deep below the buried soil (Fig. 5.19). The sides were nearly vertical and the base flat. The ditch was irregular in plan, having a lobe at each end and a narrower, shallower central portion. Similar irregularities were found in Ditches D and F to H, where they raised the issue of what we expect these ditches to look like. If we expect them to be regularly cut, then Ditch K may have been dug as two pits which were then joined up. Alternatively the ditch may have been dug irregularly in

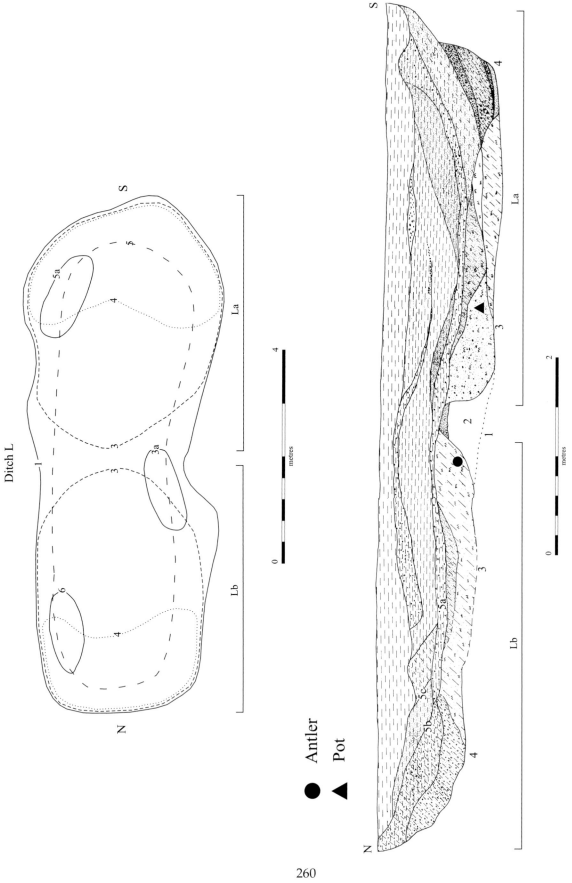

**Figure 5.18.** *HAD '87: interpretative plan and longitudinal section, Ditch L (see Fig. 5.16 for location).*

the first place. In fact these two hypotheses are similar, since the first recognizes that there was no evidence in the fills for a long period of time between the early pits and their joining into a ditch segment. The issue which does remain, however, is whether different 'gangs' were at work.

The primary fills consisted of clays, gravels and marl with sandy silts above them. Irregular large lumps of clay were found in the bottom of the ditch. These sometimes lay on the central axis (Fig. 5.19), recalling the axial mound in Ditch I. However, the longitudinal section showed that these were not continuous along the length of the ditch and may simply have been 'blocks' of clay which fell at an early stage into the ditch. Several pieces of bone and antler were found in these lower fills; these and the pottery were distributed along the central axis of the ditch.

The section across the ditch could be read to indicate a recutting into the primary fills to produce a round-bottomed linear ditch 2.7 m wide. The upper fills consisted of various sandy silt weathering horizons. There was some evidence for a pit recut in the uppermost horizon in the northern butt end with a ditch cut from the same level to the south. The northern pit was 1.7 m by 1.5 m and was 0.25 m deep. The ditch to the south had the same width and depth but continued out of the excavated area to the south. This final phase of recutting was associated with some localized concentrations of charcoal. The finds in the secondary fills were found in the southern half of the ditch.

In summary, an irregular or staggered cutting of the initial ditch was followed by a rapid primary infill which may have been associated with a marking of the central axis (by clay and finds deposition). The secondary fills showed two possible phases of recutting in a period in which deposition of finds was concentrated in the southern half of the ditch.

*Ditch L*

After the relative simplicity of Ditch K, the next ditch was overwhelming in its complexity, recalling with some clarity the sequence in the elaborate Ditch I. The recutting in Ditch L continued through a long sequence, of which only the outline will be described here (see Fig. 5.18 for details).

In overall appearance the initial ditch was 9.75 m long, 3.4 m wide and 1.5 m deep below the buried soil (Figs. 5.16 & 5.18). In final form it had near-vertical sides and a flat base but

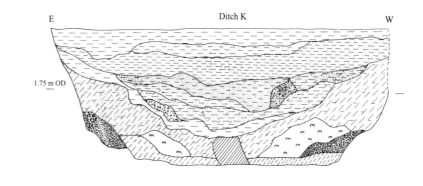

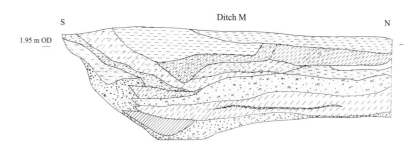

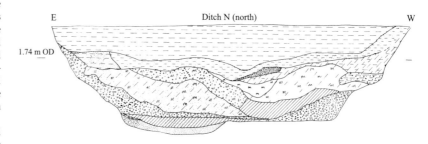

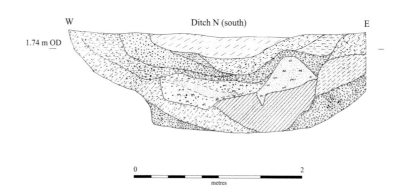

**Figure 5.19.** *HAD '87: sections, Ditches K, M & N (see Fig. 5.16 for location).*

much of this shape was produced by later recutting. The ditch was allowed to fill up at least partially with gravels before being recut to produce two shorter ditches (La to the south and Lb to the north) with a 0.35 m causeway between them. La was 4.6 m long and Lb 4.8 m. Both had vertical sides and flat bases. It is also possible that La and Lb were dug at different times with their interrelationship obliterated by later recutting in the ditch (see below). However,

their identical shape and symmetry suggest that they were probably contemporary.

The two ditch segments were then filled with a clay marl which in La contained a near-complete pot (Fig. 5.32:4) and in Lb an antler. This marl filled the ditches to the top of the causeway between them, so reproducing the original single ditch L. As if to emphasize this refound unity the northern and southern butt ends of Ditch L

261

**A**

**B**

**Figure 5.20.** *HAD '87: A) east-facing longitudinal section through Ditch Segment N (immediately north of southern terminal; note recutting across lower profile of southern half); B) human skull exposed in lower fills of Ditch Segment M. (Photographs C. Evans.)*

ends. The evidence recalls the special 'placed' deposits in the primary fills in Ditches D and I. However, the placing of the antler and the pot in Ditch L was less obviously patterned than in Ditch I. It must be recognized that the quicker initial filling and slipping of the sides of the ditches may have protected any pot or other artefact which had fallen or slipped in. The upper fills probably took a longer period of time, therefore contained more artefacts which were more likely to be disturbed, weathered or broken up. We have, then, to be very circumspect about the interpretation of 'placed' deposits.

The ends of Ditch L were then recut, shifting the emphasis to the butt ends. In similar ways Ditches I and J saw a recutting and closing of the entrance ways between the ditches. In both I and J this redefining of the ends of the ditches was closely linked in time to activities on the marl platform (in J) and the dumping of burnt material (in I) on the flat bottom of the shallow ditch. In Ditch L burnt material was also dumped along a flat-bottomed ditch. The final phase of fills may have included several recuts, but the focus of artefact discard (mainly pottery) was now at the southern butt end, making a clear contrast with the earlier more centrally located bones. This shift in time towards discard at the butt ends has been identified now in four ditches (D, I, J & L). Overall the finds in the secondary fills had now been found in the terminals rather than in the centres of the ditches in seven clear cases, and only in one case (Ditch D) in the centre. In other instances the pattern was not clear.

*Ditch M*

The bipolarity so clearly evident in Ditch L became even more marked in Ditch M, which was a long segment (12.8 m by 3.2 m wide and 1.65 m deep below the surface of the buried soil; Figs. 5.16 & 5.19). The sides sloped at about 45° down to a flat base. But the base was deeper and wider at the southern butt end and through much of its later life the ditch consisted of two pits, one at each end, joined by a narrower and shallower

were recut with small ditches rather like the kidney-shaped recuts in Ditches I and J.

After some weathering into the ditch above the butt ends, and perhaps after some clearing out or recutting of the whole ditch, a thick deposit of burnt material was deposited on top of the marl base of the ditch. The sand silts above this deposit showed several phases of recutting (perhaps as many as three or four) along the whole length of the gradually reduced ditch.

In summary, the sequence in Ditch L recalls Ditches I and J, both in the complexity of the sequence and in the specific nature of the events. After the initial infilling of an elongated ditch, the two ends were cut leaving upstanding gravel between two pits (La and Lb). This pattern recalls the recutting to form multiple ditches within Ditch F.

The deposits of marl which filled the bases of La and Lb were similar to the marl platform in J. The marl contained mainly (animal) bone with antler and one near-complete pot in La. The bone was dispersed along the ditch with no concentration near the butt

straight section.

The initial linear ditch already had a deeper and wider pit-like southern end (Fig. 5.19). It then filled up with gravel slips to a depth of 0.20–0.30 m along the sides and on the bottom. At the southern end these gravel deposits were then cut away to reform the pit (about 1 m to 1.5 m in diameter and centrally placed within the butt end). Indeed, this southern pit seems to have gone through several recuttings (perhaps three or four) as the ditch filled up with gravel and marl deposits.

On top of the basal gravel fill a clay marl had formed which was often heavily compacted and concreted (cf. Ditch J). The marl contained 20 per cent sand and 10 per cent gravel and it formed a relatively flat deposit at the bottom of the ditch, which was now only 0.35 m deep in the central portion but was 0.50 m deep at the southern end and 0.90 m deep at the northern end. Thus the bipolarity was already taking shape, with two deeper butt ends. A light distribution of bone and antler was found throughout the ditch.

On top of the marl was a thin layer (0.05–0.10 m thick) of sandy silts which contained varying amounts of charcoal. Similar horizons of burnt material have been found in other ditches (e.g. I & L) above the marl or gravel basal deposits. In the southern part of the ditch this had been cut away in the various phases of recutting of the southern pit. In the northern part of the ditch the thin layer consisted of a silty clay with sandy gravel. Within this deposit and towards the northern end of the ditch was found a human cranium without its mandible (Fig. 5.20). A number of cranial fragments were found at this point as well as a human long bone.

The ditch had thereafter continued to fill up with weathered silts, but great activity continued at both the butt ends. At the southern end a substantial pit up to 2 m in diameter and up to 1.05 m deep (below the buried soil surface) may have been dug several times (Fig. 5.19). At the northern end a pit was dug lengthways across the width of the butt end. This was 1 m wide (north–south) and about 2.2 m long (east–west) and 1 m deep (below the surface of the buried soil).

The upper fills of the ditch consisted of weathered buried soil, which sealed the ditch and both the end pits. Only a small number of finds was found in the deposits above the marl. These consisted mainly of sherds in the northern end of the ditch.

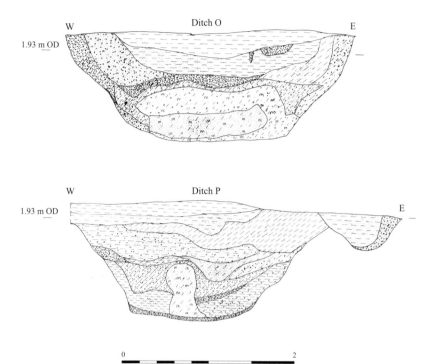

**Figure 5.21.** *HAD '87: sections, Ditches O & P (see Fig. 5.16 for location).*

In summary, as in many of the other ditches the initial gravel and clay fills were associated with animal bone. This was not concentrated at the ends of the ditch but already the southern end was being recut. Gradually through time the ends of the ditches became more important and more opposed to each other. Skull and other human bones were placed at the northern end of the marl platform or ditch base. This placing of deposits in association with the ends of a platform or ditch recalled Ditches I and L. In all cases these deposits have been associated with the primary deposits. Also like Ditches I and L, as well as J, the top of the platform in M was associated with burnt material.

As the ditch filled up, the two ends were repeatedly reformed by the digging of substantial pits. Little material found its way into the ditch at this time, although there was some pottery in the northern pit. This recutting of the ends of Ditch M took place later in the ditch's sequence than in Ditch L, but it corresponded to the later recutting of the butt ends of Ditches I and J.

*Ditch N*
This extremely long section of ditch retained a bipolarity reminiscent of that in Ditch M. The initial spatial structure was in fact similar to M in that a central section joined two deeper end pits (though see *Development trends* below p. 318; Figs. 5.16 & 5.20). And like M, the southern end pit saw more evidence of recutting. In N the finds were also concentrated at the southern end in both early and late phases.

In other ditches the evidence for early pitting had to be deduced from the shape of the base and sides of the ditch. In Ditch N, however, there was the first evidence of deposits associated with an early 'pit' or small ditch. The traces of this feature had been almost entirely removed by the main ditch, and the 'pit' was only seen in section, 9 m north of the southern terminal of the later main ditch, as a shallow hollow filled with small gravel (Fig. 5.19). The hollow was 0.15 m deeper than the main ditch, had a flat base and was only

1.20 m wide, fitting into the eastern half of the later main ditch. The length of the 'pit' remained unknown, but since it did not appear in adjacent sections it cannot have been more than 4–5 m long (unless it was elsewhere less deep and had been entirely cut away by the later ditch). It was also relevant to note that the main ditch was at its widest at this point, 9 m from the southern terminal. The bulge in this part of the ditch may have resulted from the incorporation of the earlier 'pit'.

The initial ditch was flat bottomed with sides sloping at 45°. Overall it was 25 m long, 3.5–4.25 m (at the bulge) wide and 1.20–1.50 m deep below the buried soil. Gravel ridges (0.20–0.50 m broad), which seemed to have been primary, although they could have been the result of recutting the primary fills as in M, occurred at 7 m from the northern end and 5 m from the south. The ditch as a whole was thus divided into a northern pit 6.80 m long, a southern pit 5.00 m long, joined by a central ditch 13.20 m long. The latter central segment sloped downwards gradually from south to north. Another possible gravel ridge occurred 5 m to the south of the northern pit but this is more likely to have been a fallen lump of gravel. The ditch had clearly been dug in three (or four) segments (see below).

Marl filled the ditch above the thin primary gravel and clay slips on the base and sides. In places, these slips seemed very fine, implying that the coarse primary fills had been cleaned out. Indeed, the whole of the ditch appeared to have been recut through the upper slips and basal marl down to the base of the primary ditch. A smooth round-based ditch was produced about 2.50 m wide and 1.2 m deep. In places the ditch did not follow the line of the earlier ditch with any precision. In the southern part of the ditch its central linear axis was to the west of the earlier ditch.

As the marl formed in the base of this new ditch, a 5-m-long pit was recut above the basal pit at the southern terminal. Generally the marl contained fairly high concentrations of bone and charcoal, especially in the upper 0.10 m. These finds began 4 m from the northern end of the ditch and increased in frequency towards the south, being concentrated just to the north of the southern pit. It is possible here as elsewhere that high concentrations of finds at the southern end of the ditch were removed by the recutting of the southern pit. Indeed it is possible that the recutting of the ditch ends may have been to remove deposits of bone, etc.

A layer of silt and charcoal occurred along the top of the marl, and sands and silts were found to have weathered in from the sides of the ditch as recutting continued in the southern pit. The whole southern end of the ditch was then recut, including the southern pit, in one elongated ditch 12 m long, 0.85 m deep and slightly less wide than the original ditch.

The ditch as a whole may, however, still have been visible since some recutting may have occurred in the northern part of the ditch. The evidence for this was very ephemeral and could be seen in plan but not in the sections. Clear evidence of a post-hole occurred in the northern part of the ditch. The finds at this stage (bones and pottery mainly) were concentrated in the southern end of the southern pit. Once again therefore there was evidence of a shift of activity towards the butt ends. However hardly any finds were made at the northern end. The southerly emphasis recalls Ditch H.

In summary, it needs to be re-emphasized that the data partly depend on interpretation, particularly when it comes to evidence for recuts. Where the lines on the sections were drawn could not be determined precisely by the soil colours themselves in the context of leached and iron stained deposits. Nevertheless, there was for the first time clear evidence of an early phase of ditch or pit construction. The main ditch was then dug, probably in three sections, with two pit ends separated by a central ditch. In contrast to other ditches, there was possible evidence for recuts of the overall ditch through the basal marl deposits. But as elsewhere, the top of the marl contained charcoal and bone. There was by now systematic evidence of depositional activities towards the end and immediately after the formation of the marl in the bottom third of the ditch. Recutting in the southern end of the ditch continued during and after the formation of the marl, at one point producing a 12-m-long ditch in the southern end of the main ditch. The emphasis on the south of the ditch was also seen in the southerly concentration of finds in both the primary and secondary fills. There was possible evidence for late recutting at the northern end of the ditch, corresponding to the late features at the southern end of Ditch O.

*Ditch O*
There was only the shortest of causeways between Ditches N and O. Indeed it would not be difficult to imagine Ditch O as simply another in the sequence of three (or four) early pits or ditches along the length of Ditch N. Nevertheless, Ditch O again contained an internal polarity. The ditch as a whole was 7.4 m long, 3.0–3.55 m wide, and 1.50 m deep (Figs. 5.16 & 5.21). However, in plan it had a narrower central section which corresponded to a 0.10 m rise in the central section of the base of the ditch. There was some ambiguous evidence from the complex patterning of the initial slips that the northern end of the ditch at first stopped 1.50 m short of its final position. Indeed, there was a sharp break in the basal sand slips 2.70 m from the northern terminal which may have represented the southern edge of a northern pit dug into and lengthening the northern end of the ditch. If these slight traces were correctly interpreted, they represent evidence that the segmented cutting of the ditches occurred through time rather than being the result of 'gang' labour during a single event of ditch construction.

As the initial sand and gravel slips bedded down the sides of the full-length ditch, containing a zone of burning and charcoal at the northern end, a marl deposit began forming in the base of the ditch, ultimately achieving a thickness of 0.40–0.50 m. During the formation of the marl, two pieces of (possibly the same) antler

tine 'pick' were deposited towards the centre of the northern part of the ditch.

In the deposits above the marl there were again substantial traces of burning, especially in the northern part of the ditch. The ditch then filled up with sandy silt to leave a ditch only 0.20–0.30 m deep. At this point the focus of activities unambiguously changed to the southern end of the ditch. Here in the butt end were found a post-hole containing considerable amounts of ash, a stake-hole, a pit containing charcoal and burnt flint, a linear 1-m-long hollow and two irregular linear features. The whole butt end was then covered by a layer rich in charcoal. The surrounding earth was burnt, suggesting *in situ* burning. These late features parallel those in the northern butt end of Ditch N and late features found elsewhere, as in the butt end of Ditch A. A problem that such features raise is whether they represented activities confined to the ditches or whether they were all that remained from activities spread across the ditches and into the surrounding areas. It is possible that we were seeing here residual traces of activities not confined to the ditches but surviving preferentially in soils which slumped into the ditches. Certainly, the features made little sense in themselves. Perhaps they were part of a wider area of activities, the traces of which had not survived in the leached and ploughed buried soil. The top of the ditch was filled with redeposited buried soil which would have protected the traces of activities towards the top of the ditch. Even if this hypothesis of a wider area of activities is accepted, it remains noteworthy that the features are often concentrated at the butt end of ditches.

In summary, we were now beginning to see the enclosure not as made up of a series of discrete ditches but as the product of an ever-changing process of ditch redigging and realignment. Indeed, the very existence of Ditch O as separate from N seemed to be as much accident as design. The 0.50-m-wide causeway between them could hardly have acted for long as a stable pathway. Through time there is increased evidence of 'pairing' of Ditches N and O.

The initial cutting of the ditch was complex, involving not only double (north and south) pits but also, at a late stage in this first phase of digging, a northern extension of the ditch. After this early period of digging and clearing out the ditches, the ditch was allowed partially to fill with slips and marls. At the same time traces of burning and pieces of antler tine (pick) were deposited in the northern part of the ditch. The overall density of finds at this stage was low and was even in the northern and southern parts of the ditch. Above the marls, evidence of burning was again found before the ditch largely filled up with sandy silts. Activities involving a post-hole and substantial traces of *in situ* burning then occurred in and perhaps also around the southern end of the ditch in parallel with the later events in the north end of Ditch N. The overall density of finds in the secondary deposits was low. Whatever the activities taking place here, they do not seem to have involved substantial domestic refuse deposition.

*Ditch P*
Uncharacteristically, Ditch P proved to be simple in its sequence of use, corresponding to a total lack of finds recovered. However, it was dug in appallingly wet conditions, with the sections continually collapsing, so we may have missed subtle complexities.

The northwestern edge of the ditch continued beyond our excavation area but the ditch appeared to be 5.40 m long, 2.60 m wide and 1.70 m deep (Figs. 5.16 & 5.21). The sides sloped at 40° down to a flat base. The initial fills consisted of sands, clays and silts with gravels. In the middle of the ditch a 'mushroom' of marl had welled up. The deposits around its top contained some charcoal. The secondary fills consisted of sandy silts and sandy clays with gravel and with no evidence of recutting.

In summary, this ditch showed no evidence of complex sequences of recutting and no finds were recovered from it.

*HAD IX Ditch Q*

In 1987 a small section across the causewayed enclosure ditch was obtained while digging the HAD IX Iron Age enclosure (see Volume 2, Chapter 6; Fig. 5.1). A 12-m length of ditch was uncovered in plan. A causeway immediately to the northeast of the ditch was inferred from the absence of the ditch in a cross-trench. The ditch was 4.30 m wide and the stepped sides and the fills indicated at least three phases of recutting. The primary deposits were collapsed gravels overlain by weathered sandy loam and substantial deposits of marl. The marl was sealed by deposits of sandy silty clay with charcoal, and by a terminal weathering fill of sandy silt loam.

We were beginning to find the same things over and over again. In particular, the sequences of events in the ditches were similar: even evidence that had been collected early on could be 're-read' to fit into the same pattern. Normally we had found multiple phases of early pitting at opposed ends of the ditch, associated with careful cleaning out of earlier fills. The bottom of the ditch was then allowed to fill up quickly with sands, gravels, clays and marl. During this period, items such as skulls, antler, pot and the polished axe were deposited, often on the central axis. The end of this phase of initial ditch filling was usually associated with evidence of charcoal and burning. Recuts also occurred in the secondary, slower fills and there was often evidence of marking the butt ends of the ditches and late pits and post-holes.

Other patterns which were clarified in the 1987 season were that although concentrations of finds and recutting were found to move towards the butt ends in the secondary fills (e.g. Ditches L, N & O) as had been found in 1984, such activities were also concentrated in the butt ends in primary fills (e.g. K, L, M, N & O). In addition, the tendency towards concentrations of activities at the southern ends of ditches was confirmed in many cases but also contradicted in others. It was unclear how far we would be able to argue for such patterns.

Perhaps a greater regularity would occur in relation to entrances. After all, we had excavated in this spot in order to find a major entrance. Had one been found? The answer to this question must partly await the discussion of the palisade but the only obvious 'pairing' of ditches as had been found in 1984 with I and J occurred between N and O, which had the smallest of causeways between them. Clearly this was not a major entrance. We had expected the entrance between M and N. Certainly there was a large causeway here (although no larger than that between O and P), and certainly the southern end of N, nearer the 'entrance', contained much evidence of recutting and finds deposition. But the northern 'entrance' end of M did not contain high densities of artefacts and there was more evidence of recutting at its southern end. Human bone was found in the northern butt end,

but it was difficult to argue on this basis for a major entranceway at this point.

If the variation between ditches could not be related to major entranceways alone, what other factors might be considered? The variation was after all very marked. Some ditches such as K and P were relatively simple, while others such as L, M, N and O were extremely complex in that they had many recuts and deposits of artefacts. In fact, at least in the case of Ditch P, there seemed to be a correlation between little evidence of recutting and few artefacts. This recalled the similar evidence from G and H. In addition, all these 'simple' ditches were relatively small. Perhaps the more complex ditches were larger or were nearer larger ditches than the simple ditches.

Perhaps the most important result of the 1987 season was the vindication of a sequence viewpoint. *What we were digging was not so much 'a thing' as a process.* A certain bipolarity was evident, with repeated evidence of a division of the ditches into two ends. But within this balance seemingly anything could happen. Ditches were continually being recut and realigned, joined up to adjacent ditches or 'paired' with them, divided into shorter ditches and then combined again. It was difficult to see any method in this complexity apart from the duality of ends and the sequential structure outlined above.

We had, in effect, completed the circle. A general understanding of how the ditches were organized had been built up. But archaeology is not simply a matter of amassing objective data in a linear sequence. Rather, we tend to go back, or 'round', to the data that was first collected and reinterpret them in the light of our most recent interpretations. And so all 'data' have a provisional character. We are continually circling back on them to give them new meaning, trying to find an interpretation that makes sense of the whole in terms of the parts and the parts in terms of the whole. So it is necessary to go on round the enclosure again to reconsider our early tentative results. Could we now make sense of our early mistakes?

*The 1981 area — again (the '87 season)*

Towards the end of the 1987 season we began to think that important evidence might have been missed concerning the 1981 site. We had initially tended to assume considerable variability around the enclosure, and so had accepted that the palisade did not exist in the northern part of the enclosure, as it did not seem to exist inside Ditch C in 1982. However, the palisade had now been found everywhere else except Ditch C and we also now knew that the palisade was sometimes set well back from the ditches. In 1981 we had not excavated to the base of the buried soil in the southern part of the main north–south trench. Perhaps the palisade had been missed there. Nor had a ditch been found to the east of Ditch B. Was the causeway there really so big or was it possible that the ditches did not continue around the whole enclosure?

**Table 5.2.** *Summary of the causewayed enclosure ditches (excludes Ditch Q/HAD IX; * bracketed ditch length indicates estimated total segment length). Recuts exclude initial pitting and post-holes and small pits. Finds refers to numbers of lithics and ceramics; bracketed numbers in this category marks where low numbers result from limited amount of excavation of ditch.*

| Ditch (A–R) | Length (m) | Causeway length (I–XIII) (m) | Recuts | Finds | 'Placed' | Human bone |
|---|---|---|---|---|---|---|
| A | 24.4+ (?) | | >2 | (194) | – | – |
| I | | 1.25 | | | | |
| B | c. 3.50 | | ?few | 0 | | |
| II | | 9.50 | | | | |
| R | 7.0+ | | | | – | – |
| C | 7.60+ (14.30*) | | ? | (22) | 1 | – |
| III | | 4.80 | | | | |
| D | 29.2 | | ?several | 38 | 1 | – |
| IV | | 2.60 | | | | |
| E | 6.0+ | | ?none | (12) | – | – |
| F | 6.0+ | | 1–4 | 36 | – | – |
| V | | 1.95 | | | | |
| G | 8.0 | | 1–2 | 23 | – | – |
| VI | | 2.00 | | | | |
| H | 5.8 | | 0–3 | 4 | – | – |
| VII | | 2.65 | | | | |
| I | 7.8 | | 4–7 | 172 | 2 | yes |
| VIII | | 2.80 | | | | |
| J | 13.0+ | | 5–6 | 84 | – | – |
| K | 5.0+ (6.8*) | | 3 | 89 | – | – |
| IX | | 1.60 | | | | |
| L | 9.75 | | 6 | 2 | – | – |
| X | | 2.00 | | | | |
| M | 12.80 | | 5 | 18 | 1 | yes |
| XI | | 3.90 | | | | |
| N | 25.0 | | >6 | 156 | – | yes |
| XII | | 0.50 | | | | |
| O | 7.4 | | 3–4 | 11 | 2 | yes |
| XII | | 4.50 | | | | |
| P | 5.80 | | ? | 0 | 0 | |

In order finally to settle this, in 1987 part of the 1981 trenches were reopened. The information obtained is shown in Figure 5.3. The identification of the small Ditch B had been correct and there was a substantial causeway to its east without features. What had, though, been missed was the beginning of a further ditch to the east (Ditch R, 3.50 m wide and 7.00+ m long). In addition, our trenches had not extended far enough to the south to expose the palisade.

It was also possible to reconsider other aspects of the 1981 data. For example, sense could now be made of the section drawn in the ill-fated machine slot at the western edge of the site (Fig. 5.3). This section now seemed familiar. On the basis of the knowledge from the rest of the enclosure it was realized that the upstanding central block of 'pale orange-grey sand' probably represented a deposit of what we later came to call marl. Less likely, it could have represented a central ridge or mound as in Ditch I. The lens of 'pale grey' above the marl may well have been evidence of burning just beneath or at the base of a secondary recut.

Other evidence too began to make sense. All the late features in the butt end of Ditch A were similar to those found elsewhere (e.g. Ditch O). In fact the pit containing grain in Ditch A suggested

that these later activities may have been more 'occupational' than the earlier activities.

*The ditches: overview*

In writing a summary of the results of the excavations of the ditches the aim is not to reach a point at which we can say 'that's it', except temporarily. There is no finality for a number of reasons. First, different conclusions would have been reached if more of its circuit had been excavated. Second, other data such as the palisade and the finds will need to be considered. In a sense, then, we will be able to keep going round 'the circle' of our interpretations, gradually transforming them through the adjustment to new data. Third, even without new data, interpretations will change in the future as our ideas and theories alter; as we learn to see with new eyes we will come back to the data and look at them from a different angle.

As regards temporal patterning, a 'sequence view' tended to predominate in that the sequences of activities in the ditches seemed complex, even if a minimal view was taken. And yet an overall repeated structure emerged. The early fills were associated with recutting and cleaning out and perhaps with 'placed' deposits (skulls, antler picks, pots and the Langdale axe) although, except in the case of I, these 'placements' could be unintentional products of rapid early infilling. Later fills were associated with burning and further recutting. In both, recutting concentrated at the ends of ditches. The differences between early and late fills could be seen in terms of a shift from 'ritual' practices to a wider range of activities, but again depositional factors could explain the changes observed. The pit with grain in the upper fill in Ditch A (F.15) and the often higher densities of material in the upper fills might support such a view. But it is also possible that initial rapid weathering and collapse infilling protected artefacts (which thus look 'placed') and produced lower densities of material than the upper horizons. The evidence of burning in the upper deposits, especially in the earliest upper fills, must be distinguished from post-depositional processes. The regularity of this pattern must raise the possibility that the supposed burned deposits are actually reduced soils enriched with migrated manganese. However, sufficient amounts of charcoal were identified in the basal upper fills to indicate burning, although in only one case (Ditch C) was this associated with reddened surrounding deposits indicating *in situ* burning. Most of the charcoal in the fills would appear to be secondary.

Another possible shift through time concerns closure. Many of the recuttings resulted in elongation or linkages and the closure of gaps. Ditches F and G came to be joined together and the recutting of I and J led to a narrower causeway between them. This indication of closure through time will be explored further in relation to the palisade. At least we can say that sequences of digging and redigging in the ditches were often long and complex. However, the degree of temporal sequencing in the ditches partly depends on spatial variation.

In summarizing the complex spatial data, Table 5.2 may be helpful. However, any table presents data as if they were devoid of interpretative dimensions. We looked at the 1982 ditches, for example, with a gaze different from that in 1987; consequently the data are not equivalent. The number of recuts identified in a ditch was contingent upon our knowledge and approach (i.e. the event or the sequence view). The table therefore does violence to the archaeological process. In interpreting it we must bear in mind the lower level interpretations that have already been made.

It was immediately clear from a consideration of the evidence that some ditches were more elaborate than others in that they had more recuts, greater placed deposits and finds, and further evidence of burning and human bone. Also clear was that these more elaborate ditches tended to occur together. Thus in 1984 Ditches G & H formed a pair of simple ditches (perhaps linked with F) in contrast to the more elaborate pair I & J. In 1987, the sequence started and ended with the simple Ditches K & P, whereas in between were found increasingly and then decreasingly complex ditches (L, M, N & O).

The clusters of more elaborate ditches might have been thought to relate to the position of major entrances into the enclosure. The difficulty here, in interpreting the evidence, is that our excavation strategy had been guided by the idea of entrances. We had not, therefore, excavated in areas without what looked like major entrances, except in 1981 when the evidence was in any case difficult to interpret. As is always the case, our excavation strategy had to some extent ensured that we found what we were looking for. In 1982 we had expected an entrance between Ditches C & D. The causeway between these ditches was indeed wider than many, special deposits were found in the southern terminal of C and a high density of finds in the northern half of D. These aspects of the evidence might have been taken to indicate an entrance at this point, but on the other hand, the special placed deposits in D occurred in the central part of the ditch. In 1984 the evidence for a major entrance was stronger. A wider causeway between I & J (6.80 m) was later narrowed (to 2.80 m) and a corresponding gap in the palisade was also possibly closed. Both Ditches I & J were complex, with evidence of a shift through time to parallel activities in the butt ends which faced each other across the causeway. I & J were the only very elaborate ditches in the 1984 sequence. In 1987 the evidence again initially seemed to fit the entrance hypothesis. There was indeed a larger gap between M & N and some concentration of activities in the corresponding butt ends. However, the main concentration of activities in M was at the 'wrong', southern end of the ditch. In addition, the clear pairing of Ditches N & O could not have been a major entrance since the causeway was only 0.50 m wide.

Perhaps the notion of major entranceways with activities concentrated round them would have to form part of our overall interpretation, and this possibility will be explored further by considering the palisade (see below). We had identified 'entrance ways' from the patterning of ditches on the aerial photographs. On the ground, other wide causeways might have been equally good candidates. We came across these despite our excavation strategy. The largest causeway was between Ditches B & R. Ditch R was not excavated at all and B was incompletely excavated in 1981. Nevertheless, Ditch B was carefully excavated in its upper fills and it produced few finds and none of the obvious recuts seen in Ditch A. There was also a wide causeway between Ditches O & P, and again Ditch P was one of the simplest excavated.

A major difficulty in the discussion of major entrances is that these may have been partly defined as entrances by reference to a bank system which no longer survives. Nevertheless, in terms of the evidence available to us, the entrance hypothesis seemed at least incomplete since there were pairings of complex ditches which were not entrances and other wide causeways without elaborate ditches. The evidence would not directly fit together by taking this line of reasoning. However, this is a complex issue and will be further explored at length below (see **Context and enclosure**).

The group of elaborate ditches in 1987 seemed larger than could be explained by reference to any putative entrance. Four ditches (L, M, N & O) were involved here. An alternative 'whole' which might begin to make sense of the data was that the more elaborate ditch sequences occurred in relationship to longer ditch segments. The lengths of ditches in the 1987 season gradually increased and then decreased from K to P. In the middle of the elaborate ditches was Ditch N, 25 m long. Similarly in 1984, one of the elaborate pair of ditches (I & J) was very long (J being 19 m). Indeed, we had not excavated any long ditch which was simple. In 1982 we had excavated Ditch D which was 29.2 m long and our re-interpretation of this ditch suggested that it too must have been relatively elaborate with possible 'placed' deposits and sequential digging or recutting.

The link between ditch length and complexity is shown in Table 5.2. Here it is clear that long ditches were both more elaborate themselves and were surrounded by more elaborate ditches. Of course, it is to be expected that longer ditches will produce more finds, given an even density around the circuit. However, as we shall see in the discussion of the pottery finds from the ditches, different densities occur at different levels within them. In addition there are clear differences in overall densities in different areas. For example, lower densities occur in the 1982 area so that an extremely long section of ditch (Ditch D) has a comparatively low frequency of artefacts. Also, Ditch I, which is relatively short, has a very high concentration of finds. This concentration relates not so much to the length of the ditch as to the complexity of activities and recuts in Ditch I (which, of course, was excavated almost in its entirety, thereby further biasing the representation/frequency of finds).

Artefact frequencies in ditches are thus not determined by the length of ditch as they would be if there was an even distribution of finds around the circuit. The high frequencies in I, however, awaken us to the possibility that higher frequencies of artefacts occur where more of a ditch was excavated. Certainly the complexities of Ditch I resulted in extensive excavation. However, D was also extensively excavated and produced low frequencies. Such factors, while playing a role, do not alter the fact that extremely low densities of artefacts tended to occur in less complex and smaller ditches.

Overall, the frequencies of lithics and ceramics in ditch segments are certainly affected by a range of complex factors. Even if such correlations are discounted, there is undoubtedly a link seen in Table 5.2 between ditch length or proximity to long ditches and intensity of recutting. How might we interpret this pattern, which is itself an interpretation? We need to start by establishing what type of social unit was represented by the ditches. It is difficult to argue that they simply represent work units which came together merely to dig the ditch. The process involved more than digging a lobate hollow in the ground. The

'hole' or pit was carefully cleaned out and remodelled and deposits including human bones were sometimes placed in it. This use of the ditch through time showed clear evidence of continuity. Complex primary deposits were often followed by complex secondary fills and *vice versa*. The specific uses of the ditches also showed continuities. For example the central mound was reformed in Ditch I. These various continuities through a range of different activities imply that more than a work 'gang' was involved. Rather, the ditches related to units which had a longer duration, and therefore a distinct social and structural identity.

Let us assume, therefore, that the size of the ditch, the way it was dug and maintained, and the depositional practices within it were partly a matter of social display. Larger or more successful groups were able to mobilize more labour. Perhaps the digging, care and use of the ditches helped to define social status. The ditches were not, however, independent of each other. Adjacent ditches were often similar, they often seemed 'paired' across causeways and sometimes they were physically joined or brought closer through time. Perhaps it could be further assumed, therefore, that the groups which excavated and used adjacent ditches were more closely related than those which used distant ditches. Those groups or work units which constructed and used ditches near the larger ditches may have formed a larger grouping that benefited from the greater success of the larger ditch unit. The ditch cluster as a whole was able to gain access to more labour through time to tend to cleaning and recutting of the ditches, was more able to gain access to prestigious goods (such as polished axes), and was more able to conduct depositional and burial rituals. Peripheral or smaller groups were less able to become involved in these activities.

The potentially competitive nature of ditch digging and use activities is seen clearly through time. As already noted, the enclosure was less a thing than a process. Ditches were continually being subdivided or joined. Emphasis changed from ditch centres to terminals or from one terminal to its opposite. Within the overall unity or 'whole' of the enclosure there was tension at various scales. At one scale, we could see from the aerial photographs that some ditches were larger than others, and this variability was confirmed in the excavations of the ditches. At another scale, the common structure of the ditches was continually being transformed. If a link is made between the ditches and social units, the ditch evidence seems to be telling us that social alliances were continually being realigned and renegotiated.

To some degree we have done little more than define 'elite' and 'non-elite' groups, but in relation to ditches rather than to burials or houses. However, three further important claims have been made. First, the social structure has been argued to be organized but competitive and continually negotiated and changing. Second, a basis for the definition of social groupings has begun to be defined. While access to polished axes and other exchange goods and involvement in burial rituals may have formed components of social position, the component most directly observable to us at the enclosure was the deployment of labour. The most elaborate ditches were those associated most closely with ditches in which most earth had been moved, both initially and in the later recutting. Third, we have implicitly begun to make assumptions about the ideas which lay behind the competitive display and the control of labour. These ideas involved defining and perhaps even defending the enclosure, and behind all this must be a sense of the motivating 'content' and implied 'idea' of *enclosure* itself. The contribution of the segmented labour activities was to the formation of a larger entity. But that larger entity was formed in a specific way: the movement of large amounts of soil and digging into the ground. Deposits may have been specially placed in the ditches as they were filling up. Somehow or other, in ways which remain to be explored, the digging of and deposition within the ground defined not only the larger enclosure group but also the way in which that group expressed competitive endeavours.

## The palisade

Unlike causewayed enclosure ditches, which have been the subject of much debate concerning their supposedly ritual nature, few causewayed enclosures with palisades have been excavated. It was therefore approached with very different expectations. Our initial assumptions were that this feature would be relatively simple and without obvious ritual. Functional questions concerned whether the palisade could have revetted or been part of a bank, and whether it was defensive. The major difficulty was expected to be one of dating. How could it be determined whether the ditches and palisade were contemporary? From the aerial photographs it was clear that the gaps in the palisade sometimes corresponded to the causeways between the ditches. They had to be at least partly contemporary, but were they entirely so?

It was not expected that the answer to this question would necessarily be simple. As already noted, it was initially assumed that there would be considerable variability around the enclosure and it was expected that the palisade would reflect this. It did not unduly worry us, therefore, when we did not

discover the palisade in 1981. The 1987 re-excavation of the 1981 area showed that the trenches had not extended far enough into the interior of the enclosure to pick up the palisade, which at this point lay well within the ditches (by 13.50 m). However, even if our trenches had extended far enough, we would probably have missed the palisade, which, as all the subsequent excavations showed, was not visible at the top of the buried soil.

### The 1982 exposure

Since the buried soil was removed by machine down to the underlying sands and gravels in 1982, we were able to identify the palisade to the west of Ditches D & E (Figs. 5.5 & 5.22). On average, the palisade lay 1.50 m inside the ditches. The southerly segment (F.40) was 6.35 m long but continued beyond the excavated area. There was then a small (0.70 m wide) gap before reaching the fully excavated segment (F.49).

F.49 was 31.75 m long but was actually composed of three straight segments of 11.50 m, 10.50 m and 9.75 m from south to north respectively. At the time, little was read into this; however, it is tempting to equate the tripartite division of the palisade trench with the division of Ditch D into two deeper ends and a shallower and narrower central section. Indeed, the palisade trench did not follow the alignment of Ditch D exactly. Rather, it bowed inwards, leaving a larger gap between the palisade and the ditch in the centre and north than in the south. The relationship between the ditch and palisade was clearly complex and could have been built up through time.

The trench for the palisade was very deep and regular (average depth 0.95 m below surface of buried soil). The top width varied from 0.30–0.80 m and was on average 0.50–0.60 m wide. While the upper portion of the trench was somewhat broken and sloped more gently and irregularly, with depth the sides were very steep, nearly vertical, coming down to a flat or slightly rounded base which generally was 0.25 m wide. At some points along the trench the interior (western) side sloped more gradually than the more vertical eastern profile. This difference in slope between the interior and exterior sides could have been produced by the setting or removing of the palisade timbers from the interior aspect.

Only at the northern end of F.49 was there a clear post-cut within the palisade trench. The terminal was quite bulbous, being 0.55 m across at the top and containing a sub-circular hollow at the base (0.36 × 0.48 m across and 0.08 m deep). This evidence might have been taken to support the idea of a major entrance between Ditches C & D. However, although the southern terminal of F.49 did not contain a separate post cut, it did bulge (0.65 m wide) and had a sub-circular butt-end.

The fill and packing of the palisade trench was a mixture of redeposited natural gravels and grey-brown silty clay, often quite compacted. Careful examination of the upper fills of the palisade trench revealed a number of post impressions. Very elusive and difficult to define and excavate, these consisted of a looseness of compaction and a higher proportion of clay/silt to gravel than in the surrounding packing. They were sub-circular in plan with an average diameter of 0.30 m and varied in depth from 0.35–0.70 m. When recovered in any number they were an average distance of 0.35–0.40 m apart along the centre of the trench. While it is possible that the post impressions were the products of the decay of original posts left *in situ*, the irregular impressions may have been the result of the removal of the posts at a later date. This interpretation would explain the lack of a markedly different fill in these holes which might otherwise have been present if the posts had rotted *in situ*. Moreover, the lack of definition of the sides of the post impressions could have come about through the removal of the posts and the

269

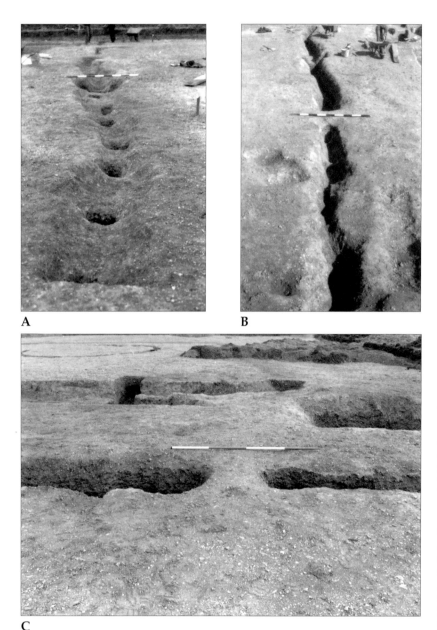

A

B

C

**Figure 5.22.** *HAD '82. The palisade: A) looking south along F.40 length with post pipes excavated; B) looking north along partially excavated profile of F.40 to segment F.49; C) looking east with the interruption F.40 and F.49 palisade segments in foreground (with the causeway between Ditches D & E behind; photographs G. Owen).*

features appeared to have been natural in origin. However, their roughly linear distribution parallel to the palisade trenches suggested some relationship with the palisade. Perhaps they represented a hedge or bushes growing at the exterior base of the palisade. It was also possible that the troughs and hollows were the remains of an insubstantial hurdle or fence.

This ephemeral evidence of more than one phase of palisade drew attention again to the complex nature of Ditch D and its relationship to palisade F.49. The overall impression from the changes in alignment of the ditch and palisade and from the possible hurdle/fence was that this part of the site had been remodelled through time.

Almost no finds were found in the palisade trench fills, implying little occupational use of the soils before and during construction. The palisade was well built but had possibly gone through phases of remodelling in line with changes to the ditches themselves. The gaps in the palisade closely followed those in the ditches, suggesting at least partial contemporaneity. No evidence was found in the fills of the palisade trench of a collapsed interior bank. If the palisade did revet a bank, what was its function? Was it constructed early or late in the use of the ditches?

*The 1984 exposure*
The most obvious difference in the character of the palisade in this area from the 1982 palisade was that it was set well back from the ditch, the distance in the south part of the excavated area being 11.0 m, and in the north 8.5 m (Fig. 5.10). Its 'line' also differed in other ways. In particular, the link between breaks in the palisade and ditch causeways was much less clear, and the palisade itself showed much greater variation along its length. There was also a high density of finds at least in part of its length.

In general terms the palisade trench had a similar form to that in 1982, with sloping upper and near vertical lower sides, and a flat to concave base. However, it varied considerably in depth from 0.50 m (below the surface of the buried soil) to 1.05 m. The trench was 0.35–0.40 m wide at the top and 0.05–0.15 m across at the base. As in 1982, the inner edge of the trench tended to have a more gentle slope at the top.

The fills typically consisted of *c.* 0.10 m of basal coarse sandy silt. Above this and along the sides of the trench was a packing of fine sand with gravel. Down the central axis of the trench was a band 0.10–0.20 m wide, presumably representing a slot for post settings since it extended down to the basal fills. In one place gravel packing had fallen in on top of the slot from the interior of the enclosure. Despite this evidence of dismantling or collapse, post impressions were seen in the central slot along the central part of the 1984 pali-

subsequent collapse of the packing. The somewhat broader and broken upper portion of the palisade trench could have been produced during this digging out of the posts.

At the northern end of the palisade trench F.49 a series of minor irregular hollows ran roughly parallel with the palisade, 0.70 m to its east. At first these appeared as a continuous strip, 7 m long and 0.20–0.40 m wide. As the fill was removed, a series of irregular shallow troughs and hollows was identified. The features were filled with silty clay. A similar irregular linear trough was found at the southern end of the site, just to the east of F.40. Owing to their irregularity and homogeneous fills devoid of cultural material, these

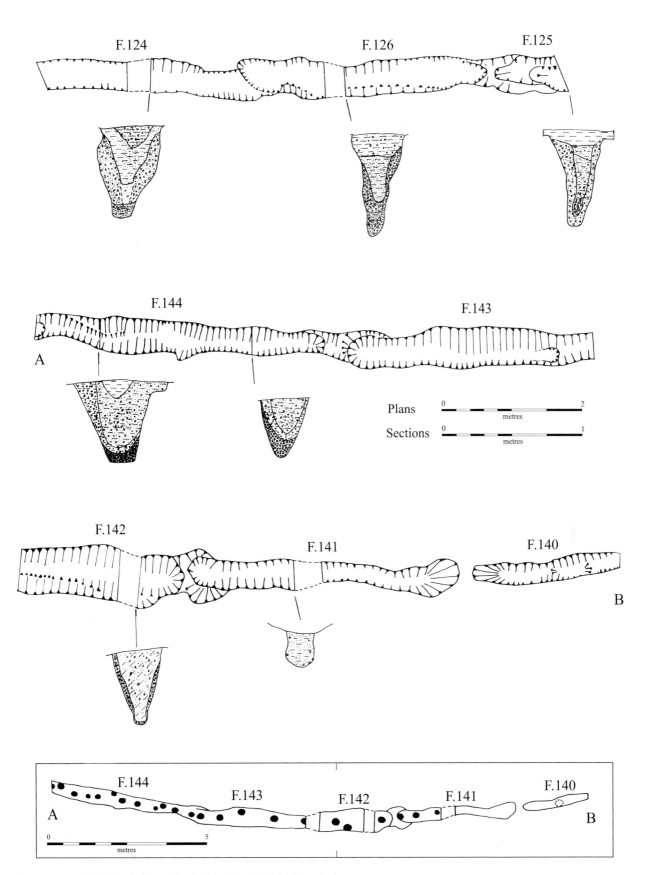

**Figure 5.23.** *HAD '84: the palisade (see Fig. 5.10 for location).*

271

sade (Fig. 5.23); 25 impressions were found. Set 0.20–0.25 m apart in well-preserved sections, these were approximately 0.10–0.20 m wide and 0.10–0.35 m deep. They were identified as darker grey clay/silt patches, difficult to define but in one case apparently representing half a timber with the flat surface facing into the interior. In some cases charcoal was associated with these post impressions.

The palisade was less substantial towards the south. Here a short segment (F.140) 2.60 m long sloped down gradually from north to south, but even at the southern end where it left the excavated area was only 0.60 m deep. There was no gravel packing and only one possible post impression. A 0.20-m gap separated the F.140 segment from F.141 to the north. This could be seen to correspond to the causeway between Ditches G & H.

F.141 may have been part of a longer section of palisade, but it was initially dug as a separate segment 3.80 m long. This was again very shallow, being only 0.50 m deep in part and having no evidence of packing. It did, however, have clear impressions of posts. A small 10-cm-wide ridge in the base of the palisade trench separated the F.141 segment from the F.142/3 segment. This ridge corresponded with a mid point on Ditch H rather than with any causeway, and the post impressions showed no gap at this point.

The F.142/3 segment was 6.20 m long although a slight ridge occurred half way along. The bulbous northern terminal had been redefined several times by recutting. The trench was up to 0.70 m deep and the fills showed evidence of gravel packing. The separation of the F.142/3 segment may again only have been constructional since the post impressions showed no gap to the north where F.144 continued the line of the palisade. However, this better defined palisade segment (F.142/3) corresponded to the shift from Ditch H to the more complex Ditch I. Indeed, the recutting at the northern end of F.142/3 was parallel with the southern part of Ditch I: palisade and ditches thus increased in complexity in tandem.

A ridge 0.40 m wide separated F.142/3 from the next palisade segment F.144. This was 6.80 m long and the base sloped downwards from 0.60 m deep at the south to 0.80 m deep near the northern, upward sloping butt end (F.125). Gravel packing was found at the sides of the trench.

A narrow ridge 0.10 m wide separated F.142/3 from the next segment F.126 and once again there was no evidence of a break in the palisade at this point. However, there was good stratigraphical evidence to demonstrate that the F.126 segment had been added later, either into a gap in the palisade or as a rebuilding. The F.126 palisade segment was 3.6 m long and up to 0.90 m deep with near-vertical sides, and had clear evidence of gravel packing. No post impressions were identified. In plan the southern end tapered to a blunt point 0.10 m wide, while the northern end was slightly bulbous and protruded slightly into the interior of the enclosure. This minor break in alignment corresponded with evidence that F.126 had cut into the gravel packing on the west side of F.124, the palisade segment to the north. There was no trace of any earlier palisade trench beneath F.126, although any earlier feature may have been entirely removed. It was of immediate interest, however, that F.126 corresponded with the southerly extension of Ditch J. Both F.126 and the late extension of Ditch J may have been involved in the same process of restricting entrances into the enclosure. The evidence from F.126 also raised the issue of whether other segments of the 1984 palisade varied in date. No evidence of this had been found so far, but it was quite possible that segments F.140, F.141 or F.142/3 had been placed in the palisade at a later date.

The F.124 segment continued north beyond the excavated area but was observed over 3 m. The trench was up to 1.05 m deep with collapsed gravel packing and central slot. There were no post impressions.

Progressing northward, the ditches had become increasingly more complex (I & J) with more recutting.

Similarly, as one moved northwards along the palisade it became deeper, with clearer evidence of gravel packing and with clearer evidence of recutting/resetting. This evidence, therefore, supported the impression gained in 1982 that the palisade and ditches were closely contemporary. There was also a certain sequential similarity in that the post impressions seemed to have been associated with burning, recalling the late posts and burning in several of the ditches.

On the other hand, evidence from 1984 suggested that the link between the palisade and the ditches was less strong than in the 1982 area. In the first place, the palisade was set well back from the ditches. Secondly, the gaps or breaks in the palisade did not appear to correspond with the causeways between the ditches.

The latter point involved several uncertainties. Superficially, all the 1984 palisade, except the small southern F.140 segment, could have been seen as one continuous stretch. The evidence from the post impressions certainly suggested that for much of its length the palisade had been continuous. Even the gap between F.140 and F.141 was only 0.20 m wide. Thus anyone entering the enclosure through this area's causeways would at some point in time have been met by a continuous barrier allowing only limited entry.

However, part of the palisade (F.126) was added later and may have filled in an earlier gap corresponding to the earlier causeway between Ditches I & J. Other segmented extensions of the palisade appeared to be constructional, but it was also possible that they too represented later closing of gaps in the palisade. For example, F. 142/3 could have filled a gap corresponding to the causeway between Ditches H & I, while F. 140 could have acted in the same way for the causeway between Ditches G & H.

The combined evidence from the 1982 and 1984 palisade indicated that the palisade and ditches were at least partially contemporary. But it was also possible that the palisade was associated with a late use of the enclosure. The 1984 ditches had provided evidence of gradual restriction of access through time. For example, Ditches F & G had been joined at a later date in their use and the gap between I & J had been narrowed. The palisade as a whole, or at least the filling in of any gaps in it, may also have played a part in this process of closure.

There was little evidence in the fills of the palisade for a substantial bank behind it. In any case, the soil from the ditches would have been unlikely to have been placed behind a palisade at such a distance from them. A close functional link between ditches and palisade was therefore not warranted.

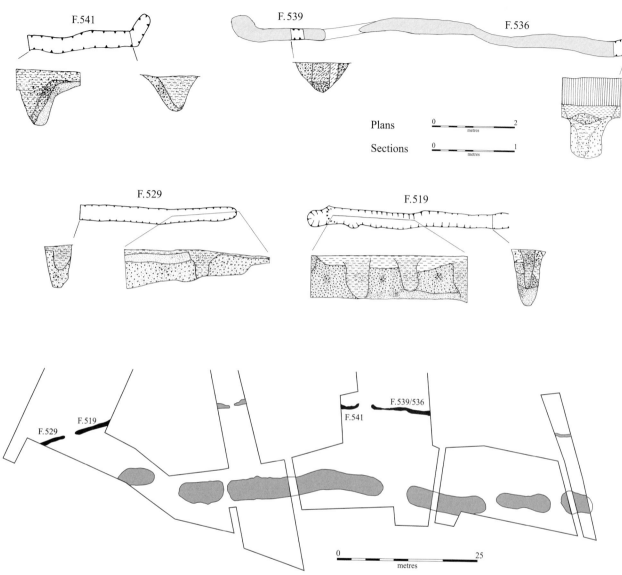

**Figure 5.24.** *HAD '87. The palisade: entranceway details.*

## The 1987 exposure

It was difficult to distinguish all the segments of the palisade trench shown in Figures 5.16 & 5.24. Even after removal of the buried soil down to the underlying Pleistocene deposits, we still could not see the palisade in the southern part of the site. This was because the fluvio-glacial deposits here consisted largely of leached clays in which features were difficult to define. Therefore, the machine had to brought back in to remove 0.20–0.30 m of the top of the Pleistocene deposits before its line could be distinguished.

The palisade trench varied from 0.70–0.90 m deep below the surface of the buried soil. The sides were generally near vertical, producing a trench 0.40 m wide at the top and 0.10 m wide at the flat to slightly concave base. The butt ends of the trenches sloped upwards more gradually. The packing fills consisted of clay silts, sandy silts or sands and gravels depending on the surrounding subsoils. In cross-section we were able to see, as before, the impressions of posts filled with darker, grey sands and silts, sometimes with evidence of charcoal, as if at least some of the posts had burnt in position. It was decided to build on the 1984 discovery of lines

of post pipes by again excavating in longitudinal sections along its length. This showed the post pipes very clearly as being 0.40–0.50 m deep (0.60–0.70 m below surface of the buried soil) and 0.20–0.35 m wide. The post pipes were set 0.28–0.45 m apart with a strong tendency to be spaced at intervals of 0.40 m.

The southern section of the palisade (F.548) was especially difficult to define. It was 3 m long, showed a slight kink in the middle but otherwise gave no indication of having been segmented at any time. To the north, the F.536 segment was 6.25 m long but was clearly divided into two sections (the northern being 2.75 m long) by a 1-m-long narrower central portion. The two sections were on different alignments. This was the longest section excavated in 1987 and was thus the only one to confirm the evidence from 1984 that the palisade was divided into smaller segments. F.536 was separated from the short (2.3-m-long) F.539 segment of palisade by a 0.75-m gap. Originally, F.539 and F.536 may have been continuous with a shallower portion between them. As already noted, in some areas such as this we had to machine deeper into the subsoil in order to define the palisade, but doing so removed its upper portion.

273

F.539 and F.541 were considered important lengths of the palisade because they both appeared to have inturned ends which formed an entrance approximately in line with the putative major entrance between Ditches M & N. F.541 was found over a 2.80 m length in the excavated area and the inward turning southern end was clear. However, the paired inturn at the northern end of F. 539 appeared on excavation to have been a tree-root hollow, although an earlier inturn could have been masked by this. The palisade trench was not particularly substantial at this point (only up to 0.78 m deep) and there was no concentration of finds. It was difficult to make a major entrance out of this evidence, especially since in fact it would not line up exactly with the causeway between Ditches M & N.

The two short excavated sections F.531 and F.530 were separated by another entrance gap, 0.90 m wide. F.530 tapered to a point at the entrance and its base sloped downwards to the north. However, in both ditches the butt ends were clearly defined, with the end wall of the trench sloping upwards at 45°. The gap at this point might have been related to the very narrow causeway between Ditches N & O, but once again the relationship was not precise.

F.519 and F.529 presented a similar pairing, with the base of the northern trench sloping downwards to the north. The gap was here 1.65 m wide.

The small section of the palisade excavated in 1987 in the HAD IX area was 10.5 m within the ditch circuit (Fig. 5.1). The base was estimated to be 0.60–0.70 m below the buried soil surface and the sides sloped steeply to a flat base 0.20–0.25 m across. The fill of the trench had a relatively high concentration of charcoal flecks and there was evidence of post pipes.

The evidence from the palisade sections F.536 and F.539 again showed that the palisade had probably been constructed in segments. But in 1987 distinct entrances were more frequent than in 1984. Two of the three openings corresponded only inexactly to the causeways. The other palisade gap occurred to the north of the excavated ditches but could have corresponded to a causeway north of Ditch P. The imprecise link between palisade interruptions and causeways may have been related to the considerable distance between the palisade and ditch circuits at this point. In this area the distance between the palisade and the ditches varied from 7.60 m to 12.0 m.

The finds densities from the palisade trench were very low in contrast to 1984. There were also other differences between the two areas. In particular, while the 1984 palisade had by the end of its life severely restricted access into the enclosure, the 1987 palisade retained more entrances, one of which was elaborated by an inturn.

*The palisade: overview*

The palisade had first been found in 1982, where it was set close to the ditches. In the same way our interpretations began by being closely linked to those of the ditches. For example, the close spatial linkages suggested a similar date for both circuits and a similar function. In addition, the segmentation of the palisade seemed to mirror that in Ditch D. But as the excavations progressed round the enclosure, interpretations of the two types of circuit began to diverge, as indeed did the interrelationship between the circuits. By the time we had returned to the 1981 excavation and re-excavated it in 1987 in order to locate the palisade, we had amassed evidence for considerable differences between palisade and ditches. The palisade at this point was a full 13.5 m within the ditches, whereas it had started at a distance of 1.5 m in 1982. In between, in 1984 and 1987 the distance varied from 7.6 m to 12.0 m.

The difference in interpretation partly concerned function and social role. On the one hand, both palisade and ditches had evidence of segmented construction. Segmentation of the palisade was seen in the F.49 section in 1982, in 1984, and in F.536 and F.539 in 1987. Both the palisade and ditches had evidence of recutting. In the case of the palisade this, for example, was perhaps represented by the 'hedge' in 1982 and was clearly evident in the F.126 insert in 1984. Despite these similarities, it was undoubtedly the case that the palisade had less evidence of recutting than the complex ditches, nor did it have 'placed' deposits and there was nothing that could be termed 'ritual'.

The difference in interpretation mainly concerned date. As we moved round the enclosure the palisade became farther removed from the ditches. In addition, the detailed correspondence between palisade gaps and ditch causeways became increasingly inexact. Already in 1982 it had been noted that the alignments of Ditch D and the F.49 palisade were different. But in 1984 and 1987 it was not always clear that specific gaps in the palisade could be equated with ditch causeways.

It was impossible to deny all association, however. The link between gaps and causeways in 1982 had been precise, and in 1984 increasing complexity of both ditches and palisade towards the north end of the excavated area was noted. It was also not to be denied that an inturned entrance in the palisade occurred at approximately the place where an entrance through the ditches had been seen on the aerial photographs (between Ditches M & N).

How is a compromise to be reached between the similarities and differences between the palisade and ditches? The 1984 evidence offered the most elegant solution. Here the closure of the palisade by F.126 related to the late narrowing of the causeway between Ditches I and J. The general nature of the palisade in the 1984 area was to close off the enclosure and this was a tendency also noted in the late joining of Ditches F and G. An overlapping, but late date for the palisade was also suggested by the evidence of burning of the palisade, perhaps associated with the burnt layers and features towards the tops of some of the ditches.

But as with the ditches it would be wrong to assume an overall unity of purpose for the palisade. In general terms, the different excavated portions of the palisade were very similar. The trench was always similar in form and the fills were comparable. In several places the inner edge of the trench sloped more markedly, implying that the posts had been set or removed from the interior of the enclosure. However, there was also considerable variation around the enclosure, not only in relation to the distance between palisade and ditches, but also, for example, in the size, depth and spacing of post impressions. In 1982 and 1987 the impressions were up to 0.50 m deep, 0.30 m wide and set about 0.40 m apart. In 1984, however, the impressions were up to 0.35 m deep, 0.15 m wide and 0.20–0.25 m apart. There was also variation in finds densities, with few finds found in the palisade in 1982 and 1987 but many in 1984.

The overall evidence supports the notion that the palisade, like the ditches, was involved in the social actions of related but distinct groups. That these were not just haphazard work gangs is suggested by the link between ditches and palisade in 1984, where the northern, more elaborate ditches were parallel with the more complex palisade sections. It was not just the construction of the palisade and ditches which were involved, but their use. Through time, then, groups built portions of the palisade as part of the endeavour to contribute to the enclosure as a whole. The palisade could be used to realign relationships between groups, sometimes restricting movement to and from the interior of the enclosure, sometimes drawing attention to major entrances.

In none of the palisade sections did the fill indicate the presence of an interior bank. In 1982, where the palisade was closest to the ditches there was no evidence from the ditch fills that the palisade had held up a substantial bank which had then slipped into the ditch. Perhaps, however, the palisade, being partially later than the ditches, had prevented such slippage. This issue was specifically addressed through the buried soil sampling programme and is discussed below.

## The interior

As outlined above, only limited areas in the interior, and those mainly adjacent to the enclosure's circuit, were investigated. The major questions here were whether there was evidence for occupation inside the enclosure, whether there was variation in activities in different parts of the enclosure, and if there was evidence of a bank.

While most of the buried soil across the interior of the enclosure had been protected in historic times by overlying peat and alluvium, we came to understand that the soil over the enclosure had been ploughed in later prehistory (see Volume 2, Chapters 2, 3 & 5). Little pottery and bone was found in the buried soil, largely because of its poor survival in highly acidic soils, and therefore the main evidence for Neolithic and Bronze Age activity was derived from flint distributions. In compensation, various then-experimental techniques were attempted, including an early use of radar in 1981, and in 1982 the buried soil horizon was subject to intense phosphate sampling. The results, however, proved negative and the causewayed enclosure's circuit failed to be distinguished through these methods (in the case of the phosphate survey this must reflect the impact of later prehistoric arable activity; see Chapter 4, Fig. 4.10).

As discussed in Chapter 4, sampling of the buried soil within and outside the enclosure had produced flint densities varying from 1 to 8 pieces per square metre, but with an overall concentration in the western central part of the enclosure (Spread A).

In 1981 much effort was expended on understanding the character of the buried soil and large numbers of flints were collected from it. Since the amount of soil excavated from different parts of the buried soil was measured, it was possible to quantify the density of worked flint in the buried soil. The densities found varied from 0.01 to >0.8 per 1500 cc (Fig. 5.2). The density of flints dropped off markedly below 0.05 m from the top of the buried soil. These 1981 densities therefore can be estimated to equate to between 0.04 and 3.2 flints per square metre. The densities, although low, were higher inside the enclosure ditches where they commonly ranged from 1–3 per sq. m, but were very low outside, where they seldom reached above one flint. These slightly higher densities inside the ditch circuit support a relationship between the flint densities and the enclosure interior, as had indeed been suggested by the sampling survey. However, very little worked flint was found in the causewayed enclosure ditches themselves in 1981, implying that there were few flints in the surrounding soil when the ditches filled up. On the other hand, high flint densities were associated with the secondary features in the butt end of Ditch A. It seems possible that the flint distribution largely relates to secondary activity, perhaps of a more domestic nature, associated with the recuts in the main 1981 ditches (A & B).

Given the overall low density of worked flint found in the 1981 area, it is not surprising that only two features were found, both outside the enclosure, which were, like the causewayed enclosure ditches, earlier than the soil and peat formation over the buried soil. A small pit or hearth (F.5) 0.91 m across and 0.41 m deep below the buried soil contained a large amount of charcoal, bone, flint flakes and a core. Also found was the butt end of a flat bottomed ditch (F.8), 0.90 m deep. In the base of the butt end was found a centrally placed stake-hole (Fig. 5.3).

In 1982, two methods were used to collect worked flints from the buried soil. First, they were recovered during the cleaning of the surface of the soil. Second, before the removal of the soil by machine, 66 1-metre square samples were excavated on a 5-m grid (Figs. 5.4 & 5.8). In the latter case densities could be adjusted by the amount of earth obtained from each square and all the sampled

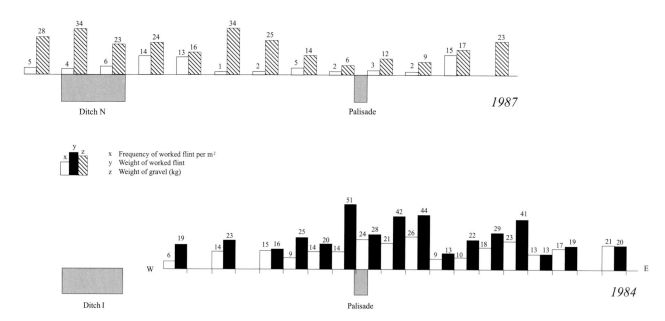

**Figure 5.25.** *HAD '84 & '87: sieve transects (see Figs. 5.10 & 5.16 for location).*

soil was sieved. As can be seen from Figure 5.8, both techniques produced the same results: very low densities of finds (0–3 flints per metre square on average, the greatest amount being 7) with little evidence of variation across the site. These densities correlated with the paucity of finds in the ditches and palisade trench fills. Given such low numbers of finds any spatial patterning was difficult to discern, but slightly higher densities were recovered over the ditch and just outside of the enclosure.

The low densities of finds in 1982 related to a paucity of features. Some 22 m west of the main enclosure ditches, within the interior of the enclosure, was found a cremation containing Collared Urn sherds (F.46). A circular pit (0.43 × 0.44 m) with nearly vertical sides and a flat base (0.12 m deep below base of buried soil) contained a black silt loam with 'peaty' pockets, frequent charcoal flecks, numerous pottery fragments, and a few small pieces of calcined bone. In the same manner as the enclosure ditch, this feature was not visible at the surface of the buried soil. (The recovery of this apparently isolated urn-accompanied cremation is paralleled both in later investigations within the Delphs environs (Flat Bridge Farm; see Volume 2, Chapter 6) and also at Over (Pollard 1998). Their occurrence clearly raises crucial issues as to who warranted, and were otherwise potentially excluded from, barrow and/or cemetery interment.)

As noted above, in 1984 the buried soil was removed by machine so that information on flint densities within it could only be obtained from a transect of 1-m squares left running across the lines of the ditch and palisade (Figs. 5.10 & 5.26). The area of excavation lay adjacent to the Spread A higher worked-flint concentration identified in the 50-m grid sampling squares (see Chapter 4; Fig. 4.8). It was thus of immediate interest that the densities of flint recovered in 1984 were much higher than in previous years. As can be seen from Figure 5.25 the densities ranged from 6–26 per sq. m and averaged 15.9 per unit. There was little evidence of spatial patterning apart from a slight rise in densities immediately behind and above the palisade. This concentration of worked flint might represent the redeposition of soil (and artefacts therein) in a slight bank behind the palisade, although no evidence of the collapse of a gravel bank into the palisade trench was identified. Alternatively, the slight concentration might have represented middening along the margins of the enclosure within the palisade.

The recovery of the highest density of flints in this area obviously related to the complexity of the ditch sequences at this point, and the fact that where the palisade had not only been reworked but had itself contained high densities of flint in its fills. The overall complexity of Ditches I and J had therefore to be related to a whole sector of the enclosure involving ditches, palisade and interior.

There were in fact more features found in the buried soil in 1984 than in any other year, although it was always difficult to distinguish natural hollows from cut features and precise dating was difficult. The only 'real' small pits and post-holes were [1949], [1961], [1962] and a cluster of comparable features within the palisade opposite Ditch I (Figs. 5.10 & 5.26). Generally having leached grey sandy loam and gravel fills these were:

[1710]: An oval pit, 0.75 × 0.65 m in size and 0.22 m deep, with a gentle concave profile.

[1713]: A probable post-hole, measuring 0.50 × 0.27 m and 0.12 m deep, with a bowl-shaped concave profile.

[1714]: A circular post-hole, 0.40 m diameter and 0.43 m deep, with near-vertical sides and a concave base.

[1715]: An oval pit, 1.00 × 0.80 m in size and 0.18 m deep, with a gentle concave profile.

[1740]: A sharply cut vertical-sided pit, 0.35–0.40 m in diameter and 0.50 m deep.

[1777]: A sub-circular post-hole, 0.25 m diameter and 0.16 m deep.

Of these, [1740] in particular deserves mention as its sandy loam fill had much evidence of charcoal and burning *in situ*, and contained two burnt flakes.

In all these cases the regular, steep sides of the cuts or the nature of the fills indicated human activity. In other cases, features could not easily be distinguished from natural hollows (part of the undulating basal profile of the buried soil horizon) even though they sometimes contained artefacts which had moved down through the buried soil. Small pits and post-holes of 'possible-only' status are: [1770], [1774], [1782], [1788], [1946] [1963], [1992/3] and [1997].

Although the [1740] cluster is suggestive of structural/building-related remains (cf. the Barleycroft Farm stake-hole structures: Fig. 4.16) and the four possible post-holes of [1963] were in a straight line, insufficient area was excavated of the interior to pick up definite post-hole patterns which might indicate structures. However, two general aspects of the patterning of internal features are clear. First, almost all the certain features are within the palisade, towards the interior and away from the edge of the enclosure. This evidence supports that from the test-pit flint densities, which shows a concentration of activities towards the eastern middle of the enclosure. Second, the internal concentration of features is in a sector of the enclosure adjacent to Ditch I with its evidence of recutting and complex activities.

In 1987 the same methods were employed as in 1984 with a transect of the buried soil carefully sieved (Fig. 5.16). In addition all the soil from each metre square was sieved through a 5-mm mesh and the recovered gravel weighed. Taking its inspiration from Bradley's sampling programme at Barrow Hills (1984), the aim of this exercise was to check whether traces of a bank could thus be identified behind the ditches or palisade.

The overall density of worked flints was 5.5 per sq. m, with a range from 0–15 (Fig. 5.25). This was lower than in 1984 but higher than in 1981 and 1982. The result related well to the lower density of finds in the palisade and the less complex ditches than in 1984. There were also fewer interior pits and post-holes than in 1984 (see below). Once again, therefore, the notion of the enclosure as being sectored seemed valid, as was also evident from the distribution of features in the 1987 area (see below). The spatial patterning showed no clear trends, although there was perhaps a slight cluster of higher readings behind the ditch (as in the 1981 area).

The distribution of gravel in the buried soil appeared to show a clearer spatial pattern (Fig. 5.25). A weak spread of higher densities of gravel occurred over and behind the ditch. No such concentration occurred in relation to the palisade. These results are difficult to interpret, since the densities of gravel in the buried soil relate at least partly to the nature of the underlying Pleistocene deposits which

**Figure 5.26.** *HAD '84. A) Looking southwest along the main northeastern arm of the area of excavation; note the alternate metre-square buried soil sampling transect left and [1740] et al. pit configuration in mid field; B) detail of pit configuration [1740] et al. looking northeast. (Photographs C. Evans.)*

A

B

277

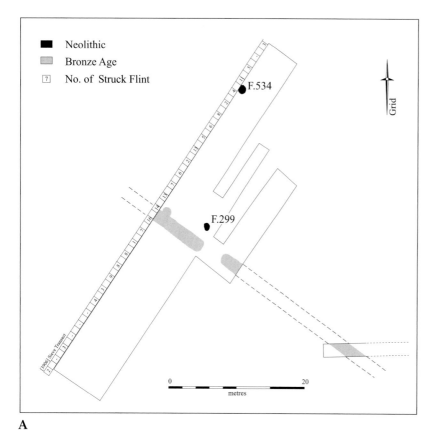

**A**

**B**

**Figure 5.27.** *HAD VIII: A) plan of area and main features (note location of sieve transect with number of flint per metre square indicated); B) pit F.534. (Photograph C. Evans.)*

concentrations of slipped material in the interior sides of the ditches.

The possible evidence of a slight bank inside the ditches but beyond the palisade confirmed the notion that the palisade was of a partly different date than the ditches. Indeed, the palisade may have been set far back behind the ditches in this area of the enclosure (in contrast to the 1982 area) partly because of the existence here of an immediately ditch-interior bank.

There were fewer features within the palisade than in 1984 and these occurred both near and at a distance from the palisade. Their dating is often insecure since diagnostic artefacts were rare. For example, near the palisade a large pit was excavated (F.516: Fig. 5.16). This was 3.50 × 3.00 m in plan and 1.20 m deep, with steeply sloping sides and a flat base. The thick primary weathering fills consisted of grey clays interweaving with collapsed sands and gravels. The few finds did not contradict a date contemporary with the enclosure and a well function might be presumed. However, of comparable size to some of the unelaborated 'ditch-pits' within the causewayed enclosure circuit (e.g. Ditch B), its occurrence raises other possibilities that will be discussed below.

Close to F.516 was a shallow pit (F.532), 0.25 m deep, containing a layer of black scorched sandy clay and burnt flint. Further to the south, F.520 was an irregularly shaped pit, 0.70 m deep, with silt and sand fills, which contained Grooved Ware and later Neolithic pottery (see Gdaniec below). In its top was a small recut pit, 0.50 m in diameter and 0.40 m deep, containing scorched black clayey silts, charcoal flecks, burnt flint and fragments of white burnt bone, indicating a probable 'cremation'. Whilst perhaps comparable to the Collared Urn cremation found within the enclosure in 1982, the burnt bone from the pit has been examined by N. Dodwell and, being of very small size, none were identifiable (i.e. neither as human or animal; see *A note concerning the burnt bone* below p. 312). F.524 was a well-defined curving 'slot' with steep sides and a flat base, 0.63 m deep and 0.56 m wide and containing a sandy silt fill. A hammerstone and 'rubber' were found in the fill as well as Early Bronze Age pottery.

All the above features were within the palisade. Three further features were found outside the palisade, immediately adjacent to the main ditches. Both F.537 and F.538 consisted of small shallow features with burnt fills. F.540 also contained evidence of burning but could more obviously be identified as a post-hole with steep sides and a depth of 0.56 m. All this evidence of burning near the enclosure's main circuit corresponds with the traces of burning present in the upper fills of the ditches.

An area of the interior away from the enclosure ditches was examined during the course of the HAD VIII investigations (see Volume 2, Chapter 3; Fig. 5.1). Although the area was cleaned by machine down to the base of the buried soil, a transect of the soil

include mixed sands, clays and gravels. However, as far as we could observe, the subsoil near the ditch did not seem to contain a higher gravel content. The gravel distribution thus provided the first indication that a bank may have stood inside the ditches. This can only have been minor since no evidence was found of higher

was once more left and was sieved through a 5-mm mesh (Fig. 5.27). The densities of 0–14 struck flints per metre square and the overall mean of 5.3 correlate well with the densities obtained for the nearby 1987 area, and again throw into relief the high densities obtained for the 1984 area. However, there is a possible concentration of higher densities of struck flint over the putative Bronze Age enclosure ditch in this area, so that some of the flints may relate to post-causewayed enclosure activity. Certainly the number of Neolithic features found in this area were low. F.299 was a roughly circular 'pit hearth', 1.20 × 1.00 m in plan and 0.28 m deep with gently sloping sides; it was sealed by upcast gravel from the Bronze Age enclosure. There was evidence of *in situ* burning and a high density of ash and charcoal within its fill. There was no bone and little pottery and flint, except for a fine blade at the base. The only other Neolithic feature was F.534, which consisted of a shallow (0.30 m deep), flat-based, circular (1.00 m diameter) cut filled with dark sandy clay silts with a high charcoal content. The large plain bowl sherds recovered from this features are described by Knight below. As detailed by Middleton (see below) it also contained 83 worked flints, including four serrated flakes. The date of 2900–2200 cal. BC (4020±110 BP; HAR-10518) obtained from charcoal from this pit must be erroneous given its assemblages, and is thought to be 500–1000 years too late.

### The F.534 pottery
by M. KNIGHT

The pit produced 85 sherds of Early Neolithic pottery, weighing 1156 g (mean sherd weight: 13.6 g). The assemblage includes six rim sherds, all of which are plain, and of which four can be refitted to make large parts of two separate vessels. The fabric appears uniform throughout the assemblage (Fabric 1e, after Gdaniec below) and has an exact equivalent at Barleycroft Paddocks (Fabric 1: Moderate to hard fabric with common small to medium sized flint and sparse sand; after Pollard, in Evans & Knight 1997). There are no decorated fragments. The two reconstructed vessels mentioned above comprise (Fig. 5.28):

P1: 'S'-profiled bowl with a slightly out-turned rim. Diameter: 0.15 m; Height: 0.11 m. The external surface of the vessel shows some traces of wiping (two sherds).

P2: 'S'-profiled with a slight shoulder, the rim ranges between simple, out-turned and externally expanded over a distance of 7 cm. Diameter: 0.20 m; Height: 0.17 m. Slight burnishing on external surface (three sherds).

The remaining two rim sherds survive as comparatively small fragments and represent two different types: simple and expanded (after Longworth 1960). These probably represent another two vessels, although as P2 illustrates, rims are not necessarily consistently executed throughout the same vessel. It is possible that the additional rims also belong to P2. Therefore the minimum number of vessels present in Pit F.534 is two. There is nothing about the 79 plain body sherds to suggest additional vessels.

The two identified vessels are comparable with the plain Mildenhall forms located at the Barleycroft Paddocks site (Pollard, in Evans & Knight 1997). Although found along with decorated forms the Barleycroft assemblage included plain shouldered bowls with 'heavy' rims which equate very well with P2. At Barleycroft the context for the pottery was also pits and the condition and quantity of material found within particular pit features also compares favourably. For instance, although caused by post-depositional processes both the Haddenham and Barleycroft material is prone to lamination. In terms of quantity the figures below serve to exemplify the number of artefacts that can be found in similar pit features:

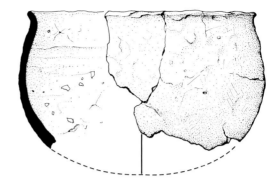

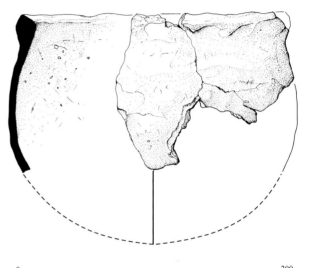

**Figure 5.28.** *HAD '84: Pit F.534 pottery. Above: P1; below: P2.*

Barleycroft Paddocks
Pit F.478: 54 sherds, 844 g (MSW 15.62 g); 11 flints
Pit F.500: 170 sherds, 823 g (MSW 4.84 g); 70 flints

Haddenham
Pit F.534: 85 sherds, 1156 g (MSW 13.60 g); 83 flints.

The dating of the Barleycroft Paddocks material relies on a radiocarbon date of 3780–3380 cal. BC (4820±40 BP: OxA-8108). A similar date range exists for another Mildenhall pit group from Broom Covert, Kilverstone, where a group of nine dates suggest the pits date to *c.* 3650 cal. BC to *c.* 3350 cal. BC (Garrow 2002; e.g. Beta-178139, 4770±50 BP, 3700–3370 cal. BC and Beta-178140, 4510±40 BP, 3360–3040 cal. BC).

The evidence from the buried soil demonstrated that the variation around the ditches and palisade corresponded to variation in the density of worked flint and features within the enclosure. Thus the complex Ditches I & J were associated with a higher density of artefacts and features in the interior. The 1981 and 1982

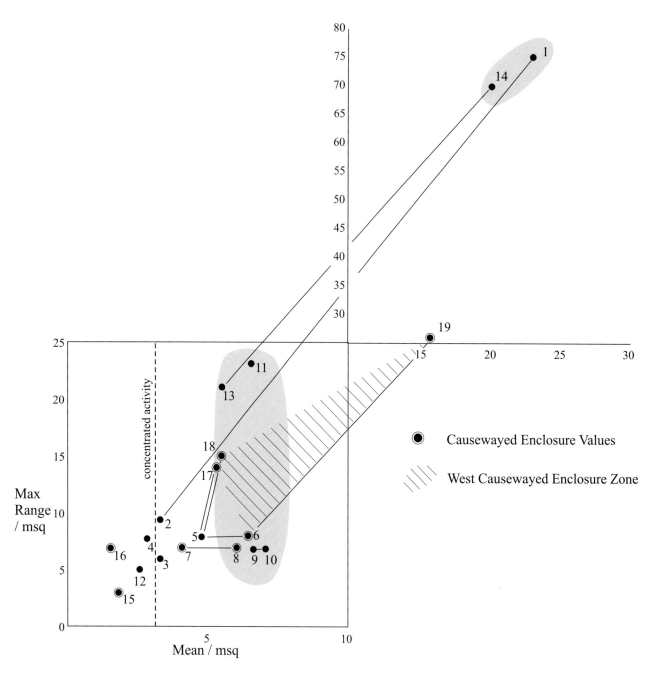

**Figure 5.29.** *Plot of site/area flint densities, including Causewayed Enclosure mean buried soil sampling values (for 1–14 see Fig. 4.14): 15) 1981; 16) 1982; 17) HAD VIII; 18) 1987; 19) 1984.*

areas in particular were less complex in all respects. From all this it appeared that the enclosure might be sectored.

Indeed, in reference to Tables 4.11 & 5.3, it is remarkable that the 1981 and 1982 worked-flint densities actually fall below the mean for the Upper Delphs test pitting as a whole and are, in fact, the lowest encountered within the project's sampling (Fig. 5.29). As established in relationship to the other site/landscape sampling densities, the values of

worked flint recovered from the 1984 sieving transect are nevertheless sufficient to count as evidence of settlement *per se*. Although not seeing the same range of high(est) values, its metre square mean of 15.9 pieces is broadly comparable to the Cracknell Farm (core area) and Foulmire Terrace-side cuttings mean values (20 & 16.8/29.1 respectively). However, equally relevant are the HAD VIII and 1987 sample transect results. With mean metre square values of 5.3 and 5.5 pieces of flint respectively, these fall into what has been identified as 'medial category' densities. They are betwixt formal 'settlement' and 'concentrated activity' levels, and directly correspond to the core values of Spread A established by the test pitting as extending through the western middle of the causewayed enclosure (see Chapter 4 above; Fig. 4.14). Regardless of whatever term is applied to these enhanced lithic densities, they suggest that much more intensive activity generally occurred throughout this swathe of the enclosure than in its other sectors.

In this context the importance of the recovery of two Neolithic settlement features, especially the F.534 pit, within the area of the HAD VIII investigations must not be underestimated. In much the same way that Ditch I uniquely speaks of a ritual content for the enclosure, in reference to the Neolithic 'pit-type' occupation sites outlined above (see Garrow, Chapter 4), so too do these features attest to domestic occupation. Admittedly, the radiocarbon determination for pit F.534 (2900–2200 cal. BC; 4020±110 BP; HAR-10518) seems some 500–1000 years too late for what appear to be its earlier/Middle Neolithic assemblages. Even if not directly contemporary with the early usage of the enclosure, their recovery raises the possibility that relatively substantial Neolithic occupation, however localized, may have evaded our sampling.

This speculation is in part engendered through the work at Barleycroft Farm and what appears to be the intentional backfilling of settlement refuse into its pits (Evans & Knight 2000). Evidencing the tidying up of the encampment, this resulted in very little register of the occupation within the extensively sampled buried soil above (Evans et al. 1999). It is equally salient that, whereas vast quantities of earlier Neolithic material occurred within the 138 shallow pits at the Kilverstone settlement (Area E; representing 17,335 litres of fill), including 1767 pottery sherds and 10,424 worked flints, the site only had a mean surface register of 6.5 flints per 'metre square' (90 litre ploughsoil samples, roughly equivalent to a metre square's buried soil representation; see Chapter 4 above; Garrow 2002). From this it can be calculated that in its pits worked flint occurred in a density eight times that of its surface deposits (see below for discussion of Runnymede's surface finds densities; see also Matthews 1976 concerning the pits from the Maiden Bower enclosure and adjacent Puddlehill site in Bedfordshire ).

Only the Etton excavations provide any basis of distributional comparison within a causewayed enclosure. Etton is accredited with having substantial evidence of interior usage (albeit seasonal) and 38 out of the 138 pits within it were of Mildenhall attribution (Pryor 1998, table 8). In the course of its excavation a

c. 0.50-m-square sample of the buried soil was sieved from the centre of each 5-m square across its interior (Pryor 1998, fig. 77). To enable direct comparison with Haddenham's metre-square sieving Etton's densities must, of course, be multiplied by a factor

| Site/Area | Average density | Range |
|---|---|---|
| 1981 | 1.8 | 0–3 |
| 1982 | 1.5 | 0–7 |
| 1984 | 15.9 | 6–26 |
| 1987 | 5.5 | 0–15 |
| HAD VIII | 5.3 | 0–14 |

Table 5.3. *Mean struck flint buried soil densities.*

of four. Though since its raw data is not available a mean value cannot be established, nevertheless its frequencies can be evaluated. It is clear that Etton's interior densities were much higher than across the interior of the Haddenham enclosure *as a whole*. However, 94% of its sieved unit had less than four pieces (13 factored value) and 37.9% produced no flint whatsoever. (Though this latter figure may be biased by the smaller sample fraction, there being only a 1 in 4 chance of recovering a flint in a 0.50 m unit from a metre that has only a single piece within it.) At Etton only 4% of its sieved units had values of between 13–24 (factored) pieces, whereas 48.3% of the metre units from HAD '84 and '87 fell within this range. This, of course, does not really compare like with like as this sampling at Haddenham occurred within the high value Spread A swathe. More direct comparison is provided by separating Etton's distributions into the halves distinguished by Pryor: 'the living and the dead', respectively the west and east. While doing this significantly increases the frequency in the 1–12 flint range (to 56.1% compared to Haddenham's 44.8%), it still does not see markedly greater densities above this level (only 6% compared to Haddenham's 51.7%). Therefore, despite Etton's much more obvious evidence of interior usage, it clearly did not result in intense 'horizontal' lithic deposition or fall-out within its buried soils.

Whilst given the limitations of Haddenham's within-enclosure exposures, the finding of the F. 534 pit (and other features) cannot amount to anything other than a cautionary tale, it has to be admitted that 'occupations' comparable to that at Kilverstone, the Barleycroft Paddocks or, indeed, Etton itself (see below) may lie somewhere within the Delphs enclosure's western sector. Detailing of the enhanced usage across that area can only occur following presentation of the finds specialist studies below. It is, however, clear that at least in part it is a product of long-term activity and probably involved some degree of both later Neolithic and even earlier Bronze Age 'occupation'.

As regards the question of whether Haddenham's ditch circuit had an accompanying upcast bank, the evidence unfortunately is ambiguous. It has been suggested from the distribution of gravels in the HAD '87 transect that a bank may have lain immediately behind the ditch circuit and exterior to the palisade, the latter being secondary to it. Yet this seems unlikely on two accounts. Firstly, there was no evidence of any bank slip within the ditch fills and, given the density of finds within its secondary/tertiary deposits, there would seem to have been no 'impediment' stopping enclosure-related material entering its circuit. Secondly there is the evidence of the palisade, for in the HAD '82 area it generally lay within 1.50 m of the ditch; insufficient space for a bank in this position. Given that the palisade seems to have been a secondary phenomenon, it could have always cut through any putative bank. There was, though, no evidence of this within its fill matrix and, therefore, the issue must remain without resolution. However, it is worth remembering that no evidence of a bank was found at Etton, which was generally better preserved than the Haddenham enclosure (Pryor 1998). There, locally, was evidence that the upcast had simply been 'spread' in an unstructured manner on the circuit's interior edge. This may well also be the case at Haddenham; certainly the evidence provides no basis by which to argue that a non-extant bank somehow provides *the* missing 'answer' to the enclosure's causewayed form.

## Artefact studies

In common with other causewayed enclosures in eastern England (e.g. Etton, Pryor 1998; Briar Hill, Bamford 1985) the Delphs enclosure's assemblages were not particularly prolific. As will be discussed below, this, combined with the scale of its construction, has major implications for the actual degree of usage of these monuments and brings into question the easy assignation of regular mass-group activities such as 'feasting'.

### Struck flint
by H.R. MIDDLETON

The assemblage consists of 2245 worked pieces of which the majority (1637, 73%) is from the buried soil (including HAD VIII and IX), and smaller amounts are from ditch (474, 21%) and palisade contexts (51, 2%), and also the HAD VIII pit (F.534; 83, 4%). Of this material, only that from the palisade, the primary ditch silts and from the F.534 pit are from truly sealed contexts, and this represents only 7% of the entire assemblage (Table 5.4). This is a significant point, as the site has Late Neolithic as well as Middle Neolithic

material associated with it and otherwise the material is thoroughly mixed in context.

*Condition* (Table 5.5)
The majority of the material was in a fresh and unabraded condition. There was little evidence for extensive damage or rounding of edges, but the material from the HAD '84 and '87 excavation areas was slightly more abraded.

The material from the upper ditch deposits and the buried soil showed a similar degree of patination, but in the pit F.534, palisade and primary ditch silts the proportion patinated was higher and the degree of patination greater. This suggests that cut features favoured the deposition of mineral salts and patination.

Some 58% of pieces were complete from the causewayed enclosure. Breakage was generally consistent throughout, but in the HAD '84 and HAD VIII areas breakage was more common, with only 49% of the pieces complete. Breakage was extensive at the thinner, non-bulbar end, suggesting a natural breakage pattern. This, together with the evidence for greater abrasion, may suggest the flint from the HAD '84 area is less well preserved. In the primary ditch deposits a high proportion of flints were broken at the non-bulbar end, while a low proportion were broken at the bulbar end. In the F.534 pit and HAD IX assemblages a higher percentage of flints were complete.

Only 5% of the assemblage had suffered from burning and this was concentrated along the western circuit of the causewayed enclosure. In the HAD '84 area 11% of the flints were burnt, while in the HAD '87 area 7% had been fired. 9.8% of the flints from the palisade were burnt, all in the HAD '84 area; of the F.534 material, 9% were burnt. The location of the burning, apart from within the pit, is closely associated with the western side of the enclosure and may suggest that the palisade was destroyed by fire in this area. As no burnt flints were found in the base of the ditch, but are associated with the upper fills, it is clear that this burning episode cannot be associated with the initial use of the enclosure but must be dated later.

*Raw material* (Table 5.13)
On 73% of cortical pieces the cortex was thin and abraded (a characteristic of gravel flint); 1.9% of pieces had a chalky unabraded cortex characteristic of flint from the chalk ridge. This material was common (4–5%) along the western side of the causewayed enclosure in the primary ditch and palisade trench contexts, and was even more common (6–8%) in the interior immediately behind the ditch in the HAD '87 and HAD VIII excavation areas. Smaller proportions

## Gathering and scattering: a horse fair
by M. Edmonds

Appleby horse fair — a handful of days in June when all roads rise to meet each other; when a field becomes a focus and a pivot for the year.

Fair Hill, once Gallows Hill, lies on the edge of things; seen from a car window if noticed at all. But for a week or so in the summer, perspectives change. The ground shifts; becomes a centre of sorts. Hundreds of travelling families move into the Eden Valley and converge on Fair Hill, setting up stalls and grazing horses brought to race and to trade. Numbers vary, but most years there's a broad range. Piebalds, Cobs, New Forest, Connemara, Welsh and even Drays; regions of Britain and Ireland mapped out in breeds and measured in hands.

Official history has it that the fair goes back to the seventeenth century, held first within Appleby itself before being moved more recently to the margins. History also records that the Fair has only rarely been suspended, once because of the plague, and again in 2001 because of foot-and-mouth disease. Beyond these instances, much is made of the continuity of proceedings, with roots traced back to the late Middle Ages. Some even claim a more extended genealogy. Talk in bars sometimes turns to pre-Christian calendars, to pagan celebrations and dimly remembered or invented gods. (A claim of distant roots does much to enhance the appeal of the fair to a burgeoning tourist market. An unbroken line between present and past is prominent in tourist brochures, in Lakeland heritage advertising and in the limited edition ceramic 'scenes' of Vardoes and deals made available to collectors in magazines.)

Like many other fairs, Appleby is an anticipated time and place, a point where paths overlap. Part of the traditional calendar, it requires an acknowledgement of a scale of community far beyond that of the everyday. And that acknowledgement is worked on, physically. Arrival, the sorting out of pitches and the setting up of stalls brings a face-to-face encounter with families that spend much of their time in other regions; some well known, others less so. For the duration of the Fair, the site draws lines together. It encourages the recognition of wider relations, webs of kinship or moral obligation addressed as people meet, talk, eat, drink and trade. The field is both common ground and a space divided along the lines of more extensive social geographies.

Gathering also brings other relations into sharp relief; with more sedentary communities and with conflicting senses of landscape and identity. These ties and tensions are worked upon, new currents added in the ebb and flow of activities on site and around town. Though the town council set certain terms and conditions, the influx of people to the site and the particular character of proceedings each year is a loose, organic process. Both casual and performative, it requires no strict hierarchy of decision making, no central authority. Things are fluid.

It is the same with trade. The selling of tools, stock and materials to other families, the stalls faced towards tourists and people from the town; barter with partners, gift giving and more alienated exchanges. Then there are the horses. Taking animals down to the Eden to be washed; running along the lanes to show form; inspection, talk, racing and gambling. There is close scrutiny, questioning of bloodlines, judgement of condition, haggling and the sealing of deals with the slap of one hand upon another. Financial but not faceless transactions. Horses can change hands several times during one fair, the movement of animals a record of ties between people. Like riding itself, talking knowledgeably, making judgements and good deals are respected skills. These take time to learn, just as it takes time to learn how biography and geography combine.

It's a pattern repeated at other fairs: the gathering and scattering days at Puck, the flux of people, the relaxation of many forms of licence. A press of faces not seen since last year, or never before. Services and blessings; the veneration of Saints. Gossip, gaming and casual indiscretion. And after the haggling, the hard trade and the horseplay. What then? Beyond the 'official' duration of the event, things disentangle in a piecemeal fashion. With deals and agreements sorted and the 'market' shrinking, families leave along different roads, departure encouraged by a tightening of attitudes in the town. Some remain for longer, but eventually, the field slips out of focus and back to the margins. All that remains is a superficial archaeology and a will to return.

**Figure 5.30.** *Appleby Horse Fair. (Photograph © Liverpool University.)*

**Table 5.4a.** *Causewayed enclosure: flint typology (based on whole assemblage).*

| Division | Ditch: Lower No. | % | Ditch: Upper No. | % | Ditch: Total No. | % | Palisade No. | % | Had VIII Pit No. | % | Site total No. | % |
|---|---|---|---|---|---|---|---|---|---|---|---|---|
| Waste flakes | 17 | 85.0 | 363 | 94.5 | 380 | 94.1 | 46 | 100.0 | 69 | 100.0 | 1874 | 93.3 |
| IWW | 1 | 5.0 | 4 | 1.0 | 5 | 1.2 | 0 | 0.0 | 0 | 0.0 | 34 | 1.7 |
| Cores | 2 | 10.0 | 17 | 4.4 | 19 | 4.7 | 0 | 0.0 | 0 | 0.0 | 96 | 4.8 |
| Micro-burins | 0 | 0.0 | 0 | 0.0 | 0 | 0.0 | 0 | 0.0 | 0 | 0.0 | 4 | 0.2 |
| **Total** | **20** | **100** | **384** | **100** | **404** | **100** | **46** | **100** | **69** | **100** | **2008** | **100** |
| Utilized flakes | 1 | 10.0 | 21 | 35.0 | 22 | 31.4 | 2 | 40.0 | 7 | 50.0 | 71 | 30.0 |
| Retouched flakes | 1 | 10.0 | 5 | 8.3 | 6 | 8.6 | 1 | 20.0 | 2 | 14.3 | 38 | 16.0 |
| Serrated flakes | 6 | 60.0 | 13 | 21.7 | 19 | 27.1 | 0 | 0.0 | 4 | 28.6 | 31 | 13.1 |
| Edge blunted flake | 0 | 0.0 | 0 | 0.0 | 0 | 0.0 | 0 | 0.0 | 0 | 0.0 | 2 | 0.8 |
| Scrapers | 1 | 10.0 | 8 | 13.3 | 9 | 12.9 | 0 | 0.0 | 0 | 0.0 | 32 | 13.5 |
| Fabricators | 0 | 0.0 | 0 | 0.0 | 0 | 0.0 | 0 | 0.0 | 0 | 0.0 | 2 | 0.8 |
| Knives | 0 | 0.0 | 4 | 6.7 | 4 | 5.7 | 0 | 0.0 | 0 | 0.0 | 15 | 6.3 |
| Knife (polished) | 0 | 0.0 | 0 | 0.0 | 0 | 0.0 | 0 | 0.0 | 0 | 0.0 | 2 | 0.8 |
| Leaf arrowhead | 0 | 0.0 | 1 | 1.7 | 1 | 1.4 | 0 | 0.0 | 0 | 0.0 | 1 | 0.4 |
| Transverse arrowhead | 0 | 0.0 | 0 | 0.0 | 0 | 0.0 | 0 | 0.0 | 0 | 0.0 | 3 | 1.3 |
| Tanged arrowhead | 0 | 0.0 | 0 | 0.0 | 0 | 0.0 | 0 | 0.0 | 0 | 0.0 | 1 | 0.4 |
| Stone axes | 1 | 10.0 | 0 | 0.0 | 1 | 1.4 | 1 | 20.0 | 0 | 1.0 | 2 | 0.8 |
| Flint axes | 0 | 0.0 | 0 | 0.0 | 0 | 0.0 | 0 | 0.0 | 0 | 0.0 | 3 | 1.3 |
| Piercer | 0 | 0.0 | 4 | 6.7 | 4 | 5.7 | 1 | 20.0 | 0 | 0.0 | 16 | 6.8 |
| Notched | 0 | 0.0 | 1 | 1.7 | 1 | 1.4 | 0 | 0.0 | 0 | 0.0 | 8 | 3.4 |
| Microliths | 0 | 0.0 | 0 | 0.0 | 0 | 0.0 | 0 | 0.0 | 0 | 0.0 | 1 | 0.4 |
| Burin | 0 | 0.0 | 3 | 5.0 | 3 | 4.3 | 0 | 0.0 | 1 | 7.1 | 6 | 2.5 |
| Truncated flakes | 0 | 0.0 | 0 | 0.0 | 0 | 0.0 | 0 | 0.0 | 0 | 0.0 | 3 | 1.3 |
| **Total** | **10** | **100** | **60** | **100** | **70** | **100** | **5** | **100** | **14** | **100** | **237** | **100** |
| Assemblage total | 30 | | 444 | | 474 | | 51 | | 83 | | 2241 | |
| Implement:by-product ratio | 1:2 | | 1:6.4 | | 1:5.8 | | 1:9.1 | | 1:4.9 | | 1:8.5 | |

**Table 5.4b.** *Causewayed enclosure: flint typology (based on whole assemblage).*

| Division Type | 1981 Area No. | % | 1982 Area No. | % | 1984 Area No. | % | 1987 Area No. | % | Had VIII No. | % | Had IX No. | % |
|---|---|---|---|---|---|---|---|---|---|---|---|---|
| Waste flakes | 522 | 90.6 | 261 | 91.9 | 240 | 97.2 | 196 | 97.5 | 149 | 90.3 | 11 | 68.8 |
| IWW | 8 | 1.4 | 4 | 1.4 | 5 | 2.0 | 2 | 1.0 | 9 | 5.5 | 1 | 6.3 |
| Cores | 44 | 7.6 | 19 | 6.7 | 2 | 0.8 | 1 | 1.5 | 5 | 3.0 | 4 | 25.0 |
| Micro-burins | 2 | 0.3 | 0 | 0.0 | 0 | 0.0 | 0 | 0.0 | 2 | 1.2 | 0 | 0.0 |
| **Total** | **576** | **100** | **284** | **100** | **247** | **100** | **201** | **100** | **165** | **100** | **16** | **100** |
| Utilized flakes | 11 | 16.2 | 3 | 12.0 | 7 | 38.9 | 8 | 53.3 | 8 | 47.1 | 3 | 60.0 |
| Retoucbed flakes | 13 | 19.1 | 7 | 28.0 | 2 | 11.1 | 2 | 13.3 | 4 | 23.5 | 1 | 20.0 |
| Serrated flakes | 2 | 2.9 | 2 | 8.0 | 4 | 22.2 | 0 | 0.0 | 0 | 0.0 | 0 | 0.0 |
| Edge blunted flake | 1 | 1.5 | 0 | 0.0 | 0 | 0.0 | 0 | 0.0 | 1 | 5.9 | 0 | 0.0 |
| Scrapers | 13 | 19.1 | 5 | 20.0 | 0 | 0.0 | 3 | 20.0 | 2 | 11.8 | 0 | 0.0 |
| Fabricators | 1 | 1.5 | 1 | 4.0 | 0 | 0.0 | 0 | 0.0 | 0 | 0.0 | 0 | 0.0 |
| Knives | 8 | 11.8 | 2 | 8.0 | 1 | 5.6 | 0 | 0.0 | 0 | 0.0 | 0 | 0.0 |
| Knife (polished) | 0 | 0.0 | 1 | 4.0 | 1 | 5.6 | 0 | 0.0 | 0 | 0.0 | 0 | 0.0 |
| Denticulates | 0 | 0.0 | 0 | 0.0 | 0 | 0.0 | 0 | 0.0 | 0 | 0.0 | 0 | 0.0 |
| Leaf arrowhead | 2 | 2.9 | 0 | 0.0 | 0 | 0.0 | 1 | 6.7 | 0 | 0.0 | 0 | 0.0 |
| Transverse arrowhead | 1 | 1.5 | 0 | 0.0 | 0 | 0.0 | 0 | 0.0 | 0 | 0.0 | 0 | 0.0 |
| Stone axes | 0 | 0.0 | 0 | 0.0 | 0 | 0.0 | 0 | 0.0 | 0 | 0.0 | 0 | 0.0 |
| Flint axes | 2 | 2.9 | 0 | 0.0 | 1 | 5.6 | 0 | 0.0 | 0 | 0.0 | 1 | 20.0 |
| Piercer | 6 | 8.8 | 3 | 12.0 | 1 | 5.6 | 0 | 0.0 | 0 | 0.0 | 0 | 0.0 |
| Notched | 4 | 5.9 | 1 | 4.0 | 1 | 5.6 | 0 | 0.0 | 1 | 5.9 | 0 | 0.0 |
| Microliths | 0 | 0.0 | 0 | 0.0 | 0 | 0.0 | 0 | 0.0 | 1 | 5.9 | 0 | 0.0 |
| Burin | 2 | 2.9 | 0 | 0.0 | 0 | 0.0 | 0 | 0.0 | 0 | 0.0 | 0 | 0.0 |
| Truncated flakes | 2 | 2.9 | 0 | 0.0 | 0 | 0.0 | 1 | 6.7 | 0 | 0.0 | 0 | 0.0 |
| **Total** | **68** | **100** | **25** | **100** | **18** | **100** | **15** | **100** | **17** | **100** | **5** | **100** |
| Assemblage total | 644 | | 309 | | 265 | | 216 | | 182 | | 21 | |
| Implement:by-product ratio | 1:8.5 | | 1:11.4 | | 1:13.7 | | 1:13.4 | | 1:9.7 | | 1:3.2 | |

**Table 5.5a.** *Causewayed enclosure: flint condition (based on whole assemblage).*

| Division | Ditch: Lower | | Ditch: Upper | | Ditch: Total | | Palisade | | Had VIII Pit | | Site total | |
|---|---|---|---|---|---|---|---|---|---|---|---|---|
| | No. | % | No. | % | No. | % | No. | % | No. | % | No. | % |
| *Condition* | | | | | | | | | | | | |
| Abraded | 8 | 26.7 | 102 | 23.0 | 110 | 23.2 | 13 | 25.5 | 14 | 20.3 | 572 | 25.8 |
| Fresh | 22 | 73.3 | 342 | 77.0 | 364 | 76.8 | 38 | 74.5 | 55 | 79.7 | 1643 | 74.2 |
| **Total** | **30** | **100** | **444** | **100** | **474** | **100** | **51** | **100** | **69** | **100** | **2215** | **100** |
| *Degree of patination* | | | | | | | | | | | | |
| Unpatinated | 22 | 73.3 | 375 | 84.5 | 397 | 83.8 | 39 | 76.5 | 52 | 75.4 | 1894 | 85.5 |
| Partially | 6 | 20.0 | 62 | 14.0 | 68 | 14.3 | 11 | 21.6 | 16 | 23.2 | 292 | 13.2 |
| Completely | 2 | 6.7 | 7 | 1.6 | 9 | 1.9 | 1 | 2.0 | 1 | 1.4 | 29 | 1.3 |
| **Total** | **30** | **100** | **444** | **100** | **474** | **100** | **51** | **100** | **69** | **100** | **2215** | **100** |
| *Breakage* | | | | | | | | | | | | |
| Complete | 18 | 60.0 | 259 | 58.3 | 277 | 58.4 | 27 | 52.9 | 47 | 68.1 | 1274 | 57.5 |
| Broken proximal end | 6 | 20.0 | 61 | 13.7 | 67 | 14.1 | 8 | 15.7 | 11 | 15.9 | 332 | 15.0 |
| Broken distal end | 2 | 6.7 | 72 | 16.2 | 74 | 15.6 | 7 | 13.7 | 8 | 11.6 | 299 | 13.5 |
| Broken both ends | 4 | 13.3 | 52 | 11.7 | 56 | 11.8 | 9 | 17.6 | 3 | 4.3 | 310 | 14.0 |
| **Total** | **30** | **100** | **444** | **100** | **474** | **100** | **51** | **100** | **69** | **100** | **2215** | **100** |
| *Burning* | | | | | | | | | | | | |
| No. burnt (worked) | 0 | 0.0 | 14 | 82.4 | 14 | 82.4 | 5 | 100.0 | 6 | 100.0 | 103 | 92.8 |
| No. burnt (cores) | 0 | 0.0 | 0 | 0.0 | 0 | 0.0 | 0 | 0.0 | 0 | 0.0 | 4 | 3.6 |
| No. burnt (implement) | 0 | 0.0 | 3 | 17.6 | 3 | 17.6 | 0 | 0.0 | 0 | 0.0 | 4 | 3.6 |
| No. burnt (unworked) | 0 | 0.0 | 0 | 1.0 | 0 | 0.0 | 0 | 0.0 | 0 | 0.0 | 0 | 0.0 |
| **Total** | **0** | **0.0** | **17** | **100** | **17** | **100** | **5** | **100** | **6** | **100** | **111** | **100** |
| % flint burnt | | 0.0 | | 3.8 | | 3.6 | | 9.8 | | 7.2 | | 5.0 |

**Table 5.5b.** *Causewayed enclosure: flint condition (based on whole assemblage).*

| Division | 1981 Area | | 1982 Area | | 1984 Area | | 1987 Area | | Had VIII | | Had IX | |
|---|---|---|---|---|---|---|---|---|---|---|---|---|
| | No. | % | No. | % | No. | % | No. | % | No. | % | No. | % |
| *Condition* | | | | | | | | | | | | |
| Abraded | 163 | 25.3 | 76 | 24.7 | 83 | 31.3 | 63 | 29.2 | 45 | 26.9 | 5 | 23.8 |
| Fresh | 481 | 74.7 | 232 | 75.3 | 182 | 68.7 | 153 | 70.8 | 122 | 73.1 | 16 | 76.2 |
| **Total** | **644** | **100** | **308** | **100** | **265** | **100** | **216** | **100** | **167** | **100** | **21** | **100** |
| *Degree of patination* | | | | | | | | | | | | |
| Unpatinated | 552 | 85.7 | 258 | 83.8 | 232 | 87.5 | 194 | 89.8 | 153 | 91.6 | 17 | 81.0 |
| Partially | 82 | 12.7 | 48 | 15.6 | 30 | 11.3 | 21 | 9.7 | 12 | 7.2 | 4 | 19.0 |
| Completely | 10 | 1.6 | 2 | 1.6 | 3 | 1.1 | 1 | 0.5 | 2 | 1.2 | 0 | 0.0 |
| **Total** | **644** | **100** | **308** | **100** | **265** | **100** | **216** | **100** | **167** | **100** | **21** | **100** |
| *Breakage* | | | | | | | | | | | | |
| Complete | 385 | 59.8 | 184 | 59.7 | 129 | 48.7 | 129 | 59.7 | 81 | 48.5 | 15 | 71.4 |
| Broken proximal end | 83 | 12.9 | 47 | 15.3 | 48 | 18.1 | 31 | 14.4 | 36 | 21.6 | 1 | 4.8 |
| Broken distal end | 85 | 13.2 | 48 | 15.6 | 31 | 11.7 | 20 | 9.3 | 25 | 15.0 | 1 | 4.8 |
| Broken both ends | 91 | 14.1 | 29 | 9.4 | 57 | 21.5 | 36 | 16.7 | 25 | 15.0 | 4 | 19.0 |
| **Total** | **644** | **100** | **308** | **100** | **265** | **100** | **216** | **100** | **167** | **100** | **21** | **100** |
| *Burning* | | | | | | | | | | | | |
| No. burnt (worked) | 19 | 90.5 | 12 | 92.3 | 28 | 100.0 | 14 | 100.0 | 5 | 71.4 | 0 | 0.0 |
| No. burnt (cores) | 2 | 9.5 | 1 | 7.7 | 0 | 0.0 | 0 | 0.0 | 1 | 14.3 | 0 | 0.0 |
| No. burnt (implement) | 0 | 0.0 | 0 | 0.0 | 0 | 0.0 | 0 | 1.0 | 1 | 14.3 | 0 | 0.0 |
| No. burnt (unworked) | 0 | 0.0 | 0 | 0.0 | 0 | 0.0 | 0 | 0.0 | 0 | 0.0 | 0 | 0.0 |
| **Total** | **21** | **100** | **13** | **100** | **28** | **100** | **14** | **100** | **7** | **100** | **0** | **0.0** |
| % burnt flint | | 3.3 | | 4.2 | | 10.6 | | 6.5 | | 3.8 | | 0.0 |

**Table 5.6a.** *Causewayed enclosure: flake technology (based on complete waste flakes).*

| Division Technology | Ditch: Lower No. | % | Ditch: Upper No. | % | Ditch: Total No. | % | Palisade No. | % | Had VIII Pit No. | % | Site total No. | % |
|---|---|---|---|---|---|---|---|---|---|---|---|---|
| *Initiation* | | | | | | | | | | | | |
| Hertzian | 10 | 100.0 | 189 | 94.5 | 199 | 94.8 | 20 | 87.0 | 31 | 96.9 | 950 | 94.1 |
| Bending | 0 | 0.0 | 11 | 5.5 | 11 | 5.2 | 3 | 13.0 | 1 | 3.1 | 60 | 5.9 |
| **Total** | **10** | **100** | **200** | **100** | **210** | **100** | **23** | **100** | **32** | **100** | **1010** | **100** |
| | | | | | | | | | | | | |
| *Termination* | | | | | | | | | | | | |
| Feather | 8 | 80.0 | 115 | 56.9 | 123 | 58.0 | 16 | 69.6 | 17 | 53.1 | 583 | 57.4 |
| Hinge | 2 | 20.0 | 65 | 32.2 | 67 | 31.6 | 5 | 21.7 | 9 | 28.1 | 303 | 29.9 |
| Plunging | 0 | 0.0 | 10 | 5.0 | 10 | 4.7 | 0 | 0.0 | 1 | 3.1 | 45 | 4.4 |
| Stepped | 0 | 0.0 | 12 | 5.9 | 12 | 5.7 | 2 | 8.7 | 5 | 15.6 | 84 | 8.3 |
| **Total** | **10** | **100** | **202** | **100** | **212** | **100** | **23** | **100** | **32** | **100** | **1015** | **100** |
| | | | | | | | | | | | | |
| *Platform preparation* | | | | | | | | | | | | |
| Plain | 6 | 60.0 | 160 | 78.8 | 166 | 77.9 | 17 | 73.9 | 19 | 59.4 | 793 | 78.3 |
| Facetted | 1 | 10.0 | 42 | 15.8 | 33 | 15.5 | 3 | 13.0 | 11 | 34.4 | 154 | 15.2 |
| Abraded | 3 | 30.0 | 11 | 5.4 | 14 | 6.6 | 3 | 13.0 | 2 | 6.3 | 66 | 6.5 |
| **Total** | **10** | **100** | **203** | **100** | **213** | **100** | **23** | **100** | **32** | **100** | **1013** | **100** |
| | | | | | | | | | | | | |
| *Platform cortex* | | | | | | | | | | | | |
| Complete | 0 | 0.0 | 49 | 24.3 | 49 | 23.1 | 5 | 21.7 | 3 | 7.9 | 216 | 21.4 |
| Partial | 2 | 20.0 | 14 | 6.9 | 16 | 7.5 | 0 | 0.0 | 4 | 10.5 | 103 | 10.2 |
| Absent | 8 | 80.0 | 139 | 68.8 | 147 | 69.3 | 18 | 78.3 | 31 | 81.6 | 692 | 68.4 |
| **Total** | **10** | **100** | **202** | **100** | **212** | **100** | **23** | **100** | **38** | **100** | **1011** | **100** |
| | | | | | | | | | | | | |
| *Striking* | | | | | | | | | | | | |
| Side | 2 | 20.0 | 89 | 43.4 | 91 | 42.3 | 4 | 17.4 | 11 | 28.9 | 467 | 45.6 |
| End | 8 | 80.0 | 114 | 55.6 | 122 | 56.7 | 19 | 82.6 | 27 | 71.1 | 553 | 54.0 |
| Bashed | 0 | 0.0 | 2 | 1.0 | 2 | 0.9 | 0 | 0.0 | 0 | 0.0 | 4 | 0.4 |
| **Total** | **10** | **100** | **205** | **100** | **215** | **100** | **23** | **100** | **38** | **100** | **1024** | **100** |

**Table 5.6b.** *Causewayed enclosure: flake technology (based on complete waste flakes).*

| Division Technology | 1981 Area No. | % | 1982 Area No. | % | 1984 Area No. | % | 1987 Area No. | % | Had VIII No. | % | Had IX No. | % |
|---|---|---|---|---|---|---|---|---|---|---|---|---|
| *Initiation* | | | | | | | | | | | | |
| Hertzian | 283 | 94.3 | 140 | 93.3 | 108 | 93.9 | 104 | 92.0 | 56 | 96.6 | 9 | 100.0 |
| Bending | 17 | 5.7 | 10 | 6.7 | 7 | 6.1 | 9 | 8.0 | 2 | 3.4 | 0 | 0.0 |
| **Total** | **300** | **100** | **150** | **100** | **115** | **100** | **113** | **100** | **58** | **100** | **9** | **100** |
| | | | | | | | | | | | | |
| *Termination* | | | | | | | | | | | | |
| Feather | 164 | 54.5 | 76 | 50.3 | 80 | 69.0 | 68 | 59.6 | 31 | 54.4 | 8 | 88.9 |
| Hinge | 90 | 29.9 | 48 | 31.8 | 27 | 23.3 | 36 | 31.6 | 20 | 35.1 | 1 | 11.1 |
| Plunging | 20 | 6.6 | 3 | 2.0 | 4 | 3.4 | 5 | 4.4 | 2 | 3.5 | 0 | 0.0 |
| Stepped | 27 | 9.0 | 24 | 15.9 | 5 | 4.3 | 5 | 4.4 | 4 | 7.0 | 0 | 0.0 |
| **Total** | **301** | **100** | **151** | **100** | **116** | **100** | **114** | **100** | **57** | **100** | **9** | **100** |
| | | | | | | | | | | | | |
| *Platform preparation* | | | | | | | | | | | | |
| Plain | 236 | 78.7 | 131 | 87.3 | 91 | 79.1 | 79 | 69.9 | 47 | 81.0 | 7 | 77.8 |
| Facetted | 50 | 16.7 | 15 | 10.0 | 15 | 13.0 | 16 | 14.2 | 9 | 15.5 | 2 | 22.2 |
| Abraded | 14 | 4.7 | 4 | 2.7 | 9 | 7.8 | 18 | 15.9 | 2 | 3.4 | 0 | 0.0 |
| **Total** | **300** | **100** | **150** | **100** | **115** | **100** | **113** | **100** | **58** | **100** | **9** | **100** |
| | | | | | | | | | | | | |
| *Platform cortex* | | | | | | | | | | | | |
| Complete | 80 | 26.8 | 31 | 21.1 | 22 | 19.3 | 17 | 15.3 | 9 | 15.5 | 0 | 0.0 |
| Partial | 31 | 10.4 | 21 | 14.3 | 11 | 9.6 | 11 | 9.9 | 6 | 10.3 | 3 | 33.3 |
| Absent | 188 | 62.9 | 95 | 64.6 | 81 | 71.1 | 83 | 74.8 | 43 | 74.1 | 6 | 66.7 |
| **Total** | **299** | **100** | **147** | **100** | **114** | **100** | **111** | **100** | **58** | **100** | **9** | **100** |
| | | | | | | | | | | | | |
| *Striking* | | | | | | | | | | | | |
| Side | 162 | 53.1 | 67 | 44.1 | 53 | 45.7 | 50 | 43.9 | 28 | 48.3 | 4 | 44.4 |
| End | 141 | 46.2 | 85 | 55.9 | 63 | 54.3 | 64 | 56.1 | 30 | 51.7 | 5 | 55.6 |
| Bashed | 2 | 0.7 | 0 | 0.0 | 0 | 0.0 | 0 | 0.0 | 0 | 0.0 | 0 | 0.0 |
| **Total** | **305** | **100** | **152** | **100** | **116** | **100** | **114** | **100** | **58** | **100** | **9** | **100** |

**Table 5.7a.** *Causewayed enclosure: platform characteristics (based on complete waste flakes).*

| Division<br>Type | Ditch: Lower<br>No. | %  | Ditch: Upper<br>No. | %  | Ditch: Total<br>No. | %  | Palisade<br>No. | %  | Had VIII Pit<br>No. | %  | Site total<br>No. | %  |
|---|---|---|---|---|---|---|---|---|---|---|---|---|
| *Platform length (mm)* | | | | | | | | | | | | |
| 0–5   | 3  | 30.0 | 60  | 28.4 | 63  | 28.5 | 16 | 69.6 | 22 | 57.9 | 341  | 33.2 |
| 5–10  | 3  | 30.0 | 64  | 30.3 | 67  | 30.3 | 5  | 21.7 | 8  | 21.1 | 310  | 30.2 |
| 10–15 | 1  | 10.0 | 48  | 22.7 | 49  | 22.2 | 1  | 4.3  | 4  | 10.5 | 209  | 20.4 |
| 15–20 | 2  | 20.0 | 17  | 8.1  | 19  | 8.6  | 1  | 4.3  | 1  | 2.6  | 94   | 9.2  |
| 20–25 | 1  | 10.0 | 9   | 4.3  | 10  | 4.5  | 0  | 0.0  | 1  | 2.6  | 38   | 3.7  |
| 25+   | 0  | 0.0  | 13  | 6.2  | 13  | 5.9  | 0  | 0.0  | 2  | 5.3  | 34   | 3.3  |
| **Total** | **10** | **100** | **211** | **100** | **221** | **100** | **23** | **100** | **38** | **100** | **1026** | **100** |
| *Platform width (mm)* | | | | | | | | | | | | |
| 0–2   | 4  | 40.0 | 90  | 42.7 | 94  | 42.5 | 16 | 69.6 | 26 | 68.4 | 464  | 45.2 |
| 2–4   | 2  | 20.0 | 50  | 23.7 | 52  | 23.5 | 6  | 26.1 | 7  | 18.4 | 252  | 24.6 |
| 4–6   | 2  | 20.0 | 35  | 16.6 | 37  | 16.7 | 1  | 4.3  | 1  | 2.6  | 157  | 15.3 |
| 6–8   | 1  | 10.0 | 13  | 6.2  | 14  | 6.3  | 0  | 0.0  | 1  | 2.6  | 68   | 6.6  |
| 8–10  | 0  | 0.0  | 4   | 1.9  | 4   | 1.8  | 0  | 0.0  | 0  | 0.0  | 33   | 3.2  |
| 10+   | 1  | 10.0 | 19  | 9.0  | 20  | 9.0  | 0  | 0.0  | 3  | 7.9  | 52   | 5.1  |
| **Total** | **10** | **100** | **211** | **100** | **221** | **100** | **23** | **100** | **38** | **100** | **1026** | **100** |
| *Platform angle* | | | | | | | | | | | | |
| –80     | 0 | 0.0  | 3  | 1.4  | 3  | 1.4  | 1 | 4.3  | 0  | 0.0  | 25  | 2.5  |
| 80–90   | 0 | 0.0  | 12 | 5.7  | 12 | 5.4  | 3 | 13.0 | 2  | 5.3  | 62  | 6.1  |
| 90–100  | 1 | 10.0 | 44 | 20.9 | 45 | 20.4 | 5 | 21.7 | 10 | 26.3 | 220 | 21.6 |
| 100–110 | 6 | 60.0 | 65 | 30.8 | 71 | 32.1 | 4 | 17.4 | 12 | 31.6 | 323 | 31.8 |
| 110–120 | 0 | 0.0  | 47 | 22.3 | 47 | 21.3 | 9 | 39.1 | 9  | 23.7 | 234 | 23.0 |
| 120–130 | 2 | 20.0 | 37 | 17.5 | 39 | 17.6 | 1 | 4.3  | 5  | 13.2 | 132 | 13.0 |
| 130+    | 0 | 10.0 | 3  | 1.4  | 4  | 1.8  | 0 | 0.0  | 0  | 0.0  | 21  | 2.1  |
| **Total** | **10** | **100** | **211** | **100** | **221** | **100** | **23** | **100** | **32** | **100** | **1017** | **100** |

**Table 5.7b.** *Causewayed enclosure: platform characteristics (based on complete waste flakes).*

| Division | 1981 Area<br>No. | %  | 1982 Area<br>No. | %  | 1984 Area<br>No. | %  | 1987 Area<br>No. | %  | Had VIII<br>No. | %  | Had IX<br>No. | %  |
|---|---|---|---|---|---|---|---|---|---|---|---|---|
| *Platform length (mm)* | | | | | | | | | | | | |
| 0–5   | 82 | 27.4 | 41 | 27.3 | 49 | 42.6 | 47 | 41.6 | 20 | 34.5 | 1 | 11.1 |
| 5–10  | 98 | 32.8 | 40 | 26.7 | 40 | 34.8 | 31 | 27.4 | 21 | 36.2 | 0 | 0.0  |
| 10–15 | 67 | 22.4 | 38 | 25.3 | 16 | 13.9 | 22 | 19.5 | 9  | 15.5 | 3 | 33.3 |
| 15–20 | 33 | 11.0 | 21 | 14.0 | 6  | 5.2  | 7  | 6.2  | 5  | 8.6  | 1 | 11.1 |
| 10–25 | 9  | 3.0  | 5  | 3.3  | 3  | 2.6  | 4  | 3.5  | 2  | 3.4  | 4 | 44.4 |
| 25+   | 10 | 3.3  | 5  | 3.3  | 1  | 0.9  | 2  | 1.8  | 1  | 1.7  | 0 | 0.0  |
| **Total** | **299** | **100** | **150** | **100** | **115** | **100** | **113** | **100** | **58** | **100** | **9** | **100** |
| *Platform width (mm)* | | | | | | | | | | | | |
| 0–2   | 117 | 39.1 | 54 | 36.0 | 66 | 57.4 | 58 | 51.3 | 32 | 55.2 | 1 | 11.1 |
| 2–4   | 75  | 25.1 | 34 | 22.7 | 29 | 25.2 | 27 | 23.9 | 18 | 31.0 | 4 | 44.4 |
| 4–6   | 58  | 19.4 | 32 | 21.3 | 10 | 8.7  | 12 | 10.6 | 5  | 8.6  | 1 | 11.1 |
| 6–8   | 25  | 8.4  | 13 | 8.7  | 4  | 3.5  | 8  | 7.1  | 1  | 1.7  | 2 | 22.2 |
| 8–10  | 10  | 3.3  | 10 | 6.7  | 2  | 1.7  | 6  | 5.3  | 1  | 1.7  | 0 | 0.0  |
| 10+   | 14  | 4.7  | 7  | 4.7  | 4  | 3.5  | 2  | 1.8  | 1  | 1.7  | 1 | 11.1 |
| **Total** | **299** | **100** | **150** | **100** | **115** | **100** | **113** | **100** | **58** | **100** | **9** | **100** |
| *Platform angle* | | | | | | | | | | | | |
| –80     | 3  | 1.0  | 6  | 4.0  | 6  | 5.2  | 5  | 4.4  | 1  | 1.8  | 0 | 0.0  |
| 80–90   | 21 | 7.1  | 11 | 7.3  | 5  | 4.3  | 4  | 3.5  | 4  | 7.0  | 0 | 0.0  |
| 90–100  | 63 | 21.2 | 27 | 18.0 | 32 | 27.8 | 20 | 17.7 | 18 | 31.6 | 1 | 11.1 |
| 100–110 | 92 | 31.0 | 50 | 33.3 | 31 | 27.0 | 40 | 35.4 | 20 | 35.1 | 6 | 66.7 |
| 110–120 | 71 | 23.9 | 41 | 27.3 | 25 | 21.7 | 27 | 23.9 | 6  | 10.5 | 0 | 0.0  |
| 120–130 | 39 | 13.1 | 14 | 9.3  | 13 | 11.3 | 14 | 12.4 | 6  | 10.5 | 2 | 22.2 |
| 130+    | 8  | 2.7  | 1  | 0.7  | 3  | 2.6  | 3  | 2.7  | 2  | 3.5  | 0 | 0.0  |
| **Total** | **297** | **100** | **150** | **100** | **115** | **100** | **113** | **100** | **57** | **100** | **9** | **100** |

**Table 5.8a.** *Causewayed enclosure: metric analysis (based on complete waste flakes).*

| Division Type | Ditch: Lower No. | % | Ditch: Upper No. | % | Ditch: Total No. | % | Palisade No. | % | Had VIII Pit No. | % | Site total No. | % |
|---|---|---|---|---|---|---|---|---|---|---|---|---|
| *Length (mm)* | | | | | | | | | | | | |
| 0–10 | 0 | 0.0 | 26 | 12.4 | 26 | 11.9 | 0 | 0.0 | 0 | 0.0 | 92 | 8.9 |
| 10–20 | 0 | 0.0 | 62 | 29.7 | 62 | 28.3 | 12 | 52.2 | 8 | 21.1 | 411 | 39.7 |
| 20–30 | 4 | 40.0 | 73 | 34.9 | 77 | 35.2 | 5 | 21.7 | 20 | 52.6 | 343 | 33.2 |
| 30–40 | 6 | 60.0 | 36 | 17.2 | 42 | 19.2 | 4 | 17.4 | 7 | 18.4 | 145 | 14.0 |
| 40–50 | 0 | 0.0 | 10 | 4.8 | 10 | 4.6 | 1 | 4.3 | 3 | 7.9 | 35 | 3.4 |
| 50+ | 0 | 0.0 | 2 | 1.0 | 2 | 0.9 | 1 | 4.3 | 0 | 0.0 | 8 | 0.8 |
| **Total** | **10** | **100** | **209** | **100** | **219** | **100** | **23** | **100** | **38** | **100** | **1034** | **100** |
| *Breadth (mm)* | | | | | | | | | | | | |
| 0–5 | 0 | 0.0 | 5 | 2.4 | 5 | 2.3 | 0 | 0.0 | 0 | 0.0 | 19 | 1.8 |
| 5–10 | 0 | 0.0 | 34 | 16.3 | 34 | 15.5 | 10 | 43.5 | 6 | 15.8 | 162 | 15.7 |
| 10–15 | 2 | 20.0 | 42 | 20.1 | 44 | 20.1 | 4 | 17.4 | 8 | 21.1 | 219 | 21.2 |
| 15–20 | 4 | 40.0 | 49 | 23.4 | 53 | 24.2 | 4 | 17.4 | 8 | 21.1 | 260 | 25.1 |
| 20–25 | 1 | 10.0 | 37 | 17.7 | 38 | 17.4 | 4 | 17.4 | 7 | 18.4 | 168 | 16.2 |
| 25–30 | 1 | 10.0 | 19 | 9.1 | 20 | 9.1 | 0 | 0.0 | 4 | 10.5 | 102 | 9.9 |
| 30–35 | 1 | 10.0 | 12 | 5.7 | 13 | 5.9 | 0 | 0.0 | 1 | 2.6 | 67 | 6.5 |
| 35+ | 1 | 10.0 | 11 | 5.3 | 12 | 5.5 | 1 | 4.3 | 4 | 10.5 | 37 | 3.6 |
| **Total** | **10** | **100** | **209** | **100** | **219** | **100** | **23** | **100** | **38** | **100** | **1034** | **100** |
| *Thickness (mm)* | | | | | | | | | | | | |
| 0–2 | 2 | 20.0 | 45 | 21.5 | 47 | 21.5 | 10 | 43.5 | 13 | 34.2 | 209 | 20.2 |
| 2–4 | 3 | 30.0 | 34 | 16.3 | 37 | 16.9 | 6 | 26.1 | 6 | 15.8 | 227 | 22.0 |
| 4–6 | 1 | 10.0 | 65 | 31.1 | 66 | 30.1 | 0 | 0.0 | 7 | 18.4 | 250 | 24.2 |
| 6–8 | 2 | 20.0 | 25 | 12.0 | 27 | 12.3 | 2 | 8.7 | 5 | 13.2 | 138 | 13.3 |
| 8–10 | 1 | 10.0 | 13 | 6.2 | 14 | 6.4 | 3 | 13.0 | 4 | 10.5 | 93 | 9.0 |
| 10–12 | 0 | 0.0 | 9 | 4.3 | 9 | 4.1 | 0 | 0.0 | 2 | 5.3 | 55 | 5.3 |
| 12+ | 1 | 10.0 | 18 | 8.6 | 19 | 8.7 | 2 | 8.7 | 1 | 2.6 | 62 | 6.0 |
| **Total** | **10** | **100** | **209** | **100** | **219** | **100** | **23** | **100** | **38** | **100** | **1034** | **100** |
| *Weight (g)* | | | | | | | | | | | | |
| 0–2 | 2 | 20.0 | 98 | 46.9 | 100 | 45.7 | 17 | 73.9 | 17 | 44.7 | 534 | 51.6 |
| 2–4 | 3 | 30.0 | 62 | 29.7 | 65 | 29.7 | 3 | 13.0 | 11 | 28.9 | 231 | 22.3 |
| 4–6 | 3 | 30.0 | 13 | 6.2 | 16 | 7.3 | 0 | 0.0 | 4 | 10.5 | 108 | 10.4 |
| 6–8 | 1 | 10.0 | 11 | 5.3 | 12 | 5.5 | 0 | 0.0 | 2 | 5.3 | 54 | 5.2 |
| 8–10 | 0 | 0.0 | 6 | 2.9 | 6 | 2.7 | 0 | 0.0 | 2 | 5.3 | 34 | 3.3 |
| 10–12 | 0 | 0.0 | 3 | 1.4 | 3 | 1.4 | 2 | 8.7 | 1 | 2.6 | 22 | 2.1 |
| 12–14 | 0 | 0.0 | 5 | 2.4 | 5 | 2.3 | 1 | 4.3 | 0 | 0.0 | 18 | 1.7 |
| 14+ | 1 | 10.0 | 11 | 5.3 | 12 | 5.5 | 0 | 0.0 | 1 | 2.6 | 33 | 3.2 |
| **Total** | **10** | **100** | **209** | **100** | **219** | **100** | **23** | **100** | **38** | **100** | **1034** | **100** |

(<3%) were found in the HAD '84 excavation area, in the HAD VIII pit (F.534) and in the upper ditch contexts; it was completely absent from the HAD '81, '82 and HAD IX excavation areas on the eastern and northern edges of the causewayed enclosure. Three cores were found with chalky cortex, all three from the HAD '87 excavation area. Two were from the ditch; one from the primary fills of Ditch H, the other from the upper deposits of N; both had narrow blade scars. The presence of these cores indicates that raw material was being imported from the chalk ridge and worked at the causewayed enclosure. The lack of cores and small quantities of chalk flint from the other Haddenham sites suggests that the enclosure may have had a special status in the working and distribution of this material.

The dominance of gravel flint compares well with the evidence from Foulmire Fen and the long barrow, but unlike this predominantly Mesolithic material the flint from the causewayed enclosure had a higher percentage of indifferent quality and medium grain (12%). In the palisade, primary ditch silts, HAD VIII and the HAD VIII pit (F.534) the percentage of poor material was much less, but this only partly reflects the higher proportion found of quality chalk flint.

Throughout the flint was largely dark brown-grey/black in colour. Only in the palisade and the

**Table 5.8b.** *Causewayed enclosure: metric analysis (based on complete waste flakes).*

| Division | 1981 Area | | 1982 Area | | 1984 Area | | 1987 Area | | Had VIII | | Had IX | |
|---|---|---|---|---|---|---|---|---|---|---|---|---|
| | No. | % | No. | % | No. | % | No. | % | No. | % | No. | % |
| *Length (mm)* | | | | | | | | | | | | |
| 0–10 | 26 | 8.5 | 5 | 3.3 | 26 | 22.4 | 7 | 6.0 | 2 | 3.3 | 0 | 0.0 |
| 10–20 | 127 | 41.6 | 62 | 40.5 | 49 | 42.2 | 54 | 46.6 | 36 | 59.0 | 3 | 33.3 |
| 20–30 | 105 | 34.4 | 58 | 37.9 | 27 | 23.3 | 31 | 26.7 | 17 | 27.9 | 4 | 44.4 |
| 30–40 | 38 | 12.5 | 23 | 15.0 | 10 | 8.6 | 16 | 13.8 | 5 | 8.2 | 2 | 22.2 |
| 40–50 | 7 | 2.3 | 5 | 3.3 | 3 | 2.6 | 6 | 5.2 | 1 | 1.6 | 0 | 0.0 |
| 50+ | 2 | 0.7 | 0 | 0.0 | 1 | 0.9 | 2 | 1.7 | 0 | 0.0 | 0 | 0.0 |
| **Total** | **303** | **100** | **153** | **100** | **116** | **100** | **116** | **100** | **61** | **100** | **9** | **100** |
| *Breadth (mm)* | | | | | | | | | | | | |
| 0–5 | 2 | 0.7 | 1 | 0.7 | 7 | 6.0 | 2 | 1.7 | 1 | 1.6 | 1 | 11.1 |
| 5–10 | 41 | 13.4 | 6 | 3.9 | 34 | 29.3 | 21 | 18.1 | 11 | 18.0 | 0 | 0.0 |
| 10–15 | 50 | 16.4 | 37 | 24.2 | 26 | 22.4 | 28 | 24.1 | 22 | 36.1 | 1 | 11.1 |
| 15–20 | 75 | 24.6 | 46 | 30.1 | 29 | 25.0 | 29 | 25.0 | 14 | 23.0 | 2 | 22.2 |
| 20–25 | 62 | 20.3 | 29 | 19.0 | 8 | 6.9 | 13 | 11.2 | 7 | 11.5 | 1 | 33.3 |
| 25–30 | 41 | 13.4 | 17 | 11.1 | 8 | 6.9 | 8 | 6.9 | 4 | 6.6 | 0 | 0.0 |
| 30–35 | 26 | 8.5 | 14 | 9.2 | 1 | 0.9 | 12 | 10.3 | 0 | 0.0 | 0 | 0.0 |
| 35+ | 8 | 2.6 | 3 | 2.0 | 3 | 2.6 | 3 | 2.6 | 2 | 3.3 | 2 | 22.2 |
| **Total** | **305** | **100** | **153** | **100** | **116** | **100** | **116** | **100** | **61** | **100** | **9** | **100** |
| *Thickness (mm)* | | | | | | | | | | | | |
| 0–2 | 38 | 12.5 | 17 | 11.1 | 39 | 33.6 | 24 | 20.7 | 22 | 36.1 | 0 | 0.0 |
| 2–4 | 61 | 20.0 | 39 | 25.5 | 30 | 25.9 | 28 | 24.1 | 17 | 27.9 | 3 | 33.3 |
| 4–6 | 85 | 27.9 | 35 | 22.9 | 16 | 13.8 | 28 | 24.1 | 10 | 16.4 | 4 | 44.4 |
| 6–8 | 50 | 16.4 | 30 | 19.6 | 6 | 5.2 | 16 | 13.8 | 3 | 4.9 | 0 | 0.0 |
| 8–10 | 27 | 8.9 | 15 | 9.8 | 17 | 14.7 | 10 | 8.6 | 4 | 6.6 | 1 | 11.1 |
| 10–12 | 25 | 8.2 | 10 | 6.5 | 0 | 0.0 | 6 | 5.2 | 3 | 4.9 | 1 | 11.1 |
| 12+ | 19 | 6.2 | 7 | 4.6 | 8 | 6.9 | 4 | 3.4 | 2 | 3.3 | 0 | 0.0 |
| **Total** | **305** | **100** | **153** | **100** | **116** | **100** | **116** | **100** | **61** | **100** | **9** | **100** |
| *Weight (g)* | | | | | | | | | | | | |
| 0–2 | 149 | 48.9 | 62 | 40.5 | 86 | 74.1 | 61 | 52.6 | 40 | 65.6 | 3 | 33.3 |
| 2–4 | 65 | 21.3 | 40 | 26.1 | 13 | 11.2 | 24 | 20.7 | 12 | 19.7 | 2 | 22.2 |
| 4–6 | 39 | 12.8 | 25 | 16.3 | 8 | 6.9 | 13 | 11.2 | 2 | 3.3 | 1 | 11.1 |
| 6–8 | 16 | 5.2 | 11 | 7.2 | 4 | 3.4 | 6 | 5.2 | 2 | 3.3 | 2 | 22.2 |
| 8–10 | 13 | 4.3 | 7 | 4.6 | 1 | 0.9 | 3 | 2.6 | 1 | 1.6 | 1 | 11.1 |
| 10–12 | 7 | 2.3 | 3 | 2.0 | 2 | 1.7 | 4 | 3.4 | 0 | 0.0 | 0 | 0.0 |
| 12–14 | 8 | 2.6 | 1 | 0.7 | 0 | 0.0 | 1 | 0.9 | 2 | 3.3 | 0 | 0.0 |
| 14+ | 8 | 2.6 | 4 | 2.6 | 2 | 1.7 | 4 | 3.4 | 2 | 3.3 | 0 | 0.0 |
| **Total** | **305** | **100** | **153** | **100** | **116** | **100** | **116** | **100** | **61** | **100** | **9** | **100** |

F.534 pit were there high proportions of flint of other colours.

*Technology* (Tables 5.6, 5.7, 5.10 & 5.11)

The assemblage was a mixture of Middle and Late Neolithic material and the technological data reflects this. The palisade, ditch and HAD VIII pit frequently stand out from the rest of the assemblage and often share features with the HAD '84 and '87 excavation areas.

The majority of the pieces have hertzian cones of percussion which suggest the use of hard hammers (Table 5.6). In the primary silts of the ditch all pieces had hertzian cones while in the palisade 87% had this trait. The average for the assemblage as a whole was 95%,

higher than most of the other Haddenham sites except Church's Drove (see Chapter 4 above). The report on the flint from the long barrow (Middleton, Chapter 3 above) links this lack of soft-hammer technique to a regional dependence on small nodules of raw material which preclude elaborate core preparation necessary for the use of soft hammers. The material from the causewayed enclosure and other Haddenham sites supports this view as most cores found were not heavily worked and were of small size (see below).

An analysis of the amount of cortex surviving on waste flakes suggests that all stages of the knapping sequence are represented (Table 5.10). The proportions differ from those from Foulmire Fen and the long

**Table 5.9a.** *Causewayed enclosure: flake characterization (based on complete waste flakes).*

| Division | Ditch: Lower | | Ditch: Upper | | Ditch: Total | | Palisade | | Had VIII Pit | | Site total | |
|---|---|---|---|---|---|---|---|---|---|---|---|---|
| Type | No. | % | No. | % | No. | % | No. | % | No. | % | No. | % |
| *Ratios (n:5)* | | | | | | | | | | | | |
| 0–1 | 0 | 0.0 | 2 | 1.0 | 2 | 0.9 | 1 | 4.3 | 1 | 2.6 | 6 | 0.6 |
| 1–2 | 1 | 10.0 | 12 | 5.7 | 13 | 5.9 | 5 | 21.7 | 5 | 13.2 | 60 | 5.8 |
| 2–3 | 4 | 40.0 | 38 | 18.2 | 42 | 19.2 | 9 | 39.1 | 11 | 28.9 | 184 | 17.8 |
| 3–4 | 1 | 10.0 | 50 | 23.9 | 51 | 23.3 | 3 | 13.0 | 5 | 13.2 | 221 | 21.4 |
| 4–5 | 3 | 30.0 | 49 | 23.4 | 52 | 23.7 | 3 | 13.0 | 6 | 15.8 | 238 | 23.0 |
| 5–6 | 1 | 10.0 | 15 | 7.2 | 16 | 7.3 | 0 | 0.0 | 4 | 10.5 | 101 | 9.8 |
| 6–7 | 0 | 0.0 | 24 | 11.5 | 24 | 11.0 | 1 | 4.3 | 2 | 5.3 | 107 | 10.3 |
| 7–8 | 0 | 0.0 | 9 | 4.3 | 9 | 4.1 | 0 | 0.0 | 3 | 7.9 | 47 | 4.5 |
| 8–9 | 0 | 0.0 | 3 | 1.4 | 3 | 1.4 | 1 | 4.3 | 1 | 2.6 | 32 | 3.1 |
| 9+ | 0 | 0.0 | 7 | 3.3 | 7 | 3.2 | 0 | 0.0 | 0 | 0.0 | 38 | 3.7 |
| **Total** | **10** | **100** | **209** | **100** | **219** | **100** | **23** | **100** | **38** | **100** | **1034** | **100** |
| % Blades | 1 | 10.0 | 14 | 6.7 | 15 | 6.8 | 6 | 26.1 | 6 | 15.8 | 66 | 6.4 |
| % Flakes | 8 | 80.0 | 137 | 65.6 | 145 | 66.2 | 15 | 65.2 | 22 | 57.9 | 643 | 62.2 |
| % Broad flakes | 1 | 10.0 | 58 | 27.8 | 59 | 26.9 | 2 | 8.7 | 10 | 26.3 | 325 | 31.4 |
| % Flakes – blade scars | 3 | 17.6 | 42 | 11.6 | 45 | 11.8 | 7 | 15.2 | 14 | 20.3 | 232 | 12.4 |
| % Flakes + brk blades | 1 | 5.9 | 39 | 10.7 | 40 | 10.5 | 11 | 23.9 | 21 | 30.4 | 200 | 10.7 |
| *Possible use* | | | | | | | | | | | | |
| Cutting | 1 | 10.0 | 5 | 2.4 | 6 | 2.7 | 1 | 4.3 | 4 | 10.5 | 21 | 2.0 |
| Awls | 0 | 0.0 | 7 | 3.3 | 7 | 3.2 | 1 | 4.3 | 4 | 10.5 | 26 | 2.5 |
| Other | 9 | 90.0 | 197 | 94.3 | 206 | 94.1 | 21 | 91.3 | 30 | 78.9 | 987 | 95.5 |
| **Total** | **10** | **100** | **209** | **100** | **219** | **100** | **23** | **100** | **38** | **100** | **1034** | **100** |

**Table 5.9b.** *Causewayed enclosure: flake characterization (based on complete waste flakes).*

| Division | 1981 Area | | 1982 Area | | 1984 Area | | 1987 Area | | Had VIII | | Had IX | |
|---|---|---|---|---|---|---|---|---|---|---|---|---|
| | No. | % | No. | % | No. | % | No. | % | No. | % | No. | % |
| *Ratios (n:5)* | | | | | | | | | | | | |
| 0–1 | 0 | 0.0 | 0 | 0.0 | 3 | 2.6 | 0 | 0.0 | 0 | 0.0 | 0 | 0.0 |
| 1–2 | 16 | 5.2 | 2 | 1.3 | 7 | 6.0 | 9 | 7.8 | 2 | 3.3 | 1 | 11.1 |
| 2–3 | 34 | 11.1 | 32 | 20.9 | 22 | 19.0 | 23 | 19.8 | 12 | 19.7 | 0 | 0.0 |
| 3–4 | 63 | 20.7 | 31 | 20.3 | 22 | 19.0 | 28 | 24.1 | 16 | 26.2 | 2 | 22.2 |
| 4–5 | 60 | 19.7 | 38 | 24.8 | 44 | 37.9 | 21 | 18.1 | 15 | 24.6 | 1 | 11.1 |
| 5–6 | 42 | 13.8 | 17 | 11.1 | 10 | 8.6 | 8 | 6.9 | 3 | 4.9 | 3 | 33.3 |
| 6–7 | 40 | 13.1 | 16 | 10.5 | 5 | 4.3 | 13 | 11.2 | 5 | 8.2 | 1 | 11.1 |
| 7–8 | 18 | 5.9 | 5 | 3.3 | 0 | 0.0 | 9 | 7.8 | 3 | 4.9 | 0 | 0.0 |
| 8–9 | 14 | 4.6 | 8 | 5.2 | 0 | 0.0 | 3 | 2.6 | 1 | 1.6 | 1 | 11.1 |
| 9+ | 18 | 5.9 | 4 | 2.6 | 3 | 2.6 | 2 | 1.7 | 4 | 6.6 | 0 | 0.0 |
| **Total** | **305** | **100** | **153** | **100** | **116** | **100** | **116** | **100** | **61** | **100** | **9** | **100** |
| % Blades | 16 | 5.2 | 2 | 1.3 | 10 | 8.6 | 9 | 7.8 | 2 | 3.3 | 1 | 11.1 |
| % Flakes | 157 | 51.5 | 101 | 66.0 | 88 | 75.9 | 72 | 62.1 | 43 | 70.5 | 3 | 33.3 |
| % Broad flakes | 132 | 43.3 | 50 | 32.7 | 18 | 15.5 | 35 | 30.2 | 16 | 26.5 | 5 | 55.6 |
| % Flakes – blade scars | 37 | 7.1 | 19 | 7.3 | 28 | 11.7 | 28 | 14.3 | 9 | 6.0 | 0 | 0.0 |
| % Flakes + brk blades | 32 | 6.1 | 14 | 5.4 | 23 | 9.6 | 9 | 4.6 | 9 | 6.0 | 1 | 9.1 |
| *Possible use* | | | | | | | | | | | | |
| Cutting | 5 | 1.6 | 3 | 2.0 | 2 | 1.7 | 0 | 0.0 | 0 | 0.0 | 0 | 0.0 |
| Awls | 4 | 1.3 | 2 | 1.3 | 4 | 3.4 | 2 | 1.7 | 2 | 3.3 | 0 | 0.0 |
| Other | 296 | 97.0 | 148 | 96.7 | 110 | 94.8 | 114 | 98.3 | 59 | 96.7 | 9 | 100.0 |
| **Total** | **305** | **100** | **153** | **100** | **116** | **100** | **116** | **100** | **61** | **100** | **9** | **100** |

**Table 5.10.** *Causewayed enclosure: flake cortex (based on complete waste flakes).*

| Division<br>Type | Ditch: Lower<br>No. | %  | Ditch: Upper<br>No. | %  | Ditch: Total<br>No. | %  | Palisade<br>No. | %  | Had VIII Pit<br>No. | %  | Site total<br>No. | %  |
|---|---|---|---|---|---|---|---|---|---|---|---|---|
| *% Cortex* | | | | | | | | | | | | |
| 0 | 1 | 10.0 | 72 | 34.1 | 73 | 33.0 | 10 | 43.5 | 14 | 36.8 | 361 | 34.8 |
| 0–25 | 5 | 50.0 | 81 | 38.4 | 86 | 38.9 | 11 | 47.8 | 19 | 50.0 | 377 | 36.4 |
| 25–50 | 2 | 20.0 | 16 | 7.6 | 18 | 8.1 | 1 | 4.3 | 2 | 5.3 | 110 | 10.6 |
| 50–75 | 0 | 0.0 | 17 | 8.1 | 17 | 7.7 | 1 | 4.3 | 2 | 5.3 | 79 | 7.6 |
| 75–100 | 0 | 0.0 | 6 | 2.8 | 6 | 2.7 | 0 | 0.0 | 1 | 2.6 | 48 | 4.6 |
| 100 | 2 | 20.0 | 19 | 90 | 21 | 9.5 | 0 | 0.0 | 0 | 0.0 | 61 | 5.9 |
| **Total** | **10** | **100** | **211** | **100** | **221** | **100** | **23** | **100** | **38** | **100** | **1036** | **100** |

| Division<br>Type | 1981 Area<br>No. | %  | 1982 Area<br>No. | %  | 1984 Area<br>No. | %  | 1987 Area<br>No. | %  | Had VIII<br>No. | %  | Had IX<br>No. | %  |
|---|---|---|---|---|---|---|---|---|---|---|---|---|
| *% Cortex* | | | | | | | | | | | | |
| 0 | 91 | 29.8 | 51 | 33.3 | 43 | 37.1 | 47 | 40.5 | 31 | 50.8 | 4 | 44.4 |
| 0–25 | 111 | 36.4 | 56 | 36.6 | 40 | 34.5 | 42 | 36.2 | 12 | 19.7 | 1 | 11.1 |
| 25–50 | 36 | 11.8 | 16 | 10.5 | 18 | 15.5 | 8 | 6.9 | 10 | 16.4 | 2 | 22.2 |
| 50–75 | 22 | 7.2 | 13 | 8.5 | 6 | 5.2 | 14 | 12.1 | 2 | 3.3 | 2 | 22.2 |
| 75–100 | 25 | 8.2 | 7 | 4.6 | 5 | 4.3 | 1 | 0.9 | 4 | 6.6 | 0 | 0.0 |
| 100 | 20 | 6.6 | 10 | 6.5 | 4 | 3.4 | 4 | 3.4 | 2 | 3.3 | 0 | 0.0 |
| **Total** | **305** | **100** | **153** | **100** | **116** | **100** | **116** | **100** | **61** | **100** | **9** | **100** |

**Table 5.11.** *Causewayed enclosure: flake typology (based on all waste flakes).*

| Division<br>Type | Ditch: Lower<br>No. | %  | Ditch: Upper<br>No. | %  | Ditch: Total<br>No. | %  | Palisade<br>No. | %  | Had VIII Pit<br>No. | %  | Site total<br>No. | %  |
|---|---|---|---|---|---|---|---|---|---|---|---|---|
| Unretouched flakes | 13 | 76.5 | 259 | 71.3 | 272 | 71.6 | 42 | 91.3 | 61 | 88.4 | 1428 | 76.3 |
| Dressing chips | 0 | 0.0 | 40 | 11.0 | 40 | 10.5 | 1 | 2.2 | 2 | 2.9 | 179 | 9.6 |
| Trimming flakes | 0 | 0.0 | 2 | 0.6 | 2 | 0.5 | 0 | 0.0 | 0 | 0.0 | 7 | 0.4 |
| Preparation flakes | 2 | 11.8 | 34 | 9.4 | 36 | 9.5 | 1 | 2.2 | 2 | 2.9 | 145 | 7.7 |
| Thinning flakes | 1 | 5.9 | 11 | 3.0 | 12 | 3.2 | 0 | 0.0 | 0 | 0.0 | 43 | 2.3 |
| Core rejuvenation flakes | 1 | 5.9 | 17 | 4.7 | 18 | 4.7 | 2 | 4.3 | 4 | 5.8 | 69 | 3.7 |
| **Total** | **17** | **100** | **363** | **100** | **380** | **100** | **46** | **100** | **69** | **100** | **1871** | **100** |

| Division<br>Type | 1981 Area<br>No. | %  | 1982 Area<br>No. | %  | 1984 Area<br>No. | %  | 1987 Area<br>No. | %  | Had VIII<br>No. | %  | Had IX<br>No. | %  |
|---|---|---|---|---|---|---|---|---|---|---|---|---|
| Unretouched flakes | 394 | 75.5 | 203 | 77.8 | 188 | 78.3 | 148 | 75.5 | 114 | 76.5 | 10 | 90.9 |
| Dressing chips | 49 | 9.3 | 17 | 6.3 | 28 | 12.0 | 29 | 15.2 | 12 | 8.1 | 0 | 0.0 |
| Trimming flakes | 2 | 0.0 | 0 | 0.0 | 2 | 0.0 | 1 | 0.0 | 0 | 0.0 | 0 | 0.0 |
| Preparation flakes | 51 | 9.3 | 21 | 7.7 | 13 | 5.2 | 7 | 3.5 | 14 | 9.4 | 0 | 0.0 |
| Thinning flakes | 9 | 1.6 | 9 | 3.3 | 5 | 2.0 | 2 | 1.0 | 5 | 3.4 | 1 | 9.1 |
| Core-rejuvenation flakes | 17 | 3.1 | 11 | 4.0 | 4 | 1.6 | 9 | 4.5 | 4 | 2.7 | 0 | 0.0 |
| **Total** | **522** | **100** | **261** | **100** | **240** | **100** | **196** | **100** | **149** | **100** | **11** | **100** |

**Table 5.12a.** *Causewayed enclosure: core typology.*

| Division Type | Ditch: Lower No. | % | Ditch: Upper No. | % | Ditch: Total No. | % | Palisade No. | % | Had VIII Pit No. | % | Site total No. | % |
|---|---|---|---|---|---|---|---|---|---|---|---|---|
| *Clarke typology* | | | | | | | | | | | | |
| A1 | 0 | 0.0 | 0 | 0.0 | 0 | 0.0 | 0 | 0.0 | 0 | 0.0 | 1 | 1.0 |
| A2 | 1 | 50.0 | 7 | 41.2 | 8 | 42.1 | 0 | 1.0 | 0 | 0.0 | 4l | 42.7 |
| B1 | 0 | 0.0 | 1 | 5.9 | 1 | 5.3 | 0 | 0.0 | 0 | 0.0 | 1 | 1.0 |
| B2 | 0 | 0.0 | 3 | 17.6 | 3 | 15.8 | 0 | 0.0 | 0 | 0.0 | 16 | 16.6 |
| B3 | 0 | 0.0 | 1 | 5.9 | 1 | 5.3 | 0 | 0.0 | 0 | 0.0 | 2 | 2.1 |
| D | 1 | 50.0 | 1 | 5.9 | 2 | 10.5 | 0 | 0.0 | 0 | 0.0 | 13 | 13.5 |
| E | 0 | 0.0 | 1 | 5.9 | 1 | 5.3 | 0 | 0.0 | 0 | 0.0 | 2 | 2.1 |
| Ill-defined | 0 | 0.0 | 0 | 0.0 | 0 | 0.0 | 0 | 0.0 | 0 | 0.0 | 2 | 2.1 |
| Damaged | 0 | 0.0 | 2 | 11.8 | 2 | 10.5 | 0 | 0.0 | 0 | 0.0 | 8 | 8.3 |
| Crude bashed pebble | 0 | 0.0 | 1 | 5.9 | l | 5.3 | 0 | 0.0 | 0 | 0.0 | 10 | 10.4 |
| **Total** | **2** | **100** | **17** | **100** | **19** | **100** | **0** | **0.0** | **0** | **0.0** | **96** | **100** |
| *Ford typology* | | | | | | | | | | | | |
| Type 1 | 1 | 50.0 | 0 | 0.0 | 1 | 5.3 | 0 | 0.0 | 0 | 0.0 | 2 | 2.1 |
| Type 2 | 0 | 0.0 | 2 | 11.8 | 2 | 10.5 | 0 | 0.0 | 0 | 0.0 | 12 | 12.5 |
| Type 3 | 0 | 0.0 | 8 | 47.1 | 8 | 42.1 | 0 | 0.0 | 0 | 0.0 | 15 | 15.6 |
| Type 4 | 0 | 0.0 | 1 | 5.9 | 1 | 5.3 | 0 | 0.0 | 0 | 0.0 | 3 | 3.1 |
| Type 5 | 0 | 0.0 | 0 | 0.0 | 0 | 0.0 | 0 | 0.0 | 0 | 0.0 | 10 | 10.4 |
| Type 6 | 1 | 50.0 | 6 | 35.3 | 7 | 36.8 | 0 | 0.0 | 0 | 0.0 | 50 | 52.1 |
| Type 8 | 0 | 0.0 | 0 | 0.0 | 0 | 0.0 | 0 | 0.0 | 0 | 0.0 | 4 | 4.2 |
| **Total** | **2** | **100** | **17** | **100** | **19** | **100** | **0** | **0.0** | **0** | **0.0** | **96** | **100** |
| *Core weight (g)* | | | | | | | | | | | | |
| 0–10 | 0 | 0.0 | 2 | 11.8 | 2 | 10.5 | 0 | 0.0 | 0 | 0.0 | 18 | 18.8 |
| 10–20 | 0 | 0.0 | 5 | 29.4 | 5 | 26.3 | 0 | 0.0 | 0 | 0.0 | 30 | 31.3 |
| 20–30 | 0 | 0.0 | 7 | 41.2 | 7 | 36.8 | 0 | 0.0 | 0 | 0.0 | 28 | 29.2 |
| 30–40 | 1 | 50.0 | 1 | 5.9 | 2 | 10.5 | 0 | 0.0 | 0 | 0.0 | 13 | 13.5 |
| 40–50 | 0 | 0.0 | 2 | 11.8 | 2 | 10.5 | 0 | 0.0 | 0 | 0.0 | 5 | 5.2 |
| 50+ | 1 | 50.0 | 0 | 0.0 | 1 | 5.3 | 0 | 0.0 | 0 | 0.0 | 2 | 2.1 |
| **Total** | **2** | **100** | **17** | **100** | **19** | **100** | **0** | **0.0** | **0** | **0.0** | **96** | **100** |
| *% Cortex* | | | | | | | | | | | | |
| 0 | 0 | 0.0 | 5 | 29.4 | 5 | 26.3 | 0 | 0.0 | 0 | 0.0 | 15 | 15.6 |
| 0–25 | 0 | 0.0 | 5 | 29.4 | 5 | 26.3 | 0 | 0.0 | 0 | 0.0 | 17 | 17.7 |
| 25–50 | 1 | 50.0 | 3 | 17.6 | 4 | 21.1 | 0 | 0.0 | 0 | 0.0 | 30 | 31.3 |
| 50–75 | 1 | 50.0 | 3 | 17.6 | 4 | 21.1 | 0 | 0.0 | 0 | 0.0 | 28 | 29.2 |
| 75–100 | 0 | 0.0 | 1 | 5.9 | 1 | 5.3 | 0 | 0.0 | 0 | 0.0 | 6 | 6.3 |
| 100 | 0 | 0.0 | 0 | 0.0 | 0 | 0.0 | 0 | 0.0 | 0 | 0.0 | 0 | 0.0 |
| **Total** | **2** | **100** | **l7** | **100** | **19** | **100** | **0** | **0.0** | **0** | **0.0** | **96** | **100** |

barrow predominantly Mesolithic sites, having few non-cortical pieces and a greater proportion of heavily corticaled pieces. This suggests more raw material was being brought to the site for primary working which is supported by the core evidence. The palisade has lower proportions of corticated material while the primary ditch silts contained a greater proportion of such pieces. This may hint at an incorporation of primary flint flakes in the base of the ditch and the incorporation of more fully worked flakes within the palisade fills.

The overall quality of the flaking (poorer than the Foulmire Mesolithic assemblages) is apparent from a number of technological traits (Table 5.6):

1. Feather terminations predominate (55%);

2. There is a large percentage of hinge terminations (32%);

3. There is a high proportion of cortical platforms (29%);

4. There is a high proportion of side-struck material (44%);

5. There is a high proportion of faceted platforms (18%).

The quality of the flaking is undoubtedly better in the palisade, ditch and HAD VIII pit, having a greater proportion of feather terminations, fewer hinged pieces, fewer cortical platforms and low proportions of side-struck material. There is also some evidence to suggest a higher quality of flaking in the HAD '84 excavation area (fewer hinge terminations) and in the

**Table 5.12b.** *Causewayed enclosure: core typology.*

| Division<br>Type | 1981 Area<br>No. | %   | 1982 Area<br>No. | %   | 1984 Area<br>No. | %   | 1987 Area<br>No. | %   | Had VIII<br>No. | %   | Had IX<br>No. | %   |
|---|---|---|---|---|---|---|---|---|---|---|---|---|
| *Clarke typology* | | | | | | | | | | | | |
| A1 | 0 | 0.0 | 0 | 0.0 | 0 | 0.0 | 0 | 0.0 | 1 | 20.0 | 0 | 0.0 |
| A2 | 21 | 47.7 | 8 | 42.1 | 1 | 50.0 | 1 | 33.3 | 1 | 20.0 | 1 | 25.0 |
| B2 | 5 | 11.4 | 5 | 26.3 | 0 | 0.0 | 1 | 33.3 | 0 | 0.0 | 2 | 50.0 |
| B3 | 0 | 0.0 | 0 | 0.0 | 0 | 0.0 | 0 | 0.0 | 1 | 20.0 | 0 | 0.0 |
| D | 9 | 20.5 | 1 | 5.3 | 0 | 0.0 | 1 | 33.3 | 0 | 0.0 | 0 | 0.0 |
| E | 1 | 2.3 | 0 | 0.0 | 0 | 0.0 | 0 | 0.0 | 0 | 0.0 | 0 | 0.0 |
| Damaged | 2 | 4.5 | 2 | 10.5 | 0 | 0.0 | 0 | 0.0 | 1 | 20.0 | 1 | 25.0 |
| Ill-defined | 2 | 4.5 | 0 | 0.0 | 0 | 0.0 | 0 | 0.0 | 0 | 0.0 | 0 | 0.0 |
| Crude bashed pebble | 4 | 9.1 | 3 | 15.8 | 1 | 50.0 | 0 | 0.0 | 1 | 20.0 | 0 | 0.0 |
| **Total** | **44** | **100** | **19** | **100** | **2** | **100** | **3** | **100** | **5** | **100** | **4** | **100** |
| *Ford typology* | | | | | | | | | | | | |
| Type 1 | 0 | 0.0 | 1 | 5.3 | 0 | 0.0 | 0 | 0.0 | 0 | 0.0 | 0 | 0.0 |
| Type 2 | 5 | 11.4 | 3 | 15.8 | 1 | 50.0 | 0 | 0.0 | 1 | 20.0 | 0 | 0.0 |
| Type 3 | 3 | 6.8 | 3 | 15.8 | 0 | 0.0 | 0 | 0.0 | 1 | 20.0 | 0 | 0.0 |
| Type 4 | 0 | 0.0 | 1 | 5.3 | 0 | 0.0 | 0 | 0.0 | 1 | 20.0 | 0 | 0.0 |
| Type 5 | 4 | 9.1 | 5 | 26.3 | 0 | 0.0 | 1 | 33.3 | 0 | 0.0 | 0 | 0.0 |
| Type 6 | 31 | 70.5 | 4 | 21.1 | 1 | 50.0 | 2 | 66.7 | 1 | 20.0 | 4 | 100.0 |
| Type 8 | 1 | 2.3 | 2 | 10.5 | 0 | 0.0 | 0 | 0.0 | 1 | 20.0 | 0 | 0.0 |
| **Total** | **44** | **100** | **19** | **100** | **2** | **100** | **3** | **100** | **5** | **100** | **4** | **100** |
| *Core weight (g)* | | | | | | | | | | | | |
| 0–10 | 6 | 13.6 | 6 | 31.6 | 1 | 50.0 | 1 | 33.3 | 0 | 0.0 | 2 | 50.0 |
| 10–20 | 19 | 43.2 | 3 | 15.8 | 1 | 50.0 | 0 | 0.0 | 2 | 40.0 | 0 | 0.0 |
| 20–30 | 11 | 25.0 | 6 | 31.6 | 0 | 0.0 | 1 | 33.3 | 1 | 20.0 | 2 | 50.0 |
| 30–40 | 6 | 13.6 | 4 | 21.1 | 0 | 0.0 | 1 | 33.3 | 0 | 0.0 | 0 | 0.0 |
| 40–50 | 2 | 4.5 | 0 | 0.0 | 0 | 0.0 | 0 | 0.0 | 1 | 20.0 | 0 | 0.0 |
| 50+ | 0 | 0.0 | 0 | 0.0 | 0 | 0.0 | 0 | 0.0 | 1 | 20.0 | 0 | 0.0 |
| **Total** | **44** | **100** | **19** | **100** | **2** | **100** | **3** | **100** | **5** | **100** | **4** | **100** |
| *% Cortex* | | | | | | | | | | | | |
| 0 | 5 | 11.4 | 4 | 21.1 | 0 | 0.0 | 0 | 0.0 | 1 | 20.0 | 0 | 0.0 |
| 0–25 | 5 | 11.4 | 5 | 26.3 | 1 | 50.0 | 0 | 0.0 | 0 | 0.0 | 1 | 25.0 |
| 25–50 | 15 | 34.1 | 6 | 31.6 | 0 | 0.0 | 2 | 66.7 | 1 | 20.0 | 2 | 50.0 |
| 50–75 | 15 | 34.1 | 4 | 21.1 | 1 | 50.0 | 1 | 33.3 | 2 | 40.0 | 1 | 25.0 |
| 75–100 | 4 | 9.1 | 0 | 0.0 | 0 | 0.0 | 0 | 0.0 | 1 | 20.0 | 0 | 0.0 |
| 100 | 0 | 0.0 | 0 | 0.0 | 0 | 0.0 | 0 | 0.0 | 0 | 0.0 | 0 | 0.0 |
| **Total** | **44** | **100** | **19** | **100** | **2** | **100** | **3** | **100** | **5** | **100** | **4** | **100** |

HAD '87 excavation area (fewer cortical platforms).

Most of the flint including that from the ditch has long (>10 mm) and thick (>4 mm wide) platforms with the majority of platform angles over 100° (Table 5.7). However in the palisade, HAD '84 and '87 areas, HAD VIII and the F. 534 pit, platforms are shorter and thinner and a high percentage have platform angles under 100°.

All stages of the core-reduction sequence were present and the proportions differ from the Foulmire sites (see Chapter 3), the main differences being a higher proportion of cores, core-rejuvenation flakes and preparation flakes and a lower percentage of dressing and trimming flakes (Table 5.11). This may suggest that more primary working of raw material occurred at the causewayed enclosure but less implement production. The primary ditch silts have the highest proportion of cores, core-rejuvenation flakes and core-preparation flakes and no evidence for implement production. The HAD '81 and '82 areas also have high proportions suggestive of core working. In contrast the palisade, HAD '81 and '84 areas have few of no cores, few core-reduction flakes (hereafter CRF) and few preparation flakes but have higher proportions of dressing and trimming flakes (except the palisade which contained mainly unretouched flakes) which suggests more implement production.

**Table 5.13a.** *Causewayed enclosure: raw material (based on whole assemblage).*

| Division Type | Ditch: Lower No. | % | Ditch: Upper No. | % | Ditch: Total No. | % | Palisade No. | % | Had VIII Pit No. | % | Site total No. | % |
|---|---|---|---|---|---|---|---|---|---|---|---|---|
| *Source* | | | | | | | | | | | | |
| Pebble | 13 | 65.0 | 191 | 77.3 | 204 | 76.4 | 13 | 56.5 | 25 | 67.6 | 919 | 73.4 |
| Abraded nodule | 6 | 30.0 | 50 | 20.2 | 56 | 21.0 | 9 | 39.1 | 11 | 29.7 | 309 | 24.7 |
| Unabraded nodule | 1 | 5.0 | 6 | 2.4 | 7 | 2.6 | 1 | 4.3 | 1 | 2.7 | 24 | 1.9 |
| **Total** | **20** | **100** | **247** | **100** | **267** | **100** | **23** | **100** | **37** | **100** | **1252** | **100** |
| *Quality* | | | | | | | | | | | | |
| Good | 29 | 96.7 | 386 | 86.9 | 415 | 87.6 | 49 | 96.1 | 62 | 89.9 | 1941 | 87.7 |
| Bad | 0 | 0.0 | 0 | 0.0 | 0 | 0.0 | 0 | 0.0 | 0 | 0.0 | 0 | 0.0 |
| Indifferent | 1 | 3.3 | 58 | 13.1 | 59 | 12.4 | 2 | 3.9 | 7 | 10.1 | 271 | 12.3 |
| **Total** | **30** | **100** | **444** | **100** | **474** | **100** | **51** | **100** | **69** | **100** | **2212** | **100** |
| *Grain* | | | | | | | | | | | | |
| Fine | 28 | 93.3 | 385 | 86.7 | 413 | 87.1 | 48 | 94.1 | 59 | 85.5 | 1942 | 88.0 |
| Medium | 2 | 6.7 | 59 | 13.3 | 61 | 12.9 | 3 | 5.9 | 10 | 14.5 | 264 | 12.0 |
| Coarse | 0 | 0.0 | 0 | 1.0 | 9 | 0.0 | 0 | 0.0 | 0 | 0.0 | 0 | 0.0 |
| **Total** | **30** | **100** | **444** | **100** | **474** | **100** | **51** | **100** | **69** | **100** | **2206** | **100** |
| *Colour* | | | | | | | | | | | | |
| Dark grey/brown | 19 | 63.3 | 229 | 51.6 | 248 | 52.3 | 27 | 54.0 | 39 | 56.5 | 1168 | 52.8 |
| Light grey | 0 | 0.0 | 51 | 11.5 | 51 | 10.8 | 5 | 10.0 | 13 | 18.8 | 191 | 8.6 |
| Light brown | 9 | 30.0 | 157 | 35.4 | 166 | 35.0 | 14 | 28.0 | 15 | 21.7 | 823 | 37.2 |
| White | 1 | 3.3 | 5 | 1.1 | 6 | 1.3 | 3 | 6.0 | 1 | 1.4 | 19 | 0.9 |
| Other | 1 | 3.3 | 2 | 0.5 | 3 | 0.6 | 1 | 2.0 | 1 | 1.4 | 11 | 0.5 |
| **Total** | **30** | **100** | **444** | **100** | **474** | **100** | **50** | **100** | **69** | **100** | **2212** | **100** |

*Metrical attributes* (Tables 5.8, 5.9 & 5.12)
The largest number of flakes were 10–20 mm long, 15–20 mm wide, 4–6 mm thick and 0–2 g in weight. This reflects the range of material present and contrasts with the Foulmire Mesolithic sites having generally smaller, broader and thicker flakes. This may in part reflect the small size and poor quality of the raw material and in part the poor quality of the flaking.

In the palisade and ditch contexts the flakes were longer, narrower, thinner and lighter. The HAD '84 and '87 excavation areas and HAD VIII (including the F.534 pit) have greater proportions of narrower and thinner flakes.

The breadth:length ratios (Table 5.9) indicated that the assemblages contained 7% blades, 61% flakes, and 33% broad flakes. When broken blades are included the percentage of blades rises to 11% and 12% of flakes had blade scars on their dorsal surfaces. The palisade, ditch, pit F.534 and HAD '84 and '87 excavation areas had the highest proportions of blades, broken blades and flakes with blade scars while the HAD '81, '82, '87, HAD VIII and HAD IX areas had the highest proportions of broad flakes. This suggests that blade technology and Middle Neolithic activity was predominantly concentrated along the western face of the causewayed enclosure and its adjacent interior.

The core typology (Table 5.12) shows a predominance of one- and two-platform cores (64%) with a high percentage of keeled forms (14%). Most of the single platform flake cores had flakes removed part way round, the two-platform cores mainly had one platform at an oblique angle and the keeled forms mainly had flakes removed from two directions. These traits and the lack of three-platform types reflect the small size of the raw material available.

An analysis of the cores following Ford's 1987 typology reveals a separation into cores with flake scars of 5:2 (30%), cores with flake scars between 2:1 and 5:2 (14%) and cores with broad flake scars (52%) reflecting the mixed nature of the assemblage. Of the 96 cores found associated with the causewayed enclosure, the majority (71%) occurred in the HAD '81, '82 and HAD VIII excavation areas and the HAD '81 area contained a high proportion of cores with broad flake scars. The highest proportion of cores with blade scars was found in the ditch contexts and in the HAD VIII area.

The average core weight was similar to the Foulmire sites (79% were under 30 g) but core weights were generally heavier in the upper ditch contexts (59% over 20 g) and heaviest in the primary

**Table 5.13b.** *Causewayed enclosure: raw material (based on whole assemblage).*

| Division | 1981 Area | | 1982 Area | | 1984 Area | | 1987 Area | | Had VIII | | Had IX | |
|---|---|---|---|---|---|---|---|---|---|---|---|---|
| Type | No. | % | No. | % | No. | % | No. | % | No. | % | No. | % |
| *Source* | | | | | | | | | | | | |
| Pebble | 310 | 78.9 | 123 | 68.3 | 112 | 79.4 | 71 | 63.4 | 52 | 61.2 | 9 | 64.3 |
| Abraded Nodule | 83 | 21.1 | 57 | 31.7 | 28 | 19.9 | 34 | 30.4 | 26 | 10.6 | 5 | 35.7 |
| Unabraded Nodule | 0 | 0.0 | 0 | 0.0 | 1 | 0.7 | 7 | 6.3 | 7 | 8.2 | 0 | 0.0 |
| **Total** | **393** | **100** | **180** | **100** | **141** | **100** | **112** | **100** | **85** | **100** | **14** | **100** |
| *Quality* | | | | | | | | | | | | |
| Good | 549 | 85.2 | 276 | 89.6 | 231 | 88.2 | 190 | 88.0 | 151 | 90.4 | 18 | 85.7 |
| Bad | 0 | 0.0 | 1 | 0.0 | 0 | 0.0 | 0 | 0.0 | 1 | 0.0 | 0 | 0.0 |
| Indifferent | 95 | 14.8 | 32 | 10.4 | 31 | 11.8 | 26 | 12.0 | 16 | 9.6 | 3 | 14.3 |
| **Total** | **644** | **100** | **308** | **100** | **262** | **100** | **216** | **100** | **167** | **100** | **21** | **100** |
| *Grain* | | | | | | | | | | | | |
| Fine | 556 | 87.1 | 274 | 89.0 | 238 | 90.8 | 188 | 87.0 | 148 | 88.6 | 18 | 85.7 |
| Medium | 82 | 12.9 | 34 | 11.0 | 24 | 9.2 | 28 | 13.0 | 19 | 11.4 | 3 | 14.3 |
| Coarse | 0 | 0.0 | 0 | 0.0 | 0 | 0.0 | 1 | 0.0 | 0 | 0.0 | 1 | 0.0 |
| **Total** | **638** | **100** | **308** | **100** | **262** | **100** | **216** | **100** | **167** | **100** | **21** | **100** |
| *Colour* | | | | | | | | | | | | |
| Dark grey/brown | 358 | 55.8 | 186 | 60.4 | 105 | 39.6 | 114 | ~2.8 | 78 | 46.7 | 13 | 61.9 |
| Light grey | 35 | 5.5 | 29 | 9.4 | 32 | 12.1 | 19 | 8.8 | 6 | 3.6 | 1 | 4.8 |
| Light brown | 244 | 38.0 | 91 | 29.5 | 123 | 46.4 | 82 | 38.0 | 81 | 48.5 | 7 | 33.3 |
| White | 2 | 0.3 | 1 | 0.3 | 5 | 1.9 | 1 | 0.5 | 1 | 0.0 | 0 | 0.0 |
| Other | 3 | 0.5 | 1 | 0.3 | 0 | 0.0 | 0 | 0.0 | 2 | 1.2 | 0 | 0.0 |
| **Total** | **642** | **100** | **308** | **100** | **265** | **100** | **216** | **100** | **167** | **100** | **21** | **100** |

ditch deposits (two examples over 30 g) and at HAD VIII. The examples from the primary ditch were not extensively worked but those from the upper ditch were (59% below 0–25% cortex). Throughout the site cores retained a high percentage of cortex, 35% having more than 50% cortex and this is in marked contrast to the Foulmire sites. This evidence suggest the primary working of cores on site and a discard pattern reflecting low levels of use. Given the small size of the nodules it suggests the exploitation of poor material and a heavy discard pattern.

*Chronological variation*
*Mesolithic*: A small number of Mesolithic artefacts were found: two edge-blunted blades, a microlith, two truncated blades and two micro-burins. This suggests there was no concentrated Mesolithic activity.

*Earlier/Middle Neolithic*: This material was dominant in the palisade and ditch contexts and within the HAD VIII pit (F.534); it formed a major element in the HAD '84 and '87 excavation areas, and occurred in the enclosure's upper ditch fills, HAD VIII, HAD IX, HAD '81 and '82 excavation areas in smaller quantities. The earlier material is defined by a higher proportion of good-quality raw material associated with a higher

quality of flaking. Cores with blade scars were found throughout the site, as were significant proportions of blades. The implement typology is consistent with sites of this type and period. Most significantly, high percentages of serrated and utilized flakes occur, and these are generally blades or narrow flakes. Four leaf-shaped arrowheads were found, two from the HAD '81 area, one from the HAD '87 excavations and another from upper ditch deposits. Short end-scrapers predominate and those associated with the ditch tend to be of good quality. The number of retouched flakes and knives is small and these tend to be on narrow flakes or blades. Two Langdale axe fragments were associated with the palisade and Ditch I in the HAD '84 area (Fig. 5.31; see also Edmonds, inset Chapter 6, p. 352).

*Later Neolithic*: This material was dominant in the HAD VIII, HAD '81 and '84 excavation areas, and formed significant proportions of the material in the upper ditch levels in the HAD IX, HAD '84 and '87 areas. The later material is defined by a higher proportion of poor quality material associated with poor quality flaking. Cores with broad flake scars were common and the metrical analysis highlighted a significant proportion of broad flakes

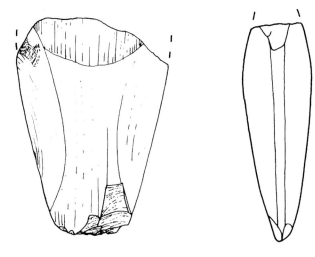

**Figure 5.31.** *The Ditch I Axe ([1705], <11500>).*

in the assemblage. An analysis of the implements supports the evidence for Late Neolithic activity. Serrated flakes are rare in the HAD VIII, HAD IX, HAD '81, '82 and '87 areas, and the proportion of utilized flakes is very low in the HAD '81 and '82 areas. By contrast, retouched flakes and knives are more common in these areas and many of these are on broad flakes in the HAD '81 and '82 areas. In these same two areas the scrapers tended to be shorter and of poorer quality and most of the notched flakes and piercers (which may be seen as 'convenience tools') were found here. A transverse arrowhead was recovered from the HAD '81 area. Both fabricators were found in HAD '81 and '82 areas. Polished flint axe fragments were found in the HAD IX, HAD '81 and '84 areas (one in each).

*Material exploitation*
All the areas of the enclosure had a preponderance of gravel flint as raw material and this was generally of poorer quality than the Foulmire sites: nodules were evidently small and were not suitable for extensive working as the high discard and high cortex pattern suggest. This is more pronounced in the later material and is associated with a decline in the quality of flaking. Chalk flint was also used in small quantities but is more frequent in the palisade and primary ditch silts of the western side of the enclosure and in the HAD VIII area. This material must have been imported from the southern chalk ridge.

The cores show fairly 'raw' material was being used on the site and this is confirmed by the high frequency of cortical flakes. This pattern could not be separated chronologically and variations across the site are more likely to reflect functional than chronological variation.

*Spatial patterning*
Ditch contexts (Tables 5.14–5.17)
In the primary ditch silts there is a pattern of segments with high numbers and segments with low numbers of flint. Ditch I in the HAD '84 area has the highest number and Ditches A & M in the HAD '87 area also have high values. High implement:by-product ratios occur in Ditches F/G (1:0), I (1:2) and M (1:1). In the secondary ditch silts a similar pattern is encountered, with large numbers of cores and implements being associated with large numbers of flakes in certain segments.

The implement:by-product ratios do not fully support this pattern as high (>1:4) values occur in most segments. Ditches A & B in the 1981 area were particularly important as they represent 43% of all the material from the upper ditch and so form an important 'clustered' deposit, but with a very low implement:by-product ratio (1:47).

Most implements were from the upper ditch contexts, although the Langdale axe (Fig. 5.13) and a significant proportion of the serrated flakes were from the primary silts. Most implements were from the HAD '84 and '87 areas, the western side of the enclosure, and some patterning is clearly apparent (Table 5.17).

19 serrated flakes (27%), 22 utilized flakes (31%), six retouched flakes (9%), nine scrapers (13%), four knives (6%), four piercers (6%), three burins (4%), a notched flake (1%) and one leaf arrowhead (1%) were recovered from ditch contexts. This is quite varied and represents a high implement:by-product ratio, especially in the primary ditch deposits.

It is important to note that half of the material in the upper ditch contexts is from the HAD '81 and '82 areas, which may largely account for the mixed nature of the upper ditch assemblage. However, most of this material is from a concentrated area in Ditches A/B; if this is discounted, it would appear that most of the material is of Middle Neolithic date and the spatial patterning predominantly reflects this period. This observation is supported by the implement distribution: 78% of the implements from the upper ditch contexts and all of the implements from the primary ditch deposits are from the HAD '84 and '87 areas. Therefore, the bulk of the ditch and palisade implement types (37% of all implements) are Middle Neolithic in date and are also associated with the primary use of the causewayed enclosure. Further support is provided by the analysis of cores from the ditch as the majority are blade cores. The implement distribution also confirms that the focus of early activity on the site was towards the western aspect of the enclosure.

## Palisade contexts

Almost all of the material from the palisade derived from the HAD '84 area (86%) and is associated with a moderate implement:by-product ratio. It is significant that the HAD '84 area exhibits a large element of early flintwork and the palisade material is also predominantly early. Finds from the palisade include an axe fragment from the HAD '84 area, suggesting a link with the Langdale axe fragment from one of the ditch segments in the same area (Ditch I). Two utilized flakes and a retouched flake were also found. The material in the façade probably dates from its erection and the material is closely linked in quality and technology with that in the ditch suggesting that they were contemporary.

## The interior

Aside from the F.534 pit within the HAD VIII area of excavation, the vast majority of this material derived from buried soil contexts:

*HAD '81*: Serrated flakes (3%), utilized flakes (16%), retouched flakes (18%), knives (11%), scrapers (18%), fabricator (1%), notched flakes (6%), piercers (9%), burin (3%), axe fragments (2%), 3 arrowheads (4%). There is a wide variety of artefacts and a low implement: by-product ratio.

*HAD '82*: Serrated flakes (8%), utilized flakes (12%), retouched flakes (28%), knives (12%), scrapers (20%), fabricator (4%), notched flakes (4%), piercers (12%). There was a wide variety and a low implement: by-product ratio (1:11.4).

*HAD' 84*: Serrated flakes (22%) utilized flakes (39%), retouched flakes (11%), knives (11%), notched flakes (6%), piercers (6%) and axe fragments (5%). There are few types and a low implement: by-product ratio (1:13.7).

*HAD '87*: Utilized flakes (50%), retouched flakes (13%), scrapers (19%), 1 arrowhead (6%). There were few types and a low implement:by-product ratio (1:13.4)

*HAD VIII* (excluding F.534): Eight utilized flakes (47%), four retouched flakes (24%), two scrapers (12%) and a notched flake (6%) were recovered; it had a low implement:by-product ratio (1:9.7).

*Pit F.534*: Four serrated flakes (29%), seven utilized flakes (50%), two retouched flakes (14%) and a burin (7%) were found within this pit. This suggests a similar composition to that of the main ditch contexts; it also has a very high implement:by-product ratio (1:4.9).

Most of the patterning already noted reflects the chronological distributions across the enclosure, but further patterning is also apparent. The primary ditch contexts exhibit high proportions of material associated

**Table 5.14.** *Ditches with high flint values.*

| Area | Ditches with high values |
|------|--------------------------|
| 1981 | A |
| 1984 | F, I, J |
| 1987 | K, N |

**Table 5.15.** *Causewayed enclosure: spatial analysis (primary ditch silts).*

| Division / Type | 1984 area: | | | | | 1987 area: | | | | | | | 1981 area: | | 1982 area: | | | |
|---|---|---|---|---|---|---|---|---|---|---|---|---|---|---|---|---|---|---|
| | F/G | H | I | J | Pal | K | L | M | N | O | P | Pal | A | B | C | D | E | Pal |
| Unretouched flakes | 0 | 0 | 7 | 0 | 37 | 4 | 0 | 1 | 0 | 0 | 0 | 1 | 1 | 0 | 0 | 0 | 0 | 4 |
| Dressing chips | 0 | 0 | 0 | 0 | 1 | 0 | 0 | 0 | 0 | 0 | 0 | 0 | 0 | 0 | 0 | 0 | 0 | 0 |
| Trimming flakes | 0 | 0 | 0 | 0 | 0 | 0 | 0 | 0 | 0 | 0 | 0 | 0 | 0 | 0 | 0 | 0 | 0 | 0 |
| Preparation flakes | 0 | 0 | 1 | 0 | 0 | 0 | 0 | 0 | 0 | 0 | 0 | 0 | 0 | 0 | 0 | 0 | 1 | 1 |
| Thinning flakes | 0 | 0 | 0 | 0 | 0 | 0 | 0 | 0 | 0 | 0 | 0 | 0 | 1 | 0 | 0 | 0 | 0 | 0 |
| Core-rejuvenation flakes | 0 | 0 | 1 | 0 | 1 | 0 | 0 | 0 | 0 | 0 | 0 | 0 | 0 | 0 | 0 | 0 | 0 | 1 |
| **Waste flakes** | **0** | **0** | **9** | **0** | **39** | **4** | **0** | **1** | **0** | **0** | **0** | **1** | **2** | **0** | **0** | **0** | **1** | **6** |
| **Cores** | **0** | **0** | **1** | **0** | **0** | **0** | **0** | **0** | **0** | **0** | **0** | **0** | **0** | **0** | **0** | **1** | **0** | **0** |
| **IWW** | **0** | **0** | **1** | **0** | **0** | **0** | **0** | **0** | **0** | **0** | **0** | **0** | **0** | **0** | **0** | **0** | **0** | **0** |
| Utilized flakes | 0 | 0 | 0 | 0 | 2 | 0 | 0 | 1 | 0 | 0 | 0 | 0 | 0 | 0 | 0 | 0 | 0 | 0 |
| Retouched flakes | 1 | 0 | 0 | 0 | 1 | 0 | 0 | 0 | 0 | 0 | 0 | 0 | 0 | 0 | 0 | 0 | 0 | 0 |
| Serrated flakes | 0 | 0 | 4 | 0 | 0 | 0 | 0 | 2 | 0 | 0 | 0 | 0 | 0 | 0 | 0 | 0 | 0 | 0 |
| Scrapers | 0 | 0 | 1 | 0 | 0 | 0 | 0 | 0 | 0 | 0 | 0 | 0 | 0 | 0 | 0 | 0 | 0 | 0 |
| Piercers | 0 | 0 | 0 | 0 | 1 | 0 | 0 | 0 | 0 | 0 | 0 | 0 | 0 | 0 | 0 | 0 | 0 | 0 |
| Burins | 0 | 0 | 0 | 0 | 0 | 0 | 0 | 0 | 0 | 0 | 0 | 0 | 0 | 0 | 0 | 0 | 0 | 0 |
| Knives | 0 | 0 | 0 | 0 | 0 | 0 | 0 | 0 | 0 | 0 | 0 | 0 | 0 | 0 | 0 | 0 | 0 | 0 |
| Notched | 0 | 0 | 0 | 0 | 0 | 0 | 0 | 0 | 0 | 0 | 0 | 0 | 0 | 0 | 0 | 0 | 0 | 0 |
| Leaf arrowheads | 0 | 0 | 0 | 0 | 0 | 0 | 0 | 0 | 0 | 0 | 0 | 0 | 0 | 0 | 0 | 0 | 0 | 0 |
| Axe fragment | 0 | 0 | 1 | 0 | 1 | 0 | 0 | 0 | 0 | 0 | 0 | 0 | 0 | 0 | 0 | 0 | 0 | 0 |
| **Implements** | **1** | **0** | **6** | **0** | **5** | **0** | **0** | **3** | **0** | **0** | **0** | **0** | **0** | **0** | **0** | **0** | **0** | **0** |
| **Total** | **1** | **0** | **16** | **0** | **44** | **4** | **0** | **5** | **0** | **0** | **0** | **1** | **2** | **0** | **0** | **1** | **1** | **6** |
| Implement:by-product ratio | 1:0 | 0 | 1:2 | 0 | 1:8 | 0 | 0 | 1:1 | 0 | 0 | 0 | 0 | 0 | 0 | 0 | 0 | 0 | 0 |

**Table 5.16.** *Causewayed enclosure: spatial analysis (secondary ditch silts).*

| Division | 1984 area: | | | | 1987 area: | | | | | 1981 area: | | 1982 area: | | |
| Type | F/G | H | I | J | K | L | M | N | O | P | A | B | C | D | E |
|---|---|---|---|---|---|---|---|---|---|---|---|---|---|---|---|
| Unretouched flakes | 24 | 0 | 38 | 13 | 24 | 2 | 2 | 20 | 1 | 0 | 122 | 0 | 5 | 5 | 3 |
| Dressing chips | 2 | 0 | 3 | 2 | 3 | 0 | 0 | 2 | 0 | 0 | 27 | 0 | 0 | 1 | 0 |
| Trimming flakes | 0 | 0 | 0 | 0 | 0 | 0 | 0 | 0 | 0 | 0 | 2 | 0 | 0 | 0 | 0 |
| Preparation flakes | 0 | 0 | 2 | 4 | 2 | 0 | 0 | 3 | 0 | 0 | 21 | 0 | 0 | 0 | 2 |
| Thinning flakes | 1 | 0 | 2 | 1 | 0 | 0 | 0 | 0 | 0 | 0 | 8 | 0 | 0 | 0 | 0 |
| Core-rejuvenation flakes | 3 | 0 | 4 | 3 | 3 | 0 | 0 | 1 | 0 | 0 | 3 | 0 | 0 | 0 | 0 |
| **Waste flakes** | **30** | **0** | **49** | **22** | **32** | **2** | **2** | **26** | **1** | **0** | **183** | **0** | **5** | **6** | **5** |
| **Cores** | **1** | **0** | **5** | **1** | **2** | **0** | **0** | **2** | **1** | **0** | **3** | **0** | **3** | **0** | **0** |
| **IWW** | **0** | **0** | **1** | **1** | **0** | **0** | **0** | **0** | **0** | **0** | **2** | **0** | **0** | **0** | **0** |
| Utilized flakes | 2 | 1 | 6 | 1 | 4 | 1 | 0 | 1 | 0 | 0 | 2 | 0 | 1 | 0 | 2 |
| Retouched flakes | 2 | 0 | 0 | 0 | 1 | 0 | 0 | 1 | 0 | 0 | 0 | 0 | 0 | 1 | 0 |
| Serrated flakes | 2 | 0 | 3 | 3 | 0 | 0 | 0 | 5 | 0 | 0 | 0 | 0 | 0 | 0 | 0 |
| Scrapers | 1 | 0 | 2 | 0 | 1 | 1 | 1 | 0 | 0 | 0 | 0 | 0 | 2 | 0 | 0 |
| Piercers | 0 | 0 | 0 | 0 | 2 | 0 | 0 | 0 | 0 | 0 | 1 | 0 | 1 | 0 | 0 |
| Burins | 1 | 0 | 1 | 0 | 0 | 1 | 0 | 0 | 0 | 0 | 0 | 0 | 0 | 0 | 0 |
| Knives | 1 | 0 | 1 | 0 | 1 | 0 | 0 | 0 | 0 | 0 | 0 | 0 | 0 | 0 | 1 |
| Notched | 0 | 0 | 0 | 0 | 0 | 0 | 0 | 0 | 0 | 0 | 1 | 0 | 0 | 0 | 0 |
| Leaf arrowheads | 0 | 0 | 0 | 0 | 0 | 0 | 0 | 0 | 0 | 0 | 0 | 0 | 0 | 1 | 0 |
| Axe fragment | 0 | 0 | 0 | 0 | 0 | 0 | 0 | 0 | 0 | 0 | 0 | 0 | 0 | 0 | 0 |
| **Implements** | **9** | **1** | **13** | **4** | **9** | **3** | **1** | **7** | **0** | **0** | **4** | **0** | **4** | **2** | **3** |
| **Total** | **40** | **1** | **68** | **28** | **43** | **5** | **3** | **35** | **2** | **0** | **192** | **0** | **12** | **8** | **8** |
| Implement:by-product ratio | 1:3 | 1:1 | 1:4 | 1:6 | 1:4 | 1:1 | 1:2 | 1:4 | 0 | 0 | 1:47 | 0 | 1:2 | 1:3 | 1:2 |

**Table 5.17.** *Ditch segment implements.*

| Area | Ditch | Artefacts |
|---|---|---|
| 1982 | D | Scrapers |
| | E | Leaf arrowhead |
| 1984 | F/G | Retouched flakes |
| | I | Langdale axe, scrapers, serrated flakes, utilized flakes |
| 1987 | K | Utilized flakes |
| | N | Serrated flakes |

with core preparation, reduction and discard, but lack evidence for implement production. This pattern is also encountered in the HAD '81 and '82 areas but is less marked. The HAD '84 and '87 areas have less evidence for core reduction but more for implement production. While the palisade and HAD VIII pit have very little core or implement production waste, they contain high proportions of unretouched flakes. The evidence suggests some functional patterning for both phases:

**Earlier Neolithic**

| | |
|---|---|
| Primary Ditch | Evidence for deposition of implements, unretouched flakes, few cores, CRF, core preparation. No evidence for implement production. Dressing and very little evidence of working. Evidence for core reduction and discard; few implement types, but specialized and specially high implement ratio. |
| Upper Ditch | Implements deposited 78% in HAD '84 and '87. CRF: mainly HAD '84 and '87. Cores mainly in HAD '84 and '87 (67%) and mainly blade cores. Many implement types and a specially high implement ratio. |
| Palisade | Evidence for deposition of implements and waste flakes (including CRF). No evidence for extensive flint working; few implement types and specialized. |
| Pit F.534 | Evidence for deposition of implements waste flakes (including CRF). No evidence for extensive flint working; few implement types and specialized (high implement ratio). |
| 1984/1987 | Evidence for all core-reduction and implement-production processes; few implement types, low ratio. |

**Later Neolithic**

| | |
|---|---|
| Ditch Contexts | Core-preparation flakes: mainly HAD '81 and '82 areas; dressing chips: mainly in HAD '81 area. |
| 1981/1982 | Evidence for all core-reduction and implement-production processes. Evidence for large quantity of core reduction in the case of 1981 area, the cores involved certainly broad flaked; many implement types, low ratio. |
| HAD IX | Evidence for large quantity of core reduction but not primary working. |
| HAD VIII | Evidence for all core-reduction processes; few implement types, low ratio. |

## The pottery assemblage
by K. GDANIEC

This report describes the basic character of the cause-wayed enclosure ceramic assemblage. It is based on an examination of the pottery, field observations and archive records. It is notable that no cases of specific deposition of pottery were noted in the field. Such deposits were noted for bone and polished axes in the ditches of the causewayed enclosure, and it is relevant that specific deposits of pots were recorded at the façade of the long barrow; the causewayed enclosure pottery generally consisted of very small and eroded fragments.

The catalogue for pottery contains sherds which were recovered as single sherds, associated sherds or numerous crumb fragments. The majority of catalogue entries contain a single sherd; where more than one sherd occurs and no difference between the fabrics could distinguish them as deriving from separate vessels they have been treated as one. Except where stated otherwise, all quantification below depends on the number of catalogue entries rather than individual sherd count (409 entries for 444 sherds; the former number will be used as the 'sherd count').

### The assemblage
The excavations recovered a total of 409 prehistoric pottery sherds and crumb fragments, or c. 3.2 kg in weight. Most of these belong to Neolithic groups not demonstrably 'late' and which have been considered as 'earlier Neolithic' pottery. This comprises 249 sherds (61% of the total number) weighing 2213 g (69% of the total weight) and with an average sherd size of 8.8 g. No sherds were found in the 1981 excavation of the ditches. The main structural components of the site as a whole were those of the segmented ditches and its internally situated palisade trench; in Table 5.18 the pottery assemblage is broken down by these components, by weight.

The overall character of the assemblage betrays its general Neolithic date, with the majority of sherds representing undiagnostic earlier Neolithic plain ware bowls or vessels in the Mildenhall style and comparable to Longworth's Hurst Fen descriptions (Longworth 1960, 228–40). Only very rarely could sherds be described as being in good condition; rather they were abraded and suffered from post-depositional staining, root channelling and other erosive surface effects. In some cases these effects masked decorative elements although such sherds were not generally common. The later prehistoric sherds were generally made from sandy, hard fabrics and resisted post-depositional damage. The Neolithic sherds contrasted with their more friable gritty fabrics and were, doubtless, prone to abrasion or erosion both before and after deposition. The sherd size was generally small and divided into three broad size groups of roughly 250–350 square millimetres in size, 650 sq. mm and 1100 sq. mm.

The usual colour ranges of buff pale browns through to reddish-browns and dark greys illustrated the mixed firing temperatures or conditions common to this period.

### Fabrics
The fabrics were studied macroscopically for tempering agents (Table 5.19). Some variability was apparent but mostly conformed to locally available materials, predominantly flint but also with other admixtures: shell, sand and/or vegetal matter (Longworth's 'Grit tempered': 1960, 228). Typically no grog was evident in the earlier Neolithic assemblage but occurred in low quantities in some of the Bronze Age sherds. The predominance of flint grits as a tempering agent may simply reflect its natural occurrence in the clay sub-soils and chalk deposits of southern Cambridgeshire. Alternatively, the huge quantities of burnt flints (river gravel derived) in the southern fens (seen in the numerous scatter sites around the fen margins: Edmonds et al. 1999; Silvester 1991) may have been used as a source for shattered flint grits for pottery temper as a by-product. By way of contrast, the Neolithic assemblage from the Etton causewayed enclosure, near Maxey in northern Cambridgeshire, was made almost entirely from shell-tempered fabrics (Kinnes, in Pryor 1998), in a region where fossil shell-rich clays occur widely in the locality.

Over half of the assemblage (58%, 238 sherds) contained flint grits as the main temper, with shell-tempered fabrics accounting for 14% (57 sherds) of the total (Table 5.20). The remaining 28% consisted of assorted sand, vegetable temper or grog tempers. Earlier Neolithic sherds of the Mildenhall style or plain bowl traditions were predominantly filled with flint grits (74%) although most of the shelly wares also occur at this time (18%). Subsequent period styles were relatively under-represented in the assemblage and while the later Neolithic group reflected the fabric preferences of the earlier potters, later prehistoric sherds became increasingly more sand and grog-tempered.

No distinctive patterning occurred in the cause-wayed ditch segments although Ditch N produced a distinct group of shelly wares (25 out of all 45 shelly sherds), which probably represented a single vessel.

### Earlier Neolithic feature sherds
The bulk of the earlier Neolithic pottery consisted of plain body sherds. However, 30 rims were recovered

**Table 5.18.** *Pottery distribution in main structures (by weight).*

| | 1982 wt (g) | 1982 % | 1984 wt (g) | 1984 % | 1987 wt (g) | 1987 % | Total wt (g) | Total % |
|---|---|---|---|---|---|---|---|---|
| Ditch segments | 134 | 27.0 | 624 | 40.8 | 1092 | 91.0 | 1850 | 57.3 |
| Palisade trench | 7 | 1.4 | 487 | 31.8 | 6 | 0.5 | 500 | 15.5 |
| Others | 355 | 71.6 | 420 | 27.4 | 102 | 8.5 | 877 | 27.2 |
| **Total (g)** | **496** | **100** | **1531** | **100** | **1200** | **100** | **3227** | **100** |
| (Sherd total) | 65 | 15.9 | 201 | 49.1 | 143 | 35 | 409 | 100 |

**Table 5.19.** *Fabric groups.*

| | Sparse | Moderate | Frequent |
|---|---|---|---|
| **Group 1** *Flint* | | | |
| Fine-medium | 1a | 1b | 1c |
| Medium-coarse | 1d | 1e | 1f |
| **Group 2** *Shell* | | | |
| Fine-medium | 2a | 2b | 2c |
| Medium-coarse | 2d | 2e | 2f |
| Dissolved / 'corky' | 2g | | |
| **Group 3** *Flint & shell* | | | |
| Fine-medium | 3a | 3b | 3c |
| Medium-coarse | 3d | 3e | 3f |
| **Group 4** *Flint & sand* | | | |
| | 4a | | |
| **Group 5** *Shell & sand* | | | |
| Fine-medium | 5a | 5b | 5c |
| Medium-coarse | 5d | 5e | 5f |
| **Group 6** *Sand* | | | |
| Fine-medium | 6a | 6b | 6c |
| Medium-coarse | 6d | 6e | 6f |
| **Group 7** *Shell & grog* | | | |
| | 7 | | |
| **Group 8** *Grog* | | | |
| | 8 | | |
| **Group 9** *Vegetable/dissolved organic* | | | |
| | 9 | | |

(12% of the total 249 sherds) of which 10 were decorated and 20 plain (Table 5.21).

Decorated rims occur in each category except in-turned, expanded and externally thickened. Simple, undecorated rims are most common, six of which are flint-based fabrics, two shell-based and one sand-based. Two of the rolled rims are from the same vessel, as are two of the everted rims, already reducing the relative number of vessels represented by the rims. A minimum number of vessels estimate is, however, not useful here since the assemblage size is so small,

fragmentary and largely undiagnostic. The rim forms conform to those typical of East Anglian assemblages (Longworth 1960, 230; Whittle 1977, 82–3), which is further corroborated by the decorative motifs that they carry.

*Decoration*
Only 53 sherds in the assemblage were decorated (13%). Of these, 28 sherds were attributable to earlier Neolithic bowls in the Mildenhall decorated style, 19 to later Neolithic decorated vessels in the Peterborough and Grooved Ware traditions, and 3 to earlier Bronze Age wares (Beaker and Collared Urn). The most common decorative motif was that of incised lines (see Table 5.22), occurring either as a sole trait or in combination with others.

Earlier Neolithic decoration
The earlier Neolithic assemblage mostly displayed the typical combinations of impressed or incised motifs, including one example of loosely twisted cord. Generally only a few incised lines or random dots were all that could be noted for the motif.

Of the Mildenhall-style sherds, seven were evidently part of a single vessel that had been deposited in the secondary fills of Ditch L. Some of these could refit along ancient breaks to form part of one vessel (Fig. 5.32:4). It is not clear how much of the vessel was present since the refitted groups did not conjoin. This reflects the nature of the vessel's deposition within the causewayed enclosure ditch where selected parts of a previously broken vessel were gathered to be placed into the ditch, perhaps in association with other material. The rest of the Mildenhall sherds from the ditch were demonstrably from different pots, confirming that not all of this decorated vessel had ever been placed in this ditch segment.

The vessel was an open bowl with a characteristically heavy rolled rim, *c.* 200 mm in diameter, which was decorated with closely spaced fine diagonal lines. The internal rim area is too poorly preserved to tell if it was ever decorated. Most of the bowl's neck was absent. A small but sharp carination ledge was emphasized by a neat row of closely spaced punctate impressions, probably fashioned with the articular end of a small bone, or a rounded stick. Below the ledge was an 8 mm zone of oblique diagonal lines above a 16 mm zone of rows (four) of punctate impressions. Below these another zone of very steep diagonal lines occurred, to the point where the sherds broke. The combination of precisely

**Table 5.20.** *Fabric types in each major period.*

| | Fabric Description | Neolithic (incl. earlier Neolithic & Mildenhall) | Later Neolithic | Bronze Age | Iron Age | Prehistoric | Total No. | % |
|---|---|---|---|---|---|---|---|---|
| 1 | Flint | 112 | 17 | 4 | 1 | 3 | 137 | 33.5 |
| 2 | Shell | 43 | 9 | 0 | 0 | 1 | 53 | 13 |
| 3 | Flint & shell | 9 | 1 | 0 | 0 | 0 | 10 | 2.4 |
| 4 | Flint & sand | 64 | 20 | 5 | 2 | 4 | 95 | 23.2 |
| 5 | Shell & sand | 2 | 1 | 1 | 1 | 1 | 6 | 1.5 |
| 6 | Sand | 7 | 7 | 2 | 10 | 6 | 32 | 7.8 |
| 7 | Shell & grog* | 0 | 0 | 1 | 0 | 0 | 1 | 0.2 |
| 8 | Grog* | 0 | 0 | 2 | 0 | 0 | 2 | 0.5 |
| 9 | Vegetable/dissolved organic | 9 | 0 | 1 | 0 | 1 | 11 | 2.7 |
| 10 | Mixed | 3 | 23 | 15 | 0 | 21 | 62 | 15.2 |
| | **Total** | **249** | **78** | **31** | **14** | **37** | **409** | **100** |

executed decoration on finely flint-gritted smoothed fabric indicates the superior skill of the potter, and may suggest that this particular vessel was chosen upon breakage (deliberate or otherwise) to be placed into the ditch.

Middle/Later Neolithic decoration

The later Neolithic pottery demonstrated the use of whipped cord in association with other motifs characteristic of Peterborough vessels (e.g. Mortlake and Ebbsfleet). Part of a Peterborough vessel, probably in the Ebbsfleet style, with a pronounced shoulder carination was recovered from a post-hole-associated terminal recut in Ditch I. The everted rim top (*c.* 240 mm in diameter) carried diagonal lengths of impressed whipped cord on both surfaces of neck (Fig. 5.32.8). The shoulder also had whipped cord diagonals, 'stopped' with dots. Almost all of the upper part of the vessel (no lower part was seen: probably plain) was covered in decoration with liberal use of tightly whipped cord common to Middle/later Neolithic decorative styles (Cleal 1984).

One sherd of Mortlake pottery was recovered from Ditch N. This 'T'-shaped rim sherd was decorated with whipped cord impressions on the rim ledge and on the external cavetto neck.

A burnt spread on the surface of Ditch O produced a large sherd of Grooved Ware with sharp, deeply incised (2 mm), large herringbone pattern on a shelly fabric (Fig. 5.32:10). The decoration looked as if it had been made with a flint blade rather than a stick or bone, and despite its incised nature the herringbone decoration suggested its Grooved Ware style. Three other, non-conjoining, sherds of Grooved Ware with irregular herringbone decoration came from 'cremation' pit, F.520 (Fig. 5.32:11), and another from just below the upper surface of the fill in Ditch N where zoned decoration of

**Table 5.21.** *Rim forms.*

| Type | No. |
|---|---|
| Simple | 9 |
| Everted | 4 |
| Expanded | 4 |
| Rolled | 4 |
| Externally thickened | 3 |
| Out-turned | 3 |
| In-turned | 1 |
| S-shaped | 1 |
| T-shaped | 1 |
| **Total** | **30** |

**Table 5.22.** *Decorative traits displayed by the prehistoric assemblage.*

| Date | Incised lines | Punctate impressions | Herring-bone | Fingertip/ finger-nail impressions | Grooves | Combinations | Total |
|---|---|---|---|---|---|---|---|
| Earlier Neolithic | 10 | 1 | 0 | 1 | 1 | 1: inc. lines & FN; 1: inc. lines + tw'd cord; 1: inc. lines & dots; 1: inc. lines and grooves; 11: inc. lines and dots (1 vessel) | 28 |
| Later Neolithic | 3 | 0 | 2 | 1 | 1 | 9: dots & wh'd cord maggots (1 vessel); 2 twisted cord & h'bone (1 vessel); 1 wh'd cord + stick imps | 19 |
| Neo/BA+LN/BA | 3 | 0 | 1 (beaker) | 0 | 1 | 1 fingernail & scored lines | 6 |
| **Total** | **16** | **1** | **3** | **2** | **3** | **28** | **53** |

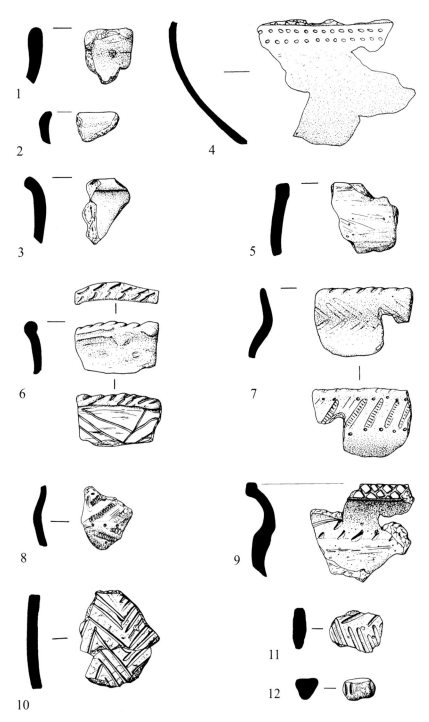

**Figure 5.32.** *Selected pottery. 1) Mildenhall-type rim, palisade F.125 ([1718], <12608>); 2) Mildenhall-type rim, Ditch K (tertiary fill; [3806], <27600>); 3) Mildenhall-type rim, Ditch O (primary fill; [3934], <28395>); 4) Mildenhall Vessel, Ditch L (primary fill; [3949], <27742>); 5) Mildenhall Ware small cup, Ditch N (F.521; [3893], <28235>); 6) 'Mildenhall style' rim, Ditch I (late recut F.120; [1888]); 7) Later Neolithic rim, Ditch I (late recut F.120; [1888]); 8) Peterborough Ware shoulder sherd, Ditch I ('late' recut F.120; [1888]); 9) Peterborough Ware rim, Ditch I ('late' recut F.120; [1888]); 10) Grooved Ware, Ditch O (surface deposit; [3992], <28378>); 11) Grooved Ware, pit F.520 ([3818], <28012>); 12) Small fired-clay plug, pit F.520 ([3818], <28013>).*

fingernail impressions was carried on shelly fabric.

One possible Beaker sherd came from a dry-sieve transect. One irregular-shaped 'plug' of fired clay with two fingernail impressions was also found in cremation pit, F.520 (Fig. 5.32:12).

*Context*
No sherds conjoined across the major features. The only two instances of cross-feature conjoins occurred between hollows at the base of the buried soil and the causewayed ditches or their recuts. Such joins occurred in relation to Ditches H & I (see Fig. 5.33).

In order to evaluate the stratigraphic context of the ceramics, the causewayed enclosure ditch fills were divided into primary, secondary and tertiary levels. The primary fills are the basal deposits within the ditches, consisting of gravels, sands, and clay marls. These often contain large lumps of collapsed material from the ditch walls and were presumably deposited fairly quickly. They may have held water, at least seasonally. The secondary fills are the loams with some sand and gravel in the upper parts of the ditches. At the base of the secondary fills there are often layers of burnt material and the fills themselves generally contain higher quantities of charcoal. Although tertiary fills have not been distinguished in other parts of this volume, the greater chronological resolution available in the analysis of pottery suggested that some attempt be made to differentiate tertiary contexts for the ceramic study. However, it should be noted that while the distinction between primary and secondary processes of infill could clearly be identified in the field, tertiary fills are less easy to distinguish. They have been defined here as those related to the final phase of recutting and realignment in each ditch segment or, where recutting of the secondary fills does not occur, the final layer of weathered fill.

Any attempt to date these different fills using the pottery is hampered by a number of factors:

(a) the inaccuracy and uncertainty involved in assigning dates to small abraded sherds and crumbs;
(b) the fact that in the 1987 season the ditches were dug in 10–20 cm spits and in the same year the palisade segments were dug in single units;
(c) the lack of ceramics from certain contexts such as the 1982 palisade and the 1981 ditches;
(d) the heavy leaching of the soil leading to a bleaching of stratigraphic relationships;
(e) problems of residuality which have been caused by recutting so that pottery from earlier layers has been incorporated into and may dominate assemblages in later layers.

Given these problems, the patterns which emerge in Table 5.23 should be viewed with some caution. It should be stressed that the Haddenham pottery assemblage consists of a relatively large proportion of crumbs and small fragments that are relatively unattributable. Thus the largest frequencies in Table 5.23 often occur in the broad date categories (Neolithic general, LN/EBA, Neo/BA).

It is, however, clear from Table 5.23 that most of the pottery derives from secondary and tertiary fills. This may largely be the result of the relative speed of infilling, the quick primary deposits offering less opportunity for sherds to end up in the ditches. It should also be noted that a high proportion of the sherds in the secondary and tertiary deposits are very small fragments which could only be identified as generalized Neolithic (Table 5.21). The higher densities of such sherds in the upper fills could again be the result of the speed of fill, the slower upper fills resulting in longer periods of weathering and fragmentation of sherds. As Table 5.24 shows, many of the smaller sherds in the upper fills are residual and could at least partly be the product of recutting into earlier fills. However, it is also possible that the greater abrasion of sherds in the upper fills results from activity of a domestic nature at the site. This notion of a change of use of the enclosure is supported by the fact that most of the features (pits and post-holes) in the surrounding buried soil are late in the life of the enclosure (later Neolithic and Bronze Age), and the

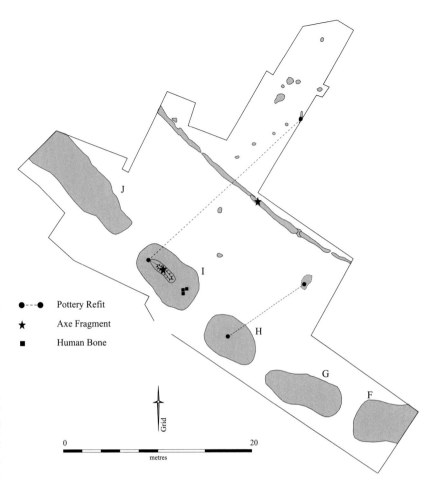

**Figure 5.33.** *HAD '84: pottery refits and location of axe and human skull fragments.*

secondary and tertiary fills are associated with much evidence of burning and post-holes, etc. This shift to a more domestic use of the enclosure is also seen in the struck flint.

In terms of the dating, the primary fills of the ditch segments are clearly associated with Mildenhall pottery (Table 5.20). The secondary fills also have much Mildenhall ware, but also some later ceramics although not as much as the tertiary fills. There is a small concentration of Early Bronze Age pottery in the secondary fills in Ditch J and a small amount of generalized later Neolithic but by far the largest amount of secondary fill ceramics is Mildenhall. Also noteworthy is that the secondary deposits do not contain the wider range of later Neolithic, early Bronze Age and Bronze Age pottery found in the surrounding pits and post-holes. In sum, it might be argued that the secondary fills fall largely into a Mildenhall phase with some overlap and use in later periods.

The ceramics in the tertiary fills are clearly different in that there is a considerable amount of

303

**Table 5.23.** *The distribution of pottery of different dates in different contexts in the causewayed enclosure. (Note pottery 'crumbs' have been counted as one sherd and sherds have been counted individually rather than by catalogue number; * indicates Collared Urn).*

| | Ditches | | | Pits etc. | | | Palisade | | | Buried |
| | Primary | Secondary | Tertiary | F520 | F.46 | Other pits | Primary | Secondary | Undiff. | soil |
|---|---|---|---|---|---|---|---|---|---|---|
| Neolithic (general) | 15 | 72 | 101 | 6 | 1 | 12 | 6 | 36 | 10 | 7 |
| Mildenhall | 24 | 32 | 13 | 6 | 0 | 0 | 6 | 1 | 2 | 0 |
| Earlier Neolithic | 0 | 10 | 1 | 0 | 0 | 0 | 0 | 0 | 1 | 0 |
| Later Neolithic | 0 | 8 | 14 | 0 | 0 | 1 | 0 | 0 | 0 | 1 |
| Grooved Ware | 0 | 0 | 1 | 3 | 0 | 0 | 0 | 0 | 0 | 0 |
| Peterborough | 0 | 0 | 12 | 0 | 0 | 0 | 0 | 0 | 0 | 0 |
| Late Neo/Early Bronze Age | 2 | 1 | 17 | 5 | 4* | 2 | 0 | 1 | 0 | 5 |
| Neolithic/Bronze Age | 0 | 2 | 14 | 0 | 0 | 3 | 0 | 5 | 0 | 2 |
| Early Bronze Age | 0 | 8 | 2 | 0 | 0 | 12 | 0 | 2 | 0 | 1 |
| Bronze Age | 1 | 0 | 5 | 1 | 0 | 3 | 0 | 4 | 5 | 2 |
| Bronze Age/Iron Age | 0 | 0 | 1 | 0 | 0 | 1 | 0 | 0 | 0 | 0 |
| Iron Age | 0 | 0 | 0 | 0 | 0 | 0 | 0 | 0 | 0 | 5 |
| Later prehistoric | 0 | 0 | 0 | 0 | 0 | 0 | 0 | 0 | 0 | 1 |
| Undiag. prehistoric | 1 | 5 | 6 | 3 | 2 | 0 | 0 | 7 | 1 | 5 |
| Romano-British | 0 | 0 | 0 | 0 | 0 | 1 | 0 | 0 | 0 | 0 |
| **Total** | **43** | **138** | **187** | **24** | **7** | **35** | **12** | **56** | **19** | **23** |

**Table 5.24.** *Average sherd size of pottery of different dates in the different ditch fills. Sherd size has been calculated as weight divided by number of sherds.*

| Ditch fills | Primary | Secondary | Tertiary |
|---|---|---|---|
| Neo. (general) | 6.6 | 76.58 | 4.07 |
| Mildenhall and E Neolithic | 11.1 | 29.48 | 9.57 |
| All later prehistoric | (8.25) small sample | 5.3 | 38.25 |
| **Average** | **9.30** | **7.25** | **6.10** |

Peterborough, later Neolithic, Late Neolithic/Early Bronze Age, Neolithic/Bronze Age pottery. No differences could be identified between the different types of tertiary deposits in the ditches (ditches connecting earlier ditches, post-holes, final recuttings, etc.). These tertiary deposits are too substantial to be the result of differential visibility: they are not simply the result of features being preserved in the subsiding ditch tops. These later deposits indicate recurrent use of the enclosure over a considerable time, and this is supported by the late date of many of the features in the surrounding buried soil away from the ditches.

The lower fills of the palisade contain Mildenhall pottery which is rarely found in the upper fills. It is also distinctive that no later Neolithic pottery was found in the palisade, although the size of the later Neolithic sample is everywhere small. While the palisade may have been built fairly early in the use of the enclosure, rotting of posts or subsidence of the trench fills must have gone on into a late phase of use. It is also possible that, given the prevalence of later

ceramics in the palisade, some construction activity went on at least into the Early Bronze Age.

The dates derived from the ceramics fit well with those obtained from the struck flint (see above). There are also acceptable fits with the radiocarbon dates obtained from the enclosure. The primary fill in Ditch J produced a date of 3610–2920 cal. BC (4560±90 BP: HAR-8093), and a primary fill in I gave a date of 3630–3100 cal. BC (4630±80 BP: HAR-8096). These dates fit well with the later part of the range of dates for Mildenhall ceramics, as do the secondary fills in Ditch C which gave a date of 3700–3130 cal. BC (4690±90 BP: HAR-10520). The date of 2320–1690 cal. BC (3620±110 BP: HAR-8094) for the primary fill of the palisade may also be acceptable given that the discussion above suggested that the palisade segment from which the date derives may have been added in later in order to restrict movement into the interior. However, the date for the tertiary fills in Ditch I ([1888]) produced a date of 3990–3530 cal. BC (4970±90 BP: HAR-8092) which is clearly out of sequence.

As regards the spatial context of the sherds, it is clear from Table 5.25 that there is considerable variation between the ditch segments in terms of frequencies of pottery. The variation correlates with the pattern already obtained from other evidence. Figure 5.42 identifies the five ditch segments containing the most pottery. These ditch segments are also those with most worked flint and animal bone. They include Ditches D, I, J & N which stand out on other grounds. In a similar vein, the palisade again shows a clear concentration in the 1984 area. Considering the palisade by area, in the 1982 area there were two

It has not been possible to find direct parallels for this object, which is assumed to be of Neolithic date. Size and form would suggest it is a projectile point, presumably an arrowhead, and there is no reason to assume that it was not intended to function as such (i.e. it is not primarily symbolic or a display piece). Why such should be made of bone when good-quality flint was likely to be readily available is unclear. While the tanged form could imply a copy of an early Bronze Age barbed-and-tanged arrowhead, once hafted it would more closely resemble early Neolithic leaf-shaped forms.

*A hide-working implement*
From primary fills of Ditch K ([3938]) was recovered a left acetabulum of *Bos*, with small parts of the ilium and ischium remaining but the pubis broken away, with the broken ends smoothed and worn (Fig. 5.34:3). The sharp dorsal margin of the bone is heavily rubbed and faceted by wear, suggesting some use akin to hide working or scraping. Besides the utilization of this piece, the surface also shows multiple cut marks across the outer face of the ischium.

## Overview discussion: material culture — displaying labour and the dead

As has been outlined above, the evidence of the finds-packed 'pit settlements' should by now have laid to waste *de facto* arguments that large-scale artefact deposition need necessarily represent the remains of mass-group feasting. Once acknowledging that earlier Neolithic settlements had clearly been tidied up and that this involved backfilling features with large fragments of 'fresh' primary/secondary refuse (pottery, flint and bone), then such explanations as 'feasting' are no longer applicable as a *deus ex machina*. Similarly, if examining the Delphs enclosure's remains with a 'cold eye', there is neither the frequency of artefacts nor the regularity of patterning to indicate that what we are seeing is the fall-out of long-term regular group meetings (i.e. mass-group fairground/exchange explanations).

Against this, in assessing what distinguishes its finds assemblages three factors stand out. The first

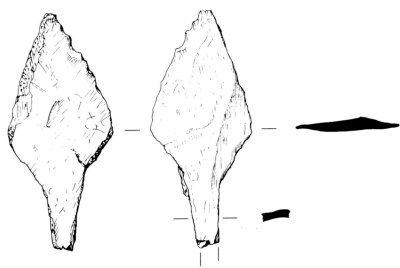

**Figure 5.35.** *Manufactured bone point; arrows in photograph highlight flaking ([094]; <1341>; photograph G. Owen).*

pertains to lithic resources, and this relates both to the acquisition of chalk flint and, also, stone axes. As stressed by Middleton, none of the other sites investigated within the course of the project have such finds and this is also true of the subsequent Barleycroft/Over and Earith investigations; the Barleycroft Paddocks flint having, for example, been only manufactured from river cobbles (Pollard, in Evans & Knight 1997). While the occurrence of chalk ridge flint would only have entailed an exchange distance of some 15 km, the displacement of the stone axes would have involved hundreds of kilometres. In this regard comparison can be made (though very much to Haddenham's detriment) to the Etton enclosure (Pryor 1998). There 24 stone axe/adze pieces and 20 polished flint axes or parts thereof were found (Middleton & Edmonds, in Pryor 1998). At Haddenham this would compare to only two and three pieces in each category respectively. Whilst seemingly low, it must be remembered

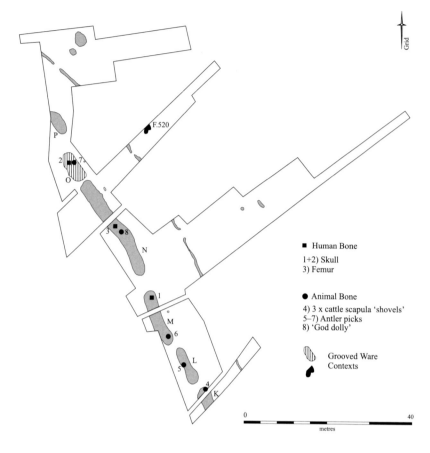

**Figure 5.36.** *HAD '87: location of human remains and animal bone special finds (and also showing Grooved Ware contexts).*

tion in terms of clearance as opposed to forest-based hunting activities. (By the same modelling as applied above the enclosure would have a population of at least 64 leaf-shaped arrowheads; see Saville 2002 concerning 'ordinariness' of causewayed enclosure flint assemblages.)

The second factor is the occurrence of human remains. Whilst the detailing of their distribution will be explored below, here what is important is that this material does not generally occur in contemporary settlements. This is demonstrated both in the testing of the contemporary Haddenham environs sites and, more tellingly, in the excavation of the Kilverstone and Barleycroft Paddocks 'pit settlements'. Together with the long barrow, and in contrast to Bronze and Iron Age settlements (see Volume 2, Chapter 5; Brück 1995; Hill 1995), this further indicates that the causewayed enclosure was also a rarefied context, albeit to a different degree than contemporary mortuary monuments. However, before proceeding it is worth noting that the survival of bone is usually poor on open Neolithic settlements and, moreover, this inference may now have to be called into question by the results from Runnymede Bridge (see concluding chapter, Discussion below).

Finally, there is the presence of the tools of the enclosure's construction. Unlike, for example, in the long barrow where such items were evidently removed, here antler picks and cattle scapula 'shovels' feature in the monument's deposits. Comparable to the long-term imprint of ditch recutting, this would seem a matter of labour 'made manifest'. The issue, given the presence of antler within the HAD '82 ditches, is whether these implements were 'placed' or simply downed and left. In other words, did tools have a special status or was it simply that, unlike the long barrow, there was little or no concern with 'cleanliness'? Evidently not employed for digging, the half-size antler pick from Ditch M (like also the bone point and 'god dolly') raises intriguing questions in this context. In some respects it is comparable to a miniature bow found in Bronze Age contexts at Isleham, Cambs. (Gdaniec 1996). These are all ambiguous objects: were they children's toys or sacred objects? What unites them is their potential for *substitution*. Whether intended for

that Etton was almost entirely excavated and to facilitate comparison the data must be factored. The average of the interior buried soil sampling cover (ranging from 0.9–5%) is 3.3%; interrelating this with the 9% ditch circuit sample approximates to an overall 6% excavation sample (ignoring the 50-m test pitting and interior features, e.g. the palisade). By this means a population of some 32 ground-stone axes and 48 polished axe fragments could be postulated for the Delphs enclosure.

While this could attest to models of causewayed enclosures relating to access to long/medium-distance resources (see Edmonds, in Pryor 1998), it would not support their role in 'high-level' redistribution networks. At least in the case of Haddenham, these materials were apparently not being exchanged 'down-the-line' to neighbouring settlements, but rather remaining within the enclosure itself. Relating to this, at a symbolic level much could be made of the 'celebration of the axe' in the placement of the Group VI axe set atop the 'long mound' in Ditch I (see Edmonds, inset Chapter 6 below; cf. the arrowheads within the long barrow), which has obvious ramifica-

play or ritual, in this case the bone miniatures (though the manufactured point does not involve reduction) could have respectively replaced or stood for a 'real' antler pick, a flint arrowhead or a person/personification (the 'dolly').

## Economic evidence

Although the data upon which the following studies are based are not particularly rich or abundant, most salient is the evidence of the animal remains and the contrast it offers with long barrow's assemblage. Nevertheless here it is largely a matter of evaluating 'negatives'.

*Animal remains*
by A.J. LEGGE

The Neolithic sites at Haddenham have presented rather poor conditions for the preservation of animal bone due to erosion in acidic burial conditions. Subsequent induration with iron salts has, in some instances, covered the bones with hard concretions of sand and gravel. As is usual in such cases, the condition of the bones varies locally from good to very poor. It is probable that a substantial proportion of the less dense bones, or more juvenile bone, has been lost from the archaeological record.

It is obvious that mammal bones deposited at sites such as causewayed enclosures represent more than the simple debris of the daily diet. Consequently the bone identifications set out below are described in a general way for the whole sample, but are also listed by both layer and ditch segment. From the causewayed enclosure, 104 bones, 23 teeth and seven fragments of antler have been identified to species level. These give the numerical proportions in Table 5.27. In addition to the specimens listed, three fox bones were identified; an atlas and a cervical vertebra in Ditch N primary fills, and a distal left humerus in Ditch H. When occasional bones of this species are found it is probable that they are intrusive.

Although the identified sample is small, the proportions conform to those found in other sites of this type and period. For example, Jackson (1934) reported that cattle bones were 'very abundant' at the Whitehawk causewayed enclosure, implying that this species was the most common, and Grigson (1965) found that cattle were the most common in all Neolithic levels at Windmill Hill (59–68% limb bones only). Legge (1981a) has found that cattle bones are 55–60% of those identified at the Hambledon Hill and Stepleton causewayed sites.

The fills of the ditch segments have been divided into two phases (see below). In each, the proportion of identified cattle bones is effectively the same; the primary fills have 80.3% cattle bones, and the

**Table 5.27.** *Overall proportions of identified bone (* 3 of 4 bones are referred to this species).*

|  | Cattle | Caprine | Pig | Red deer* |
|---|---|---|---|---|
| Bones | 88 (84.6%) | 7 (6.7%) | 5 (4.8%) | 4 (3.8%) |
| Teeth & jaws | 16 | 3 | 1 | 0 |

secondary and tertiary 83.8%. In comparison with other causewayed enclosure faunas, Haddenham has a high proportion of cattle. However, this must be considered in relation to the possibly limited survival at Haddenham of the smaller bones from the smaller species. Legge (1991) has shown that limb bones of the smaller domestic mammals survive poorly in relation to teeth and jaws at a range of Neolithic and Bronze Age sites, and that this is related to processes of bone destruction which are, as yet, poorly understood. Under very good conditions of preservation, as was found in sealed middens at Grimes Graves (Legge 1981b; 1992), 30 sheep bones were identified for each mandible or mandible fragment. Under the more severe conditions of preservation found in Bronze Age ditch fills at Down Farm (Legge 1991) this falls to an average of 2.5 bones for each jaw or jaw fragment identified. The Haddenham causewayed enclosure bone survival obviously falls at the lower end of this range of variation, so that the proportion of the smaller mammals identified is very probably skewed by poor preservation.

In spite of the problems of bone survival, the importance of cattle in the earlier Neolithic of southern Britain is probably real as they are found to be the most common species at causewayed enclosures with all conditions of bone preservation. It has been argued elsewhere (Legge 1981a; 1989) that the bone remains in causewayed enclosures cannot be taken as indicative of the prevailing domestic economy or environment, as there is little doubt that the sites have a social rather than a purely economic function. However, the quantity of cattle bones is indicative of a substantial wealth in this species among earlier Neolithic communities. It would be surprising to find a contrary situation in the bone remains of domestic sites in this same region.

Cut marks, canid gnawing and articulated bones
Of the bones listed opposite, 12 show cut marks from flint knives and 10 were gnawed, probably by domestic dogs; five specimens were both cut and gnawed. As outlined above (see **Worked bone and antler**), burning is found only on one antler pick (from Ditch L). It has been argued that animal bones from causewayed enclosures show features which distinguish them from

**Bone measurements**

*Cattle*

| | | | | | | | | | |
|---|---|---|---|---|---|---|---|---|---|
| P scapula | L | SLC = 40.5 | | | | | | | |
| D humerus | R | BT = 67.5 (E) | HT = 41.4 | | HTC = 30.4 | | Bd = 75.0 | | |
| D humerus | L | | HT = 43.3 | | | | | | |
| P radius | R | BFp = 61.3 (E) | Bp = 69.0 (E) | | | | | | |
| P radius | L | BFp = 70.0 (E) | | | | | | | |
| acetabulum | L | LA = 77.6 | | | | | | | |
| D tibia | R | Bd = 54.0 | Dd = 42.2 | | | | | | |
| tibia | L | GL = 368.0 | Bp = 113.0 (E) | | Bd = 68.4 | | Dd = 44.9 | | |
| P metacarpal | R | Bp = 53.9 | Dp = 33.4 | | | | | | |
| P metatarsal | L | Bp = 46.1 | | | | | | | |
| D metatarsal | R | Bd = 51.6 | Td = 25.6 | | | | | | |
| D metatarsal | R | Bd = 50.7 | Td = 29.3 | | | | | | |
| astragalus | L | GLM = 52.8 | GLl = 63.5 | | Bd = 38.5 | | | | |
| phalanx | | 1GL = 57.6 (E) | Bp = 31.6 | | Dp = 32.1 | | | | |
| phalanx | | | 1Bp = 28.1 | | Dp = 31.9 | | | | |

domestic waste, in particular a lesser extent of bone processing, in part shown by more common finds of articulated bones (Legge 1981a).

This argument is difficult to sustain in the virtual absence of Neolithic domestic settlement debris from England; comparison must be made with Bronze Age settlement site bone remains where, in the writer's experience, articulated bones are rarely found. One such instance of articulated cattle bones is found at Haddenham in the primary fills of Ditch K. The specimen is a distal tibia of *Bos*, having the astragalus and the lateral malleolus cemented in place by mineral accretions. The specimen cannot therefore have been disturbed after its deposition. The astragalus has multiple fine cuts across its medial face of the type TA-2 (Binford 1981), which are typically associated with dismemberment of the lower limb at this point, cutting through the thick medial ligaments to allow separation of the joint. Even if bone processing by humans was less at causewayed enclosures, dogs obviously had access to the bones, although it cannot be determined whether this was before or after the bones were deposited in the ditch segments.

A note concerning the burnt bone

Amounting to some 60 fragments, though only weighing in total 160 g, the burnt bone from the HAD '84 area was subsequently assessed by C. Swaysland, an undertaking with the specific aim of trying to establish whether these derive from human or animal sources; unfortunately due to their small size none was identifiable. It warrants notice, however, that evidently attesting to different practices of food cooking/preparation, the investigations at Barleycroft/Over have shown that burnt animal bone is a feature of later Neolithic sites. Therefore, there seems no basis to attribute this material to the cremation of human remains. Perhaps like the F.520 'cremation' pit from the HAD '87 area (which was also found not to include any identifiable human remains) the many pits at Etton that were also originally assigned as being cremation-related proved to consist of burnt animal bone alone (Pryor 1998).

*Charred plant remains*
by G. Jones

Soil samples collected from the causewayed enclosure ditch, palisade trenches, other features (e.g. pits) and the buried soil were processed using a water-separation machine (cf. French 1971; Kenward *et al.* 1980) with flot sieves of mesh sizes 1 mm and 300 $\mu$m and with a 1-mm mesh for collecting the heavy residue. In 1981, *c.* 150 samples from *c.* 100 different units were processed. Every unit was sampled at least once and units from the buried soil were sampled on a 'checkerboard' system taking alternate 5-m squares for processing. A minimum of 40 litres of soil was processed for each sample except for the buried soil, where the minimum sample size was 20 litres per square, and small features which were processed in their entirety. After the minimum sample had been processed, the 1-mm flot sieve was examined and, if charred remains were observed, the rest of the unit (sometimes over 200 litres) was processed. In 1982, the minimum sample size was reduced to 10 litres of soil and sample size was no longer based on scanning of the flot, although nearly all the 130 units excavated were sampled. In 1984, soil was processed from 23 units out of a total of 260 excavated, although 40 litres of soil were usually processed from each of the sampled units (less for small units). In 1987, 40 out of 176 units were sampled and usually 40 to 60 litres of soil were processed per unit.

While the heavy residues were sorted by members of the excavation team, only material from the residues collected in 1981 was available for the present study. The >1-mm flots were all sorted for charred plant remains. The <1-mm flots were collected primarily for the recovery of weed seeds associated with crops and so these were sorted only from units with 10 or more crop 'items' (grains, glume bases, rachis internodes and straw nodes) in the >1-mm fractions. Plant remains were identified (at magnifications of ×10 to ×40) by comparison with modern reference material and the results are presented in Table 5.28. As no clear difference was

## Species distribution

The ditch fills were divided into Level 1 (primary) and Level 2 (secondary and tertiary). The following designations describe particular conditions that have been seen on bones: gnawed = gnawed by dog or other canid; cut = fine cut marks on surface of the bone; burnt = bone charred; referred = identification not wholly certain and the specimen is referred to this species. A number in brackets refers to the number of identical specimens where more than one was found in that context. It must be remembered that the rather poor condition of some bones makes the frequency of gnawing or the pattern of cut marks uncertain.

| Ditch segment | Species | Elements |
|---|---|---|
| C (1) | cattle | metacarpal shaft fragment (referred) |
| D (1) | red deer | fragment distal right radius |
| | | fragment mandibular bone (referred) |
| | cattle | distal humerus, right, fused |
| | | distal humerus, left, fused (cut) |
| | | proximal radius, right |
| | | proximal radius, left |
| | | proximal metatarsal, left |
| | | navicular-cuboid, right |
| | | upper M1 and M2, left, young adult |
| D (2) | red deer | metatarsal shaft, right |
| | | large, unshed antler base |
| | cattle | distal humerus, fused, right (cut) |
| | | proximal shaft, radius/ulna, left |
| | | proximal radius, right |
| | | acetabulum, left |
| | | distal tibia, left, fused |
| | | proximal tibia, left, fused (cut) |
| | | proximal tibia, left, fused |
| | | proximal tibia, shaft fragment |
| | | astragalus, left |
| | | rib fragment, left |
| | | horn core, fragment |
| | | upper P4, left, young adult |
| | | upper M2, right, adult |
| F (1) | cattle | proximal humerus fragment, immature, right |
| F (2) | cattle | distal humerus, fused, right (gnawed) |
| | | radius shaft fragment |
| | | phalanx 1 fragment |
| | | upper M3, right, sub-adult |
| G (1) | cattle | proximal ulna fragment, fused, right |
| | | proximal radius, right |
| | | part calcaneum, right (gnawed) |
| | | phalanx 2, fused |
| | | horn core fragment |
| | | lower M1, left, broken |
| | | upper M2 |
| H (1) | cattle | scapula fragments |
| H (2) | fox | proximal humerus, left |
| | pig | proximal humerus fragment, left |
| | cattle | distal tibia fragment, left |
| | | acetabulum, right |
| | | phalanx 2, fused |
| | | skull fragment, left |
| I (1) | cattle | distal humerus, fused, left |
| | | distal humerus, fragment, left |
| | | part humerus shaft, juvenile, right |
| | | proximal ulna fragment, right |
| | | proximal radius fragment, left |
| | | distal tibia, fused, right |
| | | proximal metacarpal, right (3, plus shaft fragments) |
| | | navicular-cuboid, left |
| | | phalanx 1, fused (2) |
| | | lumbar vertebrae, fused (3) |
| | | skull fragment, right |
| | | horn core fragment (2 - large) |
| J (1) | cattle | distal radius fragment, fused |
| J (2) | cattle | radius shaft fragment |

| Ditch segment | Species | Elements |
|---|---|---|
| K (1) | cattle | scapula fragment, right |
| | | scapula, left (gnawed) |
| | | acetabulum, left (gnawed, cut, utilized: see Pollard above) |
| | | distal tibia, astragalus, lateral malleolus, right (bones in articulation) |
| | caprine | lower dp4 , left, juvenile |
| K (2) | cattle | distal humerus, fused, right (gnawed) |
| | | ilium of pelvis, left |
| L (1) | red deer | rib fragment (referred) |
| | cattle | distal metatarsal, fused, right |
| | | vertebra fragment |
| L (2) | red deer | antler beam fragment and tine |
| | cattle | distal humerus, fused, right |
| | | distal radius, fused, left |
| | | acetabulum, left |
| | | navicular-cuboid, left |
| M (1) | red deer | antler pick (partly burnt) |
| | cattle | proximal ulna fragment, left |
| | | proximal radius, left |
| | | astragalus, left |
| M (2) | cattle | tibia shaft fragment, left (gnawed, cut) |
| | | calcaneum, right |
| | | ramus of mandible, right |
| | | lumbar vertebra |
| | | part mandible, lower M2 and M3, right, sub-adult |
| | | molar fragment |
| | caprine | distal tibia, fused, left (cut) |
| N (1) | fox | axis vertebra and cervical vertebra (probably originally articulated) |
| | pig | distal humerus shaft, left |
| | cattle | proximal scapula, left, fused |
| | | proximal tibia fragment, right |
| | | metatarsal, fused, right (worked: see below) |
| | | fragment of mandibular bone, left |
| | | lower M3, right, adult |
| | caprine | calcaneum, fused, right |
| | | rib fragment (2) |
| N (1/2) | cattle | proximal tibia fragment, left |
| | | thoracic vertebra, fused |
| | | rib fragment |
| N (2) | cattle | proximal tibia shaft fragment, right |
| | | tibia shaft, right |
| | | proximal metacarpal, left (cut) |
| | | rib fragment (2) |
| | | part mandible, M2 and M3, left, adult |
| | | upper M9, broken, young |
| | caprine | distal humerus fragment, right (referred) |
| | | distal tibia, fused, left |
| O (1) | pig | humerus shaft, left (gnawed, cut) |
| | | skull fragment, left |
| | red deer | fragment distal femur, left (referred) |
| | | antler fragments (2) |
| | cattle | distal humerus, left, fused |
| | | right and left upper M3, young adult |
| | | condyle of mandible |
| O (2) | pig | distal humerus, left, fused (gnawed, cut) |
| | cattle | acetabulum and pubis, right (gnawed, cut) |
| | | rib fragment |
| | caprine | distal humerus, fused, right (gnawed) |
| Interior F.520; ('87 pit) | cattle | upper M3, right, young adult |

Table 5.28. *Charred plant remains. + = 1 fragment of nutshell; ++ = several fragments of nutshell.*

| Feature no. | Main causewayed ditch | | | | | Recuts | | Palisade | Pit | Prehistoric | | | Roman ditch | A horizon | | |
|---|---|---|---|---|---|---|---|---|---|---|---|---|---|---|---|---|
| | 10 | 36 | 42 | 132 | 522 | 11 | 15 | 49 | 520 | 5 | 8 | 46 | 1 | 18 | 22 | – |
| *Hordeum vulgare* grains | – | – | – | – | – | 2 | – | – | – | – | – | – | – | – | – | – |
| *Hordeum* sp. grains | – | – | – | – | – | 352 | 33 | – | 1 | – | 2 | 3 | 1 | – | 2 | 3 |
| *Hordeum* rachis internodes | – | – | – | – | – | 1 | – | – | – | – | – | – | – | 1 | – | – |
| *Triticum dicoccum* grains | – | – | – | – | – | 20 | 3 | – | – | – | 1 | – | – | – | – | – |
| *Triticum* sp. grains | – | – | – | – | – | 37 | 6 | – | – | – | 1 | 2 | – | – | – | – |
| indet. cereal grains | 1 | – | – | – | – | 153 | 17 | – | – | – | 1 | – | – | – | – | – |
| *Linum usitatissimum* | – | – | – | 1 | – | – | – | – | – | – | – | – | – | – | – | – |
| *Coryllus avellana* (nutshell) | – | – | – | – | – | – | – | – | + | ++ | – | + | – | – | – | – |
| *Veronica hederifolia* | – | – | – | – | – | – | – | – | 1 | – | – | – | – | – | – | – |
| *Chenopodium album* | – | – | – | – | – | – | – | – | 1 | – | – | 4 | – | – | – | – |
| *Bilderdykia convolvulus* | – | 2 | – | – | – | 5 | – | – | – | – | – | 2 | – | – | – | – |
| *Polygonum aviculare* agg. | – | – | – | – | – | 1 | – | – | – | – | – | – | – | – | – | – |
| *P. lapathifolium* | – | – | – | – | – | 1 | – | – | – | – | – | – | – | – | – | – |
| Polygonaceae | – | – | – | – | – | – | – | – | – | – | – | 1 | – | – | – | – |
| *Rubus* sp. | – | – | – | – | – | – | – | 1 | – | – | – | – | – | – | – | – |
| cf. *Malus sylvestris* | – | – | – | – | 1 | – | – | – | – | – | – | – | – | – | – | – |
| cf. Labiatae | – | 1 | – | – | – | – | – | – | – | – | – | – | – | – | – | – |
| *Galium* cf. *aparine* | – | – | 1 | – | – | – | – | 2 | – | – | – | – | – | – | – | – |
| *Malva* sp. | – | – | – | – | – | 1 | – | – | – | – | – | – | – | – | – | – |
| *Bromus* sp. | – | – | – | – | – | – | – | 1 | – | – | – | – | – | – | – | – |
| Gramineae | – | – | – | – | – | 1 | – | – | – | – | – | 1 | – | – | – | – |
| indet. | – | – | – | – | 6 | – | 1 | – | – | – | – | 2 | – | – | – | 1 |
| vol. soil processed (litres) (1981 samples only) | 10 | – | – | – | – | 1000 | 220 | – | – | 60 | 130 | – | 40 | 40 | 50 | 1500 |

observed between units from the same feature, these have been combined in the table.

It is clear from Table 5.28 that only two features (F.11 & F.15) produced significant quantities of charred plant remains, and it is interesting to note that both these features were excavated in 1981 when sampling was both widespread (covering every unit) and flexible (processing larger volumes where indicated by the results of scanning). Moreover, both features were amongst those selected for further processing because charred remains were observed in the >1 -mm flot (1000 litres of soil was processed from F.11 and 220 litres from F.15). It is apparent, therefore, that breadth of sampling and scanning of flot were useful in the detection of these rare productive deposits and that flexibility in the amount of soil processed was useful for maximizing the information obtained from such deposits. The heavy residues from 1981 yielded charred remains in addition to those found in the flot. These included cereal remains and, in the residue from one feature (F.5), significant quantities of hazelnut shell, though this species was absent from the flot (and from most of the rest of the site). The recovery of hazelnut shell predominantly from the heavy residues is a common phenomenon (cf. Jones & Moss 1993;

Jones in press) and emphasizes the need to collect and study material from these residues.

Species represented

The range of cereal species represented at Haddenham presents no surprises. Barley (the hulled variety where this could be determined) predominates and two twisted grains from F.11 indicate that this includes the six-row species (*Hordeum vulgare* L.). Wheat, including emmer (*Triticum dicoccum* Sch-bl.), was also present though in smaller numbers. Six-row hulled barley and emmer are both well documented from other Neolithic sites in Britain (Hillman 1981; Moffett *et al.* 1989; Greig 1991; Palmer & Jones 1991; Fairweather & Ralston 1993; Jones in press).

Wild fruits and nuts were represented by hazel-nut shell (*Corylus avellana* L.) and one possible apple pip (cf. *Malus sylvestris* Mill.). Again, this is consistent with other Neolithic finds (Hillman 1981; Moffett *et al.* 1989; Greig 1991; Palmer & Jones 1991; Fairweather & Ralston 1993; Jones in press). The single seed of cultivated flax or linseed (*Linum usitatissimum* L.) is of some interest as, until recently, flax was known in the British Neolithic only from impressions at Windmill Hill (Helbæk 1952). Quantities of charred flax seeds have recently been identified, however, at Balbridie (Fairweather & Ralston 1993) and at Lismore Fields, Buxton (Jones in press).

## Discussion

All the units from F.11, a pit cut into the main enclosure ditch, were of very similar composition with (hulled) barley heavily predominating over wheat (including emmer). This deposit represents one of the largest 'caches' of charred barley grain from the British Neolithic, being comparable in terms of numbers of grains to the six-row barley cache from the Late Neolithic henge at Coneybury, Wiltshire (Moffett *et al.* 1989), several samples of barley from Early Neolithic Scord of Brouster and a larger barley cache from Ness of Gruting, both in Scotland (Milles 1986). The sample from F.11 differs from the Coneybury cache, however, in three respects. First, the Coneybury barley comprised approximately equal numbers of hulled and naked grains (similar to Ness of Gruting, where the naked form predominated), whereas all the grains which could be determined at Haddenham were of the hulled variety (as also were most of the grains from Scord of Brouster). Secondly, the density of grain in F.11 is considerably lower (*c.* 0.5 grains per litre) than at Coneybury (*c.* 13 grains per litre), perhaps suggesting secondary or tertiary deposition in F.11, whereas the Coneybury barley is more likely to represent primary or secondary deposition. Thirdly, the Coneybury barley (like that from Ness of Gruting) was not contaminated by other cereals, unlike that from F.11 (and Scord of Brouster), which was mixed with smaller quantities of wheat, though it is difficult to establish whether this represents field contamination or was the result of a separate accident.

The Haddenham, Coneybury and Ness of Gruting caches exhibit a low level of weed contamination (1.5 per cent for the English sites and <0.1 per cent at Ness of Gruting) and are virtually free of chaff. Like the Ness of Gruting and Coneybury barley, therefore, the grain from F.11 probably represents cleaned grain in the final stages of processing (presumably burnt accidentally). This is in contrast with samples from Scord of Brouster, which contain variable amounts of weeds and significant quantities of chaff in the form of rachis internodes, and apparently represent various stages in the crop processing sequence (Milles 1986).

F.15, a pit of similar date and also cut into the main enclosure ditch, contained similar plant remains at similar density (*c.* 0.2 grains per litre) to those in F.11. It is likely, therefore, that both F.11 and F.15 were filled with debris from the same accident or accidents. Charred hazelnut shell was recovered from only three features (F.5, and a single fragment from each of F.46 and F.520).

Very few identifiable charred remains were recovered from the main enclosure ditch or palisade trench, which may be a recovery problem as they were excavated in later seasons (see above). Such remains as were found were mainly from species which could have become charred in a number of different ways and are not necessarily indicative of any human activity other than the use of fire. However, the single flax seed and possible apple pip both came from the main enclosure ditch (from F.132 and F.522 respectively).

The buried soil was similarly largely devoid of identifiable charred remains and, in this case, may represent a real absence as it was sampled extensively (though in one area only) in 1981. If so, this contrasts with the observation by Murphy (1988) that buried soils often yield a greater concentration of charred remains than pits from settlement sites or ditches associated with ritual structures.

In conclusion, there is no positive evidence for crop processing waste at Haddenham, though many of the wild species commonly occur as weeds of crops. The samples are, however, too small to enable a distinction between crop-processing waste and chance occurrences. The only large sample available is of cleaned cereal grain. On the basis of this evidence, it is difficult to determine whether grain was brought into the enclosure in a fully cleaned state or whether it was processed at the site (cf. Legge 1989).

It has been suggested that wild plant foods may have been of greater importance than cereals in the British Neolithic (Moffett *et al.* 1989; Entwistle & Grant 1989) and this has been held to support the suggestion that Neolithic settlement was of an essentially mobile nature (Entwistle & Grant 1989; Moffett *et al.* 1989; Thomas 1991). It has been pointed out, however, that the wild plant foods (notably hazelnut) produce more durable and visible remains (nutshell) than cereals (chaff and accidentally charred grain) and are therefore more likely to survive and be recovered (Legge 1989; Jones in press; Rowley-Conwy 2000). Cereal grains were found more frequently than wild plant foods at Haddenham which, at least in 1981, may be the product of the intensive recovery programme. In later seasons, the relative paucity of remains may be a product of the reduced sampling and, in the case of hazelnut especially, the unavailability of the heavy residues (see above). Overall, the number of productive samples from Haddenham is rather too small to make any significant contribution to this debate.

**Table 5.29.** *The frequency of animal bone in the ditches in the different areas of the enclosure.*

|  | 1982 | | 1984 | | 1987 | |
|  | No. | % | No. | % | No. | % |
|---|---|---|---|---|---|---|
| Cattle | 22 | 84.6 | 38 | 95.0 | 46 | 69.7 |
| Other | 4 | 15.4 | 2 | 5.0 | 20 | 30.3 |
| Total | 26 | 100 | 40 | 100 | 66 | 100 |

**Overview discussion: a cattle economy**

Poor preservation limits the conclusions that can be drawn from the animal bones, but the low occurrence of articulation and the significant presence of gnawing perhaps suggests that, on the whole, the bones were not being specially 'placed' in the ditches. Consisting of 85% cattle, and very much in contrast to the long barrow's more diverse assemblage, the enclosure would seem to reflect the standard cattle economy of the earlier Neolithic (e.g. Kinnes 1988; Thomas 1991). In terms of the site's broad distributions (aside from its construction tools noted above: Table 5.29), one point that warrants particular notice is that pig bones were only found along the western ditch segments (H, N & P), with none being found in the HAD '82 excavations. This, however, may be affected by preservation, as caprine bone also only occurred in the western areas (Ditches K, M, N & O); red deer bone (as opposed to antler), while occurring in the western exposures, was also present in the HAD '82 ditches. But even in this context there would seem no evidence to suggest the totemic deployment of 'the wild', as no red deer remains occurred with the 1984 assemblage: an obviously 'interesting' and intensively utilized area.

For reasons outlined above, the project's environmental sampling was insufficient to enable any reasonable analysis of the enclosure's charred plant remains as a whole. This is regrettable, especially concerning the issue of whether processed cereals were being brought into the enclosure; given its size (and the low artefact densities within its eastern and northern sectors) it is even conceivable that arable plots actually occurred within the enclosure's interior. Nevertheless, such evidence would always remains ambiguous, as broadly contemporary settlements are known within the enclosure's immediate Delphs terrace environs (e.g. the Cracknell Farm scatter). It is reasonable to presume that the terrace itself saw arable activity at that time. In other words, any transportation of processed crops may have only been a matter of a kilometre or less.

**Context and enclosure: breaking the circle**

Before progressing to any kind of concluding discussion of the site those major factors that frame its interpretation must first be outlined. There comes a point in any site's analysis when it is necessary to stand back from the chronicle of its excavation and immediate fieldwork-generated interpretations, and effectively *break the narrative*. Such a perspective is particularly relevant in the case of the causewayed enclosure, for examining the individual ditch segments in too much micro-detail leads to a quality of almost photographic pixilation and risks losing any sense of the larger picture. In this section of the text, unlike for the long barrow, we will not attempt to address 'how the enclosure *worked*', but rather whether broad distributional patterns and principles of its development can be distinguished. Here issues of the organization, duration and character of its labour are also paramount: can its construction traces be differentiated from its usage? Although liberally applying statistics in an effort to envisage 'the problem', there is no hard-edged security in these matters, and it is a matter of propensity and not rule.

*Resourcing and labour*
Gauging the labour involved in the construction of the causewayed enclosure is crucial to the understanding of its use. Unlike, for example, the long barrow, its function is ambiguous and it is reasonable to query to what extent construction was itself its prime purpose. In order to evaluate such proposals we need to establish some measure of the numbers involved in its building, the duration of these works and thereby the 'stay' of the workforce at the site. Only by doing so will it be possible to explore the extent of the enclosure's usage as distinct from the 'act' of its construction.

It is estimated that approximately one-fifth of the enclosure's main circuit (1113 m) consisted of causeways, thereby leaving some 890 m of ditch segments. Calculating that each metre of its length represents on average a capacity of *c.* 4.2 m$^3$, its perimeter equates to 3738 m$^3$. Once more employing Startin's figures that a team of four could dig between 5.43 and 8.15 m$^3$ of gravel per day, its construction would therefore have entailed between 14,688 and 22,016 person-hours. The key issue, of course, is how many 'teams'/'communities' participated in this, and a range of gang sizes is shown in Table 5.30.

The same issues arise in relation to the nature of labour and its 'sustainability' at the site as were explored for the long barrow (see Chapter 3 above). Presuming that it is unlikely that such an ambitious project would have been embarked upon by a small gang-unit (i.e. one or two four-person teams) and that it would be difficult to maintain a large (and socially diverse) workforce for a considerable period of time, the number of approximately month-long seasons needed for its annual building is shown in brackets in Table 5.30. From this it can be seen that theoretically five four-person teams could have constructed the ditch circuit over three–five annual month-long seasons. However, this implies a discipline of eight-hour long work days and takes no account of various 'breaks', both ceremonial and pragmatic. Therefore, given this, and in the light of frequency of the enclosure's pattern of recut construction, it would be much more likely that it was built over approximately the same period but involving a workforce upwards of twice that number (i.e. 10 four-person teams). However, when modelling the construction it would not just be a matter of some 40 adults as a socially isolated unit (i.e. a work gang), but rather a community with a full array of attendants involving children, spouses and individuals assigned to tend the stock, etc. In all likelihood this would, in total, entail upwards of 100 individuals staying at the site. If so many were resident for a period of approximately a month *per annum* over three to five years the issue then becomes, given the relative paucity of the enclosure's finds and the quantity of refuse their presence would generate, just how much scope there is for enclosure-specific activities apart from its construction itself.

Of course, the monument consisted of more than just the ditch circuit alone. Although the labour expended for the cutting of the palisade trench would not have been as great, it was still considerable. Accounting for its interruptions, it is estimated that the 950 m trenched length of its *c.* 1020 m perimeter would represent *c.* 237.5 m³ of spoil. In Table 5.31 the same figures that are used above have been employed. In that table the bracketed numbers provide an estimate of the length of time it would take, in addition, to set and backfill the posts; here thought together to equate roughly with the same time as the digging of the trench itself. Representing in total 1864–2800 person-hours of labour, using 5–10 four-person teams, the palisade could therefore have easily been erected within a single month-long season.

Yet the actual erection of the palisade would not encompass all the labour that its construction would have demanded. Its perimeter would have involved *c.* 0.30 m diameter posts set an interval of two per metre (0.30–0.40 m distance). By this, 1800 3.00-m-long poles would have been required. At a minimum each would demand 1.5 'cuttings' (two 3.00-m lengths possibly cut from a 6.00+ m long length); by applying

**Table 5.30.** *Labour required to construct the ditch circuit (bracketed figures indicates number of month-long seasons per annum required).*

| | Work days | |
| | 5.43m³ per day | 8.15 m³ per day |
| --- | --- | --- |
| 1 four-person team | 688 (23) | 459 (15) |
| 5 four-person teams | 138 (5) | 92 (3) |
| 10 four-person teams | 69 (2) | 46 (1.5) |

**Table 5.31.** *Labour input for digging palisade trench (bracket number includes backfilling and setting of posts).*

| | Work days | |
| | 5.43m³ per day | 8.15 m³ per day |
| --- | --- | --- |
| 1 four-person team | 44 (88) | 29 (58) |
| 5 four-person teams | 9 (18) | 6 (12) |
| 10 four-person teams | 4 (8) | 3 (6) |

Darrah's estimates for stone axe felling of timbers, the cutting of the palisade would therefore represent an additional 4050 person-hours of labour (calculated on basis of 1.5 hours per cut). To this would need to be added the haulage of the wood. Here a minimal distance has been envisaged (see below), requiring an average of 15 minutes per pole. Coming to a total of 450 person-hours, the distances involved and time thus expended obviously could have been much greater. By this means the palisade would represent 6364–7300 person-hours' labour in total, approximately a third to a half that required for the ditch circuit. It can, therefore, be estimated that two circuits of the causewayed enclosure would have involved 21,052–29,316 person-hours; approximately three to seven times that required for the long barrow.

Behind this lies what is perhaps the most important factor of all: the character of the palisade's timber and the investment it entailed. By appearance it would seem to have consisted of *c.* 50-year-old oak poles. In other words, exactly the kind of timber used in 'robust' building frame construction. However, as outlined above (Chapter 4), the period's domestic architecture generally did not seem to draw upon timbers of this size. Therefore, does the use of large poles for the palisade imply a 'reservation' of timber to ensure its adequate scale and survival from the browse grazing of herds (and deer)? If so, requiring approximately a half-century's protection and nurturing (Darrah pers. comm.), albeit incalculable this could actually represent the greatest investment within the construction of the causewayed enclosure.

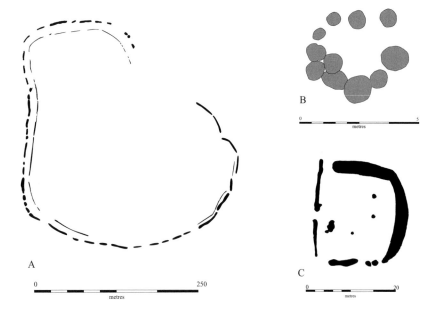

B

A

0                    250
        metres

C

0              20
      metres

**Figure 5.37.** *Design principles: A) the Upper Delphs, Haddenham Causewayed Enclosure; B) 'A Necklace of Pits': Mildenhall pit cluster, Kilverstone, Suffolk (see also Garrow 2002 and Chapter 4, Fig. 4.17); C) façade construction: mortuary structure, Grendon Barrow, Northants (see also Fig. 3.75; after Gibson 1985).*

*Emergent structures: development trends and design principles*

Figure 5.37 effectively amounts to a caricature of what have been seen as the main sources of 'design' analogies for causewayed enclosures. On the one hand, based on the interruption of their circuits is the sense that their plan amounts to no more than a 'necklace' or string of pits equally accessible on all aspects, with their implied segmented gang-labour being the key to their organization. The other model, largely based on analogy to the mortuary monuments of the period, relates towards façade-type principles, the sense that there is 'front space' (and, *de facto*, a 'back'). This is a crucial issue as behind it sits the question of whether the layout of such enclosures was a matter of purposeful 'style' and intent, or if instead they were some sort of broad cultural 'blueprint'. The latter, of course, largely arises from the near pan-European distribution of enclo-

As is evident at Etton, short coppicing was clearly practised during the earlier Neolithic for a range of wooden implements (e.g. axe handles and hurdles: Taylor, in Pryor 1998). Yet unless especially planted from seed, it is unlikely that coppicing was the source of the palisade timbers (it being impossible to coppice from felled ancient woodland, which may well have been cleared by the pulling downs of trunks rather than cutting: M. Taylor pers. comm.) The most probable source is rather from secondary growth following clearance (and perhaps arable and pasture usage: R. Darrah pers. comm.). It is thereby conceivable that the interior of the causewayed enclosure was itself the source of this timber. (Estimating a 10.00-m canopy cover, *c.* 100 trunks and 200 poles could theoretically be available from a hectare, and an area of *c.* 9 ha might produce some 1800 poles.) By this, following its construction and initial usage, the enclosure could, in effect, have become a reserved forest stand awaiting the maturation of the palisade timbers. Whatever the attraction of such arguments (the symbolic clearance becoming a delineated woodlot) and having resonance with the in-ditch coppicing at Etton (Taylor, in Pryor 1998), such speculation is unjustified, given the site's lack of palynological analyses (there was also insufficient detailing of its treeholes). This, nevertheless, does not detract from what an investment of timber (as a nurtured resource) the palisade represents.

sures of this type and the notion that they somehow embody the Neolithic experience: in other words, the sense that as 'first enclosures' they are a model of the Neolithic collective and of life in woodland clearances.

Usually in archaeology we are able to side-step issues of enclosure 'design' by vague recourse to tradition, but of course this is not valid in the earlier Neolithic. Occurring in a world without monument reference or fabric, as regards issues of how *the idea* and, thereby, *the form* of 'enclosure' was transmitted the immediate social group's landscape experience would surely have predominated over any sense of formal design *per se* (such criteria being more appropriate in the later Neolithic with its obvious sense of absolute geometries and 'tighter' monument typologies; though see McAvoy's 2000 claims concerning the Rectory Farm, Godmanchester complex.) The problem here is that to deny precepts of formal planning to such enclosures, privileging instead landscape experience as their source, is in effect to relegate their construction to the equivalent of bee hives or beaver lodges (see e.g. Ingold 1995) and as almost a biological response to environment. Equally we must be wary of casting the basic causewayed form of these enclosures into an evolutionary perspective, as if somehow enclosures were destined to be uninterrupted (apart from formal entrances) and that causewayed circuits were effectively only half-achieved. As indeed is the case with the contemporary Foulmire Fen long barrow, these communities were evidently quite capable of completing fully finished 'design projects' (including uninterrupted ditch circuits). The interrupted circuits of causewayed enclosures, however much drawing inspiration from clearance situations, were clearly intended, and an integral part of their content. Given these factors our concern here is to try to determine what, if any, 'design' or organizational principles underlay the Upper Delphs enclosure.

As has been already alluded to, the enclosure does seem to have been organized according to a 'façade-type' principle, that is from off its straight western side or front. Its definition is based on a number of factors. First there is a much higher quantity of finds throughout this area. Initially detected through test-pit sampling as the Spread A 'core zone' (see Chapter 4 above, Fig. 4.8), with the results of the transect sampling this swathe must now be enlarged to encompass an area of 1.8 ha (Fig. 6.9, below). Secondly, at least in contrast to the HAD '82 site and as shown on aerial photographs, around the eastern half of the enclosure there is the much greater stand-off of the palisade from the ditch perimeter (c. 1.50 m vs 12.00 m). Finally, there is the evidence of the 'special deposits'. Not only would this include the 'ditchwork' mound in Ditch I, but the inclusion of human remains in that ditch and also in M, N & O. As is proverbially the case, we excavated insufficient portions of the circuit off this side to be absolutely assured of this interpretation, and human remains could always be found elsewhere. Yet there is no escaping the fact that, in contrast to the remainder of its circuit, the western side of its perimeter runs straight for some 165 m, and the evidence of greater artefact densities throughout that area is unequivocal.

Following upon the 1984 season a means of phasing the ditch circuit's development was devised (Fig. 5.38; see Evans 1988a). In that portion of its perimeter, although the length of the ditch segments varied from 5.80–13.0+ m, the extent of the causeways seemed relatively standard and only ranged from 1.95–2.80 m. What the analysis demonstrated, however, was that this interval was only emergent through the sequence. Aside from Ditch I (that was always 'special' with its internal mound and placed deposits) the three southern ditches (F–H) began as large sub-circular/-ovoid pits (c. 3.00–5.00 m) and in this Phase I.1 the causeway interval was irregular and varied from 2.65–6.30 m in length. It was only with the subsequent Phase I.2 lateral extension of each segment (including Ditch I southwards) that the 'standard' c. 2.00 m causeway interval was achieved. In contrast, in relation to the

original Phase I southern terminal of Ditch J, the c. 6.80 m gap between it and Ditch I was ascribed as being a major entranceway: an interpretation that was in part engendered by the 'special' character of Ditch I on its southern side. Thereafter, it was only with the Phase II ditch-like recutting of Ditch J that this entranceway was reduced to a regular causeway length of 2.80 m.

In the 1988 interim (Evans 1988a) it was proposed that a length of the palisade opposite Ditches I/J's causeway had been secondarily inset. Yet, while segments of its trench were indeed somewhat later additions, this no longer seems valid. It was essentially promoted to further argue that the enclosure had major entrances and the originally wide Ditch I/J gap or 'crossing' was one of these. At that time it was thought that the palisade was, in effect, a primary feature of the enclosure, rather than probably relating to Phase II long-segment digging (see below). This is not to disavow the major entrances-interpretation, but that the ditches did not act in direct unison with the palisade. Based on the subsequent analysis, the primary I/J causeway does indeed mark a formal entranceway, but it was cut off with the extension of Ditch J in Phase II.

Having established this broad phasing 'model', the 1982 excavations can be reviewed (Fig. 5.38:D); with its ditch segments largely excavated in alternative longitudinal sections (i.e. quadranted segments) some degree of reappraisal of the results is possible. Although given its limited exposure Ditch E has no potential for sub-division, the lobate plan of C would suggest its later recut expansion. However, it is the very long, c. 29.00 m middle ditch segment (D) where recutting was always thought to be likely. This is based on its plan configuration and the varying basal depth along its length; any earlier recuttings were not really apparent in its lower fills. In all likelihood, it originally consisted of two distinct segments:

*D1*: In total, 13.00 × 4.70 m and 1.40 m deep throughout. Based on its lobate plan it would, in fact, be possible to sub-divide into two components: D1a being the original c. 7.00 m long (4.70 m wide) ovoid pit at its southern end that was laterally extended northward (D1b) to its full 13.00 m length.

*D2*: Lying at the southern end of Ditch D this was 10.00 m long, 4.00 m wide and 1.20 m deep; no further sub-division was apparent.

There would, therefore, have been an approximately 6.40-m wide causeway between these two segments that was eventually cut through by the more ditch-like recut along the combined length of the segment (D3). At its shallowest this was only 0.80 m deep across the spine that originally separated the D1 and D2 seg-

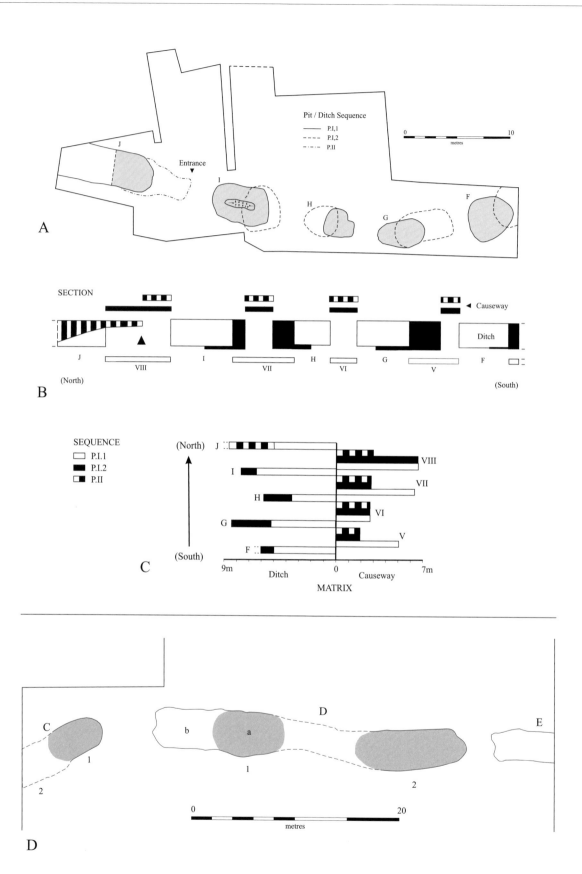

**Figure 5.38.** *Enclosure phasing. A–C) HAD '84: A) plan showing lateral expansion of small primary pits; B) schematic section; C) phasing/development 'matrix'; D) HAD '82 with grey tone indicating primary pit segments.*

ments. (Such a long causeway would not, of course, coincide with the 'standard' interval unless it has been further impinged upon by unrecognized recutting.)

At least in part, this sequence would correspond to the HAD '84 phasing scheme. The long D3 ditch-like recut would equate with Phase II; the D1 and D2 lobate segments being attributable to Phase I, with the D1b expansion of the original D1a ovate pit corresponding to the Phase I.1 and I.2 distinctions. Given this, two points are particularly noteworthy. The first is the fact that the causeway distance between Ditches D and E is of the same basic *c.* 2.00 m length that was distinguished as being the paramount interval in 1984. Second is the interrelationship between the ditch circuit and the palisade line. As has been mentioned, the 0.70 m 'interruption' between palisade segments F.40 and F.49 occurs at the same point as the causeway between Ditches D and E (Figs. 5.5 & 5.22). More important is what seems to be the close correspondence between the extent of the long F.49 palisade segment and the combined Phase II ditch-like recut length of Ditch D (Fig. 5.5). From this it could be inferred that the palisade was indeed a secondary addition to the enclosure and was only added as part of the Phase II activities.

Why the palisade should not continue across the northern quarter of the '82 area is unknown, but it must be presumed that it related to the deflection in the alignment of Ditch C (i.e. diverging in towards the enclosure's interior; see below). Given this, and the somewhat wider causeway interval between Ditches C and D (4.80 m), it is possible that this marks a major entrance. Whilst this could be supported by the evidence of the burning and post-holes at the terminal of C, perhaps more likely is that an entrance actually lay on the north side of that ditch, between it and the next seemingly long segment visible on aerial photographs (Fig. 5.1).

It is surely telling of the character of the enclosure as a whole (and its variability) that it has proved impossible to apply the HAD '84 phasing structure directly to the 1987 area of excavation. As is apparent in the greater variability of the latter's ditch lengths (5.40–25.00 m), this portion of the circuit was generally more complicated and saw intense recutting. Nevertheless, as far as is possible, its 'original' pit divisions have been distinguished (Fig. 5.39 & Table 5.32).

The problem of applying the HAD '84 analysis method to this area also relates to the basic character of how the ditches were originally dug and extended. Instead of lateral extension from an original pit, here they do not so much overlap but within each segment were set successively side-by-side; their characteristic

longer term 'bi-polarity' evidently also being a primary feature. Thereafter, their upper portions eventually merged, or were otherwise recut to form the elongated ditch segments. The problem is that, aside from Ditch N, it is impossible to determine whether the elongated merging/recutting of the individual pit tops was the equivalent to the Phase I.2 cutting, as in the HAD '84 sequence, or the Phase II ditch-like recutting (the final form of Ditch N being securely ascribed to the latter). Although not abetting site-wide analyses, the recognition of these differences is crucial as it demonstrates, at the most basic level, how the execution of labour was performed varied by sector.

A 'matrix' has been duly constructed for the HAD '87 area (Fig. 5.39). Despite phasing/sequence caveats, by assuming that broadly circular pit-digging relates to Phase I.1 and the elongated pit/ditch forms (equivalent to the HAD '84 *c.* 8.00-m lengths) were assigned to the Phase I.2 phenomenon, a certain degree of comparison is possible. Along the length of Ditch N four elongated ovate 'pits' could be distinguished, 4.20–8.30 m in length; a *c.* 0.50-m-wide upstanding ridge of natural separated pits N2 and N3 (0.20 m high above the base of ditch, its top was truncated at a depth of *c.* 0.85 m). The size of these individual pits would, however, approximately correspond to that of the basic HAD '84 ditch segments (F–H; i.e. in their final Phase I.2 form) and would, for example, also correlate to the *total length* of Ditch O immediately to the north. However, in the case of the latter segment, it was recognized that it actually consisted of two 'side-by-side' pits, each *c.* 3.60 m in diameter: in other words comparable to the primary Phase I.1 pits in the HAD '84 area. In all likelihood, the four Ditch N elongated segments also probably began as sub-circular pits (?two per segment), but due to the season's high watertable we simply could not distinguish the full subtlety of their recutting (the final long ditch cutting/'grooming' eradicated most of their traces).

This kind of primary, dual or 'side-by-side' pit pattern of Ditch O was also apparent in the three southern segments (K–M). As outlined above, those that made up L were separated by a slight gravel ridge (comparable to that noted in Ditch N), whereas between M's original two pits there must have been a more substantial causeway. Some 3.60 m across, this was later largely eradicated by segment-long ditch-like recutting. This is the only 'true' or major causeway in the HAD '87 area that subsequent recutting had removed. Others may, however, simply not have been 'distinguishable' through the intensity of recutting.

Given this logic, rather than being solely based on stratigraphic observation, the tripartite division

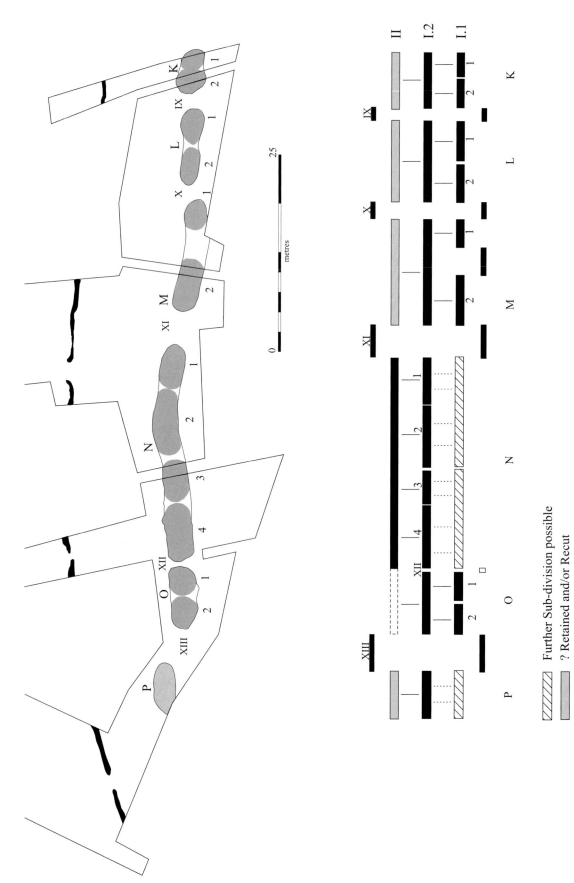

**Figure 5.39.** *HAD '87: phasing matrix; note that in the plan above grey tone indicates primary pit segments.*

**Table 5.32.** *HAD '87: ditch segment sub-divisions.*

| Ditch/pit divisions | Length (m) |
|---|---|
| *Ditch K* | *6.80* |
| 1 | 3.00 |
| 2 | 3.50 |
| | |
| *Ditch L* | *9.75* |
| 1 | 4.40 |
| 2 | 4.50 |
| | |
| *Ditch M* | *12.80* |
| 1 | 3.50 |
| 2 | 6.00 |
| | |
| *Ditch N* | *25.0* |
| 1 | 5.50 |
| 2 | 8.30 |
| 3 | 4.30 |
| 4 | 7.40 |
| | |
| *Ditch O* | *7.40* |
| 1 | 3.60 |
| 2 | 3.60 |
| | |
| *Ditch P* | *5.80* |

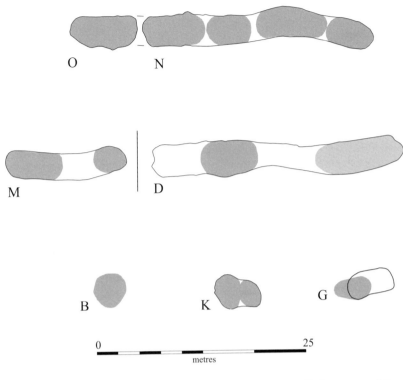

**Figure 5.40.** *The techniques of labour: illustrating basic ditch types and the variability of their combinations (grey tone indicates primary pit segment): Ditch B ('81), simple pit form; Ditch K ('87), side-by-side pit technique; Ditch G ('84), lateral pit expansion.*

recognized in the HAD '84 area does seem to be broadly valid: pits (I.1) becoming elongated ovate segments (I.2) that were locally recut as longer ditches (II). The point of the contrast between the HAD '84 and '87 areas is that there was more than one way to achieve the I.2 segments, either by later expansion or merging the tops of 'side-by-side' pits (Fig. 5.40).

The 0.50-m interruption between Ditch N/O in the HAD '87 area probably indicates that at the level of the buried ground surface there was no break between these ditches. The Ditch O length would then be equivalent to the four elongated 'pit' sub-divisions within Ditch N and together: in Phase II they thus constituted one continuous 33-m-long ditch. Against this, the 1.60- and 2.00-m wide causeway lengths respectively found between Ditch M/L and L/K would match the 'standard' *c.* 2.00-m-interval established in the course of the HAD '84 analysis. Therefore, by contrast, the 3.90- and 4.50-m gaps between Ditches M/N and O/P would mark formal entranceways and here it is relevant that human skull fragments occurred in the ditch terminals flanking the southern side of both (Fig. 5.36). The M/N entranceway would have had a staggered entrance access between the inturned entrance gap in the palisade between F.539/541 (though see below); unfortunately the portion of the palisade corresponding to the O/P entrance was not

exposed. Given these arguments, and the postulated Phase II merger of Ditches N and O, it is likely that the ditch-like recutting resulted in a continuous ditch length between major entranceways across the circuit, from M/N to O/P. This thereby attests to a formality of the 'enclosure process' and perhaps suggests a basic entrance interval.

Having established a basic causeway interval of *c.* 2.00 m (1.25–2.80 m), which was regularized by Phase I.2, major entranceways are therefore essentially defined by markedly greater causeway lengths. As shown in Figure 5.41, these fall between HAD '81 Ditches B/R (9.50 m), I/J in '84 (*c.* 7.00 m; Phase I only) and, in the '87 area, Ditches M/N (3.90 m) and probably also O/P (4.50 m). The determination of the latter three on the western side of the enclosure is furthered by the recovery of human skulls in the terminals of the ditch segments on the southern side (Ditch R in HAD '81 was not excavated whatsoever). More problematic is whether Ditch C in the HAD '82 area marked an entrance; if so, it probably fell on the northern side of that ditch. Equally, as mentioned, given the wide 'break' in the palisade trench between F.519/529 it is possible that still another entrance fell on the north side of Ditch P (in the HAD '87 area) at

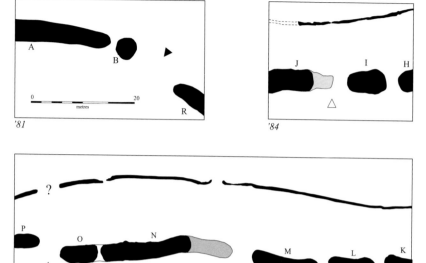

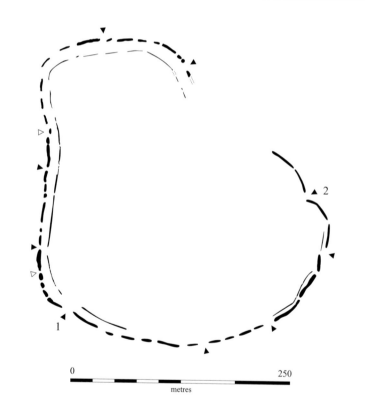

**Figure 5.41.** *Enclosure entrances: with blackened arrows indicating definite access points; open triangles, 'possible' (only).*

act in absolute unison. In the instance of the HAD '84 entrance (Ditches I/J), in concert with the Phase II extension of the northern ditch, the palisade also seems to have cut off this entrance. In the case of Ditches B/R (HAD '81) and O/P (HAD '87) entrances, the corresponding portion of the palisade was not exposed. Falling midway along the western side of the enclosure, given a 'façade logic' the Ditch M/N entrance would in effect have been the central point of access on the side and *the* main entrance into the enclosure, and would correlate to the uniquely inturned terminals of the palisade entrance at this point (Fig. 5.41). Yet against this the fact that the palisade entrance is staggered in relationship to that crossing of the ditch circuit (Ditches M/N) does not seem terribly 'formal'. Whilst recourse could also be made to the independence of the palisade circuit, a more likely explanation relates to broader enclosure dynamics. At this point the straight western side actually kinks somewhat in its alignment, this being much more apparent in the line of the ditch circuit than the palisade, which is somewhat more 'rounded' in its layout. This divergence actually occurred along the Ditch O/N segment length, the kinking happening at the point of the Ditch N.2 pit. If the northern length of this originally stopped at the point of this change of alignment (admittedly not distinguished in excavation) then the resultant terminal (in relationship to Ditch M) would be symmetrical in relationship to the F.541/539 palisade entrance. It is furthermore relevant that a human femur and the 'god dolly' would then have occurred in its northern ditch terminal (Fig. 5.36).

Variously due to work 'stoppages' (i.e. interruptions) around its perimeter, it is otherwise impossible to know just how many entranceways were present in the line of the palisade within the four areas investigated. Nor is this situation abetted by the fact that (apparently a secondary phenomenon within the development

the point of the perimeter's kinking (see below; the northern half of the ditch was not excavated, so it is not known whether it held skull pieces).

The relationship of these ditch entranceways to the palisade is complicated and generally they did not

of the causewayed enclosure, Phase II) there is not necessarily a direct relationship between entrances across the ditch circuit and the palisade. Despite its staggered relationship with the ditch circuit's entrance (see above), having formally inturned terminals the 2.30-m-wide gap between F.539/541 in the HAD '87 area certainly marks an entrance across the line of the palisade. Within that same area the 0.90-m wide gap between the F.530/531 would seem just to be a 'work-' or segment-related interruption that is essentially equivalent to the 0.70-m-wide break between F.40/49 (neither of which corresponded to a major ditch circuit entrance). More difficult within the HAD '87 area is knowing whether the 1.60-m break between F.519/529 palisade lengths marked an entrance or an interruption. Unlike the ditch circuit, the determination of this issue is not furthered by the fact that the palisade clearly did not see any 'special' entrance-related deposition (human remains, etc.). Against this, that the palisade clearly stopped in relationship to Ditch C in the HAD '82 area would also probably denote an entrance. The issue there is whether this lay on the northern or southern side of that ditch segment.

Having a 0.30–0.40 m interval between its uprights it is difficult to comprehend just what kind of barrier the palisade would have constituted. Whilst its posts were potentially set close enough to corral large stock (i.e. mature cattle), their gaps are such that it would not have had an effective defensive function (i.e. individuals could have squeezed through at a number of points). Rather, in many respects the palisade seems comparable to the ditch circuit. It would have been *a permeable boundary* in which the interval of posts, in much the same ways as the ditch circuit's causeways, was as important as their impediment as a barrier.

Finally we need to consider the awkward layout of the enclosure's northern perimeter. Here the status of the large pit F.516, set behind the palisade along the northern edge of the 1987 area, is intriguing (Fig. 5.16). Provisionally ascribed as being a well, it was not dated with certainty and can only generally be assigned to the causewayed enclosure's 'usage'. What is particularly interesting is how akin to the HAD '84 Phase I.1 enclosure ditch/pits it is, and it could equally be compared to Ditch B in the HAD '81 area. Given this, the feature's broader situation in relation to the enclosure's circuit warrants attention; it occurs at a point where the perimeter kinks from the line of the western front and from where it begins to arc away to the northwest. From this evidence it is just possible that F.516 pit represents an attempt at another primary northern circuit, which would then have never been completed and/or was superseded by the enclosure's

extant northern side (aerial photographs give no indication of such an earlier northern line). Reminiscent of the northwestward perimeter-divergent alignment of Ditch C on the eastern side opposite, it is conceivable that it was F.516's intended junction (Fig. 5.46). Alternatively, the four long segments of the northeastern perimeter that are visible north of the HAD '82 area could equally have been part of this original plan, which in either case would then have been more typically ovoid. It is the northwestern 'corner' that gives the enclosure its almost 'heart-shape' plan, as if the circuit there deflected to include something or had been extended as an afterthought.

*Distributional patterning and populations*

The fluid nature of the processes producing ditch variation is evident in that the frequencies of finds within them (Fig. 5.42). For example, Ditch K had the equal highest sherd frequency in the secondary fills, and then one of the lowest in its tertiaries. Similarly, Ditch D had a high frequency in the secondary fills but very little in its tertiary deposits. Such evidence fits well with the overall evidence from the ditches of their continual redigging and their relationships one with another.

Of course, in order to facilitate ditch-by-ditch analysis a means must be achieved to compensate for variations in their length and the proportion of each that was excavated. Although more sophisticated methods could have been adopted (e.g. cubic capacity), in an effort to further inter-enclosure comparison a simple density per metre length of ditch segment fill has been applied. By this, pottery respectively occurred with a mean density of 4.6 and 4.65 per metre in the HAD '84 and '87 areas of excavation, which is in marked contrast to the 2.0 sherd mean within the HAD '82 area (where none of the segments achieved the HAD '84/'87 means: Table 5.33).

A similarly complex picture is obtained from the flint distributions, with much evidence of variation in production, use and discard. But some general patterns emerge which resonate with other evidence, both in terms of the spatial sectors identified within the enclosure and the sequencing of activities over time. The enclosure's earlier usage, especially in the 1984 and 1987 areas, was associated with the importing of flint from the chalk ridge. In comparison with other early sites in the locality, the enclosure may have played a central role in the exchange and production of flint. The evidence for flint working, including the initial working of cores and implements, comes in the early phase from inside the causewayed enclosure. Overall levels of deposition at this time are quite low and the very low frequencies of struck flint in the

**Table 5.33.** *Mean artefact densities per metre length of excavated ditch segments; shading indicates densities above area-mean (\*\* includes teeth and antler).*

| | Ditch segment | | | | | | | | | | | | | |
|---|---|---|---|---|---|---|---|---|---|---|---|---|---|---|
| | C | D | E | F | G | H | I | J | K | L | M | N | O | P |
| **Pottery** (no. sherds) | 10 | 29 | 3 | 16 | 2 | 3 | 88 | 56 | 42 | 25 | 10 | 121 | 9 | 0 |
| Per metre | 2.6 | 1.9 | 1.6 | 4 | 0.5 | 1.0 | 11.3 | 6.2 | 9.3 | 5.1 | 1.5 | 8.9 | 3.1 | – |
| Area mean | | 2.0 | | | | 4.6 | | | | | 4.65 | | | |
| **Flint** (no.) | 12 | 27 | 8 | 21.5 | 21.5 | 2 | 84 | 28 | 48 | 5 | 9 | 34 | 2 | 0 |
| Per metre | 3.2 | 1.8 | 1.66 | 5.4 | 5.4 | 0.7 | 10.8 | 3.1 | 10.6 | 1.0 | 1.4 | 2.5 | 0.5 | – |
| Area mean | | 2.2 | | | | 5.1 | | | | | 2.7 | | | |
| **Bone** (no.)** | 1 | 25 | 0 | 5 | 8 | 8 | 15 | 2 | 9 | 9 | 11 | 22 | 14 | 0 |
| Per metre | 0.3 | 1.7 | – | 1.2 | 2 | 2.7 | 1.9 | 0.2 | 2 | 1.8 | 1.6 | 1.6 | 3.8 | – |
| Area mean | | 0.6 | | | | 1.6 | | | | | 1.8 | | | |

primary fills may suggest that the site was then only used intermittently. The primary ditch and palisade contexts (and pit F.534) have less evidence for implement production. The special nature of the early activities in the ditches has been demonstrated by the complex recutting and depositional activities. Such activities and the higher densities of flint concentrate in the 1984 and 1987 areas and their adjacent interior swathes.

As indicated in Table 5.33, the mean per metre ditch density of struck flint was again higher in the HAD '84 and '87 areas as opposed to the 1982 length. However, it is in this one finds category alone that, complementing the buried soil sampling (see Table 5.3), the HAD '84 area is singularly distinguished. Having a mean of 5.1 pieces per metre, this is generally twice that of the HAD '87 and '82 areas (2.7 and 2.2 pieces respectively).

In many of the ditch sequences the initial phase of formalized activity was brought to an end by a phase of burning, just as the upper fills and the final use of the ditch and the palisade were again associated with burning. This evidence is supported by the distribution of burnt struck flint which is concentrated in the upper fills and palisade especially in the 1984 area. Firing was associated with the long barrow's closure. A similar interpretation may be made for at least some of the burning at the enclosure, since here too there is evidence of closing gaps between ditches and between palisade sections towards the end of their use.

In the later Neolithic there are greater quantities of flint and denser concentrations of activity. This occurred especially within the enclosure since much of the material from the 50-m-grid sampling squares is of this attribution (and continuing into Early Bronze Age), concentrating in the southwestern part of the enclosure. However, activity also focused in the north and east of the enclosure: the 1982 and 1981 areas. As well as the spatial shift in focus, there is a change in the nature of activity in the ditches. In the upper levels there is evidence for core reduction and implement production. Such a change in the nature of the use of the enclosure is supported by the occurrence of small pits, post-holes and the 'grain pit' in association with the upper fills of the ditches. We may be able to posit an overall transformation towards more domestic activity through the use of the enclosure. It may also be the case that the shift occurs as the south and west areas were increasingly 'closed'.

There is other evidence of variation between ditches which changes through time. High frequencies of struck flint are found in the more elaborate and longer ditches as defined above. Thus I, J & N have high frequencies of total struck flint. However, the pattern is not as clear as for ceramics in that D (a relatively long ditch segment) has low quantities of struck flint, whereas the simpler F/G and K ditches have large quantities of flint, as does A. But, as with the pottery, with the ditches' recutting and realignment there is much fluidity and change through time. In the primary fills of the ditches, most struck flint is found in I, whereas of the secondary fills Ditch I retains high frequencies but A is dominant; other secondary fills, F/G, N and K, also have high frequencies.

It should be emphasized that the more elaborate ditches are not necessarily those with least evidence for discard or implement production, as is clear from the implement:by-product ratios in Tables 5.15 & 5.16. The samples from the primary fills are too small to allow useful discussion, but in the secondary fills there are if anything larger amounts of by-products relative to implements in the more elaborate ditches (I, J, N, D & A, if the latter is assumed to be a longer ditch). However, the differences are very slight.

Few conclusions can be drawn from the charred plant remains and residues with any security. The low densities of charred plant remains in the intensively sampled 1981 buried soil are of interest in relation to the overall evidence from the site of low frequencies of flint and ceramics, and of intermittent use, at least in the earlier phases. The 1981 ditches (A & B) had very low densities of ceramics and animal bone. There were also relatively low densities of struck flint in the buried soil in that area and in the primary fills of its ditches. However, high densities of struck flint were found in the secondary fills in Ditch A, which include the pits, F.11 & F.15, from which the highest concentrations of charred plant remains were recovered. Charred plant remains were also recovered from late pits. This very limited evidence parallels that of other materials of which larger quantities were recovered, in that a wider range of more intense uses of the enclosure seems to develop through time.

Poor preservation equally limits the conclusions that can be drawn from the animal bones, but the low occurrence of articulation and the significant presence of gnawing perhaps suggests that, on the whole, the bones were not being specially 'placed' in the ditches. As previously outlined, while in its faunal assemblages the 1987 ditches had a mixture of animal species represented including pig, caprines and deer, the 1984 area had almost exclusively cattle, as is seen in Table 5.29. The absolute amount of bone in the different areas correlates with the size of area opened and the amount of soil excavated. In Table 5.33 it is apparent that the HAD '84 and '87 bone densities within the

**Figure 5.42.** *A) Frequency of struck flint in primary and secondary ditch fills; B) frequencies of struck flint and animal bone in the ditches, with the five ditches with the highest frequencies of ceramics also indicated. (Note in both plottings 'lined' open circles indicate factored densities of Ditch I in compensation for its total excavation.)*

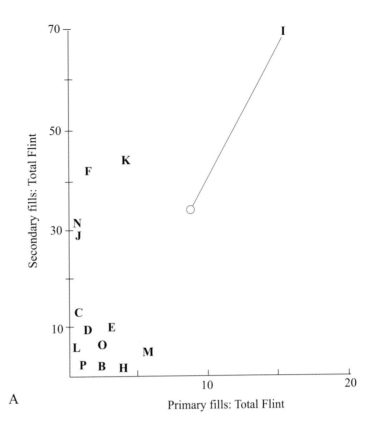

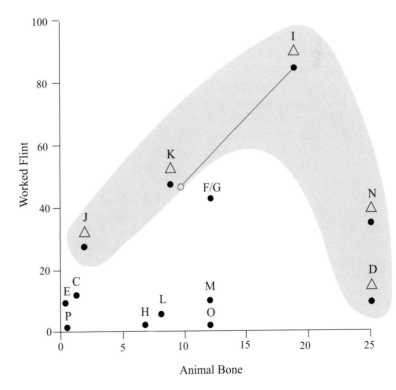

**Table 5.34.** *Minimum number of individuals per species from ditch contexts and estimated total populations.*

|          | Cattle | Caprine | Pig | Red deer |
|----------|--------|---------|-----|----------|
| MNI      | 5      | 2       | 2   | 1        |
| Factored | 55     | 22      | 22  | 11       |

ditches are roughly comparable (1.6 and 1.8 pieces), in contrast with the much lower HAD '82 ditch mean of 0.6 pieces. Nevertheless, the proportions of cattle support the distinctiveness of the 1984 area, which has the densest flint in the ditches, palisade (and there also pottery) and buried soil, and which has the most complex evidence of recutting. (As indicated in Table 5.33, in all categories Ditch I has the highest overall finds values, with Ditch K in HAD '87 also only having consistent above-mean levels.)

Insofar as it reflects upon the usage of the enclosure the minimum number of individuals per species has been calculated (MNI, by C. Swaysland: Table 5.34). Given that 9 per cent of the enclosure's circuit was excavated, in Table 5.34 the factored figures indicate the estimated total number of individuals by species that could be expected from the enclosure circuit as a whole. Such extrapolations are, of course, fraught with difficulties concerning recovery bias and the problems of representation/fragmentation within the record (see Evans 2003a for further discussion). They are, nevertheless, salient (in the light of their paucity) in terms of the intensity of the enclosure's usage and sequence. With a total population of *c.* 55 cattle, even if this figure is doubled in recompense this does not attest to intense usage. Postulating the butchery of only one animal in this category *per annum* (much too low a figure, given the human labour involved in the enclosure's construction alone) a duration of only a century could be postulated, and half or less of that span would be far more realistic. Even if every time a cow-sized animal was slaughtered it was, in effect, a matter of sacrifice and, *de facto*, a 'feast', from these estimates arguments of regular group feasting would be difficult to justify. In short, the MNI figures would have to be factored by at least ten-fold to approach the kind of *en masse* 'behaviours' (and then only over the course of a century) that have been postulated for causeway enclosures (see below).

The same conclusions would also have to be drawn from the enclosure's pottery. Based on the same factoring, the 32 rims of earlier Neolithic attribution that were recovered (see Gdaniec above, plus two from the HAD VIII pit F.534) would only attest to a total population of some 350 vessels; although this figure might have to be adjusted upwards in compensation

for the lack of coverage within the enclosure's interior and, thereby, take the total to, perhaps, some 400–500 vessels.

It is not a straightforward matter to estimate the frequency of vessel breakage within a 'monumental' context (see also e.g. Avery, in Case & Whittle 1982, 24–5), as domestic criteria of wear/usage need not apply. 'Placement' and the potential 'sacrifice' of vessels might be relevant factors. Nor is it known, for example, whether a residential/familial group's total ceramic assemblage was brought with them to the causewayed enclosure. Equally, in a similar manner as postulated for the terrace's Romano-Celtic shrine (see Volume 2, Chapter 7), it is conceivable that vessels brought to the enclosure were not subsequently removed. These caveats aside, such speculation does further thinking about the scale of the participatory communities involved. We will start by approaching this problem with the 100-person 'working community' described above, which might represent 10–20 familial groups. If, on the one hand, none of the vessels brought to the enclosure were removed then a 'loss rate' of five per visit would seem reasonable. If there is a total population of 400 vessels, this would only leave scope for 5–8 'visits'. Given the period needed to construct the enclosure this would only allow for 1–4 additional episodes/seasons of its actual 'usage'. Alternatively, taking a more minimal figure (assuming that complete vessel 'placement' was rare and that each group otherwise only broke on average one vessel per visit) then this would imply that there could have been upwards of 15–35 non-constructional episodes of the enclosure's (primary) use. Obviously doubling the size of the participatory community would halve these figures.

Reconstruction modelling of this kind is not possible for the enclosure's struck flint. Certainly, the 608 pieces recovered from its cut features alone could only compare very poorly to the 10,424 and 1212 pieces respectively recovered from the Kilverstone and Barleycroft Paddocks pit settlements. Yet, for reasons of post-depositional survival, it is the flint that offers the greatest potential for comparative analysis, as pottery and bone undergo far greater attrition and decay in buried soil 'surface' contexts. It is estimated that approximately 428.4 m³ of the enclosure's circuit was excavated in total. From these deposits 474 pieces of worked flint were recovered, which equates to only 1.12 flints per cubic metre. Although even this is less than the mean square metre test pit densities across the terrace as a whole (1.8 pieces; see Chapter 4), to achieve volumetric consistency this figure should still be further divided by approximately a quarter to relate to the depth of the test pit buried soil samples: 0.28

pieces. In order to appreciate this comparison it must, of course, be understood that the buried soil finds attest to a palimpsest of Mesolithic to Iron Age activity and its densities result from long-term cumulative usage. The earlier Neolithic, of course, occurred early in its 'sequence' and therefore background or area-wide flint densities would have then been substantially less than their ultimate values. Nevertheless, confirming the evidence of the bone and pottery distributions, these figures also suggest that the enclosure's ditches only saw very low artefact densities.

Taking the evidence as a whole this seems a very different kind of communal monument than is usually envisaged for causewayed enclosures, especially in the light of the Delphs' grand scale. It must be imagined that it was built and used by only upwards of 100–200 individuals or 10–40 residential/familial groups (or 3–7 'lineages') and that its primary usage did not last longer than a century and was potentially less than 10–50 years. To whatever degree *sequence* may be emphasized in terms of the realization of the enclosure's construction, to all intents and purposes from a 'long' archaeological perspective it was effectively *an event* or at least a series of short-lived episodes.

### Dating evidence: an episodic sequence

As outlined by Gdaniec above, earlier Neolithic Mildenhall Ware bowls occur throughout the ditches' primary and secondary fills. Based on precedent, this dates the enclosure to the mid fourth millennium BC. The low quantity of their decoration could, in fact, suggest an 'early' affinity, but in all honesty the numbers are so low and the sherds generally too abraded to sustain this argument. Middle/later Neolithic Peterborough Wares were recovered from late ditch recuts (Ditch I) and more extensively from the ditches' tertiary fills. Generally dating to the late fourth/early third millennium BC, the issue then becomes whether the enclosure continued in use uninterrupted throughout the second half of the fourth millennium. A later Neolithic presence was also recognized in the site's flint assemblage (see Middleton above). Occurring in all areas, it was present in the upper fills of the HAD '84 and '87 (and HAD IX) ditches and was dominant in the HAD '81, '82 and HAD VIII assemblages.

Weighing the evidence as a whole, there seems no conclusive evidence to suggest the actual 'use' of the enclosure at that time. As attested to by the character of the enclosure's upper/tertiary ditch assemblages, it surely then survived as a relic earthwork and would have been recognized as a distinct 'historical place' within the local landscape. It could still, on occasion,

even have hosted group gatherings, but it seems unlikely that it was actively maintained. As alluded to above, amongst the underlying reasons for this interpretation is the general paucity of the enclosure's finds. When compared to contemporary (short-lived) settlements such as the Barleycroft Paddocks or Kilverstone, there is simply insufficient material to postulate that the enclosure hosted regular/annual usage stretching uninterrupted over centuries. It can, therefore, be imagined that its original usage was short-lived, probably less than a century's duration and, as discussed, most of the primary Mildenhall-associated material could in truth be accounted for in the act of construction itself.

The evidence of the enclosure's Grooved Ware activity, with pottery of this attribution found in pit F.520 and in the burnt spread across the top of Ditch O in the 1987 area (Fig. 5.36), would seem to attest to a 'post-usage' occupation episode within that area of the enclosure. Probably dating to the mid/later third millennium BC, comparable evidence of Grooved Ware activity was found sealed beneath the Snows Farm barrow excavated in 1983 (see Volume 2, Chapter 2).

The occurrence of a singe Beaker sherd recovered in one of the sieving transects can only be considered 'incidental'. (A major Beaker assemblage was recovered from a hollow excavated during the course of the HAD VII investigations; see Volume 2, Chapter 3).

Finally, the recovery of a few Early Bronze Age sherds from the upper fills of Ditch J is intriguing, given the late radiocarbon date from a burnt length of the palisade in the same HAD '84 area (HAR-8094; see below). This could suggest still another episode of activity that might even have involved resetting part of the palisade, however implausible that may seem given the time-scale involved. Nevertheless, this activity may well have related to the HAD VIII Bronze Age enclosure. Fully described in Volume 2 (Chapter 3), the line of a slight gravel embankment with which it was evidently associated (extending north through the eastern end of the HAD '87 trenches) appeared to respect the causewayed enclosure's circuit. Again undoubtedly a relic earthwork relationship, it seems that it was only in the Iron Age that the causewayed enclosure was 'lost to history' and its traces finally eradicated through agricultural activity; the buried soils' phosphate and magnetic susceptibility results discussed above (Chapter 4, Fig. 4.10) and the plotting of the tighter interval sampling across the enclosure's southwestern sector (Volume 2, Chapter 3, fig. 3.10) indicate that it no longer influenced land use.

Seven radiocarbon dates were achieved for the enclosure's sequence (Table 1.1). In addition, four

### Great Wilbraham 1975–76

Located *c.* 4 km east of the River Cam, on the chalk east of Cambridge and close to the County's downlands, the causewayed enclosure at Great Wilbraham was excavated over three seasons in the mid 1970s as part of a University of Cambridge training excavation. Originally the fieldwork occurred under the joint direction of John Alexander and David Clarke. With the latter's untimely death, in 1976 Ian Kinnes (then recently appointed to the British Museum) stepped in to accompany Alexander.

As yet the excavations are unpublished (and un-synthesized) apart from a few terse 'fieldwork notes'. In response, knowledge of their work has largely been anecdotal, for example, the great quantities of its assemblages (Mildenhall-associated), and it has accumulated much rumour (e.g. much of the first season's energies went to carefully digging off-terrace Iron Age fen carr horizons in the belief that its fallen trunks were part of a lake village platform). Set against this, the main enclosure features were also clearly 'sealed' by a buried soil, and in the later seasons this was obviously dealt with in an appropriate manner (alternate metre square excavation prior to its removal; as regards the HAD '81 efforts to this end, this tells of the 'loss of knowledge' when work is left unpublished).

The responsibility for publishing the enclosure has now been shouldered by the British Museum and Cambridge Archaeological Unit, and the recent arrival of the site's archives and assemblages in Cambridge does indeed attest to how prolific were its finds. It is hoped to be able to re-open the original trenches in the course

of 2005 to retrieve dating and environmental samples — like Peacocks Farm, another case of re-visiting sites (and establishing excavation 'genealogies': see Chapter 2, Peacocks Farm inset).

Not least amongst the site's attractions is the fact that it was David Clarke's only excavation, occurring respectively seven and two years after the publication of *Analytical Archaeology* (1968) and his 1973 'Loss of Innocence' paper. One imagines that a causewayed enclosure would have appealed to his research interests, providing an opportunity to model both local/regional exchange systems and patterns of land-use. Whilst perhaps reflecting something of Grahame Clark's legacy of regional fieldwork (both were at Peterhouse), the choice of the site probably also attests to Clarke's own local interests. Living at Shelford, south of Cambridge, he is known to have discovered a major Neolithic flint scatter at Duxford and he drew, for example, upon Alexander and Trump's excavations at Arbury Camp as a parallel for Somerset's wetland transhumant systems in his 'Glastonbury Model' of 1972. (Chris Tilley, a student of Clarke's, published his undergraduate thesis, *Post-glacial Communities in the Cambridge Region*, in 1979. Essentially applying site catchment analysis to a number of the region's sites, this topic further suggests Clarke's local interests; see also Volume 2, Chapter 1.)

Aside from general historiographic interests concerning the construction of the archaeological record, as the only 'near-chalkland' causewayed enclosure excavated in Eastern England (with all that it implies for access to flint resources), analysis of their excavations should provide key insights into the region's enclosures and broader scale patterns of Neolithic land use.

**Figure 5.43.** *Left, John Alexander with David Clarke (roofing the site hut; cf. Fig. 5.17); right, 1977 season with inner circuit being excavated in mid-ground with outer circuit at far end of trench. (Photographs G. Owen.)*

further groups of animal bone were subsequently submitted, but these samples failed due to a lack of collagen. Generally we were not well served by the results, and further dates should have been obtained. As has been discussed above, two of them seem extraordinarily late. The HAR-10518 assay from

the F.534 pit at HAD VIII (4020±110 BP; 2900–2200 cal. BC) must at least be 500–1000 years too late, given the attribution of its assemblages. Similarly the HAR-8094 sample (3620±100 BP; 2320–1690 cal. BC) from a burnt length of the palisade trench in the HAD '84 area must either attest to late resetting of the palisade or else be 1000–1500 years too late for the true date of this feature.

Of the remaining five dates, whilst bracketing the fourth millennium and therefore generally acceptable, there are problems with individual samples. On the one hand, the two samples from primary ditch contexts, HAR-8093 (4560±90 BP; 3610–2920 cal. BC) and HAR-8096 (4630±80 BP; 3630–3100 cal. BC), are later than the two assays from ditch recuts. Of the latter, one seems reasonable, HAR-10520 (4690±90 BP; 3700–3130 cal. BC). More spurious, however, is the HAR-8092 assay from a late recut of Ditch I in the HAD '84 area (4970±90 BP; 3990–3530 cal. BC). Although including Peterborough Ware sherds, the fill of this deposit consisted of a burnt charcoal-rich matrix, but there was no evidence of burning *in situ*. Therefore, this early assignation may reflect primary enclosure-related midden deposits scraped up and redeposited within this later recut. By this, and in relationship to the other recut-derived sample (HAR-10520) and to the dates of comparable earlier Neolithic assemblages in the region (e.g. the Barleycroft Paddocks pits), in all likelihood the primary usage of the enclosure occurred between *c.* 3750–3400 cal. BC.

## Concluding discussion: acts of construction

Only in part engendered by the scale of the project's excavations, it would have to be said that the enclosure's finds assemblages (and environmental results) were too sparse to contribute greatly to the detailing of the operational dynamics of causewayed enclosures in general. Instead, in this section we will largely concentrate on those facets of the site that provide significant insights. Primarily, these are the character of its layout in relationship to other enclosures of this type as regards issues of formal planning (i.e. 'intention'), and the organization of communal labour. Of course, given the enclosure's scale, the very paucity of finds from it does itself directly reflect upon the actual usage of causewayed enclosures (*vs* their construction) and the entire idea of *monuments as projects*.

Let us reiterate that within the hermeneutic of the enclosure's excavation at one point it became apparent that what we were digging was not so much 'a thing' as *a process*. This verges on a truism for monuments in general, as it is in their character to draw allied or secondary constructions; they are inherently cumulative and, like landscape itself, are ultimately 'unfinished' (Evans 1988c; Bradley 1993a, 91–104). Here, for example, arguments relating to the 'performance' of Iron Age hillfort construction (e.g. Bowden & McOmish 1987), themselves influenced by 'Neolithic modes' of interpretation, are pertinent. Yet there

are major differences in kind between causewayed enclosures, henges and hillforts. Often involving as much backfilling as ditch-digging, can causewayed enclosures actually be considered as monuments in any normative sense of the term? Comparing the Delphs enclosure to the Foulmire Fen long barrow (or for that matter Stonehenge) can we be assured that it was ever completed, or did the builders simply stop its elaboration (adding further circuits, etc)? Moreover, taking the wide range of site-types that were encountered within the course of the project (see Volume 2), surely it is telling that the causewayed enclosure is the only one that cannot be adequately phased. ('Phasing' in this context attests to a fundamental grasp of functional purpose and presumes a degree of site-wide developmental uniformity.) Causewayed enclosures seem so fundamentally different from any other types of prehistoric monuments that we do an injustice to their open-ended character simply to subsume their complex constructional dynamics within a vague spectrum of long-term monument 'ambiguity'.

Accordingly, there is no question here of striving towards *an* answer or singular explanation for the enclosure. Indeed, as was raised in this Chapter's introduction, it clearly included both ritual and settlement components. Its interpretation is therefore not a matter of 'either/or', but of elucidating the nature of their interrelationship. What, for example, was the character of the enclosure's rituals and their relationship to those of the long barrow? Equally, what was the duration and/or rhythm of its associated occupation? Especially relevant for the latter are advances that have recently been made in the understanding of contemporary settlement. As outlined in Chapter 4, in the two decades since the site's excavation there is now simply a much greater sense of context and a domestic 'base-line' by which to evaluate the role played by causewayed enclosures, and it is imperative that this evidence be brought to bear. In this capacity there may, in fact, now be a lesson to learn from Iron Age studies. With the impact of Neolithic-inspired modes of interpretation during the later 1980s and '90s the recognition of the importance of placed deposition and manipulated human remains on settlements did not cause it to deny 'settlement' in sole favour of ritual, but rather broaden how occupation was conceptualized. Accordingly, some redress towards the 'archaeology of the living' may now be required for the Neolithic.

Finally it should be stressed that this discussion of the Delphs enclosure is just that: discursive. Pryor, in the recent Etton volume, has thoroughly summarized the evidence of the region's excavated enclosures and there is no need for repetition (see Pryor 1998, chap. 16). Enjoying the freedom that this situation accords, here other aspects of the 'enclosure question' will be explored, with Etton serving as something of a foil. This is particularly appropriate, given the overlap of their excavation and, whereas Etton was dug in its entirety, the Delphs was only sample investigated and in many ways its results are best considered in contrast.

*Building communities (and categories)*
The Delphs enclosure's straight western side, while oriented towards the palaeochannel of the Ouse, perhaps more importantly cut across the 'high ground' spine of the terrace and in all probability this was how it was approached. Seemingly based on a *façade* principle (there being a front and back-space) this indicates that the enclosure shared basic organizational principles with the long barrow. This would be to the point of also having human remains deployed along its front, with access to the dead being after all a prime source of ritual authority and thereby social organization (i.e. the ability to compel the labour of others). Against this, the orientations of these monuments differed greatly. Yet what is also surely relevant is that whereas the long barrow seems to reflect a sense of absolute alignment that had little basis within the immediate landscape (apart from the generic course of the river), and that occurs, at least, region-wide (see Fig. 3.74), the orientation of the causewayed enclosure seems to arise out of immediate topographic factors: *the lie of the land* (see also Pryor 1988 concerning the organization of lowland Neolithic landscapes).

The recognition that basic organizational principles underlay the enclosure (effectively that it was *oriented* and was not accessible across each causeway, but had major entranceways) is not to advocate any kind of formalized mathematical design. Indeed, the human body was probably its 'yardstick'. The basic *c.* 2.00-m causeway interval may well have roughly equated with a double-arm span (i.e. two yards) and the posts of the palisade could have substituted for people (if so then they may well have included ancestors, both fictive and real, as their number seems much too great to allot each participant a single upright; see Mawson in Volume 2 concerning 'people as posts' and also Evans & Knight 2001). In a comparable manner, individual ditch segments/pits may themselves have represented immediate families and been places of 'domestic' identity and ceremony. Nevertheless, a degree of organized design is equally apparent in the enclosure's development. Cross-cutting any sense of it being group-sectored, long ditch segments (*c.* 25+ m) occur at various points around its perimeter and even in portions which saw little depositional activity (e.g. the HAD '82 area). Though achieved by diverse modes of pit-digging, there still remains a sense of a

unified structure (however partial its final execution may have been).

Based on the diverse patterns of the ditches' recutting and artefact frequencies, it could be argued that the enclosure effectively amounts to a *dialogue of power* and the dispersed residual groups and lineages competitively deployed labour (and ritual) to further social prestige and authority. However, unless long barrow burial (or enclosure-building itself) was the goal of this social competition, there would otherwise be little evidence of such *difference* and the period's settlements give no indication of any kind of elite distinction. Moreover, whatever the 'everyday' factors that compelled the social organization of the enclosure's construction, a sense of cultural content would still have underlain its operation. The point stressed throughout is that construction alone may have in fact provided its *raison d'être*. Regardless of whether competition motivated its execution, the enclosure nevertheless was an integrating structure that intermeshed (but did not subsume) the participation of diverse groups to build what was, in effect, a larger community.

In contrast to the long barrow, which was very much a 'finished' monument, the causewayed enclosure effectively amounts to a proclamation of collective labour. Its ditches were left ragged and bulbous, directly telling of the input of diverse work groups. Equally the tools of its construction (antler picks and scapula shovels) were left in place and in instances even appear to have been utilized as 'special deposits' (e.g. the Ditch M half-size pick). This is in marked contrast to the long barrow where such implements played no part in its ritual deposits, and that it was evidently cleared of such 'waste debris' thereby tells of the contextual specificity of ritual. The barrow was, of course, much smaller and as a ritual space more easily distanced from the everyday. Its 'closed' ditch surround clearly acted as a barrier, whereas the 'penetrated' circuit of the causewayed enclosure was an inclusive boundary.

Whilst within the Delphs' enclosure sequence, and also, for example at Etton (see below), the establishment of longer ditch segments is evident, circuit 'interruption' was clearly maintained. For whatever reason, segmented construction was clearly an intentional choice. Despite the evidence of uninterrupted long barrow ditch circuits or the similarly continuous perimeter around Rectory Farm, Godmanchester (see Chapter 3 above and McAvoy 2000), circuit 'completion' or infilling was not a matter of an evolutionary design process; ditch perimeters were not somehow destined to be uninterrupted. There is no known instance, for example, of a Neolithic enclosure that had all its causeways eradicated into a continuous circuit and, in most, the point of recut 'coalescence' (the ratio of short and longer segments) seems broadly comparable. It can only therefore be assumed that ditch segmentation was itself meaningful and the enclosure-form modelled or expressed something.

Yet contradictions underlie our reasoning in this matter. It has generally been understood that ditch segmentation reflects the deployment of gang labour and social segmentation: in short, the participation of otherwise dispersed groups. These inferences may be valid for large enclosures such as the Delphs, but are surely challenged by the fact that even the smallest enclosures have comparable circuit interruptions (e.g. Roughton; see below). It is one thing to see a huge enclosure like the Delphs as the result of inter-group gathering, but quite another to presume this for those less than a hectare.

Cultural symbolism would surely have underpinned any meaning of causewayed enclosures. Balancing them as a metaphor of competitive social processes is the principle of concentricity, and the 'ripple-like' arrangement of some enclosures has been seen as reflecting a cosmological ordering of culture and nature (see e.g. Windmill Hill's *harmony of symbols*: Whittle *et al.* 1999). Here it is essential to appreciate just what kind of barrier the enclosure would have presented; the ditch circuit could have been crossed between any of its segments, but there were major entrances. Passing this line, the palisade would have presented a similar front: defined entranceways, but if necessary each post could have been transgressed. All this suggests both a sense of 'agreed' passageway and perhaps also sorting, and in many ways evokes the elaborated access into the long barrow. Woodland traverse might offer another generic symbolic parallel, being a space that could be moved through with staggered interruption wherever, but within which there are easier paths. This itself recalls the idea of the woodland clearance as a 'primary' model of this enclosed space, with its edges delineating a permeable barrier. Yet in this, contradiction is again encountered, for the enclosure's palisade 'enfolds' this symbolism. Like the long barrow's façade, its widely spaced uprights may have been suggestive of a forest front — the 'wall of wood'. Progressing across the ditch you symbolically arrive at the clearing, only to be confronted by a 'woodland' barrier (i.e. the palisade). Here the possibility that its timbers were a 'cultivated' or least curated resource seems relevant. The causewayed enclosure may have epitomized or bridged both a sense of *woodland as environment* (i.e. 'the world') and its delineation, at least locally, as *a category* or resource.

*Settlement and seasonality*

As has been suggested, in some respects the interpretation of the Delphs enclosure (and others of its type) hinges upon arguments relating to 'feasting'. In other words, the display and hosting of *en masse* consumption. Often drawn from ethnographic references (usually Northwest American Coast potlatching and New Guinea pig banquets), this was a major piece of interpretative baggage we brought to the site's excavation. Yet, in many instances, such evidence seems essentially to relate to post-depositional factors and large animal bone is often preserved within causewayed enclosure ditches in contrast to its deterioration in 'open' settlement contexts (see below). In the light of this, and taking account of the other Delphs finds data, there is simply not the evidence of sustained mass-group consumption. Here we must be equally wary of being blinded by amassed statistics and limited to only a 'vulgar materialism'. Communities may well have continued to gather at the enclosure long after its initial construction for brief stays to exchange marriage partners, goods and/or animals and participate in cross-group interactions that left little material trace (see Edmonds, Appleby Fair inset above). Ritual action need not have depositional correlates; rather the point is that we do not see evidence of 'potlatched' or 'New-Guinea-type' behaviours (though the in-ground or depositional traces of these activities have never themselves been detailed).

The mis-identification of feasting may largely be a product of the fact that sites clearly were being 'tidied up' (see Evans *et al.* 1999). It was argued in Chapter 3 that such factors were in play at the long barrow, where the paucity of deposition upon the mound and within its ditched perimeter behind the front façade suggests that 'cleanliness' was appreciated and perhaps held as a spatial quality/category. Equally, the evidence of the pit sites outlined in Chapter 4 would attest to the intentional backfilling of settlement refuse into their pits. Given this, it is difficult to see how causewayed enclosure ditch deposits differed. Could not these find-rich horizons simply represent, at least for the better part, backfilled occupation debris? Whilst perhaps relating to general prohibitions concerning occupation 'waste', such attitudes may have been more pronounced in cases of seasonal usage. When not occupying a site (be it a pit settlement or causewayed enclosure) there may have been obvious reasons to avoid having subsequent visitors to the locale (i.e. 'strangers') accessing one's refuse. What has been interpreted as feasting may, therefore, amount to little more than the hiding of occupation.

Before further exploring the role and affinities of the enclosure, its artefact frequencies should be

**Table 5.35.** *Causewayed enclosure mean artefact densities (per metre length of ditch circuit): * estimated figure based on information supplied by K. Gdaniec; ** indicates limited circuit excavation and thereby risk of unrepresentative figures; *** as before, pottery frequencies from Abingdon are not detailed beyond imperial weight in Avery in Case & Whittle 1982 and in Case 1956; the figure estimates here assume a 7.5 g mean sherd weight; ^^ figure represents average of material from all the enclosure's main Neolithic ditch contexts (e.g. enclosures, outworks and cross-dykes, but not its long barrow; based on information provided by F. Healy; Healy forthcoming).*

| | Flint (no. per m) | Pottery (no. per m) |
|---|---|---|
| **Eastern enclosures** | | |
| 1 *Upper Delphs, Haddenham* | 4.6 | 4.0 |
| 2 *Etton** | 6.3 | 7.7 |
| 3 *Briar Hill* | 8.5 | 5.3 |
| Outer | 3.2 | 0.9 |
| Middle | 7.2 | 3.9 |
| Inner ('spiral') | 15.3 | 11.8 |
| **Thames enclosures** | | |
| 4 *Orsett*** | 13.1 | 21.8 |
| Outer | 3.2 | 10.9 |
| Middle | 2.9 | 7.1 |
| Inner | 33.1 | 47.4 |
| 5 *Staines* | 31.8 | 19.3 |
| Outer | 18.0 | 17.7 |
| Inner | 45.7 | 20.9 |
| 6 *Abingdon**** | 16.1 | 38.2 |
| Outer | 1.3 | 30.6 |
| Inner | 31 | 45.9 |
| **Wessex enclosures** | | |
| 7 *Hambledon Hill^^* | 73.8 | 22.4 |
| Main enclosure | 68.3 | 37.3 |
| Stepleton enclosure | 46.8 | 41.8 |
| 8 *Windmill Hill* | 204.0 | 27.6 |
| Outer | 176.3 | 28.9 |
| Middle | 256.1 | 40.4 |
| Inner | 181.0 | 13.4 |

gauged. Accordingly, in Table 5.35 and Figure 5.44 the average densities of flint and pottery from a range of causewayed enclosure circuits are compared. As determined by the character of publication (and a lack of standard analytical format), these can only be approximate. Indicating average densities per metre length of the circuits excavated, while half-sectioning is compensated for, the diverse scale/cubic capacity of their ditches are not taken into account; nor have specific phase-related criteria been factored. (The Etton pottery is, for example, somewhat unrepresentative due to the fact that almost all derived from its western arc of ditches and very little post-primary deposition occurred along the eastern side of the enclosure as a result of later stream over-flooding: Pryor 1998, fig. 12

and K. Gdaniec pers. comm.) Despite these caveats, the figures demonstrate that the Delphs enclosure indeed has the lowest densities of any excavated enclosure. Equally apparent is the paucity of material within the eastern enclosures in general. For example, the averaged circuit densities of Windmill Hill are 32–44 times greater for flint and 4–9.5-fold more for pottery than the two Fenland enclosures. This being said, on comparing the Thames Valley enclosures it is clear that the main distinction relates to worked flint. The density of pottery within the inner circuit of Orsett exceeds the Windmill Hill mean (this may be biased by the former's very limited exposure, though the latter also includes significant quantities of later material) and Abingdon's estimated pottery densities are directly comparable to that site and also Hambledon Hill. Yet, Windmill Hill still saw worked flint densities 6.4–15.6 times that of the Thames enclosures, with Hambledon having densities 2.3–5.6 times greater. This would resonate with the idea that amongst the key roles of causewayed enclosures was the exchange of lithic resources. In this regard the analysis of the Great Wilbraham material (see inset above; after superficial appraisal the site seems to have a very rich flint assemblage) could prove crucial, as it is the one fen-edge enclosure located near chalk lands: could it, for example, have been the source for the Delphs chalk ridge flint?

Given the range of these densities (which is equally as much a matter of comparing the Thames Valley and Wessex enclosures), this does not just seem to reflect the 'marginality' of the Fenland enclosures (or 'Midland' in the case of Briar Hill). Low intensity monument usage, such as at Maxey (Pryor & French 1985), has been cited as a long-term regional tradition (Bradley 1993b). Yet regional marginality is itself essentially a construction, and in a Fenland context has often been encouraged by the very framing of our maps. Cropping distributions plots tightly on the fen basin invariably leaves a scatter of enclosure 'dots' along the left-hand side of the page (i.e. the western fen-edge) with the remainder being blank (i.e. the fens). However, viewed in a larger perspective this is not the case (Fig. 5.45). Taking the east as a whole, if overlooking the Lincolnshire, Norfolk and fen basin 'blank spots', the distribution of enclosures is comparable to that across southern England, including Wessex (the Midland's clays having a markedly lower representation: Butler *et al.* 2002). When set against this, the variability of enclosure artefact densities suggests something more, their great range making it difficult to envisage that these enclosures performed the same role. Yes, they may have shared broadly similar spatial structures, but it is hard to see how they could have fulfilled a comparable long-term function.

Partially as a result of Mercer's Hambledon excavations (Mercer 1980; 1988; Mercer & Healy forthcoming), but also prompted by Isobel Smith's interpretation of Windmill Hill (1965 and 1971), over the last two decades a ritual focus has come to dominate the interpretation of causewayed enclosures (and Neolithic studies in general). Only in part engendered by an emphasis on placed deposits and the recovery of human remains, it has equally been encouraged by the apparent paucity of 'normative' occupation evidence, in other words the expectation of a robust settlement architecture. It is precisely in this regard that advances have recently been made in the period's study. As outlined in the preceding chapter, it must now be accepted just how slight Neolithic settlement traces truly are. While still maintaining a dichotomy between domestic and ritual 'spheres' (now with the balance very much in the latter's favour), this evidence has yet to inform our understanding of causewayed enclosures.

Attributed to the enclosure's earlier Neolithic usage (Phase 1), some 125 'small filled pits' were recovered across Etton's interior. Many were packed with finds (often with quantities of Mildenhall and/or Fengate wares) and had a distinct charcoal-rich matrix, including small fragments of burnt bone (Pryor 1998, 102–3, fig. 103, table 8). Despite the fact that the latter all proved to be animal-derived, the interpretation of these features remained linked to funerary rites ('people as pits') and was associated with putative ritual pyres/bonfires detected through magnetic susceptibility survey. Although only three contained unequivocally placed deposits (a complete stone axe, a quartzite *polissoir* and a saddle quern with its rubber, respectively in pits F.263, F.786 & F.711), all these features were essentially assigned a ritual function, the excavator

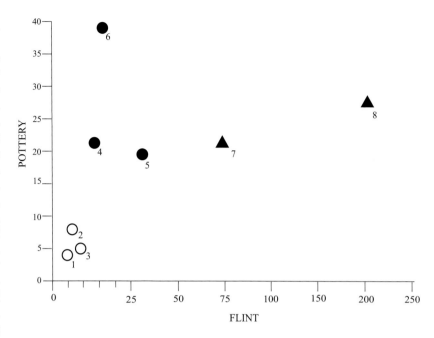

**Figure 5.44.** *Mean causewayed enclosure artefact densities. Eastern enclosures (open circles): 1) Upper Delphs, Haddenham; 2) Etton; 3) Briar Hill; Thames enclosures (blackened circle): 4) Orsett; 5) Staines; 6) Abingdon; Wessex enclosures (triangles): 7) Hambledon Hill; 8) Windmill Hill.*

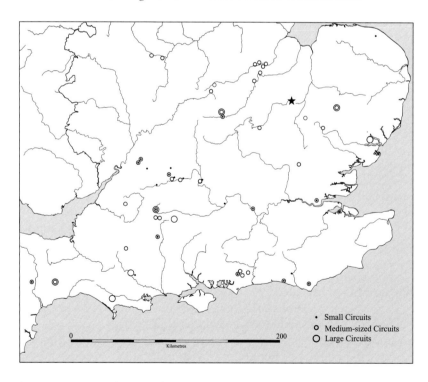

**Figure 5.45.** *Distribution of causewayed enclosures, with the Delphs enclosure shown starred (after Oswald et al. 2001, fig. 4.24).*

being emphatic that they were not 'rubbish pits' on the grounds that there was no evidence of settlement (Pryor 1998, 353–5). The three critical features aside, there essentially seems to be no intrinsic difference between them and constituent features at the Hurst Fen, Kilverstone and Barleycroft Farm pit settlements (see Garrow, Chapter 4 above), nor for that matter F.534 at the Delphs. The charcoal-rich (with fine burnt bone) matrix of their fills might equally be compared to the upper ditch deposits found in the HAD '84 and '87 areas. Apart from these distinctive pits, the interior of Etton also included a number of 'suggestive' post settings, though no definite structures were identified (Pryor 1998, fig. 102). In short, by the measure of the pit settlements Etton itself must also have hosted some degree of occupation. This is not to imply that this presence need have been permanent or particularly intensive, and the same problems of the determination of the duration/rhythm of its occupation (i.e. seasonality) equally apply to the 'open' pit sites.

What is particularly relevant in this context is that the area of Etton (with its 'occupation') is roughly comparable to the higher-density finds spread ('A') extending over 1.8 ha across the western south-central swathe of the Delphs enclosure. Though admittedly, in part, a product of later Neolithic and Early Bronze Age activity, it also attests to more intense enclosure-contemporary usage. It could, therefore, be the case that this area saw the longer-term seasonal occupation of the enclosure's main 'host' community, that may itself have been the equivalent of Etton's social unit. Proportional to its size, the Haddenham enclosure should theoretically have involved four such groups (?lineages). Yet the sectoring of the enclosure's artefact densities would not support this and, instead, the issue becomes what occurred in the remaining three-quarters of the enclosure. A variety of uses could be envisaged, from the corralling of stock and even enclosed arable plots. Yet, at best, these could have been incidental or secondary activities and they would not explain the scale of the enclosure in the first place.

In this context two points warrant stressing. Firstly, no earlier Neolithic settlement is known to extend continuously across an area as large as the Delphs enclosure. Evidence of densities aside, on the basis of its scale alone it is therefore unlikely just to have been a settlement. However, the same is not necessarily true of small-scale enclosures, those with an area of a hectare or less, which amongst eastern enclosures would include Roughton and the innermost single circuits of Orsett or Briar Hill (see Evans 1988c and Oswald et al. 2001, 75–7, fig. 4.26 concerning concentric expansion and enclosure phasing). Given the insubstantial nature of contemporary occupation traces, and that the greater survival of bone (both human and animal) in causewayed enclosures need not be accounted as reflecting anything other than

post-depositional survival, is there anything that would prevent these small sites from representing enclosed (seasonal) settlements? Certainly a number of contemporary open settlement spreads of this size are known, and the fact that the innermost rings at both Orsett and Briar Hill had markedly higher finds densities than their outer circuits (Table 5.35) could also be enlisted in support. (Apparently Runnymede Bridge's alluvium-sealed 'open' and pit-accompanied Middle Neolithic occupation horizons included 10 deposits of human bone (Needham 1991 & 1996 and pers. comm.). This could indeed suggest that the paucity otherwise of human remains on Neolithic settlements relates to survival/preservation and, if so, would thereby erode what has been amongst the most significant distinctions between causewayed enclosures and contemporary settlements. Equally, whilst perhaps also reflective of post-depositional loss, the artefact densities from Runnymede's Neolithic horizons are truly staggering. Stuart Needham has kindly provided the figures for four of its trenches that collectively amount to 138 sq. m. Although also including the material from a few cut features, these largely derive from surface strata: pottery, range 52–125 sherds per square metre, 96 mean; flint, range 50–199 pieces, 79 mean; bone, range 261–390 fragments, 309 mean.)

Yet a site like the contemporary Honey Hill, Ramsey scatter (c. 1 ha) would equally suggest that inter-group gathering may have occurred but without any ditched surround (Edmonds et al. 1999). There, the evidence of collectivity is the opposite of what is usually applied in the case of causewayed enclosures: the structured burnt flint-ringed arrangement of the core scatter and its remarkably high flint densities (but apparently without associated features). (Set perched on a marked fen rise, the site could be considered as being naturally enclosed by the surrounding wetlands (see also Healy 1992); however, see arguments in Chapter 6 concerning enclosure and attendant island-size.)

Whilst admitting that temporary settlement was a component of its usage, surely the scale of the Delphs enclosure related to the 'event' of its construction and those occasions of larger group gathering (i.e. inter-communal/-lineage meetings), as at such times an enormous tract may have been necessary to hold livestock. The evidence of the site's finds densities would indicate that either such gatherings were rare or that the impetus behind this greater collectivity was short-lived.

The frequency of causewayed enclosure recutting has itself been enlisted as evidence of their annual seasonal occupation. Based on the excavated evidence, however, is this really a valid argument? Certainly we want to be able to feel that we can detect annual rhythms in prehistoric 'life-cycles' analogous to historical fairs and other events in the agricultural calendar. Yet if the use of enclosures spanned centuries, why is it that only c. 5–10 phases of recutting are usually distinguished? Either this must suggest that their annual usage was much more short-lived or that their redefinition was more episodic and related to a longer temporal cycle (cf. the mass-group 'Feasts of the Dead' held on a 10-year cycle by the Huron and Iroquois of Great Lakes of North America). Alternatively these recut frequencies might represent a 'plateau' in our ability to recognize specific actions in the archaeological record. The issue of calendrical rhythms of ritual deposition, its limited span and potential 'translations', is discussed for the Delphs Romano-Celtic shrine in Volume 2 (Chapter 7).

*The permeable barrier: regional affinities*
Figure 5.46 shows the Delphs enclosure in relationship to the neighbouring monuments of this type. They seem diverse with little obvious affinity. Whilst, like the Delphs, Etton had only a single circuit (though without an accompanying palisade), extending only over 2 ha it is less than a quarter of its size. By scale alone Etton would be more comparable with Great Wilbraham on the River Cam (2.4 ha), though it has a double-ditch circuit.

Located at a distance of c. 45 km from Haddenham upstream on the Ouse, the enclosure at Cardington, Bedfordshire is considerably larger. Having, at least locally, a triple ditch circuit, it extends over 5.1 ha. As a type and by its size it would seem more comparable to a number of the enclosures within the marked cluster now known to lie close to the fen-edge reaches of the Rivers Nene and Welland (Fig. 5.45). Extending over 1.8–4.3 ha, aside from Etton these have closely set multiple ditch perimeters (see below) and superficially seem very different to the Delphs enclosure. Here, however, the proposal that the latter may have originally had a different primary northern perimeter could be relevant (Fig. 5.46). If so, this would have resulted in a more 'egg-shaped' plan and have been only 6.5 ha in area (cf. the enclosures at Mavesyn Ridware and Alrewas, Staffordshire: Oswald *et al.* 2001, figs. 4.9 & 4.18). The nearest known causewayed enclosure to the Delphs (11 km distant) was only discovered in the early 1990s, and after our fieldwork. Located on the west side of the Cam at Landbeach (TL 483654), a length of its interrupted circuit had first been identified by the RCHME (Oswald *et al.* 2001, 150, Gaz. no. 10), and only subsequent flying by the Cambridge University Committee for Aerial Photography in 1995

revealed its southwestern sector (Fig. 5.47). Although as yet unplotted, it appears to consist of two or more circuits and, if symmetrical (i.e. circular) upon the arc that has been exposed (the eastern half of the enclosure has been destroyed through quarrying), would be at least 5 ha in area. While its plan-morphology is far from definite, it would seem more comparable to Cardington than to the Haddenham enclosure.

By its scale, within Eastern England the Delphs enclosure would only compare to those of Freston and Fornham All Saints in Suffolk. The former, 8.3 ha in area, is further discussed below; the latter consists of two conjoining double-circuit enclosures and, if projected, extends in total over c. 15.5 ha, the northern of which alone would be over some 11 ha (Fig. 6.2). Of course, with their multiple ditch circuits the labour invested in many of the other smaller eastern enclosures would have exceed that of the Delphs enclosure. This is clearly apparent in Table 5.36 and Figure 5.48 (which excludes Fornham All Saints due to the extreme degree of reconstruction required to project its circuits). If taking both of Great Wilbraham's circuits, the combined length of its double-ditch perimeter would approach that of Haddenham's single circuit. Equally, though the overall area of the Orsett enclosure is less than a quarter of the Delphs, the collective length of its three ditch perimeters (1038 m) would actually exceed the Delphs, as would also Briar Hill's (3.1 ha area; 1150 m collective perimeter). Similarly, by this measure, with its two double-ditch circuits (four complete 'circles' in total) the 3.2 ha Northborough enclosure would actually have the longest perimeter in the region (1875 m), though it is closely rivalled by Cardington (1859 m); it is only with the inclusion of their palisades that the two larger enclosures, Freston and the Delphs, surpass this perimeter length.

As outlined elsewhere (Evans 1988c; Oswald *et al.* 2001, 76–7, fig. 4.26) and will be further discussed below, such concentric plan enclosures probably represent cumulative constructions. The crucial issue here is that what distinguishes the large enclosures (without markedly smaller internal rings; e.g. the Delphs, Freston or Fordham North) is that their ultimate scale was obviously intended from the outset. Accordingly, was their size a product of their attendant populations and territorial 'pull', or a matter of greater monumental ambition?

Six other causewayed enclosures within England are known to be palisaded (with three further 'possibles'). Including the Delphs enclosure, four out of the seven 'definites' have an eastern distribution, with three in this category all lying near the present-day coast: Roughton in Norfolk, Freston, Suffolk and Orsett, Essex (Figs. 5.45 & 5.49: Oswald

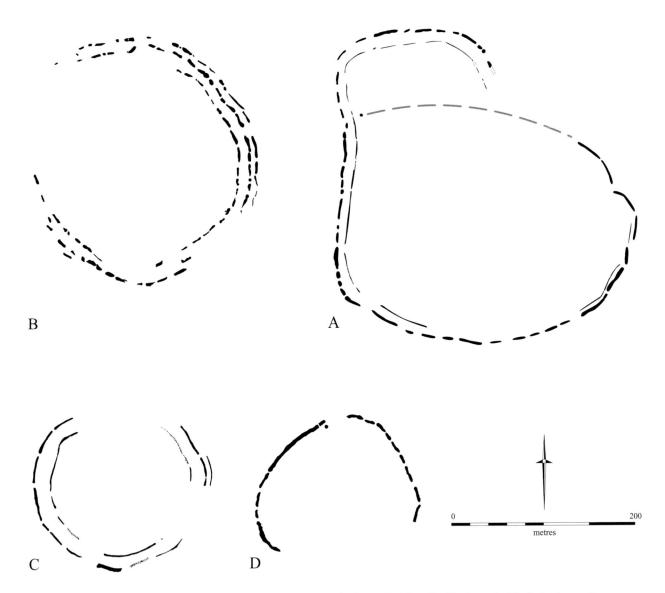

**Figure 5.46.** *Selected Fen-edge ('neighbouring') enclosures: A) Upper Delphs, Haddenham (with dashed grey line indicating possibly 'intended' original northern perimeter); B) Cardington; C) Great Wilbraham; D) Etton.*

*et al.* 2001, fig. 3.15). Apart from their accompanying palisades, these share few affinities. The small Roughton enclosure (0.75 ha) has its palisade set immediately interior to its single circuit. In the case of Orsett it is not the comparably smaller inner ditch circuit (*c.* 0.7 ha) that the palisade was associated with, but rather it was immediately interior to the outer double-ditch perimeter (1.9 ha). In the much larger Freston enclosure (8.3 ha), the palisade is set between its closely spaced double-ditch circuit. By this it is clear that enclosure size was not a factor and palisades accompany the full small- to large-size range of causewayed enclosures.

Neither the Roughton nor Freston enclosures have been excavated, and Orsett's exposures were only very limited. Therefore, any appreciation of the layout of their palisades must essentially derive from aerial photography. One trait that all three share is that in each the palisade is closely set to a ditched perimeter and they do not constitute separate circuits. However, whereas at some points interruptions in the palisades correspond to ditch causeways, at others they extend continuously between adjacent ditch segments.

In the light of the Delphs '87 palisade plan (Fig. 5.41), in both the Orsett and Freston plottings inturned palisade terminals are also apparent (Fig. 5.49). Those visible along the northwestern perimeter of the Freston enclosure offer a salient parallel. The southern, seemingly marked by a pair of major post pits on the exterior of the circuit, directly corresponds to the alignment of causeways across the double-ditch perimeter (Fig. 5.49: B). The same, however, is not true of the northern ('2' Fig. 5.49:C). There, again apparently accompanied by a large exterior post pit, the palisade terminals only relate to a major causeway in the outer ditch circuit. A short length of palisade trench appears to have been inset into the inturned entrance, and within the corresponding portion of the inner circuit a ditch segment blocks cross-circuit movement. Whilst access at that point may always have been staggered, like the Delphs enclosure the relationship of the palisade to the ditch circuit is ambiguous; there are both points of complementary access and circuit discontinuity.

Orsett provides the only other instance of an excavated cause-wayed enclosure palisade within Britain. Trench-built, its line lay c. 3.00-m interior to the enclosure's outer double-ditch circuit. In the excavated portion (Area B) it would seem comparable to the Delphs, being c. 0.80 m wide and c. 0.40–0.60 m deep (from machined surface). Similarly there was not a continuous post line, but rather individual post pipes were identified (0.20–0.25 m in diameter: Hedges & Buckley 1978, 237–44, figs. 14 & 15). Although no regular interval was established, their spacing would seem quite wide (c. 0.50–0.80 m). Within the area of excavation a 5.60-m-wide gap in the palisade's circuit directly corresponded to aligned causeways across the main double-ditch perimeter, and together these clearly constituted a major entranceway. It may be relevant that a large post pit (F. 14) was set centrally within the palisade 'gap' and that it was thought that a number of individual post-holes (continuing the line of the palisade but not trench-footed) later blocked the western half of the entrance. Other apparently

**Figure 5.47.** *Aerial photograph showing southwest sector of Landbeach causewayed enclosure (arrowed; note that the eastern half of the enclosure has been destroyed through quarrying; CUCAP 70Kn 34).*

**Table 5.36.** *Comparison of enclosure areas and collective/cumulative length of their ditch and palisaded perimeters (NB for the latter a 10% 'interruption interval' has been presumed; for the ditch circuits a 20% causeway factor has been applied; i.e. subtracted from the perimeter total).*

| Enclosure | Area (ha) | Ditched perimeter (m) | Perimeter with palisade (m) |
|---|---|---|---|
| 1 Roughton | 0.75 | 248 | 494 |
| 2 Uffington | 1.8 | 739 | – |
| 3 Orsett | | | |
|    A Innermost | 0.70 | 289 | – |
|    B Outer Double Circuit | 1.9 | 1038 | 1390 |
| 4 Etton | 2.0 | 426 | – |
| 5 Wilbraham | 2.4 | 819 | – |
| 6 Briar Hill | | | |
|    A Inner 'Spiral' | 0.72 | 305 | – |
|    B Outer Double Circuit | 3.1 | 1150 | – |
| 7 Northborough | | | |
|    A Inner Double Circuit | 2.1 | 805 | – |
|    B Outer Double Circuit | 3.2 | 1875 | – |
| 8 Cardington | 5.1 | 1859 | – |
| 9 Freston | 8.3 | 1609 | 2514 |
| 10 Upper Delphs, Haddenham | 8.75 | 890 | 1840 |

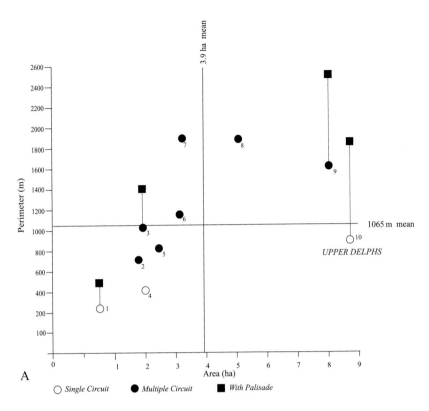

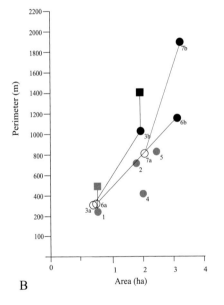

contemporary 'miscellaneous' postholes were also found in the area of Orsett's entrance. While some appear to form a second, if more irregular, post alignment behind the palisade, others were aligned within the entrance and appeared, almost reminiscent of Sarup (see below; Andersen 1997), to 'box' one of the ditch terminals (F.2; Hedges & Buckley 1978, fig. 66) and recall the post settings within the HAD '84 and '87 areas (see also the north–south Phase 1 fence line that was aligned on the main northern entrance into the Etton enclosure: Pryor 1998, 100, fig. 103).

Though admittedly from only a single sample, given its late radiocarbon date (HAR-8094, 2620±110 BP, 2320–1690 cal. BC) a certain degree of ambiguity is unavoidable as to the attribution of the Delphs palisade, despite its sympathetic arrangements with the main ditch circuit. By this it could be argued that the palisade was a later Neolithic or even Early Bronze Age construction, and rather related to such third millennium BC palisaded sites as Mount Pleasant, West Kennet or Greyhound Yard, Dorchester. Yet the latter are truly monumental constructions that involved substantially heavier posts. In recognition of this Gibson has relegated the flimsier Orsett and Haddenham palisades as 'fenced sites', though he suggests that they might provide a typological link between causewayed enclosures and the later palisaded complexes (Gibson 2001, 73–5, fig. 6.6). (The equally slight posts of the later

**Figure 5.48.** *Scaling the eastern causewayed enclosures. A) Plot showing area against collective perimeter length (with blackened boxes indicating addition of palisade circuits; enclosure enumeration as Table 5.35); B) As 'A' but with open circuits indicating innermost rings of Orsett (3) and Briar Hill (4). Note that in addition to the 10 plotted enclosures, the mean area figure also takes into account seven other enclosures: Kedington (1.4 ha), Husbands Bosworth (1.5 ha), Barholm (2.4 ha), Southwick (3.3 ha), Upton (4.3 ha), Dallington (5.4 ha) and Fornham All Saints (north circuit only, 11 ha); it does not include those enclosures whose plans are only very partially known (Sawbridgeworth, Maiden Bower and Springfield Lyons) and the 'suspect-only' and/or partial cropmarks at Landbeach and Stapleford, Cambs (Oswald et al. 2001 Gazetteer nos. 10 & 13; hereafter OG), Saffron Walden, Essex (OG no. 28), Buxton with Lammas, Norfolk (OG no. 53) and Bentley, Suffolk (OG no. 78).*

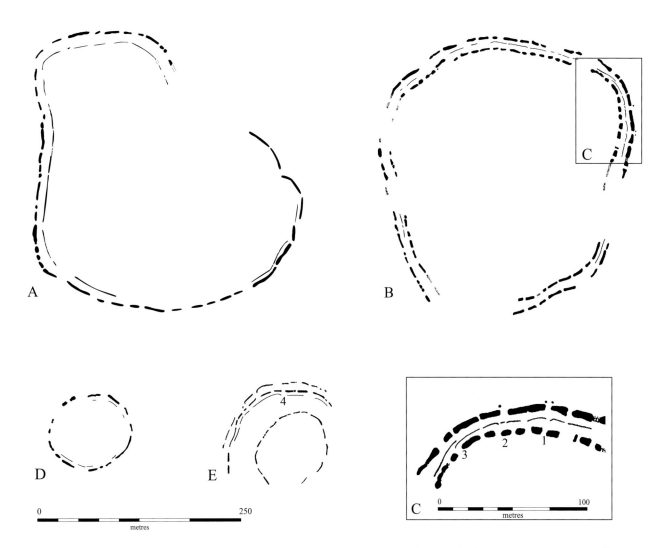

**Figure 5.49.** *Eastern palisaded causewayed enclosures: A) The Upper Delphs, Haddenham; B & C) Freston, Suffolk with inset below showing inturned palisade entranceways; D) Roughton, Norfolk; E) Orsett, Essex (B–D after Oswald et al. 2001, figs. 3.11, 3.14 & 6.7).*

Bronze Age fence 'screen' alignments at Barleycroft Farm were individually set and not trench-built: Evans & Knight 2001.)

Set against this background, what does it imply that the Delphs' neighbouring enclosures have such disparate plans? Perhaps more telling is what is implied by this question itself. Do we really expect that enclosures acted as some manner of cultural blueprint, bearing the distinct imprint of socio-cultural groupings and readily accessible to typological modes of spatial analysis? Surely local factors, both contingent/historical and topographic, would have intervened. Yet it is equally reasonable to presume that in the case of 'first enclosures' the transmission of their 'idea' would itself have implied (or, better, have had embedded) similarities beyond a basic interrupted ditch form.

Sample recovery must be a significant factor. In lowland river valley situations, and especially in the fens, due variously to masking by alluvium and peat it would be naive to think that aerial photography has now achieved the total population of the region's causewayed enclosures. Others could still be undetected between the Delphs and Cardington on the Ouse or, for that matter, either lie deeply buried below the Delphs along the river's lower Fenland reaches or southeast between the Delphs and Great Wilbraham.

In this context it is surely relevant that the one area of Eastern England where enclosure-plan regularities are apparent (the aforementioned Welland/Nene cluster) is where such enclosures are known in their greatest density. There, through aerial photography seven enclosures have been identified over an area of only some 170 sq. km. Lying at an interval of 2.5 to 9.5 km along their respective rivers, aside from the single-circuit 'pairing' of the two Etton enclosures, these otherwise show a remarkable degree of plan similarity (Oswald *et al.* 2001, 109–10, fig. 6.3). All are ovoid and essentially seem a variation on a basic type. Situated on slight rises in their respective river valleys, only at Southwick does topography seem to have influenced the layout (a stream course appears to have determined the line of its eastern side). Yet subtle differences can be discerned which suggest that their interrelations were, in fact, riverine. The two enclosures on the Nene, Southwick and Upton, are both slightly larger (3.3 and 4.3 ha respectively) and have a greater interval between their double-ditch perimeters. Of the Welland enclosures, whereas those at Uffington (1.8 ha) and Barholm (2.4 ha) essentially match each other, in having two double-ditch circuits that at Northborough is more elaborate (3.2 ha in total). Applying developmental logic, it may be the case that the latter originated in a small double-ditch 'circle' (the inner *c.* 2 ha perimeter) which could then be considered an Uffington/Barholm equivalent, with the outer perimeter being a secondary addition.

Proximity alone would not seem to explain the similarity of this grouping; their seemingly pristine qualities might also reflect limited 'outside' influence. In some contrast, the one other area where enclosures are known in comparable densities, the Middle/Upper Thames Valley by Reading and Swindon, shows greater plan variability. With the layout of its low-lying enclosures appearing to be more directly influenced by adjacent river courses, there both more wide-zone concentric types (e.g. more 'Windmill Hill-type') and also those with closely set multiple ditch perimeters occur (Oswald *et al.* 2001, 110–11, fig. 6.4).

Based on the evidence of Eastern England it would be difficult to argue for any kind of hierarchical interrelationship between causewayed enclosures. Size may been a factor of territorial or population pull, but amongst themselves large and small enclosures do not occur in groupings that suggest their tiered interrelationships. Within, for example, the Welland/Nene cluster, whereas the Northborough enclosure displays greater elaboration this was probably the result of a greater continuity of 'enclosure impetus'. No single enclosure amongst them otherwise seems out-of-the ordinary and none, for example, achieves the 'large-size-category'. Equally, elsewhere within the region, whilst not occurring in the same density, small and large enclosures occur in a seemingly random mix. This could suggest a uniformity of basic process, though admittedly of widely different ambitions.

*Planning and enclosure resolution*

Not least among the key results of Etton's excavation was the recovery of the enclosure's near-complete plan (across the northern two-thirds that were available for excavation). Its 14 ditch segments ranged in size from 8.80–81.00 m, with most being 10–20.00 m in length (see Fig. 4.17). Whilst generally comparable to the Delphs' ditch lengths, in Figure 5.50 it is evident that Etton has a tendency for somewhat longer segments; the longest ditch visible on the aerial photographic plotting of the Delphs' perimeter is *c.* 40 m and none would approach the 81-m length of Etton's Ditch 5. The evidence could therefore suggest that the latter's circuit saw a greater frequency of recutting, that was perhaps reflective of its more intense usage.

Etton's causeways varied from 1–3.75 m, with an average of 2.58 m (see Pryor 1998, table 1). Three main entranceways were identified across its circuit and, displaying strong formal tendencies, these were located on each of its cardinal axes (any corresponding southern entrance was not available for investigation). That in the east, Causeway M, was 6.60 m across; the eastern, Causeway B/C, that was essentially distinguished by the Structure 1 'guardhouse', was subsequently blocked by Ditch 2 but was thought to have originally been *c.* 15.00 m wide. The main entrance, Causeway F opening northward, was initially 25.00 m across, but in Phase 1C was reduced to 10.00 m. The latter was marked not only by a fence line, but also a parallel timber slot 'gateway' on its interior aspect (Pryor 1998, 98–102, fig. 103).

Given the apparently greater frequency of Etton's 'placed' deposits, it is difficult to distinguish any entrance-specific patterning (e.g. human bone occurred in eight of its ditches, including five skulls in four segments). Nevertheless, human skeletal remains did occur in ditch segments flanking each of the main entranceways (Armour-Chelu, in Pryor 1998; note that despite the complete excavation of Etton's interior, human bone (15 pieces in total) was recovered from ditch contexts alone).

Questions of access have been considered paramount to the interpretation of causewayed enclosures, it being after all causeways or circuit interruptions (i.e. a negative attribute) that define them as a monument type. In response, earlier researchers turned to a diverse range of sources for analogical inspiration, from the hundred gates of Troy to the plans of Zulu encampments (Fig. 5.51:3; see Evans 1988b for overview). Although Etton's 'compass point' arrangement would have no known parallel, it is no longer generally held that causewayed enclosures were equally accessible between each ditch segment, and the existence of major entranceways is widely accepted. Leaving aside those instances when knowledge of entrance locations can be supplemented by bank survival, as present within the Delphs enclosure (apart from markedly wider causeway intervals) entrances are generally distinguished by a slight inturning of ditch circuits. As shown on Figure 5.41, nine such plan-based entrances can be seen around the Delphs circuit. The most obvious are those along its southwestern and northwestern aspects (Figs. 5.41:1 & 5.41:2). Other major entrances probably evade superficial detection; those that have been identified seem to fall at distances of *c*. 75–100 m around the circuit, and this may indicate a basic 'interval of access' (though based on the HAD '87 evidence the inclusion of 'lesser' entrances could suggest access on a *c*. 35–40 m interval).

Such inturned entrance arrangements have been identified on a number of other enclosures (Oswald *et al*. 2001, 49–53, fig. 3.16) and are particularly obvious in the case of the small innermost circuits at Windmill Hill and Eastleach, Gloucestershire and also the Stepleton enclosure at Hambledon Hill. In all three instances the inturned entranceways occur centrally along one somewhat flattened side of their circuits. In addition, within the outer circuit of the Eastleach enclosure antenna-like ditches project as if to funnel access; out-turned entranceworks are also apparent in the possible enclosure at Norton, Glamorganshire (Oswald *et al*. 2001, figs. 3.18 & 3.19). Complicated enclosure entranceways are also known in areas of the Continent, particularly west-central France (e.g. Scarre 1998; Burnez & Louboutin 2002) and Denmark (Andersen 2002; Madsen 1988). Of the latter these include complex palisade/fence systems, the most renowned, of course, being those at Sarup (Andersen 1997). Of a later date than most British causewayed enclosures, in the context of this volume the importance of Sarup is not so much a matter of providing direct structural parallels but rather how it generally attests to Neolithic design process and the organization of labour.

Sarup's frequently reproduced reconstruction drawing (Oswald *et al*. 2001, fig. 3.13; Andersen 2002, fig. 1.8; and the splendid model of the same scene in Moesgaard Museum, Århus) goes far to naturalize its extraordinary maze-like layout. Timber screens frame ditch segments and flank tunnel-like passages, some leading to points of access while others are simply blocked. Undoubtedly, in part, a product of phase construction, it has a highly organic character (i.e. cumulative). Yet in reference to arguments pertaining to human architecture as opposed to the works of animals, how 'organic' is this? Whilst arguably having distant affinities to warren or burrow networks, most animal constructions display a far greater symmetry (e.g. bee hives) and/or functional intent (e.g. beaver

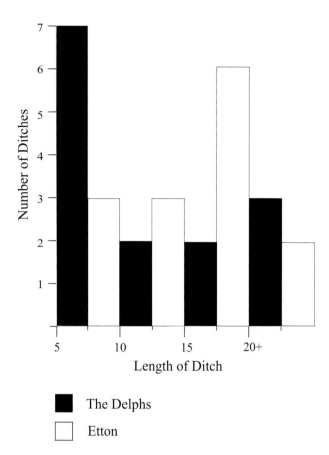

**Figure 5.50**. *Comparison of 14 ditch segment lengths from each of Etton and the Delphs enclosures. (Due to their 'non-reconstructability' the HAD '81 segments are not included; otherwise the full length of only partially exposed ditches at the extremes of the three areas of the excavations have been estimated through reference to the aerial photographic plotting.).*

lodges). There is something singularly human in the apparent chaos of Sarup's layout. Akin to the various examples of non-aligned entrance causeways across ditch and palisade circuits, there is a sense of underlying structure but with a lack of sustained 'guidance' or authority to maintain its intentions.

Continuing this volume's allusions to the works of Pieter Bruegel, Sarup (and with it causewayed enclosures in general) could be gainfully compared to his *Tower of Babel* of 1563 (Fig. 6.1). This is not only a matter of spatial structure: its tower rises to the clouds as if in concentric rings (its actual spiralling ziggurat-like form largely being lost in perspective; cf. the undated 'Rotterdam version' of the same): but rather of intent. Attended in the foreground by a kingly overseer, the construction scene is one of ant- or termite-like industry, displaying structure amidst intense, if superficially chaotic, activity. The sin of mankind was to build a tower to rival God's

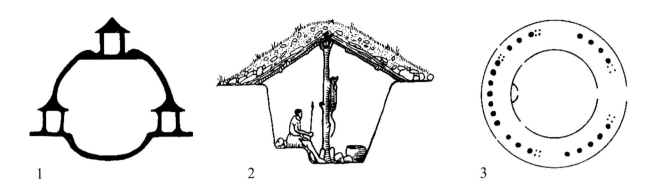

1                                    2                                         3

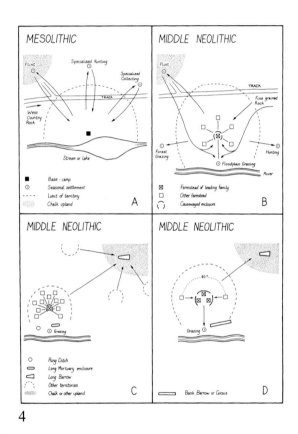                 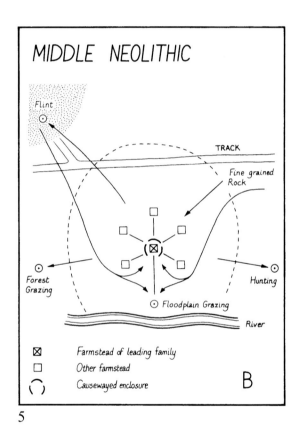

4                                    5

**Figure 5.51.** *Neolithic settlement models and analogies: 1) symbol for 'Habitation-sites (Windmill Hill-type)' from Map of Neolithic Wessex, Ordnance Survey 1932; 2) Piggott's reconstruction of a 'long pit-dwelling' found beneath Kemp Howe barrow (Piggott 1935, fig. 7); 3) plan of Zulu kraal (after Krige 1936,* The Social Structures of the Zulus *cited in Case 1956); 4 & 5) Case's Mesolithic and Middle Neolithic Abingdon land-use models ('5' being an enlargement of 4.B; in Case & Whittle 1982, diagram 1).*

omnipotence; in retribution they lost the ability of common speech and in the ensuing cacophony the project failed. On the one hand, its moral could be read as warning of the potential volatility of any *en masse* gathering, where a greater collectivity always risks inter-group rivalry and unforeseen fractures. On

the other hand, Babel, the awe-inspiring construction born out of a broad-based understanding and shared language (see Renfrew 1987 concerning the potential spread of an Indo-European mother language during the earliest Neolithic), could equally substitute for causewayed enclosures as 'first monuments' and a pan-European phenomenon (in whose wake followed diverse regional traditions). Of course, it is ultimately in the nature of the social fabric that these things are simultaneous. In mass-group endeavour and meetings beyond the everyday community, upon the verge of coalescence lurk the seeds of sub-sector self-interest and jealousies that may eventually undermine (over-) aspiring collective enterprise.

Ultimately the Delphs causewayed enclosure cannot itself be accounted for by purely immediate circumstances. By the variability of enclosure-artefact densities demonstrated in Figure 5.44 (and Table 5.35), it becomes doubtful whether a single suite of factors can adequately explain causewayed enclosures as a phenomenon. In relation to the control of territory and/or resources, it would have to be questioned whether population densities would have been sufficiently uniform throughout southern Britain or comparable

lineages simultaneously needed to express themselves in competitive display so that the enclosures independently arose in such numbers. In short, given what seems to be the close bracketing of the dates of their construction and widespread grammar of layout, in most instances they are unlikely to have arisen from strictly local conditions. The possibility that the distribution of some enclosures potentially reflects an 'in-roads-type' patterning is raised in Chapter 6 below and certainly it would have to be suspected that, at the very least, *emulation* may have been a major factor. Perhaps involving cult-like attributes, ultimately it would have come down to the dissemination of *an idea of enclosure*. Causewayed enclosures relate to a different way of organizing 'the world' and formally demarcating (and fostering) modes of broad communal interaction, and in different areas were evidently sustained to a greater degree beyond their initial impetus.

*Chapter 6*

# Concluding Discussion:
# Constructing Identities (and Landscapes)

'The only universal is the local'

William Carlos Williams

Following Ingold's lead, references to paintings by Pieter Breughel have punctuated this volume: *The Harvesters* of 1565, *The Fall of Icarus* (*c.* 1558) and, finally, *The Tower of Babel* (1563). In a manner unforeseen by the Late medieval painter these can be read as a commentary on the European Neolithic. Ignoring their contemporary context and relative chronology, on the basis that (akin to trees and plants) in a western canon 'paintings are good to think with (too)', in Figure 6.1 they have been arranged as if they were a triptych. Underpinned by agriculture and trade (the harvest and *Icarus'* ploughman and ship), with the forest always lurking in the background, these enable the great collective project of mankind / culture: Babel. With its ensuing failure came linguistic misunderstanding and the disunity of localism, what Manguel has ironically referred to as 'God's curse of multi-culturalism' (1996, 177).

This convenient parable ultimately comes down to the operation of *metaphors*. This is more than just a matter of comprehending something distant through similarities to something more familiar, be it a bird, tree-type, catch-phrase or a construction. Simultaneously sharing key characteristics, these can effectively become interchangeable, though 'outside' a cultural system such associations can seem entirely arbitrary. Such diverse linkages would equally have underpinned the Neolithic experience of the world (see Tilley 1996; 1999). Variously involving physical and conceptual *transformations*, let us explore at least some of those which seem materially manifest within the context of the project's fieldwork.

They start with clearance in woodland, with which the causewayed enclosure may have resonated. For whatever interval, people lived in these clearings, and the trapezoidal longhouses of the earlier Continental European Neolithic were echoed in the layout of the Foulmire long barrow. Yet this monument inverted this association, having at its core a passage into the mound / ground, going 'into the earth' that may well have evoked the digging of ditches (and potentially even flint mining), and, instead of celebrating the fruits of domestication, referenced 'the wild' (deer deposits and arrowheads). Similarly, interment within the dismembered oak trunk of the long barrow's chamber may, in effect, have been to be buried within a / *the* tree, just as the monument's façade may have suggested the mass 'wood wall' of clearance edges and later played against the 'stand' of the causewayed enclosure's palisade.

Other, more specific associations may also be traced. For example, the cremation-related activity preceding the long barrow may have been linked with the 'crematoria' closing of the monument's usage and, too, the burnt fills of the causewayed enclosure's terminal deposits: all of which may have resonated in relationship to domestic hearths and concepts of cleansing / purity. Turf cutting and the stripping of flesh may been another. Equally, there were associations with axes, variously evoking mounds, genitalia and torsos (see inset below and e.g. Thomas & Tilley 1993; Edmonds 1999), and a number of the worked bone objects from the causewayed enclosure suggest further 'substitutions'.

This is not a matter of easy structural associations, but slippery contexts and transformational metaphors. In fact, what was probably the prime 'identifier' amongst Neolithic communities, *cattle* (evoking a sense of parallel descent-/age-group categories, colour sets and other characteristics: see e.g. Tilley 1996, 183–4), had no obvious material-symbolic content within the project's fieldwork. Add to this what seems to have been an over-arching concern with ancestors — *the dead* (burnt, loose or interred) — and what might approximate to a cultural framework of Haddenham's Neolithic here comes to the fore. Only thereafter is it appropriate to explore its expression within the immediate cultural landscape and 'harder edged' concerns (e.g. territory, settlement densities, environmental change and authority).

## Abstracting landscape: marking edges

The cropmark complex at Fornham All Saints, Suffolk, shows a startling interplay of monuments: the 'double' causewayed enclosure overlain by the 1.3+ km length of a cursus (Fig. 6.2). Such an interaction of monuments of these types is paralleled elsewhere (e.g. Etton: Pryor 1998). It is not, therefore, their juxtaposition that is so remarkable, but the fact that the Fordham cursus bends in relationship to the river and, in effect, mimics it. This has implications for associations between cursuses and procession (e.g. Tilley 1994), and a sense of 'coursed' movement that they would have in common with rivers. The Fordham landscape, therefore, effectively sees the succession of two monuments and, arguably, metaphors: *the woodland clearance* (the causewayed enclosures) and *the river* (the cursus).

Not only does the Etton landscape demonstrate a comparable interrelationship between monuments of this type, but also its cursus lies closely parallel to a river, in that case a palaeochannel of the Welland (Oswald *et al.* 2001, fig. 8.2). Though of much later date, upstream on the Ouse at Meadow Lane, St Ives, a Middle Iron Age pit alignment has been excavated running along the edge of what was then an active channel of the river (Pollard 1996). It seems remarkable that a river (a ready natural boundary) should require such 'active' cultural delineation. The cases of the Etton and Fordham cursuses may not so much involve a sense of territorial riverside demarcation as a symbolic duplication of the river itself. Why should it seem extraordinary that early monuments may have duplicated, or at least embodied, natural

phenomena such as rivers or forest clearances (Bradley 1993a, 26–9; 2000)? Is this any different a category of reference than between long barrows and Neolithic longhouses (whether knowingly or not in Britain)? Much of the power of monuments lies after all in their resonance and reference to cultural myths. Consider Neolithic monuments, occurring in a world where human constructions had still to impact significantly on the landscape and a monumental fabric had yet to be established. In this context it should not be unexpected that the 'natural' environment, or at least the human experience of being in the world, should itself provide models for the organization of monuments and their 'design'. The Haddenham landscape (as indeed all cultural landscapes) also involves these elements (delineated places and 'alignments') which in an earlier Neolithic context would essentially come down to forest clearances and routeways (see also Pryor's 1988 & 2001a discussion of Fengate's primary Neolithic axis).

The layout of the Over/Haddenham/Sutton barrow field raises crucial issues concerning the resolution of culture/tradition in nature (Figs. 6.3 & 6.5B). Generally the barrow field's alignment is northeast–southwest and it appears to follow the river. In some respects it is reminiscent of, for example, the Barrow Hills round barrow cemetery which extends northeast from the Abingdon Causewayed enclosure on a straight axis (with a lesser parallel alignment on its southern side: Bradley 1993a, fig. 55). Yet where the Haddenham (*et al.*) cemetery differs is that it was laid out in two- and three-barrow clusters on staggered axes sharing the same approximate orientation, but

**Figure 6.1.** *'This much is already known: for every sensible line of straightforward statement, there are leagues of senseless cacophonies, verbal jumbles and incoherences ... For a long time it was believed that these impenetrable books corresponded to past or remote languages. It is true that the most ancient men, the first librarians, used a language quite different from the one we now speak; it is true that a few miles to the right the tongue is dialectal and that ninety floors farther up, it is incomprehensible' (J. Luis Borges,* The Library of Babel*).*

*The Bruegel 'Triptych'. Left: the agricultural labours of* The Harvesters *(1565) and trade (the galleon in* The Fall of Icarus *of c. 1558, right) support the greater collective enterprise of 'unified' mankind:* The Tower of Babel *(1563). Note that the Harvesters' great tree and Icarus' 'splash' have been highlighted.*

not on a continuous line. Though it seems to echo the orientation of the area's long barrows, this is not precise (see below) and it can be questioned to what degree this pattern was actually locally determined. (Raising issues of 'mapping knowledge', if only mimicking the course of the river would 'they' have been able to appreciate the overall trend of its course from the sweep of its immediate 'S'-bends?)

In the case of the Neolithic, although for the region as a whole it is difficult to argue for a dominant axis, along the western Fenland-edge and its East Midlands hinterland this northeast–southwest orientation was shared by the Rectory Farm, Godmanchester enclosure, the Raunds long barrow and the 'small' monuments on the Nene (see Chapter 3 above). Equally, for the Bronze Age this orientation is common to field systems (e.g. Barleycroft/Over and Fengate, and the HAD VIII 'enclosure'). It therefore becomes difficult to know just how local was this orientation, however sympathetic it may seem with the immediate stretch of the river. (As discussed below and in Volume 2, unlike for the Neolithic, the Bronze Age orientation did not seem actually to 'face' in either of these directions and rather the prime orientation of 'objects' within its landscape, houses and barrows, was southward.) Moreover, whilst within the immediate Haddenham environs this axial orientation was common to the Haddenham Site 7 barrows in Foulmire Fen (roughly extending the line of the Haddenham 6 long barrow; see below) and the Haddenham Sites 2 and 3 clusters on the Hermitage Farm terraces (Figs. 6.3 & 6.5), other barrows did not follow it. There seems no obvious layout to the Site 9 pair or the northern Over

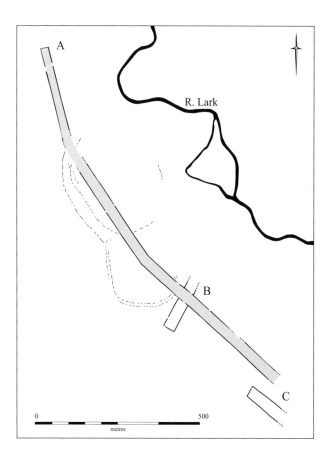

**Figure 6.2.** *Landscape passage and mimicry. The Fornham All Saints enclosure(s) and 'cursus' (A–C), with the main cursus (A; grey toned) clearly mimicking the course of the River Lark (after Oswald* et al. *2001, fig. 8.2).*

349

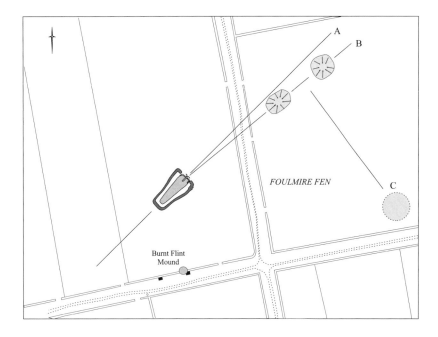

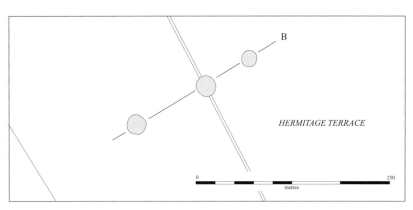

**Figure 6.3.** *Landscape axes: A) the long barrow's 47° east-of-north orientation; B) the round barrows' 53° east-of-north orientation (with 'C' its right-angle return). Note, however, that while the B axis of the Site 9 barrows on the Hermitage Terraces approximates that of the Foulmire Fen round barrows (Site 7) there is a 7° discrepancy between them (i.e. approximately equivalent to the difference between axes A & B).*

screens and complicated ring-ditches that there occur on the northwestern floodplain. (Together, in its scale and mixed components, the Over/ Barleycroft grouping is in some respects reminiscent of the Fengate/ Flag Fen complex, and clearly was some manner of significant 'centre' during the Bronze Age: Evans & Knight 2001.) In this capacity mention needs finally to be made of the Snows Farm barrow (Haddenham Site 1). The only barrow sited on the Upper Delphs proper, it outlies the main barrow cemetery by some 900 m and is rather situated adjacent to the causewayed enclosure (Fig. 6.5: B). Its status and subsequent development (a Romano-Celtic shrine was later constructed upon it) are the central theme of Volume 2, and it highlights the entire issue of ritual distance and context. The crucial question is obviously whether that barrow's apparent association with the causewayed enclosure (then still surely a prominent earthwork) was a matter of intentional reference.

All this attests to the complexity of long-term cultural landscape interactions (see also Evans 1985 and Hodder 1999b concerning Haddenham's *longue durée*). Certainly there were 'ideal' alignments, but the ultimate impetus of their orientation we can only guess at (e.g. an immediate length of the river echoing a mythical river; see e.g. Turner 1967, 61–5 concerning the 'mystery of the three rivers' and colour classification amongst the Ndembu). Over time

barrow group (Over Sites 2 & 3). Equally, in the same way that the Haddenham Site 11 barrow at Foulmire Fen seems laid on an axial return south of the Site 7 aligned pair (Fig. 6.3), so too in the main southern Over barrow cemetery (Sites 4 & 5) the dominant arrangement is in two northwest–southeast alignments: that is the opposing axis and at right-angles to the river. This river-perpendicular layout is uncommon and may actually mark the southwestern end of this portion of the barrow cemetery as a whole, though of course barrows do occur further upstream (there on both banks). This pattern could also denote a major point of river crossing and relate to the series of timber

some monument groups duplicated and extended this system, whether or not their builders knew of any originally structuring precepts or were only vaguely referencing an immediate landscape 'past'. Other subsequent monuments alternatively outlay the prime orientation or, indeed, followed another. This may have been due to the 'lie of the land' or the intentional following of other meaningful alignments, stories or myths. In short, against ideal-system precepts through time/history the possibilities of land, other mythical pasts and active 'presents' intervened. Nevertheless within the local Haddenham landscape a sense of river-sympathetic orientation pervades amidst elaboration. Yet even this was not stable as the river itself in this portion of the fen came, over the course of the later third and earlier second millennium BC, to mark the southern edge of the great marsh embayment: the dead being set close to the water's edge (no barrows are known on the river's northern side at this point).

## Land loss and appraisal

In attempting to model land use in such a complexly subtle environment we must be wary of thinking that *the* wet/dry edge has been found, as if somehow it was a distinctly stable divide instead of a 'fluid' boundary (cf. Heraclitus' 'you cannot cross the same river twice'). Equally the depth that sampling procedures could successfully achieve is influential, as is also the subsequent scouring away of lithic scatters through later flooding. In the case of the project's investigations, just because in two instances (at Cracknell Farm and Foulmire Fen) Early Neolithic occupation was found at around sea level/0 m OD does not imply that both spreads do not descend further, nor that other sites do not lie below this datum. Here, for example, it is relevant that the crest of the Peacocks Farm sand ridge lies at 1.50–0.50 m *below* sea level (with the nearby Letter F Farm Early Neolithic site falling at *c.* 1.00 m OD: Smith *et al.* 1989) and much of the Dutch coastal Neolithic occurs well below 'zero' (e.g. Louwe Kooijmans 1987). We should not, therefore, be lured into thinking that the Delphs causewayed enclosure nor the Foulmire long barrows need represent the lowest monuments of these types in Britain, and others may lie out in the fens too deeply buried for conventional detection.

More immediately at hand, our understanding of the land-use history of the low terraces north of the Upper Delphs and west across the Lower Delphs is undeveloped. It would be convenient, but erroneous, to infer from the fact that only earlier Neolithic material seems to have been recovered from the two areas of test pitting across this northern swathe that these lower terraces were thereafter subsumed by marsh. Our sampling was unfortunately too limited to justify such a sweeping interpretation and this would, moreover, fly in the face of other stands of evidence. There is the occurrence of later Neolithic/earlier Bronze Age activity at just above the 0 m OD level at Foulmire Fen (*c.* 0–0.30 m OD) and also the very construction of the round barrows at that height. Equally there is the evidence of the dated environmental cores, both Cardiff's at 900/50 and the Fenland Survey's from Willingham Mere. Further discussed in Volume 2 (Chapter 3), the results of both of these indicate that the lower terraces (at *c.* 0.50–0.85 m OD) were not

inundated before the later second–early first millennium BC. (The Cardiff core in fact suggests that cereal production was undertaken at this level during the Early/Middle Bronze Age.)

In this context B. Coles's observations concerning the potential survival of portions of the Doggerland land-bridge to the Continent as islands into the fourth millennium help to situate the fieldwork (1998; 1999, fig. 10.2). This would effectively make the Continent closer or at least more readily accessible (and Haddenham fall further inland). Yet Coles conversely argues that the marshy environment of this drowned archipelago would have promoted the survival of Mesolithic groups, who could have impeded the westward progression of the Neolithic. Be this as it may, perhaps even more compelling is the degree that the loss of Doggerland (and ensuing population retreat) could have featured in local cultural myths, providing 'a place' of lost origins.

Admittedly only grasped in cartoon-like caricature and lacking in topographic subtlety (see though also Volume 2, Chapter 3), Figures 6.5 & 6.6 provide a measure of the area's loss of land to marsh between the Neolithic and Iron Ages. It cumulatively represents an 83 per cent loss of the raised terraces, so that by the Iron Age dryland usage would effectively have been restricted to surfaces above 2.00 m OD. Although there was widespread loss of land north of the Ouse channel during the later Neolithic through marine inundation (Waller 1994), this does not seem to be the case across the southern, Haddenham level. It is only during the earlier Bronze Age, when the local environs experienced the maximum extent of these marine floods, that the area first suffered any significant land loss. As suggested by Cloutman above (Chapter 4), this would probably have seen the saturation of the low grounds of the Lower Delphs and left its raised Hermitage Farm terrace spine as an elevated ridge (Fig. 6.5:B). Thereafter, the trajectory of loss was from north to south. First ground at or just above sea level (Newlyn) would have been given over to marsh by the later Bronze Age, and by the Middle/later Iron Age all the land below *c.* 2.00 m OD would have been inundated (Fig. 6.6:D). In fact, the single greatest loss of land would have occurred between the later Bronze and Iron Ages, when there was a 66 per cent loss from *c.* 197 ha to 67 ha (Fig. 6.7).

This sense of loss and retreat could in some respects be compared with the Block Fen, Chatteris landscape. There a low plain of *c.* 14 sq. km lying at *c.* 1.00–2.00 m OD, dotted by round barrows and with a major Bronze Age field system, was inundated in the early centuries of the first millennium BC leading to a concentration of population on the immediate high

### The axe and the mound
by M. EDMONDS

'... Stone celts are held to preserve from lightning the house in which they are kept. They perspire when a storm is approaching; they are good for diseases of man and beast; they increase the milk of cows; they assist the birth of children; and powder scraped from them may be taken with some advantage for various childish disorders. It is usually nine days after their fall before they are found on the surface ...' (Evans 1897, 58)

The idea that enclosure ditches could be pulled into focus for considered acts of deposition has a long and varied pedigree. From Isobel Smith's *ritual rubbish* to the *structured* and *formal* deposits of more recent literature, work often starts from the premise that the patterned deposition of material can be a product of tacit cultural values or, on occasion, of more explicit statements. Such arguments are easily overstated; we don't deal particularly well with either the mess of routine life nor the confusion that can attend what we term ritual. Contemporary values draw lines that are far too sharp, with the result that both the context and the circumstance of events are often lost. That said, there are some deposits where elements and settings invite close attention and broader comparison; where an event can be followed at more than one scale.

The deposit consists of a low mound of redeposited material which runs along part of the base of a single ditch segment (Ditch I). Halfway along the mound, an axe blade was laid to rest. Macroscopic inspection suggests that the blade is made from a fine-grained epidotized tuff which has its geological source in the central fells of Cumbria (Fell & Davis 1988). Though ground and polished over most of its surface, it retains a number of flake scars (Fig. 5.31). These are most common towards the butt and some have themselves been reworked, their edges smoothed and eroded by grinding. It has also been burnt, hence the pattern of angular fractures across the surface of the lateral break and the chaotic pattern of cracks across the

body. At the broader end of the blade, there are few, if any, conchoidal fractures and this suggests that the absent cutting edge was either lost during burning, or was broken off after the stone had cooled. The blade has distinct side facets, one of which is truncated towards the butt, and the start of the slope towards the cutting edge is visible on both faces.

Beyond the head of the Ditch I mound, three human skull fragments were also interred (Figs. 5.13 & 6.4).

There is a play here with shape and alignment. The mound, like the ditch in which it is set, maintains a longitudinal axis, as does the blade. The morphology of the blade and the mound also bears some relation to the form of the nearby long barrow. That the pattern is repeated suggests an opportunity for connections to be made even if it does not prove them: there is a suggestion of 'model' sources, interplay and marked transformation (in their form axes offer another near-trapezoidal exemplar, one closer at hand than distant Continental longhouses). There are also the elements; skull fragments and an axe blade that has been broken by fire and perhaps by hammering. What we have is the body of a blade without its cutting edge, perhaps its head, laid on a mound at the end of which were fragments of a human skull. The idea of a composite, if fragmented, body; a scarred torso of stone and a head of bone.

Whatever its specific metaphoric content, the idea that the arrangement was both considered and evocative gains weight from broader comparison. The deposit is one of a number identified on enclosures in which axe blades of non-local origin were interred with some formality. The closest parallels are to be found at Etton, where blades from the same source were also buried, some deliberately broken (Pryor 1998). Axes were not the only objects to be given special treatment. But they were important, and this was most likely because of associations that were both practical and biographical. Axes were implicated in many skilled tasks. They were also statements in stone, acknowledged in passing, on the shoulder, in use and in talk. (Originating in a quarries hundreds of kilometres away, whatever arguments may be rehearsed concerning

ground (Langwood Ridge: Hall 1992; Evans 2003b). As outlined in Volume 2, as a result of marshland encroachment settlement appears to have become locally focused upon the Upper Delphs during the second half of the first millennium BC. Equally the number of later Neolithic sites, especially those of Grooved Ware attribution, encountered in the course of the project and more markedly in the subsequent Barleycroft/Over investigations, could also suggest a degree of flood-determined high ground retreat. However, in this instance the loss does not seem to have occurred within the immediate Haddenham Level environs itself, but from further out in the fen and the deeper terraces north of the Ouse palaeochannel, that would have suffered marine inundation during the third millennium BC. The effect of this flooding on the dispersed land-use patterns of mobile economies would have been particularly acute and could well have led to increased population densities on higher fen islands, fen-edge terraces and, too, along the lower/middle reaches of the rivers

flowing into the fen basin. Yet there seems no evidence to think that such flood-related dynamics were a significant factor during the earlier Neolithic and 'the explanation' for the region's causewayed enclosures and long barrows is unlikely to relate to strictly local environmental conditions.

Challenging any one-to-one identification between conceptual territories and actual (dry) land-masses, a recent publication concerned with the Iron Age of the southern Fenland explores the idea of island territories in critique of the application of Thiessian polygon modelling (Evans 2003a). It is not surprising that the islanded character of the region is not applicable to 'ideal' (i.e. uniform) land-use modelling. Nevertheless, despite obvious caveats, the differential histories of its individual islands allows us to explore the appraisal of land as regards the siting of monuments and settlement sequences. As shown in Figure 6.8, there clearly was a relationship between the size of islands and their monuments. The causewayed enclosure was not, for example, sited on the Hill Row

investigation. Otherwise, apart from the Barleycroft Farm pit cluster, the other sites lay immediately adjacent to palaeochannels of the River Ouse. This includes the Foulmire Fen and Cracknell Farm scatters, the Early Neolithic activity now known to occur on the Over 1 sand-ridge complex and the Fen Drayton sites. Although suggesting a propensity for riverside occupation, by no means does this constitute any kind of 'closed' picture of Early Neolithic land use. On the one hand, as demonstrated through the much more extensive Barleycroft/Over investigations, we know that low-density traces of Neolithic activity (occasional minor flint spreads and/or isolated pits) are widely dispersed across the landscape (Evans & Knight 2000) and, to a lesser degree, this was also evident in the Haddenham project sampling (e.g. the earlier Neolithic material in the HAD III & V/VI flint assemblages). Certainly it is imperative that this sense of a dispersed landscape 'presence' is seen as more than just a ubiquitous lithic background, but it is variously reflective of landscape traverse and short task-related 'stays' (Edmonds *et al.* 1999; Evans 2002). On the other hand, concerning the recovery of patterns of earlier Neolithic land use, given the deep overburden soil cover across most of the terraces it would be naive to think that we have found anything other than a small fraction of the period's sites in the area.

In relation to questions of the degree of 'tethered' settlement mobility, as attempted in Figure 6.10 the key issue is the scale of landscape movement that is envisaged. Questions of chronology are also relevant: whether non-feature associated scatters such as at Foulmire Fen or Cracknell Drove represent an earlier mode of Early Neolithic (and later Mesolithic) settlement than the pit occupations. Alternatively, were the pit sites base-camps and, in relation to this, do the 'open' scatter sites and 1–2 pit groupings only

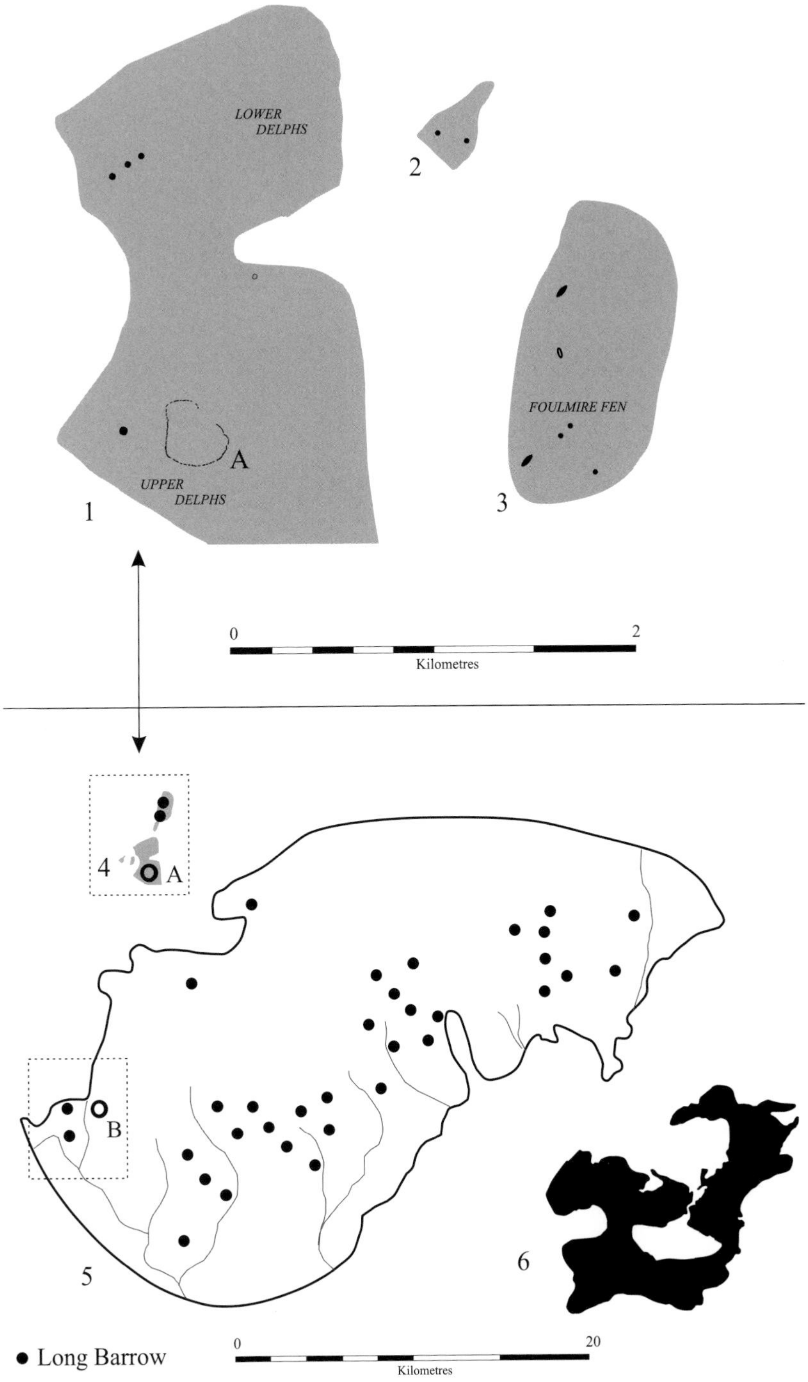

**Figure 6.8.** *Islands and territories. Top: 1–3) Haddenham area terrace islands ('A' indicates Upper Delphs causewayed enclosure); below: the Haddenham terrace islands shown to scale (with the causewayed enclosure and long barrows indicated); 4) in comparison to Renfrew's 570 sq. km Hambledon Hill territory (5; B indicates its causewayed enclosure; after Renfrew 1973, fig. 3) and the Isle of Ely (6; blackened).*

attest to off-site tasking? Due to the poor survival of economic/environmental evidence, the data are not

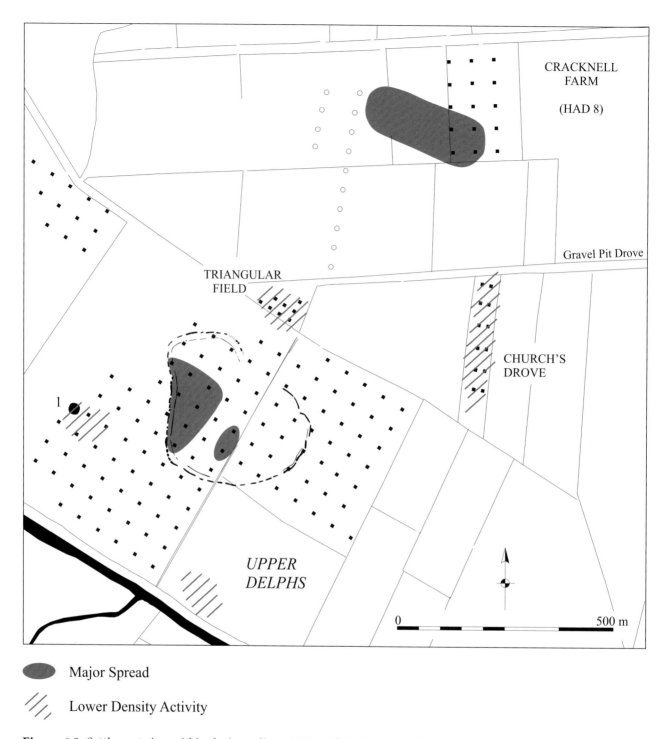

Major Spread

Lower Density Activity

**Figure 6.9.** *Settlement sites within the immediate vicinity of the Upper Delphs enclosure.*

currently available to adjudicate this. Be this as it may, the evidence of the recent earlier Neolithic settlements suggests a spectrum of 'light' occupation that must include causewayed enclosure usage. Equally, no hard or fast line can be drawn between ritual and settlement activities, and to practise sustained ritual at a locale would *de facto* imply some degree of residence.

In Figure 6.8 Haddenham's island terraces (and their attendant monuments) are shown in comparison to Renfrew's postulated Hambledon Hill territory (1973). Covering some 570 sq. km, the latter would be 200 times greater than the area of the Delphs terraces and, if draped onto the region by superimposing the relative location of the causewayed enclosures (Fig.

358

6.11), would extend for 35 km along the southern fen-edge and continue as far east as Mildenhall. This seems truly massive and its application helps to off-set the localism of much of the region's archaeology. It is, of course, unlikely that causewayed enclosures had *a* territory of whatever scale, and rather they were probably situated within a web-work of overlapping socio-spatial 'zones'. Nevertheless, reference to Renfrew's Hambledon territory highlights the problem of how large is 'the local' and, by extension, demonstrates just how limited are most research strategies/areas in the face of social units of this potential scale. This is not, however, to say that this is an appropriate comparison. Whereas attesting to much greater 'lineage display' (if not higher population densities in general), 34 long barrows are known within the putative Hambledon territory; this is as opposed to only two when imposing its plot onto the fen. Furthermore, in demonstration that immediate environs (even within 'islanded' landscapes) should not be confused with broader territorial 'pull', it is clear in Figure 6.8 that the Delphs terrace setting of the causewayed enclosures is only the equivalent of the immediate two long barrow environs of the Hambledon enclosure itself. It is most unlikely that this could have represented the total population 'catchment' of the Delphs enclosure.

'Closed' modelling of enclosure territories is not easily achieved for the east of the country, primarily due to the paucity of long barrows whose distribution underpins the putative Wessex territories (Renfrew 1973). Accepting caveats concerning the partial aerial photographic sample recovery, tentative patterns are nevertheless apparent that encourages speculation. Most striking in the Fenland is the complete absence of enclosures within the north and around its eastern edge. Against this, enclosures are known at the junction of the fen basin and all the major rivers debauching into its southern and western side: the Delphs on the Ouse, Upton and Southwick on the Nene, the aforementioned foursome on the Welland, and Landbeach and Wilbraham on the Cam. Again, while recognizing that other enclosures may still lie more deeply buried and evade detection, this distribu-

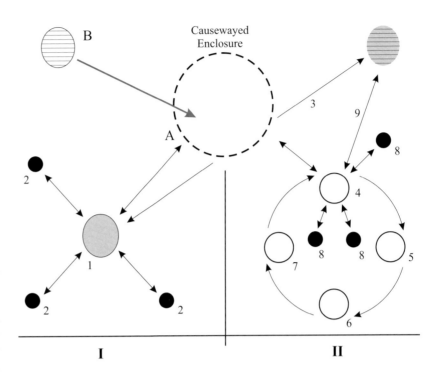

**Figure 6.10.** *Settlement 'cycling'. Land-use patterns shown in relationship to the causewayed enclosure (A): I) Swidden/Base-Camp Model: 1) Barleycroft Farm-type pit settlement (year-round occupancy) with both short-stay resource 'tasking' in local environs (2) and more distant 'expeditions' (3); II) Annual Round Model: successive annual occupancy of a series of Barleycroft Farm-type 'camps' (4–7) with immediate landscape resource tasking occurring from each (e.g. 8) and occasional longer distance forays (9); B indicates lithic resources coming into causewayed enclosure.*

tion nevertheless suggests the cognitive recognition of the fens as a geographical entity: in other words, a distinct region.

Can we, however, go further in the interrogation of enclosure distributions? One way would be to take a concept common to both earlier palaeo-economic site catchment analysis (e.g. Higgs & Vita-Finzi 1972; Barker & Webley 1978; see also Volume 2, Chapter 1) and current phenomenological approaches (Tilley 1994), that of *walking land*. Accordingly, on Figure 6.11 a 20-km radius is shown centred upon Haddenham. (Upwards of 30–40 km could easily be traversed in a day but this reduced estimate takes account of river crossings and the slowed pace of young/old members of communities and also the group's herds.) Yet the resultant catchment is not very satisfactory when seen in a larger perspective. It neither complements the broader distributions (e.g. Haddenham's radius would overlap with both the Landbeach and Wilbraham's enclosures) and nor does it acknowledge that this was a 'corridored' landscape crossed with communication routes (i.e. river valleys). Therefore returning again to

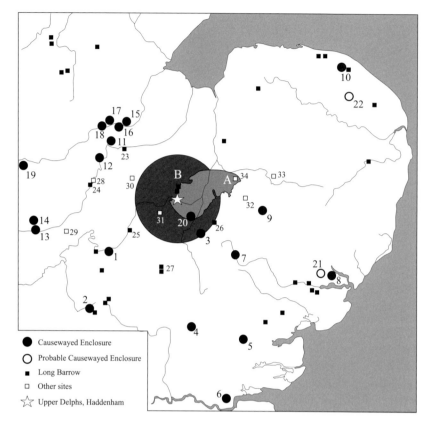

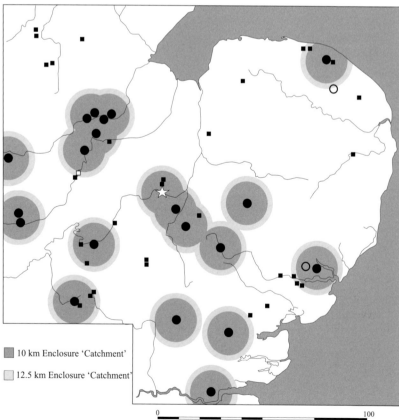

**Figure 6.11.** *Walking land and territorial 'catchments'. Top: map indicating Renfrew's Hambledon Hill territory ('A'; see Fig. 6.8) with position of its causewayed enclosure superimposed upon the Upper Delphs, Haddenham; B) 15 km 'walking' radius centred upon the Delphs.*

*Definite/probable causewayed enclosures:*
*1) Cardington; 2) Maiden Bower; 3) Great Wilbraham; 4) Sawbridgeworth; 5) Springfield Lyons; 6) Orsett; 7) Kedington; 8) Freston; 9) Fornham All Saints; 10) Roughton; 11) Upton; 12) Southwick; 13) Briar Hill; 14) Dallington; 15) Northborough; 16) Etton; 17) Barholm; 18) Uffington; 19) Husbands Bosworth; 20) Landbeach.*

*Possible causewayed enclosures:*
*21) Bentley; 22) Buxton with Lammas. Selected long barrows: 23) Orton Meadows; 24) Raunds; 25) Eynesbury, St Neots; 26) Swaffham Prior; 27) Therfield (after Oswald* et al. *2001, fig. 6.8).*

*Other selected sites:*
*28) Alwincle Barrow; 29) Grendon Barrow; 30) Honey Hill, Ramsey; 31) Fen Drayton; 32) Kilverstone; 33) Hurst Fen; 34) Peacock Farm, Shippea Hill.*

*Below: the region's causewayed enclosures with 10 and 15 km radius 'catchments' indicated. Note that these are strictly conceptual units intended for the purposes of representation only. Territorial catchments surely were not perfectly circular and may well have been linear along river valleys or ridgeway routes.*

the distribution plot, two patterns rather seem apparent. (To facilitate this analysis paired enclosures, e.g. Briar Hill/Dallington and Upton/Southwick on the Nene, and Wilbraham/Landbeach on the Cam, and the four-enclosure Welland cluster are considered as a result of immediate 'historical' circumstances and are, for these purposes, counted as one: see Oswald *et al.* 2001, 112–13, fig. 6.5.) On the one hand, amongst the riverine distributions a *c.* 40-km interval can be distinguished. This would include Husbands Bosworth to the lower Welland 'foursome'; the Briar Hill/Dallington to Upton/Southwick 'pairs' on the Nene; and, on the Ouse, Maiden Bower to Cardington to the Delphs, Haddenham. This distance could have been easily afforded in a day's boat journey and, if so, *communication* may have been their determining factor. On the other hand, amongst the 'off-river' or hinterland enclosures another pattern seems evident. This would relate to the two three-enclosure groupings of Kedington/Fornham All Saints/Great Wilbraham and Sawbridgeworth/Springfield Lyons/Orsett, in which they all seem to approximately fall at a 20–25 km distance from each other and could suggest a potential 10–12.5 km 'catchment' radius. In other words, they occur at roughly half the interval of the riverine enclosures, and as a minimal basic distance it is worth exploring its implications. This is by no means to adopt this figure in a mechanistic manner; *no territory would be symmetrical* and the distributions of resources/population in 'hinterland zones' are unlikely to have been the equivalent of those in river corridors (and the resource-exchange 'spheres' of enclosures may have been substantially larger than their population catchment). It does, nevertheless, seem much more appropriate in terms of the populations participating in the construction of the causewayed enclosure, a figure in the lower hundreds (or less) being more realistic than one of thousands.

A 10–12.5 km catchment would, furthermore, encompass the majority of the region's long barrows (at least in those parts where enclosures occur: Fig. 6.11). The most marked discrepancy is that there is no enclosure to accompany the Therfield barrows and, indeed, no causewayed enclosure is known along the headwaters of the Cam (though one has long been suspected, though with little obvious basis, adjacent to Wandlebury). In this regard it is relevant that some years ago Rog Palmer identified a truly unusual enclosure nearby (Fig. 6.12; TL 3766391) which, while lacking ditch interruptions, otherwise has the plan-form of a causewayed enclosure. Other atypical enclosures are also known within the vicinity: the uniquely henge-suggestive one at Melbourn (Palmer 1976, no. 39; Oswald *et al.* 2001, fig. 8.1) and what is probably a

palisaded site at Stapleford (Evans 1988a; Oswald *et al.* 2001, 150, Gaz. no 13). In short, the Royston environs seem another special case ('place'), whose understanding will only be furthered by fieldwork.

Figure 6.13 attempts to portray what may have been the 'paths' or means of mediation between the study area's causewayed enclosure and its long barrows. The crucial question is whether the face-to-face community of settlements (presumably largely consisting of extended families) had direct access to the enclosure or if it was mediated by a higher level grouping (i.e. long barrow lineages). There is obviously no way of definitely proving that long barrows directly related to lineages; it is a reasonable and attractive inference, but awaiting the widespread application of DNA analyses, this we cannot 'know'. However, based on the evidence of the sectoring of labour around the circuit of the Delphs enclosure, it can be determined that an intermediate level grouping did exist between the immediate family and the greater enclosure community. This comes down to something so basic as how ditch segments were dug. If individual lengths had been the responsibility of single families and if no organizational grouping intervened between their participation and the 'enclosure whole', then considerably greater ditch-to-ditch variability might be expected. The fact that their digging technique varied by sector rather than by segment (e.g. side-by-side vs lateral expansion 'styles' respectively in the HAD '87 and '84 areas) does indeed suggest a medial-scale collective that was probably, but not necessarily, lineage-based.

The 'triangular relationship' of settlement, long barrows and causewayed enclosures is an abiding framework of the Neolithic. However it is an 'ideal package', whose latter two components also evidently occurred quite independently of each other. The layout of the Delphs enclosure would, for example, suggest the participation of more than two such 'medial'/lineage groups, despite the fact that only two long barrows are known in the area (and that three is the minimum number of lineages required for sustained group reproduction: see Zubrow, Volume 2, Chapter 6 concerning pre-modern/prehistoric population dynamics). Recognizing what would have been the relatively small scale of the causewayed enclosure's community raises crucial issues concerning the concept of 'being' Neolithic (e.g. Thomas 1999). It strikes at the heart of British archaeology's now predominant concern with monumentality, as if only by participating in monuments did communities somehow become Neolithic. Based on the eastern evidence this simply cannot be true. Here we face the dual problems of having to model

A

B

**Figure 6.12.** *The Royston enclosure and Fen Drayton cursus: A) aerial photograph of double-circuit enclosure at Royston (photograph R. Palmer); B) looking southwest along line of the possible Fen Drayton cursus and long enclosure (arrowed); note a possible 'Barford-type' enclosure in central foreground (CUCAP BJD 44).*

earlier Neolithic settlement densities and the total number of causewayed enclosures within the region: neither of which are 'knowns'. Given the riverine distribution of the west-of-fen causewayed enclosures and accepting that the Delphs enclosure did not involve a community of more than 100–200 individuals, then it seems likely that this membership could theoretically have been drawn from quite a small 'territory'. Here, whilst acknowledging caveats that there may not have been a one-to-one relationship between enclosure participation and physical territories (and membership need not have been exclusive to a geography), to sound this problem further Table 6.1 gives an indication of the variability of population densities amongst a selection of the world's sedentary 'horticulturalists' and swidden cultivators. (The figures are drawn, in part, from Sahlins's 1974 arguments concerning the lower-than-carrying capacity of 'affluent' swidden-based societies. See Layton & Barton 2001, 19–20; Kelly 1995, 221–32, table 6-4 concerning hunter-gatherer densities, the vast majority of which fall well below 1 per sq. m, the highest level known being 8.4 per sq. m amongst the Chumash of California.)

Again, it should be stressed that such ethnographic densities are not offered as any kind of absolute basis of modelling, and local conditions will always vary from means. Nevertheless, statistics, like plants, trees and paintings, are also 'good to think with'. The amassed figures display a considerable range, with densities of 1–111 persons per square kilometre. The uppermost figure, indicative of swidden cultivators in New Guinea's tropical highlands, is obviously unreasonably high and, at face-value, the Huron density of 24 persons seems much more appropriate (living in temperate North American forests their lifestyle was probably more

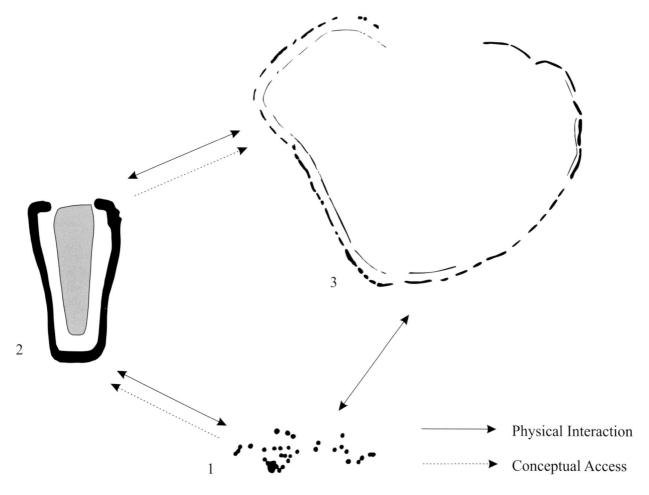

**Figure 6.13.** *A triangular relationship. Early Neolithic settlement (1; Barleycroft Farm pit site; see Fig. 4.16); 2) the Foulmire Fen long barrow; 3) the Delphs causewayed enclosures (not to standard orientation or scale).*

generally applicable to the European Neolithic). However, if being still more conservative and only applying a figure of 10–20 (the equivalent of a pit-settlement's population) per square kilometre to a 10-km causewayed enclosure catchment (314 sq. km) would generate what seems to be enormously high population levels (a community of 3000–6000) and a 5-km catchment (19.6 sq. km) would provide more than adequate numbers (200–400). These estimates raise further possibilities. The first is obvious; just because in parts of the region causewayed enclosures seem to display a regular 20–25 km interval need not necessarily imply that their 'territories' maximally filled the intervening swathes and 'territorial stand-off' could have promoted smaller catchments between

**Table 6.1.** *Population densities (per sq. km).*

| Group | Location | Economy | Population density |
|---|---|---|---|
| *Ndembu* (Turner 1967) | Zimbabwe | Swidden | 1 |
| *Swaka* (Sahlins 1974) | Zimbabwe | Swidden | <1.5 |
| *Lamet* (Sahlins 1974) | Laos | Swidden | 2.9 |
| *Iban* (Sahlins 1974) | Sut Valley, Borneo | Swidden | 8.8 |
| *Dogomba* (Sahlins 1974) | Ghana | Swidden | 9.6–19.3 |
| *Huron* (Heidenreich 1978) | Canadian Great Lakes | Horticulture | 24 |
| *Yagaw Hanoo* (Sahlins 1974) | Philippines | Swidden | 30 |
| *Gurung* (Macfarlane 1976) | West-Central Nepal | Rice agriculture/ woodland pastoralism | 45.2 |
| *Naregu Chimbu* (Sahlins 1974) | New Guinea | Swidden | 111.2 |

them (e.g. 5 vs 10–12.5 km). The second point returns us to the issue of landscape 'cycling' and the degree of contemporary settlement mobility. If practising a mobile forest pastoralism involving regular shifts of residence (and with dispersed arable stands), then these 10–20 person camp-units may have annually 'occupied' areas of 10 sq. km or more. Ignoring the question of any overlap between pastoral/settlement ranges, then in relationship to a 10 km enclosure-catchment this would generate a population of 300–600 persons. This is quite in keeping with the estimates for the causewayed enclosure's construction, though by most normative standards both the 10/12.5 and 5 km catchments would be considered small for enclosure territories (though the latter is the unit that Barker & Webley used for their strictly economic land-use determined 1978 study).

There is no question of resolving these many population/enclosure estimates. Rather the hinge point of these analyses is that they suggest that upwards of half or more of the region's population may not have been amongst the 'membership' of causewayed enclosures. Even more directly telling here is the complete absence of causewayed enclosures from eastern Norfolk and its fen-edge. What this surely indicates is that the character of Neolithic communities must have been much more diverse than has been credited, and, in this manner, pocketed '*monument enclaves*' may be a more valid concept or terminology than 'territories'.

These arguments become pronounced in the case of the region's long barrows, whose distributions seem very localized. For example, though the fen-ward reaches of the Nene/Welland have causewayed enclosures they have no long barrows (the anomalous Orton Meadows barrow aside), whereas eastern Lincolnshire has a high density of long barrows but no enclosures. Further aerial photographic reconnaissance is likely to alter this picture and, of course, communities may have had other mortuary practices than long barrow interment (e.g. both smaller unmounded and round barrow-associated mortuary structures such as has been found along the Nene). Nevertheless the evidence suggests a sense of *social mosaic*. Here the moot question becomes whether this was a matter of only partial or 'non-monumental' Neolithic groups as opposed to lingering quasi-Mesolithic communities who had yet to take up 'the package'. Alternatively, 'being Neolithic' may been a matter of local responses to change and differed according to both immediate conditions and historical factors (i.e. adopting only facets of *the* lifestyle). This seems a key issue; archaeology must itself guard against projecting a 'pre-Babel' holism onto the earlier Neolithic: advocating the virtues of a life in symbolic harmony, balanced with nature and mediating emergent social authority through 'open' monuments and ritual (see Levi-Strauss's 'Virtuous Savage'; 1973). We should be wary of our own 'myths of origins' and a desire to impose a pristine ethnography upon prehistory, as there will have always been degrees of social conflict, competition, hierarchies and *difference*.

## Locality and place-values

In reference to the Carlos Williams citation that introduces this chapter, concepts of 'place' potentially cross-cut the formal distributional analyses rehearsed above. Are significant locales deemed such by the qualities or associations of their immediate cultural landscape or larger scale factors? Of course, there always would have been a tension between that which is locally 'recommended' (i.e. long-term resonance) as opposed to what was more broadly sustainable. These issues are of singular importance when trying to understand Haddenham's Neolithic. Situated at the northward bend of the Ouse's palaeochannel with its 'great' causewayed enclosure and 'classic' long barrows, it seems a very distinct place-grouping. Although seeming special, both of these monument categories have pan-European exemplars, and it is clearly a matter of 'introductions' taking root. Crucial here is the *translation* or *transformations* this involved, both in terms of distant Continental models and the dominant Wessex expression of southern British prehistory. Whilst not overlooking the Mesolithic impact upon the landscape, it would have to be suspected that in a context of earlier Neolithic 'first monuments' (and their arrival) that broader landscape factors would predominate over local sequences. Long-term place-values would not as yet have had a significant impact and there is nothing to suggest that the Delphs themselves were a particularly favoured Mesolithic locale. Here, although related, perhaps the most important result of the study of the region's causewayed enclosures is not so much their potentially 'small territories' but that their riverine interval should be so great, especially given that river valleys were then clearly such a focus of settlement. This does indeed imply that communication rather than territory may have been the prime factor. It is a kind of patterning suggestive of 'in-roads' colonization and 'coming into land', and it further tells that this monumental expression of the Neolithic did not arise locally, whatever its source.

The post-Neolithic history of the Delphs and Haddenham level is the concern of the second volume of this series. This is not so much a matter of a narrative as a charting of the ebb and flow of settlement. It is argued that the area only again became 'significant' during the earlier Bronze Age with the establishment of the round barrow cemetery, though the focus of Bronze Age activity was then clearly along the Barleycroft/Over reaches of the river itself. Thereafter, the Delphs saw substantive occupation during the Iron Age, only to the relegated to the status of 'outlands' (relative to higher ground settlement at Willingham/Over) during the Roman era, before eventually being 'lost to the fen' in the Saxon/medieval period.

More critical in the context of this volume is the status of the area during the later Neolithic, in the aftermath of its earlier monumentality. Although Grooved Ware-related settlement clusters have been identified, especially within the Barleycroft/Over investigations (Evans & Knight 2000; 2001), in marked contrast to the Maxey landscape on the River Welland (Pryor & French 1985) no cursuses or henges have been convincingly identified along the lower reaches of the Ouse (Jackson & Potter's putative Stonea cursus being highly suspect; 1996; see though Fig. 5.47 and Chapter 5 above). As opposed to Etton, the Delphs evidently saw no monument construction during the third millennium BC and the 'lowest' known candidate for a cursus (and with an associated mortuary enclosure) along the Ouse Valley is at Fen Drayton (northwest–southeast orientation: Fig. 6.12:B), with the Huntingdon/Godmanchester area apparently then becoming a significant ritual nexus (see Malim 2000 for overview).

These developments and the apparent up-river shift in the focus of monument construction were, no doubt, largely engendered through the third-millennium marine flooding and the ensuing disruption of regional-scale patterns of land use. Promoting the concentration of Grooved Ware settlement within the area of the Ouse's lower/middle reaches (which seem to occur at densities at least two or three times that of the earlier Neolithic sites) the lack of accompanying monuments may be attributable to the fact that this was then still held to be a 'landscape of risk' (i.e. in fear of further inundation). Yet local monument traditions could also be evident. Despite the scale of recent fieldwork along the river's lower reaches and the fen-edge at Somersham/Earith (leading to the recovery of many second millennium BC mortuary-associated ring-ditches: e.g. Evans & Knight 2000), no henge monuments have been discovered. The nearest lies some 20 km upstream at Brampton, near Huntingdon (Malim 2000, 66–70, fig. 8.6), and downstream on the Ouse their absence is conspicuous (a triple-circle cropmark at Chatteris seems more likely to be an elaborate ring-ditch rather than a henge: Hall 1992, 89–90, pl. IX). While possibly reflecting different intensities of fieldwork (and this kind of broad patterning can be overturned by a single discovery), there may have

been a relationship between the number of henges known on the Nene/Welland and the earlier Neolithic round barrow-associated mortuary complexes that also occur in that area. The latter are again thus far absent from the Ouse and it may be the case that the one tradition fostered the other.

It is appropriate to conclude this volume with themes that were announced from the outset — *the river* and *life in woods*. These tell of different cognitive dynamics, respectively change and loss. Of the latter, it is surely reasonable to presume that, as attested to by the 'tree-sympathetic' arrangement of the long barrow's timbers (and probably developing from Mesolithic antecedents), trees and woods were probably imbued with symbolic attributes. If so, by increased inroads into forest over the course of the Neolithic a way of life would have effectively destroyed much of the matrix of these cognitive systems (see Macfarlane 1976 & Bloch 1995 concerning the relentless pace of cattle browse and swidden slash-and-burn; see also Krech 1999 concerning current mythologies of the 'Ecological Indian'). It is relevant to speculate whether elements of this symbolic language were retained and later found expression in, for example, the 'rarefaction' of wood in the Holme timber circle (i.e. 'Sea Henge': Pryor 2001b; Brennand & Taylor in press) or the Barleycroft 'screens' (Evans & Knight 2001). Simultaneously, new cognitive systems would have developed relating to the descriptive meaning of open pastures, arable plots and *discrete* forest stands. Woodland (and with it hunting) would, over the course of the fourth to second millennia BC, have changed from being the matrix of life (in which clearance was something to define and symbolize) to itself becoming a category: something prescribed and limited.

The river would have been a different matter, not something of loss but drastic change, and is appropriately a constant throughout both of the volumes. From being a corridor through densely forested landscape, with the third/earlier second-millennium BC marine flooding it would have lost any clear northern edge and effectively come to mark the southern edge of open wetlands. With the sea or at least estuarine marsh lapping against the southern Ouse-side terraces, and perhaps involving ancient cultural myths concerning land-loss and water, the barrow cemeteries came to delineate this wet/dryland divide (however much the land behind was permeated by backwater channels). Adaptation to this increasingly wet environment, the advent of marshland communities, is the central theme of Volume 2.

# References

Adams, J.C., 1981. *Outline of Orthopaedics*. Edinburgh: Churchill Livingstone.

Andersen, N.H., 1997. *The Sarup Enclosures*. (Jutland Archaeological Society Monographs 33:1.). Århus: Jutland Archaeological Society.

Andersen, N.H., 2002. Neolithic enclosures in Scandinavia, in Varndell & Topping (eds.), 1–10.

Andersen, S.H., 1987. Tybrind Vig: a submerged Ertebølle settlement in Denmark, in Coles & Lawson (eds.), 253–81.

Andersen, S.T., 1970. The relative pollen productivity and pollen representation of northern European trees, and correction factors for tree pollen spectra. *Danmarks Geologiske Undersøgelse* (2nd series) 96, 1–99.

Andersen S.T., 1979. Identification of wild grasses and cereal pollen. *Danmarks Geologiske Undersøgelse Årbog* 1978, 69–92.

Andrews, P. & J. Cook, 1985. Natural modifications to bone in a temperate setting. *Man* 20, 675–91.

Ashbee, P., 1966. The Fussell's Lodge long barrow excavations, 1957. *Archaeologia* 100, 1–80.

Ashbee P., 1984. *The Earthen Long Barrow in Britain*. 2nd edition. Norwich: Geo.

Ashton, N., F. Healy & P. Pettitt (eds.), 1998. *Stone Age Archaeology*. (Oxbow Monograph 102.) Oxford: Oxbow.

Atkinson, R.J.C., 1965. Wayland's Smithy. *Antiquity* 39, 126–33.

Atkinson, R.J.C., C.M. Piggott & N.K. Sanders, 1951. *Excavations at Dorchester, Oxon.*, vol. 1. Oxford: Ashmolean Museum.

Austin, P., 2000. The emperor's new garden: woodland trees and people in the Neolithic of southern Britain, in Fairburn (ed.), 63–78.

Avery, B.W., 1980. *Soil Classification for England and Wales*. (Soil Survey Technical Monograph 14.) Harpenden: Soil Survey.

Baby, R.S., 1954. *Hopewell Cremation Practices*. Columbus (OH): The Ohio Historical Society.

Badeslade, T., 1725. *The History of the Ancient and Present State of the Navigation of the Port of King's-Lynn and of Cambridge*. London: Roberts.

Baillie, M.G.L., 1982. *Tree-ring Dating and Archaeology*. London: CroomHelm.

Baillie, M.G.L., 1989. Do Irish bog oaks date the Shang Dynasty? *Current Archaeology* 10, 310–13.

Baillie, M.G.L. & D. Brown, 1988. An overview of oak chronologies, in Slater & Tate (eds.), 543–8.

Baillie, M.G.L. & J.R. Pilcher, 1973. A simple cross-dating program for tree-ring research. *Tree-Ring Bulletin* 33, 7–14.

Baillie, M.G.L. & J.R. Pilcher, 1988. Make a date with a tree. *New Scientist* 117(160), 448–51.

Bakkevig, S., 1980. Phosphate analysis in archaeology — problems and recent progress. *Norwegian Archaeological Review* 13, 73–100.

Bamford, H., 1982. *Beaker Domestic Sites in the Fen-Edge and East Anglia*. (East Anglian Archaeology 16.). Norwich: Norfolk Museums Service.

Bamford, H., 1985. *Excavations at Briar Hill*. Northampton: Northampton Development Corporation.

Banks, H.V., 1934. Incidence of third molar development. *Angel Orthodont. Chicago* 4, 223–33.

Barker, G. & D. Webley, 1978. Causewayed camps and early Neolithic economies in central southern England. *Proceedings of the Prehistoric Society* 44, 161–86.

Barrett, J.C. & I. Kinnes (eds.), 1988. *The Archaeology of Context in the Neolithic and Bronze Age: Recent Trends*. Sheffield: J.R. Collis and University of Sheffield, Department of Archaeology and Prehistory.

Barringer, C. (ed.), 1984. *Aspects of East Anglian Prehistory*. Norwich: Geo Books.

Bartholin, T.S., 1978. Alvastra pile dwelling: tree studies. *Fornvännen* 73, 213–19.

Barton, R.N.E., 1987. Vertical distribution of artifacts and some post-depositional factors affecting site formation, in Rowley-Conwy *et al.* (eds.), 55–64.

Barton, R.N.E., 1992. *Hengistbury Head, Dorset*, vol. 2: *The Late Upper Palaeolithic and Early Mesolithic Sites*. (Oxford University Committee for Archaeology Monograph 34.) Oxford: Oxford University Committee for Archaeology.

Barton, R.N.E., 1998. Long blade technology and the question of British late Pleistocene/early Holocene lithic assemblages, in Ashton *et al.* (eds.), 158–64.

Barton, R.N.E. & A. Roberts, 1996. Reviewing the British Late Upper Palaeolithic: new evidence for chronological patterning in the late glacial record. *Oxford Journal of Archaeology* 15, 245–65.

Bass, W.M., 1992. *Human Osteology: a Laboratory and Field Manual*. Columbia (MO): Missouri Archaeological Society.

Becker, B., 1983. Prehistoric dendrochronology for archaeological dating, in *C14 and Archaeology*, eds. W.G. Mook & H.T. Waterbolk. *PACT* 8, 503–10.

Behre, K.E., 1981. The interpretation of anthropogenic indicators in pollen diagrams. *Pollen et Spores* 23, 225–45.

Bersu, G., 1936. Rössener Wohnhäuser vom Goldberg, O.A.

Neresheim, Württemberg. *Germania* 20, 229–43.

Bersu, G., 1938. Excavations at Woodbury, near Salisbury, Wiltshire. *Proceedings of the Prehistoric Society* 4, 308–13.

Binford, L.R., 1981. *Bones: Ancient Men and Modern Myths.* London: Academic Press.

Birks, H.J.B., 1973. *Past and Present Vegetation of the Isle of Skye.* London: Cambridge University Press.

Bloch, M., 1995. People into places: Zafimaniry concepts of clarity, in Hirsch & O'Hanlon (eds.), 63–77.

Bloch, M., 1998. Why trees, too, are good to think with: towards an anthropology of the meaning of life, in Rival (ed.), 39–55.

Bloch, M. & J. Parry, 1982. *Death and the Regeneration of Life.* Cambridge: Cambridge University Press.

Bloomfield, C., 1951. Experiments on the mechanism of gley formation. *Journal of Soil Science* 2, 196–211.

Bonsall, C. (ed.), 1977. *Gazetteer of Upper Palaeolithic Sites in England and Wales.* (Council for British Archaeology Research Report 22.) Norwich: CBA.

Borges, J.L., 1973. New refutation of time, in *Other Inquisitions.* London: Souvenir Press.

Bowden, M. & D. McOmish, 1987. The required barrier. *Scottish Archaeological Review* 4, 76–84.

Bradley, R., 1984. Sieving for soil marks. *Oxford Journal of Archaeology* 3.3, 71–6.

Bradley, R., 1993a. *Altering the Earth.* Edinburgh: Society of Antiquaries of Scotland.

Bradley, R., 1993b. Where is East Anglia? Themes in regional prehistory, in *Flatlands and Wetlands*, ed. J. Gardiner. (East Anglian Archaeology 50.) Norwich: Scole Archaeological Committee, 5–13.

Bradley, R., 1998a. *The Significance of Monuments.* London: Routledge.

Bradley, R., 1998b. Interpreting enclosures, in *Understanding the Neolithic of North-Western Europe*, eds. M. Edmonds & C. Richards. Glasgow: Cruithne Press, 188–203.

Bradley, R., 2000. *An Archaeology of Natural Places.* London: Routledge.

Bradley, R. & J. Gardiner (eds.), 1984. *Neolithic Studies: a Review of some Current Research.* (British Archaeological Reports, British Series 133.) Oxford: BAR.

Bradley, R., R.A. Chambers & C.E. Halpin, 1984. *Excavations at Barrow Hills, Radley, Oxfordshire, 1983–84.* Oxford: Oxford Archaeological Unit.

Brennand, M. & M. Taylor, in press. The survey and excavation of a Bronze Age timber circle at Holme-next-the-Sea, Norfolk 1998–9. *Proceedings of the Prehistoric Society.*

Bridge, M., 1983. The Use of Tree-ring Widths as a Means of Dating Timbers. Unpublished PhD thesis, Portsmouth Polytechnic.

Bridges, E.M., 1978. Interaction of soil and mankind in Britain. *Journal of Soil Science* 29, 125–39.

Brommage, T.G. & A. Boyde, 1984. Microscopic criteria for the directionality of cutmarks on bone. *American Journal of Physical Anthropology* 65, 359–66.

Brothwell, D.R., 1971. Forensic aspects of the so-called skeleton Q1 from Maiden Castle, Dorset. *World Archaeology* 3, 233–41.

Brothwell, D.R., 1981. *Digging up Bones.* 3rd edition. London: British Museum.

Brown, A.E., 1983. Orton Longueville. *Northamptonshire Archaeology* 18, 171–2.

Brown, A.G., 2000. Floodplain vegetation history: Clearings as potential ritual spaces?, in Fairburn (ed.), 49–62.

Brown, D., M.A.R. Munro, M.G.L. Baillie & J.R. Pilcher, 1986. Dendrochronology — the absolute Irish standard. *Radiocarbon* 28, 279–83.

Brück, J., 1995. A place for the dead: the role of human remains in Late Bronze Age Britain. *Proceedings of the Prehistoric Society* 61, 245–77.

Buikstra, J.E. & D.H. Ubelaker, 1994. *Standards for Data Collection from Human Skeletal Remains.* (Arkansas Archaeological Survey Research Series 44.) Fayetteville (AR): Arkansas Archaeological Survey.

Bullock, P. & C.P. Murphy (eds.), 1983. *Soil Micromorphology.* Berkhamsted: AB Academic.

Bullock, P., C.P. Murphy & P.J. Waller, 1985a. *The Preparation of Thin Sections of Soils and Unconsolidated Sediments.* Albrighton: Waine Research.

Bullock, P., N. Fedoroff, A. Jongerius, G. Stoops & T. Tursina, 1985b. *Handbook for Soil Thin Section Description.* Wolverhampton: Waine Research.

Burgess, C., P. Topping, C. Mordant & M. Maddison (eds.), 1988. *Enclosures and Defences in the Neolithic of Western Europe.* (British Archaeological Reports, International Series, S403.) Oxford: BAR.

Burl, A., 1981. *Rites of the Gods.* London: J.M. Dent & Sons.

Burnez, C. & C. Louboutin, 2002. The causewayed enclosures of western-central France from the beginning of the fourth to the end of the third millennium, in Varndell & Topping (eds.), 11–27.

Butler, A., P. Clay & J. Thomas, 2002. A causewayed enclosure at Husbands Bosworth, Leicestershire, in Varndell & Topping (eds.), 107–9.

Buttler, W. & W. Haberey, 1936. *Die bandkeramische Ansiedlung bei Köln-Lindenthal.* Berlin.

Cambridgeshire SMR = Sites and Monuments Record for Cambridgeshire, Cambridgeshire County Council.

Caple, C. & W. Murray, 1989. *The Composition and Conservation Potential of the Charred Structural Timbers from the Haddenham Long Barrow.* Durham Archaeological Conservation and Research Report. Archive report.

Care, V., 1982. The collection and distribution of lithic materials during the Mesolithic and Neolithic periods in southern England. *Oxford Journal of Archaeology* 1, 269–85.

Case, H., 1956. The Neolithic causewayed camp at Abingdon, Berks. *Archaeological Journal* 36, 11–30.

Case, H.J. & A.W.R. Whittle, 1982. *Settlement Patterns in the Oxford Region: Excavations at the Abingdon Enclosure and Other Sites.* Oxford/London: Council for British Archaeology.

Cassen, S., C. Audran, S. Hinguant, G. Lannuzel & G. Marchand, 1998. L'habitat Villeneuve-Saint-Germain du Haut Mée (Saint-Étienne-en-Coglès, Ille-et-Vilaine). *Bulletin de la Société Préhistorique Française* 95, 41–75.

Childe, V.G., 1936. Review of Buttler & Haberey 1936. *Antiquity* 10, 502–4.

Childe, V.G., 1949. The origin of Neolithic culture in northern Europe. *Antiquity* 23, 129–35.

Childe, V.G., 1957. *The Dawn of European Civilisation.* 6th edition. London: Routledge & Paul.

Clark, J.G.D., 1932. *The Mesolithic Age in Britain.* Cambridge: Cambridge University Press.

Clark, J.G.D., 1936. The Köln-Lindenthal excavations. *Proceedings of the Prehistoric Society* 2, 245–6.

Clark, J.G.D., 1939. *Archaeology and Society.* London: Methuen.

Clark, J.G.D. 1955. A microlithic industry from the Cambridgeshire fenland and other industries of Sauveterrain affinities from Britain. *Proceedings of the Prehistoric Society* 21, 3–20.

Clark, J.G.D., 1989. *Prehistory at Cambridge and Beyond.* Cambridge: University Press.

Clark, J.G.D. & H. Godwin, 1962. The Neolithic in the Cambridgeshire fens. *Antiquity* 36, 10–23.

Clark, J.G.D., H. Godwin, M.E. Godwin & W.A. MacFadyen, 1933. Report on an Early Bronze Age site in the south-eastern Fens. *Antiquaries Journal* 13, 266–96.

Clark, J.G.D., H. Godwin & M.H. Clifford, 1935. Report on excavations at Peacock's Farm, Shippea Hill, Cambridgeshire. *Antiquaries Journal* 15, 283–319.

Clark, J.G.D., E.S. Higgs & I.H. Longworth, 1960. Excavations at the Neolithic site at Hurst Fen, Mildenhall, Suffolk, 1954, 1957 and 1958. *Proceedings of the Prehistoric Society* 26, 202–45.

Clarke, D.L., 1968. *Analytical Archaeology.* London: Methuen.

Clarke, D.L., 1972. A provisional model of an Iron Age society and its settlement system, in *Models in Archaeology*, ed. D.L. Clarke. London: Methuen, 801–85.

Clarke, D.L. 1973. Archaeology: the loss of innocence. *Antiquity* 47, 6–18.

Cleal, R., 1984. The later Neolithic in eastern England, in Bradley & Gardiner (eds.), 135–58.

Cleal, R., K.E. Walker & R. Montague, 1995. *Stonehenge in its Landscape.* London: English Heritage.

Clutton-Brock, J., 1984. *Excavations at Grimes Graves 1972–76*, fascicule 1: *Neolithic Antler Picks from Grimes Graves, Norfolk, and Durrington Walls, Wiltshire.* London: British Museum Press.

Coles, B.J., 1990. Anthropomorphic wooden figurines from Britian and Ireland. *Proceedings of the Prehistoric Society* 56, 315–33.

Coles, B., 1998. Doggerland: a speculative survey. *Proceedings of the Prehistoric Society* 64, 45–81.

Coles, B., 1999. Doggerland's loss and the Neolithic, in *Bog Bodies, Sacred Sites and Wetland Archaeology*, eds. J. Coles & M.S. Tørgensen. Exeter WARP.

Coles, B., 2001. Wood species for wooden figures: a glimpse of a pattern, in Gibson & Simpson (eds.), 163–73.

Coles, B. & J.M. Coles, 1986. *Sweet Track to Glastonbury: the Somerset Levels in Prehistory.* London.

Coles, J.M & D.D.A. Simpson, 1965. The excavation of a Neolithic round barrow at Pitnacree, Perthshire, Scotland. *Proceedings of the Prehistoric Society* 31, 34–57.

Coles, J.M. & A.J. Lawson (eds.), 1987. *European Wetlands in Prehistory.* Oxford: Clarendon Press.

Coles, J.M., F.A. Hibbert & B.J. Orme, 1973. Prehistoric roads and tracks in Somerest: 3. The Sweet Track. *Proceedings of the Prehistoric Society* 39, 256–93.

Coles, J.M., *et al.* 1983. *Somerset Levels Papers No. 9.* Cambridge and Exeter.

Conneller, C., forthcoming. Two Cambridgeshire Mesolithic sites. *Proceedings of the Cambridge Antiquarian Society.*

Cook, J., 1986a. Marked human bones from Gough's Cave, Somerset. *Proceedings of the University of Bristol Spelaeological Society* 17(3), 275–85.

Cook, J., 1986b. The application of scanning electron microscopy to taphonomic and archaeological problems, in *Studies in the Upper Palaeolithic of Britain and Northwest Europe*, ed. D. Roe (British Archaeological Reports, International Series, S296). Oxford: BAR, 143–62.

Cook, J., 1991. Preliminary report on marked human bones from the 1986–1987 excavations at Gough's Cave, Somerset, England, in *The Late Glacial in Northwest Europe*, eds. N. Barton, A.J. Roberts & D.A. Roe (CBA Research Report 77). London: CBA, 160–68.

Cotterell, B. & J. Kamminga, 1979. The mechanics of flaking, in *Lithic Use-Wear Analysis*, ed. B. Hayden. New York: Academic Press, 97–112.

Cotterell, B. & J. Kamminga, 1987. The formation of flakes. *American Antiquity* 52, 675–708.

Courty, M.A. & N. Fedoroff, 1982. Micromorphology of a Holocene dwelling, in *Proceedings of the 2nd Nordic Conference of Scientific Methods in Archaeology, Denmark, 1981*, 2, 7, II, 257–77.

Crone, B.A., 1988. Dendrochronology and the Study of Crannogs. Unpublished PhD thesis, University of Sheffield.

Crowson, A., 2000. Feltwell Anchor, Feltwell, in Crowson *et al.* (eds.), 182–7.

Crowson, A., T. Lane & J. Reeve (eds.), 2000. *The Fenland Management Project: Summary Volume.* (Lincolnshire Archaeology & Heritage Reports Series No. 3.) Norwich: Norfolk Archaeological Unit.

Daniel, G., 1950. *The Prehistoric Chamber Tombs of England and Wales.* London: Hutchinson.

Darby, H.C., 1940. *The Draining of the Fens.* Cambridge: Cambridge University Press.

Darby, H.C., 1956. *The Draining of the Fens.* 2nd edition. Cambridge: Cambridge University Press.

Darvill, T., 1996. Neolithic buildings in England, Wales and the Isle of Man, in Darvill & Thomas (eds.), 77–112.

Darvill, T. & J. Thomas (eds.), 1996. *Neolithic Houses in Northwest Europe and Beyond.* Oxford: Oxbow.

Dawson, M., 2000. The Mesolithic interlude, in Dawson (ed.), 45–50.

Dawson, M. (ed.), 2000. *Prehistoric, Roman and Post-Roman Landscapes of the Great Ouse Valley.* (Council for British Archaeology Research Report 119). York: CBA.

de Laet, S.J., 1958. *The Low Countries.* London: Thames & Hudson.

Degerbøl, M. & B. Fredskild, 1970. *The Urus and Neolithic Domesticated Cattle in Denmark.* (Det Kongelige Danske Videnskabernes Selskab Biologiske Skrifter 17(1).) Copenhagen: Munksgaard.

Drew, C.D. & S. Piggott, 1936. Excavation of long barrow 163a on Thickthorn Down, Dorset. *Proceedings of the Prehistoric Society* 2, 77–96.

Duchaufour, P.L., 1982. *Pedology*. London: George Allen & Unwin.

Dugdale, W., 1772 [1662]. *The History of Imbanking and Draining of divers Fens and Marshes*. London. (2nd ed. by C.N. Cole).

Dumont, J.V., 1987. Mesolithic microwear research in Northwest Europe, in Rowley-Conwy *et al.* (eds.), 82–92.

Edmonds, M., 1993. Interpreting causewayed enclosures in the past and the present, in Tilley (ed.), 99–142.

Edmonds, M., 1997. Taskscape, technology and tradition. *Analecta Praehistorica Leidensia* 29, 99–110.

Edmonds, M., 1999. *Ancestral Geographies of the Neolithic: Landscapes, Monuments and Memory*. London: Routledge.

Edmonds, M., C. Evans & D. Gibson, 1999. Assembly and collection — lithic complexes in the Cambridgeshire fenlands. *Proceedings of the Prehistoric Society* 65, 47–82.

Elstobb, W., 1793. *An Historical Account of the Great Level of the Fens*. London: Crowder.

Ellis, C.J., forthcoming. *A Prehistoric Ritual Complex at Eynesbury, Cambridgeshire: Excavation of a multi-period Site in the Great Ouse Valley, 2000–2001*. East Anglian Archaeology.

Entwistle, R. & A. Grant, 1989. The evidence for cereal cultivation and animal husbandry in the southern British Neolithic and Bronze Age, in *The Beginnings of Agriculture*, eds. A. Milles, D. Williams & N. Gardner. (British Archaeological Reports, International Series, S196.) Oxford: BAR, 203–15.

Evans, C., 1984. A shrine provenance for the Willingham Fen hoard. *Antiquity* 58, 212–14.

Evans, C., 1985. Tradition and the cultural landscape: an archaeology of place. *Archaeological Review from Cambridge* 4, 80–94.

Evans, C., 1987. 'Nomads in Waterland'? — Prehistoric transhumance and Fenland archaeology. *Proceedings of the Cambridge Antiquarian Society* 76, 27–39.

Evans, C., 1988a. Excavations at Haddenham, Cambridgeshire; A 'planned' enclosure and its regional affinities, in Burgess *et al.* (eds.), 127–48.

Evans, C., 1988b. Monuments and analogy: the interpretation of causewayed enclosures, in Burgess *et al.* (eds.), 47–73.

Evans, C., 1988c. Acts of Enclosure: a consideration of concentrically-organised causewayed enclosures, in Barrett & Kinnes (eds.), 85–96.

Evans, C., 1989b. Perishables and worldly goods: artefact decoration and classification in the light of recent wetlands research. *Oxford Journal of Archaeology* 8, 179–201.

Evans, C., 1992. Commanding gestures in lowlands: the investigation of two Iron Age ringworks. *Fenland Research* 7, 16–26.

Evans, C., 1993. Sampling settlements: investigations at Lingwood Farm, Cottenham and Eye Hill Farm, Soham. *Fenland Research* 8, 26–30.

Evans, C., 1997a. Hydraulic communities: Iron Age enclosure in the East Anglian Fenlands, in *Reconstructing Iron Age Societies: New Approaches to the British Iron Age*, eds. A. Gwilt & C. Haselgrove. (Oxbow Monograph 71.) Oxford: Oxbow, 216–27.

Evans, C., 1997b. Sentimental prehistories: the construction of the Fenland past. *Journal of European Archaeology*, 105–36.

Evans, C., 1998. Constructing houses and building context: Bersu's Manx Roundhouse Campaign. *Proceedings of the Prehistoric Society* 64, 183–201.

Evans, C., 1999a. The Lingwood Wells: a waterlogged first millennium BC settlement at Cottenham, Cambridgeshire. *Proceedings of the Cambridge Antiquarian Society* 87, 11–30.

Evans, C., 1999b. Cognitive maps and narrative trails: fieldwork with the Tamu-mai/Gurung of Nepal, in *Shaping Your Landscape: the Archaeology and Anthropology of Landscape*, eds. R. Layton & P. Ucko. London: Routledge, 439–57.

Evans, C., 2000a. Wardy Hill, Coveney, in Crowson *et al.* (eds.), 44–51.

Evans, C., 2000b. Langwood Farm West and environs, in Crowson *et al.* (eds.), 25–36.

Evans, C., 2000c. Testing the ground — sampling strategies, in Crowson *et al.* (eds.), 15–21.

Evans, C., 2000d. Megalithic follies: Soane's 'druidic remains' and the display of monuments. *Journal of Material Culture* 5, 347–66.

Evans, C., 2002. Metalwork and 'cold claylands': pre-Iron Age occupation on the Isle of Ely, in *Through Wet and Dry: Proceedings of a Conference in Honour of David Hall*, eds. T. Lane & J. Coles. Lincolnshire Archaeology and Heritage Reports Series No. 5/WARP Occasional Paper 17, 33–53.

Evans, C., 2003a. *Power and Island Communities: Excavations at the Wardy Hill Ringwork, Coveney, Ely*. (East Anglian Archaeology 103).

Evans, C., 2003b. Britons and Romans at Chatteris: Investigations at Langwood Farm, Cambridgeshire. *Britannia* 34, 175–264.

Evans, C. & I. Hodder, 1984. Excavations at Haddenham. *Fenland Research* 1, 32–6.

Evans, C. & I. Hodder, 1985. The Black Fen-edge. *Popular Archaeology* 6(10), 32–40.

Evans, C. & I. Hodder, 1988. The Haddenham Project — 1987: the Upper Delphs. *Fenland Research* 5, 7–14.

Evans, C. & M. Knight, 1997. *The Barleycroft Paddocks*. (Cambridge Archaeological Unit Report 218.) Cambridge: Cambridge Archaeological Unit.

Evans, C. & M. Knight, 2000. A Fenland delta: later prehistoric land-use in the lower Ouse Reaches, in Dawson (ed.), 89–106.

Evans, C. & M. Knight, 2001. The 'community of builders': The Barleycroft Post Alignments, in *Bronze Age Landscapes: Tradition and Transformation*, ed. J. Bruck. Oxford: Oxbow, 83–98.

Evans, C. & M. Knight, 2002. 'A great circle': investigations at Arbury Camp, Cambridge. *Proceedings of the Cambridge*

*Antiquarian Society* 91, 23–53.

Evans, C. & D. Serjeantson, 1988. The backwater economy of a fen-edge community in the Iron Age: the Upper Delphs, Haddenham. *Antiquity* 62, 381–400.

Evans, C. & L. Webley, 2003. *A Delta Landscape: the Over Lowland Investigations II.* (Cambridge Archaeological Unit Report 556.)

Evans, C., J. Pollard & M. Knight, 1999. Life in woods: Tree-throws, 'settlement' and forest cognition. *Oxford Journal of Archaeology* 18, 241–54.

Evans, J., 1881. A dug out canoe from Sutton, Cambridgeshire. *Committee of the Cambridge Antiquarian Society* 4, 195–6.

Evans, J., 1897. *The Ancient Stone Implements of Britain.* London: Longmans.

Evans, J.G. & D.D.A. Simpson, 1986. Radiocarbon dates for the Giants' Hills 2 long barrow, Skendleby, Lincolnshire, in *Archaeological Results for Accelerator Dating*, eds. J. Gowlett & R. Hedges. Oxford: Oxford University Press, 125–31.

Evelyn, J., 1664. *Silva, or a discourse of Forest-Trees.*

Faegri, K. & J. Iversen, 1975. *Textbook of Pollen Analysis.* Oxford: Blackwell Scientific Publications.

Fagan, B., 2001. *Grahame Clark: an Intellectual Biography of an Archaeologist.* Oxford: Westview Press.

Fairburn, A.S. (ed.), 2000. *Plants in Neolithic Britain and Beyond.* (Neolithic Studies Group Seminar Papers 5.) Oxford: Oxbow.

Fairweather, A.D. & I.B.M. Ralston, 1993. The Neolithic timber hall at Balbridie, Grampian region, Scotland: the building, the date, the plant macrofossils. *Antiquity* 67, 313–23.

Fedoroff, N., 1968. Genèse et morphologie des sols à horizon B textural en France atlantique. *Science du Sol* 1, 29–65.

Fedoroff, N., 1982. Soil fabric at the microscopic level, in *Constituents and Properties of Soils*, eds. M. Bonneau & B. Souchier. London: Academic Press.

Fell, C. & V. Davis, 1988. The petrological identification of stone implements from Cumbria, in *Stone Axe Studies (II)*, eds. T.H.M. Clough & W.A. Cummins. (CBA Research Report 67.) London: CBA, 71–7.

Fernandez, J. W., 1998. Trees of knowledge of self and other in culture: on models for the moral imagination, in Rival (ed.), 81–110.

Field, K., 1974. Ring-ditches of the upper and middle Great Ouse Valley. *Archaeological Journal* 31, 58–74.

Field, N., C. Matthews & I. Smith, 1964. New Neolithic sites in Dorset and Bedfordshire, with a note on the distribution of Neolithic storage pits in Britain. *Proceedings of the Prehistoric Society* 30, 352–81.

Fisher, P.F., 1982. A review of lessivage and Neolithic cultivation in southern England. *Journal of Archaeological Science* 9(3), 299–304.

Fisher, W.F., 2001. *Fluid Boundaries: Forming and Transforming Identity in Nepal.* New York (NY): Columbia University Press.

Ford, S., 1987. Chronological and functional aspects of flint assemblages, in *Lithic Analysis and Later British Prehistory*, eds. A.G. Brown & M.R. Edmonds. (British

Archaeological Reports, British Series, 162.) Oxford: BAR, 67–86.

Fox, C., 1926. A dug-out canoe from South Wales with notes on the typology and distribution of monoxylous craft in England and Wales. *Antiquaries Journal* 6, 121–51.

French, C.A.I., 1994. *Excavation of the Deeping St Nicholas Barrow Complex, South Lincolnshire.* Lincolnshire Archaeology and Heritage Report Series, No. 1.

French, C.A.I. & F.M.M Pryor, 1993. *The South West Fen Dyke Survey Project, 1982–86.* (East Anglian Archaeology 59). Peterborough: Fenland Archaeological Trust.

French, D.H., 1971. An experiment in water sieving. *Anatolian Studies* 21, 59–64.

Fulcheri, E., E. Rabino Massa & T. Doro Garetto, 1986. Differential diagnostics between palaeopathological and non-pathological post-mortem environmental factors in ancient human remains. *Journal of Human Evolution* 15, 71–5.

Garrow, D., 2002. *Archaeological Excavations at Norwich Road, Kilverstone, Norfolk.* (Cambridge Archaeological Unit Report 463.)

Garrow, D., 2003. *Excavations at Kilverstone: Broom Covert (Area E).* (Cambridge Archaeological Unit Report 518.)

Garthoff-Zwann, M., 1987. An ethnohistorical perspective in archaeology, in *Assendelver Polder Papers 1*, eds. R.W. Brandt, W. Groenman-van Waateringe & S.E. van der Leeuw. (Cingula 10.) Amsterdam: Amsterdam University, 333–8.

Garton, D., L. Elliott & C. Salisbury, 2001. Some fieldwork in Derbyshire by Trent and Peak Archaeological Unit in 1998–99: Aston-upon-Trent, Argosy Washolme (SK431291). *Derbyshire Archaeological Journal* 121, 196–200.

Gdaniec, K., 1996. A miniature antler bow from a Middle Bronze Age site at Isleham, Cambridgeshire, England. *Antiquity* 70, 652–7.

Gell, A., 1995. The language of the forest: landscape and phonological iconism in Umeda, in Hirsch & O'Hanlon (eds.), 232–54.

Gibbard, P. L., 1986. Flint gravels in the Quaternary of southeast England, in Sieveking & Hart (eds.), 141–9.

Gibson, A., 1985. A Neolithic enclosure at Grendon, Northants. *Antiquity* 59, 213–19.

Gibson, A., 2001. Hindwell and the Neolithic palisaded sites of Britain and Ireland, in Gibson & Simpson (eds.), 68–79.

Gibson, A. & A. McCormick, 1985. Archaeology at Grendon Quarry, Northamptonshire, part 1: Neolithic and Bronze Age sites excavated in 1974–75. *Northamptonshire Archaeology* 20, 23–66.

Gibson, A. & D. Simpson (eds.), 2001. *Prehistoric Ritual and Religion.* Stroud: Sutton.

Gilks, J.A., 1989. Cave burials of northern England. *British Archaeology* 11, 11–15.

Godwin, H., 1938. The origin of roddons. *Geographical Journal* 91, 241–50.

Godwin, H., 1978. *Fenland: its Ancient Past and Uncertain Future.* Cambridge: Cambridge University Press.

Greig, J.R.A., 1991. The British Isles, in *Progress in Old World*

*Palaeoethnobotany*, eds. W. van Zeist, K. Wasylikowa & K.E. Behre. Rotterdam: Balkema, 299–334.

Griffiths, D.R., N.J. Seeley, H. Chandra, G.V. Robins, D.A.C. McNeil & M.C.R. Symons, 1982. Trapped methyl radicals in chert. *Nature* 300, 435–6.

Griffiths, D.R., N.J. Seeley & M.C.R. Symons, 1986. Investigation of chert heating conditions using ESR spectroscopy, in Sieveking & Hart (eds.), 258–62.

Grigson, C., 1965. Measurements of bones, horn cores, antlers and teeth, in Smith (ed.), 145–67.

Grigson, C., 1982. Porridge and pannage: pig husbandry in Neolithic England, in *Archaeological Aspects of Woodland Ecology*, eds. M. Bell & S. Limbrey. (British Archaeological Reports, International Series, S146.) Oxford: BAR, 287–95.

Grinsell, L.V., 1975. *Barrow, Pyramid and Tomb*. London: Thames & Hudson.

Grygiel, R., 1986. The household cluster as a fundamental social unit of the Lengyel culture in the Polish lowlands. *Prace i Materialy Muzeum Archeologicznego i Etnograficznego w Lodzi, Seria Archeologiczna* 31, 43–334.

Gurney, D.A., 1985. *Phosphate Analysis of Soils: A Guide for the Field Archaeologist*. (Institute of Field Archaeologists Technical Paper 3.) Birmingham: Institute of Field Archaeologists.

Hall, D.N., 1992. *The Fenland Project No. 6: the Southwestern Cambridgeshire Fenlands* (East Anglian Archaeology Report 56.) Cambridge: Cambridgeshire Archaeological Committee.

Hall, D.N., 1996. *The Fenland Project Number 10: Cambridgeshire Survey, The Isle of Ely and Wisbech* (East Anglian Archaeology Report 79.) Cambridge: Cambridgeshire Archaeological Committee.

Hall, D.N. & J.M. Coles, 1994. *Fenland Survey: an Essay in Landscape and Persistence*. London: English Heritage.

Hall, D.N., C. Evans, I. Hodder & F. Pryor, 1987. The fenlands of East Anglia, England: Survey and excavation, in Coles & Lawson (eds.), 169–201.

Hammond, F.W., 1983. Phosphate analysis of archaeological sediments, in *Landscape Archaeology in Ireland*, eds. T. Reeves-Smyth & F. Hamond. (British Archaeological Reports, British Series, 116.) Oxford: BAR, 47–80.

Hassan, F.A., 1973. On the mechanics of population growth during the Neolithic. *Current Anthropology* 14 (5), 535–40.

Healey, E. & R. Robertson-Mackay, 1983. The lithic industries from Staines causewayed enclosure. *Lithics* 4, 1–27.

Healey, E. & R. Robertson-Mackay, 1987. The flint industry, in The Neolithic causewayed enclosure at Staines, Surrey: excavations 1961–63, R. Robertson-Mackay. *Proceedings of the Prehistoric Society* 53, 95–118.

Healy, F., 1984. Farming and field monuments: the Neolithic in Norfolk, in Barringer (ed.), 77–140.

Healy, F., 1988. *The Anglo-Saxon Cemetery at Spong Hill, North Elmham*, part VI: *Occupation during the Seventh to Second Millennia BC* (East Anglian Archaeology 39.) Norwich: Norfolk Archaeological Unit.

Healy, F., 1991. Lithics and pre-Iron Age pottery, in *The Wissey Embayment and the Fen Causeway*, R.J. Silvester.

(East Anglian Archaeology 52.) Dereham: Fenland Project Committee.

Healy, F., 1992. Neolithic and Bronze Age — A shopping list (Regional Research Priorities Special Section). *Fenland Research* 7, 3–6.

Healy, F., 1996. *The Fenland Project Number 11: The Wissey Embayment: Evidence for Pre-Iron Age Occupation* (East Anglian Archaeology 78.) Dereham: Norfolk Museums Service.

Healy, F., forthcoming. Hambledon Hill and its implications, in *Monuments and Material Culture: Papers on Neolithic and Bronze Age Britain in Honour of Isobel Smith*, eds. R.M.J. Cleal & J. Pollard.

Healy, F. & J. Harding, forthcoming. *Raunds Area Project: the Neolithic and Bronze Age Landscapes of West Cotton, Stanwick and Irthlingborough, Northamptonshire*. English Heritage Archaeological Monograph.

Hedges, J., 1983. *Isbister: a Chambered Tomb in Orkney*. (British Archaeological Reports, British Series, 115.) Oxford: BAR.

Hedges, J. & D. Buckley, 1978. Excavations at a Neolithic causewayed enclosure, Orsett, Essex, 1975. *Proceedings of the Prehistoric Society* 44, 219–308.

Heidenreich, C.E., 1978. Huron, in *Handbook of North American Indians: Northeast* (vol. 15), ed. B. Trigger. Washington (DC): Smithsonian Institution, 368–88.

Helbæk, H., 1952. Early crops in southern England. *Proceedings of the Prehistoric Society* 12, 194–229.

Henderson, J., 1988. Factors determining the state of preservation of human remains, in *Death, Decay and Reconstruction*, eds. A. Boddington, A.N. Garland & R.C. Janaway. Manchester: Manchester University Press.

Herne, A., 1988. A time and a place for the Grimston Bowl, in Barrett & Kinnes (eds.), 9–29.

Higgs, E.S. & C. Vita-Finzi 1972. Prehistoric economies: a territorial approach, in *Papers in Economic Prehistory*, ed. E.S. Higgs. Cambridge: Cambridge University Press, 27–36.

Hill, J.D., 1995. *Ritual and Rubbish in the Iron Age of Wessex*. (British Archaeological Reports, British Series 242.) Oxford: BAR.

Hillam, J., 1985. Theoretical and applied dendrochronology: how to make a date with a tree, in *The Archaeologist and the Laboratory*, ed. P. Phillips. (CBA Research Report 58.) London: CBA, 17–23.

Hillam, J., 1987. Dendrochronology — 20 years on. *Current Archaeology* 9, 358–63.

Hillam, J., R.A. Morgan & I. Tyers, 1987. Sapwood estimates and the dating of short ring sequences, in *Applications of Tree-Ring Studies*, ed. R.G.W. Ward. (British Archaeological Reports, International Series, S333.) Oxford: BAR, 165–85.

Hillam, J., C.M. Groves, D.M. Brown, M.G.L. Baillie, J.M. Coles & B.J. Coles, 1990. Dendrochronology of the English Neolithic. *Antiquity* 64, 210–20.

Hillman, G.C., 1981. Crop husbandry: evidence from macroscopic remains, in *The Environment in British Prehistory*, eds. I. Simmonds & M. Tooley. London: Duckworth, 183–91.

372

Hirsch, E. & M. O'Hanlon (eds.), 1995. *The Anthropology of Landscape: Perspectives on Place and Space*. Oxford: Oxford University Press.

Hodder, I., 1984. Burials, houses, women and men, in *Ideology, Power and Prehistory*, eds. D. Miller & C. Tilley. Cambridge: Cambridge University Press, 51–68.

Hodder, I., 1990. *The Domestication of Europe*. Oxford: Blackwell.

Hodder, I., 1992a. *Theory and Practice in Archaeology*. London: Routledge.

Hodder, I., 1992b. The Haddenham causewayed enclosure: a hermeneutic circle, in Hodder 1992a, 213–40.

Hodder, I., 1994. Architecture and meaning: the example of Neolithic houses and tombs, in Parker Pearson & Richards (eds.), 73–86.

Hodder, I., 1999a. *Archaeological Process: an Introduction*. Oxford: Blackwell.

Hodder, I., 1999b. The wet and the dry: symbolic archaeology in the Wetlands, in *Ancient Lakes: Their Cultural and Biological Diversity*, eds. H. Kawanabe, G.W. Coulter & A.C. Roosevelt. Ghent: Kenobi Productions, 61–73.

Hodder, I. & P. Shand, 1988. The Haddenham long barrow: an interim statement. *Antiquity* 62, 349–53.

Hodge, C.A.H. & R.S. Seale, 1966. *The Soils of the District around Cambridge*. Harpenden: Agricultural Research Council.

Hogg, A.H.A., 1940. A long barrow at West Rudham, Norfolk. *Norfolk Archaeology* 27, 315–31.

Holgate, R., 1988. *Neolithic Settlement of the Thames Basin*. (British Archaeological Reports, British Series, 194.) Oxford: BAR.

Houlder, C., 1963. A Neolithic settlement on Hazard Hill, Totnes. *Transactions of the Devon Archaeological Exploration Society* 21, 2–31.

Humphrey, C., 1995. Chiefly and shamanist landscapes in Mongolia, in Hirsch & O'Hanlon (eds.), 135–62.

Ingold, T., 1993. Conceptions of time and ancient society. *World Archaeology* 25, 152–74.

Ingold, T., 1995. Building, dwelling, living: how animals and people make themselves at home in the world, in *Shifting Contexts: Transformations in Anthropological Knowledge*, ed. M. Strathern. London: Routledge, 57–80.

Ingold, T., 2000. *The Perception of the Environment: Essays in Livelihood, Dwelling and Skill*. London: Routledge.

Jackson, D.A., 1976. The excavation of Neolithic and Bronze Age sites at Aldwincle, Northants, 1967–71. *Northamptonshire Archaeology* 11, 12–70.

Jackson, J.W., 1934. Report on the animal remains from Whitehawk Neolithic camp. *Antiquaries Journal* 14, 127–9.

Jackson, R.P.J. & T. Potter, 1996. *Excavations at Stonea, Cambridgeshire, 1980–85*. London: British Museum Press.

Jacobi, R.M., 1973. Aspects of the 'Mesolithic Age' in Great Britain, in *The Mesolithic in Europe*, ed. S.K. Kozlowski. Warsaw: Warsaw University Press, 238–65.

Jacobi, R.M., 1984. The Mesolithic of northern East Anglia, in Barringer (ed.), 43–76.

Jacobsen, T.W. & T. Cullen, 1981. A consideration of mortuary practices in Neolithic Greece: burials from Franchthi Cave, in *Mortality and Immortality: the Archaeology and Anthropology of Death*, eds. S.C. Humphrey & H. King. London: Academic Press, 79–101.

Jane, F.W., 1970. *The Structure of Wood*. London: Black.

Johnson, A.H., 1954–56. Examination of soil from Corrimony chambered cairn, Glenurquart, Inverness-shire, with special reference to phosphate content. *Proceedings of the Society of Antiquaries of Scotland* 88, 200–207.

Jones, D., 1998. Long barrows and Neolithic elongated enclosures in Lincolnshire: an analysis of the air photographic evidence. *Proceedings of the Prehistoric Society* 64, 83–114.

Jones, G., in press. Charred plant remains from the Neolithic settlement at Lismore Fields, Buxton, in The excavation of a Mesolithic and Neolithic settlement area at Lismore Fields, Buxton, Derbyshire, by D. Garton. *Proceedings of the Prehistoric Society*.

Jones, G. & R. Moss, 1993. The charred plant remains, in *Beeston Castle: a Report on the Excavations by Peter Hough and Laurence Keen, 1968–1985*, by P. Ellis. (HBMC Archaeological Report 23.) London: HBMC, 80–83.

Jongerius, A., 1970. Some morphological aspects of regrouping phenomena in Dutch soils. *Geoderma* 4, 311–31.

Jongerius, A., 1983. The role of micromorphology in agricultural research, in Bullock & Murphy (eds.), 111–38.

Jørgensen, S., 1985. *Tree-felling with Original Neolithic Flint Axes in Draved Wood*. Copenhagen: National Museum of Denmark.

Keeley, L. & D. Cahen, 1989. Early Neolithic forts and villages in north-east Belgium: a preliminary report. *Journal of Field Archaeology* 16, 157–76.

Kelly, R.L., 1995. *The Foraging Spectrum: Diversity in Hunter-Gatherer Lifeways*. London: Smithsonian Institution Press.

Kenward, H., A. Hall & A. Jones, 1980. A tested set of techniques for the extraction of plant and animal macrofossils from waterlogged deposits. *Science and Archaeology* 22, 2–15.

Kinnes, I., 1975. Monument function in British Neolithic burial practices. *World Archaeology* 7, 16–28.

Kinnes, I., 1979. *Round Barrows and Ring-Ditches in the British Neolithic*. London: British Museum Press.

Kinnes, I., 1988. The Cattleship Potemkin: the first Neolithic in Britain, in Barrett & Kinnes (eds.), 2–8.

Kinnes, I., 1992. *Non-megalithic Long Barrows and Allied Structures in the British Neolithic*. (British Museum Occasional Paper 52.) London: British Museum Press.

Kinnes, I. & I. Longworth, 1985. *Catalogue of the Excavated Prehistoric and Roman Material in the Greenwell Collection*. London: British Museum Press.

Kinnes, I., T. Schadla-Hall, P. Chadwick & P. Dean, 1983. Duggleby Howe reconsidered. *Archaeological Journal* 140, 83–108.

Kinnes, I., A. Gibson, J. Ambers, S. Bowman, M. Leese & R. Boast, 1991. Radiocarbon dating and British Beakers: the British Museum programme. *Scottish Archaeological Review* 8, 35–68.

Krech, S. (III), 1999. *The Ecological Indian: Myth and History*.

London: W.W. Norton & Co.

Kroeber, K.L., 1948. *Anthropology*. New York (NY): Harcourt Brace Jovanovich.

Kromer, B. & B. Becker, 1993. German oak and pine 14C calibration, 7200–9400 BC. *Radiocarbon* 35, 125–36.

Kromer, B., M. Rhein, M. Bruns, H. Schoch-Fischer, K.O. Münnich, M. Stuiver & B. Becker, 1986. Radiocarbon calibration data for the sixth to the eighth millennia BC. *Radiocarbon* 28, 954–60.

Last, J., 1996. Neolithic houses: a central European perspective, in Darvill & Thomas (eds.), 27–40.

Last, J., 1997. *Neolithic Activity Near Blaby's Drove, Sutton: an Archaeological Evaluation* (Cambs. County Council Archaeological Field Unit Report 131.)

Layton, R. & R. Barton, 2001. Warfare and human social evolution, in *Ethnoarchaeology and Hunter-Gatherers: Pictures at an Exhibition*, eds. K.J. Fewster & M. Zvelebil, (British Archaeological Reports, International Series, 955.) Oxford: Hadrian Books, 13–24.

Legge, A.J., 1981a. Aspects of cattle husbandry, in *Farming Practice in British Prehistory*, ed. R. Mercer. Edinburgh: Edinburgh University Press, 169–81.

Legge, A.J., 1981b. The agricultural economy, in *Grimes Graves, Norfolk: Excavations 1971–72*, by R. Mercer. (Department of the Environment Research Reports 11.) London: HMSO, 79–103.

Legge, A.J., 1989. Milking the evidence: a reply to Entwhistle and Grant, in *The Beginnings of Agriculture*, eds. A. Milles, D. Williams & N. Gardener. (British Archaeological Reports, International Series, S496.) Oxford: BAR, 217–42.

Legge, A.J., 1991. Animal remains from Neolithic and Bronze Age sites at Down Farm, in *Papers on the Prehistory of Cranbourne Chase*, eds. J. Barrett, R. Bradley & M. Hall. Oxford: Oxbow, 54–100.

Legge, A.J., 1992. *Excavations at Grimes Graves, Norfolk 1972–1976, fasc. 4: Animals, Environment and Bronze Age Economy*. London: British Museum Press.

Lethbridge, T.C., 1935. Investigation of an ancient causeway in the fen between Fordey and Little Thetford. *Proceedings of the Cambridge Antiquarian Society* 35, 86–9.

Leuschner, H.H. & A. Delorme, 1986. Verlangerung der Göttinger absoluten Eichenchronologie bis 6255 v. chr. *Archäologisches Korrespondenzblatt* 16, 481–4.

Levi-Strauss, C., 1973. *Tristes Tropiques*. London: Jonathan Cape.

Limbrey, S., 1975. *Soil Science and Archaeology*. London: Academic Press.

Linick, T.W., H.E. Suess & B. Becker, 1985. La Jolla measurements of radiocarbon in south German oak tree-ring chronologies. *Radiocarbon* 27, 20–32.

Longworth, I.H., 1960. The pottery, in Clark *et al.* (eds.), 202–45.

Longworth, I., G. Wainwright & K. Wilson, 1971. The Grooved Ware site at Lion Point, Clacton. *British Museum Quarterly* 35, 93–124.

Louwe Kooijmans, L.P., 1987. Neolithic settlement and subsistence in the wetlands of the Rhine/Meuse Delta of the Netherlands, in Coles & Lawson (eds.), 227–51.

Loveday, P., 1989. The Barford ritual complex: further excavations (1972) and a regional perspective, in *Midlands Prehistory*, ed. A. Gibson. (British Archaeological Reports, British Series, 204.) Oxford: BAR, 51–84.

Lucas, C., 1930. *The Fenman's World*. London: Jarrold.

Lucas, G. & G.A. Wait, 1996. *Archaeological Investigations at Fen Drayton Reservoir, Fen Drayton, Cambridgeshire*. (Cambridge Archaeological Unit Report 195.)

Lynch, F., 1969. The contents of excavated tombs in North Wales, in *Megalithic Enquiries in the West of Britain*, ed. T.G.E. Powell. Liverpool: Liverpool University Press, 107–74.

Macfarlane, A., 1976. *Resources and Population: a Study of the Gurungs of Nepal*. Cambridge: Cambridge University Press.

Mackreth *et al.*, forthcoming. *Two Neolithic and Bronze Age Burial Sites in Orton Meadows, Peterborough*. East Anglian Archaeology.

Macphail, R.I., 1985a. *Soil Report on Balksbury Camp, Hants*. London: AMLR 4621.

Macphail, R.I., 1985b. *Soil Report on Hazleton Long Cairn, Gloucestershire*. HBMC 1 AM ARCH (3SP) 186.

Macphail, R.I., 1986. Palaeosols in archaeology: their role in understanding Flandrian pedogenesis, in *Palaeosols: their Recognition and Interpretation*, ed. V.P. Wright. Oxford: Blackwell Scientific, 263–90.

Macphail, R.I., 1987. A review of soil science in archaeology in England, in *Environmental Archaeology: a Regional Review* vol. II, ed. H.C.M. Keeley. London: HBMCE, 332–77.

Macphail, R.I., J.C.C. Romans & L. Robertson, 1987. The application of micromorphology to the understanding of Holocene soil development in the British Isles; with special reference to early cultivation, in *Soil Micromorphology*, eds. N. Fedoroff, L.M. Bresson & M.A. Courty. Plaiser: AFES, 647–56.

Madsen, T., 1988. Causewayed enclosures in southern Scandinavia, in Burgess *et al.* (eds.), 301–37.

Malim, T., 2000. The ritual landscape of the Neolithic and Bronze Age along the middle and lower Ouse Valley, in Dawson (ed.), 57–88.

Manby, T.G., 1974. *Grooved Ware Site in Yorkshire and the North of England*. (British Archaeological Reports, British Series 9.) London: BAR.

Manchester, K., 1983. *The Archaeology of Disease*. Bradford: University of Bradford.

Manguel, A., 1996. *A History of Reading*. Toronto: Alfred Knopf.

Martin, E., 1988. Swales Fen Suffolk: a Bronze Age cooking pit? *Antiquity* 52, 358–9.

Masters, L., 1973. The Lochhill long cairn. *Antiquity* 47, 96–100.

Matthews, C.L., 1976. *Occupation Sites on a Chiltern Ridge: Excavations at Puddlehill and Sites near Dunstable, Bedfordshire*, part I: *Neolithic, Bronze Age and Early Iron Age*. (British Archaeological Reports, British Series, 29.) Oxford: BAR.

McAvoy, F., 2000. The development of a Neolithic monument complex at Godmanchester, Cambridgeshire, in Dawson (ed.), 51–6.

McKeague, J.A., 1983. Clay skins and argillic horizons, in Bullock & Murphy (eds.), 367–88.

McKinley, J., 1989. Cremation: expectations, methodologies and realities, in *Burial Archaeology; Current Research and Development*, eds. C. Roberts, F. Lee & J. Bintliff (British Archaeological Reports, British Series, 211). Oxford: BAR.

Mercer, R., 1980. *Hambledon Hill — a Neolithic Landscape*. Edinburgh: Edinburgh University Press.

Mercer, R., 1988. Hambledon Hill, Dorset, England, in Burgess *et al.* (eds.), 89–107.

Mercer, R. & F. Healy, forthcoming. *Hambledon Hill, Dorset, England, Excavation and Survey of a Neolithic Monument Complex and its Surround Landscape*. English Heritage Archaeological Report.

Messerschmidt, D.A., 1976. *The Gurungs of Nepal: Conflict and Change in a Village Society*. Warminster: Aris & Phillips.

Middleton, H.R., 1990. The Walker Collection: a quantitative analysis of lithic material from the March/Manea area of the Cambridgeshire Fens. *Proceedings of the Cambridge Antiquarian Society* 79, 13–38.

Miller, S.H. & S.B.J. Skertchly, 1878. *The Fenland Past and Present*. London.

Milles, A., 1986. Charred remains of barley and other plants from Scord of Brouster, in *Scord of Brouster: an Early Agricultural Settlement on Shetland*, by A. Whittle, M. Keith-Lucas, A. Milles, B. Noddle, S. Rees & J.C.C. Romans (Oxford University Committee for Archaeology Monograph 9.) Oxford: Oxford University Press, 119–24.

Mills, C., 1988. Dendrochronology: The long and the short of it, in Slater & Tate (eds.), 549–66.

Milsom, S.J., 1979. Within- and Between-tree Variation in Certain Properties of Annual Rings of Sessile Oaks, Quercus petraea (Mattuschka) Liebl., as a Source of Dendrochronological Information. Unpublished PhD thesis, Liverpool Polytechnic.

Moffet, L., M.A. Robinson & V. Straker, 1989. Cereals, fruit and nuts: charred plant remains from Neolithic sites in England and Wales and the Neolithic economy, in *The Beginnings of Agriculture*, eds. A. Milles, D. Williams & N. Gardner (British Archaeological Reports, International Series, S496). Oxford: BAR, 243–61.

Morgan, F. de M., 1959. The excavation of a long barrow at Nutbane, Hampshire. *Proceedings of the Prehistoric Society* 25, 15–51.

Morgan, R.A., 1988. *Tree-ring Studies of Wood Used in Neolithic and Bronze Age Trackways from the Somerset Levels*. (British Archaeological Reports, British Series, 184.) Oxford: BAR.

Morgan, R., 1990. Reconstructing a Neolithic mortuary chamber from the Fens in eastern England through tree-ring study, in *Experimentation and Reconstruction in Environmental Archaeology*, ed. D. Robinson. Oxford: Oxbow, 101–17.

Morgan, R.A., C.D. Litton & C.R. Salisbury, 1987. Trackways and tree trunks — dating Neolithic oaks in the British Isles. *Tree-Ring Bulletin* 47, 61–9.

Morris, M.G., & F.H. Perring (eds.), 1974. *The British Oak: its History and Natural History*. Faringdon: Classey.

Mortimer, R., 1995. *Archaeological Excavations at Low Fen, Fen Drayton, Cambridgeshire*. (Cambridge Archaeological Unit Report 156.)

Mortimer, R., 2000. Village development and ceramic sequence: the Middle to Late Saxon village at Lordship Lane, Cottenham, Cambridge. *Proceedings of the Cambridge Antiquarian Society* 89, 5–33.

Murphy, J. & J.P. Riley, 1962. A modified single solution method for the determination of phosphate in natural waters. *Anal. Chim. Acta* 27, 31–6.

Murphy, P., 1986. *Thin Section Preparation of Soils and Sediments*. Berkhamsted: AB Academic.

Murphy, P., 1988. Carbonised Neolithic plant remains from the Stumble, an intertidal site in the Blackwater Estuary, Essex, England. *Circaea* 6, 21–38.

Needham, S., 1991. *Excavation and Salvage at Runnymede Bridge, 1978: The Late Bronze Age Waterfront Site*. London: British Museum.

Needham, S., 1996. *Refuse and Disposal at Area 16 East Runnymede*. London: British Museum.

Northamptonshire Archaeology, 1998. Proposed Quarry Extension at Maxey, Cambridgeshire: Archaeological Assessment.

Okasha, M.K.M., 1987. Statistical Methods in Dendrochronology. Unpublished PhD thesis, University of Sheffield.

Olausson, D.S., 1983. Lithic technological analysis of the thin-butted flint axe. *Acta Archaeologia* 53, 1–87.

Olsen, S.L. & P. Shipman, 1988. Surface modification on bone; trampling versus butchery. *Journal of Archaeological Science* 15, 535–53.

Ortner, D.J. & W.G.J. Putschar, 1985. *Identification of Pathological Conditions in Human Skeletal Remains*. Washington (DC): Smithsonian Institution Press.

Oswald, A., C. Dyer & M. Barber, 2001. *The Creation of Monuments: Neolithic Causewayed Enclosures in the British Isles*. London: English Heritage.

Palmer, C. & M. Jones, 1991. Plant resources, in *Maiden Castle: Excavations and Field Survey 1985–6*, by N.M. Sharples. (HBMC Archaeological Report 19.) London: HBMC, 129–39.

Palmer, R., 1976. Interrupted ditch enclosures in Britain: the use of aerial photography for comparative studies. *Proceedings of the Prehistoric Society* 42, 161–86.

Paret, O., 1942. Vorgeschichtliche Wohngruben? *Germania* 26, 84–103.

Parker, R., 1983. *Town and Gown*. Cambridge: Stephens.

Parker, S., 1985. An Experimental and Comparative Study of Cremation Techniques. Unpublished MA dissertation, University of Sheffield.

Parker Pearson, M. & C. Richards, 1994. Ordering the world: perceptions of architecture, space and time, in Parker Pearson & Richards (eds.), 1–37.

Parker Pearson, M. & C. Richards (eds.), 1994. *Architecture and Order: Approaches to Social Space*. London: Routledge.

Pearson, G.W., 1986. Precise calendric dating of known growth period samples using a 'curve fitting' technique. *Radiocarbon* 28, 292–9.

Pearson, G.W. & M. Stuiver, 1986. High-precision calibration of the radiocarbon time scale, 500–2500 BC. *Radiocarbon* 28, 839–62.

Pearson, G.W., J.R. Pilcher, M.G.L. Baillie, D.M. Corbett & F. Qua, 1986. High-precision 14C measurement of Irish oaks to show the natural 14C variations from AD 1840–5210 BC. *Radiocarbon* 28, 911–34.

Phillips, C.W., 1935. A re-examination of the Therfield Heath Long Barrow, Royston, Hertfordshire. *Proceedings of the Prehistoric Society* 1, 101–7.

Phillips, C.W., 1936. The excavation of the Giants Hills long barrow, Skendleby, Lincolnshire. *Archaeologia* 85, 37–106.

Phillips, C.W., 1970. *The Fenland in Roman Times.* (Royal Geographical Society Research Series 5.) London: Royal Geographical Society.

Piggott, S., 1935. A note on the relative chronology of the English long barrows. *Proceedings of the Prehistoric Society* 1, 115–266.

Piggott, S., 1954. *The Neolithic Cultures of the British Isles.* Cambridge: Cambridge University Press.

Piggott, S., 1973. The Dalladies long barrow, NE Scotland. *Antiquity* 47, 32–6.

Pignede, B., 1993. *The Gurungs: a Himalayan Population of Nepal.* Kathmandu: Ratna Pustak Bhandar.

Pilcher, J.R., M.G.L. Baillie, B. Schmidt & B. Becker, 1984. A 7272-year European tree-ring chronology. *Nature* 312, 150–52.

Pitt Rivers, A., 1898. *Excavations in Cranborne Chase,* vol. 4. Privately published.

Pitts, M.W. & R.M. Jacobi, 1979. Some aspects of change in flaked stone industries of the Mesolithic and Neolithic in Southern Britain. *Journal of Archaeological Science* 6, 163–77.

Pollard, J., 1996. Iron Age riverside pit alignments at St Ives, Cambridgeshire. *Proceedings of the Prehistoric Society* 62, 93–115.

Pollard, J., 1998. *Excavations at Over: Late Neolithic Occupation (Sites 3 & 4).* (Cambridge Archaeological Unit Report 281.)

Pollard, J., 1999. 'These places have their moments': thoughts on settlement practices in the British Neolithic, in *Making Places in the Prehistoric World: Themes in Settlement Archaeology,* eds. J. Bruck & M. Goodman. London: UCL Press, 76–93.

Pollard, J., 2000. Neolithic occupation practices and social ecologies from Rinyo to Clacton, in *Neolithic Orkney in its European Context,* ed. A. Ritchie. (McDonald Institute Monographs.) Cambridge: McDonald Institute for Archaeological Research, 363–9.

Pollard, J., 2001. The aesthetics of depositional practice. *World Archaeology* 33(2), 315–33.

Pollard, J., 2002. The nature of archaeological deposits and finds assemblages, in *Prehistoric Britain: The Ceramic Basis,* eds. A. Woodward & J.D. Hill. (Prehistoric Ceramics Research Group Occasional Publication 3.) Oxford: Oxbow, 22–33.

Porter, E., 1969. *Cambridgeshire Customs and Folklore.* London: Routledge & Kegan Paul.

Price, J., 1992. Retrieving the larger structure. Ideas and case studies in lifting technology, in *Retrieval of Objects from Archaeological Sites.* Denbigh: Archetype Publications, 61–76.

Price, J. & M. Macqueen, 1988. Reflections on lifting Neolithic structures: a tale of two archaeological sites, in *Conservation Today. Papers Presented at the UKIC 30th Anniversary Conference.* London: United Kingdom Institute of Conservation, 117–22.

Pryor, F.M.M., 1974. *Excavation at Fengate, Peterborough, England: the First Report.* (Royal Ontario Museum Archaeology Monograph 3.) Toronto: Royal Ontario Museum.

Pryor, F.M.M., 1978. *Excavation at Fengate, Peterborough, England: the Second Report.* (Royal Ontario Museum Archaeology Monograph 5). Toronto: Royal Ontario Museum.

Pryor, F.M.M., 1982. Problems of survival: later prehistoric settlement in the southern East Anglian Fenlands. *Analecta Praehistorica Leidensia* 15, 125–43.

Pryor, F.M.M., 1988. Earlier Neolithic organised landscapes and ceremonial in lowland Britain, in Barrett & Kinnes (eds.), 63–72.

Pryor, F., 1998. *Etton — Excavations of a Neolithic Causewayed Enclosure Near Maxey, Cambridgeshire, 1982–7.* London: English Heritage.

Pryor, F.M.M., 2001a. *The Flag Fen Basin: Archaeology and Environment of a Fenland Landscape.* London: English Heritage.

Pryor, F.M.M., 2001b. *Seahenge: New Discoveries in Prehistoric Britain.* London: HarperCollins.

Pryor, F.M.M. & C.A.I. French, 1985. *Archaeology and Environment in the Lower Welland Valley.* (East Anglian Archaeology 27.) Cambridge: Cambridgeshire Archaeological Committee.

Pryor, F., C.A.I French & M. Taylor, 1985. An interim report on excavations at Etton, Maxey, Cambridgeshire, 1982–1984. *Antiquaries Journal* 65, 275–311.

Rackham, O., 1980. *Ancient Woodland: its History, Vegetation and Uses in England.* London: Edward Arnold.

Renfrew, C., 1973. Monuments, mobilization and social organization in Neolithic Wessex, in *The Explanation of Culture Change: Models in Prehistory,* ed. C. Renfrew. London: Duckworth, 539–58.

Renfrew, C., 1987. *Archaeology and Language: the Puzzle of Indo-European Origins.* London: Jonathan Cape.

Reynier, M.J., 1998. Early Mesolithic settlement in England and Wales, some preliminary observations, in Ashton *et al.* (eds.), 174–84.

Richards, C. & J. Thomas, 1984. Ritual activity and structured deposition in Later Neolithic Wessex, in Bradley & Gardiner (eds.), 189–218.

Rival, L., 1998. *The Social Life of Trees: Anthropological Perspectives on Tree Symbolism.* Oxford: Berg.

Robertson-Mackay, M., 1987. Excavations at Staines, Middlesex. *Proceedings of the Prehistoric Society* 63, 1–147.

Roe, D.A., 1968. *Gazetteer of British Lower and Middle Palaeolithic Sites.* (CBA Research Report 8.) London: CBA.

Romans, J.C.C. & L. Robertson, 1983. The general effects

of early agriculture on the soil, in *The Impact of Aerial Reconnaissance on Archaeology*, ed. G.S. Maxwell. (CBA Research Report 49.) London: CBA, 136–41.

Rowley-Conwy, P., 1999. Sir Grahame Clark, in *Encyclopaedia of Archaeology: the Great Archaeologists* (II), ed. T. Murray. Oxford: ABC-CLIO, 507–29.

Rowley-Conwy, P., 2000. Through a taphonomic glass darkly: the importance of cereal cultivation in prehistoric Britain, in *Taphonomy and Interpretation in Environmental Archaeology*, eds. J. Huntley & S. Stallibrass. Oxford: Oxbow, 43–53.

Rowley-Conwy, P., 2003. No fixed abode: nomadism in the Northwest European Neolithic, in *Formal Disposal of the Dead in Atlantic Europe during the Mesolithic–Neolithic Interface, 6000–3000 BC*, ed. G. Burenhult & S. Westergaard. (British Archaeological Reports, International Series, S1201.) Oxford: Archaeopress, 115–44.

Rowley-Conwy, P., 2004. How the west was lost: a reconsideration of agricultural origins in Britain, Ireland and southern Scandinavia. *Current Anthropology* 45(54), 83–113.

Rowley-Conwy, P., M. Zvelebil & H.P. Blankholm (eds.). 1987. *The Mesolithic of Northwest Europe: Recent Trends.* Sheffield: Sheffield University.

Russell, M.D., 1987. Mortuary practices at the Krapina Neanderthal site. *American Journal of Physical Anthropology* 72, 381–97.

Sahlins, M., 1974. *Stone Age Economics*. London: Tavistock Publications.

Saville, A., 1980a. On the measurement of struck flakes and flake tools. *Lithics* 1, 16–20.

Saville, A., 1980b. Five flint assemblages from excavated sites in Wiltshire. *Wiltshire Archaeological Magazine* 72/73, 1–27.

Saville, A., 1981a. Honey Hill, Elkington: a Northamptonshire Mesolithic site. *Northamptonshire Archaeology* 16, 1–13.

Saville, A., 1981b. Mesolithic industries in central England. *Archaeological Journal* 138, 49–71.

Saville, A., 1981c. *Grimes Graves, Norfolk, Excavations 1971–72 (II).* (Dept. of the Environment Archaeological Report No. 11.)

Saville, A. 1982. Carrying cores to Gloucestershire: some thoughts on lithic resource exploitation. *Lithics* 3, 22–5.

Saville, A., 1990. *Hazelton North: the Excavation of a Neolithic Long Cairn of the Cotswold–Severn Group.* London: English Heritage.

Saville, A., 2002. Lithic artefacts from Neolithic causewayed enclosures: character and meaning, in Varndell & Topping (eds.), 91–105.

Scaife, R.G. & R.I. Macphail, 1983. The post-Devensian development of heathland soils and vegetation, in *Soils of Heathland and Chalk Grasslands*, ed. P. Burnham. Ashford: Wye College, 70–99.

Scarre, C., 1998. Arenas of action? Enclosure entrances in Neolithic western France *c.* 3500–2500 BC. *Proceedings of the Prehistoric Society* 64, 115–37.

Schama, S., 1995. *Landscape and Memory*. London: Harper-Collins.

Scruton, R., 1982. *A Dictionary of Political Thought*. London: Macmillan.

Seaby, S.A., 1989. The Hillsborough Logboat, Cruimghlinn. *Bulletin of Experimental Archaeology* 10, 17–24.

Seale, R.S., 1975a. *Soils of the Ely District*. Harpenden: Soil Survey of Great Britain.

Seale, R.S., 1975b. *Soils of the Chatteris District of Cambridgeshire* (Sheet TL 38). Harpenden: Soil Survey of Great Britain.

Seale, R.S., 1980. Ancient courses of the Great and Little Ouse in Fenland. *Proceedings of the Cambridge Antiquarian Society* 69, 1–19.

Shell, C., 2002. Airborne high-resolution digital, visible, infra-red and thermal sensing for archaeology, in *Aerial Archaeology*, eds. R.H. Bewley & W. Raczkowski. Amsterdam & Oxford: IOS Press, 181–95.

Shennan, S., 1988. *Quantifying Archaeology*. Edinburgh: Edinburgh University Press.

Sherratt, A., 1990. The genesis of megaliths: monumentality, ethnicity and social complexity in Neolithic north-west Europe. *World Archaeology* 22, 147–67.

Shipman, P. & J. Rose, 1983. Early hominid butchering and carcass-processing behaviours: approaches to the fossil record. *Journal of Anthropological Archaeology* 2, 57–98.

Sieveking, G. de G. & M.B. Hart (eds.), 1986. *The Scientific Study of Flint and Chert*. Cambridge: Cambridge University Press.

Silvester, R.J., 1991. *The Fenland Project Number 4, Norfolk Survey. The Wissey Embayment and Fen Causeway.* (East Anglian Archaeology 52.) Dereham: Fenland Project Committee.

Skertchly, J.B.S., 1877. *The Geology of the Fenland*. Memoir of the Geological Survey of Great Britain.

Slager, S. & H.T.J. van de Wetering, 1977. Soil formation in archaeological pits and adjacent soils in southern Germany. *Journal of Archaeological Science* 4, 259–67.

Slater, E.A. & J.O. Tate (eds.), 1988. *Science and Archaeology, Glasgow, 1987.* (British Archaeological Reports, British Series, 196.) Oxford: BAR.

Smith, A.G., A. Whittle, E.W. Cloutman & L. Morgan, 1989. Mesolithic and Neolithic activity and environmental impact on the south-east fen-edge in Cambridgeshire. *Proceedings of the Prehistoric Society* 55, 207–49.

Smith, I., 1965. *Windmill Hill and Avebury, Excavations by Alexander Keillor, 1925–1939*. Oxford: Oxford University Press.

Smith, I., 1971. Causewayed enclosures, in *Economy and Settlement in Neolithic and Early Bronze Age Britain and Europe*, ed. D.D.A. Simpson. Leicester: Leicester University Press, 89–112.

Smith, P., 1997. Grahame Clark's New Archaeology: the Fenland Research Committee and Cambridge prehistory in the 1930s. *Antiquity* 71, 11–30.

Startin, W., 1982. Prehistoric earthmoving, in Case & Whittle (ed.), 153–6.

Startin, W. & R. Bradley, 1981. Some notes on work organisation and society in prehistoric Wessex, in *Astronomy and Society During the Period 4000–1500 BC*, eds. C. Ruggles & A. Whittle (British Archaeological Reports,

British Series, 88). Oxford: BAR, 289–96.

Steele, D.G. & C.A. Bramblett, 1988. *The Anatomy and Biology of the Human Skeleton.* Texas: A&M University Press.

Stuiver, M. & G.W. Pearson, 1986. High-precision calibration of the radiocarbon time scale, AD 1950–500 BC. *Radiocarbon* 28, 805–38.

Stuiver, M. & H.A. Polach, 1977. Reporting of $^{14}$C data. *Radiocarbon* 19, 355–63.

Stuiver, M. & P.J. Reimer, 1986. A computer program for radiocarbon age calculation. *Radiocarbon* 28, 1022–30.

Stuiver, M., B. Kromer, B. Becker & C.W. Ferguson, 1986. Radiocarbon age calibration back to 13,300 years BP and the $^{14}$C age-matching of the German oak and US bristlecone pine chronologies. *Radiocarbon* 28, 969–79.

Summers, D., 1976. *The Great Level.* London: Newton Abbot.

Tainter, J.A., 1978. Mortuary practices and the study of prehistoric social systems. *Advances in Archaeological Method and Theory* 1, 105–41.

Taylor, M., 1998. Wood and bark from the enclosure ditch, in Pryor 1998, 115–59.

Taylor, M., 2001. The wood, in Pryor 2001, 167–228.

Thomas, J., 1991. *Rethinking the Neolithic.* Cambridge: Cambridge University Press.

Thomas, J., 1996a. *Time, Culture and Identity.* London: Routledge.

Thomas, J., 1996b. Neolithic houses in mainland Britain and beyond — a sceptical view, in Darvill & Thomas (eds.), 1–12.

Thomas, J., 1999. *Understanding the Neolithic.* London: Routledge.

Thomas, J. & C. Tilley, 1993. The axe and the torso: symbolic structures in the Neolithic of Brittany, in Tilley (ed.), 225–324.

Thompson, E.P., 1968. *The Making of the English Working Class.* Harmondsworth: Penguin.

Thurnam, J., 1869. On four leaf and lozenge shaped javelin heads from an oval barrow near Stonehenge; and on the leaf-shaped type of flint arrowhead and its connection with long barrows. *Wiltshire Archaeological Magazine* 11, 40–49.

Tilley, C., 1979. *Post-glacial Communities in the Cambridge Region.* (British Archaeological Reports, British Series, 66). Oxford: BAR.

Tilley, C. (ed.), 1993. *Interpretative Archaeology.* Oxford: Berg.

Tilley, C., 1994. *A Phenomenology of Landscape.* Oxford: Berg.

Tilley, C., 1996. *An Ethnography of the Neolithic: Early Prehistoric Societies in Southern Scandinavia.* Cambridge: Cambridge University Press.

Tilley, C., 1999. *Metaphor and Material Culture.* Oxford: Blackwell.

Tringham, R., G. Cooper, G. Odell, B. Voytek & A. Whitman, 1974. Experimentation in the formation of edge damage: a new approach to lithic analysis. *Journal of Field Archaeology* 1, 171–96.

Turner, J., 1962. The *Tilia* decline: an anthropogenic interpetation. *New Phytologist* 61, 328–41.

Turner, V., 1967. *The Forest of Symbols: Aspects of Ndembu Ritual.* New York (NY): Cornell University Press.

Ubelaker, D.H., 1974. *Reconstruction of Demographic Profiles from Ossuary Skeletal Samples: a Case Study from Tideswater Potomac.* (Smithsonian Contributions to Anthropology 18.) Washington (DC): Smithsonian Institution Press.

Ubelaker, D.H., 1978. *Human Skeletal Remains: Excavation, Analysis, Interpretation.* Chicago (IL): Aldine.

Ucko, P.J., 1989. Ethnography and archaeological interpretation of funerary remains. *World Archaeology* 1, 262–80.

Ullrich, H., 1982. Artificial injuries on fossil human bones and the problem of cannibalism, skull-cult and burial rites. *Anthropos Brno* 21, 253–62.

Varley, G.C., 1978. The effects of insect defoliation on the growth of oaks in England, in *Dendrochronology in Europe,* ed. J.M. Fletcher. (British Archaeological Reports, International Series S51.) Oxford: BAR, 179–84.

Varndell, G. & P. Topping (eds.) 2002. *Enclosures in Neolithic Europe.* Oxford: Oxbow.

von den Dreisch, A., 1976. *A Guide to the Measurement of Animal Bones from Archaeological Sites.* Harvard (MA): Peabody Museum of Archaeology & Ethnology.

von Hugel, A., 1887. Some notes on the gold armilla found in Grunty Fen. *Communications of the Cambridge Antiquarian Society* 6, 96–105.

Vyner, B.E., 1984. The excavation of a Neolithic cairn at Street House, Loftus, Cleveland. *Proceedings of the Prehistoric Society,* 50, 151–95.

Wainwright, G., 1972. The excavation of a Neolithic settlement on Broome Heath, Ditchingham, Norfolk. *Proceedings of the Prehistoric Society* 38, 1–97.

Wait, G.A., 1992. *Archaeological Investigations at Fen Drayton Reservoir, Fen Drayton, Cambridgeshire.* (Cambridge Archaeological Unit Report 73.)

Wait, G., 2000. Stocking Drove Farm, Chatteris, in Crowson *et al.* (eds.), 36–9.

Wakely, J. & S.J. Wenham, 1988. Use of scanning electron microscopy in the study of trauma in human skeletal material from archaeological sites. *Journal of Anatomy* 158.

Waller, M., 1994. *The Fenland Project Number 9: Flandrian Environmental Change.* (East Anglian Archaeology 70.) Cambridge: Cambridgeshire Archaeological Committee.

Warren, S.H., S. Piggott, J.G.D. Clark, M. Burkitt & H. & M. Godwin, 1936. Archaeology of the submerged land-surface of the Essex coast. *Proceedings of the Prehistoric Society* 2, 178–210.

Weir, A.H., J.A. Catt & P.A. Madgett, 1971. Post-glacial soil formation in the loess of Pegwell Bay, Kent (England). *Geoderma* 5, 131–49.

Wells, C., 1974. Osteochrondritis dissecans in ancient British skeletal material. *Medical History* 18, 365–69.

Wells, S.H., 1830. *The History of the Drainage of the Great Level of the Fens.* London.

Wessex Archaeology, 2001. *Barford Road, Eynesbury, St. Neots, Cambridgeshire: Assessment Report.*

Wheeler, R.E.M., 1943. *Maiden Castle, Dorset.* Oxford: University Press.

Whittle, A., 1977. *The Earlier Neolithic of Southern England*

*and its Continental Background.* (British Archaeological Reports, British Series, 35.) Oxford: BAR.

Whittle, A., 1997. Moving on and moving around: Neolithic settlement mobility, in *Neolithic Landscapes*, ed. P. Topping. (Oxbow Monograph 86/Neolithic Studies Group Seminar Papers 2.) Oxford: Oxbow, 15–22.

Whittle, A., 1999. The Neolithic period, in *The Archaeology of Britain: an Introduction from the Upper Paleolithic to the Industrial Revolution*, eds. J. Hunter & I. Ralston. London: Routledge, 58–76.

Whittle, A., J. Pollard & C. Greigson, 1999. *The Harmony of Symbols: the Windmill Hill Causewayed Enclosure.* Oxford: Oxbow.

Willis, E.H., 1961. Marine transgression sequences in the English Fenland. *Annals of the New York Acadamy of Science* 95, 368–76.

Wyman Abbot, G., 1910. The discovery of prehistoric pits at Peterborough. *Archaeologia* 62 (1), 333–40.

Wysocki, M. & A. Whittle, 2000. Diversity, lifestyles and rites: new biological and archaeological evidence from British earlier Neolithic mortuary assemblages. *Antiquity* 74, 591–601.

# Index